D0894107

EXOTICS AT HOME

WOMEN IN CULTURE AND SOCIETY

A series edited by Catharine R. Stimpson

Micaela di Leonardo

EXOTICS AT HOME

Anthropologies, Others, American Modernity

The University of Chicago Press

Chicago and London

MICAELA DI LEONARDO is professor of anthropology and women's studies at Northwestern University. A sometime contributor to the *Nation*, she is the author of *The Varieties of Ethnic Experience*, editor of *Gender at the Crossroads of Knowledge: Feminist Anthropology in the Postmodern Era*, and coeditor of *The Gender/Sexuality Reader: Culture, History, Political Economy*.

Credit information will be found at the end of this book.

The University of Chicago Press, Chicago 60637
The University of Chicago Press, Ltd., London
© 1998 by The University of Chicago
All rights reserved. Published 1998
Printed in the United States of America
07 06 05 04 03 02 01 00 99 98   1 2 3 4 5

ISBN: 0–226–47263–9 (CLOTH)

Library of Congress Cataloging-in-Publication Data

Di Leonardo, Micaela, 1949–
    Exotics at home : anthropologies, others, American modernity /
Micaela di Leonardo.
        p.   cm.—(Women in culture and society)
    Includes bibliographical references and index.
    ISBN 0-226-47263-9 (cloth : alk. paper)
    1. Ethnology—Philosophy. 2. Ethnology—Authorship. 3. Ethnology—
United States. 4. Ethnocentrism—United States. 5. Cultural relativism—
United States. 6. Exoticism in literature. 7. Women anthropologists—
United States. 8. Feminist anthropology—United States. 9. Women—
Cross-cultural studies. 10. Women—United States—Social conditions.
11. United States—Social life and customs.   I. Title.   II. Series.
GN33.D5   1998
305.8'001—DC21   97-48475
                                                                      CIP

♾ The paper used in this publication meets the minimum requirements of the American National Standard for Information Sciences—Permanence of Paper for Printed Materials, ANSI Z39.48–1992.

Eppure, si muove. [Anyway, it (the earth) moves.]
Galileo

Power concedes nothing without a demand.
It never has and it never will.
Frederick Douglass

My country is the whole world.
Virginia Woolf

When will there be a harvest for the world?
Ronald Isley

America I'm putting my queer shoulder to the wheel.
Allen Ginsberg

CONTENTS

ILLUSTRATIONS

FOREWORD

Exotics at Home is a fearless work. Micaela di Leonardo writes with passion as well as scholarship. Witty, pungently clear, fiercely eloquent, often severely critical in tone, she offers her readers two visions. The first is that of a more democratic world; the second is that of radically altered anthropology. This discipline matters because it is a "gathering place" of concerns that are "central to national and global politics in this century" (p. 22). If American anthropology goes wrong, it drastically blurs and impedes a genuinely global democracy.

For di Leonardo, American anthropology has gone wrong. Far too often, it has forgotten it cannot understand a culture, including that of modern America, without understanding its political economy. In brief, anthropology has isolated culture from power and, as a result, from the processes and changes of history itself. So doing, anthropology over the course of this century has permitted, indeed encouraged, America to construct its identity through destructive representations of race, ethnicity, and gender. For example, the figure of the Dusky Maiden, one of an array of Exotic Others, dominates the popular imagination—with the complicity of anthropology.

Di Leonardo is too ambitious to limit her scholarship to anthropology itself, ambitious though this would be. She also offers a bold, panoramic survey of the ways in which Americans have used ideas about culture, anthropology, and the anthropologist who symbolizes the study of cultures and serves as the messenger from alien cultures to America. Margaret

Mead, whom di Leonardo analyzes skeptically, embodies both the errors of the discipline and the error-endorsing symbol the anthropologist has become.

Modern scholarship has often progressed through big, passionate, provocative books. I think, for example, of the influence of *Sexual Politics* by Kate Millett. Di Leonardo is calling on American anthropology to attend far more self-consciously and broadly to its home and this home's connections with the world. Here are home truths and arguments aplenty from a scholar who takes the study of women and men seriously enough to work fearlessly.

Catharine R. Stimpson
New York University

ACKNOWLEDGMENTS

So many friends, colleagues, and loved ones aided me on this project that the crowded stage of my indebtedness resembles one of the ditzier musical comedies analyzed in the pages that follow. As the curtain drops, though, I stand alone on the boards in taking responsibility for any flaws in the play.

Without the intelligence, warm support, and wit of my bicoastal anthropological sisters, Brett Williams and Patricia Zavella, I could not have finished this book. Williams, sharing my concerns with Afro-American and urban studies and anthropological history, has been my constant intellectual and emotional companion throughout the years of writing. She provided invaluable readings of early chapters, and I have been inspired by her own work on the culture of debt and on D.C. history. She and her family, as well, have had the grace and forbearance to laugh at all my jokes. The *confianza* Zavella and I have developed over nearly a quarter-century is precious to me, as is the warm hospitality she and her family have extended to me. A significant portion of this book was composed *en su casa que es mi casa también.* Her evolving work on race, gender, and Mexican/American political economy has been vital to my scholarly development.

Catherine Lutz sacrificed time from her important research in Fayetteville, North Carolina, to review the manuscript. I have benefited enormously from her work and from her responses to mine—even when we disagree. Roger Lancaster, having seduced me temporarily from this project to coedit *The Gender/Sexuality Reader* with him, more than recouped his debt through providing me an extraordinarily detailed and thoughtful set of responses to the draft manuscript. I have learned much from our Stakhanovite comradeship. Michel-Rolph Trouillot revealed himself only toward the end of the writing process as Chicago's Mystery Reviewer. His elegant and incisive evaluations have been of much use, even as I disregarded some of his suggestions.

I have been very fortunate in my colleagues and students at Northwestern. Africanist anthropologists Karen Hansen, Robert Launay, Jane Guyer, and Caroline Bledsoe helped me greatly from the vantage of their specialties, as did my fellow Americanist anthropologist Helen Schwartzman. Historian, linguist, and Internet expert Josef Barton has been an unfailingly helpful friend and colleague, as has fellow historian James Oakes. In the Department of English, Christopher Herbert and Madhu Dubey provided early and late critical readings. Dwight Conquergood, of Performance Studies, has been a dear friend and enthusiastic supporter—and helped in the construction of my title. The Alice Berline Kaplan Humanities Center provided me a year's leave, during some of which I reworked this book instead of writing another. Dean Frank Safford provided expert adminstrative interventions at crucial moments.

The women of my feminist graduate reading group—Michelle Boyd, Leslie Dunlap, Cathy Flynn, Diane Gross, Jacalyn Harden, Shannon Jackson, Celia Marshik, Michele Mitchell, Heather McClure, and Gina Pérez have provided crucial critical responses and support over the years. As well, Harden, Flynn, and Pérez, with the addition of the redoubtable Jacqueline Pegg, and Patricia Silver of American University, worked serially as research assistants on the project. Dunlap, in addition, took time out from her important research to review the entire manuscript from the perspective of American women's history.

William Roseberry (with Jay O'Brien) first commissioned me to write a piece that, much transformed, has taken its place in chapter 2. I value his work and our ongoing colleagueship. He and Nicole Polier also read the entire draft manuscript and offered invaluable suggestions. I have appreciated Elsa Dixler's intelligent editing and incisive political analyses over the near-decade that we have worked together on my pieces for *The Nation*. My piece for her on cultural relativism appears in much expanded form in chapter 6.

Five old friends from New Haven have been of inestimable help. Kathryn Oberdeck has brought her sharp intelligence repeatedly to bear on American studies issues, as has William Munro on my African politics material. They both, also, have been enduring friends in hard times. Mary Summers and Rogers Smith have given me important insights on American history and contemporary politics, warm hospitality, and my adorable god-daughter Carolyn. Last, Jacqueline Dirks offered detailed and thoughtful responses to my women's history material in chapter 2.

Adolph Reed Jr. shared New Haven fieldwork and many of the difficulties of the early framing of this project with me. This book, with my other work over the past decade, bears the imprint of our long and fruitful intellectual and political association.

Many individuals provided early critical readings, popular cultural references, crucial expertise, and/or citations at various stages of the project. Especially important here were Anne Allison, Ruth Andris, Arjun Appadurai, Mark Auslander, Giulia Barrera, James Bellis, Niko Besnier, John Bodnar, Timothy Burke, John Comaroff, Michael Curtin, Miguel Diaz-Barriga, Diane Dillon, Paul Durrenberger, Amal Hassan Fadlalla, Norma Field, Susan Gal, David Givens, Robert Gordon, Linda Hurwitz, James Jatczynski, Leola Johnson, David Joravsky, Ivan Karp, Corinne Kratz, Hank Leland, Elise Levin, Chris Lowe, Peter Mamakos, Bruce Mannheim, Sam Marts, Sidney Mintz, Kathleen Morrison, Clare O'Shea, Angela Palermo, James Peacock, Elizabeth Povinelli, David Price, Jeffrey Rice, David Roediger, Roberta Spalter-Roth, Ellen Schattschneider, Gavin Smith, Werner Sollers, Susan Sperling, Gil Stein, Stephen Steinberg, Alaka Wali, Kenneth Warren, Kath Weston, Edwin Wilmsen, Carter Wilson, and Carl Woideck.

I have presented parts of this book at schools and conferences around the country. Many thanks for responses and enthusiasm to colleagues at the University of Chicago, Colby College, Columbia University, Brooklyn College, the CUNY Graduate Center, the University of California at Santa Cruz, Duke University, Emory University, the University of Iowa, the University of Kansas, Marquette University, MIT, the University of Michigan, the University of Minnesota, Northwestern, Notre Dame, the University of North Carolina, Rutgers, Swarthmore, Wake Forest, Wesleyan, the University of Wisconsin, Yale, and the American Anthropological Association and American Studies annual meetings.

Staffs at Yale University Library, Northwestern University Library (especially Mette Shayne), the Evanston Public Library, and the Harold Washington Library in Chicago (especially Andrea Mark) were unfailingly helpful. At the University of Chicago Press, I was fortunate in my first editor, Karen Wilson, and have greatly appreciated the intelligence, competence, and sharp wit of her successor, Susan Bielstein. I have also benefited from Paige Kennedy-Piehl's help, Erin Hogan's work on publicity, and Jill Shimabukuro's excellent design work.

Finally, there are those who played no active part in the making of this book but who are nevertheless crucial to its existence. George Stocking's long labors in the establishment of the history of anthropology as a field made my work within it possible—even allowed me to dissent from some of his conclusions. My women's studies colleague at Yale, Nancy Cott, profoundly influenced my understanding of American women's history. My California support system, including my mother Audrie di Leonardo, my cousins Kevin McRae, Kelly McRae, and Michael Vanderlan, my nephew Ian Kwei McRae, my uncle Jim Tucker, and my friends Wayne Maeda, Robin Wells, and Cary Zeitlin all deserve great thanks. I appreciate the warmth and hospitality of old and new neighbors in New Haven and Evanston, and that of my many friends on Dempster Street. My stay in the Heartland has been sweetened by Chicago Bulls victories and live Chicago jazz, but it is Chicago jazz and black radio, especially V103 and Herb Kent (the cool gent), that made bearable the long night and weekend hours at the computer this project necessitated. Finally, the support, concern, and witty conversation provided by my mother-in-law, Clarita MacDonald Reed, has buoyed my spirits over these many years.

HIDDEN IN PLAIN SIGHT

ex·ot·ic . . . *adj.* 1. From another part of the world; not indigenous; foreign. 2. Having the charm of the unfamiliar; strikingly and intriguingly unusual or beautiful . . . — *n.* One that is exotic.—The American Heritage Dictionary of the English Language, *1969*

The American present is another country. My walk to work in Evanston, Illinois—a white-bread, Midwestern college town known for good schools, clean beaches, and the Women's Christian Temperance Union—runs along a small-business stretch of Dempster Street bustling with stores merchandising the charm of the unfamiliar. Crowded cheek by jowl up against Navajo and Pueblo pots, rugs, and jewelry are tarot cards and crystals, Southeast Asian guardian figures, Mexican *santos,* and a small forest's worth of books on women's primitive goddess nature written by self-styled "cantadoras" or devotees of Australian aboriginal or Latin American Indian or rural Japanese "wise women." Store names celebrate Otherness: Nomads, Ltd., Primitivo, East Meets West, The Light of the Moon, The Jade Monkey. Even the recently opened futon shop displays furniture whose fabric covers vaguely evoke Indonesian batik and Indian design motifs from the Southwest. Incense billows out onto the sidewalk, and curbside cars sport "Native American" dream catchers—string, hide, and feather constructions—hanging from rearview mirrors.

Dempster Street's Otherness is innately part of contemporary American selfhood. College towns across the nation since at least the 1950s have been

1. On Dempster Street, the gauntlet of ethnological antimodernism. (Photo by the author.)

staging grounds for selling the offbeat, developing merchandising meccas
not just for students and hangers-on eager to display sophistication
through the consumption of the exotic, but for outlying suburbanites as
well. Particular commodities—folk music, Indian import women's wear,
Balinese jewelry—succeeded first in college town test markets before becoming standard American mall merchandise.

But the present is always linked to many pasts. Contemporary Dempster
Street's fin de siècle gauntlet of ethnological antimodernism, of escape from
the contemporary West through refuge in the "timeless" exotic, evokes as
well earlier elites' widespread sense of inauthenticity, futility, "experiencing life at a remove." At the end of the last century, members of the American bourgeoisie made equally widespread efforts to escape modernity
through immersion in the lives of those Others considered organically

2. East meets West on Dempster Street. (Photo by the author.)

whole by virtue of their distance, in time and/or space, from the etiolated world of Western logic and progress.[1] Medieval Europeans, South Sea islanders, southwestern Native Americans—even the impoverished southeastern Europeans resident in northern industrial cities—were grist for the antimodernism mill of the Gilded Age and Progressive Era. The ghosts of Mabel Dodge Luhan and Henry Adams are at home among the exotics of Dempster Street, and Jane Addams's spirit has found a new clientele just down the road in Chicago around Hull House.

Antimodernists, whether past or present, construct noble savages for their personal salvation. But joined to the hip of every noble savage is its nasty savage twin, proof of Western modernity's superiority and legitimation of Western white domination. Addams was fulfilled through her European immigrant clients, acknowledged learning from them, but also settled among such "primitive people" to uplift them, to "keep whatever of value their past life contained and to bring them into contact with a better class of Americans."[2]

WHITE CITY, MIDWAY, DEMPSTER STREET

Four years after the founding of Hull House, in fact, an unholy combination of elites, entrepreneurs, and anthropologists gave birth to Dempster

Street's dark twin at the Chicago World's Columbian Exposition of 1893. The American fin de siècle was a political fulcrum. It was, at one and the same time, the period of the consolidation of capitalist industrialization, of a bloody war against a significantly European immigrant labor force, and of federal abandonment of Reconstruction in the South and the establishment there of a white reign of terror against black Americans. (*Plessy v. Ferguson*, the landmark Supreme Court case establishing "separate but equal" uncivil rights, would be decided in 1896.) It was as well the end of the war of expropriation against Native Americans—the exposition opened only three years after the massacre at Wounded Knee—the heyday of American imperialist expansion into the Caribbean, Latin America, and the Pacific; and the period of an ongoing Victorian woman movement still twenty-seven years short of the achievement of female voting rights and tinged by racist and classist response to short-lived post–Civil War black male suffrage.[3] The complicated politics of this fulcrum period were exceedingly well represented in the structures and process of the Chicago fair.

Opening in a largely immigrant city, in the midst of a financial panic only seven years after the Haymarket uprisings, hosting more than 21 million visitors, and closing only a season prior to the great Pullman railroad strike, the Chicago World's Columbian Exposition enacted a local and national elite "search for order" in the industrial triumph over labor unrest and the celebration of technological and cultural progress. Banking on congressional support, handsome returns to their original investment, and the financial ripple effect of massive positive publicity, wealthy individuals bought more than 18 million dollars in stocks and bonds to support fair construction. Like those who lived in the model workers' town built by Pullman just outside Chicago, the labor force building the fair was isolated, regimented, and driven—more than thirty workers were killed on the job—and force-fed "improving culture" in the form of nightly classical music and lantern-slide programs. Despite concerted protest, however, local Afro-Americans failed to gain a foothold in even that regimented body and were frozen out of almost all exhibits, the mass of white-collar jobs opened by the fair, even excluded from the fair's police force, the Columbian Guards. On the token concession and condescendingly planned Colored Jubilee Day, during which fair organizers distributed free watermelons, Frederick Douglass hauntingly described antiblack discrimination at the exposition as "a world in miniature."[4]

Within the official fairgrounds—the White City—science and progress held sway in a heavily planned, electrified Beaux Arts environment with

3. The White City, Chicago World's Columbian Exposition, 1893. (Courtesy of the Chicago Public Library.)

its own railroad, water, and sewage system. The vistas of soaring white neoclassical buildings—lit with fairy lights at night—of statues, lagoons, and fountains, inspired a veritable flood of popular and high-cultural praise. Harvard philosopher William James wrote to his brother Henry in England that "everyone says one ought to sell all one has and mortgage one's soul to go there, it is esteemed such a revelation of beauty." State exhibits lauded technological breakthroughs and the industrial marvels they made possible. New York senator Chauncey Depew, in a Dedication Day oration, linked "the flower and fruitage of this transcendent miracle" to the necessity of disciplining European immigrants and prohibiting further immigration: "We must have a national quarantine against disease, pauperism and crime. . . . We cannot admit those who come to undermine our institutions, and subvert our laws."[5] The theme of teleological progress was further underlined by anthropological exhibits that, through life-size statues, presented obviously Anglo-Saxon Harvard and Radcliffe students as ideal human types and various Native American populations as illustrating "lower races in costume."

Entirely separate from the White City but extending its "nasty savage" ideology was the highly profitable Midway Plaisance, the sideshow entertainment and refreshment area that fair architect Daniel Burnham described as the "lighter and more fantastic side of the Fair" but that Harvard historian Charles Eliot Norton denominated "an immense border of vulgarities." The Midway—which had been permitted by fair organizers only because a like institution at the recent Paris Exposition had been highly profitable—operated officially under the aegis of Department M, the anthropological wing headed by F. W. Putnam, director of Harvard's Peabody Museum. It was in reality run by San Fransisco entrepreneur (and later congressman) Sol Bloom, who later remarked about Professor Putnam that "to have made this unhappy gentleman responsible for the establishment of a successful venture in the field of entertainment was about as intelligent a decision as it would be today to make Albert Einstein manager of the Ringling Brothers and Barnum and Bailey Circus." Along the Midway, the first Ferris wheel vied with hootchy-cootchy dancers, and sideshow barkers and refreshment stand operators competed for visitors' cash. And on the Midway, in extension of the Anthropology Building in the White City, living humans—Native Americans, Africans, Pacific islanders, Middle Easterners, and Southeast Asians—were displayed to a buying public in ethnological zoos and widely perceived as representing various lower stages of ascending human social evolution. In an official Smithsonian "Summary of Progress in Anthropology," Otis T. Mason remarked with satisfaction of the Midway and "the bazaars everywhere throughout the grounds" that "indeed, it would not be too much to say that the World's Columbian Exposition was one vast anthropological revelation." Historian Robert Rydell observes that "the Midway provided visitors with ethnological, scientific sanction for the American view of the nonwhite world as barbaric and childlike and gave a scientific basis to the racial blueprint for building a utopia."[6]

But some barbarians are more barbaric than others. Within an overarching racist disourse, popular magazines nevertheless lauded the Japanese, the "Yankees of the East," at the fair; the Javanese, described as "about the color of a well-done sweet potato"; and the Samoans, whom the *Nation* denominated "fine specimens of humanity . . . the aboriginal note in its purity." As well, although Native Americans' petitions for proper representation were ignored, and they were often placed near the bottom of the "grand sliding scale of humanity" that white fair visitors imposed on its

4. Dahomean "village," Midway Plaisance, Chicago World's Columbian Exposition, 1893. (Courtesy of the Chicago Public Library.)

human ethnological exhibits, compared to the Dahomeans, a souvenir booklet affirmed, they were to be seen as "a thing of beauty and joy forever."[7]

Women of "the savage races" were perceived equally variously. In the common orientalist parlance, Asian and Middle Eastern women were largely apprehended as embodiments of exotic beauty and sexuality. One account described a dancer who "revels in all the glory of oriental colors and barbaric jewelry . . . [and] displays her charms, dimly hidden by a gauze nothing; a narrow zone of gauze silk through which the warm flesh tints are distinctly visible." Black African women, however, were frequently portrayed as offensively ugly and frighteningly savage. One journalist asserted that "a Dahomean mother is, in feature and figure, the incomparable nightmare of the human race," while another asserted that the Dahomeans were "blacker than buried midnight and as degraded as the animals which prowl the jungles of their dark land. It is impossible to conceive of a notch lower in the human scale than the Amazon, or female warrior, represents."[8]

But even white Anglo-Saxon American women were liminal figures in the eyes of the elite males who planned the fair. Socialite Bertha Palmer had to fight for a role for women beyond fund-raising—indeed, activist women had been derided and excluded from both of the earlier world's fairs in New York and Philadelphia. Palmer capitalized on Susan B. Anthony's quiet organizing among the wives and daughters of Washington, D.C., elites and turned to the "separate but equal" strategy of a free-standing Woman's Building when it became clear that male planners would neither fund nor properly label women's exhibits in the White City. Planners, too, positioned the Woman's Building at the very gateway to the Midway Plaisance. Robert Rydell points out the double message of this siting: "Women, in the eyes of the exposition's male sponsors, came close to slipping into the category of 'otherness' reserved for 'savages' and 'exotics.' They were redeemed only by their capacity to serve as mothers of civilization—a stereotype that some upper- and middle-class white women were only too happy to embrace to advance their own reform agenda."[9]

From Hull House, to the White City and Midway, to Dempster Street today, we see evidence of the paramount American studies themes of the ubiquity of a heavily classed and gendered therapeutic/punitive discourse on self and Other and of the increasing commodification of American identities with the maturation of corporate capitalism. We see also the linkage of that discourse and commodification, since the late nineteenth century, both to "noble savage" ethnological antimodernism and to Calvinist-inflected morality plays in which the dominance of good self over bad Other provides the trope for legitimizing domestic and international racial and ethnic stratification.[10]

ANTHROPOLOGISTS & OTHERS

In these sites we see not only the centrality of "exotics" (about whom anthropologists claim and have claimed expertise) to that commodification and that discourse, but the increasing importance of anthropology itself, as practice and as polyvalent symbol, to twentieth-century American structures of feeling. Anthropologists on the American scene have over the decades become liminal, highly cathected cultural figures, guardians of the offbeat—exotics at home. Indeed, anthropologists' public personae have come to mirror college town entrepreneurship: wittingly or unwittingly, we often function on the "lighter and more fantastic side," as test marketers for new trends in the acceptably strange, for new, consumable cultural difference.

And those American Others often studied by anthropologists—racial, religious, sexual, occupational minorities, the stigmatized, the poor—are also marked as domestic exotics. "Culture," the concept arguably most central to the discipline, has long been repatriated for home use—with dire results. Like one of its alternate definitions, "culture" is a foreign microbe run wild, an invisible Frankenstein monster of the discipline's own making, rampaging across the body politic. To extend the Columbian Exposition metaphor: Department M has always existed under putative anthropological guardianship, *but not under its control.* Increasingly since the 1960s, "culture" stands in for "race" in distorting, victim-blaming visions of class, mobility, power, and poverty in America and elsewhere. Behind anthropologists' own backs, "cultures" have become characters in our national morality play, theological archetypes representing Good and Evil for the commonweal.

This evolving script is unsurprising, in retrospect, since "culture" and "biology" are the two major ways in which Americans historically launder politics from public sphere inspection. Anthropology, sententiously self-described as the most humanistic of the sciences, the most scientific of the humanities, is the ground zero discipline representing both of these domains in American public life. It thus has seemingly naturally developed into a key locus for the production of the notion of rational, authoritative discourse on political issues. It is then equally unsurprising that anthropology, as trope and practice, has become a cynosure of political approbation and attack, both refuge and refuse in contemporary contestations over power. Foolish multiculturalists lauding the Midway's "immense border of vulgarities" (defending infidels against the beleagured West) arrogant imperialists misrepresenting subaltern peoples, sensitive interpreters of cultural difference and primitive wisdom, disinterested "human scientists" tracing our genetic inheritance—anthropologists wear all these hats and more in our contemporary fin de siècle discourse. They are broadly invoked to authorize liberal and rightist, racist and progressive, feminist and antifeminist politics in the contemporary public sphere.

Two 1980s upsurges of political uses of anthropological interpretation, indeed, served as the locus classicus for this project. Marjorie Shostak's 1981 life history of Nisa, a woman of the southern African !Kung San, was ecstatically reviewed in middlebrow, especially feminist journals, became a runaway bestseller, and has been widely adopted, as an anthropological, multicultural, and women's studies classic, for college classroom use. Two years later, Derek Freeman's attack on Margaret Mead's 1928 ethnography, *Coming of Age in Samoa,* spurred a veritable conservative media feeding frenzy over the "documented proof" that Mead had seriously misinterpreted Samoan life—had in fact been lied to by her own female informants—and thus that all liberal political convictions were based on false science. The spectacle of white Western women ethnographers being alternately celebrated and reviled for their cultural interpretations of the lives of exotic brown-skinned women—combined with the complete failure to consider the historical and political economic placement of those ethnographers and those female Others—extraordinarily mirrored the contested sexual and racial politics, the overarching Orwellian and very public bad faith of the Reagan era. It spurred my investigation of the public functions of anthropology, of the neglected history of the popular reception of ethnographies foregrounding "dusky maidens," and of the unnoticed embeddedness of those ethnographies in shifting American gender, race, and class politics over three generations.

This book,then, is about these ideological elements which, like the stores lining Dempster Street, are hidden in plain sight around us—and about the heretofore relative invisibility of a form of knowledge production fantastically central to apprehensions of American selfhood. It is simultaneously about other key American phenomena also hiding in plain sight, populations and processes that are either little represented in scholarship and popular culture or most represented in their least typical forms.

EMBEDDED GENDER

Certainly no one would now claim that women, or gender relations, after a quarter-century of renascent feminism, are the least bit invisible in American life. It is equally clear that questions of race and ethnicity hold center stage in American scholarship and popular culture. But which considerations of gender and race are most common, and how do they tend to be linked? Dempster Street offers an abundance of "Great Goddess" texts and other commodities harnessing notions of exotic brown women, past and present, to the self-help project of increasing largely white, largely middle-class American women's self-esteem, enhancing their therapeutic discourse on themselves and their relations with others. (There really is a New Age kit labeled "Goddess Guide Me: The Oracle That Answers Questions of the Heart.") Late-twentieth-century cultural feminist notions of women's benevolent, nurturant *Ur*-nature, which flow effortlessly from the very familiar image of women as "the nice gender" and mothers as naturally loving into the slightly outré, "exotic" practice of goddess worship, derive ultimately from the Victorian construction of the Moral Mother, the Angel on the Hearth that Virginia Woolf longed to murder—but that Jane Addams revered. Progressive Era women reformers in general relied on notions of women's innate moral superiority to men, their home-based probity and unselfishness, to legitimate their efforts to gain public political power. Thus Addams's famous coinage, "social housekeeping."

But the noble savage always coexists with her nasty twin, and there is simply no possible analysis of gender divisions in any time or place without a consideration of the social stratifications crosscutting them. The women who fought for the Women's Building at the Chicago Columbian Exposition had no qualms in excluding their petitioning Afro-American sisters from their Board of Lady Managers with the excuse that the two local middle-class women's organizations made different demands for representation. Although Frances Harper, Anna Julia Cooper, and four other accomplished black American women spoke at the World's Congress of Representative Women held in conjunction with the fair, and although Ida B. Wells, with Frederick Douglass and F. L. Barnett, wrote and distributed ten thousand copies of the pamphlet "The Reason Why the Colored American Is Not in the World's Columbian Exposition" from the fair's Haitian pavilion, white power and capital prevailed. Racist representations, buttressed by social evolutionary anthropology, overwhelmed the most vigorous Afro-American efforts. Emphasizing its assent to social evolutionary models, the Board of Lady Managers commissioned two allegorical murals, representing "Primitive Woman" and "Modern Woman," for its main interior court. *Harper's Weekly* even published an insulting cartoon series on efforts by the uncomprehending Southern black "Johnson family" to interpret fair exhibits. On the Midway, Mr. Johnson clasps hands with a Dahomean, at which Mrs. Johnson exclaims, "Ezwell Johnson, stop shakin' hans wid dat heathen! You want de hull Fair ter t'ink you's found a poo' relation?" The white establishment asserted the "reason why" Afro-Americans were not represented in the White City: blacks were to be exhibited in ethnological zoos, and women of the "savage races" were incapable of the White City's civilization. They belonged only on the Midway, representing the lowest levels of evolution, forbidden sexuality, unwomanly labor, and scandalous lifeways. Mason, the Smithsonian anthropologist, noted his reactions to a White City bas-relief in which a "forlorn savage woman . . . at one end of a series of weary burden bearers was in strange contrast with the spirituelle painting of angels on the walls above her head." As Frederick Douglass stormed in the "Reason Why" pamphlet, tellingly using the New Testament reference, the White City was in reality a "whited sepulcher."[11]

Plus ça change. While, as we shall see, the functions Dusky Maidens fulfill in the white Western mind have altered considerably over the succeeding century, some structural connections between representations and political economic realities remain brashly unmediated. On Dempster Street in the multicultural present, few "cantadoras" report studying with

African or *Afro-American* "wise women" to bring back primitive truths. The store selling African artifacts opened and shut down within months, unlike those retailing commodities associated with the "right" exotics. (On the west side of town, and on Chicago's South and West Sides, though, African commodities are steady sellers in boutiques and black nationalist bookstores.) On the national scene, Catherine Lutz and Jane Collins find that white Americans approve photographs of "bronze" people in *National Geographic,* but react negatively to those of darker humans, misidentifying them as largely African and falsely perceiving a disproportionate number of stories on Africa in the magazine itself.[12] In Jane Addams's old haunts, University of Chicago sociologists retool discredited "culture of poverty" arguments to blame the black poor for their victimization by state and capital—and some even separate out Chicago's Mexican population as the local "model minority."[13]

Like the noble/nasty savage, ethnological antimodernism and imperialist racism are twins, and equally deeply gendered. Neither allows for an analysis of anthropology's engagement with—and exploitation by—American popular culture in its shifting constructions of race, class, gender, and nationality, the subject of this volume's first chapter. Nor can they account for the complicated and changing politics embedded in ethnographic representations of the "exotic woman" in American structures of feeling (chapters 3–5). Anxieties and equivocations about modernity fuse with distorted representations of American ethnic, women's, and racial history and economic functioning in the invented traditions of "the white ethnic community," "women's culture," and the invented nontradition of "the underclass" (chapters 2 and 6).

Invented traditions veil actualities, allow millions of human beings and ubiquitous quotidian processes to hide in plain sight. And the popular and scholarly avalanche of "underclass" rhetoric of the Reagan years into the present fuses with essentializing visions of race literally to deny the statistical reality that the majority of black America is neither impoverished nor well off—the key representations allowed onto the American stage—but precariously working-class. The Dempster Street panhandlers, the boys in their baggies on the west side of town, Michael Jordan—nasty versus noble exotics on the current Midway—excite all the representational interest. The nurse living next door to me in Evanston and the bus driver down the street are nearly invisible Americans. "Inner cities" are regularly limned as hearts of darkness, while the shifting working-class neighborhoods abutting them—like the one in which I lived for five years in New Haven, Connecticut—waste their historical fragrance on the desert air.

5. Samoan "village," Midway Plaisance, Chicago World's Columbian Exposition, 1893. (Courtesy of the Chicago Public Library.)

PLACE, POWER, MEMORY

Ethnographic writing famously relies on the fiction of the "ethnographic present," the time period during which research was conducted in a particular place. Imprisoned in time like flies in amber, objects of anthropological study, critics have contended, seem all the more to be denied the flux, change, and historical agency inseparable from the lives of "Westerners," those who undertake studies on others.[14] Just as Columbian Exposition anthropologists "assisted" Native Americans in redonning the correct costumes for exhibit, and just as their horrified fair manager demanded that the boatload of disembarking Samoans who had cut their hair and adopted American dress "resume their natural state of barbarism" for appropriate display, so we continue to read about a "timeless" Nuer—who had been conquered by the British just prior to Edward Evan Evans-Pritchard's study, and whose land has been for years the site of civil war—or to argue over a "Samoan culture" deemed somehow unaffected by American and European occupations, capital penetration, war, tourism, and mass emigration.[15] As a graduate student in the mid-1970s, I had a fantasy of writing a "red tour" of anthropological classics: disrupting their ethnographic presents through providing a series of historical and political economic contex-

tualizations of the Nuer, the Tallensi, the Navajo, the Tepoztecos, the Tro-
brianders, and the Samoans from before the point of study into the present.

But certain Americans—domestic exotics—have also been subjected to
the operations of the ethnographic present. Those same years in which I
fantasized historicizing Mead's Samoa and Evans-Pritchard's Sudan, hundreds of thousands of college students were reading about Italians in Boston in the late 1930s and late 1950s and blacks in Washington, D.C., in the
early and mid-1960s, for all the world as though the Good War were still
hovering in the wings, or Ike or Camelot or LBJ were still with us—or
merely as if there were something so essential to "Italian" or "black culture" that Whyte and Gans, Liebow and Hannerz had captured them for
all time, and all places, in their "ethnographically present" case studies.[16]

The facts that black and Italian-Americans, like the Nuer and the Samoans, vary among themselves and have their own histories are not the only
points to be discerned here. It is not only those upon whom the ethnographic present has been imposed who should be considered, but those
who have imposed it. That is, anthropologists and others have frequently
portrayed foreign and domestic exotics as, in Eric Wolf's felicitous formulation, "people without history."[17] But we tend as well to see ourselves
as unchanging observers, our epistemological frames, our methodological
toolkits unaffected by changing political regimes, war, demography, movements of capital, or material interest.

Or rather, there are three tendencies now abroad in the land in considerations of anthropology and historical change. The first is the positivist
assumption of an unchanging, scientific, anthropological eye. Thus, as we
shall see, the bulk of commentary on Freeman and Mead focused on
whether Mead had "got it right," in abstraction from how much "it"—
Samoans, us, and our notions of good anthropology—may have changed
over nearly a half-century. The second tendency is positivism's mirror image. Here a heterogeneous group of postmodern-influenced anthropology
bashers assume, indeed, a materially interested anthropology—but one of
unchanging imperial focus, of Michel Foucault's single oppressive panopti-
con, of an inherently criminal, timeless, objectifying eye. Finally, those who
specialize in the history of anthropology or the precincts of American cultural history that intersect with anthropological work have produced a
wealth of careful, nuanced work contextualizing that shifting set of individual lives, discursive practices, and material traces labeled as a singular
anthropology (thus the pluralization in my title).

But the very clustering of these historical contextualizations around the
fin de siècle, and their thinning out as we move through the decades of
the twentieth century, implies a set of practices less and less in need of

contextualization, more and more impervious to their own political economic and cultural embeddedness, the closer we approach the present. In particular, we hear almost nothing of our own historical blind spot, of the tumultuous years of radicalism and backlash from the 1960s to the present, the last two academic generations in which most currently practicing American anthropologists were trained—years in which the discipline as a whole, mirroring the country itself, closely approached and then decisively withdrew from an official stance of speaking truth to American imperial power. And the explicitly political roles anthropologists have played and play—rather than the political implications of anthropological work—have been nearly uniformly ignored. American anthropology, like the United States in general, embraces its own culture of forgetting and of convenient remembrance.

I have thus ended up writing the ironic obverse of my 1970s fantasy book. Instead of detailing the changing, power-saturated worlds of anthropology's Third World objects (although I have attempted some responsible sketching-in here), I have written a Red Tour of the changing and connected worlds of American anthropological production as they have—and have not—intersected with the histories and popular representations of racial, ethnic, and gendered exotic and domestic Others.[18] These linked histories provide an alternative Archimedean standpoint from which we then can envision American and all other social realities anew. In the following pages, indeed, such central twentieth-century public cultural figures as W. E. B. Du Bois, H. L. Mencken, Freda Kirchwey, Diana Trilling, Leonard Bernstein, Gore Vidal, and Susan Sontag will make fresh cameo appearances as they consume and interpret varying anthropological scripts for American audiences. As Dorothy remarked in another context, there's no place like home.

And home is very much the issue here. In a wonderfully cranky 1986 piece, Arjun Appadurai comments on the extraordinary power of locality in anthropological theorizing. He notes that "places become showcases for specific issues over time." With his eye on the Indian subcontinent, Appadurai points out that, because "the ethos of anthropology has been driven by the small, the simple, the elementary, the face-to-face . . . the anthropology of complex non-Western societies has, till recently, been a second-class citizen in anthropological discourse." Denominating India an "anthropological black hole" because of the invisibility of theoretical concerns separate from "hierarchy and its twin—purity/pollution" to "the metropolitan gaze," Appadurai calls for us to "examine the peculiar complicities between subject and object in anthropological activity."[19]

But the United States, a complex *Western* society, is an even more dense and light-consuming black hole in anthropology, even more a second-class citizen, than is the Indian subcontinent. Appadurai warns that interpretations of particular societies run "the risk of serious distortion" through overemphasis on locality-based theorizing. American anthropology, as we shall see—despite the vigorous and careful efforts of some—relies on an implicit, and therefore entirely untheorized, American "home." Its metropolitan gaze misses its own reflection. It thus proceeds, whether its eye focuses upon the near or the far away, in casual disregard of the "America" known to other scholars, and its own specifically American history, most importantly its growth in conjunction with the rise to hegemony of the American imperial state. (Postmodernists tend to skip lightly across the American Century to a "postcolonial" and "poststate" present that we have not yet seen.)[20]

This serious interpretive distortion is then compounded by anthropology's central role in American popular political culture and, ironically, by the recent tropism of other scholarly disciplines, particularly history, toward anthropology's deceptively life-giving theoretical star.[21] It is, indeed, no overstatement to say that the blind eye anthropology has turned toward America has blurred our focus, as scholars and citizens, on the entire globe. Just as David Harvey has demonstrated that postmodernists often work from mistaken visions of modernity, so many of those who theorize Otherness work from partial and historically uninformed visions of American selves. I once noted, critically, that Otherness is in the details.[22] So is selfhood. If our country is to be the whole world, we would do well to attend to what is still the world's major imperialist power.

To disrupt our own compacted and imprisoning ethnographic presents, then, we need to theorize, to historicize the home of American anthropology. And this practice involves not only engagement with the linked histories of American race, class, and gender politics and anthropological practice, but also a concerted focus on the changing American public sphere and on the anthropologists who have played key roles on that stage.

THE UBIQUITOUS MARGARET MEAD

Anything by Margaret Mead that relates to tribal habits.—*Katie Ford, CEO of Ford Models, responding to a query about "summer reading to change your life"*[23]

As professional anthropologist and popular cultural figure, Margaret Mead runs like a sturdy thread through this narrative, and by no means only because of Freeman's Reagan-era attack on her Roaring Twenties ethnography. In fact, Mead has threatened to take over this book—even popping up on a poster in a Dempster Street store window—as she inevitably takes over the life of anyone with the temerity to try to read much by and about her. She has hovered over the project and haunted my dreams, throwing her cloak over my books and papers and following me, stumping her staff and uttering sibylline fatuities, up and down stairs. "The poet Keats died when he was 25; and he wrote all his work before that," wrote the youthful Virginia Woolf to a friend, satirizing her own boobish efforts to teach working men and women at Morley College.[24] Lucky, lucky Virginia Woolf. Margaret Mead turned in her master's thesis to Columbia University in 1924 at age twenty-two, died in 1978 at age seventy-six, and simply *never shut up* in all the long years of economic crisis, war, political protest, and cultural shift in between. Although, as we shall see, *Coming of Age in Samoa* had little to do with feminism or the analysis of gender relations (nor was Mead ever much of an antimodernist, despite the dominant tendency to read her work in terms of "sex under the palm trees"), it has certainly been interpreted as a feminist book since the second-wave era, and Mead produced no dearth of texts explicitly about gender, race, the American ethos, and international relations, from *Sex and Temperament* to the wartime *And Keep Your Powder Dry,* from *Male and Female* to her *Rap on Race* with James Baldwin, from her memoir *Blackberry Winter* to popular pieces in women's magazines.

But more than all that, Margaret Mead is and has been the most well-known anthropologist across this century in the United States, and probably the world. Not only did she produce an endless stream of anthropological text and film; she acted, for much of her adult life, as a pundit in the public sphere, American anthropology's happy Polonius, using the authority conferred on her through "exotic fieldwork" to declaim on American and world culture and politics for a full half-century. Quite simply, she represents the genus *Anthropologicus* to the public, and even anthropologists who despise her work must deal with her presence in popular culture. There are, for example, no fewer than three hagiographical children's biographies of Mead in the Evanston Public Library, two of whose subtitles—*World's Grandmother, The World Was Her Family*—faithfully reflect Mead's own canny late-in-life self-marketing. There is even a set of children's stamps that rather smudgily illustrate "celebrated heroines," including Florence Nightingale, Amelia Earheart, Harriet Tubman, Susan B. Anthony, Eleanor Roosevelt—and Margaret Mead.[25]

Four recent vignettes—pieces of inadvertent fieldwork—further illustrate Mead's iconic public sphere status. First, inside the guild: At the 1993 meetings of the American Anthropological Association in Washington, D.C., an older woman standing by the elevators walked from group to group, repeatedly thrusting a staff in people's faces and commanding "Touch it," then confiding in a portentous whisper, "It's Margaret Mead's." A few months later, in Evanston's Barnes and Noble bookstore, graduate student Jacalyn Harden observed a cluster of well-heeled North Shore matrons listening in approval as one of their number expounded on Mead as a "great woman," a "pioneer for all of us." Shortly thereafter, in the bar of a Chicago Ethiopian restaurant, I eavesdropped on two men who capped one another's Freeman-originated criticisms of Mead: "She didn't even know the language." "And all her claims were false." Finally, in 1996, a young man in a Thai restaurant just off Dempster Street, overhearing my mention of Mead to my lunchtime companion, approached our table literally trembling with emotion: "You want to know what Margaret Mead was? She was the greatest fraud of the twentieth century." Avatar, guru, or fraud—manna, or shoddy goods. From the stale air of hotel conference rooms to crystals and incense on Dempster Street, Margaret Mead is the public sphere's *Ur*-anthropologist, the condensation symbol of both the properly "gone native" merchant of primitive wares and the con artist hawking false exotic merchandise.

And yet this mixture of adulation of and visceral repugnance against Mead is no recent popular invention. Inside academic anthropology, aside from a corps of long-term associates and defenders, Mead has long had fervent detractors, and for a congeries of unassorted reasons. Some male anthropologists have engaged, in the classic sexist move to discredit ambitious women, in depreciation of her personal appearance, as did a Berkeley professor in an introductory course in the mid-1970s. Looking for an easy laugh, he editorialized on a slide of the young Mead in Samoa, "She should have thought twice about adopting native dress with those legs." His own legs were not such as to bear the light of day, a point that the phalanx of female teaching assistants who visited him to protest his remark forbore from mentioning.

Then, many anthropologists have been made queasy by Mead's embrace of publicity. Clifford Geertz, for example, in his recent study of anthropological writing, *Works and Lives,* adds the less influential Ruth Benedict rather than Mead to his male triumvirate of Bronislaw Malinowski, Evans-Pritchard, and Claude Lévi-Strauss. He does so not only, I would contend, because he is thus able to include an American and a woman in his lineup while ignoring the issue of gender as an analytic category in anthropological history—Benedict's treatment of the topic, as we shall see, is highly mediated—but also because his ivory tower sensibility is not then offended by contact with the hoi polloi. (Although, in fact, Benedict sought publicity for her work, and her *Patterns of Culture* has sold millions of copies, she died a half-century ago. Her popularity is now sanitized through her status as a classic.)

Unable, however, actually to leave Mead alone, Geertz scatters a series of revealing swipes against her through his text: Mead is "inevitable," "larger-than-life," and exaggeratedly self-conscious; she is Benedict's "custodian" and "proprietor," who attempted "to incorporate [Benedict's] persona into her own" and whose work does not deserve to be read alongside that of her friend and former teacher. She has a "loose-limbed, improvisational style, saying seventeen things at once and marvellously adaptable to the passing thought," all of which mean, to Geertz, that she exemplifies "save-the-world anthropology."[26] While all of these characterizations except the last (Benedict was far more clearly politically engaged than Mead, in work and life) can be defended, what is noteworthy is Geertz's skirts-lifted distaste for Mead's contaminating public presence in anthropology. As I will demonstrate, this sense of unease with anthropological popularization has its own, extremely interesting historical contingency, one relating directly both to the changing political economy of the discipline and to unnoticed shifts in the American Fourth Estate and larger public sphere.

In fact, overcoming one's distaste for popular culture's tabloid versions of anthropological truths—and some anthropologists' engagement with them—long enough to analyze them in context is a key heuristic of this study. Here I try to steer an analytic course between the Scylla of our Frankfurt school inheritance of eyes-averted, pessimistic disgust with mass culture and the Charybdis of some more recent cultural studies practitioners' rather promiscuous embrace and celebration of the popular as pleasure and "resistance." Instead, I have been inspired by Stendhal's Lucien Leuwen, who, faced with the spectacle of an irrational, bullying, intransigent provincial aristocracy during France's post–Revolutionary Louis Phillipe regime, determined to "study them the way one studies natural history": "M. Cuvier used to tell us in the *Jardin des Plantes* that to study methodically, carefully noting down all the differences and resemblances, was the surest way of curing oneself of the repulsion that worms, insects, and hideous sea-crabs inspire."[27] Thus in the following pages I dissect the uses of anthropology as trope in a variety of popular and high-cultural genres—whether allegory, pastoral, morality play, or jeremiad. Representations may be literarily unpalatable, may be loose-limbed, may say seventeen things at once, may engender disgust in mandarin scholars—and yet may be politically consequential. And consequentiality is what must concern us.

Finally, many individuals have objected specifically to Mead's academic anthropology, and to her anthropological politics. Here I have benefited much from the work of others, but have come to my own rather heterodox conclusions. Contra her Boasian training and popular image as a liberal feminist, Mead's entire career, in fact, was based on the consistent efface- ment or sheer denial of American class, race, and gender stratification and of the sequelae of American and other capitalist imperialisms abroad. De- spite her sometime endorsement of progressive causes, Mead spent a half- century lecturing Americans and others on changing cultural patterns while sedulously avoiding dealing with the harsh realities of power, dis- crimination, oppression, exploitation. In this way, she centrally embodied the legacy of unconcern with the contours of power that Eric Wolf, a gener- ation ago, discerned as the hallmark of American anthropology.[28] And this legacy is directly connected to American anthropology's elision of political economy, an elision made necessary by its dominant historic reduction of human social reality to the narrow-compass notion of individual psycholo- gies, *mentalités*, writ large.

DIFFERENCE/POWER

The elision of historical political economy in anthropology, as in popular culture, has taken a dizzying kaleidoscope of forms over the American Century. Many of these incarnations reduce in the end, though, to the prob- lematic and enduring antinomy in Western thought between cultural dif- ference and the operations of power. Since the 1960s, we have seen a high culture/lowbrow split in anthropological expressions of this antinomy. Popular culture has taken over that product of Boasian anthropology, the notion of cultural relativism, and made it over into a vacuous and commer- cialized Disneyland-doll, Benetton-ad, *Family of Man* multiculturalism—a trope that works unceasingly against its own humanist intentions to veil the very processes of the enforcement of power. (Even this bowdlerized and seemingly inoffensive trope, as we shall see in the last chapter, has come in for wild attacks from the Right.)

High theory, on the other hand, has been inspired by Clifford Geertz's famous "linguistic turn" declaration that "the culture of a people is an ensemble of texts . . . which the anthropologist strains to read over the shoulders of those to whom they properly belong."[29] The process of anthro- pologizing then becomes, by extension, the "translation of culture," of the society-wide *mentalités* of Others, in effacement of contestations over meaning and thus power *among* those Others, and in neglect, as Talal Asad has pointed out, of the power-laden relations between the society from which the straining anthropologist comes and that whose text she attempts to read.[30] (Never mind, for the moment, the problematics involved when the two societies are one.)

Each vision of culture, whether high or low, *creates* the culture/power antinomy through its epistemic denial of the historical operations of power in apprehensions of cultural or biological difference, through turning its blind eye on the functioning of the White City, the Midway, Dempster Street. It is necessary, then, to recognize both terms of the trope, to avoid the reduction of human social reality to one pole or the other. (It is precisely the plumping for the "difference" pole that allows the counterempirical stance of contemporary cultural feminism, which further exacerbates our tendency to imagine that there is a singular, nonadjectival feminist stance.) It is especially important, in the current theoretical and political conjuncture, to overcome the too-common cultural studies declaration that, to paraphrase another aestheticizing idealist,

> "Culture is politics, politics culture"—that is all
> Ye know on earth, and all ye need to know.

Collapsing power into particularity in this manner leads to finding resistance in all the wrong places—most especially in cultural production—and thus to a failure really to come to terms with the changing contours of hegemony, the leitmotif of this study. Particular historical moments may allow "multiple public spheres," as when Ida B. Wells, Frederick Douglass, and many other Afro-Americans vigorously protested their exclusion from the Columbian Exposition's representations of American progress.[31] But protest and victory are not isomorphic, and the black protesters won then neither the representational war nor the return of Reconstruction civil rights. Celebration of their actions and productions—as in "expanding the canon" in humanities curricula—is obviously valuable, but can take us only so far. Denial of the triumph of fin de siècle imperialist racism, or of the recent solidification of the Right and its national and international entailments, prevents emancipatory analysis altogether. Only forthrightly investigating the hideous sea-crab of hegemony gives us the tools to prevent its reproduction in a world without end.

Representations are authorized inside the symbiotic relationship between official scholarship and popular interpretation, in the hidden trafficking between the White City and the Midway. This book is about the shadowed bridges between the two sites, the often unacknowledged relationship between vulgar popular political culture and high scholarship, and the collective human daily lives they join in depicting. As such, it takes decidedly partisan stands. In the first place, the "turn to language" that has so affected the academy over the past two decades has been salutary in some key ways. But it has also functioned as a Trojan horse, smuggling rigid idealisms, false intellectual histories, an evisceration of the political, and new rationales for shoddy scholarship into the groves of academe. In anthropology, for example, as I show in chapter 1, many postmodernists continue the tradition of earlier, less sophisticated colleagues in feeling perfectly free to expatiate on "American culture" in ignorance of much American history, sociology, economics, &c. Discourse analysis need not play this role, and does not in the work of those who retain a political economic vision. It is precisely the denial of political economy as "just another discarded Victorian grand narrative" that allows so much of the contemporary United States—and the world—to be hidden in plain sight.

Then, relatedly, following Marx and other nineteenth-century grand theorists, I argue that the writing of theory must be embodied in the empirical. In a little-noticed introductory section of her magisterial *Primate Visions*, Donna Haraway asserts the necessity of keeping the "four temptations"—positivism, Marxism, feminism/antiracism, and poststructuralism—in tension with one another, without allowing any one of these epistemological frames to silence the others.[32] In the contemporary progressive academy, the last two temptations speak most frequently, their loud voices often drowning out the vital contributions of the realist and Marxist traditions. The way, for example, out of the "race-class-gender conundrum" is not the coinage of ever more abstract theoretical neologisms, nor a series of clever but uncontextualized readings of popular cultural artifacts, but the enactment of theory in empirically detailed, hands-on historical and contemporary studies—studies that may "front stage" one or two phenomena but always allow the others room in the script. I try to practice the stagecraft I preach in each of the following chapters.

Finally, I hope to accomplish a paradoxical task with reference to anthropology itself. I write largely about cultural anthropology, but, unlike many recent commentators, from the perspective of ethnography's historical embeddedness in the other three epistemic frames of the American "four fields"—physical anthropology, archaeology, and linguistic anthropology. I want to draw rigorous attention to the discipline as a gathering place (for good and ill) of particular concerns—"human nature," cultural "difference," ethnic "resurgence," "tribalism," multiculturalism, the "origins" of asymmetric gender relations—central to national and global politics in this century. In the following pages, I appear both as defender and fierce critic of my disciplinary guild. I underline the importance of the ethnographic, culture-sensitive eye to social analysis, at home and abroad, and at the same time try to kill the Frankenstein monster—to focus away from certain overly valued anthropological visions and to showcase other, more compelling ones. But I also attempt to "dissolve" anthropology, to escape guild-bound solipsism, the poisoned heritage of turn-of-the-century disciplinary imperialisms, into the larger ground of responsible interdisciplinary scholarship, into the rebirth of the unified nineteenth-century political economy from which our balkanized social sciences and humanities descended. Such an escape and such a practice are, after all, the aspirations if not always the accomplishments of women's studies, race scholarship, and American and cultural studies. In fact, in ironic parallel to the plight of organized labor at home, we live and work in an America suffused with "anthropology without anthropologists," and would do well to be honest about the paradoxical implications for practitioners with—and without— the union card designating that most imperialist and imperialized of scholarly fields.

I have thus written a work of "blurred genres" not as an escape from a troubled discipline, nor as a solipsistic technique for creating textual *jouissance*, but in the belief that the simultaneous engagement here of cultural criticism, historical political economy, intellectual history, and ethnography does the work of making a cogent argument and documenting its empirical rationale. Finally, in analyzing representations, I focus more on texts than graphic art and film. I do so not because literature is necessarily more important than these other media, but because it has been, for these purposes, far less well studied.

I have begun this book on my current home ground, and the 1893 Chicago exposition, the long ideological arm of the Chicago School with its visions of American modernity steeped in social ecology, and contemporary local urban and suburban life make that starting point particularly appropriate. But as Robert Rydell points out, world's fairs of the Gilded Age and Progressive Era were staged all over the United States as well as Europe. They took place in slightly different historical eras, they responded to local political economies and racial demographics, but they all picked up and extended the same thread of imperialist racism. Similarly, there were and are widely varying ethnological antimodernisms. *Women Who Run with the Wolves* is not *Das Mutterrecht*. There is no necessary contradiction between regional and temporal grounding and detail and sweeping national and transhistorical analysis. Each, in fact, can enhance the other. The following chapters are arranged slightly out of chronology in furtherance of analytic clarity: beginning in the present with a nailing-the-theses-to-the-church-door bastinado, then working in successive recuperative loops across the century to return to the starting point. They by no means exhaust their topics, but instead hover at abstract levels or zoom down to detailed analyses in the process of building an overall synthetic argument. They are based on close readings of texts in political and historical context; on local and national primary sources; on ethnographic research in the Midwest, in the West, and on the East Coast; on much "exotic" anthropological and historical work; and on a wealth of excellent Americanist work across the disciplines. As the end of this century approaches, with its alarming political parallels to the last, I hope that they help to counter contemporary hegemonies, to work against dominant structures of feeling on Dempster Street, on the Midway, and in the White City, to disclose not an "other" America, but the one right before our eyes.

one

ANTHROPOLOGY AND
AMERICAN MORALITY PLAYS

Who is the Proust of the Papuans? The Tolstoy of the Zulus?—*Saul Bellow*

Bring out number, weight & measure in a year of dearth.—*William Blake*[1]

"L'hai trovato la tua America" runs the Italian immigrant-era saying. You have found your America, your golden fleece, your cornucopia. And in a similar Columbian flurry of recognitions and effacements, of discoveries that deny prior residencies, recent American popular culture celebrates anthropology's "turn" to research at home.

Business Week, for example, announces that anthropologists are now "Studying Natives on the Shop Floor": "American business is suddenly finding a more practical use for this largely academic pursuit. To help cut costs and improve competitiveness, companies are employing anthropologists to study the interactions and working habits of the natives down in the factory, or even in middle and upper management. Where Margaret Mead went to Samoa six decades ago, anthropologists today are heading for places like Detroit and New York."[2]

The *New York Times*, less interested in profit margins and more concerned with the middlebrow's "big picture," repeats the Margaret Mead cliché while adding inferential history: anthropologists are now turning "us" into "natives" because decolonized Third World states make it harder for them to do research, and because progressively lazier ethnographers no longer want to endure the rigors of the bush.

By studying other societies, Western anthropologists have sought to derive lessons about their own, as Dr. Margaret Mead did in her classic 1928 study, "Coming of Age in Samoa." In a significant new trend, some anthropologists in this country are focusing on coming of age here at home, using the same methods of ethnography they would apply in an exotic land. . . . The new effort casts anthropology in the role of cultural critic, able to examine and lay bare the hidden assumptions that shape the main institutions of American culture. . . . Conveniently, in a day when tight money and hostile regimes make it more difficult for anthropologists to study people in distant and often discomfiting places, the new approach allows them to ply their trade amid the comforts of home.[3]

Or, from the *Times Book Review,* a more snide example with an Alexandrian imperial reference:

Pity the poor anthropologist. She has trekked the highlands, machetied the jungles, sifted the sands for new tribes to study. But the Ik have been exposed, the Tasaday tallied. What's left? Increasingly, today's would-be Meads and Benedicts are turning in their bush jackets for tweeds, for some easy poking around in their own backyards—where, lo and behold, they unearth practices as alien to Western norms as any found in the heart of New Guinea.[4]

This trope has become almost race memory for reviewers, witness a *Nation* writer's unconscious mimicry eight years later: "Pity the poor anthropologist. The ceaseless progress of capitalism across the globe has nearly eliminated the last remains of 'primitive' societies, the assigned subject of the field, forcing its practitioners either to become students of the modernization process or to do their fieldwork in 'modern' society itself."[5]

In a survey piece, the *Chronicle of Higher Education* trumpets, "Many Anthropologists Spurn Exotic Sites to Work Territory Closer to Home": "Cultural anthropologists have long been expected to do work in exotic, faraway sites. . . . Serious anthropologists trekked to distant places like Micronesia or Nepal. They considered American culture too neat and too familiar, hardly worth studying."[6]

Some popular media play with anthropologists' liminal, quasi-primitive symbolic status to reverse "traditional" images of ethnographer and native, as in a *Chicago Sun-Times* story: "Adorning themselves with jackets of tweed or gaily colored beads, puffing on elaborately carved pipes, ears pierced and decorated with rings, members of a national tribe are holding their potlatch in Chicago this week. . . . Once anthropologists focused their ethnographies on tiny tribes in South America. Today they are just as likely to study bowling leagues or Cub Scout packs or bridge groups."[7]

There is only one problem with this picture: anthropology's America wasn't born yesterday. It is not simply, for example, that anthropologist Lucy Suchman, who is profiled in a 1991 *New York Times* article on the "recent" anthropological hires in American corporations, began working at Xerox twelve years earlier. (And on the West Coast, corporate hiring dates at least back to the mid-1970s.)[8] Nor is the issue as transparent as pointing out that contemporary popular cultural accounts of anthropology's "sudden" United States focus ignore the florescence of Americanist urban anthropology in the 1960s and 1970s, wiping from history the best-selling work of Oscar Lewis (on whom the *New York Times* published a three-column obituary in 1971) and that of James Spradley, Charles and BettyLou Valentine, John Gwaltney, Americo Paredes, John Szwed, Carol Stack, Eleanor Leacock, Ulf Hannerz, and Elliot Liebow.[9] Popular culture, in fact, has effaced its own history: In 1974, *Time* magazine "discovered" that "the gimmick is that anthropologists, after decades of following Margaret Mead to Samoa and Bronislaw Malinowski to the Trobriand Islands, have staked out new territory—the nonexotic cities and rural byways of the U.S. . . . U.S. anthropology, it seems, must recognize that the primary tribe to study is the Americans."[10] The weight and progressive political implications of that era's American work (and research on cities in the Third World) were sufficient to sting Robin Fox in 1973 to the extraordinarily antiempirical and racist comment that contemporary urban anthropology was the "undignified scramble to find substitute savages in slums."[11]

But Fox was also wrong about the recency of urban anthropology. British urban anthropological research in southern Africa dates from the 1930s—can one scramble for four decades? And then the American Chicago School (among whom it is impossible to distinguish anthropologists from sociologists without a scorecard) of Lewis Wirth, Ernest Burgess, W. I. Thomas, Lloyd Warner, E. Franklin Frazier, Charles Johnson, Allison Davis, Harvey Zorbaugh, Horace Cayton, St. Clair Drake, and others was nearly entirely urban and began in the 1910s. That makes a more than half-century "scramble." Urban or not, the titans of both American and British anthropology were and are involved in self-study. The most well-known British work is Elizabeth Bott's 1957 network study, and although Michael Young and Peter Willmott of *Family and Kinship in East London* fame were sociologists, they had studied with anthropologist Raymond Firth. Firth himself published the London-based *Families and Their Relatives* in 1969. Max Gluckman and his students put out *Closed Systems and Open Minds*, based on 1957 work, in 1964. And Marilyn Strathern in 1981 finished and published Audrey Richards's 1962 village study, *Kinship at the Core*.[12]

On this side of the Atlantic, beyond the continuous flood of texts on Native Americans from the mid–nineteenth century on, Franz Boas himself, Zora Neale Hurston, Robert Lowie, Ralph Linton, Paul Radin, Hortense Powdermaker, Elsie Clews Parsons, and even Margaret Mead did Americanist work and commented on the American scene long prior to World War II—when there were fewer than two hundred Ph.D. anthropologists in the country.[13] Despite this fact, Clyde Kluckhohn in 1950 was moved to comment on what he saw as a brand-new phenomenon. "Anthropology," he declared, "has returned from the natives. . . . Some anthropologists are undoubtedly a bit intoxicated by the heady wine of a little power over the here and now, for, until recently, they had drunk only the chaste nectar of detached contemplation of the long ago and far away."[14]

Nor has this anthropological scholarship on the United States been so recondite as to be known only to specialists. When George and Louise Spindler started the Holt, Rinehart and Winston series "Case Studies in Cultural Anthropology," a group of thin, photo-rich course-adoption ethnographic paperbacks in 1960, they included two United States non–Native American studies in their list of twenty-eight. By 1970 the tally was fourteen of eighty-seven, and the proportion has wavered between 14 and 25 percent in the years since. When George Spindler in 1970 chose authors from the series to write first-person accounts for *Being an Anthropologist: Fieldwork in Eleven Cultures,* he found Lincoln Keiser's narrative of work among a Chicago gang and John Hostetler and Gertrude Huntington's story of research on Hutterites to be integral to delineating the profession.[15] There is, then, no such thing as American anthropology's "turn" to work in the United States. Quite simply, anthropology has always been at home in America.

And yet Robin Fox is by no means alone as an anthropologist in complicity with popular culture's repeated "discovery" of newly self-studying ethnographers. Historian of anthropology George Stocking claims "a distinguishing feature of modern anthropology" to be "participant-observation," which he defines as "entering as a stranger into a *small and culturally alien* community" (my emphasis). Clifford Geertz, arguably the contemporary American anthropologist most intellectually influential outside the profession, ended his 1983 "Distinguished Lecture" to the American Anthropological Association, "If we wanted home truths, we should have stayed at home." And lest we imagine that Geertz was merely playing with metaphor, his 1988 *Works and Lives* has chapters jokily titled "Being There" and "Being Here," referring respectively to field site and academic and social home. For Geertz, as for Stocking, anthropology, despite abundant evidence to the contrary, is definable solely as "engaging others where they are and representing them where they aren't."[16]

This effacement of anthropology's actual historical engagement with the United States allows the definition of anthropologists as specialists only on "exotics" abroad—"merchants of astonishment," Geertz labels his colleagues, just as Clyde Kluckhohn boasted in the 1940s that anthropologists were all "eccentrics" "interested in bizarre things." Like other falsifying histories, this narrative performs multiple functions for varying interested parties. In fact, this fundamental denial of actual history is integral to the growing character of the discipline as the symbolic shatterbelt of contemporary American political tensions and debates, as an important element of modernist and antimodernist arguments in the American public sphere.[17]

Certainly, as we shall see, anthropology as trope has long been an element of American cultural baggage. Progressive Era novelist Edith Wharton, for example, has her male protagonist in the 1913 novel *The Custom of the Country* label his relatives "the Aborigines," and likened them to "those vanishing denizens of the American continent doomed to rapid extinction. . . . He was fond of describing Washington Square as the 'Reservation,' and of prophesying that before long its inhabitants would be exhibited at ethnological shows, pathetically engaged in the exercise of their primitive industries." In the later *Age of Innocence,* Wharton envisions Newland Archer feeling that his in-laws are showing him off "like a wild animal cunningly trapped" and, shocked at his reaction, supposing "that his readings in anthropology caused him to take such a coarse view of what was after all a simple and natural demonstration of family feeling."[18] Wharton's references to social evolutionary theories of primitive life, however, are made as much to evoke the earlier era in which the novels take place as for any other purpose. More current uses of the discipline tend to be much more obviously political.

This delineation of the contemporary and recent past's multiply layered and chiasmic "anthropology's America, America's anthropology" reaches beyond currently modish disciplinary solipsism. The analysis that follows is not about anthropology for anthropology's sake, but for the purpose of "finding America"—and the rest of the world—within and behind the representations of Dempster Street, the White City, and the Midway.

A DISCIPLINE IN DRAG

Central to the icon's construction is the traditional slippage of identities among anthropology's objects of study: "primitives" (cultural anthropology), prehistoric populations (archaeology), and monkeys and apes (primatology). In too much past and present scholarship, and ubiquitously in the public mind, the past is not another country. Rather, other societies and species are *our* (white, Western) past. Anthropologists then become the specialists on, in Eric Wolf's phrase, "people without history," human (and even nonhuman primate) populations that exist not in their own stream of time and change, but simply to embody our prehistory. Michel-Rolph Trouillot names the discursive location we have been assigned "the savage slot."[19] This social evolutionism, which dominated Victorian social thought, and which was resoundingly rejected by anthropologists on both sides of the Atlantic in the early decades of this century, keeps turning up like a bad penny in too many—but by no means all—popular and anthropological visions of the discipline's past and present. Bernard Cohn delineates the model in which "the anthropologist posits a place where the natives are authentic, untouched and aboriginal, and strives to deny the central historical fact that the people he or she studies are constituted in the historically significant colonial situation, affirming that they are somehow out of time and history."[20]

Thus, the most common American lay reaction to an individual identifying herself as an anthropologist, that she must "go on digs"—much remarked upon in-house—makes perfect sense. (Despite its minority status in the field as a whole, about three-quarters of all *New York Times* anthropology stories from 1930 to the present focus on archaeology alone.) Johannes Fabian has commented with some acerbity on this phenomenon: "I am surely not the only anthropologist who, when he identifies himself as such to his neighbor, barber, or physician, conjures up visions of a distant past. When popular opinion identifies all anthropologists as handlers of bones and stones it is not in error; it grasps the essential role of anthropology as a provider of temporal distance."[21]

When American University anthropologist Brett Williams responded to one such layperson, "No, I study real live people," her confused interlocutor exclaimed, "What? You dig up *live people?*"[22] A clearer-sighted respondent's alternative guess retains the pith helmet and simply switches from the past in the past to the past in the present: "So you're like Margaret Mead—you study primitive people." Neolithic tribes, Stone Age people, ancient customs, barbaric rituals—the "provider of temporal distance" will give you access to this measure of your modern selfhood.

This provision of access, as well, carries a religious connotation. As George Stocking has documented, nineteenth-century anthropology's debates began as frankly theological exercises and continued, for many, as a "substitutionary atonement"—with scientific taking the place of religious revelations. E. B. Tylor, the first labeled professor of anthropology at Oxford, wrote anonymously,

> Theologians all to expose,
> 'Tis the *mission* of Primitive Man.[23]

Christopher Herbert argues that in fact the epistemological frame of Wesleyan Methodism "was invested with so much affective and imaginative power . . . that it could hardly be purged altogether." Late-Victorian ethnographic theories of culture then appear as "insidious refigurings of these very principles and as reinscriptions of the moral rhetoric which they specifically claim to banish."[24]

And indeed, archaeologists, biological, and cultural anthropologists appear particularly in the American popular imagination as marked, in the linguistic sense, by the religious origins of their discipline. Fieldwork or the dig—even life among "innocent" gorillas or chimps—takes on the aura of a religious pilgrimage; the process of "culture shock" is framed as the rebirth of the soul. The returning anthropologist is often regarded, and may regard herself, as having gained charisma—and, like a prophetic figure, as having the right, with or without furnishing empirical evidences, to proffer new behavioral commandments. David Riesman, for example, in 1964 commended Laura Bohannan's *Return to Laughter* as a "kind of modern *Pilgrim's Progress*" and compassionated her "emotional hegira" among the Nigerian Tiv. More recently, in a classic "call the witch doctor" move, a frustrated corporate executive reported to *Personnel Journal*, "We were stuck. So at one meeting, I said, 'We've tried everything else, why not bring in an anthropologist?'"[25]

Like the "paradoxical double image of savagery,"[26] though, the anthropologist as evangelist might also be a false prophet, a seducee of the Devil rather than Divinity. "Going native" can mean, in this context, "giving in to the worst." Tabloid newspapers, lacking subtlety, express this view most succinctly: "A noted anthropologist has given up his job, home and family to join a tribe of bloodthirsty South American cannibals."[27] Shades of Conrad in the supermarket. And as anthropology is more than ever in the public sphere—both at the behest of some practitioners and as a result of deliberate abductions—anthropologists more than ever wear multiple black and white hats in popular and middlebrow discourse. The next stage, in fact, can only be the establishment of standard "anthropologist" Halloween costumes to join "beatnik," "fairy," "ghost," and "witch."

But how many costumes would be needed? Because of their key position as quasi-religious "clinching" figures brought on stage by various producers of long-running American morality plays—and the fact that narratives of modern American selfhood always, finally, hook into some notion of *Ur*-human nature based on a vision of primitive/past life—anthropologists could now command the full-time labors of a wardrobe mistress. As Christopher Hill has remarked of the Bible in seventeenth-century Britain, "It was a huge bran-tub from which anything might be drawn."[28] Consider the following lucky dips of popular and scholarly anthropological roles demanding appropriate raiment, which can be organized according to their positive, neutral, or negative valuation of anthropologist and "primitive." (Of course, in taxonomizing this cultural field I simplify the pragmatics of use in which elements of individual costumes, in life as in fashion, may be combined for strategic use.) These characterizations, as well, are not just integral to the denial of Americanist anthropology. Nor are they simply annoying popular misconstructions of scholarly work, or merely occasions for banal contemplation of ourselves in the mirror of the Other. No, the function of anthropological drag in the public sphere is fundamentally political.[29] That is, these costumes are elements of structures of feeling in use to "find" particular Americas—to organize accommodation to or protest against contemporary stratifications by race, class, gender, and nationality. They are fighting words and images.

Noble Savage, Noble Anthropologist: Ethnographers as Technicians of the Sacred[30]

Contemporary ethnological antimodernism has been in the making since the 1960s and bears the marks of four major political debates of our era— American racism at home and imperialism abroad; the environmental crisis; women's status and aspirations; and the American "crisis of meaning," including the role of religion and irrational experience in a secular, rationalist state, and concern over social inequality. Primitives, whether "there" or "here," appear in these arguments (but rarely all at once) as our innocent victims who themselves are nonviolent and cooperative; as people who live in harmony with nature, the "original ecologists"; as practitioners of sexual equality or even female rule; and as custodians of ancient religions that "work" and that include a role for ecstatic (and possibly drug-enhanced) experience.

Our role as modern Westerners, then, is to let primitives teach us their "tribal wisdom"—and incidentally to stop killing them off and destroying their homelands, as that will cut off our supplies (and latterly—because it

6. North State Street, Chicago. (Photo by the author.)

will destroy the global environment). Anthropologists are the go-betweens in this process, the time travelers who return from pilgrimage with comparative ratings of quality ethnological commodities so that we can buy our salvation as informed consumers. As if to underwrite this point, Urban Outfitters now runs a line, and a chain of stores, featuring "casual, vaguely ethnic, sort of rustic" clothing, crafts, and furniture labeled "Anthropologie."[31]

Consider Colin Turnbull's popular 1961 ethnography of Congolese (then Zairean, now again Congolese) Pygmies who "are infinitely wise and who taught me something of their wisdom . . . their intense love for the forest and their belief that it is better and kinder than the outside world that threatens to destroy it."[32] Then there is Carlos Castañeda's string of best-selling fictions, beginning in 1968 with *The Teachings of Don Juan: A Yaqui Way of Knowledge*. Castañeda, who received an anthropology Ph.D. from the University of California at Los Angeles, claimed to have apprenticed himself to the cryptic and elusive Don Juan, to have taken hallucinogenic drugs under his direction, and to have returned with a "fragment of Don Juan's teachings" about "becoming a man of knowledge."[33] Then there is the "discovery" of the Filipino Tasaday, a world press sensation—the *New York Times* alone ran thirteen stories on them in 1971–73—who were reported to have lived in Stone Age isolation and to be so gentle that they had no word for war.[34]

The most blatant recent example of the commodification of the noble savage and anthropological midwife, though, is the *Millennium* phenomenon. *Millennium: Tribal Wisdom and the Modern World* is Harvard anthropologist David Maybury-Lewis's book and Public Broadcasting series, which is underwritten in part by Anita Roddick's corporate empire, The Body Shop.[35] Roddick based a major advertising campaign on her benevolence and on her (ecologically sound) employment of rain forest Indians to provide raw materials for her cosmetics. The Body Shop catalog makes it clear that the tribal wisdom indigenous peoples have to offer includes profitable beauty tips: "While travelling through Sri Lanka, Anita noticed that local women rubbed their faces with pineapple . . . Voila! Pineapple Facial Wash! . . . The Body Shop developed Mamatoto, our impressive collection of mother and baby products, by studying pregnancy and childbirth practices from many cultures." The catalog also offers *Millennium*, "this big, beautiful hard-cover book, complete with over 100 pages of gorgeous color photographs." The Public Broadcasting System goes one step further in its catalog ad for the video: "Sex, love, work, play, art, spirit—the fabulous panorama of human life brought to you in *Millennium*. . . . At the threshold of the third millennium, the humanity of tribal values may be the only hope for the future."[36]

Maybury-Lewis's vision of contemporary small-scale societies fits this "salvation through consuming the primitive" model well. Although his text bristles with caveats (he even has a critical section on the eighteenth-century construction of the noble savage), his portrayal homogenizes quite varying populations; pulls them out of their own complicated histories of Western colonialism and intercultural contact and hostilities; and offers them up to us as cooperative, unalienated, ecological, and sexually egalitarian actors to plug into our salvationist play: "By examining the roads they took that we did not, we can get a better insight into the choices we ourselves make, the price we pay for them, and the possibilities of modifying them."[37] As T. O. Beidelman insightfully complains, "Reviewing the film series *Millennium*, a writer for the *New York Times* remarked that seeing it was like doing penance. In fact, reading the book is a comparably glum experience, like being preached glib sermons oblivious to problematical experience."[38]

And what is more glib and sermonic in contemporary American life than prescriptive literature on health and diet? Here as well we see the primitive invoked as the romantic exemplar of correct living from which we have departed, with disastrous results. Marjorie Shostak (of *Nisa* fame), her husband Melvin Konner, a medical anthropologist, and S. Boyd Eaton published *The Paleolithic Prescription* (*The Stone Age Health Programme* in Britain) in 1988 as a "plan for recapturing certain features of our ancestors' lives." Even prior to this work, *New York Times* food and health columnist Jane Brody made use of some anthropologists' work which collapsed archaeological evidence with that from some contemporary foragers to proclaim "dietary lessons from human evolution . . . modern tribes eat mostly plant foods."[39]

Tell that to the Eskimos. But collapsing wildly differing societies in one mushy "tribal" image is the least of the intellectual confusions of the "technicians of the sacred" construct. Whether it encompasses all "primitives" or simply one population, it presumes that contemporary human beings are literally living in the past, that cultural anthropologists *correctly* provide temporal distance. But whether described by others in 1928 or 1954 or the 1990s, "primitives" have all lived as many years in the stream of history as have "civilized" populations. They may have low levels of technology, and they may have very small populations. Those factors do not imply, however, "simpler" societies or "more direct" lives "more in touch with nature." They certainly do not prove higher levels of spirituality (negative interpretation: superstition) or lower levels of rationality (positive interpretation: nonlinear thinking) than among "us." Nor, as we shall see, can we say in any meaningful way that "primitive women" have it better (or worse) than the rest of us.

The one provable fact about "primitives" across many populations is precisely the point that the assertion of their temporal distance from us disallows: that they have been, and are, entangled on the losing ends of the varying institutions of international political economy. Whether individuals or groups are dealing with the Brazilian state, the United Nations, or Anita Roddick, with the Australian court system or tourists from all over the world, with anthropologists, art dealers, or New Age types eager to cash in on Primitive Wisdom, they simply have less power and fewer resources than their interlocutors—and often because of their interlocutors' ancestors' depredations.[40] Anthropological assertions of the moral worth, the charisma of these groups may help, in some cases, to ameliorate current exploitation or expropriation; in others, to enhance their abilities to sell themselves and their wares. Such assertions do not, however, help us raise awareness of or protest against the larger world system that expands the gulf between haves and have-nots with each passing year. Since they hinge on notions of primitive authenticity as well, they also function to delegitimate further the human rights and innate interest of the vast mass of the globe's population, which is spread across despoiled countrysides, shanty-towns, and inner cities. The noble savage is a character in the drama of the Fall, and while "we" strut on that stage as post-Adamic seekers, we can find our redemption through antimodernist engagement with the not-yet-fallen. There is no role, save that of the Devil, for the desperate, "inauthentic" world's poor caught as pawns in the internationalization of capital and labor.

Of course, the primitive's anthropological midwife is not always needed. Mass media and salvationist hucksters can often induce labor on their own. Witness the immensely successful 1972 Advertising Council's antipollution "crying Indian" commercial and poster, which rely on inducing environmental guilt in Americans through the use of homogenizing and romantic notions of Native Americans' benign stewardship of the land.[41] Or there is the more recent and equally romantic film *Dances with Wolves*. Preliberation South Africa contributed the comedy *The Gods Must Be Crazy*, which portrayed the !Kung San—a population with a complicated and politically fraught position—as Rousseauian natural people.[42]

Then, finally, there is the prescriptive New Age genre, which sells one-hundred-proof ethnological antimodernism without overmuch worry about bothersome ethnographic facts. A stroll down Dempster Street, or indeed, through any chain bookstore, reveals commodities like *Sacred Path Cards: The Discovery of the Self through Native Teachings*. The feminist Great Goddess subset of this genre has evolved from the angry, political 1970s texts like *When God Was a Woman* and *The First Sex*—which were concerned with institutional power for women, however batty their notions of prehistory. The current plethora of titles, instead, like the dreadful women's self-help literature of which they are a part, admonish women not to challenge the outer world, but to get in touch with the goddess within, through learning from one or more types of female noble savage—of the "correct" race/ethnicity, of course.

Lynn Andrews, for example, who offers expensive "shamanic initiation

7. 1970s Technician of the Sacred: the Crying Indian. (By permission of Keep America Beautiful, Inc.)

seminars" and has published eight books (she is so popular that chain bookstores have whole shelves labeled for her) detailing her claimed apprenticeship to Native American, Australian, and Japanese female shamans, writes: "I'm spending my life writing about my experiences with ancient women that are part of the sisterhood. My work has to do with becoming a bridge between the primal mind and white consciousness: we as a people . . . have lost our sense of Mother Earth and Nature. . . . [We need to] learn about a high art that has enabled indigenous people to live in harmony on this planet for over 10,000 years." This high art involves, for example, learning "how to prepare your body and energy field to work with crystals" and undertaking "a ceremony for finding and dancing your power animal."[43] It is no accident that her jacket blurbs compare Andrews to Carlos Castañeda. She has polished his profitable 1970s multibook formula into a 1990s snake-oil empire.

Even travel agents have gotten into the act. The "On the Trail of the

Great Goddess" tour of Turkey, home of ancient "matriarchal" societies, claims to be "particularly appealing for those interested in women's spirituality, ancient religions, and the role of women in history and in society." They offer "opportunities to connect with the Goddess in her many forms," although, as they note that one of these forms "brings death," this gives the brochure an inadvertently Agatha Christie-ish character.[44]

But there is nothing inadvertent in the evocation of Christie's world in the second major anthropological costume mode:

Nasty Savage, Noble Anthropologist: Shadows of Forgotten Imperialisms

In this role, anthropologists wear the pith helmet with a vengeance. The Other is terminally orientalized—a proven inferior who must be forced to cooperate in studying his or her own present or past, an exotic individual who, in the aggregate, can provide the mise-en-scène for an infinite series of dramas of modern Western selfhood. Anthropologists participate in this "colonial chic" or "imperialist nostalgia," as the phenomenon has been labeled, as archetypes of tough, smart colonials who know how to handle the natives, who can return from the Heart of Darkness unscathed but also have a higher calling beyond administration of the empire—the correct rape of the Other for treasure/knowledge. "That thing", exclaims Indiana Jones of the lost ark, "represents everything we got into archaeology for in the first place!"[45] And Dian Fossey, in *Gorillas in the Mist* (and in real life), protected innocent apes, our stainless cousins and the repositories of priceless scientific information, from "evil African poachers." Ivan Karp and Corinne Kratz note that a recent traveling exhibition on African gorillas represents Africans, even African children, as voracious, evilly proliferating threats to the true Africans—wildlife. So much for the primitive as natural environmentalist.[46]

Of course, anthropologists are often dispensable characters in this "last macho raiders" script, which is really just a modern subset of Edward Said's Western imperial structure of feeling. In *Romancing the Stone,* Michael Douglas plays a rifle-toting hippie entrepreneur, fluent in Spanish, wise to the ways of Colombian wogs, who reads the treasure map, courts the female lead, dispatches a number of superfluous Latin Americans, and experiences spiritual renewal, all in 106 minutes. The list of films includes *Out of Africa, Passage to India, The Flame Trees of Thika*—or, for the less pretentious imperialist, Stallone's endless series of low-rent morality plays on steroids.[47]

And then of course, colonial chic *sells,* as witness the Banana Republic chain store phenomenon, in which make-believe safari and bush wear are purveyed in make-believe safari and bush (my last sighting was a jeep "broken down" in desert sand). The Bombay Company offers mahogany-veneer furniture, bibelots, and pictures imitating the look of a retired Indian Service officer's cottage in Surrey. The latest entry in the lists of selling blatant, unashamed imperialist nostalgia, and old money, though, is the J. Peterman catalog—one edition of which unashamedly labels itself "Booty, Spoils & Plunder":

> Buffet supper at Masai Mara. Out of the bush comes Grace in that singular, civilized dress . . .

> . . . this is silk *twill:* the same weave used not only in the uniforms of British officers in India . . .

> It was the last summer before income taxes. A young man stood facing the sea, with all the 75-room cottages of Newport behind him . . .

> There, in the distant sub-Himalayan hill stations . . .

> Between the years 1906 and 1939, a trickle, then a light rainfall, then a downpour, of Englishmen, Germans, Scots, and some remarkable women, began to fall upon the immense gorgeous plateau of East Africa. . . . It was paradise. It lasted three decades. There will never be anything else like it again.[48]

Many other social types, then, can play the anthropological imperialist role.

And a good thing too. Because whether we consider American or British popular films, Christie's 1930s archaeologists in the Middle East (her husband, Max Mallowan, was one such and provided her with the model and the exotic locales), or Kipling's wise ethnologist character, Creighton, in *Kim,* precursors and contemporary images all partake of the past, for the simple reason that little in contemporary anthropological writing fits the model.[49] Certainly it is true, however, that many still-read anthropological classics provide rich costuming for contemporary imperialist nostalgia. Edward Evan Evans-Pritchard (whose *Nuer* certainly rivals Bronislaw Malinowski's *Argonauts of the Western Pacific* as most classic ethnography), was, as Clifford Geertz concedes, "possessed (as he certainly was, and even defiantly) of a colonial mentality."[50] Laura Bohannan's 1954 anthropological novel, *Return to Laughter,* which quickly became and has remained a standard American classroom introductory text, is literally structured by colonialist nostalgia—the neophyte egalitarian American's admiration for colonial British sang-froid and infinite knowledge of the ways of the bush:

> Then the carriers began to sing, and my momentary depression vanished. Seeing them file down the path, boxes on their heads, made me feel like something out of an old explorer's book. . . . My relief lasted only through the soup.

Then I realized that there was a slit between the thatch and the veranda wall and that, in the lamplight, I was fully displayed. Impervious to the stares of natives, generations of empire-building Englishmen in jungles and deserts have sat down in full evening dress to eat their custard and tinned gooseberries. An American like myself can only feel that she has been somehow tricked into going on a picnic in high heels.

Bohannan not only longs to embody a colonialist British anthropological character; she believes that she is narrating "the sea change in oneself that comes from immersion in another and savage culture," and incidentally proving that there is such a thing: "'Quite.' My voice was as cold as my heart, and, as always seemed to happen here when I was deeply upset, I spoke English. 'Quite. Typical peasant humor, but I am not a peasant, and you are a bunch of savages.'"[51]

But for some, it is both the savage and the anthropologist who are Other, who together threaten the West with certain decline, who are the

Barbarians at the Gates

When Saul Bellow asks rhetorically, "Who is the Proust of the Papuans? The Tolstoy of the Zulus?" he defines the non-West, through its failure to produce "great art," as innately inferior, unworthy of equal rights or respect. (The argument, of course, parallels the old "Where are the great women artists?" chestnut so well answered by twentieth-century feminists.)[52] In his best-selling *Closing of the American Mind*, Bellow's friend and political ally, the late Allan Bloom, completes the thought with its anthropological link:

> Sexual adventurers like Margaret Mead and others who found America too narrow told us that not only must we know other cultures and learn to respect them, but we could also profit from them. We could follow their lead and loosen up, liberating ourselves from the opinion that our taboos are anything other than social constraints. We could go to the bazaar of cultures and find reinforcement for inclinations that are repressed by puritanical guilt feelings. All such teachers of openness had either no interest in or were actively hostile to the Declaration of Independence.[53]

Note Bloom's unconscious evocation, in "the bazaar of cultures," of the Chicago Columbian Exposition's Midway, a ghostly presence just around the corner from his University of Chicago office. For Bloom, anthropologists and those they are presumed to study and uphold are first among equals in the evil attempted takeover of academe by social sciences and history: "Philosophy, not history or anthropology, is the most important human science. . . . Anthropologists have tended to . . . be susceptible to infatuations with experiments tending to correct or replace liberal democracy."[54]

Others, as well, have objected to anthropology's contaminating offerings of inferior, non-Western cultural materials. This rooted distaste, in fact, seems to crop up particularly among conservative classicists (not necessarily a redundancy). One writes that "scholars of the early 20th century . . . taking their cue from anthropology . . . stressed the otherness of the ancient world, viewing the Greeks as alien, primitive and bizarre," noting thankfully the demise of such interpretations. Another claims that classicists "of an anthropological turn have ascribed peculiar attributes to Homer's heroes: they had no selves and no souls, they were not agents and made no decisions; one scholar has even urged, in a memorable moment of folly, that Homeric men had no bodies." In a wonderfully effete, unconscious echoing of Dante's treatment of ancient Greeks in the *Inferno* as "noble pagans"—not to mention their place on the Victorian social evolutionary scale—he approves a vision in which "Greeks are not Trobriand Islanders, nor yet are they Fellows of Balliol; they are betwixt and between."[55]

One need not be an aggrieved right-wing novelist or classicist to engage in such sleights of logic. A reviewer for the *Chicago Tribune,* blaming "popular sociology" but obviously meaning anthropology, complains bitterly about visions of "distant and vaguely described 'other cultures' where the sexes are more equal and where child-rearing is 'shared,'" which prevent us from focusing on family values in America.[56]

The "barbarians at the gates" formulation, then, concerns more than sour grapes at the collapse of enrollments in university classics and philosophy courses, or annoyance that now one is being asked to read Lady Murasaki, Ibn Khaldūn, Garcia Marquez, and Chinua Achebe as well as Plato, Shakespeare, Dickens, Proust, Tolstoy, and Bellow. It is specifically political, ruling out of order the notion of the equal humanity, the equal rights, the equally intrinsic interest, of non-Western populations. ("Forget the Pygmies!" exclaimed a political theorist to me in a 1980s feminist reading group. "Now let's get back to Plato.") In this argument, anthropologists join with liberal humanists as wimpy multiculturalists, attempting to foist a dangerously standard-less—"cultural relativist"—world on us in the misguided name of equality. And this political argument has pragmatic functions in the charting of American scripts for both domestic and foreign policy.

In fact, eerily echoing Bellow's specific population obsession, Pat Buchanan, on the 1992 presidential campaign trail, asked whether "if we had to take a million immigrants in, say, Zulus, next year or Englishmen and put them in Virginia, what group would be easier to assimilate and would cause less [*sic*] problems for the people of Virginia?" There are multiple ironies operative here: the historically racist political character of Virginia, and Northern Virginia's postwar development as a segregationist bedroom community for white federal government workers—including Pat Buchanan; and the fact that currently neither the English nor *any* Africans, unlike Latin Americans and Asians, are migrating to the United States in considerable numbers. And then, why Zulus? Of all African populations, Zulus were perhaps the best politically organized and the most militarily successful against European colonists. A significant proportion of Zulus were, from the 1920s to the arrival of self-rule, the select group which (through the Inkatha party) was allied with and paid off by the apartheid government to embody "tribal division," to hold the line against the African National Congress. By rights, Buchanan should have been begging Zulus to migrate as his natural political allies.[57]

There is a persuasive explanation for the Bellow/Buchanan Zulu obsession, one that does not rely—as one should not, despite Bellow's graduate work in Northwestern's anthropology department—on their mastery of any of these political facts. The transcript of a *Crossfire* program in which Robert Novak, Sam Donaldson, Michael Kinsley, and Richard Cohen wrestle with the implications of Buchanan's statement gives us a clue:

NOVAK: —pedophiles. For example, there was on Pat's—on Sam's program, Pat Buchanan said that it would—this is an example, if you're going to bring a million immigrants into Virginia, it would be easier to assimilate people from England than a million Zulus, and everybody—you have been upset about that but you said something. You said he probably has a point, in your column you said that, a point.

MR. COHEN: I—

NOVAK: He may have a point, you said, but the question is—

KINSLEY: I don't think he has a point. I think that was a racist remark, don't you, Sam?

NOVAK: No, but I'm—just let me finish. Mr. Cohen said—

MR. DONALDSON: By definition it was a racist remark.

NOVAK: But Mr. Cohen—

MR. DONALDSON: You can argue whether it's true or not.

NOVAK: If I could ever get to my question—

MR. COHEN: When we elect a man—

NOVAK: Mr. Cohen said he had a point. You just don't think that the word Zulus is politically correct. If he had said blacks you'd be happy, right?

MR. COHEN: No, no, no. If you want to make the point that some people are culturally closer to Americans than other people, fine, I have no problem with that.

MR. DONALDSON: Buchanan makes that point often.

MR. COHEN: *But when you use the word Zulu and you know damn well what you're saying.* (My emphasis)[58]

What do you know damn well you're saying? If we return to the era of high imperialism, of American world's fairs, traveling ethnological exhibits, sideshows, and vaudeville, we see that since the nineteenth century, "Zulu" has been the modal Western folk category into which most "primitive, tribal" Africans have been shoved. V. G. Kiernan states flatly that "no other people caught the Western . . . imagination so powerfully." One hundred Zulus were imported for the 1904 St. Louis World's Fair to serve as the savage Other over whose land the Boers and British fought, and a remnant continued to perform at Coney Island after the fair closed.[59] "Zulu," to neoliberal columnist Richard Cohen, is the term white Americans shouldn't use because it reminds black Americans of their "embarrassing, savage" origins. The *New Yorker*'s James Wolcott criticizes Ted Danson for making the 1992 Los Angeles riots "sound like a Zulu uprising."[60] "Zulu" is one measure of the failure of twentieth-century anthropology to shift popular political discourse, to extinguish the antiempirical, xenophobic construction of the barbarian at the gates, to kill the nasty savage. Together with shadows of forgotten imperialisms, this construction is always used with retrogressive political intent. Both at home and abroad, each functions to dehumanize nonwhites and non-Westerners, preparing and maintaining the ideological ground for our invasions, bombings, police actions, and the less visible but in aggregate more harmful International Monetary Fund, World Bank, and other financial depredations of the Third World and domestic minority poor. Each fits into a City on the Hill morality play, in which "our" precious group of the elect, who alone hold the key to right— Western democracy—are threatened and seduced by the Devil in multiple and perplexing forms. Each is part of a rightist holding action against progressive attempts to undo imperial structures of feeling in American public culture and thus to bring about progressive political change.

But a large group of recent critics do not believe that anthropologists have ever tried to act against "nasty savage" ideology. For them, anthropologists and their presumed subjects are

Good Subaltern, Evil Imperialist Anthropologist

"The anthropologist" is the favorite new demon for a wide array of progressive cultural commentators. This particular "good subaltern, evil anthropologist" script may have first been copyrighted in the 1960s by Vine Deloria in his justifiably angry, but object-less, chapter in *Custer Died for Your Sins*, "Anthropologists and Other Friends": "Into each life, it is said, some rain must fall. Some people have bad horoscopes, others take tips on the stock market. McNamara created the TFX and the Edsel. Churches possess the real world. But Indians have been cursed above all other people in history. Indians have anthropologists."

Deloria turns wonderful phrases—"the most prominent members of the scholarly community that infests the land of the free, and in the summer time, the homes of the braves"—but fails to cite a single real anthropologist or a single actual article or book. He objects (and before Foucault, too) to the regime of surveillance, warning the white middle-class that they will be the next unwitting population under the microscope. Primarily, though, he objects that anthropologists have repeatedly misrepresented Native American life, and that they ought, in any event, to be materially assisting Indians rather than studying them. Deloria's inheritors have maintained his stance of vague, sweeping denunciation but, in keeping with the depoliticization of progressive public culture, have jettisoned the material demands.

Nowadays, a sneering reference is often simply tossed off, as when an anonymous *New Yorker* reviewer declaims that "anthropology, having heroically defined itself as the study of man, has sunk into a deserved moral crisis," and castigates Richard and Sally Price for having neglected "to examine the racial assumptions of their field of study."[61] More commonly, though, the evil imperialist anthropologist is brought on stage for a full-dress morality play to stand in for the bad, white (and often male) West before a (usually) belletristic audience. The examples of Marianna Torgovnick, Trinh Minh-Ha, and Edward Said are noteworthy of the genre. I treat Said last because his anthropological solecisms are such a clear departure from the genuinely scholarly tenor of his work as a whole.

Literary critic Torgovnick's *Gone Primitive* attempts to delineate a Western "primitivist discourse" on the analogue of Said's orientalism: "A genealogy of thinkers would perpetuate ideas about primitive life that would affect an entire culture's imagination of the primitive."[62] While this is a laudable enterprise, her accounts of this "genealogy of thinkers," particularly the anthropologists, egregiously fail to engage with the facts at hand. She hinges a discussion of Malinowski's sexism (which was real enough) on an extended critique of the iconography of the 1968 cover of *The Sexual Life of Savages*. Malinowski died in 1942, a point she rather disingenuously admits in a footnote. (She then goes on, in reaction to Malinowski's posthumously published personal diaries, to offer up an essay on "Malinowski's body": "It's a small body, well-fed, but not kindly disposed enough toward itself to put on flesh." She gives no evidence of having read Clifford Geertz's much-reprinted essay on the diary.) Considering lesbianism, she declares roundly of Margaret Mead's *Coming of Age in Samoa* that "the text itself makes no mention of lesbian relations. . . . In 1928, Mead, perhaps prudently, avoided any explicit reference to what was then an unmentionable topic." Too taken up with Catherine Bateson's revelations of her mother's bisexual experiences to attend to the actual text, Torgovnick fails to note that Mead discusses girls' (and boys') homosexual experiences at length in *Coming of Age,* and pronounces that "they are simply *play,* neither frowned upon nor given much consideration" (emphasis in original).[63] Torgovnick is in general less critical of Mead than of male anthropologists. She sees her as "a complicated case," marking "a half-way point" between "masculine values and attitudes" and "some other relationship to the primitive." But her cultural feminist charity does not lead her to attend any more seriously to Mead's actual writing than to other anthropologists'.

Having misread individual anthropologists, Torgovnick is ready to pronounce on the profession as a whole: "The anthropologist ages but remains tied, always, to the experience of youth, immortalized in a classic text of anthropology. Unlike the face and body of the anthropologist, this classic text . . . can never change, since anthropologists resist revision as a process that might falsify original observations."[64] Which anthropologists are the reverse Dorian Grays of this peculiar passage? And what other sorts of writers do not "resist revision"? Novelists? Historians? Political scientists? Literary critics? Torgovnick, self-described progressive critic of anthropology, energetically manufactures her object of deprecation.

Trinh Minh-Ha, filmmaker and poststructuralist, does the same in the fractured, hermetic prose of her calling:

> The further I disentangle social anthropology, the deeper I entangle myself. Where is the ethnic me? the Other? The more I accept his word-prescriptions, the more my *competences* shrink. . . . The goal pursued is the spread of a hegemonic dis-ease. Don't be us, this self-explanatory motto warns. Just be "like" and bear the chameleon's fate, never infecting *us* but only yourself, spending your days muting, putting on/taking off glasses, trying to please all and always at odds with myself who is no self at all. . . . The language in which *I perceive* (quite a deception) myself—cultur-ally, psychologic-ally, physic-ally, and spiritu-ally (What hasn't he contaminated? Can you name it?) . . . *Anthropo Logical Hegemony,* a non-universal homocentrism that brings in light where obscurity reigns.[65] (Emphases in original)

Like Torgovnick, Trinh assumes that personal responses to a few carelessly read anthropological texts constitute a critique of an entire discipline: "One of the conceits of anthropology lies in its positivist dream of a neutralized language that strips off all its singularity to become nature's exact, unmisted reflection. . . . Anthropology reified as the study of man which never comes close to a general definition of man by identifying in him a single quality that is at the same time specific, irreducible, and universal. . . . The anthropologist, as we already know, does not *find* things; s/he *makes* them. And makes them up."⁶⁶ Both women, as well, are obsessed with Malinowski—whom Trinh repeatedly addresses as The Great Master—and Lévi-Strauss and see anthropology as a particularly phallocentric domain.

Torgovnick, however, at least attempts to deal with feminist work in anthropology through consideration of Margaret Mead, while Trinh instead simplifies the task with a sweeping reference: "Other voices of theories. Attempts have been made recently, for example, by some women anthropologists, and, more noisily, by Ivan Illich to distinguish *sex* from *gender*" (emphases and punctuation in original). Trinh is remarkably obedient to Illich's male noisiness: she considers his work on sex and gender at length, and fails to do the same for any feminist, or female, anthropologist, of any color. In fact, nowhere in her text does Trinh offer more than a trivial, passing reference to any woman anthropologist, not even in a footnote.⁶⁷

While any woman of color in the United States can complain legitimately about racism and sexism in a variety of institutions, Trinh, like some others, substitutes complaint for scholarship. Thus, having determined the bankruptcy of anthropology without actually having engaged with it, she ends in echoing Lynn Andrews and the other huckster cultural feminists selling a cynical ethnological antimodernism: "Humidity, receptivity, fecundity. Again, her speech is seen, heard, smelled, tasted, and touched. Great Mother is the goddess of all waters, the protectress of women and childbearing, the unweary sentient hearer, the healer and also the bringer of diseases. She who gives always accepts, she who wishes to preserve never fails to refresh. Regenerate."⁶⁸ Bring on the Great Goddess oracle kit!

Edward Said is a wonderful change from this brand of postmodernist poseur—but even Said nods, and in nodding, clothes all of anthropology in the "evil imperialist" costume. At the founding session of the "Anthropology and Its Interlocutors" series at the American Anthropological Association annual meetings in 1987, Said represented all anthropology as

explicitly or implicitly laboring in the toils of imperialist ideology. He justified this claim through the operations of the synechdochic fallacy, identifying the entire field either with past, clearly colonial work or with recent
postmodernist texts. Respondents angrily and vigorously pointed out the
vast radical literatures and personal political histories that contradicted
Said's vision, and his revised article "Representing the Colonized: Anthropology's Interlocutors" thanks them and claims to have "silently incorporated" them.[69]

Rather too silently. Although Said has interpolated sections into his text
listing "various forms of Marxist or anti-imperialist anthropology" that is
"admirably partnered by feminist anthropology," "historical anthropology," "work that relates to contemporary political struggle," "American anthropology," and "denunciatory anthropology" (each category with one or
more exemplary texts listed), he comes back around to his original argument in the end:

> I am impressed that in so many of the various writings on anthropology, episte-
> mology, textualization, and otherness that I have read . . . there is an almost total
> absence of any reference to American imperial intervention as a factor affecting
> the theoretical discussion. . . . In the recent works of theoreticians who deal with
> the almost insuperable discrepancy between a political actuality based on force,
> and a scientific and humane desire to understand the Other hermeneutically
> and sympathetically in modes not always circumscribed and defined by force,
> modern Western anthropology both recalls and occludes that problematic nov-
> elistic prefiguration [Kipling's ethnologist and British spy Creighton]. . . . If
> we seek refuge in rhetoric about our powerlessness or ineffectiveness or indif-
> ference, then we must be prepared also to admit that such rhetoric finally
> contributes to one tendency or the other. The point is that anthropological repre-
> sentations bear as much on the representer's world as on who or what is repre-
> sented.[70]

Having listed various radical anthropologists only to ignore them, Said
returns to the synecdochic misidentification of the entire field—"modern
Western anthropology"—with a few recent "linguistic turn" practitioners.
Said "ha trovato la sua America," he has found his American anthropologist, who is always and forever a postmodernist.

The example of the one radical anthropologist whom Said does not entirely ignore, Eric Wolf, helps to clarify just what this seemingly unconscious set of effacements involves. Said recognizes that Wolf, the éminence
grise of American Marxist anthropology, is "resourcefully original" but
complains that in his most recent large work, *Europe and the People without*

History, "the problematic of the observer" is "remarkably underanalyzed": "Someone, an authoritative, explorative, elegant, learned voice, speaks and analyzes, amasses evidence, theorizes, speculates about everything—except itself. Who speaks? For what and to whom? . . . The histories, traditions, societies, texts of 'others' are seen either as responses to Western initiatives—and therefore passive, dependent—or as domains of culture that belong mainly to 'native' elites."[71] But Wolf's actual text, and his entire career, refutes these assertions. In 1964, he described the thrust of postwar American anthropology as "a reflex of a falsely confident movement of American society towards global hegemony . . . in disregard of the historical context which underwrote that hegemony and of all the unrequited pasts which would rise up to challenge its progression." In 1969 he published *Peasant Wars of the Twentieth Century,* pretty obviously a work that protested against the notions that the societies of Others are passive, dependent, and in any event belong to native elites. In 1970, with Joseph Jorgensen, Wolf risked his reputation in publishing "Anthropology on the Warpath in Thailand" in the *New York Review of Books,* an angry, document-driven denunciation of anthropological complicity with the United States armed forces in Southeast Asia. This is certainly a voice speaking about and analyzing itself. In 1972, in Dell Hymes's radical anthology *Reinventing Anthropology,* his pointed polemic "American Anthropologists and American Society" thundered against a history of disciplinary accommodation to American imperial power and called for a historical "sociology of anthropological knowledge." At the end of the piece, Wolf admitted that

> someone who diagnoses an illness should also prescribe remedies. If I am correct in saying that anthropology has reached its present impasse because it has so systematically disregarded the problems of power, then we must find ways of educating ourselves in the realities of power. One way I can think of to accomplish this is to engage ourselves in the systematic writing of a history of the modern world in which we spell out the processes of power which created the present-day cultural systems and the linkages between them. . . . We stand in need of such a project . . . as a responsible intellectual contribution to the world in which we live, so that we may act to change it.[72]

Wolf took on the burden of this remedy himself, and the result is the monumental *Europe and the People without History,* which title Said willfully misinterprets in *Culture and Imperialism* as "somewhat self-congratulatory . . . [as it implies] people on whom the economy and polity sustained by empire depend, but whose reality has not historically or culturally required attention."[73]

Nothing could be further from the case. As Wolf writes in his introduction, "But Europeans and Americans would never have encountered these supposed bearers of a pristine past if they had not encountered one another, in bloody fact, as Europe reached out to seize the resources and populations of other continents. . . . The tacit anthropological supposition that people like these are people without history amounts to the erasure of 500 years of confrontation, killing, resurrection, and accommodation."[74]

Said's mistaken pronouncements on Wolf's work, based on misreadings and, more importantly, sheer failure to read, are merely part of his failure to admit the existence of radical anthropology *tout court.* In *Imperialism and Culture,* Said goes to some pains to give detailed descriptions of "subaltern" scholars' work. He points out in "Representing the Colonized" that "little of this material reaches the inner chambers of and has no effect on general disciplinary or discursive discussion in metropolitian centers" and complains that anthropologists, among others, "shut and block out the clamor of voices on the outside asking for their claims about empire and domination to be considered."[75] We can easily revise this sentence to point out that *Said,* in his role as prominent public intellectual, repeatedly has acceded to the academic and popular blackout of radical work in favor of attending at length to the postmodernists whose work he so deplores. It is Said who "shuts and blocks out" the work of American anthropologists who, although largely ignored by middlebrow media, repeatedly speak and write against empire and domination; who, at home and all over the globe, work with "native" radical scholars and activists; who are his true allies.[76]

One reason for such willful blindness, and thus the reductive use of anthropological Halloween costumes in place of analysis, may be an unthinking, reflexive anti-Marxism, a stance common to the conservative establishment and postmodernists alike. And Said's mode of anti-Marxist argument gives us a clue to the mirrors-within-mirrors, falsehood-atop-falsehood state of affairs that is anthropology's intersection with American public culture.

The operations Said engages in are simple: the previously mentioned synecdochic fallacy, and what Johannes Fabian labels the denial of "coeval time," or the lumping together of present and past. Said defines Marxist work in a part-for-whole manner repeatedly in *Culture and Imperialism.* On one slippery page, for example, he scores "much of Western Marxism, in its aesthetic and cultural departments" for being "blinded to the matter of imperialism." But his "Western Marxists" are nearly all World War II–era names, and thus the veritable global flood of Marxist work on imperialism—including all the key texts on which Said relies—is rhetorically defined out of court. Then, Said repeatedly indicts more than a century of Marxist work on the basis of the failings of its nineteenth-century founders: "Even Karl Marx succumbed to thoughts of the changeless Asiatic village, or agriculture, or despotism . . . much as Marx and Engels spun out their theories of Oriental and African ignorance and superstition."[77]

What Said does to Marxism, he and many others do to anthropology, indicting the present through citing the past, and selectively choosing representative anthropologists. Torgovnick feels perfectly free to claim that "we have become accustomed to seeing modernism and postmodernism as opposed terms marking differences in tone, attitude, and forms of economic and social life between the first and second halves of the twentieth century. Yet with regard to views of the primitive, more similarities exist than we are used to acknowledging."[78] But how can she claim this of anthropology, when she takes so little account of writings in the field, and almost none of post–World War II work? Why, it must be that all anthropology is the same, and all of it was published yesterday. Were we to deal with literary criticism in this manner, for example, we would expatiate on the horrific racist (and sexist) conservatism of Matthew Arnold and T. S. Eliot as defining the field and its potential for all time, and/or use a trendy but clearly unrepresentative figure like Stanley Fish as a synecdoche for all literary critics in the present.

There is also abundant documentary evidence concerning ties between native anticolonial politicians and theorists and anthropologists that show up the adherents of the "evil imperialist anthropologist" as ignorant of anticolonial and antiracist history. While it is often noted, for example, that Zora Neale Hurston studied with Franz Boas, this connection can be wished away because she moved off in the direction of imaginative writing. But W. E. B. Du Bois, perhaps the most influential Afro-Americanist theorist, also acknowledged Boas's importance:

> As a boy I knew little of Africa save legends and some music in my family. The books we studied in the public school had almost no information about Africa, save of Egypt, which we were told was not Negroid. I heard of few great men of Negro blood, but I built up in my mind a dream of what Negroes would do in the future, even though they had no past.
>
> Then happened a series of events: In the last decade of the nineteenth century, I studied two years in Europe, and often heard Africa mentioned with respect. Then, as a teacher in America I had a few African students. Later at Atlanta University a visiting professor, Franz Boas, addressed the students and told them of the history of the Black Sudan. I was utterly amazed and began to study Africa for myself.

Faye Harrison reminds us that Du Bois and other Afro-American antiracist scholars of his generation were "vigilant consumers" of Boas's and other "progressive anthropological research."[79]

Across the Atlantic, Jomo Kenyatta studied with Bronislaw Malinowski and took his degree in anthropology at the London School of Economics. He also established warm relations with Raymond Firth and corresponded with him until Kenyatta's death. Richard Brown, Henrika Kuklick, and Jack Goody have documented the disfavor and sheer discrimination many British anthropologists faced at the hands of colonial and industrial officials who disliked them (a dislike often exacerbated by anti-Semitism), quite rightly suspecting that they did not necessarily hold the interests of empire close to their hearts. In what seems a hilarious parody of Blimpishness, one Colonial Office civil servant wrote quite seriously that an anthropologist working in Nigeria was "a recognized maniac in many ways. He wore sandals, even in this country, lived on vegetables, and was generally a rum person. I can quite understand that the people of Nigeria did not want to have an object like that going about and poking into the private affairs of the native communities."[80]

And yet in one sense anthropology deserves this rhetorical treatment (although Johannes Fabian has remarked, ruefully, that given the subsequent scene, he is sorry he ever published his "anthropology-bashing" study).[81] In that critics are doing to anthropology what some anthropologists have done to Others, the discipline, justly, is hoist by its own petard. Because, despite vigorous and repeated internal protests and a significant body of countervailing work, the protesters have not yet won the representational war. The anthropology that is allowed into the public sphere does too often define the Other as timeless, part of "our past"—think of the *Millennium* phenomenon alone—and does frequently delineate whole populations synecdochically, through the use of what George Marcus and Dick Cushman have labeled "common denominator people." Those of us in opposition are being hit by friendly fire.

But there is yet one last mode in which anthropology appears in American public culture, one in which there is neither applause nor censure. In this vision, anthropologists are neutral

Human Nature Experts

The dispassionate scholar who just gives us the facts, the scientist whose laboratory is all of humankind, the representative of knowledge on human origins and cross-cultural possibilities—such is the mantle many anthropologists have sought and have been granted in the American public sphere. In such an epistemological universe, there is no problem with the limits to any one scholar's knowledge, with the denial of coeval time, no concern with the field's colonialist heritage, no worry over the political construction of research questions. Anthropologists are simply the omniscient go-to guys on origins, culture, and human nature, the experts on the more abstruse of human practices. Phil Donahue consulted with seven anthropologists to produce *The Human Animal,* a book and NBC television series explaining "What determines human behavior? Why is there so much violence in our society? Why are male-female relationships such a struggle? Where did we come from? Where are we going? How does the human mind work?" The women's magazine *Mirabella* recommends a soul music album "that doesn't require a degree in anthropology in order to groove to it." Lance Morrow, in *Time* magazine, uses Colin Turnbull's portrait of the African Ik to expatiate on the need for "family values" in America.[82] Margaret Mead had a regular column in *Redbook* in the 1960s and 1970s; more recently, cultural materialist Marvin Harris and sociobiologists Lionel Tiger, Robin Fox, and Sarah Hrdy claim the mantle of human nature expert in popular culture. E. D. Hirsch, Jr., uses anthropology as a mantra to claim authority for his rote-memorization vision of proper American education: "In contrast to the theories of Plato and Rousseau, an anthropological theory of education accepts the naturalness as well as the relativity of human cultures. . . . The anthropological view stresses the universal fact that a human group must have effective communications to function effectively." Serious scholars also treat anthropology as the ultimate woodlot, the site to repair to for definitions of pan-human phenomena. Historian Michael Kammen, for example, begins *Mystic Chords of Memory* with a discussion of American myth based on Malinowski and Lévi-Strauss.[83]

The notion of "an anthropological study," too, has taken on a widespread popular cachet. Journalists use it to indicate the process of making the familiar strange as one observes the human comedy, as does Dennis Dermody in the *Utne Reader.*" Of course, sitting for 30 minutes watching a theater fill up is pretty boring, but through the years I've amused myself with a Margaret Mead–like study of the way people come in and take their seats and their antics during a movie." Or here, as columnist Bruce Feirstein defamiliarizes the lives of upper-middle-class New Yorkers:

And so it is high summer. A time when the Japanese beetles descend on the rose bushes . . . and thoughts turn to beach house anthropology, and the myth, symbolism and cosmology of the Weber grill. . . . "Every Friday night, a vast tribe of English-reading peoples would migrate over a hundred miles out into Long Island," an anthropologist will explain in the year 2525. "And as the men gathered around the black kettle, the house elder would sacrifice either a swordfish or a chicken to the God of second-home mortgage deductions. After that, there would ensue much drinking, and many attempts at mating, sometimes even between spouses."

And, of course, there is therapist Oliver Sacks's patient's comment that he feels like "an anthropologist on Mars."[84]

New York Times writers, in particular, have become wildly attracted to "anthropological study" references. Reporter Trip Gabriel claims that "a latter-day Margaret Mead might note . . . the land that is Fifth Avenue is populated by two tribes, two groups with distinct markings, customs and mythologies." Book reviewer Michiko Kakutani praises a nonfiction memoir for its "anthropological flair for recording the mores of the downtown drug scene," while Sven Birkerts describes belletrist John Leonard as "the anthropologist come to have a careful look at his subject"—American television. Art critic Herbert Muschamp decides that a Metropolitan Museum *Cartier* exhibit "may belong more to the realm of anthropology than to art." And columnist Maureen Dowd claims disgustedly that the "yuppie" television series *Seinfeld*, pays "anthropological attention . . . to relationship anxiety, frozen yogurt, muffins, tony mail-order catalogues . . . bodily functions . . . onanism, yada yada yada."[85]

Articles focusing on shifts in styles of self-representation are particularly likely to use the "anthropologist views the tribe" conceit. Take Mary Tannen's photographic essay "War Paint," from the *New York Times Sunday Magazine*:

> "It's Saturday night in Alphabetland. . . . The amateur anthropologist is standing in a bathtub taking notes as Bekah and her friends are putting on makeup. . . . The anthropologist is testing a theory that while the original purpose of makeup may have been to render the female more attractive to the opposite sex, it has evolved far beyond that primitive impulse, into a vast array of products and rules . . . whose primary focus . . . is the female, for whom such variations are clues to tribal identity. . . . The purpose of this ceremony is to develop a look that will distinguish the Bekah tribe from the Rave Kids, the Homegirls and various undifferentiated Bridge-and-Tunnel tribes."[86]

Or, from the *San Francisco Examiner,* a liberal columnist comments on modern youth mores, with the requisite reference to their cross-cultural ubiquity: "You don't have to be an urban anthropologist to know that body piercings and tattoos are a booming form of self-expression among the young, combining the art of the Maoris, native Americans and traditional American tattoo artists."[87]

Often, however, the defamiliarization exercise has deprecatory intent, as in Glen Garvin's conservative polemic against National Public Radio in the Chicago *Reader*, which portrays his sister as the native with strange customs: "Every few years I make an anthropological visit to my sister's home out west. My sister—her name is withheld to protect the guilty—is a lifelong bureaucrat who's never worked for anyone who had to show a profit, and she is deeply suspicious of the whole concept. . . . Needless to say, she listens to National Public Radio."[88]

In the current public sphere, then, anthropology and its presumed relations to primitives, whether lauded, derided, or neutrally noted, are tools at hand for a wide variety of actors with varying political intents. Moreover, even when the label is absent, key political issues in the present—immigration, language policies, multiculturalism, family functions, women's status—bear on squarely anthropological domains. Finally, serious journalism on race, poverty, and crime in recent years has borrowed the appearance—but not the discipline—of ethnographic work. In pieces in the *New York Times* and other major urban newspapers, in *Harper's*, the *Atlantic*, and the *New Yorker*, the extensive use of first-person, life history accounts and the placing of the investigator in the text both provide human interest and lay claim to ethnographic authority. But this is "fake ethnography." Its anthropological costume acts to disguise both its thin knowledge base and its deprecatory intent. Fake ethnography is one current American morality play in which the minority poor are cast as the Devil.

This crescendo of intellectual pilgrimage to and popular use of anthropology—including appearances in novels and mysteries (Irving Wallace, Kurt Vonnegut, Saul Bellow, Garcia Marquez, Frank Parkin, Barbara Pym, Tony Hillerman, Aaron Elkins, Peter Dickinson, Robertson Davies, William Gibson, Donald Westlake), cartoons and comics (see figs. 8–10), even television sitcoms (viz., the sluttish "feminist anthropologist" on *90210*)—takes place, ironically, in an era in which the discipline itself is in some disarray. It is the best and worst of times for anthropology. Intellectual historians of the 1970s and 1980s, such as Christopher Lasch and Rosalind Rosenberg, considered anthropological work central to twentieth-century constructions of American selfhood—although Lasch's assessment was dour while Rosenberg's was celebratory. But by the 1990s, fashions had shifted sufficiently so that Dorothy Ross could comfortably write a monumental history of American social sciences without considering anthropology at all. At the same time, the guru status of Clifford Geertz outside the discipline, particularly among theory-hungry historians, has been augmented by the intense extradisciplinary popularity of several best-selling volumes by postmodernist anthropologists. Some sociologists have embraced "ethnography" with the fervor of religious converts, outdoing the postmodernists in their "more Catholic than the Pope" claims for participant-observation's unique virtues.[89] Several departments have literally split over intellectual fights between physical and cultural anthropologists. Course enrollments, after a 1970s free fall, a 1980s trough, and gradual 1990s recovery, have not yet regained their Vietnam-era strength. The job market has been unreliable since the 1980s, and voices attempting to fashion ethnography as a neutral "methodological tool" to be sold, mercenary-fashion, to the highest (often corporate) bidders have grown in strength and respectability through the years of economic decline, funding droughts, and associated right-wing consolidation.

Chain bookstores reflect the simultaneous overloading and evacuation of the "anthropology" label in their progressive reduction of anthropology shelves to archaeology and Joseph Campbell–type myth and folklore texts. The last time I checked, Barnes and Noble, although they had an anthropology shelf, had placed books on Inca Peru, Australian aborigines, the highland Maya, Papua New Guinea, several African populations—and even *Coming of Age in Samoa,* Lévi-Strauss, Maybury-Lewis, and Sir James Frazier's *Golden Bough*—in "sociology." The American Anthropological Association *Newsletter* reflects desperation and crisis in trumpeting headlines such as "Public or Perish" and "Selling Ourselves: Our Future May Depend on It" accompanied by gloomy statistics and a youthful photo of Margaret Mead, "unquestionably the most visible of modern anthropologists."[90] Bring out number and measure in a year of dearth.

Disciplinary self-consciousness is certainly heightened under material duress, just as Samuel Johnson noted that the prospect of hanging concentrated the mind. But bringing out number and measure in attempts to sell anthropology has by and large exacerbated the wrong sort of mental concentration. The tendency has been to try to close ranks, after the fact, through retrospective guild copyrighting of concepts and methods. Thus the claim reviewed and disproven at the beginning of this chapter—that ethnography in exotic Third World settings is constitutive of cultural anthropological work—has been rigidified in the current climate. Voices are raised claiming anthropological ownership of all notions of culture, difference, Otherness, and any use of ethnographic methods. Perhaps the nadir of this tendency is James Cifford's unusually arrogant claim that the genres of oral history, journalism, and travel writing are "para-ethnographic." Chronological considerations alone would lead us to reverse the statement.[91] The silliness of trying to warn others off the guild's patch is self-evident. What is less clear, though, is how much is lost, both as insight and responsibility, through this narrow territorialism.

First, defining anthropology as the guardian of "culture," of "difference," dooms the discipline and larger intellectual community to a reductionist idealism. It splits human apprehensions of the world from the world itself. Whether this disjunction is the result of a midrange effort to demarcate a special expertise or the product of a poststructuralist epistemology that literally denies the reality of the material world, it gives permission to/commands anthropology to ignore economy, environment, human biology, politics, and history except as they are "represented." And in the absence of the need to consider the messiness of real human social relations in history, "difference" anthropologists succumb to the discipline's tendency to reify and dehistoricize cultural boundaries.[92] Eric Wolf has argued forcefully that "the concept of the autonomous, self-regulating and self-justifying society and culture has trapped anthropology within the bounds of its own definitions. . . . By endowing nations, societies, or cultures with the qualities of internally homogeneous and externally distinctive and bounded objects, we create a model of the world as a global pool hall in which the entities spin off each other like so many hard and round billiard balls."[93] He calls for a reapprehension of political economy, in the holistic nineteenth-century sense, to reknit the sundered social sciences and history, and to enable us to see that the cultural "billiard balls" we apprehend are in reality historically contingent *processes*, parts of ongoing interactions of populations living in shifting political economies. William Roseberry articulates the contemporary Marxist "culture and political economy" vision well: it attempts to "place culture in time, to see a constant interplay beween experience and meaning in a context in which both experience and meaning are shaped by inequality and domination," and to understand "the emergence of particular peoples at the conjunction of local and global histories, to place local populations in the larger currents of world history."[94] George Marcus, a central figure in postmodern anthropology, ignored most work in the field when he dismissed political economy as "a continuing commentary upon world conditions in terms most relevant to Western officialdom and statecraft."[95]

The denial of political economy includes the failure to see our own embeddedness in history, power, economy. Thus even the most anxious and principled postmodernist misses the full political contours of the process of knowledge production. James Clifford, for example, delineates "the ethnographic encounter" as "a garrulous, overdetermined, cross-cultural encounter shot through with power relations and personal cross-purposes."[96] But this lyrical yet hagridden definition limits itself to the immediate sites of ethnographic interaction, leaving out wider circles of acquaintance for both parties to the encounter. Clifford misses both informants' and ethnographers' institutional connections, up to the level of differing citizenships and differential power (by class, race, gender) as citizens. For any American anthropologist in Central America, for example, of no matter what orientation, United States–trained death squads, State Department pronouncements, International Monetary Fund measures, United States–owned multinational factories, and radical American groups like the Committee in Solidarity with the People of El Salvador must be, inevitably, also part of the ethnographic encounter.

The problematic sole focus on difference can be seen as part of a larger effort at product differentiation in American universities with the separate growth and professional consolidation of the social sciences, particularly after the Second World War. In a climate in which anthropology justifies its existence through "owning" exotic societies, Americanist research becomes a dirty little disciplinary secret.

Tackling the secret head-on—in terms both of its functioning in academe and the actual history of Americanist scholarship—can provide unlooked-for benefits. Just as laying out the anthropological Halloween costumes in current use provides us with a new critical lens on American rationales for and protests against domestic and foreign policy, so laying bare the actual internal workings of the discipline and of its intersections with popular and high culture over time will help to clarify the complicated process of "finding America"—and the Americas that are not found. Revealing the functions of one shifting but recognizable thread of argument, the "anthropological gambit," is central to this task.

Primitives "R" Us

Everything [in *The Family of Man*] aims to suppress the determining weight of History: we are held back at the surface of an identity, prevented precisely by sentimentality from penetrating into this ulterior zone of human behavior where historical alienation introduces some "differences" which we shall here quite simply call "injustices."—*Roland Barthes*[97]

The anthropological gambit has both an intellectual and an affective component. The intellectual point is that "we" are like primitives; the emotional layering is whimsical and pseudo-profound—primitives "R" us. The attribution of "our" characteristics to "them," and vice versa, is always good for a laugh in popular culture, is indeed the point of the "anthropology" cartoons printed here. The anthropological gambit, with the inclusion of putative prehistoric humans and nonhuman primates, is a major component of cartoonist Gary Larson's entire oeuvre and of course supplies the

"I'm already seeing an anthropologist."

8. The anthropological gambit, take one. (Drawing by Victoria Roberts; © 1992 The New Yorker Magazine, Inc.)

underlying logic for older cartoons and television shows like *Alley Oop* and *The Flintstones*. It is the conceit of Frank Parkin's novel, *Krippendorf's Tribe*, in which the eponymous protagonist invents a shockingly savage population, the "Shelmikedmu," through describing his own children's normal behavior.

But this state of affairs is not an uninvited slur on the discipline—even if we leave aside for the moment the fact that much-appreciated Larson cartoons decorate anthropology faculty doors from coast to coast. Anthropologists *institutionalized* the gambit early on in Americanist and exotic work and continue to make lavish use of it. Whether appearing as an apothegm or buried more deeply in text or iconography, the gambit is much of the substance conveyed by the rhetorical devices—allegory, fables of rapport, "marking," common denominator people—analyzed by postmodernist anthropologists. After all, the process of claiming ethnographic

THE FAR SIDE   By GARY LARSON

"Anthropologists! Anthropologists!"

9. Take two. Larson cartoons adorn anthropology faculty offices from coast to coast. (The Far Side by Gary Larson is reprinted by permission of Chronicle Features, San Franciso, CA. All rights reserved.)

authority—the cynosure of postmodernist eyes—is also *about* making ethnographic points. And a key point made through use of the gambit is that anthropologists can understand their own home societies simply through ethnographic observation, without reference to any extant scholarship or primary sources that might give access to statistical patterns or historical depth.

In keeping with the quasi-religious image of fieldwork, the gambit celebrates the anthropologist's ability to see what others do not: We are only Others. An *x* is only a *y*. In 1924, Ralph Linton published a serious article in the *American Anthropologist* on totemism among the American Expeditionary Forces in World War I: "a series of beliefs and practices which show a considerable resemblance to the totemic complexes existing among some primitive peoples." The dignified E. E. Evans-Pritchard complained in 1940, with bumptious humor, that exchanges with Nuer men had given him "Nuerosis." Clyde Kluckhohn exclaimed in 1944 that "we know less [of American culture] than of Eskimo culture." Laura Bohannan made extensive use of the gambit in her descriptions of Tiv social types:

> Cholo had been very much the cynical man of the world; Ihugh's viewpoint was very much like a medieval friar's. . . . Udama might dress in a single ragged waist cloth and smoke a pipe; she was, nevertheless, a *grande dame*. Yabo, I felt, needed but a change in outward appearance to be recognized as the crusty old man who disinherited his daughter for an imprudent marriage. Kako, the reserved elder statesman; Lam, a very Mr. Milquetoast, and a host of other familiar types: the gossip, the flirt, the steady young man, the devoted mother, the scholar and gentleman (though his subjects were genealogies and magic), the canny horse trader (though he dealt in goats), the henpecked husband (though it took five wives to do it), the young ne'er-do-well, and the giddy matron.[98]

Horace Miner wrote, tongue in cheek, in the *American Anthropologist* in 1956 about "Body Ritual among the Nacirema" (Americans), thus fixing the ideal type of the anthropological gambit as a set of cute references to how we as "the natives" can be seen to have irrational foibles (about which perhaps we ought to think more carefully):

> The anthropologist . . . is not apt to be surprised by even the most exotic customs. . . . the magical beliefs and practices of the Nacirema present such unusual aspects that it seems desirable to describe them as an example of the extremes to which human behavior can go. . . . the fundamental belief underlying the whole system appears to be that the human body is ugly and that its natural tendency is to debility and disease. . . . man's only hope is to avert these characteristics through the use of the powerful influences of ritual and ceremony. Every household has one or more shrines [bathrooms] devoted to this purpose. . . . the rituals associated with it are not family ceremonies but are private and secret. The rites are only discussed with children, and then only during the period when they are being initiated into these mysteries.[99]

And so on. Miner's piece unleashed a veritable flood of precious references to our tribal ways and how American culture is just like that of the Ponapeans or the Ainu. The late James Spradley, who wrote a number of influential textbooks as well as the highly regarded ethnography, *You Owe Yourself a Drunk*, actually titled one text *The Nacirema: Readings on American*

Culture. Jack Weatherford published a study of Congress, *Tribes on the Hill,* in which each chapter opened with a simplistic discussion of some "primitive" group's rituals or social organization which are then shown to be the same as Congress's:

> Many tribes attack, torture, and kill Western missionaries, explorers, traders, and anthropologists, but few have been as consistently bold or ferocious as the Shavante of Central Brazil. . . . But the ferocity of the Shavante warriors does not come naturally even to such a tribe; instead, it must be inculcated into young men in much the same way that Western men must go through basic training to become soldiers. . . . Just as Shavante men are always known by the name of the cohort with whom they spent their formative years in the bachelor hut, congressmen are always known by the name of the cohort with whom they spent their formative years in the Longworth Building. . . . Similarly, most congressmen in the bachelor building are also technically married, but the wife is usually back home in the district serving tea and leaflets, trying desperately to help her husband keep his job in the hope that one day he will move up to the Rayburn Building, thus securing their district enough for her to escape Gopher Prairie and move to Washington with him.

To identify and attack the anthropological gambit is not, however, to stand against cross-cultural comparison, or to deny that citizens of advanced industrial societies perform rituals, attach themselves to totems, &c. The "destructive analysis of the familiar," as Edward Sapir framed it, is one element of a liberatory cultural critique in use in the West at least since Montaigne's ironized cannibals. It is rather to point out the ideological functions of ahistorical, noncontextual "defamiliarization"—crosscultural vignettes which reify the pool hall vision of cultural difference, place Others at temporal distance, and thus efface the questions of history and power on both poles of the contrast.

Consider, for example, Miner's Nacirema piece, which also discusses the irrational behavior of the natives when they are ill, undergoing the "harsh ceremonies" of the "latipso," "that may even kill the neophyte."[100] Not only does the language trivialize hygiene and medicine in small-scale societies, from which, as the "technicians of the sacred" literature makes haste to inform us, we have learned and continue to learn a great deal; it also effaces the colonial encounter through which we have developed notions of "witch doctors" and "exotic rituals." Miner's whimsical frame also denies stratification and power dynamics on the American end. Had the American studies pioneers of "commodification of culture" research taken Miner's stance, they would never have considered the rise of American advertising and its efforts to enhance anxiety about bodily acceptability (tied to notions of class and race), nor would they have thought to investigate how gendered that advertising and its effects have been—not to mention that it was and is largely women who clean those amusing shrines. Nor would historians and social scientists have thought to consider the guild power of the American Medical Association and the insurance and drug company monopolies, and the resulting high price of, demographically skewed practice of, and inequitable access to American medicine by class, race, and gender.

Miner, of course, wrote in the 1950s, and so perhaps we should not evaluate him anachronistically. But then, C. Wright Mills, Eric Hofstader, Erich Fromm, Frantz Fanon, Simone de Beauvoir, Jean-Paul Sartre, and a host of other radicals and anticolonialists also were writing—and widely read—in the 1950s. Roland Barthes published his materialist critique of the homogenizing, falsely humanist *Family of Man* exhibit in 1957. No, it is the anthropological gambit, rather than simply the era, that effaces considerations of power and history. Witness Weatherford's recent exercise of the trope (he did research during the Carter administration), which treats the Shavante and other populations in as billiard-ball-ish a manner as any 1950s text, and which also serves to deny the actual complex constellations of power that Congress represents. Moreover, if we consider Weatherford's treatment of gender, we can see in some detail the ways in which the gambit both encourages an unthinking naturalization of power differentials through focusing away from actual social relations in the round and seems even to dictate an avoidance of scholarly research.

Tribes on the Hill notes the history of poor female representation in Congress, and insightfully discusses the ways in which token women, over time, have played maverick roles—such as taking antiwar stands—that were allowed by their "marked" status. But Weatherford also introduces the whole question of female members of Congress in a section entitled "Amazons on the Potomac," which likens the repeated declaration that "now" women have power in Congress to repeated Western mythic claims of the existence of "women warriors." He ends his discussion with the speculation that women may never achieve American political power until they assimilate the "peculiarly masculine styles of interaction in locker rooms and men's clubs," or until men abandon them. Not only is this analysis a reduction to a psychological microlevel of a complex political economic process involving levels of feminist ideology and organizing, sources of campaign financing, and exigencies of particular issues; it also misrepresents the facts about women's status in so-called primitive societies. That no cases of primitive female rule have ever been documented does not mean that small-scale societies offer us a smooth series of examples of uncomplicated male dominance. And then Weatherford makes use of *no* scholarly work on American women's historical fight for political power, nor any on women's statuses in small-scale societies—both abundantly available literatures at the time he was writing.[101]

Other Americanist anthropologists have made partial, limited use of the anthropological gambit—a cute title, for example—as did Michael Moffatt in his ethnography of Rutgers University undergraduate life, *Coming of Age in New Jersey.* I myself resorted to it twice in *The Varieties of Ethnic Experience.* In the first instance, I incorporated it into a fable of rapport in which I likened the middle-aged Italian-American men I had interviewed to the Nuer in their skills in avoiding answering my questions while repeatedly insulting me, as the Nuer had Evans-Pritchard:

> I was amused and impressed by these spontaneous, witty lunges at my professional neck; how could I blame these men for protecting themselves from my intrusions? But they also drew blood: few researchers are immune to the suspicions that they have not really understood anything about their topic, that they are imposing their own distorting grid on reality. And these men, unlike the Nuer with Evans-Pritchard, shared sufficient culture with me to perceive this vulnerability and to attack it with skill and verve.

Later, I commented on my informants' ubiquitous feelings of inauthenticity:

> "Real" Italian-Americans were to be found in books; one found out about them by reading, not by examining or talking with others. . . . Ripetto was particularly maddening: he interlarded his lectures on the "old community" in the East Bay with references to Alistair Cooke's *America.* At one point, he offered to answer one of my questions about his childhood by looking it up! To comfort myself, I imagined Trobriand Islanders answering Malinowski's questions by referring to their *Fielding Guides.*[102]

These examples of humorous, self-conscious use of the anthropological gambit seem harmless fun, a way of livening up texts and titles, of sparking reader interest—and also of gently reminding one's audience, in classic cultural relativist fashion, that all humans have institutions, rituals, patterned apprehensions of reality. *The Family of Man.* We Are the World. An *x* is only a *y.* But which *x*s are allowed to be only *y*s? The anthropological gambit is only usable on relatively privileged Americans, never on those

"A field anthropologist from the new Museum
of American Financial History, sir."

10. Take three. An x is only a y. (Drawing by W. Miller; © 1992 The New Yorker Magazine, Inc.)

who are in some way stigmatized. Imagine an ethnography of Spelman College, Howard, or Tuskegee University with a cute "tribal" title. No, it's not funny anymore. Nor do ethnographers of Americans of color or of other stigmatized statuses make amusing references to their informants' likenesses to Australian aborigines or the Masai. Patricia Zavella, who shared field site, fieldwork period, and publisher with me, nevertheless felt no temptation to gambit use in her *Women's Work and Chicano Families*. Nor did Brett Williams in *Upscaling Downtown,* her study of working-class and impoverished blacks and Latinos in inner-city Washington, D.C. Nor did Kath Weston in her ethnography of San Francisco gays and lesbians, *Families We Choose.*[103]

Thus affirming that an *x* is only a *y* unintentionally exacerbates the trivialized and stigmatized statuses of "primitives," the global poor, and racial, sexual, and other minority Americans alike. It literally defines a significant proportion of Americans as "outside the circle of the we," in historian David Hollinger's apt phrase. "We" can only be like "them" if we are white, middle-class or above, heterosexual, &c. Primitives "R" Not Us if we are domestic exotics. Or rather, there would be no frisson of recognition in such a claim, no hiccuplike series of instances of delighted self-congratulation that *x*s are, after all, just like *y*s, since the notion that stigmatized domestics and exotics resemble one another—witness Zulus—is already a component of imperial structures of feeling.

A non-American example further illustrates this point. In 1974, Claude Lévi-Strauss was inducted into the company of the forty "immortals" of the French Academy. His offical speech on that occasion, headlined by the *New York Times* as "We Are We Are You Are You Are We Are You," is a masterpiece of use of the gambit simultaneously to efface and to assert power. Predictably, Lévi-Strauss compares the ritual surrounding his induction to that of a group of Canadian Indians:

> Now, similar to the initiates who are covered from head to foot in a thick hooded cloak, who go through the motions of learning to walk again and, as they accomplish the first steps of their new life, test the ground before them with a staff studded with sharp points like a lightning-conductor, here I am, in my turn, arrayed in a special uniform—a suit of armor as much as an adornment—and equipped with a sword, both uniform and sword being appropriate for the defense of the wearer against those evil spells of social or supernatural origin which threaten any person undergoing a change of status.

But aside from a jocular exercise in pointing out that we all undergo rites of passage, Lévi-Strauss's speech also claims parallels between the Indians' situation and the Academy's:

> Had there been any need, that night among the Indians would have sufficed, then, to make me understand and marvel at the fact that, in spite of the divisions within our society, forty individuals should be prepared to forget the differences between them in order to form a community whose members pledge themselves to remain faithful to certain very simple values: love of their language, respect

for their culture and for very old customs that have been bequeathed to them over the centuries.

I appear before you, gentlemen, like those old Indians of my acquaintance who are determined to bear witness to the end to the culture which has fashioned them, even if that culture has been undermined and, above all, if there are people who complacently forecast its doom.[104]

This droll likening of a powerful, state-sponsored intelligentsia to a powerless group of Native Americans is an example of chutzpah as obscenity.

But the anthropological gambit—even when its use is more abstract and solemn than these examples—has further implications, for work at home and abroad, and for popular cultural notions of American life that live in symbiosis with anthropology. These implications are most easily seen in the historical actualities and influence of United States–based ethnography.

THRIVING ON A RIFF

While this chapter began in bemoaning the repeated historical denial of Americanist anthropology, one can, at times, sympathize with the impulse to draw a veil across what is often an embarrassment to the discipline. Too many United States ethnographies are just that: slapdash, ahistorical slabs of prose about artificially circumscribed "subcultures" described in isolation from larger society, politics, economy—yet simultaneously overgeneralized to claim a "key" to American culture. Worse yet, they often address their subjects condescendingly or, just as bad, with anxious, lady-doth-protest-too-much advocacy.

Even pioneering, largely admirable texts commit one or more of these crimes. James Spradley's insightful but time-and-space-bound studies claim to represent the billiard-ball, Platonic essence of what are after all very regionally and historically contingent occupations: *the* urban nomad, *the* cocktail waitress. Carol Stack, in *All Our Kin,* based on research among impoverished black Americans in one midwestern city, does, uniquely for the era, place her informants in history and political economy. But she also overgeneralizes with a vengeance in claiming to represent all of black American culture and bowdlerizes her data—she offers no evidence of petty crime or other participation in the informal economy, one means through which people that poor can reproduce daily life and raise children. Constance Perin, in the feminist Freudian *Belonging in America,* complains about racism and class stratification but nevertheless decides that she can represent American life (not a part of American life, not even one thread of ideological hegemony in American life) through studying only white suburbanites: "Wanting to hear 'American ideas,' I listened to men and women living in what is generally regarded as the 'mainstream,' those who have at least reached the suburban, single-family-detached episode of the American Dream." Perin ends her study with a set of comparisons of apprehensions of the meanings of human excretion among "Americans" and "other cultures." [105]

At the end of World War II, Charlie Parker and Dizzy Gillespie together wrote "Anthropology," a piece that has since become a jazz standard. But the first title of "Anthropology" was "Thriving on a Riff."[106] Anthropological work on the United States has too often been based on a single riff, but it has not thrived. Problematic Americanist research is locked in a vicious cycle with the second-rank, residual status of United States research in anthropology departments. Despite the fact that the American Anthropological Association estimates that half of all anthropologists work on the United States, there is a pervasive sense that those who engage in it cannot or will not go abroad, and therefore no special training for them is necessary—mere residence is deemed sufficient. The United States, from the vantage of anthropology departments, is too often considered a playground, an R&R site. Students are rarely directed to learn American history, sociology, politics, economics—their professors, in any event, would be unable to gauge their mastery of the topics. And the less one knows of American historical political economy, the easier it is to believe that there are circumscribed populations in the United States with identifiable "cultures" that are one's professional property to inscribe. To engage with American scholarly literature on one's topic, then, would be to "contaminate" one's insights from fieldwork among the folk. It follows that just as "key" informants reveal entire "exotic" cultures to some ethnographers working abroad, so a presentist ethnographic study of some small population is assumed to reveal the key to American life. Dissertations are too often "passed through"—any old sloppy pastiche of casual observation and unanalyzed opinion will do.

Too often, established anthropologists with "exotic" credentials move into the American field without sufficient effort to gain new expertise. Renato Rosaldo, for example, after a career of meticulous fieldwork on the Filipino Ilongot fully embedded in extant literature, in *Culture and Truth* adds the United States to his purview but barely acknowledges the wealth of scholarship on American imperialism and race and racism and their connections to cultural production in America, his major thematic concerns.[107]

This two-tier situation is not unlike Stendhal's observation of the difference between bourgeois marriage and an affair in nineteenth-century France: a serious matter of kin, property and children versus the frivolous feathering of a little ballerina's nest in one's prosperous (male) old age. Or, to shift the analogy to home ground, the situation brings to mind Ralph Ellison's angry denunciation of white writing on black Americans, where "as long as their hearts are in the right place they can be as arbitrary as they wish in their formulations. . . . they can air with impunity their most private Freudian fantasies as long as they are given the slightest camouflage of intellectuality. . . . they write as though Negro life exists only in the light of their belated regard."[108]

The Ellison parallel is meaningful in another sense. A significant proportion of Americanist anthropology concerns racial minorities and is often undertaken by scholars of color. Domestic exotics are, ironically, simultaneously too important and not important enough. That is, white faculty and colleagues wishing not to be thought racist often fail to apply the same stringent standards they would automatically apply to work on, say, Borneo. What is even more important is that they often *cannot* do so, since they actually know something about Borneo but frequently little about the nation in which they reside, the home country of most of their students, the very source of their paycheck—not to mention the state that is still the globe's major imperial power.

Students and colleagues of color in Americanist anthropology are often, then, simultaneously overpraised, condescended to, and ignored—treatment that gives rise, quite logically, to widespread bitterness, separatism, a scattering of poseurs—and a variety of exits. Individuals may move to extra-American research or may retain a United States specialty but take ethnic studies or other positions outside anthropology departments. Lee Baker and Thomas Patterson note that, historically, nonwhite and white anthropologists who have addressed issues of race and racism usually have done so from sociology, education, or citizen-activist positions. And Faye Harrison has summarized pioneer Afro-American anthropologists Allison Davis's and St. Clair Drake's largely extra-anthropological careers. Finally, most commonly, potential anthropologists of color may simply avoid the discipline. American sociology, for example, has twice the percentage of Afro-American full-time faculty, and currently produces more than twice anthropology's percentage of black American Ph.D.'s.[109]

This unhappy state of affairs is overdetermined, as it also obtains in a substantive sense outside anthropology, and outside the academy—throughout, in fact, most discourse on race and ethnicity in America.[110]

Nonanthropologists do not have the excuse for their ignorance of "specializing in Borneo," but, oddly enough, in a sense we all have been specializing in Borneo when it comes to American race and ethnicity, acting as if they exist only in the light of our belated regard. That is, the anthropological gambit and its sequelae have had a profound influence on the ways in which we apprehend racial/ethnic difference—class and culture—in America. Let me illustrate the character and strength of this influence through the case of Harvard historian Stephan Thernstrom's fight against and yet ultimate capitulation to it.

In 1964, Thernstrom published *Poverty and Progress,* an iconoclastic study of social mobility in nineteenth-century Newburyport, Massachusetts. Thernstrom contended that, contrary to received wisdom, mobility opportunities in America had not contracted after a nineteenth-century heyday. The reality, instead, was a continuous thread of "petty success stories" across time.[111] Moreover, mobility was more complicated than previous commentators had realized. In the first place, individuals and households might or might not attempt to rise solely through achieving the highest-paying, highest-status jobs for themselves or their children. Alternatively, they might focus on investment in property—largely home ownership in the nineteenth century. Second, scholars had confused the issue of who had been mobile by failing to take geographical movement into account. Thernstrom established, both for Newburyport and on the larger American scene, the realities of extremely high geographic mobility across the nineteenth century. Individuals measured as stuck in particular economic slots from one decade to the next were most likely not the same individuals.

In considering social history "from the bottom up" and in making extensive use of census material, city directories, and other primary sources, Thernstrom was in the vanguard of both the "new social history" and "cliometrics," or the extensive use of quantification to answer historical questions. But—and this point has been far less remarked—he also wrote explicitly to refute "ahistorical social science," most particularly the monumental five-volume study of Newburyport published over the 1940s and 1950s by Chicago School anthropologist W. Lloyd Warner.

In a lengthy appendix, Thernstrom notes Warner's previous work among Australian aborigines and scathingly quotes Warner's intentions to "use the techniques and ideas which have been developed by social anthropologists in primitive society in order to obtain a more accurate understanding of an American community." To consult the historical record, Warner averred, would "be to fall victim to the biases and preconceptions of the historian, a man necessarily 'unscientific,' 'culture-bound,' 'ethno-centric.'" Thernstrom not only contends that in relying on the apprehensions of his informants alone, Warner was led to "accept uncritically the community's legends about itself—surely the most ethnocentric of all possible views!" He also scores Warner for devoting "an inordinate amount of space" to and overaccepting the opinions "of informants from a particular social group with very special biases—Yankee City's 'upper uppers.'" Thernstrom himself refers repeatedly and with refreshing sarcasm to deliberate employer discrimination against immigrants.[112]

Thernstrom found Warner not only ahistorical and elitist, but possessing a "sterile definition of class": facilely claiming representative status for what turns out not to be a very representative American city and treating Newburyport's ethnic populations as static groups and thus missing evidence of high geographic mobility: "A more serious flaw marred Warner's treatment of both residential mobility and occupational mobility: he advanced quantitative measures of the changing status of various ethnic groups over time without understanding that the composition of these groups was steadily changing. . . . Warner believed it reasonable to treat 'the Irish' as an entity."[113]

Finally, Thernstrom ends with a ringing rejection of the anthropological gambit, both as used on the United States and among "exotics": "Interpretation of the present requires assumptions about the past. The actual choice is between explicit history, based on a careful examination of the sources, and implicit history, rooted in ideological preconceptions and uncritical acceptance of local mythology. . . . It is by no means clear that [social anthropological presumptions] are valid even for primitive societies; Leach's recent study, *Political Systems of Highland Burma,* makes a strong case for a dynamic, historically oriented approach to the primitive community."[114] And to counter the seemingly conservative implications of his findings that mobility opportunities have been more consistently available than progressive critics have contended, Thernstrom ends in suggesting that we set our sights higher: "Whether the presence of opportunity of this kind is a sufficient test of the good society, however, may be doubted."[115]

Between 1964 and 1973, though, the siren song of the anthropological gambit overcame Thernstrom's youthful logic and flirtation with the new historicist anthropology, and the billiard balls came to the fore. In *The Other Bostonians,* he displays a conservative hardening of the arteries specifically connected to an assertion of ahistorical, essential American "ethnic cultures" that explain populations' economic experiences. In articulating his own grading system of the American "ethnic report card," as I have labeled it, Thernstrom engages in both positive and negative stereotyping with little empirical reference. Jews had a "special commitment to education" which explained their superior performance. But the Irish "lacked any entrepreneurial tradition," and Italians "lived in a subculture that directed their energies away from work." The poor showing of Irish and Italians was due in part also to the dreadful cultural effect of Catholicism: "Large numbers of Boston's Irish and Italian Catholics attended parochial schools, and one wonders how effective these institutions were in providing the kind of training that was conducive to occupational success. . . . this may have meant . . . that the parochial system, although it offered the security of the familiar, muted rather than heightened aspirations and fostered a sense of alienation from the larger society."[116] One wonders, indeed. Only blacks escape this onslaught of barroom bromides, being segregated off from the main text in a chapter noteworthy for its anxious liberalism. Thernstrom considers blacks' "rural background handicaps," "alleged educational deficiencies," residential segregation, the Negro family as a "tangle of pathology," and "discrimination and the nature of black culture" as explanations for blacks' standing on the bottom of the Boston occupational ladder. He energetically rejects all but the last set of factors: "In virtually every other area of the economy it appears that the main barriers to black achievement have been not internal but external, the result not of peculiarities in black culture but of peculiarities in white culture."[117]

But Thernstrom leaves an escape hatch open to blame blacks too: "If it is admitted that the nature of Irish culture and Jewish culture had something to do with the different occupational trajectories followed by these two groups, how can we dismiss differences between black culture and white culture as an explanation of the economic differences between the races?"[118]

We need, however, make no such admission. There are simply no such entities as Irish and Jewish culture, any more than there is such a thing as a monolithic black culture, and Thernstrom's very statistical measures of relative occupational and income achievement across groups are both so poorly constructed as to prove nothing and easily disproven by simple replication for another urban area, as I show in some detail in *The Varieties of Ethnic Experience*. (Thernstrom also refuses to consider ethnic women's occupational experiences at all, claiming there is insufficient material. I do so, and show how his refusal further distorts his findings.)[119]

Having defined and excoriated "implicit history, rooted in ideological preconceptions and uncritical acceptance of local mythology," having identified and rejected the anthropological gambit, Thernstrom ended in embracing it—specializing in Borneo. But he later moved even further inside its orbit. In 1980, Thernstrom published *The Harvard Encyclopedia of American Ethnic Groups,* an apotheosis of the billiard ball vision of American race/ethnicity by its very presuppositions and organization. Moreover, in the introduction to the work, Thernstrom and his coeditors, Ann Orlov and Oscar Handlin, warn the reader about "the biases characteristic of the ethnic literature" (that is, their own contributors):

> Few groups as described have rivals, much less enemies. Prejudice and discrimination typically seem always to emanate from "the dominant society," though tensions and conflicts among rival ethnic groups do receive some attention. Little is available about dislocation and disappointment. Poverty, crime, alcoholism, racism, anti-Semitism, mental illness, and social pathology are generally absent. . . . Authors are eager to recount the achievements of the groups about which they write, but they provide little insight into the ethnic origins of the poor.[120]

In other words, the authors, ethnic/racial cheerleaders all, wouldn't come clean and identify the inferior billiard balls for us. Thernstrom has traveled far, from language worthy of Martin Luther King, Jr., to locutions only more formal than those of the scandalous Reagan administration appointee Mary Ann Mele Hall, who wrote that black Americans had experienced "10,000 years of jungle freedoms" before arriving in the United States, and thus were incapable of civil behavior.[121]

Thernstrom, then, is not simply one historian fallen victim to a foolish vision of culture and economy in America traceable to bad, old anthropology. He is an exemplar of the American academic establishment, and his personal intellectual trajectory mirrors that of the larger entity. There was an opening, a generation ago, to a complex historical account of shifting American populations and their intersections with one another and with the evolving political economy. Anthropologists were part of that movement, but failed as a group to break decisively with the anthropological gambit, as did scholars across the disciplines. Those whose work is resolutely historical and political economic are less read, less attended to. The end result in the present, as I will show, below, is an appalling national discourse on "the minority underclass"—the villain in our current morality play that blames the poor for their impoverishment—and a separate script about the "American temperament," meaning that of white middle-class Americans.

Meanwhile, however, we need to consider the presumption of recent postmodernist anthropologists that they have escaped "specializing in Borneo" in representing a new, improved mode of dealing with "writing culture"—to borrow the title of one of the main postmodern texts. Have these sophisticated theorists gone beyond the anthropological gambit through their hyperawareness of the discipline's central role in inscribing the Other to the West? Although I have referred several times, glancingly, to this recent school, it is only fair to the reader not already conversant with it to offer a précis of its development and claims before I attempt to answer this question.

Poststructuralism is a movement deriving largely from literary criticism that foregrounds language over all other social phenomena and that particularly foregrounds textual art. It construes all texts—whether private letters, op-ed pieces, *Das Kapital,* advertisements, or scientific reports—as more or less persuasive fictions. This iconoclastic stance advances our understanding of relations among seemingly unrelated genres of writing, throws presumptions of realist representation into a cocked hat, allows us to apply the analytic tools of literary criticism to nonliterary productions, and decenters pious certainties concerning artistic and "high-cultural" canons.

Postmodernism is often used interchangeably with poststructuralism. The term originally referred to particular architectural innovations that mixed stylistic elements from different eras (Greek columns on a Bauhaus skyscraper), muddying formerly clean modernist lines. Postmodernism then expanded to refer to any example of cultural production that violates modernist conventions, particularly those of linearity and realist representation. Such experimentation can enhance communication, or it can disguise lack of knowledge and illogic, as in Trinh Minh-Ha's example and in Torgovnick's excursus on Malinowski's body.[122] Finally, use expanded to the extent that postmodernism now refers to all social life and politics in the West and, even more generally, to our historical era, which has apparently obliterated all modernist conceptions of linear evolutionary change.

In anthropology, poststructuralist/postmodern work descended from the "interpretive" school associated with Clifford Geertz, an antipositivist trend that "refocusses attention on the concrete varieties of cultural meaning, in their particularity and complex texture, but without falling into the traps of historicism or cultural relativism in their classical forms. For the human sciences both the object of investigation—the web of language, symbol, and institutions that constitutes signification—and the tools by which investigation is carried out share inescapably the same pervasive context that is the human world."[123]

Interpretation thus made use of phenomenology's contention that "knowers" cannot stand outside "the known" in order to refuse the analogy between "hard" and human sciences. Interpretive social scientists not only declared that they were *not* scientists at all, but moreover, that "there is no privileged position, no absolute perspective, no final recounting." While this stance helped to underline the obviously ideological character of social knowledge, it also paved the way for what Benedict Anderson labels the "finally unbridled subjectivity" of poststructuralism. Interpretive scholars, as well, defined social science's object as "meaning"—not including the social processes about which humans construct meaning—thus setting the stage for the terminal idealism of poststructuralism/postmodernism in anthropology.[124]

This school, most appropriately labeled "ethnography as text" after the article of that title by George Marcus and Dick Cushman, focuses attention away from doing fieldwork—interacting with and trying to interpret the thoughts and actions of a group of others—to the product of the fieldwork experience, the ethnographic text. Just as poststructuralists in other fields blur the boundaries among types of texts, so these anthropologists abandon the notion that ethnographies are scientific reports that concern humans and culture rather than whales, bacteria, or black holes, and see them instead as fictions, texts that are carefully constructed to have particular effects. Anthropologists lay claim to ethnographic authority through the use of allegory, "marking" texts with signs of professional expertise (maps, statistics, photographs), or constructing "common denominator people."

Such observations are certainly true, and useful. Postmodern anthropology's problems arise from its overweening arrogance. Postmodern work is only a set of new, groundbreaking research tools; it is not an overarching epistemology to which all others must be relativized. To "unfix, by literary therapy, the narrow frames in which ethnographies have typically been read" is an accomplishment, but one with limits.[125] Postmodernist anthropologists have tended instead to treat these new insights, this new literary framing, with the fervor of religious converts. I walked into an American Anthropological Association ballroom panel in the late 1980s only to hear one of the field's leaders repeatedly intone "Chiasmus!" from the lectern as if he were disclosing a new name for the Godhead.

Ethnographies are fictions, but they are also about material realities, realities that may be socially apprehended and historically contingent but can be checked, challenged, debated, and reconsidered. Some ethnographies really are better than others—and not merely as art. They concern more than human cognitive apprehensions—"culture"—they also concern the material life of which culture is an inseparable part, that it interprets and, as material fact itself, acts upon. William Roseberry points out that postmodernist anthropologists tend to invoke rather than to analyze colonialism and capitalist functioning: "There is no attempt to conceive [them] in active and particular terms—particular problems or periods, particular policies or powers, particular capitals or states—in specific relations to processes of social and cultural formation."[126]

And anthropology is about much more than *writing* ethnography. Producing text is only the end point of a series of activities, activities that postmodern anthropologists tend to ignore. In so doing, they solipsistically focus in on an impoverished "ethnographic encounter" that excludes all the historical and institutional impedimenta in which any such encounter is embedded, reading, as Michel-Rolph Trouillot complains, "the anthropological product as isolated from the larger field in which its conditions of existence are generated." We are back to xs and ys, locked inside the anthropological gambit. We are also locked inside a cognitive universe in which all politics must arrive from without and cannot be interrogated, by the very terms of poststructuralist theory. Thus the notorious sexism of the first set of texts produced by the "pomo boys," which coexisted oddly with their anxious, strained anticolonialism.[127]

The ways in which various postmodern anthropologists deal with the United States provide an illustration of these contentions. Off-the-cuff, cocktail party assertions are common. Witness Stephen Tyler's outburst in *Writing Culture:* "... the exploitative pseudo-narrative of *Dallas,* with its insidious hiss in the ears of the poor of: 'See, the rich are rich but miserable.'" Tyler here is of course vaguely expressing an analysis first sharply posed in the 1950s by the exiled Frankfurt School Marxists in their fulminations against mass culture. Recently, other Marxists have noted that this a priori stance denies working-class people independent consciousness and historical agency and greatly oversimplifies the processes of popular cultural production and consumption.[128] But because, according to postmodernists, Marxism is a discredited grand narrative, Tyler feels no need acknowledge the ground he treads. And because he is writing about the United States, not Borneo (or India, where he originally did fieldwork), he does not consult other scholars' work on the production and reception of television programs.

A more substantive example of postmodern bumbling in finding America is Marcus and Fischer's guild defense at the end of *Anthropology as Cultural Critique* in laying out research areas for anthropologists to colonize in "repatriating ethnography": the critique of professional cultures, critical legal studies, &c. Extraordinarily, they advise psychoanalytic "inquiry into the cultural constructions" of ethnic identities, because

> in the late twentieth century, for many Americans, questions of group mobility or assimilation are no longer burning issues, or are easily identified and acknowledged problems with more or less satisfactory modes of accommodation within the ideology and programs of the liberal state. What seems to be far more compelling an issue are the deep emotional ties to ethnic origins, which are obscurely rooted and motivated, and which are transmitted through processes analogous to dreaming and transference rather than through group affiliation and influence. Ethnography [done in the manner they suggest] would contribute better understandings of accommodations to American pluralism.[129]

Only by ignoring Americans of color and all post-1965 immigrants altogether can Marcus and Fischer make such a statement. Even then, they miss the political functions of white ethnic ideology, as I will show below. And the most cursory review of economic evidence would indicate that American class relations are tightly intertwined with race and ethnicity. Which Americans exactly, in the Reagan years when Marcus and Fischer wrote these lines, felt that race and ethnicity were "no longer burning issues" and that they had "satisfactory modes of accommodation"? Domestic exotics, unlike the foreign Others upon whom so much postmodern ink has been spilled, get short shrift from this school of anthropologists. Their vision of the United States recalls Mrs. Jellyby, Dickens's *Bleak House* character who exercised herself over foreign missionizing and viewed the stark poverty of Victorian London with perfect equanimity.[130]

Sherry Ortner continues the Marcus and Fischer mode (she refers to them explicitly) as she moves from work on Nepal to the United States. She claims that Americanist work in anthropology is quite recent, and then asserts that research on social class is a marginal American anthropological concern, a contention she supports through defining out work on black and other Americans of color as "working around the (class-) edges of society." She ignores ethnographies written by Louise Lamphere, Patricia Zavella, Brett Williams, Mercer Sullivan, Constance Sutton, Ida Susser, and Rayna Rapp, among many others—all centrally concerned with the ethnography and political economy of American class relations. Part of Ortner's willful blindness may arise from her postmodern interpretation of what anthropological work on class should be. It should tackle "the complex dynamics that reproduce the American class structure" through investigation of the "discourse of class"—but not actual lives and social relations. Terminal idealism, again.[131] For all their seeming sophistication, when it comes to anthropology's America, postmodern anthropologists compare poorly to Horace Miner in the 1950s.

These postmodern failings, and those of the larger anthropological gambit in which they are embedded, arise not only from "billiard balls," from ahistorical and essentializing constructions of human social life—constructions that are shared widely in and out of academe. They are also due to non-Marxist anthropology's choice of particular, narrow slices of the academic pie of knowledge. Outside archaeological concerns, and those of no-longer-read neoevolutionists, such anthropologists tend to concern themselves with all aspects of human life *beneath* state structures, away from the corridors of material power. This play for safety is understandable, perhaps, among those who work abroad: offend the powers that be and your visa may be revoked. And as anthropologists tend to be more reliant on fieldwork than other scholars, perhaps one can justify greater prudence than shown by historians, political scientists, economists, or sociologists—who often work purely from archives and data sets.

But a partial methodological necessity should not be blown up into a disciplinary epistemological virtue. "Culture" is never separate from, and cannot be understood apart from, politics and economy. And whether we have chosen them with intent or had them thrust upon us, the multiple Halloween costumes anthropologists wear in the public sphere are political garments. If we anthropologists do not speak our own lines, our clothing will speak for us. To insist upon a bounded knowledge domain of idealist-defined culture is simply to claim a kind of permanent adolescence, or court jester status, among intellectuals—to restrict ourselves to an unambitous terrain, to refuse to take responsibility as adults for the world in which we live and work.

The evisceration of the political in recent postmodern anthropological work is different from standard anthropological procedure, then, only in that it has political pretensions. It is a difference something like that between a class clown and a clown who is also a bully. Aside from James Clifford's interesting ethnographic essay on the Massachusetts land trial of the Mashpee Indians, the closest American postmodern work of recent years has gotten to the corridors of power is Paul Rabinow's treatment of generational shift and the rituals of hiring in the Berkeley anthropology department.[132]

Ironically, only a generation ago Marxist sociologist Alvin Gouldner made exactly these criticisms of a then-trendy school of sociology, ethnomethodology. In the form practiced by Harold Garfinkel (Gouldner ignored the much more politically conscious Aaron Cicourel), ethnomethodology, derived from phenomenology, revealed "the invisible common-place by violating it in some manner until it betrays its presence." Thus, Garfinkel and his students gleefully phoned friends and then refused to make sensible conversation, repeatedly claimed ignorance of fundamental locutions in American English—"What do you mean, flat tire?"—staged scenes in public places in order to note reactions, &c. Gouldner points out both the juvenile quality of this work and its inherent political quietism in the guise of militance: "It is a way in which the alienated young may, with relative safety, defy the established order and experience their own po-tency. . . . It is a substitute and symbolic rebellion against a larger structure which the youth cannot, and often does not wish to, change."[133] The paral-lels are obvious: the use of phenomenology in the absence of political econ-omy, revolutionary pretensions without substance, refusal to engage with institutional power, juvenile enjoyment in flouting conventions (the ethno-methodological experiment, postmodern experimental prose). This is not to say—not quite—that postmodern anthropology is ethnomethodology returning as farce. But we need a genuine sociology of knowledge to pre-vent further historical repetitions, one that squarely confronts what Eric Wolf has labeled a continuous thread in American anthropology: the leg-acy of unconcern with the phenomenon of state power.[134] We need to fol-low the anthropological gambit's use by anthropologists and others, across decade after American decade, and assess its political meanings to varying publics as its actual material implications alter.

But before we enter further into anthropology's America, we need to delineate the America that is no longer ours, the world we have "lost"—that of contemporary American exotics at home.

two

THE THREE BEARS, THE GREAT GODDESS, AND THE AMERICAN TEMPERAMENT

Anthropology without Anthropologists

Somebody has been sitting in my chair!—*Baby Bear, "Goldilocks and the Three Bears"*

INTRODUCTION

Despite anthropology's prominence as trope, its central "savage slot" role in debates on Otherness in American academic and popular culture, the discipline is most notable for its recent absence in a key symbolic arena— the dynamics of race, ethnicity, and gender in modern American life. Like Sherlock Holmes's dog that did not bark in the night, this absence of anthropological casting is meaningful, a diagnostic of the ways in which domestic exotics are represented—and represent themselves—on the American stage. To see this stage in the round, we need to consider how recent morality plays deploy notions of "tradition" and "culture" in order to narrate self, Other, modernity, and redemption. Laying out this cultural and political economic tale will in turn clarify why it is that this contemporary stage is one upon which largely other sorts of scholars—and journalists and politicians—strut and play. But more important, it will help us to find America, a stage of complicated and constantly shifting inequity, behind the painted scrim of benevolent and maleficent Otherness.

Recent commentary on the American temperament portrays contemporary United States citizens as a people without traditions, except perhaps the tradition of invented and individualizing social orders. Thus Frances Fitzgerald chooses recently established communities with narrow membership criteria—an affluent white retirement development, a Christian cult, San Francisco's gay neighborhoods—as exemplars of a broad-scale and continuous American turn against both the past and the larger society in attempts to establish utopian orders for a narrow elect.[1] Allan Bloom excoriates American popular culture, and thus America's young, as vulgar, tradition-less, and not coincidentally subject to the illogical and unnatural "fads" of leftist and feminist thought and action.[2] On the other end of the political spectrum, Russell Jacoby deplores the dying-off of an early-to-mid-twentieth-century tradition of American public intellectual life and the retreat of radical intellectuals into an arid and hermetic scholasticism.[3] In the final and most instructive example, sociologist Robert Bellah and his coauthors in their multiple-interview study *Habits of the Heart*, and in the subsequent *Good Society*, determine that Americans primarily conceive the self as unencumbered by dependent others, by community obligations, by institutions, by history.[4] These authors' analyses underscore current images of protean American individualism, and the Bellah group has endorsed a new communitarian political movement calling for mandated "encumbering."

Habits typifies recent evaluations of American cultural perceptions in other ways as well. The unencumbered selves—such as those making use of "therapeutic" or "managerial" modes of apprehending reality—with which the authors find their informants struggling and which the authors adjure us to discard, are significantly white, male, and middle-class. This narrow conception of American selfhood is unsurprising when we consider both the authors' demographically skewed choice of interviewees and the prototypically elite primary historical American studies texts—Winthrop, Jefferson, Franklin, Tocqueville—to which they turn to flesh out their interviewees' hesitant statements.

Indeed, if we shift the focus to include all Americans, both as agents and as objects of the cultural construction of the self, we perceive instead an American landscape littered with images of very cumbered selves. While the myth of the nineteenth-century pioneer or frontiersman lives on, it has been joined by those of rebellious black slaves, the planners and sojourners on the Underground Railroad, and the cooperative and contentious struggles of the suffragists. Contemporary mass media images include working mothers who notoriously face a double day of obligations to others, and the native and migrant poor living, of necessity, cheek by jowl and heavily dependent on one another.

Despite the fact that the very notion of an unencumbered self is, as the Bellah group points out, a traditional American invention, scholars and popular cultural commentators associate tradition in the United States with gemeinschaft—groupness, interdependence, responsibility—with the state of cumberedness.[5] Two American groups have popular cultural "traditions" in this sense: foreign peasantry and their descendants, and women. But these associations themselves have a history. Just as anthropology's recent political economic radicalism has become a dim disciplinary memory, so the 1970s—aside from stylistic markers like bell-bottoms, Afros, disco, and Fleetwood Mac—have entered our historical blind spot. In that era, as we shall see, Chicago School obsessions with social order and anthropology's false focus on monolithic "cultures" merged with the complicated politics of the times to produce our contemporary fissioned and falsifying discourses of American race, class, and gender relations.

Here, then, I examine the two current, competing, and related images uniting these two population groups and notions of a cumbered self: ethnic community and women's culture. I connect these two American invented traditions, both historically and in terms of their symbolic logics, to our contemporary version of "blame the victim" ideology, the new barbarian *within* the gates. This newly hegemonic construction is the mythology of the (unencumbered or overcumbered, depending on analyst) minority "underclass"—which itself is not an invented tradition and yet shares features with them. In so doing, I suggest not only that there are multiple inventions of tradition in American life and many versions of the self, but also that all invented traditions, as anthropologist Frederick Barth noted in 1969 concerning ethnicity, are historically contingent and constructed on the boundaries of group membership. Even (or especially) the various mainstream notions of white, male unencumbered selves exist in unadmitted relation to raced, classed, and gendered Others and in contexts of power and domination. Male frontiersmen relied on wifely help and displaced and expropriated land from male and female Native Americans. The new white male entrepreneurs of, say, Silicon Valley, rely on a vast army of white female clerical labor and of Third World female factory labor both inside and outside the United States. The myth of the unencumbered self is thus a construction that exists in part to disguise material realities, and we need to consider, as Bellah et al. and other commentators do not, the historical, political economic foundations of invented traditions.

But images of cumbered selves are not themselves free of mystifying functions, nor do they operate monolithically. Notions of ethnic communities and of nurturing women are used by many cultural agents (political parties, commercial interests) for diverse purposes. And the process of inventing traditions is deeply intertwined with American and, indeed, Western intellectual history.

As used by different social actors, these contemporary inventions of ethnic community and women's culture, and the mythology of the underclass, implicate two related themes in Western social thought: the nature/nurture dichotomy and the ambiguous functions and meanings of human community. Women and ethnic/racial Others, in fact, are often envisioned as "temporally distant" from and thus more natural than "ordinary" Americans—as domestic exotics. These Others are primitive, traditional, folk, natural, and underdeveloped—those who will save us from modernity, those whose primitiveness proves our worth and justifies our domination. Western tropes used on exotics abroad have been thriftily recycled for home use—and vice versa. While these points have been made before, scattershot, here I consider more carefully their interrelationship and their specific connections to changing political economy and to larger intellectual and political debates in the contemporary United States.

The "American temper" or "ethos" is continually reinvented, constructed, and reconstructed without reference to changing demographics and political economy. It is "hidden in plain sight." And, in configuring America from the Progressive Era to the present, "non-Other" Americans have added to notions of primitiveness and civilization the righteous theological language of morality plays and the Gradgrind terminology of neoclassical economics. What is useful is good and good, useful—but the calculus of utility and goodness is only applied to Others, never to "ourselves." Again and again, when Others have attempted to wrest free the right to inclusion, to find an America that allows them equal citizenship, they (we) are driven to justify the claim with reference to the utility calculus. We raise your moral tone. We make contributions. Let us in.

PIZZA, KNISHES, SODA BREAD

While certain popular works (such as the World War II era's *Streetcorner Society* and the Camelot Years' *Urban Villagers*) foreshadowed it, the American concept of the white ethnic community coalesced in the early 1970s, the period in which the term "white ethnic" itself gained currency. A "white ethnic," of course, exists in contradistinction to those ethnics defined as nonwhite, and thus white ethnics came into existence as a labeled group in response to the Civil Rights/Black Power movements and the allied organizing of Latinos, Asians, and Native Americans.[6]

Populations we now label white ethnic—those whose antecedents arrived from (largely southeastern) Europe from the 1840s and increasingly after the 1880s—were subject to intensive, largely deprecating or patronizing public scrutiny particularly through the Reform and depression eras. Popular representations of Irish, Italians, Poles, Jews of every nationality, and others as mentally deficient, dirty, diseased, and/or innately criminal were widespread, and because knowledge of those representations—and the discrimination that underlay and arose from them—has fallen down the national memory hole, it may be useful to review the record here.

The *New York Tribune* commented in 1882 on the uncouth nature of Jewish immigrants in language strongly parallel to contemporary white New Yorkers' characterization of the minority poor:

> Numerous complaints have been made in regard to the Hebrew immigrants who lounge about Battery Park, obstructing the walks and sitting on the chains. Their filthy condition has caused many of the people who are accustomed to go to the park to seek a little recreation and fresh air to give up this practice. The immigrants also greatly annoy the persons who cross the park to take the boats to Coney Island, Staten Island and Brooklyn. The police have had many battles with these newcomers, who seem determined to have their own way.[7]

IQ testing was actually institutionalized as an effort to evaluate various immigrant populations' fitness for World War I military service and thus right to remain in the United States, and Jews, despite subsequent popular representations, were frequently defined with other southeastern Europeans as mentally inferior. In 1913, Henry Goddard applied mental tests to newly arrived immigrants and reported that 83 percent of the Jews (but only 79 percent of Italians!) were feeble minded. Margaret Mead's 1924 master's thesis compared intelligence test scores of English- and non-English-speaking Italian-American children in her home town, Hammonton, New Jersey. She concluded that the much higher scores of English speakers indicated the power of cultural factors, contra the arguments of eugenicists.[8]

Stanford University president David Star Jordan, in 1922 Senate testimony, distinguished northern from southern Italians on eugenic grounds. The southerners displayed "the incapacity of those hereditarily weak."[9] The official *Dictionary of Races or Peoples,* drawn up by the Dillingham Commission of the Sixty-first Congress, described the southern Italian as "excitable, impulsive, highly imaginative, impracticable; an individualist having little adaptability to highly organized society," and Slavs as representing "fanaticism in religion, carelessness as to the business virtues of punctual-

ity and often honesty, periods of besotted drunkenness among the peasantry, unexpected ferocity and cruelty in a generally placid and kind-
hearted individual."[10]

As to crime, University of Wisconsin sociologist E. A. Ross, contradicting Henry Goddard's findings, wrote in 1914 that "The fewness of Hebrews
in prison has been used to spread the impression that they are uncom-
monly law-abiding. The fact is that it is harder to catch and convict criminals of cunning than criminals of violence. The chief of police of any large
city will bear emphatic testimony as to the trouble Hebrew lawbreakers
cause him. Most alarming is the great increase of criminality among Jewish
young men and the growth of prostitution among Jewish girls."[11] This assessment is extremely mild compared to his treatment of Italians and Slavs.
Ross goes on to quote from "the Jewish press" to the effect that Jews *had*
been protesting Gentiles' exaggeration of their crimes, but now found
themselves forced to admit the "nests of theft, robbery, murder, and law-
lessness that have multiplied in our midst." Sounding hauntingly like contemporary black sociologist William Julius Wilson, as we will see, this Yid-
dish text laments: "But when we hear of the murders, hold-ups and
burglaries committed in the Jewish section by Jewish criminals, we must,
with heartache, [agree with our critics]."[12]

Ross's estimate of the Irish, whose great period of immigration was three
to four generations past on the eve of World War I, was relatively benign:
"'Tonio or Ivan now wields the shovel while Michael's boy escapes competition with him by running nimbly up the ladder of occupations." Nevertheless, "the children of the immigrant from Ireland often become infected
with the parental slackness, unthrift, and irresponsibility."[13]

All of these representations, and the more positive but equally condescending liberal appraisals of the time, such as Jane Addams's in the prologue, share several interrelated elements. They assume that southern and
eastern European migrants and their descendants are "outside the circle
of the we," in David Hollinger's phrasing; that therefore well-off white professionals have the right to speak for and about the character of those less
well off; and that there is an inextricable connection between cultural Otherness and (presumably self-caused) poverty.[14] Where commentators differ—then and now—is in their evaluation of that cultural difference. Eugenicists presumed it was genetically determined, while others used more
or less plastic notions of culture, leaving the door open for "assimilation"
to erase unpleasant traits.

Feminist theorists, following Simone de Beauvoir (who herself appro-
priated the immanence/transcendence distinction from Jean-Paul Sartre's

existentialism), have commented on Western political theory's pervasive functionalist orientation in interpreting women's lives. Susan Okin notes succinctly that "philosophers, in laying the foundation for their political theories, have asked 'What are men like?' 'What is man's potential?' have frequently, turning to the female sex, asked 'What are women *for?*'"[15] We can see an analogous orientation in discourse of the Gilded Age and Progressive Era on "strangers in the land"—the title of John Higham's classic study of American nativism. "We" WASPs simply *are* Americans; there is no need to interrogate our utility to the nation. But "they" may or may not be of use. And for many Americans of (non-Irish) northwest European origin, the meaning of "use" was nakedly obvious. The vast immigrant influx was an economic bonanza for transportation interests—particularly steamship and railroad companies—for tenement owners, for manufacturing, mining, and agricultural firms, and for many other employers of unskilled labor. It was a recurrent nightmare for union organizers and a wide variety of already resident workers whose wages employers could beat down with the specter of immigrant competition. Nativist sentiments were thus filtered (as they are now) through sets of interests—labor under threat and elements of capital who either profited little from new immigration or for whom profit could not override racist repugnance.

In 1930, Madison Grant and other racist eugenicists published an anti-immigration compendium whose title, *The Alien in Our Midst, or, Selling Our Birthright for a Mess of Industrial Pottage,* clearly comments on the contemporary tension between perceived economic self-interest and eugenics theory. Of the 1911 Dillingham Commission's forty-one volumes of reports, fully twenty-three deal with immigrant representation, skills, and pay in a wide variety of American industries. A color chart produced by the Pittsburgh branch of the National Urban League in 1925 grades thirty-six groups on their "racial adaptability to various types of plant work," including such categories as "smoke and fumes" and "night shift" (see fig. 11). E. A. Ross himself was fired from Stanford University by Jane Stanford, widow of the university's founder and sole trustee, for his racist speeches against Chinese immigration. Stanford's motives, however, were not particularly antiracist. As Rosalind Rosenberg notes, "Stanford's fortune had been built on the backs of Oriental labor and she did not wish to see this diligent labor supply cut short."[16]

The populations that would come to be called white ethnics were thus the first American groups classically defined as "urban poor," both by the nascent reform movement and by the developing field or urban sociology in the 1920s and 1930s.[17] As such, these domestic exotics were heirs to a

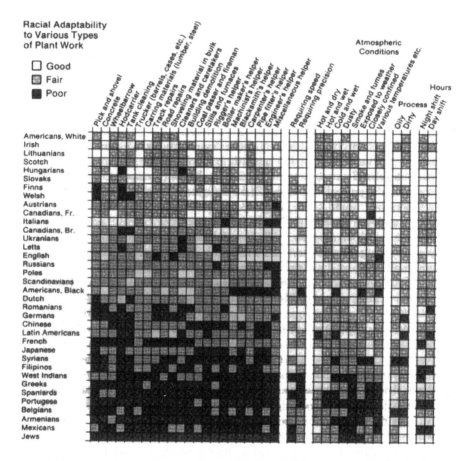

11. Naked racism, 1920s. Employment chart of the Central Tube Company, Pittsburgh, 1925. Reprinted in John Bodnar, Roger Simon, and Michael P. Weber, *Lives of Their Own: Blacks, Italians, and Poles in Pittsburgh, 1900–1920* (Urbana: University of Illinois Press, 1982), p. 240.

profound Enlightenment ambivalence about the nature of communities. Since at least the time of Rousseau and his critics, "community" has explicitly or implicitly contained the images both of equality, order, and civility and of ignorance, hidebound tradition, and narrowness. This dichotomy was first inscribed as a country/city contrast and was transposed, in the urban American context, into a contradictory vision of the functioning of newly arrived European peasantry in United States cities.

Thus the work of the Chicago School sociologists and anthropologists could describe migrants to the city both as the inheritors of gemeinschaft— the simple, humanly satisfying, face-to-face, traditional rural world that was giving way to the complex, anomic, modern urban world of strangers—and as rude, uncivilized peasants who must modernize, assimilate, Americanize in order to rise to the level of work and social life in the new industrial city. And these urbanizing peasants, as the first populations of impoverished Americans studied by social scientists, would inevitably be used as templates against which to compare other groups, especially black Americans, despite the fact that blacks were also present, and subject to even worse treatment than European migrants, in Progressive Era northern cities. The "noble versus nasty peasant" construct is, of course, directly connected to that of the noble versus nasty savage.

Robert Park, a founding Chicago School sociologist, and Herbert Miller reflect this ambivalence well in their 1921 volume, *Old World Traits Transplanted:* "At home the immigrant was almost completely controlled by the community; in America this lifelong control is relaxed. . . . All the old habits of the immigrant consequently tend to break down."[18] They argue for assimilation, but in orderly stages, because "a too rapid Americanization is usually disastrous." Immigrant crime, in their vision, is due to culture loss: "There is among [Jews], indeed, a great variety of disorder and personal demoralization—gambling, extortion, vagabondage, family desertion, white slavery, ordinary and extraordinary crime—as a consequence of the rapid decay in America of the Jewish traditions and attitudes."[19] But crime also arises from imperfectly comprehended American customs, a "misapprehension of the motives of the American models they think they are imitating":

> On October 20, 1911, Walter Shiblawski, Frank Shiblawski, Philip Suchomski, Thomas Schultz, Philip Sommerling, and Frank Keta (all boys) held up and killed Fred Guelzow, a farmer, who was bringing a load of vegetables to Chicago. They had two revolvers, a bread knife, a pocketknife, and a large club. They had been reading novels and planned a hold-up. When Guelzow was ordered to hold up his hands he promptly did so. They took his silver watch and chain, then killed him, mutilated him horribly with bullets and knives, and cut off a piece of his leg and put it in his mouth.[20]

Despite such often harrowing details—no less harrowing than current accounts of "underclass" crimes—Park and Miller end in a credo for then-contemporary European immigrant populations. They affirm their assimilability: "If the immigrant possesses already an apperception mass corresponding in some degree to our own, his participation in our life will, of course, follow more easily." And, unlike E. A. Ross and other eugenicists, Park and Miller—and with them the Chicago School in general—an-

nounce that the southeastern European "does not differ from us pro-
foundly."[21] Indeed, historians David Roediger and James Barrett and Noel
Ignatiev have documented the historical "achievement of whiteness" that
Euro-American populations have undergone.[22]

But other Others *are* unassimilable, fated to remain outside the circle of
the we. In an uncanny foreshadowing of Pat Buchanan in the 1990s, Park
and Miller warn that "if we should receive, say, a million Congo blacks and
a million Chinese coolies annually, and if they should propagate faster than
the white Americans, it is certain that our educational system would break
down."[23] They use a free-floating list of unattributed grotesqueries to define the truly Other:

> If the immigrants practiced cannibalism and incest; if they burned their widows
> and broke the necks of their wayward daughters, customarily; if (as in a North
> African tribe) a girl were not eligible for marriage until she had given her older
> brother a child born out of wedlock, to be reared as a slave; if immigrant families
> limited their children by law to one boy and one girl, killing the others . . . if
> immigrant army recruits declined target practice because the bullet would go
> straight anyway if Allah willed it—then the problem of immigration would be
> immensely complicated.[24]

Finally, in the clinching argument for "our" contingent acceptance of white
ethnics into probationary citizenship, Park and Miller assert their ancestral
temporal distance: "In comparison with these examples immigrant heri-
tages usually differ but little from ours, probably not more than ours differ
from those of our more conservative grandfathers. Slavery, duelling, burning of witches, contempt of soil analysis [!], condemnation of the view that
plants and animals have been developed slowly, not suddenly created, are
comparatively recent values and attitudes."[25] Invocation of the grandparent, as we shall see, has become a widespread and revealing trope in American race/ethnic discourse. But first we need to follow that discourse into
the present.

With the coming of World War II and through the 1960s, there was a
general hiatus in both scholarly and popular attention to the non-American
origins of this large segment of the American population. This was in part
an epiphenomenon of restrictive immigration legislation in 1924; by the
end of World War II most immigrants had been resident in the United
States at least twenty years and had children and often grandchildren.
(Many Irish, of course, were at that point marking nearly a century of
United States residence.) It was also in part a result of the conscious efforts
(assisted, of course, by capital and state) of migrants and their children to

"modernize" and "Americanize." In addition, it was in part the result of social scientists' interests in the changing physical features of the postwar American landscape, such as increasing suburbanization (*The Levittowners*), and in emerging social types and characteristic social relations related to the maturation of corporate capitalism (*The Lonely Crowd, The Organization Man, Workingman's Wife, Blue-Collar Marriage*). Even research specifically concerned with ethnic and racial life in the United States during this period (such as Milton Gordon's 1964 *Assimilation in American Life*) continued to use the Progressive Era melting pot metaphor and was more concerned with negative than with positive aspects of "unmelted" populations.[26]

This era of public and scholarly quiescence ended abruptly in the early 1970s as white ethnicity suddenly became a topic of key national concern. Across the nation, moribund ethnic voluntary associations revived and countless new ones were formed. Popular books celebrating white ethnic experience, such as the second edition of Nathan Glazer and Daniel Patrick Moynihan's *Beyond the Melting Pot,* Michael Novak's *Rise of the Unmeltable Ethnics,* Andrew Greeley's *Why Can't They Be like Us?* and Richard Gambino's *Blood of My Blood,* became best-sellers. And a stream of scholarly books and articles began to flow from the academy. Werner Sollors has noted that "ethnicity truly was in vogue in the 1970s."[27]

Journalistic and scholarly accounts alike parlayed the notions that white ethnics were an unjustly [repressed, maligned, ignored—take your pick] segment of the American population, were just beginning to rediscover their own histories and cultures, and deserved respect and attention in the public arena. Michael Novak, among many others, threw down the white ethnic gauntlet: "In the country clubs, as city executives, established families, industrialists, owners, lawyers, masters of etiquette, college presidents, dominators of the military, fund raisers, members of blue ribbon communities, realtors, brokers, deans, sheriffs—it is the cumulative power and distinctive styles of WASPS that the rest of us have had to learn in order to survive. WASPS have never had to celebrate Columbus Day or march down Fifth Avenue wearing green. Every day has been their day in America. No more."[28]

Tied to these notions of the nature of white ethnic Americans was the construct of the white ethnic community, which journalists, academics, and individual white ethnics themselves proclaimed to be an endangered but surviving inner-city institution. White ethnic communities past and present were characterized in terms reminiscent of Chicago School interpretations of interwar immigrant populations—with the negative end of the pole removed.

Social life in white ethnic neighborhoods is largely rooted in the family. . . . Most people know or at least recognize one another. There is a sense of community integrity and group identity.[29]

The pattern of Italian-American life is continuous with that of their ancestors. Its verities continue to demonstrate that family, community and work mean survival and that outsiders are threats to neighborhood stability which is necessary to the close-knit life and culture of the people.[30]

Within the geographic boundaries of the Italian Quarters the *connazionali* gave life to a closely woven community within which the Italian way of life flourished.[31]

What the [New York Jewish] East Side lacked in sophistication, it made up in sincerity. It responded to primal experiences with candor and directness. It cut through to the essentials of life: the imperative to do right and the comfort of social bonds.[32]

As Stephen Steinberg and I have argued, these claims concerning white ethnic communities rest upon unexamined presuppositions that there *were* in fact such discrete phenomena: long-term, self-reproducing, ethnically homogenous inner-city neighborhoods.[33] In reality, American white ethnic populations throughout the nineteenth and twentieth centuries, no matter how abused or discriminated against by majority society, lived in ethnically heterogeneous and shifting urban and suburban neighborhoods— and moved often. Indices of residential segregation for European populations in the United States fell steadily from 1910 on. White ethnics also took flight to the suburbs in concert with their urban WASP neighbors. Thus, for example, by the mid-1970s, in the height of publicity on the white ethnic renaissance, California's prototypical Italian-American community, San Francisco's North Beach, had more than 90 percent Chinese residents, and California's Italian-American population was in reality scattered far and wide across the state's urban, suburban, and rural areas.[34]

If such popular claims about white ethnic communities were untrue— were, in fact, a newly invented tradition—what was the purpose and meaning of this ideological construct? Clearly the assertion of self-worth had psychological benefits for individual white ethnics, but why did these assertions arise at that particular historical moment, and why were they so attentively heeded? In other words, how did the rise of "white ethnic community" ideology intersect with other contemporary political, economic, and cultural forces? Why did the various social actors who made use of it find it salient?

BEHIND THE AFROS AND BELLBOTTOMS

The late 1960s and early 1970s in the United States were characterized by continuing economic expansion, the ongoing war in Vietnam, and a linked set of social movements directly related to these two key political economic realities: the Civil Rights and Black Power movement, the antiwar movement, the student/youth movement, and the revived feminist movement.[35] The connections among these social movements and their links to larger political economic realities have been exhaustively documented, but can be summarized as follows: The unrealized prospect of partaking in the benefits of postwar economic expansion, protests against being victimized by urban renewal displacement, and anger at the disproportionate induction of black youth for war service helped to fuel Black Power activism. The antiwar and feminist movements drew inspiration and personnel from contemporary black movements. Economic expansion and the demographic bulge of a 1960s college-age cohort laid the material basis for college- and then high-school-located youth rebellion—including civil rights, antiwar, and feminist protests but also involving demands for increased autonomy and sexual freedom. Finally, postwar economic expansion led to American capital's greatly increased demands for labor, and thus American women's rising employment rate. The very possibility of supporting themselves without reliance on father or husband allowed many women to challenge male societal dominance, while the low pay, low status, and minimal prospects for advancement that characterized most "women's jobs" in that era stimulated feminist reaction.

These multiple movements for reform and liberation challenged both the federal, state, and institutional structures—such as those of colleges and universities—and individuals who perceived themselves to be threatened by particular demands for social change. The Nixon administration in particular sought to exploit and enhance these social divisions through the use of the polarizing discourse about the "silent majority"—as opposed to the protesting antiadministration "minority." Between administration rhetoric and media response, an image grew of this stipulated entity: the silent majority were white—implicitly white ethnic—largely male, blue-collar workers. They were held to be "patriotic" and to live in "traditional" families—ones in which males ruled, women did not work outside the home for pay, and parents controlled their children.

This media image, of course, did not reflect an aggregate social reality. This was the era, after all, in which married working-class women were entering the labor force at record rates and in which their additions to family income maintained working-class living standards in the face of declining real incomes. White labor support for the Democrats actually peaked in 1948—the party's loss of the white working-class had begun long before Watts, Woodstock, and Gloria Steinem. And sexual adventurism and drug use in the late 1960s and early 1970s were the property of working-class no less than middle-class youth. Nevertheless, as a media construct, as a symbol of the hemorrhaging of Democratic voters to the Republican party, the conservative white ethnic blue-collar worker gained salience in this period. This salience was much enhanced by the shifting populations and power relations in American cities.[36]

In the 1960s, poor black Americans became newly visible, and newly defined as a social problem in Northern cities. The two great waves of black migration from the South, during the First and Second World Wars, had each resulted in cohorts of permanent northern black urban residents. These men and women had come north (often through employer recruitment) both to take advantage of lucrative war jobs and to flee Jim Crow and the effects of the mechanization of southern agriculture. They had then often been laid off and largely had become part of a permanent army of reserve labor. Urban renewal projects in the 1950s and 1960s—an employment boondoggle for white ethnic blue-collar workers—destroyed countless urban black neighborhoods, replaced them with office blocks and sports complexes, and shifted and concentrated the poor black population in areas dominated by inhospitable, poorly built, and badly maintained government housing projects. Ninety percent of the housing destroyed by urban renewal was never replaced, and two-thirds of those displaced were black or Puerto Rican. The Federal Housing Authority deliberately fostered segregated white housing and refused loans to blacks until the passage of the Fair Housing Act in 1968. Douglas Massey and Nancy Denton have noted that the "highest [residential] isolation index ever recorded for any ethnic group in any American city was 56 percent (for Milwaukee Italians in 1910), but by 1970 the *lowest* level of spatial isolation observed for blacks anywhere, North or South, was 56 percent (in San Francisco).[37] Big-city governments refused to shift budgetary resources to basic services for these impoverished areas. Northern white populations, contra contemporary received wisdom, discriminated against, refused to patronize public establishments with, rioted against, attacked, and killed blacks in the North from the World War I era on. There was no "era of northern amity" prior to the Civil Rights movement and Black Power.

Neighborhood deterioration, increased crime, and urban uprisings— combined with intensive political organizing—stimulated the establishment of highly visible federal Great Society programs. (But the late-1960s explosion of welfare rolls was of almost exclusive benefit to poor *whites*.)[38] At the same time, a small cohort of socially mobile blacks, emboldened by the Civil Rights movement, attempted to buy homes in formerly white urban and suburban neighborhoods. The resulting "white flight" greatly enriched the real estate speculators who fanned its flames and exacerbated inner-city white racism. Black (and Latino) struggles for higher-quality public education, neighborhood services, and civil service and union jobs led to increased friction between white, often white ethnic, and minority citizens in northern urban environments, friction only furthered by the newly oppositional rhetorical style of Black Power advocacy. The first scattered fringe of desuburbanizing bourgeois whites entered into this polarized and often dangerous environment, benefiting, of course, from its resulting low real estate values.

Thus, the "white ethnic community" construct arose from an extraordinarily complex historical ground, and this complexity was reflected in its multiple expressions and political uses. Key to all expressions and uses, though, was its reliance upon the basic ideological tropes of the Civil Rights and black cultural nationalist movements as structural templates, and thus its posture of competition through emulation. This ideology posited blacks as a unitary, identifiable group who had experienced and were experiencing extreme forms of discrimination, and who therefore were entitled not only to cessation of discriminatory laws and behaviors but also to financial and other sorts of recompense (affirmative action, Head Start, CETA, &c.). Thus, ironically, key expressions of white ethnic resentment were couched in language consciously and unconsciously copied from blacks themselves—Werner Sollors comments on this mimicry, but as a cultural, not fundamentally political phenomenon. Notions, for example, of the strength and richness of white ethnic cultures and their repression by WASPs mimicked black cultural nationalists' (and white scholars') celebrations of black culture's endurance despite white domination.[39] Even Andrew Greeley admitted that "what the blacks have done is to legitimate ethnic self-consciousness."[40] When I was doing fieldwork among California Italian-Americans in the mid-1970s, many individuals identified my documentation of their and their antecedents' life histories as "our *Roots*," after the book and television film series on Alex Haley's Southern black family history.

Deliberate denigration of blacks vis-à-vis white ethnics relied as well on the ideological frame of entitlement used by black Americans. Both popular journalistic accounts and grassroots white ethnic discourse, for example, focused on the strength and unity of white ethnic families as opposed to those of black Americans—whose popular image had been shaped in the early 1960s as a "tangle of pathology" by the Moynihan report. (Linda Gordon's study of early-century family violence among Boston's poor Irish, Italians, Jews, and others reminds us that narratives of drunkenness, wife battery, child abuse, desertion, incest, and prostitution could be and were constructed for white ethnics.)[41] In my own study, many Italian-Americans' racist expressions against blacks focused on inferior black family behavior as both explaining and justifying widespread black poverty. Thus the argument that, as the undeserving poor, blacks were not entitled to the largesse of Great Society programs and the approval of elite sponsors, which should instead flow to "deserving" white ethnics:

> The ethnics believe that they chose one route to moderate success in America: namely, loyalty, hard work, family discipline, and gradual self-development. They tend to believe that some blacks, admittedly more deeply injured and penalized in America, want to jump, via revolutionary militance, from a largely rural base of skills and habits over the heads of lower-class whites. Instead of forming a coalition of the black and white lower classes, black militants seem to prefer coalition with intellectual elites. Campus and urban disorders witness a similarity of violence, disorder, rhetoric, ideology and style.[42]

This relative entitlement frame is attached, as I have argued, to a "report card mentality," in which shifting American class divisions are seen as caused by proper and improper ethnic/racial family and economic behavior rather than by the differential incorporation of immigrant and resident populations in American capitalism's evolving class structure. And proper and improper behaviors are related to notions of cumbered and unencumbered selfhood and to "provisions of temporal distance." The cumberedness that Chicago school social scientists saw southeastern European immigrants as inevitably losing in the gesellschaft of modernizing urban America was rediscovered in the 1970s as a surviving feature of white ethnic selfhood. Scholarship, journalism, and grassroots expressions celebrated white ethnics for their family loyalties and neighborhood ties. In fact, advertising in this period began to exploit "cute" white ethnic imagery—the pizza-baking grandmother, the extended family at the laden dinner table—in order to invest frozen and canned foods with the cachet of the gemeinschaft.

This gemeinschaft, cumberedness—this community—was delineated as an urban phenomenon existing alongside and in opposition to urban black populations. Stephen Steinberg has pointed out sardonically that "the Poles and Slavs in Chicago, like the Irish in Boston and the Jews in Forest Hills, rarely experience their ethnicity so acutely as when threatened with racial integration."[43] In fact, there was the distinct flavor of a "three bears" analogy in much 1970s and 1980s rhetoric on white ethnicity. (And this trinity, based in the eastern seaboard and the industrial Midwest, neatly wrote nonblack Latinos, Asians, and others right off the American stage.) While WASPs were "too cold"—bloodless, modern, and unencumbered—and blacks "too hot"—wild, primitive, and overcumbered—white ethnics were "just right." They could and did claim to represent the golden historical mean between the overwhelming ancientness and primitiveness of gemeinschaft and the stripped-down modernity of gesellschaft. In a flurry of do-it-yourself domestic antimodernism, white ethnics were constructed, and constructed themselves, as homegrown noble savages, sufficiently temporally distant from WASP modernity to embody the charm of Dempster Street. For a hot minute in the 1970s, American white ethnics commandeered Baby Bear's chair.

This new vision of white ethnics as the proper urban residents, those who maintain stable neighborhoods that nevertheless have "character"—ethnic restaurants, delicatessens, and other small businesses—was a major ideological component of growing gentrification. Ironically, of course, the more urban professionals were attracted to inner-city neighborhoods, the more real estate prices rose and the less could *any* working-class urban residents and shopkeepers, white ethnic, black, or other, continue to afford to live or to do business in those neighborhoods. Thus, the economic logic of Third World tourism came to characterize many American inner-city neighborhoods—the more successful one is in commodifying oneself, the less one is able to reproduce the self that has been commodified.

But in the midst of the excursions and alarums of the era, not everyone located white ethnics in Baby Bear's chair. Margaret Mead, for example, in *A Rap on Race,* a retrospectively embarrassing 1970 book based on two days of tape-recorded conversations with James Baldwin, articulated the self-assured limousine liberal's contempt for white ethnic "materialism"—as opposed to the correct, ideal-based Americanism of WASPs in condescending coalition with blacks. She also embodied the American anthropological tradition of pronouncing on American culture in deep ignorance of United States history and political economy and, as we will see, prefigured contemporary identity politics in lodging her superior understanding of race in her northern WASP upbringing:

> MEAD: I learned about race as a child. . . . In the North, in Bucks County, Pennsylvania. I have completely Northern ancestry, and my grandfather fought in the Civil War on the Northern side. My father bought a farm that had been

a station on the underground railroad. . . . But most people who came here were terribly poor and wanted things.

BALDWIN: To prove they existed.

MEAD: To prove they could get them at all. They had been eating the black bread of poverty, so they came over here and they wanted to eat the white bread that was eaten in the castle. So instead of eating good, nourishing whole wheat bread—

BALDWIN: They started eating white bread. Yes, indeed, look at the results.

MEAD: They began eating too much sugar too; that's what the people in the castle had. So that what we have here, and I think this had to be remembered, is not an old American style. Old Americans were frugal. The style in this country. . . . I still—you know, I was brought up to untie each package carefully, untie the knots in the string and roll it up and put it away to use again.

BALDWIN: Yes, I still do that too. And I hate myself for it.

MEAD: Still, there were all these people who thought they were coming to a land where the streets were paved with gold, and that is the reason they came. Now, if you go somewhere and suffer quite a lot trying to get there, being poor and digging roads, living in slums when you first come, and you only came because the streets were paved with gold—

BALDWIN: That describes a great deal of the black man's ironical amusement when he watches white people. You know, he did not have that illusion. He didn't want to come.

MEAD: He didn't come with that illusion at all. Now, most of the people who came to this country were poor. We had very, very few people who came to this country who had anything. . . . I think you have to discriminate between the people who came here early for political and religious reasons—the ones whom we still think made the country and whom we still talk about and use as ideals, and who did come here to live their kind of life the way they believed in—and the great many millions of immigrants who came here in the nineteenth century— . . . you see, we have now an enormous amount of people in this country who didn't come here to dream. They didn't have dreams, except just security for their children. And these are the people we call the silent majority, and they are terribly frightened.[44]

Central to the new construction of white ethnic community was the Madonna-like (in the older sense) image of the white ethnic woman. Early-1970s popular writers extolled her devotion to home and family, and many of the more conservative Italian-Americans in my late-1970s study echoed this fusion of ethnic chauvinism and antifeminism. Clelia Cipolla, a middle-aged civil servant, said, in describing her elaborate cooking for family holidays: "I've always thought of Thanksgiving as the only holiday the American wife really cooks for. . . . maybe that's a wrong idea of it, but that's the way my feelings are."[45] Part of the appeal of this construction was the notion that white ethnic mothers, unlike "selfish" WASP and "lazy" black mothers, could control their children and thus were exempt from blame for then-current youth protests. Clelia Cipolla exclaimed to me in response to my narration of a recent Thanksgiving holiday's activities: "You mean Mommy and Daddy *allowed* you to have Thanksgiving away from home?"[46]

But in fact, white ethnic women were no less than other women subject to the pressures and opportunities of the shifting American political economy of the 1970s, and many more of the Italian-American women with whom I worked actively altered or rejected the popular image of the self-sacrificing, kitchen-bound ethnic mother. What is important to note is not whether white ethnic women fit the model—by and large, they did not and do not—but that the model has been so hegemonic as to command belief and influence the construction of identity. Linda Mornese, for example, judged her own immigrant grandmother insufficiently ethnic because she did not conform to the nurturant peasant model: "I remember my aunt's mother, she was really the old Italian: white hair, never any makeup, the old dresses, wine barrels in the basement. I always thought: there's a *real* Italian lady. I don't see an Italian lady as one with her hair done. My grandmother's always kept herself, she's always dressed very well, she puts her jewelry on—she's better at it than I am!"[47]

In an era of rising feminist activism, the sudden celebration of a group of women socially labeled as backward, stolid, and possessive wives and mothers functioned very clearly as antifeminist rhetoric—particularly rhetoric against women's workforce participation. In addition, in focusing on women's "duties" to husband and children, it worked against prevalent civil rights imagery of heroic women of the black movement whose duties lay in the public sphere. But like all symbols, the white ethnic woman is polyvalent and was and is subject to feminist and progressive interpretation:

> As Barbara Mikulski of Baltimore points out, the white ethnic woman in America is not a dingbat, however warm and humanistic may be the character of Edith Bunker, nor is she limited to "tacky clothes," "plastic flowers," *True Confessions,* and an "IQ of 47." Rather, she is Maria Fava and Ann Giordano, who travelled to Albany to express parent and community concern over limitations on day care. She is Rosemarie Reed, who attended a Washington conference on community organizing. She is Marie Anastasi, who is working with senior citizens as well as a "mothers' morning out" group. She is one of dozens of women who have joined with Monsignor Gino Baroni of the National Center for Urban Ethnic Affairs to deal with housing, redlining by banks, and neighborhood preservation.[48]

Many feminist scholars celebrated the strength and endurance of "traditional" ethnic women and used, for example, narratives of past union and strike activities, or consumer protests, in order to suggest a vision of innately progressive, rebellious ethnic womanhood.[49] This attempt to wrest the white ethnic woman from the antifeminist Right overlapped with another prominent invented tradition of the same period, the notion of women's culture.

JANE ADDAMS MEETS THE GREAT GODDESS

In 1975, American historian Carroll Smith-Rosenberg published "The Female World of Love and Ritual: Relations between Women in Nineteenth-Century America" in the first issue of the feminist scholarly journal *Signs*.[50] In this article, using extracts from letters between female friends and kinswomen, Smith-Rosenberg contended that (at least white, literate) American women in this period constituted a mutually supportive society separate from the world of their fathers, brothers, and husbands. Smith-Rosenberg's larger point was a critique of our reductionist Western visions of sexuality. Her letters between women provided evidence of passionately romantic relations among schoolgirl friends that lasted lifetimes and were unaffected by the women's heterosexual courtships and marriages.

Smith-Rosenberg's article heralded a highly influential trend in burgeoning American feminist scholarship. Historians, literary critics, and social scientists began to focus more on relations between women, tipping the balance over from work on relations between women and men, the prime concern of early second-wave feminist writing. This shift in emphasis coincided with the institutionalization of feminist work in the academy (witness the founding of *Signs*) and with the related relative decline of grassroots feminist activism.

The focus on women's relations with one another and its attendant assumptions of female nurturance and cooperativeness reflected a growing phenomenon in academic and popular feminist circles—and one not limited to feminists, as I will show—a phenomenon I label "women's culture."[51] While actual expressions of "women's culture" ideology vary greatly, the following is an ideal typical description. There is an entity, women's culture, which represents an *Ur*-form of women's nature and has the same characteristics across time and space. These characteristics include moral superiority to men, cooperative rather than competitive social relations, selfless maternality, and benevolent sexuality. Thus, women's culture embodies the notion that there is an authentic global feminine self-

hood that has been distorted, encrusted by the accretion of male domination. While many of these tenets also fit radical or now cultural feminism,
I would distinguish between women's culture and these theoretical strands.
Women's culture is not a political or theoretical perspective, but a protean
set of claims which may be (and are, as I shall demonstrate) used to construct varying arguments, including antifeminist ones, concerning women's
nature, rights, and duties. But whatever the argument, one point is always
clear: women in their relations to one another and to children are utterly
unlike—and better than—men.

Feminist scholars across many disciplines from the mid-1970s into the
present have taken to the notion of women's culture. Consider the following extracts:

> Literary criticism: "Women's culture forms a collective experience
> within the cultural whole, an experience that binds women writers to
> each other over time and space."[52]
> Political theory: "There is always a women's culture within every
> culture."[53]
> Social theory: "The bedrock of women's consciousness is the obligation
> to preserve life. Now as in the past, women judge themselves and one
> another on how well they do work associated with being female."[54]
> Political history: "Women's culture is the ground upon which women
> stand in their resistance to patriarchal domination and their assertion
> of their own creativity in sharing society."[55]
> Psychology: "Women not only define themselves in a context of human
> relationship but also judge themselves in terms of their ability to
> care."[56]

Three elements are common to all scholarly deployments of women's
culture. The first is the aforementioned intrawomen emphasis. Second,
"women's culture" writers plump resolutely for "difference" in what historian Nancy Cott has analyzed as the "two logically opposing poles"—
sameness and difference from men—that have animated feminist political
argument since the nineteenth century. Finally, all scholars' usages "cum-
ber" women with some combination of home, children, community—what
historian Temma Kaplan labels a "shared sense of obligation to preserve
life"—or what is now often labeled "women's ethic of care."[57]

Equally important are the different ways this protean bundle of descrip-
tors is used. In the first place, the very meaning and implications of wom-
en's culture vary depending on disciplinary context. A literary critic de-

scribing a number of Western women writers divided by time, space, and class, a historian investigating proletarian Spanish women's protests, and a psychologist working with white middle-class American girls and women are drawing from very different intellectual traditions and have different scholarly agendas—they mean different things by "women's culture." One contrast alone, Carol Smith-Rosenberg versus Carol Gilligan, illustrates this point. Gilligan, inheriting the essentializing and ahistorical psychological notion of "moral development," describes women's culture, their judging themselves in terms of their ability to care, in a transhistorical, transcultural present. This is what women are like. Smith-Rosenberg, in contrast, describes a nineteenth-century female world we have lost and a "more flexible and responsive" ethos than that characterizing our own modern times. This is what women were channeled to be like—much less so now, more's the pity. (But see her development from this position, below.)

Indeed, because their discipline's raison d'être is historical change, feminist historians have written most self-consciously and prolifically about women's culture, both as historiographical taxonomy and as changing popular ideology. They have provided a multiplicity of terms to describe particular, contingent constellations of received wisdom and political argument concerning cumbered, nurturing women—republican motherhood, social feminism, moral motherhood, true womanhood, woman's sphere. Nancy Cott and Linda Kerber, most notably, have reviewed and criticized the accuracy of historians' efforts to construct and apply terminology to different populations and different eras.[58]

Among all these feminist scholars who made use of it, nevertheless, the shift to women's culture reflected a political shift in the larger society. Alice Echols's historical study, *Daring to Be Bad*, documents this general trajectory from radical to cultural feminism, or from "a political movement dedicated to eliminating the sex-class system" to "a countercultural movement aimed at reversing the cultural valuation of the male and devaluation of the female."[59] In a 1980 *Feminist Studies* symposium on politics and culture in women's history, Ellen Carol DuBois and Caroll Smith-Rosenberg faced off in classic articulations of critique and defense of women's culture. "The dominant tendency in the study of women's culture," DuBois declared, "has not been to relate it to feminism, but to look at it in isolation and to romanticize what it meant for women. . . . there is a very sneaky kind of antifeminism here, that criticizes feminism in the name of the common woman." Smith-Rosenberg countered roundly, accusing DuBois of "elite focus" and "bourgeois analysis," and stating that "'the pressing historical questions about women's culture,' I would argue do not 'center on its relation to feminism,' but rather the pressing questions about feminism center on its relation to the existence of the female world."[60]

This cultural feminist shift is equally visible in feminist activism from the 1970s forward, particularly in peace and environmental politics. Consider, for example, the popular feminist antimilitarist slogan: "Take the toys away from the boys." The implicit meaning is that morally superior, maternal women will discipline male warriors who are responsible for world militarism. Or consider the popular T-shirt and bumper sticker slogan, "When God created man, He was only practicing." Posters sternly ordering us to "Love your mother" (a photo of the earth) have been staples for years in ecology-minded circles. Popular feminist slogans from the 1980s such as "stop raping, stop warring," "mothers save your children," and "father state makes mother earth kaput" are all cut from "women's culture" cloth.

Perhaps more important to the growing hegemony of feminist "women's culture" tropes, given the progressive demobilization of peace and environmental activism through the 1980s and 1990s, has been the continuous stream of matriarchy and Great Goddess writing from the 1970s on. These popular works are based on old, often Victorian anthropology—although one woman archaeologist of European prehistory, Marija Gimbutas, turned, late in her career, to discerning prior matriarchies in potsherds and claiming women's defeat at the hands of violent invaders: "We are still living under the sway of that aggressive male invasion and only beginning to discover our long alienation from our authentic European heritage—gylanic, nonviolent, earth-centered culture."[61]

Such claims of the existence of prior matriarchies always identify them as benevolent, humane states, often associated with the worship of female supernatural beings. Early works such as *When God Was a Woman* and *The First Sex* have been superseded by a veritable flood of texts. Contemporary writers have produced feminist utopias incorporating "women's culture" claims, such as Sally Gearheart's *Wanderground.* Older texts, such as Charlotte Perkins Gilman's *Herland,* have been reprinted and have become staples of the women's studies classroom.[62] The institutionalization of feminist witchcraft (or wicca, or neopaganism) inspired by medieval Europe further underlines "women's culture" themes. Cultural feminist magazines like *Chrysalis* and *Womanspirit* serve these overlapping audiences and also provide a bridge to the New Age/Great Goddess texts and commodities available on Dempster Streets and suburban malls throughout the United States.

These widespread feminist constructions of prior perfect women's states are strikingly parallel to the pristine ethnic community of the white ethnic renaissance's imagination and the superior precolonial societies of Africa invoked by black cultural nationalism. Adolph Reed, in fact, in 1979 labeled the historical relation of cultural feminism to black cultural nationalism the "feminist photocopy of the black journey on the road to nowhere."[63] This feminist photocopy, like its black nationalist original, has also appeared in forms more academically respectable than the Great Goddess genre. Throughout the 1980s and into the 1990s, two major waves of respectable women's culture lapped through major media from the ivory tower. The first was the enormous hoopla surrounding the publication of Carol Gilligan's *In a Different Voice*. Gilligan's feminist purpose, in narrow academic terms, was exemplary: to discredit cognitive psychologist Lawrence Kohlberg's claim that women's moral and ethical development over the life course lagged behind men's. But in so doing, Gilligan replicated Kohlberg's epistemological and methodological frames—that is, she assumed that a small population of elite heterosexual whites could stand as synecdoche for all Americans, that stories told in response to hypothetical problems could stand for lifetime patterns of behavior, that there is such a thing as gender-universal moral and ethical growth culminating in adulthood. Gilligan hedged some—but by no means all—of her universalizing, generalizing statements, witness the "judging themselves on ability to care" quotation above. Despite extensive critiques of her work from academic feminists, she was widely apprehended as the scholar who had provided definitive proof of women's moral superiority, their relational "caringness" when compared to individualistic, rule-governed, rational men.[64] Gilligan was read and allowed herself to be used as a psychological vindicator of "women's culture" ideology. Her subsequent, more oppositional, collaborative research on girls and schooling has been much less attended.

In the meantime, however, linguist Deborah Tannen has become American popular culture's Gilligan redux. In a series of lively, highly accessible books and articles (e.g., *You Just Don't Understand*)—even a *Reader's Digest* piece—Tannen has parlayed a thesis first propounded by the late Ruth Borker and Daniel Maltz into a minor self-help industry. Borker and Maltz suggested that male-female communication in the modern United States was in part *mis*communication because girls and boys tended to learn differing communicative styles in their single-sex play groups: "We argue that American men and women come from different sociolinguistic subcultures, having learned to do different things with words in a conversation, so that when they attempt to carry on conversations with one another, even if both parties are attempting to treat one another as equals, cultural misunderstanding results."[65] Tannen relabeled this phenomenon "cross-cultural communication" and tapped an enormous reading market of women desperately trying to understand their male intimates: "If women speak and hear a language of connection and intimacy while men speak and hear a language of status and independence, then communication between men and women can be like cross-cultural communication, prey to a clash of conversational styles."[66] She was even invited to address an informal congressional "gender dynamics" group that came together in the wake of the Clarence Thomas/Anita Hill publicity on sexual harassment.[67] But Tannen's claims of male-female differences in communicative styles in standard American English are not borne out by reputable sociolinguistic studies. Neither she nor Borker and Maltz before her escaped overgeneralizing from small data bases to create unwarranted models of gendered language use. There are wide varieties of "gendered communicative styles" in American English. Much soi-disant "miscommunication" across sex is in fact the communication of male social power over women. And so-called female linguistic features are often exhibited by low-status male speakers.[68]

Although in subsequent work both Gilligan and Tannen have acknowledged differential male/female power in American society, each made her name—and is known for—academic popularizations of notions of gendered difference that deny the connection between differences in male and female behavior and male social and political power. The extreme popularity of each—despite extensive scholarly critiques—the ease with which they became media icons, indexes the porous boundary between oppositional, feminist "women's culture" interpretations and nonfeminist notions of women's separate, cooperative worlds. Crudely put, such interpretations let men off the hook while allowing women to feel morally superior about their lack of power. They are tailor made to succeed as what James Scott labels "the public transcript," the official, "common sense" narrative of human social reality.[69]

Indeed, the bulk of "women's culture" emanations in popular discourse are not at all feminist. Most everyday American expressions incorporating a sense of women's innate difference from men, their superior, benevolent maternality, in fact accept and defend the status quo. Cetta Longhinotti, a middle-aged, working-class woman in my first ethnographic study, unselfconsciously avowed, "I think women are superior. . . . I think God helps us," to explain her martyred familial role. Less pietistic but equally fatalistic assessments infuse American popular culture. Middlebrow entertainment often simply assumes a world of caring women—if not always separate women's worlds. The ubiquitous "Cathy" cartoons gently satirize intimate mother-daughter ties and women's worlds of shopping and food consumption. Popular women's magazines, from the working-class *Family Circle* and *Women's Day* to the higher-register *Victoria* and *Martha Stewart's Living*, cater to notions of women's innately warm interior worlds, their loving ties with other women and children, their heroic self-sacrifices for others. (And media hysteria over obvious counterexamples—"bad women"—only serves to underline happy face "women's culture" images, as we shall see.)

Even the Great Goddess trope is easily stripped of all oppositional content and infused with self-help ideology, as in best-selling New Age author Marianne Williamson's appalling *Woman's Worth*. Williamson, battening on women readers' needs to think well of themselves, bathetically suggests that we are all goddesses: "'What' you say. 'Me, a goddess?' Yes, I say, and don't act so surprised."[70] Williamson assures us that "we have a job to do reclaiming our glory," but that glory is a 1990s version of the 1890s women's pedestal. Apparently we are to approve other women's (Williamson's, obviously) speeches at dinner parties, but to eschew any effort to gain more social and political power: "As long as we focus on the outer world, which is not our home base, and try to wield power of the kind only known there (power so crude, by the way, the angels can't help but laugh), we will remain in the weaker, slightly confused position."[71]

Whether women are told to "run with the wolves" by "returning to their instinctive lives, their deepest knowing," or lectured that "men are from Mars, while women are from Venus," the non- (really anti-) feminist New Age message is the same: women are indeed superior goddesses, more connected and caring than men.[72] That's the way it is. Double day? Violence against women? Feminization of poverty? Glass ceiling? Let us avert our eyes, look within, accept, and celebrate. No struggle in the real world, no political change is needed.

Political commentator Katha Pollitt, following Nancy Cott's historical analysis, has labeled feminist "women's culture" interpretations "difference feminism." In the witty tour-de-force piece "Marooned on Gilligan's Island," printed in the *Nation* and reprinted in the *Utne Reader* (with an angry response from Deborah Tannen), Pollitt sends up academic and popular denials of women's equal personhood with men and false claims of mothers' superior morality. She understands the functionalism operating within "women's culture" discourse: "It asks that women be admitted into public life and public discourse not because they have a right to be there but because they will improve things." Pollitt goes on to claim that "no other oppressed group thinks it must make such a claim in order to be accommodated fully and across the board by society. For blacks and other racial minorities, it is enough to want to earn a living, exercise one's talents, get a fair hearing in the public forum. Only for women is simple justice an insufficient argument."[73] But in fact, functionalist arguments are the staple of historical American discourse on *all* Others, not just women. They have, if anything, become more central in the era of "underclass" ideology, part of the entwined rhetorics of identity politics and of the New Right. And the absurd recent American "men's movement," amid its tom-toms and homoerotic bonding in the woods, also makes the functionalist claim, but in reverse: only the return of patriarchal power will allow fathers to control and heal a ruined world.[74]

"Women's culture" ideology, then, whether feminist or nonfeminist, is like "white ethnic community" ideology in that it makes claims that are simply false. Women, like men, are members of the human species, and nothing human is alien to them. Women's culture denies the closer allegiances to men than to women (what 1970s radical feminists scored as "male identification") that many women form. It denies various forms of female cruelty—the reality of female participation in theft, torture, murder, in the abuse, sale, and/or abandonment of children—activities that have been carried on by at least some women in most past and present societies, activities that are not necessarily explained away by prevalent male domination. It denies what is even more prevalent: female apathy and laziness. And it denies the realities of women's self-seeking strategizing *within* their "nurturant," "unselfish" activities of caring for home and children. Children, after all, until very recently in the industrialized West, labored for their parents and as adults owed them—often especially their mothers—loyalty, labor, and cash.

Clearly, the "women's culture" concept exists in complex relation to recent political economic shifts and the ideological constructions of contemporary political movements. Women's culture, in its feminist incarnation, responds to antifeminist accusations that feminists are selfish—that they do not, in other words, accept their proper load of cumberedness—through embracing an a priori functionalist moral high ground. All women are innately morally superior to all men because they are naturally cooperative and nurturant. They are automatically cumbered, but by responsibility for other women and children, not necessarily for men. This feminist essentialist stance, as Janet Sayers labels it, by appeal to biological or near-biological differences between the sexes, neatly preempts accusations that feminists and/or lesbians have lost their femininity.[75] They cannot lose that which is innately theirs, which is ascribed, not achieved. In this vision, all women are goddesses, and goddesses automatically sit in Baby Bear's chair.

The "women's culture" construct, then, is structurally related to "white ethnic community" ideology in two ways. First, it attempts to transform extant polarized notions of its subjects (warm and orderly versus primitive and insular European migrants, Madonnas versus harridans and sluts) by chopping off and denying the existence of the negative pole. This operation has been relatively successful for the "white ethnic community" construct. The historical version of the negative pole—the stolid, backward, crime-ridden, socially immobile ethnic community, Stephan Thernstrom's "sub-culture that directs energies away from work"—has been superseded in the public mind by the black and brown poor whose segregation, poverty and high crime rates are presumed to be self-caused. The more recent historically negative vision, that of the racist, conservative white ethnic community, has not been revived, despite abundant recent examples of popular racism, property crime, and violence.

The negative pole of women's culture, in contrast, is alive and kicking in popular culture. Recent journalistic coverage—not to mention the behavior of courts and police—of reproductive issues such as surrogate motherhood and prenatal care have tended toward automatic blame of women caught in difficult circumstances. Thus, women who agree to be surrogates are deemed selfish, as was the woman who agreed and then wished to back out of her agreement. And pregnant women who do not follow doctors' orders have been arrested and charged. Negative stereotypes of women abound in popular culture, from the psychotic rejected woman in *Fatal Attraction*, to the evil upper-class boss in *Working Girl*, to the hypersexual murderess in *Basic Instinct*, to the selfish, unmaternal bourgeois witches of John Updike's recent fiction. American popular press coverage of "rich bitches" such as Ivana Trump, Imelda Marcos, and Leona Helmsley—consuming wives of far richer and/or more directly evil men—is characterized by a populist venom not aimed at wealthy or powerful men since Nixon and Watergate.

There are a number of obvious reasons for the relative failure of explicitly feminist "women's culture" ideology. The first is that it transmutes so easily into its much more prevalent antifeminist form. "Revaluing the female sphere" can be, and is, a contemporary argument for backlash against gender equity. Then, it is easier to maintain a counterfactual vision of an elusive ephemeral community—particular neighborhoods and individuals can be labeled inauthentic—than of half the human race. In addition, the social base for sentiment against white ethnic communities is small. The Nixon era is long over; Reagan and Bush's three electoral victories cannot be ascribed to crossover white ethnics alone. And Clinton won the 1992 election with Rust Belt and eastern seaboard "white ethnic" votes, while largely losing the good-old-boy South that the Democratic Leadership Council was convinced he had sewn up. In contrast, the key mainstream feminist goal of the 1980s—ratification of the Equal Rights Amendment— failed, and antifeminist ideologies have been strongly represented since the 1980s from the White House down. It is in the current interests of a large number of politically active groups to blame some population of American women—those seeking abortions, those who have children without "men to support them," those who do not have children, those who leave husbands, those who attempt to be attractive to men, those who do not, those attracted to women, those on welfare, those in the labor force, those who protest sexual harassment, those who put their children in day care—for all social ills.

The second relation between women's culture and white ethnic community is not emulation but annexation. In the 1970s context of rising feminism and the first antifeminist construct of the white ethnic woman, feminists responded, as I have noted, by claiming the white ethnic woman for themselves and their discourse. But the feminist "women's culture" construct also emulates the white ethnic community's annexation of the symbolic structures of the Civil Rights movement, "swallowing" not only the beleaguered white ethnic Madonna but the oppressed, heroic woman of color.

It is in this context that the linked phenomena of feminist academic work and popular feminist cultural production have taken on a distinctive shape and thrust. American universities, by default, as Russell Jacoby has noted, have become in the recent conservative era important havens for progressive social thought. Faculty in explicitly new, interdisciplinary programs, such as women's and Afro-American studies, frequently have taken a beleaguered, circle-the-wagons stance. This defensiveness is often justified, given the stalled feminist and civil rights agendas in the larger society and recent eruptions of racist, sexist, and homophobic behavior on American campuses. Such a beleaguered sensibility, combined with evidences of aggregate male danger and irresponsibility (high rates of violence against women, little change in indices of occupational segregation by sex, aggregate male failure to pay child support) enhance essentializing cultural feminist interpretations of women's common lot irrespective of their differences and also encourage the presumption of female moral superiority upon which the construct of women's culture rests. Thus the tendency of "women's culture" writers to annex the notion of the heroic "triply op-pressed" woman of color—which is of course the obverse of the hegemonic popular cultural vision of the feckless, welfare-dependent, drug-taking, black or Latina teenage mother.

This tendency to illogical inclusion has not gone uncriticized within feminism. Nancy Hewitt has incisively noted the ways in which scholars' accounts of nineteenth-century "women's culture" do not account for the realities of nineteenth-century black women's lives. Phyllis Palmer has criti-cized the tendency of white feminists to rely on the heroic images of such past black women activists as Sojourner Truth without acknowledging the financial gap, exacerbated by prevalent race endogamy, between black and white women today.[76] And more impressionistic, "literary" women writers of color have indicted white feminists' race-blind inclusionary stance.[77]

SHIFT CHANGE AT BABY BEAR'S CHAIR

American culture, then, contrary to the assumptions of many observers, has historically abounded in visions of cumbered selves. Two of these, the white ethnic community and women's culture, have salience and sufficient institutional impedimenta—books, journals, festivals, associations—to constitute full-blown invented traditions. How do these cultural constructs function today in the contested space of the national political arena?

White ethnic community, since the late 1970s, has not been a hot topic for academic papers and popular cultural accounts. Festivals and meetings of ethnic historical associations and social groups do not receive the public attention they once did. In Andy Warhol's phrase, white ethnicity had its fifteen minutes of fame in the mid-1970s, and other social groups and is-sues have since captured the public stage.

Nevertheless, the transformed construction of white ethnic community remains "on hold"—Bellah et al., for example, pay it lip service before hurrying on to their (presumably nonethnic) interviewees. To switch the metaphor back, white ethnic community stands backstage, ready to reenter stage left or right at a given cue. Recently, for example, a series of Demo-cratic politicians have attempted to make use of notions of family, stability, and tradition now associated with white ethnicity to bolster their appeal to the electorate. This strategy backfired for Geraldine Ferraro, of course, when both her husband and son fell foul of the law. It was ultimately use-less in insulating the originally progressive Jim Florio from full-scale right-wing attack in New Jersey. But it was quite successful for Mario Cuomo and was one of the few winning elements of Michael Dukakis's ill-fared presidential campaign.

The relative weakness of "white ethnic community" ideology since the 1980s is also, I would contend, related to Reagan era script revisions in the national ethnic and racial morality play. As Debora Silverman has compellingly argued in *Selling Culture,* the Reagan White House, the Metropolitan Museum, *Vogue* magazine, and a number of clothing designers formed a sinister interlocking directorate that simultaneously flattered the administration, lauded wealth and aristocracy, and used museum resources to flout any art historical considerations while shamelessly advertising the work of those designers who pandered most openly to wealth.[78] I would add that at the same time, paralleling the rise of colonial chic in popular culture we saw a renaissance of positive images of the wealthy West at home. Public television fare shifted significantly to reruns of BBC productions most nostalgic for the Edwardian upper classes—*Upstairs, Downstairs, Brideshead Revisited, The Treasure Houses of Britain. Good Housekeeping* began its "New Traditionalist" advertising campaign featuring obviously affluent, nonworking blond women and their well-groomed children on the spacious grounds of their suburban or country estates: "She knows what she values—home and family." And her Rolex watch.[79] Wealthy whites took back Baby Bear's chair with a vengeance, and a new romantic halo was constructed over the image—embodied by Nancy Reagan—of the elegant, dignified, adorned, and (publically at least) devoted wife and mother, the curator of the proper WASP bourgeois home and children.

Meanwhile, popular representations of white ethnics, which in the 1970s had teetered between pious "world we have lost" images of authentically warm, close families and communities, and an *All in the Family* condescension, tipped over in the 1980s into permanent condescension and even minstrelsy. Take Italian-Americans as an example. In popular film, the ambiguous *Godfather* phenomenon, which lent glamour and gravitas to an organized crime family, gave way to *Moonstruck, Married to the Mob, True Love, Working Girl*—all films that represented working-class and better-off Italian-Americans as philistines, tasteless boobs, Guidos, and Big Hair girls, the kind of people who would have mashed potatoes dyed blue to match the bridesmaids' dresses. White ethnicity, in some venues at some times, came to mean the inelegant, disorganized enactment of others' life dramas for our condescending amusement—minstrelsy. The media hoopla surrounding the Amy Fisher/Joey Buttafuoco case denied the tragic realities of the emotionally disturbed young girl and the betrayed and wounded wife in sniggering references to the "Long Island Lolita," the auto parts store, and vulgar-sounding Italian names. The apotheosis of the new Italian-American minstrelsy, though, is the long-running (in New York, Los Angeles, San Francisco, Philadelphia, Chicago) environmental theater piece, *Tony n' Tina's Wedding*, in which the audience is encouraged to interact with the low-rent wedding party. The usually racially progressive women's magazine *Glamour* threw all self-consciousness to the winds in its reaction to the production:

> Off-Broadway's most innovative play satirizes a garish New York Italian wedding, and it's all the more fun when the audience joins in: Pin a dollar on the groom (to fund their Poconos honeymoon) and he'll dance with you to Donny Dolce and Fusion's rendition of "We Are the World." Chow down baked ziti and elaborately tiered wedding cake. Watch aqua-eye-shadowed Tina and her tarty, gum-chewing bridesmaids (dressed in red) break into an interpretation of Michael Jackson's "BAD," complete with crotch-grabs. Kissing our way through the reception line, Tina said she had a cute cousin she wanted to fix us up with. Tony whispered, "Don't call me at home no more!" [80]

This arch narrative, with its voyeurist's emphasis on intriguing, inferior, transgressive sexuality, startlingly parallels the text accompanying a photograph of an exotic Other on the 1893 Columbian Exposition Midway: "The Singhalese lady, the subject of the above illustration, should be happier than her white sisters, in one respect at least, for by the laws of her people she has the right to possess as many husbands as she can find room for in her accommodating heart. Graceful in every movement, with flashing dark eyes, and robed in the picturesque dress of her country, the Singhalese maiden no doubt has many aspirants to her hand, and is in the happy position that she can accept them all." [81]

Explicitly feminist women's culture, though, as I have noted, is of more recent vintage and has never gained broad popular appeal, remaining an invented tradition in use only within sections of college and nonacademic feminist populations. Among this group, however, and despite intragroup criticism, militant belief makes up for small numbers. Along with the avalanche of New Age pap, a steady stream of emphatic cultural feminist tracts flows from the mainstream and alternative presses. In 1985, for example, St. Martin's published Elinor Lenz and (anthropologist) Barbara Myerhoff's *Feminization of America*, which argued that "women's values" were taking over American culture and promised a "bright and peaceable future." [82] In 1986, Basic Books published the multiply authored *Women's Way of Knowing*, which claimed that all women experienced male domination as "silencing" and thus perceived "male" schooling entirely differently

12. Singhalese lady, Midway Plaisance, Chicago World's Columbian Exposition, 1893.

from males and had unique modes of learning. In 1988, New Society Publishers brought out Pam McAllister's *You Can't Kill the Spirit*, which narrates "inspiring stories" of women's nonviolent action going back to "thirteenth century BC Egypt."[83]

Women's culture has had specific recent political effects. In 1985, feminist historian Rosalind Rosenberg gave expert testimony on behalf of Sears Roebuck in the 1985 affirmative action case brought by the Equal Employment Opportunity Commission (under the directorship of Clarence Thomas). Rosenberg argued that nineteenth-century American women had established a separate women's culture based on nurturance and cooperation, and that commitment to those values has limited their desires and attempts to be competitive in the American labor market into the present.[84] More recently, at the 1993 United Nations World Conference on Human Rights, Catherine MacKinnon, Kathleen Barry, and other cultural feminists succeeded in focusing the press spotlight on the sexual abuse of women—with pornography as a major cause and symptom—and allowed the final Vienna Declaration to avoid addressing gendered economic inequity. As Laura Flanders notes, "in a global women's movement rent by class, race, age, and national divisions, the experience of violence provides powerful common ground. It's also sexy: sexier than labor rights, illiteracy, self-determination or poverty. . . . Given a choice between humanity and equality, the world conference gulped down humanity. . . . The anti-permissive, pro-control, pro-action-now approach of the new Victorian feminists seems suited to the dominant current in international affairs."[85]

In summary: women's culture, which is based upon our inheritance of nineteenth-century constructions of moral motherhood, is vulnerable to a politics that reduces women to beings subject to male abuse and thus in need of social regulation, but morally responsible for children and home and thus not fundamentally in need of economic rights. It lends itself with ease to synecdochic interpretations of womanhood that mask the gulf of privilege between well-off white Westerners and others, both Western and non-Western. And masking that gulf of privilege, "spinning" any and all narratives about economic inequity to rationalize the status quo—even to argue for the necessity of greater economic stratification—has been increasingly the work of the American public script since the 1970s. The construct of the minority underclass is the crystallization of that work, the apotheosis of the painted scrim of the new hegemonic conservatism. But in order to comprehend "the underclass" fully, we need first to sketch in the changes in the American political, economic, and cultural landscape since the 1970s that conservative "spin doctors " worked so hard, and so successfully, to obscure.

OF MR. WILLIAM J. WILSON AND OTHERS[86]

The mid-1970s energy crisis, so profitable to the big oil companies, was the first of a series of shocks to the economy that helped to usher in the new public ideology that we had entered an "era of limits." During the Carter administration, rapidly escalating inflation, particularly in the rising real estate market, set the symbolic stage for the dismantling of Great Society programs which were newly seen as "too expensive." Welfare cutbacks under Carter became wholesale shrinkage of the federal social welfare budget under Reagan. Concomitant recession drove unemployment figures into double digits. Numbers of individuals and families made homeless by unemployment, real estate speculation, and the federal abandonment of low-cost housing programs grew rapidly.[87]

With the economic recovery of the middle and late 1980s, unemployment shrank to early-1970s levels, then rose again with the Bush-Clinton recession, but it shrank less for minority Americans, and of those successively reemployed, many work part-time or at jobs with lower status and pay. As a combination of these shifts and regressive tax legislation, over the Reagan-Bush years the numbers of both the very poor and the very rich rose. (We now have the most poor and the smallest middle class, proportionately, in the First World.)[88] Despite local grassroots organizing against obvious inequities such as plant shutdowns, toxic waste dumping and other environmental disasters, farm foreclosures, and continuously increasing homeless populations—and despite the 1993 replacement of a Republican with a conservative Democratic administration—popular political discourse has shifted significantly rightward since the 1970s. Keynesian economic apprehensions of the utility and ease of deficit financing, of deficits as subject to state planning and manipulation, have eroded. Neoclassical terror of "handing down debt to our grandchildren" rules the day. In this shrunken universe of kindergarten economics, all social claimants except corporations, already well-off whites, and the military are derided for "demanding entitlements instead of accepting social responsibility." Civil rights, women's, gay, and labor groups are labeled "special interests." But most crucially: public discourse on the poor, particularly poor blacks and Latinos, has turned nearly hegemonically to automatic deprecation and "blame the victim" rhetoric.

This rhetoric, as historian Michael Katz has documented, has a long American pedigree. Since the colonial era, American elites have engaged in three obfuscations with regard to domestic poverty. The first is the denial that the normal functioning of protocapitalist and capitalist economies actually produces impoverished classes, independently of individuals' or groups' cleverness or willingness to work. Second, elites tend to create artificial distinctions between the "deserving" and "undeserving" poor: those whom we should pity and help versus those—"sturdy beggars" as they were labeled—who must be punished, forced to work. Finally, Americans have repeatedly denied the history of state involvement in social welfare, from state subsidy of private philanthropy since its inception to governmental control of all aspects of economic life that both produce and ameliorate poverty.[89]

Thus, the "blame the victim" trope is hardly new in American history (although the phrase itself was enshrined in American popular consciousness through William Ryan's wonderfully furious early-1970s polemic).[90] The particular symbolic strands that coalesced as full-blown "underclass" ideology in the 1980s were, however, historically specific to our era, and uniquely symbiotic with notions of white ethnic community and women's culture.

The term "underclass" is a loose translation of Karl Marx's phrase *Lumpenproletariat*, which referred specifically to individuals thrown not only into poverty by capitalist development but onto the fringes of legitimate employment. *Lumpen* were then the wandering impoverished and those who embraced "illegitimate" means of livelihood: prostitution, thievery, robbery. Marx held no romantic brief for *Lumpen*, whom he described as a "disintegrated mass."[91] His analysis focused not on their varying behaviors, but on the political economic transformations that created them as a social category.

As Frances Piven and Richard Cloward demonstrated in *Regulating the Poor*, American social welfare policy from the depression into the 1970s evolved into an instrument to deal with the urban reserve army—those poor people who, depending on the business cycle and other economic factors, were periodically employed, then unemployed—but always on the bottom rungs of the economic ladder. Federal spigots opened and closed in response to employers' desire for cheap labor, business cycle downturns, urban unrest, and, in the 1960s, "to reach, placate and integrate a turbulent black constituency" into the Democratic party.[92] From the mid-1970s on, however, the Democratic party increasingly abandoned minority, poor, and labor constituencies, and the federal government pulled out of the business of regulating the poor. First Carter, then Reagan drastically cut back social program spending, abandoned federal commitments to low-cost housing while allowing rapid-fire real estate speculation, and continued policies that encouraged rather than slowed big-city deindustrialization as firms relocated both regionally and internationally in search of the lowest possible labor costs.

The new "underclass" ideology functioned specifically, as had older "culture of poverty" formulations, to focus attention away from this political economic production of poverty to the "pathological" behavior of the poor whose characteristics were presumed (in the hard version) to cause or (in the soft version) merely to reproduce poverty. *Time* magazine threw down the gauntlet in a 1977 cover story, *Minority within a Minority: The Underclass:* "[The underclass is] a group of people who are more intractable, more socially alien and more hostile than almost anyone had imagined." The structure of *Time*'s narrative followed the historical obfuscations laid bare in Katz's work, with two additions. First, members of "the underclass" were unlike previous impoverished American populations, an obvious reference to white ethnics and to black Americans' "heritage of slavery," which somehow unfitted them for full citizenship: "Successive generations of aspiring Americans have lifted themselves well above [poverty and despair]. . . . The underclass will find that harder to do, given its painful heritage."[93] Second, in an American exceptionalism argument—yet another use of noble against nasty savage—the new American underclass had even fallen below the level of the Third World poor: "Almost anyone who has lived in or near the crowded *barrios* of South America knows that looting on the scale that occurred in New York [during the electric blackout] could almost never happen there. . . . Family structure has not broken down . . . nor has the idea of neighborhood."[94]

Time's Carter-era rhetorical treatment of poor Americans of color appropriately frames the next two decades of popular and academic discourse. First, in denial of ongoing discrimination in employment, housing, and education, *Time* pronounced Jim Crow long over, the recent recession irrelevant, the War on Poverty won. Why, then, were there minority poor? Because "the brightest and most ambitious have risen . . . leaving the underclass farther and farther behind."[95] In an implicitly genetic argument, continued into the present by Charles Murray and Richard Herrnstein, *Time* hints that those black Americans still poor must be an innately inferior social detritus, "good for nothing" in the prevalent functionalist parlance.

Ironically, *Time's* yellow journalist vision, coming at the end of a period of intense radical American political activism, was far more conservative than anthropologist Oscar Lewis's heavily attacked "culture of poverty" formulations of the late 1950s to mid-1960s. Since Lewis is now remembered only for his phrase, not the substance of his claims, and since William Julius Wilson, the architect of academic "underclass" theory, has repeatedly distanced himself from Lewis, it is worthwhile to return to the culture of poverty before moving forward to the underclass.

Oscar Lewis, who did fieldwork among Native Americans and in Mexico, Puerto Rico, Cuba, New York, and India (not simply "in Latin America" as Wilson would have it),[96] was a prolific and widely read anthropologist in his time. Born in Manhatten to poor Polish Jewish emigrants, Lewis—named Yehezkiel Lefkowitz—grew up in his parents' upstate New York boardinghouse. He attended the City College of New York in the 1930s, and then Columbia Teachers College, studying in the post-Boas era with Ruth Benedict and Ralph Linton.[97] After establishing himself in academic venues in the 1940s and 1950s, he wrote in the 1960s a series of highly accessible, novelistic ethnographies—*Five Families, Pedro Martinez, A Death in the Sanchez Family, La Vida.*[98] He attracted a large popular following—I was urged, for example, to read *Five Families* by a classmate in an ordinary middle- and working-class California public high school in the mid-1960s. He published articles in *Harper's*, *Commentary*, even *Redbook*, and influenced Michael Harrington's analysis in *The Other America*, the book popularly credited with inspiring the War on Poverty. Lewis instantiated his notions of the culture of poverty in many of these texts but published his explicit theoretical model simultaneously as a chapter of *La Vida* (which received a National Book Award) and in *Scientific American*.

By "culture of poverty" Lewis actually meant "subculture"—"both an adaptation and a reaction of the poor to their marginal position in a class-stratified, highly individuated, capitalistic society." Only a percentage of impoverished populations ever display the culture of poverty, but "once it comes into existence, it tends to perpetuate itself from generation to generation."[99] It "can be described in terms of some seventy interrelated social, economic, and psychological traits," but rarely are all of them present in any one case. The key themes are "lack of integration of the poor in the major institutions of the larger society," a "minimum of organization beyond the level of the nuclear or extended family," a "trend toward female- or mother-centered families," and "a strong feeling of marginality, of helplessness, of dependence, and of inferiority."[100]

Lewis's key concern, then, was what he saw as the lack of self-organization and cultural richness of some proportion of the globe's poor, lacks that prevented concerted political organization for social change. He approved tightly organized primitive and peasant societies, despite their very low standards of living, because they provided lives rich in meaning to their members. He endorsed the Cuban Revolution and the American Civil Rights movement, because he characterized each as self-organization leading to dramatically improved standards of living. "In effect, we find that in primitive societies, and in caste societies, the culture of poverty does not develop. In socialist, fascist, and highly developed capitalist societies with a welfare state, the culture of poverty tends to decline. I suspect that the culture of poverty flourishes in, and is generic to, the early free enterprise stage of capitalism and that it is also endemic in colonialism."[101]

Lewis was fundamentally engaged, in the Chicago School tradition, with the specter of social disorganization, the breakdown of then-contemporary anthropology's notion of culture, a "design for living." Despite the "positive aspects" of the culture of poverty, such as "the enjoyment of the sensual" and the "indulgence of impulse," it was a roadblock to world betterment.[102] Lewis, a left-liberal American intellectual of his times, assumed that global economic and social progress were occurring both through capitalist growth and socialist revolution. He was concerned that cultures of poverty at various sites would slow down that progress: "The elimination of physical poverty *per se* may not be enough to eliminate the culture of poverty which is a whole way of life."[103] Lewis wanted poor people to be *properly* cumbered, and saw that cumbering as necessary to active political engagement.

Lewis was, in the common social science practice of that era, both rather crudely numerate and enamored of trait lists. He claimed that his work was scientific (although he also claimed it for art), because he focused on patterns of social behavior among the poor rather than on individual morality. But—postmodern before the postmodernists—he did few surveys, and rarely attempted to justify the typicality of individuals with whom he worked and from whom he took life histories.

Anthropological critics of the culture of poverty, most notably Charles Valentine and Eleanor Leacock, focused on Lewis's methodological sloppiness and his abundant internal contradictions. But they principally objected to Lewis's blaming the victim, his ascription of causality to the behavior of the poor rather than the larger economic and social forces overdetermining the reproduction of poverty. They were harshly critical of his and others' middle-class arrogance that both prescribed "lifting" or "curing" poor people psychologically when what they needed were jobs, housing, and access to political power and presumed, without investigation, a sharply divergent, idealized middle-class behavior pattern.[104]

The critics by and large prevailed in anthropology—and among intellectuals who attended to them—although not, obviously, in popular culture. Aside from a few recognized conservatives like George Foster, who claimed that an "image of limited good" ensured fatalism and prevented poor Mexican peasants from progressive risk taking—a mentality more commonly operative in Congress, in General Motors, and among university faculties than among Mexican peasants—most American anthropologists, a fairly liberal crowd, attended to the rebuttals and eschewed the "culture of poverty" framework.[105] Unfortunately, some of this virtue was simply the result, as I argued in the last chapter, of anthropological avoidance of politics and poverty as issues. In the United States, as we shall see, this avoidance merely left the field open to conservative sociologists and yellow journalism.

Nevertheless, when sociologist William Julius Wilson published *The Truly Disadvantaged* in 1987, he felt constrained to distance his analysis of the "ghetto-specific behavior" of "the underclass" from the culture of poverty: "The notion of a ghetto subculture is not to be equated with the popular conception of the culture of poverty. . . . what distinguishes the two concepts is that although they both emphasize the association between the emergence of certain cultural traits and the structure of social constraints and opportunities, *culture of poverty,* unlike *social isolation,* places strong emphasis on the autonomous character of the cultural traits once they come into existence"(italics in original).[106] Wilson claimed instead to be emphasizing the structural factors that led to ghetto-specific behaviors—crime, drug use, unwed motherhood, female-headed families, and welfare dependence—and the policy changes that would alter them. He focused particularly on the new "social isolation" of poor black Americans that he asserted resulted from a combination of middle-class black exodus from inner cities after the lifting of Jim Crow and the deindustrialization of American cities: "The exodus of middle- and working-class families from many ghetto neighborhoods removes an important 'social buffer' that could deflect the full impact of the kind of prolonged and increasing joblessness that plagued inner-city neighborhoods in the 1970s and early 1980s. . . . the very presence of these families during such periods provides mainstream role models."[107]

Wilson prescribed "macroeconomic policy designed to promote both economic growth and a tight labor market" and "measures such as on-the-job training and apprenticeships to elevate the skill levels of the truly disadvantaged." He repeatedly stressed the need for public (white) support that would "address the problems plaguing the ghetto underclass" and called for a "hidden agenda for liberal policymakers": "emphasizing programs to which the more advantaged groups of all races and class backgrounds can positively relate."[108]

Wilson's focus is on rising indices of "pathological" inner-city behavior, most particularly men's unemployment and therefore involvement in the informal economy, crime, drug use, and rising rates of births to unwed adolescents. (He fudges the birthrate issue through the use of the adjective "unwed"; otherwise, he cannot claim that rates have risen, because they have been falling since 1960.) He has no particular interest in women's access to education, housing, good jobs, or child care, focusing primarily on the need to engineer a more orderly social setting in which inner-city men avoid illegal activities, accept whatever low-wage employment is available, and marry the mothers of their children.

Rarely have two individuals so well illustrated political and social devolution, the decline from the 1960s to the 1980s, from the bang to the whimper. Both analysts reflect the social control heritage of the Progressive Era, the visceral need to organize the poor to a fare-thee-well, while assuming the "social integration" of their betters. But for Lewis the ultimate end is transcendent: a politicized, forward-looking citizenry that forces the equitable redistribution of wealth. Wilson's goal, instead, is purely functionalist and clearly sexist (while gender was largely irrelevant for Lewis, writing in an era between the first and second waves of feminism). Elite policymakers will cleverly fool the compassion-weary (white racist) American public into endorsing Keynesian welfare state measures that, with the rising tide, will lift underclass boats too. With low-wage male jobs newly available, young minority men will forsake drugs and crime and marry the mothers of their children—a functionalist plan that critic Adolph Reed satirized as a "macroeconomic dating service." Then they will be, as Reed further sardonically put it, "safely tucked away in stable, two-parent families, quietly waiting for the zephyrs of intergenerational upward mobility that somehow always seem to be blowing in some other neighborhood."[109]

Ironically, then, the professionally vilified Oscar Lewis was a far more interesting and progressive thinker (not to mention a better writer) than is the feted Wilson (past president of the American Sociological Association, chair of his department at Chicago and now in an endowed chair at Harvard, invitee to Clinton's White House). Condescending and sloppy though he was, Lewis had a global and comparative vision. He apprehended the role of states and financial interests in creating and maintaining poverty, and the role of politics—the self-organization of the oppressed—in reducing it. He had fits of middle-class *pudeur* over the poor lying around in despair and wasting money on lottery tickets, but to his credit, he wanted them to quit these behaviors for purposes of their own human transcendence, not so that they would stop being an eyesore and a menace to the elites of their countries.

For Wilson, the purview is radically shrunken to black inner-city America. Advanced capitalism is assumed, and assumed benignant. Writing in Reagan's second term, Wilson took the end of Jim Crow as a given, and simply ignored the political struggle that had been necessary to bring about that minimal recognition of black Americans' civil rights. (This erasure of struggle is all the more astonishing because Wilson himself is black.) He also neglected to attend to the voluminous radical "community power" scholarship that documents the ways in which government and private elites plan, and profit from, the continuous disenfranchisement of the poor. Thus, it follows logically that he has consistently refused to consider the role of *politics* in bringing about the social change he claims, as a self-described "social democrat," to desire. Passive-verb political economy is the order of Wilson's day: blacks "get concentrated" in inner cities, jobs just happen to leave. He scorns "racism" as an explanation for any social change—interpreting it narrowly as malign dyadic encounters in which individual whites do dirt to individual blacks.[110] To put it bluntly, Wilson is effectively saying, "It's nobody's fault, but poor blacks got screwed and now they're acting ugly."

There is no more crystalline example of Wilson's failure to comprehend the connection of politics to analysis and ideology than his treatment of the related decline of liberal and rise of conservative interpretations of racialized poverty in the 1980s. Blithely ignoring the federal government's well-documented war of disinformation against the minority poor and radical causes and movements, long-term racist urban policy and its immiserating effects despite the Civil Rights movement's legislative successes, and overt white racist backlash from coast to coast, Wilson sees the rise of the Right as due entirely to liberals' pusillanimous refusal to face "blacks getting ugly": "By 1980 . . . the problems of inner-city social dislocations had reached such catastrophic proportions that liberals were forced to readdress the question of the ghetto underclass, but this time their reactions were confused and defensive. The extraordinary rise in inner-city social dislocations following the passage of the most sweeping antidiscrimination and antipoverty legislation in the nation's history could not be explained by the 1960 explanations of ghetto-specific behavior."

Thus, according to Wilson, "by the end of the 1960s, the most forceful and persuasive arguments on the ghetto underclass had been provided by liberals, not conservatives. A few years later, just the opposite would be true."[111] But it was not the rhetorical force or persuasion of conservative texts, which were notoriously shoddy productions, or a new intensity of "ghetto-specific behavior" that led to the decline in attention to liberal and radical (not just liberal, as Wilson would edit the record) interpretations of changing urban American realities. It was the political defeat of organized left-liberalism, a defeat that was in part due to racial minorities' and others' loss to white ethnics, then to rich WASPs, in the symbolic fight to sit in Baby Bear's chair. For the short period in which political arguments for civil rights and redress of unfair policies could be couched in the symbolism of minority moral superiority (martyred leaders, bombed churches, the spectacle of dogs and fire hoses set on nonviolent demonstrators), blacks could contest for stardom in the national morality play. But with economic turndown, political shift, and associated media hysteria over "welfare queens" and racialized drug and crime issues, with crack cocaine as the *diabolus ex machina,* the national dramatis personae were recast, and no hyperbole was any longer unthinkable in describing the redemonized minority poor.

With fine disregard for not-so-distant history, commentators—many of them journalists, and many of them white ethnic—used, and use, exactly the unconscionable language of racist "Othering" that was used against white ethnics. This ethnic/racial morality play was profoundly illogical (as well as immoral) then; it is so now. Human populations should not have to prove their moral worth, their equal species-being, simply to demand equal rights. And demanding equal rights for a population simply does not constitute the approbation of every action of every member of that group. There is no Baby Bear's chair, and—to switch fairy tales—there is no (collective) wolf. Instead, there are patterned daily lives, and lifetimes, enormously influenced by policies, and money trails, but those are all less easy and fun to report on than "urban jungles," "feckless welfare mothers," and "lost youth."

Here anthropology has bequeathed to the public sphere what Stephen Steinberg labels the ethnographic fallacy: "Too often—not always—ethnography suffers from a myopia that sharply delineates the behavior at close range but obscures the less proximate and less visible structures and processes that engender and sustain that behavior."[112] American anthropology's psychologizing heritage and pool hall tendencies have provided no brake to journalistic "ethnography" of urban hearts of darkness.

Ken Auletta's *New Yorker* series, later published as a book, flippantly meanders among unproven assertions and grievances against minority youth on the order of daring to "monopoliz[e] the sidewalk"![113] (I cannot even estimate how many times, in my years on the Yale faculty, I was shoved off into the gutter by pink-cheeked Ivy Leaguers.) Nicholas Lemann's *Promised Land* blames a poor South Side Chicago woman for laziness and labor market avoidance when, by his own evidence, she worked consistently throughout her life. Brett Williams points out that "Ruby Haynes has worked as a sharecropper, household servant, waitress, laundress, and hotel maid. She has sewn awnings and cleaned office buildings and hospitals at night. She knows industrial restructuring and the increasingly polarized service economy firsthand. She has served as a Democratic precinct captain and enthusiastically attends church. Yet in this book she is always at home, most often fighting with a husband, lover, or child." Lemann retails her narrative of her husband's period of abusive behavior as though it lasted his lifetime. That man, who has now been remarried for more than a quarter-century, is a homeowner, a church deacon, and a doorman for a Chicago high-rise building and has sued Lemann for invasion of privacy.[114] Alex Kotlowitz's poignant, concerned *There Are No Children Here*, on the Henry Horner projects in Chicago, just happens to focus on a household with eight children, representative of a big 1 percent of households in the

Aid to Families with Dependent Children (AFDC) program.[115] The *Chicago Tribune* staff titled its collection of appalling misreportage *The American Millstone: An Examination of the Nation's Permanent Underclass.*[116] The *New York Times* had its own shameless tearjerker series, "Children of the Shadows" (which it explicitly peddled to high schools as an "educational module"), about minority (and a few token poor white) youth attempting to escape worlds described only in terms of endogenous disorganization and abuse, never as the result of deliberate withholding of resources by state and capital: "They are the children of the shadows: the impoverished youth who live in the tumbledown neighborhoods of the American inner city; the children of often desperate and broken families, where meals are sometimes cereal three times a day; the young people who daily face the lures of drugs, sex, fast money and guns; the unnoticed youths who operate in a maddening universe where things always seem to go wrong."[117] And the often-implicit argument that white ethnics were the good, innocent, oppressed poor, while today's impoverished minorities are somehow a different species, truly deserving the hatred and scorn of them now woven into American structures of feeling, finds its apotheosis in sociologist Philip Kasinitz's glowing review of Wilson's *Truly Disadvantaged:* "The long unfashionable notion of social disorganization may have been inappropriately applied to immigrant communities by the early Chicago sociologists. Yet Wilson argues convincingly that it has a place in the discussion of the underclass today."[118]

In other words, that was then, this is now. My grandparents are above criticism, but yours are beneath it. (Somehow I am haunted here by the vision of farmer Fred Guelzow's leg cut off and stuck in his mouth—now why is that?) Similarly, journalists wax eloquent on the difference between their charming ethnic ancestors and how they all deserved a leg up (and a wink of the eye at occasional illegalities)—and all those subhuman Others today who cannot possibly be apprehended similarly, even when they occupy the same space and are engaged in the same activities. The late Mike Royko, for example, the *Chicago Tribune* columnist who played big-shoulders, salt-of-the-earth Joe Six-Pack, wrote in his response to the threat to the historic inner-city (now largely black and Mexican) open-air Maxwell Street market, "Don't Shed a Tear for Maxwell Street": "It's easy to get nostalgic about Maxwell Street. . . . I share some of this nostalgia . . . the first suit I ever bought . . . there was some [stolen goods] . . . but not as much as people thought . . . the old Jewish ghetto produced business tycoons, powerhouse politicians, federal judges . . . [but today] this area is a major catalyst for stolen goods, drugs, prostitution, etc. . . . It's also a myth that Maxwell Street is an incubator for small businessmen. . . . Maybe in the old days, but not anymore."[119]

Or take Francis Clines of the *New York Times* waxing lyrical over a Sinatra-worshipping pizza restaurant owner who has observed the great man himself peeling off one-hundred-dollar bills for down-and-out paesans, and whose disabled son "got a spot in this great place" after he "put in one call to Sinatra".[120] Nowhere in the text is a hint of Sinatra's unsavory reputation—or of the basic inequity of a system where one has to "put in a call" to Frank Sinatra to get a place in a publically financed residential program. In another Dante-quoting puff piece on an Italian neighborhood in the Bronx, Clines not only seats white ethnics solidly in Baby Bear's chair, but literally denies the humanity of the minority poor: "Just a few blocks west in the noontime sun last Wednesday, a man lay handcuffed across the hood of a police car. The wild-eyed man seemed a mundane slab of precinct produce, a footnote far beyond the world of Belmont where Joe Cicciu . . . is busy maintaining a range of subdsidized housing for old Italians and working poor families."[121]

Sam Roberts, one of the more liberal reporters for the *New York Times,* actually openly refers to "the propensity toward violence among black Americans"—not impoverished, young, inner-city, male, black (and Latino, Asian, white) Americans in recent years since high-powered weapons (neither manufactured nor sold by or for the profit of the poor) have become so widely available, and since increased government-created poverty has greatly enhanced the desirability of engaging in illegal, and therefore violent, economic activities.[122] No—"black Americans." The biologically inflected racist language of the Victorian and Progressive Eras, so often beaten back by political and intellectual will over the course of the post-World War II decades, returned as the public transcript of the 1990s.

The academic analysts following and, in essence, cleaning up after Wilson have helped little to counter this new received wisdom—in part because many of them are largely in agreement with him. Isabel Sawhill, David Ellwood, and Christopher Jencks, for example, whatever their differences, all posit a banal set of values in which Americans believe, which must then be imposed on "them."[123] The nonwhite poor are conspicuously outside their circle of the we. Then, the more militant critics of "underclass" ideology and their more damning points are overtly excluded from mass and middlebrow media. Finally, the overly polite dissensus of some critics guarantees public inattention to their points. Michael Katz, for example, in distinct departure from his earlier angry, combative work, writes quietly that "underclass" does not refer to an observable group but is actually a "metaphor of social transformation," part of a larger contemporary American elite cultural refusal to admit the political economic shifts that "degrade all our lives." He notes the extraordinarily ahistorical character of academic "underclass" writing, and stresses that the key shift in recent years is not Wilson's "increase in ghetto-specific behavior," but the fact that the "connection between race, urban poverty, and dissociation from the labor market is new in American history." Housing specialist David Bartelt puts the point as a sardonic query: "Were everyone in the underclass to establish appropriate kinship behavior, search for employment, take whatever jobs were available at whatever pay, and cease any form of addictive or illegal behavior, would the underclass disappear? Would the heritage of entrenched housing segregation and institutionalized differentials in housing market mechanisms according to race simply dissolve?"[124]

Countering other elements of "underclass" mythology, scholars have noted that black adolescent childbearing rates began falling in the 1960s, and that "teenage pregnancy," in any event, only became an issue in the 1970s: up until then it was a norm. Public health statistician Arline Geronimus has done careful work with national data sets and come up with results that are surprising and defy "common sense." First, having a child while still an adolescent actually has little effect on a girl's life chances—instead, her prior economic position has high predictive value here. Second, young black women, as opposed to young white women, are much more likely to have health problems during pregnancy and to die as a result of childbirth the older they are (possibly because of health problems of poverty increasing with age). In other words, poor black women may be better off having their children very young.[125]

In any event, most poor Americans are white, American blacks have never been the majority recipients of welfare, and—prior to the enactment of welfare "reform"—40 percent of welfare mothers worked for pay as well. Despite media portrayals, most welfare recipients had few, not many, children—the average was two—and most cycled off the dole whenever they could line up job, child care, and health insurance. (Further, it was welfare for the often financially stable elderly [Social Security] not for poor mothers [AFDC] that took up the bulk of the federal social welfare budget.) Black and white pregnant women consume illegal substances that may be injurious to their fetuses at the same rates—but doctors report black women to law enforcement authorities ten times more often. The exception to the above rule is cigarettes, which of course are legal. A government study indicates that black mothers smoke much *less* than white mothers. And medical research now indicates, after years of hysteria over "crack babies," that children born to crack-addicted mothers are not conspicuously medically or behaviorally different from others. A final note on the "family values" front: despite received wisdom on abandonment of family responsibilities by poor minority males, federal data indicate that the higher a man's income, the *less* likely he is to make his court-ordered child support payments.[126] To paraphrase F. Scott Fitzgerald, it is the rich, not the poor, who are different from you and me.

Federal government studies indicate that black adolescents actually consume illegal drugs at *lower* rates than whites. They have admitted that blacks now graduate from high school at close to the same rates as whites, but that "returns to education" (job remuneration and status), at all educational levels, are significantly lower for both male racial minorities and all women than for white men. Employers openly admit to interviewers that they discriminate against minorities in hiring, and federal studies indicate that minorities with the same resources and credit records as whites are denied mortgages at twice the rate. Minorities are more frequently harassed by police, arrested for crimes when whites are not, convicted more frequently, and given heavier prison sentences.[127]

Finally, Wilson's "world we have lost" vision of safe ghettos in which individuals could sleep on fire escapes in the summer, and in which the middle classes provided role models and leadership to the rest, is based on two common mythologies about the past and the present. First, it is a "ritualistically reconstructed community," according to Brett Williams, for which there is a great deal of counterdata indicating black middle class contempt for, social distance from, and exploitation of the black poor— "offering shabby services at inflated prices"—among whom they were forced to live under Jim Crow.[128] Then, it is a vision contrasting a luridly described journalist's snapshot of defiant, dangerous ghetto youth of color, the urban jungle, the latest version of "domestic nasty savages," to a mass-mediated picture of a 1950s white, suburban, middle-class Ozzie and Harriet universe of social order and obedient, polite youth. In fact, suburbs were never so orderly or law abiding; and American young people in general, over the course of the twentieth century, have increasingly disrespected, defied, and done less for their elders, whether the issue is educational or career choice, financial help, sexual, reproductive, or marital behavior, or simple courtesy.[129] These facts are widely known and represented broadly in mass media—think of *Beavis and Butthead* alone—but always in venues separate from descriptions of the "vicious, immoral, underclass youth who don't respect their elders." The separation of these two discourses parallels that of "the underclass" versus "the American ethos," and enacts the structure of feeling George Lipsitz labels the "possessive investment in whiteness."[130]

The sign of the grandparent appears again, as an emblem of the past in the present, in "model minority" rhetoric. Model minorities—construed as various Asian groups and, more recently, some Latinos—are those who "work hard," have "traditional family values," "respect their elders," and thus succeed in the United States without "extra help." "Model minority" discourse is thus simply an extension into the present, and onto different populations, of the ahistorical and antiempirical "ethnic report card" model. Stephen Steinberg, in fact, has pointed out how the "theory of Asian success is a new spin on earlier theories about Jews, with whom Asians are explicitly compared."[131]

Political scientist Claire Kim has charted two waves of "model minority" mythology in American popular political discourse. The first, in the 1960s, is associated with anti-civil-rights politics. By "the rules of ideological triage," Kim argues, citing the long history of American anti-Asian racism, Asians were for the first time defined as good citizens for being *nonblack* and *non-Communist*. This new mythology was furthered by the 1965 Hart-Cellar Immigration Act's encouragement of well-off professional migrants, a significant "class drain" from the Third World. The 1980s Reagan revolution heralded the second wave, in which Asian-Americans' "success" was used to legitimate "moving back the clock" on civil rights. Kim points out that "model minority" rhetoric is not only racist against blacks and Latinos, but against Asians themselves: it obscures their heterogeneous national origins, their actually limited professional success, the widespread economic difficulties of nonelite Asian migrants (heavier users of welfare than whites in California, for example), and continuing American violations of Asian-American civil rights.[132] Suzanne Model, in her historical analysis of ethnicity and economy in New York City, effectively destroys the "why can't blacks be entrepreneurs like Jews/Asians?" line of argument. Stephen Steinberg starkly lays out the issue of privilege obscured by "model minority" claims:

> In demystifying and explaining Asian success, we come again to a simple truth: that what is inherited is not genes, and not culture, but class advantage and disadvantage. If not for the extraordinary selectivity of the Asian immigrant population, there would be no commentaries in the popular press and the social science literature extolling Confucian values and the "pantheon of ancestors" who supposedly inspire the current generation of Asian youth. After all, no such claims are made about the Asian youth who inhabit the slums of Manila, Hong Kong, and Bombay, or, for that matter, San Francisco and New York.[133]

The "model minority" trope, then, like that of the white ethnic community, of women's culture and of the underclass, is fundamentally relational, about the denigration of either *a* or *not-a*. Park and Miller's Italians and Slavs and Jews were to "Chinese coolies" as "Asians" today are to blacks and Puerto Ricans.

THE PARADOX OF THE UNION CARD

So where *are* the anthropologists in this picture? Where were the barking dogs of ethnography as "white ethnic community," "women's culture," "underclass," and "model minority" discourses arose, developed, and were challenged on the American scene? What did the guardians of "culture" have to say about these important political deployments of the sacred concept? The answer is a complicated shaggy-dog story: there were lots of anthropologists around, but they didn't bark as loudly on the public stage, they were barking about different issues, and, in any event, people weren't attending to their noise as much anymore.

The sheer amount of Americanist anthropological work (as measured by Ph.D. dissertations) increased over these years. But, after a flurry of public interest in urban ethnography in the radical 1970s, work on the United States rapidly lost cachet both inside and outside the discipline. The reasons are as complicated as the political economic shifts of the period. With the economic downturn and rightward political drift, anthropology departments under duress slipped back into their tradition of merely allowing, while devaluing, research on the United States. They stopped hiring Americanists (and foundations and agencies stopped funding them), who were increasingly perceived internally as "inauthentic" anthropologists, "really sociologists," and externally as "poaching on sociology's terrain." Minority anthropologists, as I have noted, were doubly vulnerable to this treatment, and many chose to work in the Caribbean, Africa, or elsewhere in the "exotic realm."

But even without these bottom-line professional shifts, Americanists in the discipline were left poorly dressed as the fashion of 1960s radicalism became passé, caught in the contradictions of the anthropological wardrobe. Faye Harrison has noted this surprising hiatus in insightful anthropological race research.[134] Radicals and liberals, whether writing about the urban minority poor, migrating farmworkers, or multiracial women factory workers, almost inevitably donned the "technicians of the sacred" costume, advocating for the downtrodden and pointing to their "cultural richness" to define "what they were good for" in American life. Such were the confusions of the period that many of us both understood that the public transcript was ceding "culture" to the poor in lieu of redistributing wealth and yet found ourselves talking about the "richness" of our informants' lives so much that our teeth ached. John Gwaltney, for example, a black (and blind) student of Margaret Mead's, published *Drylongso* in 1980, an evocative account of northeastern black American discourse. Within this single text, Gwaltney manages to chide other anthropologists for "romanticism" about black Americans, asserts the reality of a "core black culture," calls for "native anthropology"—meaning insider studies—and has an informant comment sardonically that "I think this anthropology is just another way to call me a nigger."[135]

But with the renaissance of the Right, noble once again became nasty savage, and ethnographic advocacy for the poor and stigmatized appeared foolish—at the very least uninteresting. More complicated, "costume-less," political-economy-based work on race, ethnicity, class, and gender was simply ignored, or ghettoized within "race studies" and "women's studies," of great interest neither inside the discipline nor on the public stage. And when urban ethnographic work with a political economic frame, like sociologist Terry Williams's *Cocaine Kids*, did make the leap to middlebrow culture, its indictment of elites for their creation of the illegal drug industry was simply erased, and an indictment of ghetto families and community read in.[136] The "last macho raiders" stance of the "underclass" journalists and social scientists was unappealing to most in a still-liberal profession.

While anthropologists writ large were still considered human nature experts, "human nature" was either "in our genes"—and thus not in the United States—or clinched by temporal distance, and thus evidenced only by exotic Others.[137] (The indexing system of the *New York Times* is a fascinating reflection of shifting politics, culture, and the purviews of academic specializations. The "Anthropology" entry traditionally included a "see Negroes" line. But with the rise of the 1960s Civil Rights movement, "Negroes," less and less exotic and increasingly political, were dropped from anthropology's liberal stewardship.) The icing on this cake was the rise of postmodernist anthropology, which, in shrinking ethnography to the "textualization" of the dyadic encounter between Western self and Third World Other, both reified being there—not here—as "doing anthropology" and snobbishly turned away from real engagement with politics and economics as working within modernist narrative illusions.

To illustrate how this anthropological conundrum worked itself out on the public stage, consider the contrast between the only two fieldwork-based books on American white ethnics from the late 1970s on that made the leap to relative popularity (sold more than ten thousand books and received multiple reviews in the middlebrow press). The late anthropologist Barbara Myerhoff's *Number Our Days* is an elegant, elegiac account of storytelling and ceremony among elderly Jews in a center in Venice, California. Myerhoff's message is clear: Let us praise these impoverished old Jews and consider how their cultural richness and inventiveness allow them to triumph over material adversity and memories of the Holocaust. (She also collaborated with a documentary filmmaker, whose work on the group won an Academy Award.) The text fits squarely within the "technicians of the sacred" model: it is sheer romantic celebration, a warm and fuzzy ethnographic transmutation of an Isaac Bashevis Singer novel:

> MOSHE: Questions, questions. Always the Jews are asking questions. Sholem Aleichem said, "The real Jewish question is this: From what can a Jew earn a living?" In my own mind the question is this, when will the Jews stop asking themselves questions?[138]

Victor Turner, in his foreword, claims that Myerhoff is in the "vanguard of anthropological theory" because she is studying her own society and documenting how people give meaning to their lives through ceremony. But the former act, as we have seen, was hardly novel, and the latter, at this level of particularity, is banal. The book is in fact theoretically thin, literally only an instantiation of "let us honor our grandparents." Myerhoff fails to acknowledge, for example, sociologist Arlie Hochschild's earlier *Unexpected Community*, also a study of the creation of community among the (in this case white non-Jewish) elderly in an apartment house in California.[139] She textually foregrounds "culture," but never indicates how Jewishness makes a difference in the larger postwar American phenomenon of old-age residence far from adult children. If center members' socially mobile children were estranged from them because of "assimilation," why didn't they at least send them money? These are not questions answered by celebration, by endless references to "rich, highly developed culture," "intricate and rich culture," "robust and impudently eclectic" culture.[140]

Nor are questions of gender differences, with which Myerhoff deals at length, adequately addressed with vague, unattributed generalizations about women's innate nurturance: "Women in the shtetl (and some writers say, women in all cultures) were emotional leaders in their family and community. They were responsible for nurturance, for interpersonal relations. . . . Let us consider biology, too. Perhaps women in general are more prepared for the inevitable infirmities of old age by a lifetime of acceptance of their bodily limits and changes. Initially, the little girl observes herself to be physically weaker than her brothers and nothing she does can alter that."[141] It should come as no surprise, then, that Myerhoff, as we have seen, was coauthor of one of the most antirational, anthropologically naive "women's culture" books of the 1980s, *The Feminization of America.*

If Myerhoff's study was noticed and valorized for its portrayal of "culture"—celebrating, ruffling no feathers, ignoring the politics and policies of her fieldwork period, finding her uncontroversial niche beneath state power—sociologist Jonathan Rieder's *Canarsie: The Jews and Italians of Brooklyn against Liberalism* was attended to and gained admirers for its tough-minded consideration of politics. *Canarsie,* in fact, claims to explain the rise of Reaganism through the prism of one area's negative and defensive white ethnic response to school and housing integration efforts. Rieder notes that he "adopted the stance of the ethnographer" in order to gain entrance to the lives and feelings of his working- and middle-class Italian and Jewish informants, and that statement is precisely accurate. Unlike sociologist Terry Williams, for example, he does not actually *practice* ethnography— chart daily life, gather life histories, analyze informants' social relations as part of a larger system. Nor, as a sociologist, is Rieder constrained by the anthropological costume conundrum. In fact, he defines his own work through sneering at the notion of being a technician of the sacred: "The last thing most Canarsians would respect is an academic gone native, sentimentalizing their nasty side and getting trapped in a folk romance. These folks are not romantic. Naturalism, not romanticism, is the appropriate aesthetic for capturing the culture of Brooklyn white ethnicity."[142]

"Culture" is a key concept in Rieder's analysis, and he makes ritual obeisance to Clifford Geertz and Mary Douglas. But Rieder actually reads the culture of white ethnicity through the racist, sentimentalizing, largely non-academic white ethnic renaissance literature, with its condescending and cartoonish 1950s notions of stereotyped ethnic billiard balls huddling in colorful neighborhoods: "Something characteristically Italian clung to her plainspoken words: unpretentious warmth, evoking a world divided neatly between loyal kin and perfidious strangers, with an implicit threat of swift reprisal for betrayal."[143] And on he goes, from amoral familism to people of the book to the pathological underclass—there is even a set of photos contrasting older Italians and Jews in their gardens, parks, and delis to black and Latino kids hanging out in graffiti-emblazoned concrete environs—no white ethnic boys on the corner with beer and baseball bats, no old black guys playing chess in the park or Puerto Rican girls in Catholic school plaid for Rieder.

Rieder is, in fact, an "underclass" ideologue, and *Canarsie* is Nixon's invocation of the silent majority, updated for new times. Rieder claims to distance himself from his informants' overt racism and even uses some faceless black interviewees to comment on it. But simultaneously he buttresses it through his own descriptions, so unconsciously evocative of Progressive Era elite descriptions of white ethnic urban neighborhoods, in which even evidences of art and religion are seen as part of social disorder:

> Much of Brownsville and East New York is now a desolate place. Junkies nod, social clubs blare soul and salsa, hookers preen for tricks at stoplights, rococo storefront tabernacles ring with the sound of tambourines, and decrepit tenements create a surrealist's landscape. When a police car cruised down one street on a sultry summer evening in 1976, milling blacks glowered at the white intruders. A man reputed to be a cannibal symbolized the seemingly alien lifestyles that rankled the white residents a mile away in Canarsie.[144]

Like Wilson before and after him (*Canarsie* comes between Wilson's *Declining Significance of Race* and *Truly Disadvantaged*), Rieder uses a political economic frame of the passive-verb variety: "The origins of many of those problems lay in national migration flows and regional patterns of economic growth and disinvestment."[145] No one is at fault, but these shifts happened, blacks and Latinos started pushing white ethnics, and it's no wonder they responded as they did and the liberal coalition fell apart.

And just as the Nixonian silent majority was held to be resentful of feminism, so Rieder, while simultaneously claiming to be for women's rights, uses his informants as mouthpieces for racist misogyny:

> Many Catholics in Canarsie . . . felt alienated from a Democratic party that seemed in thrall to the feminist enthusiasms of the upper middle classes. . . . If men and women were truly liberated from their traditional duties, what would bind them to families? And what would hold them together if they could enjoy sexual pleasure without commitment, get divorced without stigma, terminate pregnancies at will? Many Canarsians merged these fears in part because they glimpsed a real unity in all the diversity: the freeing of the self from communal duties. Liberation, they reasoned, could only dim the precious line between nature and culture as surely as did the odd mating practices of ghetto families.[146]

Note how Rieder moves, in the paragraph, from describing the thoughts of his informants as separate from his own, to merging with them and endorsing them, to a final rhetorical flourish in which he demonizes "ghetto families" (and links them with feminists) both as barbarians within the gates, threatening to collapse our frail cultural accomplishments into the undifferentiated soup of nature, and as classic exotic Others whose intimate lives are properly described as "odd mating practices."

THRIVING ON THE CULTURE RIFF

Such is the sad and dangerous use and abuse of "culture" in contemporary American political morality plays. Commentators feel free, for political purposes, to put on and to switch anthropological costumes at will, playing now the heroic colonialist, now the adventurous and respectful counterculturalist, now the neutral human nature expert. Americanist anthropologists have lost their key to the wardrobe room, or rather, ceded it through two fatal moves. The first is conspiring with the morality play, taking the stage to advocate the "cultural richness" of one stigmatized population after another. After all, if culture can be rich, it then also can be poor, or lacking altogether. The second is delimiting anthropology's purview to a truncated "culture" in the first place, as if human beings' apprehensions of reality can be studied apart from the reality they are apprehending. Despite their lofty intentions, anthropologists' idealized concept of culture, torn from history and political economy, has come to serve as a fetish, a systematic falsification in public political discourse.

Thus, the dreadful, misshapen culture of our own making, like Dr. Frankenstein's monster, has escaped from anthropologists and lays waste to the ideological landscape. The "white ethnic community," "women's culture," and "underclass" constructs could not exist without notions of culture and of anthropology—and yet they exist, by and large, without anthropologists. The narration of their overlapping developments and symbiosis is the narration of the increasing culturalization of American political discourse, now including debates about the canon, multiculturalism, and new immigration. And yet these constructs also build on other national, particularly Western pasts, build on historical modes of apprehending nations, peasantry, women, and "savages." We need to loop back, to stand on that history as well, in order to come back to current debates about "the American ethos."

QUESTIONS OF NATIONALISM

White ethnic community and women's culture share the claims of unjust oppression, moral superiority—to the oppressor group and/or others— and the possession of a unique and valuable cultural heritage. These characteristics were borrowed from black cultural nationalism and ultimately from the history of modern nationalist movements. (A key distinction between nationalism and cultural nationalism is the absence of a claim to territory, except for such symbolic intrastate sovereignty claims as the Chi cano renaming of the American Southwest as Aztlan or the creation of women-only spaces in concerts, demonstrations, bookstores, or houses.)

Modern nationalism, as Benedict Anderson notes, is an "invention of community" that, once constructed simultaneously in a number of European states and their rebellious Latin American and Caribbean colonies, provided a new ideological template that native elites in other colonized and semicolonized Third World territories could borrow.[147] The rise of European nationalism was a complex process involving multiple constructions of self and other: the nation versus other European states, versus Third World colonies, and national populations vis-à-vis one another. Most particularly, European (and later Third World) nationalisms relied—and still rely, to some extent—on constructed notions of national peasantries and on distinctive images of vulnerable national womanhood.

In European state after state, national enthusiasts discovered the unique characteristics of "their" countrypeople. The "folk" had particular customs of dress, food, dancing, and music which reflected specific national virtues and must be selected, documented, and if possible preserved. Thus, the discipline of folklore—in journals, such as Britain's *Notes and Queries,* collections such as the brothers Grimm's *Kinder- und Hausmärchen,* and historical folk museums from Wales to central Europe to Greece—arose in concert with European nationalisms.[148]

Women in this era were newly defined as more traditional ("priest-ridden" in the French revolutionary rhetoric) than men. They were thus often seen as the most folk of the folk, natural, outside history in their housebound maternality, needing both the modernizing guidance and the preservationist protection of "their" men.[149] This cultural phenomenon continued in the rhetoric and reality of Third World nationalisms: male nationalists in state after state determined that some female customs must be sacrificed for an appearance of modernity in tune with national aspirations while others, particularly those relating to women's wifely and maternal duties, must be preserved to embody national distinctiveness and worth.[150]

Thus, white ethnic community and women's culture stand in ironic relation to the historic crucible of modern nationalism. Their models of human social reality mimic the structures and characteristics of historic claims to national recognition and fealty. At the same time, their very subjects— the descendants of European peasants and "natural" womanhood—are constructs formed by that same historical process, and formed not for the purposes of peasant and female liberation but in the furtherance of male bourgeois and aristocratic political objectives.

Weaving through these historical processes is another set of symbolic associations—that between the European urban (and often rural) poor and colonized Others and their mutual need of instruction from their betters. The voluminous writings of missionaries, writers, and reformers in Victorian Britain provided a template for later American constructions of "urban jungles" filled with the "near-savage" poor. Christopher Herbert finds so many references to South Seas missionary writings in Henry Mayhew's *London Labor and the London Poor* that he christens it "Mayhew's Cockney Polynesia." He declares that Mayhew "does not invent the London poor out of whole cloth ... but out of existing ethnographies of primitive peoples (themselves highly prejudicial, ideologically and textually saturated inventions to begin with)."[151]

John and Jean Comaroff write from a different colonial direction about the Africanization of impoverished Britons, the "effort by bourgeois reformers to mobilize Africa in the cause of remaking the British underclasses—to hold up the 'dark continent' as a negative image with which to devalue its own peasants and proletarians."[152] This negative image was fundamentally gendered, basically about the reconstruction "of the home lives of both ... the primitive and the pauper." They note the unitary trope of the intrepid, civilizing voyage, of exploring a savage wilderness, in the varying writings of travelers, colonial missionaries, urban reformers. As with the later "model minority" construct, we can see the fundamentally relational, algebraic quality of this trope: the bourgeois Western eye sees the connections between domestic and exotic savages. At some points the domestic factor will have a higher value, at times the savage—the Comaroffs note that one text relates the astonished reactions to London poverty of a "young Caffre." And Jack London, in *People of the Abyss,* his nonfiction account of life among East London's homeless at the time of Edward's coronation, declared passionately that "if this is the best that civilization can do for the human, then give us howling and naked savagery. Far better to be a people of the wilderness and desert, of the cave and the squatting-place, than to be a people of the machine and the Abyss."[153]

In this discourse sphere, domestic and foreign exotics each exist in the other's equation, forever fixed as inferior in value to the bourgeois West. Thus the imperial, patriarchal source of the anthropological gambit, the structural reason for the inevitable low value assigned to the not-we end of the algebraic formula. The gambit is alive and well and functioning in contemporary American commentary on our national ethos.

THE NEW CUMBERING OF AMERICAN TEMPERAMENTS

As the Reaganite 1980s marched into the 1990s, "culture," in both the classic anthropological and the Arnoldian senses, came more and more to dominate popular discussion on the nature of the American polity. As we have seen, commentators weighed the comparative "cultural values" of differing groups, nominating one population after another "model minorities." At the same time, even these populations were the subject of a new wave of doubting xenophobia as the middlebrow press raised concerns about the assimilability of one or another non-European group. "America: Still Melting Pot?" asked a 1993 *Newsweek* cover in the classic locution requiring a negative answer. That was then, this is now. Neatly folding the denial of rights to long-resident minority citizens into a diatribe against new immigration, the article concludes that "group rights"—involving policies such as affirmative action and minority voting rights—lead to "tribalism," destroying America's "unique civic culture."[154]

Varying versions of the barbarians at the gates (or in our midst already) lament the destruction of the fabric of American culture not only by domestic exotics—immigrants and resident racial minorities—but by homosexuals and feminists, construed as "bearers of bad culture." Much of the debate has taken place in the domain of art, Arnold's "high culture," and in the art-linked venues of humanistic higher education. This is no historical accident, no transparent reflection of an autonomous shift in American public opinion. Ellen Messer-Davidow has documented the long-planned and corporate-funded rightist takeover of national "cultural politics," including the manufacturing—in the sense of the open-handed use of capital for the deliberate mass production of propaganda—of the "academic standards versus multiculturalism," "political correctness," and "obscenity in art" controversies. Allan Bloom, for example, received more than 3 million dollars from the rightist Olin Foundation, and Pat Buchanan has been a well-funded inner-circle new rightist for a quarter of a century. Since the 1970s, conservative activists have been strategically repackaging their unpopular, inegalitarian economic goals as a nostalgic return to an earlier, better American way of life. New rightist Paul Weyrich wrote that "the politics that carry us into the twenty-first century will be based not on economics, but on culture."[155]

Thus, the progressive culturalization of American political discourse is neither simply the logical product of developments in intellectual history nor only a "hall of mirrors" historical mimicry from the rise of nationalisms in general to black, then white ethnic, then women's structural reflections.

It is instead a messy amalgam of valuable new intellectual insights about the role of language/discourse, of liberal bad faith (one element of which is the anthropological gambit), of well-funded conservative politics, and of a weak opposition—"identity politics"—that operates within the pool hall vision bequeathed to it by anthropology and further evacuated of all economic content by postmodernism.

Identity politics is a political stance based on essentializing notions of membership in particular, cross-class social categories (racial and ethnic, gender, sexual orientation). It fails to acknowledge historical change, intragroup economic differences, and a larger progressive vision and in addition is structurally weak, as historian Barbara Epstein has pointed out: "A politics based on identity encounters not only the problem of the fragility of particular categories of identity, but the fact that everyone occupies various categories at once. One may be female but white, or black but male; virtually everyone is vulnerable to some charge of privilege."[156] In this confusing but conservative-controlled Tower of Babel, middlebrow and more scholarly actors have come together in a call for a reanimation of the center, an endorsement of a key vision of the meaning of American life, an American ethos. Two separable groups (but with interlocking directorates) are of particular interest for their harmonic responses to the query, How wide the circle of the we?

The first group consists of above-the-fray commentators not closely associated with the New Right who cry out against the centrifugal forces of "multiculturalism." In order to make this charge, they ignore the weak, defensive nature of identity politics—white women, racial minorities of both sexes, and homosexuals are, after all, denied equal rights on a daily basis in the United States. They also ignore the vast production of revisionist, and thus more accurate, American political, economic, intellectual, and cultural histories. These narratives, for example, chronicle both the role of labor struggle in the achievement of decent working conditions and higher pay for Americans and the prominence of race and gender exclusion in the American labor movement. The above-the-fray group instead identifies multiculturalism with billiard-ball accounts of the separate "contributions" of different American populations, the related neglect of "the basics" of "Western civilization," and the crazier fringes of cultural feminism and black and other minority cultural nationalisms. E. D. Hirsch has parlayed making lists of Western knowledge bytes children should not leave school without into a publishing industry. *Time* art critic Robert Hughes writes cholerically of the decline of America into a contemporary "culture of complaint" identified with therapeutic and consumption modes of apprehending reality—in astonishing ignorance of the lengthy American studies tradition of analyzing precisely the rise of this gestalt since the *turn of the century*.[157] Old Cold Warrior historian Arthur Schlesinger, Jr., launches a jeremiad against the "disuniting of America" through the operations of identity politics: "A cult of ethnicity has arisen both among non-Anglo whites and among nonwhite minorities to denounce the idea of a melting pot, to challenge the concept of 'one people,' and to protect, promote, and perpetuate separate ethnic and racial communities."[158] Schlesinger manages to make this claim not only through focusing on a few cranks and ignoring all real historical scholarship of the past two decades—not a single reputable academic book or article is cited in his footnotes—not only through collapsing the past thirty years of American history into an endless ethnic and racial essentialist moment, but also through attentively, obsessively heeding the polemics of multitudes of commentators brought onto the public stage only by checkbook cultural conservatism. He approvingly cites heavily funded rightists Dinesh D'Souza, Roger Kimball, and Allan Bloom as well as the less well provisioned Diane Ravitch, Richard Rodriguez, and Stephan Thernstrom—and closes the money circle through publishing his book first as a heavily subsidized "Whittle Book" complete with corporate advertising.

For the avuncular Schlesinger, the American Creed, true democracy, is immanent in the European Enlightenment and increasingly finds its realization over the course of the American Century. "The steady movement of American life has been from exclusion to inclusion." Colonialism, imperialism, the Cold War are all justified peccadillos because "whatever the particular crimes of Europe, that continent is also the source—the *unique* source—of those liberating ideas of individual liberty, political democracy, the rule of law, human rights, and cultural freedom that constitute our most precious legacy and to which most of the world today aspires. These are *European* ideas, not Asian, nor African, nor Middle Eastern ideas, except by adoption" (emphases in original).[159]

This is simply the American morality play writ large and lying: it falsely frames the debate as technicians of the sacred versus barbarians at the gates. The work of political scientist Rogers Smith more accurately describes the simultaneous and interactive nature of *multiple* American, ultimately European, political traditions—liberalism (individual rights), republicanism (communalism, civic virtue), and Americanism (racism, sexism, nativism). Smith demonstrates that American history is not at all a Whig narrative. Rather than steady social progress, we have seen, and are seeing, punctuated struggles and setbacks. He thus points out that "new intellectual systems and political forces defending racial and gender inequalities may yet gain increased power in our own time."[160]

Schlesinger also essentializes "Europe" versus "the Rest." He relies (very successfully) on the reader's ignorance of world history to deny indigenous evidences of all these "European" political virtues—and more— in other parts of the globe. Schlesinger even has the nerve, in the face of the horrors of Christian, Hindu, and Jewish fundamentalisms, to pretend both that Islam is the only world religion with fundamentalist forms and that contemporary Muslims are all fundamentalists. He lumps the entire, vastly heterogeneous African continent into "African traditions" to which "competitive political parties, an independent judiciary, a free press, [and] the rule of law are alien."[161] The logical extension of these claims is the rightist Paul Johnson's call, in the *New York Times Sunday Magazine,* for a reimposition of colonialism on the Third World.[162] Schlesinger gazes in wonder at the White City, and in ignorant contempt as he strolls the Midway. But he is magnanimous: if the denizens of the latter are very obedient, and assimilate according to his program, he will certify them for entrance into the circle of the we.

If Schlesinger's spiritual era is the 1890s, that of the new communitarians is the 1950s. This political call for reanimation of the American center, a new republican argument against liberalism, confuses "democracy" with a nostalgic, and false, vision of a past in which individuals were better integrated into society through family, church, and town meeting. But which Americans? "The heritage of trust that has been the basis of our stable democracy is eroding," declares the communitarian Bellah group in its second opus, *The Good Society.* "By the mid-sixties . . . faith [that Americans could create a better world] had begun to falter."[163] But for minority Americans—not to mention for Americans fighting for a just foreign policy—such a heritage of trust, such a faith only *began* in the 1960s, in response to multiple challenges to state power. And indeed, the Bellah group is no more interested in minority and poor Americans now than they were in *Habits of the Heart.* Their circle of the we is drawn around only middle-class whites. Domestic exotics can be sighted occasionally in the distance, in relation to their three imagined functions vis-à-vis those inside the boundary. The first function is the provision of spiritual blessing (with insurance against accusations of racism). Thus, the only minority American citizen attended to in *Habits of the Heart* is Martin Luther King, Jr., and the only three representatives in *The Good Society* are King, Jesse Jackson, and Louis Farrakhan (negatively). The second function is constituting an object for white middle-class spiritual development, for good works: church-based soup kitchens and social service provision. The third function, despite the authors' distaste for cost-benefit analysis, is their parenthetical admission that acting as moral Americans to ameliorate minority poverty would also reduce our experience of street crime outside "expensive townhouses and suburban homes."[164]

In a fascinating division of scholarly/political labor, then, communitarians are "underclass" ideologues' obverse. Both groups want to reform and reorganize populations, to get everyone lined up and properly cumbered. Neither group cares to disturb the contemporary operations of capital and states that schizmogenetically create greater poverty and wealth with each passing year. Each group feels nostalgia for a world it never lost, an imagined social body prior to the onset of present-day disease. But for "underclass" pundits the minority poor are the patients to be cured, while white middle-class America is the ghostly exemplar of social health. For communitarians, well-off whites are spiritually sick, in crisis, and need extensive treatments, while the minority poor, who never even make it into the doctor's waiting room, are told to expect trickle-down medicine.

What is the bourgeois white spiritual sickness? Over-emphasis on individual rights and pleasures, competition for status, for the accumulation of consumer goods. Communitarians scorn "rights talk" and want to alter laws to force Americans to be more responsible to their families, communities, and the larger society—but particularly their families. An underlying argument here, little noticed by critics, is a polite but persistent antifeminism. The Bellah group is the most polite. They elaborately admit that American women in the labor force work a double day, and that men should do more housework and child care. They endorse homosexual couples. But they also question the wisdom of espousing family leave, flex time, job sharing, and nonexploitative part-time work—all feminist and liberal goals since the early 1970s—until we have "an extended national discussion of what we expect from the family," and even argue for restricting women's access to abortion.[165] Mary Ann Glendon (the Bellah group's source for anti-abortion-rights ideology) and the late, explicitly antifeminist Christopher Lasch (their resident expert on community) are less polite. Both question the ease of divorce—Lasch wanted to forbid it altogether for couples with children.[166]

Heretofore I have used "morality play" as a mordant metaphor, a means of enabling the reader to see how frequently commentators on the American scene use "exotic" types to motivate a theologically inflected narrative that elides political economy and real history. But the Bellah group is not simply theologically inflected; they are purely theological. Theirs is a genuine morality play, a call for a new Great Awakening for inward-looking middle-class whites, in which "the modern," rather than a particular combination of exotics, plays the part of the Devil. Nevertheless, they do as good a job as the rest of substituting moralizing for actually attending to political economy. Their rooted distaste for money leads them to bizarre observations concerning the operations of institutions both at home and abroad. They think that the American government only recently has become involved in the economy, that the main thing wrong with corporations is that they "propagate consumption," that American involvement in the immiseration of Latin America and Africa has been "inadvertent."[167] They fail to join the largest church-based reform movement in the United States—the ongoing campaign to cut the military budget and increase social spending. They are entirely unable to see that the cultural phenomenon that most disturbs them—the unrestrained, rapacious individual pursuit of status, money, and consumer goods—coincides with untrammeled capitalist growth and was enhanced by governmental *deregulation* during the Reagan years. And while by no means all of their political allies agree with each of these particular points, in general, communitarian arguments for a "politics of meaning" are one section of the post-Reagan painted scrim that veils actual Americans, actual American inequalities, and the institutions that maintain them.[168]

So warped is the "American ethos" discourse frame, so distorted by the false culturalizing of our language, that often even the good guys, like Homer, nod. David Hollinger, for example, the intellectual historian whose "circle of the we" I have borrowed, makes his way very successfully through the "problem of the ethnos" in American history. He navigates past false universalisms, past Michael Walzer's version of the American Creed that just happens to exclude racial minorities as overcomplicating the narrative, past Richard Rorty's confused arguments for a new ethnocentrism. Hollinger calls for a "postethnic perspective" that "invites critical engagement with the United States as a distinctive locus of social identity mediating between the human species and its varieties, and as a vital arena for political struggles the outcome of which determine the domestic and global use of a unique concentration of power."[169] Thus, Hollinger stands for the United States' multiracial polity while claiming neither its uniqueness nor its perfection and avoids both the communitarians' false naïveté on American global power and the postmodernists' empty oppositional gestures about the West and the rest. But Hollinger founders when he reaches the treacherous cross-currents of gender and the exotic Other.

Hollinger catechizes Rorty and others for using hypothetical cases in their attempts to engage with politics, ethics, and cultural difference. In his own efforts to consider a "living, viable community" in such an argument, he turns to "the more challenging problem represented by Masai women":

> If these women are but breeding stock and, when barren of sons, are treated by their warrior masters as inferior to cattle, who are we to criticize? It is part of Masai culture, after all. And we probably should not even talk about it, as such talk might flatter Western prejudice and might lead us to forget how much violence and injustice are suffered by women in the United States and Western Europe. But if the Masai peoples eventually die off amid the economic, political, and ecological transformation of East Africa, we could, on ethnocentric principles, rescue the last surviving Masai woman as she crawls starving across the Ogaden. The price of her emancipation would then be the death of her culture, which we are restrained from countenancing by our principled anti-universalism and our healthy suspicion of Western imperialism. . . . Some feminists would be less timid about the matter and might even dare to be judgmental. Whether or not such a program has been devised that might actually help the Masai women . . . the value of a critical perspective on the plight of women world-wide is affirmed by some feminists.[170]

What's wrong with this picture? Everything—paint and canvas too. Although elsewhere in his article Hollinger makes use of interpretive and postmodern anthropological work, when it comes to real people's lives, it's time for anthropology without anthropologists. Hollinger's source on Masai women is a single letter to the *New York Times* (and his source for "some feminists" is a single op-ed piece in the *Los Angeles Times*). In reality, Masai, a transhumant herding population who live in both Kenya and Tanzania, have operated historically with a complicated gendered and age-graded system that guarantees the transfer of property rights in cows from fathers to sons. Women *do* have low status in this sense—they cannot own cows and their husbands are known to beat them—but so do boys and men until about age thirty, when they are finally allowed to marry, have their own homes, and own cows. Boys are set to herding early, whereas girls' lives are carefree, according to Melissa Llewelyn-Davies, an ethnographer of Masai in Kenya in the 1970s. Both sexes are circumcised. Women make strong bonds with their cowives (Masai are polygynous), working together and even giving up children to one another. They will gang together to beat men believed to have engaged in behavior threatening to women's fertility. They also support one another to the hilt in their ceaseless adulterous affairs with unmarried young men (*moran*), and one major Masai musical genre is women's love songs about the physical and romantic properties of their lovers. Sons owe their mothers love, respect, and lifelong sustenance, and women's agnatic relatives (members of their own patrilineage) maintain lifelong contact and support.[171] We can no more say that Masai women are mere chattel of men, then (which men? at what point in the life course?), than we can claim that American women have high status "in the workplace" or have achieved freedom from male violence.

Moreover, Raymond Bonner has documented the ways in which, over the course of this century, first the British colonizers and then the Kenyan and Tanzanian states, under duress from Western conservationist money, have thrown Masai off more and more of their land, confiscated their herds—and even, when they attempted to farm, destroyed their crops and fences. All of these actions were justified with spurious Western scientific "evidence" that Masai were ruining the habitat for wildlife—as Western tourism was wreaking increasing ecological degradation on their former lands. Thus, there are facts to back up a "healthy suspicion of American imperialism." It is a safe bet that these conditions of continuous displacement and economic decline have not had particularly equalizing effects on gender relations among the Masai any more than recessions and depressions have had in the West.[172]

So we probably should "talk about it," but we probably should know something about it before we do. As the old leftist political slogan put it, "No investigation, no right to speak." Hollinger's very stance of humanistic concern emanates from the "nasty savage" frame through which he apprehends the Masai's existence. Linked to that vision, of course, is that of the noble savage—and it just so happens that the Pottery Barn catalog was advertising "Masai flatware"—"inspired by the wrapped wire collars worn by Masai tribeswomen"—as Hollinger's piece was going to press. A decade earlier, cartoonist Gary Larson used a male Masai in an anthropological gambit set piece: little boy runs away, gets ridiculously far—but they, equally ridiculously, have phone booths. An American debutante on a Tanzanian tour in the mid-1990s kept a journal in which she exclaimed that Masai are "truly wild like animals and I enjoy them in every way. . . . I think I long so much . . . to be a Masai in my own right." Ralph Lauren launched a "Masai-inspired" advertising campaign. And Hillary and Chelsea Clinton's 1997 Africa tour included the requisite posed collar-wearing photo opportunity with Masai women. The First Lady confided to *Vogue* magazine her expert understanding that the Masai's "simple, pastoral way of life is at odds with Africa's push for development."[173] An *x* is only a *y*. Objects of modernist pity, objects of consumptive lust and antimodernist redemption, objects of the anthropological gambit—objects.

THE FAR SIDE　　By GARY LARSON

Larson 1-5

"Mrs. Harriet Schwartz? This is Zathu Nananga of the Masai . . . Are you missing a little boy?"

13. Ringing the Masai changes. Gary Larson cartoon, 1981. (The Far Side by Gary Larson is reprinted by permission of Chronicle Features, San Franciso, CA. All rights reserved.)

While it may be one fertile site for doing anthropology without anthropologists, the intersection of gender and the exotic Other—Hollinger's Waterloo—is never untenanted by the discipline for want of trying. In fact, American anthropologists have themselves participated in fascinating and varying ways, since the establishment of the discipline in the early years of the century, in deploying varying notions of the dusky maiden for popular consumption. But neither the Great Goddess nor the nasty female savage, neither the downtrodden burden bearer nor the vicious sexual reprobate is a timeless construction. Each female Other admits and effaces gendered power dynamics and implies a specific contrastive self, a particular kind of American womanhood, including some but not necessarily all resident women. The "dusky maiden" construct has shifted over time, moved frontstage and backstage, in conjunction with shifts in Western women's lives and statuses—and with changing American economy and empire, and anthropology's role therein. It is time to chart women's roles in the morality scripts, time to foreground gender on the stage of anthropology's America.

three

WILD WOMEN DON'T HAVE THE BLUES

The American Pragmatics of the Primitive Woman

Our ancestors are very good kind of folks, but they are the last people I should choose to have a visiting acquaintance with.—*Sheridan, The Rivals*

PROLEGOMENON

Now begins a tale of two ethnographies. Or, more accurately: the following three chapters outline a historical narrative that opens up like an accordion from the consideration of two recent anthropological texts. In the early 1980s, Harvard University Press published both Marjorie Shostak's *Nisa: The Life and Words of a !Kung Woman* and Derek Freeman's *Margaret Mead and Samoa: The Unmaking of an Anthropological Myth.*[1] Harvard promoted each book heavily, and each received strong academic and popular response. *Nisa* is the translated, edited, and arranged autobiographical narrative of a middle-aged woman of the San, a foraging population now living in parts of Botswana, Angola, and Namibia. (It is the !Kung San who play the Rousseauian "natural people" in *The Gods Must Be Crazy*, the popular comedy film from South Africa.) Shostak is one in a long line of Harvard anthropologists who have worked among the San since the 1960s, but *Nisa* differs from most earlier anthropological writing on the group in its emphasis on women's lives and on Nisa's personal evaluation of stages in her life. Shostak openly acknowledged feminist influence in her choice of research topic and the sorts of questions she encouraged Nisa to address.

"The Women's Movement had just begun to gain momentum, urging re-examination of the roles Western women had traditionally assumed. . . . !Kung women might be able to offer some answers; after all, they provided most of their families' food, yet cared for their children and were lifelong wives as well."[2]

Shostak portrayed the !Kung as having an "intact traditional value system" "distilled from thousands of years of experience."[3] Making use of Harvard project research, she suggested both that !Kung lives and those of other known contemporary foragers were very similar and that an "undeniable 'master plan'" among foragers, a common set of social adaptations, probably characterized life for "our prehistoric ancestors." Shostak chose to have a visiting acquaintance with our ancestors, and she pronounced them admirable: "Their skill in exploiting their environment allows them free time in which to concentrate on family ties, social life and spiritual development. Their life is rich in human warmth and aesthetic experience and offers an enviable balance of work and love, ritual and play."[4] Moreover, "women's status in the community is high and their influence considerable."[5] !Kung women thus represented for Shostak both *Ur*-women, living as prehistoric humans must have, and—excellent news—high-status females whose lives might serve as models for Western feminists.

A scant two years later, however, Derek Freeman's attack on Margaret Mead's interpretation of the lives of Samoan adolescents would rapidly become a print and broadcast *cause celebre*. This second Harvard Press book claimed, *contra* Mead's 1920s evocation of Samoan girls' easy transition to adulthood, replete with love affairs under the palm trees, that the true Samoan story involved stringent parental guard over girls' virginity, high rates of male violence—including rape—and a generally rank- and anxiety-infused social atmosphere. Freeman strongly argued that the "liberated young American," "only twenty-three years of age," who was "smaller in stature than some of the girls she was studying," was simply duped: "The girls . . . plied Mead with these counterfeit tales." Moreover, even if their information had been truthful, Freeman claimed that adolescent girls simply could not function as a "true and accurate lens" on Samoan life.[6]

In other words, as ethnographer of Samoa Bonnie Nardi has pointed out, Freeman determined that Mead's informants' accounts were "rendered untrustworthy simply by virtue of their age and sex." And, as we can see from Freeman's descriptions of Mead, what is sauce for the Samoans is sauce for the ethnographer. Freeman argued that his attack on the late

Mead (dead five years at publication) was motivated not by personal spite of an unknown against an American icon, but against the theoretical stance of "cultural determinism" that he claimed she espoused. That is, Freeman believed that in attacking Mead's Samoa findings he would support a "more anthropological paradigm" that recognized "the radical importance of both the genetic and exogenetic and their interaction."[7]

Two deliberately accessible anthropological works, then, each very well known, each bearing strongly on female lives in small-scale societies, each weaving together notions of gender and of "our ancestors" or human nature, but to opposing effects, each published by the same university press, each an intentional player in the long-running drama of anthropology's America.

Here we arrive at the nub of the issue. In the Western popular mind, people living in small-scale societies are primitives, with all the symbolic baggage collected over more than three centuries of Western exploration, exploitation, missionizing, colonialism, and neocolonialism. Primitives are ourselves, or our worst or best selves, or our former selves, undressed: human nature in the buff.[8] We have seen the ways in which members of small-scale societies have served as Rorschach blots, mirrors, litmus tests, lenses—either rose colored or dark—for American audiences. Living populations are merged with prehistoric ones, enhancing the tie between exoticism and temporal distance. And women primitives, in the Western mind, are *Ur*-women: who we really are, or cannot escape being, or perhaps the selves we have lost, for good or ill, on the road to civilization.

Western political debates on women's status, from the nineteenth century forward, have ineluctably referred to the primitive lodestone to clinch the argument. Ronald Reagan made notorious use of a Victorian-derived, evolutionist, "women's culture" frame in his 1983 apology for earlier sexism to the Business and Professional Women's Association: Ungrammatically identifying women as the uplifting bearers of civilization, men's redeemers, Reagan declared, "Because I happen to be one who believes that if it wasn't for women, us men would still be walking around in skin suits carrying clubs."[9] On the other hand, "primitive woman," since at least the Gilded Age, is also a woodlot to which Americans have repaired continuously to glean vigorous, redemptive narratives of escape from the burdens of patriarchal civilization. "Wild women don't worry"—sang blueswoman Ida Cox in the 1920s—"wild women don't have the blues," and we can see echoes of Cox in Shostak's portrayal of Nisa.[10]

And yet *Nisa* and *Margaret Mead and Samoa* inhabited nearly entirely separate discourse spheres in American popular culture. Since the 1960s, in fact, we have seen an increasing fissioning of attentive political publics in America, particularly with reference to gender—an adult version of children picking up their marbles and leaving the game in a snit. In general, liberal feminists and conservative antifeminists nowadays simply tend to read different books and magazines, listen to different radio and watch different television programs, bring back different gleanings from the cultural woodlot, socially accept certain costumed anthropologists, and cut the others dead.

Shostak and Freeman reached, and were interpreted by reviewers for, almost entirely different audiences—there is very little overlap in either reviewers or venues for discussions of the two texts. Conservatives saw the Freeman book as proof of the fraudulence of a liberal feminist agenda. It did indeed function, as George Marcus noted, as "a work of great mischief." *Fortune* gleefully reported that Freeman's book "could reshape the intellectual landscape," because Margaret Mead "contributed mightily to still current and widely held liberal views." *Time* magazine concurred, claiming that Mead, a "feisty, energetic scholar, political activist . . . feminist and author," was the "natural ally of those who promoted free education, relaxed sexual norms and green-light parenting intended to give American youngsters the trouble-free adolescence enjoyed in Samoa."[11] As the group on the political downslide, though, liberal feminists in the end did respond to the media circus surrounding the Freeman book—illustrating Hegel's apothegm that the slave must study the master's thought, while the master can afford to ignore the slave's perceptions. And, of course, American anthropologists—and those of other nationalities as well—weighed in on the controversy, largely in a circle-the-wagons defense of the scholarly guild against the raging ignorant hordes.

Thus, considering the "primitive woman" domain makes even more clear the falsehood of ivory tower interpretations of American anthropological functioning. Only a small percentage of anthropological work is deliberately written to be accessible to the public—few ethnographies average more than five hundred copies in lifetime sales. But those key texts both constructed to be and successful at passing through the scholarly mesh into the agora are profoundly influential. They affect not only popular culture but also subsequent anthropological work, even if only in dialogue in absentia.

This symbiosis of the scholarly and the popular, though, exists not in a static realm but in history. Deliberately accessible "primitive woman" ethnographies—and all texts—are written in particular historical contexts. Gender politics, the roles of anthropologists and the state of the discipline, the political economic surround—all have shifted over the American Century. And since the dusky maiden is exactly that—nonwhite and female—such ethnographies are not only about some sliced-off realm of gender (a logical impossibility in any event) but also about changing American race and class relations and United States foreign policy—the state of the American empire.

In fact, as we shall see, for most of the twentieth century the state of gender politics led anthropologists to merge their representations of dusky maidens into "larger" ethnographic concerns. And then, the actual representations they did craft—insofar as they were drawn against the grain of the times—were repeatedly overrun, misread, "overdetermined," by shifting images of "primitive" women in general popular culture. Ironically, *Nisa*'s great popularity and the media uproar surrounding Freeman's book on Samoa and Mead—both phenomena presupposing "timeless" primitive societies and an unchanging anthropological expertise on them—occurred at precisely the moment that, as we shall see, anthropology as a discipline was historicizing with a vengeance. Thus the two major phenomena through which the American middlebrow public was aware of cultural anthropology in the 1980s were profoundly unrepresentative of actual movements in the field.

Two final ironies characterize the twentieth-century history of Western representations of the dusky maiden. First, patterns of male dominance, West and rest, have tended to restrict the study of "exotic" women to female ethnographers—both because female Others often were not deemed important enough for male anthropologists to study, and because non-Western female worlds were often off-limits to strange males. Then, women anthropologists themselves, insofar as they came to public notice outside academic cloisters, have been and are often deemed "fair game" for popular cultural exoticization—for stigmatizing sexualization. Thus Allan Bloom's unfootnoted, tossed-off reference to Margaret Mead as a "sexual adventurer" quoted above. Thus the hypersexual and unethical "feminist anthropologist" on the television series "90210." In the 1970s, feminists declared memorably that "the personal is political." So are the Primitive Woman and her ethnographer.

And then, shifting American representations of race, class, and gender have been examined in most domains of popular culture—world's fairs, theater, museum exhibits, television, film, magazines (especially in the recent *Reading National Geographic*)—but not popular ethnographies. Postmodernists have provided narrow *readings*, à la 1960s New Criticism, of a variety of ethnographic texts' internal literary structures. But few have taken up the challenge of Talal Asad's 1973 anthology, *Anthropology and the Colonial Encounter*, to consider the historical, political contexts of ethnographic production. Fewer still have dealt with popular reception of ethnographic writing—and indeed, no one has yet remarked on how badly wrong both journalists and anthropologists have been in their accounts of contemporary responses to *Coming of Age in Samoa*. The realities of intertextuality—that work escapes the author's intentions, is read differently in the present and across time—further complicate any analysis of popular reception. But the difficulty of a task is no index to its necessity. The processes of constructing, receiving, and enacting (as did Reagan) narratives of the primitive woman constitute an important political pragmatics, one that we ignore at our peril.

Opening with the frame of the two American fins de siècle, I have engaged the question of anthropology, Others, and the changing public political sphere first in terms of the developing anthropological wardrobe from the 1960s to the present, and then through a consideration of certain domains of ethnicity, race, and gender in the United States from the Progressive Era on. The only way, however, to gain real access into the Mead-Shostak-Freeman gestalt, and through them to a broader sense of the changing American pragmatics of the primitive woman, is first to loop back behind the turn of the century, to start with that great crucible of modernity, the Victorian era. Once that ingot has been forged, I turn to Margaret Mead's Progressive training ground, lay out text, context, and reception for *Coming of Age*, and follow her and others, especially her teacher and friend, Ruth Benedict, through the interwar years and World War II. In chapter 4, Laura Bohannan's best-selling *Return to Laughter* then grounds anthropological considerations of gender, race, and class in the postwar, Cold War, decolonizing era. Janet Siskind's *To Hunt in the Morning* and Robert and Yolanda Murphy's *Women of the Forest* exemplify constructions of the dusky maiden influenced by the early second wave of American feminism and the associated political movements of the 1960s and 1970s. Finally, in chapter 5, I return to Shostak's *Nisa* and Freeman's attack on Mead, both published during Reagan's first term, to explore our era of ongoing feminism in the context of overarching reaction.

I have deliberately lodged this political economic analysis of anthropology's and public culture's symbiotic role in changing American empire inside a motif usually imagined to concern "just" gender, in order to counter the all-too-common ghettoization of feminist research from "hard" political economy. These pages, then, are booby-trapped: the reader cannot engage with changing constructions of primitive womanhood without stumbling over the trip wires of corporate capitalism and the advertising industry, fascism and antifascist organizing, McCarthyism, UNESCO, Vietnam, South Africa, the New Right. Nor can she follow the trail of emerging and shifting American empire without running headlong into simulacra of dusky maiden after dusky maiden. (Should the reader be both female and of color, she will experience the trip as a series of exasperating, distorting funhouse mirrors.)

A complete synthetic narrative of American cultural, political, gender, race, and anthropological history coupled with these close readings would fill several volumes. For this reason, and because Mead's own coming of age has been so distortingly portrayed—not least by herself—I provide here a selective, dumbbell-shaped chronological account. I focus most heavily on the first three decades of the twentieth century, and then on the recent past, and provide only basic connecting bridgework for the years between the onset of the depression and the renaissance of Western feminism. But really to understand the road to Mead's contemporary public Janus face, we need to begin the story in the era prior to the full-scale twentieth-century selling of the primitive. We must start with the Victorian gender wars—must even back up a bit to the early sex role skirmishes in the Enlightenment.

EVOLUTIONARY MAIDENS

The Victorian culture was one of very great diversity, defying monolithic explanations; and the one thing everybody is right about is that we must find in it the origins of our own complexities.—*Frank Kermode*[12]

Recent scholarship has remarked on the extraordinary florescence of the issue of human gender relations in European Enlightenment thought. This new, and newly constructed, interest has been linked to French revolutionary rhetoric and realities—anticlericalism overturning prior religious certainties concerning proper roles for women and men, the simultaneous opening afforded by Dissenting religious activism in Britain, the logical extension of democratizing "rights of man" proclamations to women, and the efforts of women of varying social positions to take advantage of social ferment to advance their own interests. As the eighteenth century rolled to its end, however, women's efforts and writings were soon turned back, both by French revolutionaries and by forces of reaction on both sides of the Channel and across the Atlantic in the infant Republic. Asserting female inferiority and the necessity of male rule became part of the rhetoric of reimposition of order, whether Tory, republican, Napoleonic, or American revolutionary. Mary Wollstonecraft, whose 1792 *Vindication of the Rights of Woman* had thrown down the gauntlet against Jean-Jacques Rousseau's patriarchal misogyny, was pilloried after her death as a "hyena in petticoats." Her calls for equal education for women, foreshadowing twentieth-century feminist socialization theories, were discredited and forgotten and had to be reinvented by John Stuart Mill and other mid–nineteenth century women's rights theorists and activists.[13]

Rousseau and Wollstonecraft, however, shared a discourse frame that would be largely overthrown by the time Mill and Harriet Taylor collaborated on *The Subjection of Women* in 1869. As Maurice and Jean Bloch have pointed out, late-eighteenth-century European theorists newly posited "nature" as a category of challenge "rather than an element in a stable binary contrast," a floating signifier put to use in critique of the present. "Nature" could refer to a presocial state, human corporeal processes, the "natural" order of plants and animals, the reported or imagined lives of "primitives"—or a mixture of one or more of these elements.[14] Rousseau's "state of nature" was accordingly ambiguous, as was Wollstonecraft's notion of women's "natural state." "Primitive Others" could be used to illustrate an ideal social order—as did Tahitians for Encyclopedist Denis Diderot. Or they might function as the exemplary depraved from which the Enlightenment writer adjured us to distinguish ourselves—as did the Muslim world for Wollstonecraft, in her numerous scathing references to seraglios, harems, sultans, odalisques, and the rest of the orientalist baggage so well excoriated by Edward Said. What Others were *not*, however, until the Victorians, were calibrated stepping-stones on a path illustrating evolutionary progress from "savagery" through "barbarism" to the apotheosis of white, male Western "civilization."

Much has been written about the "hold that the idea of social evolutionism had upon the minds of Victorian intellectuals," as J. W. Burrow put it.[15] Suffice it here to say that it was during the nineteenth century that—despite much theological dissent—the twin notions of ineluctable human progress and the placement of dead *and living* populations on a ladder of social development took root and grew as dominant structures of feeling in Europe and the United States. It was not so much the influence of Darwinism as a growing zeitgeist that Charles Darwin breathed in along with the intelligentsia of his era.

Thus it was that not only those who would now be labeled anthropologists but all writers concerned with issues of "primitive" life were, by the late nineteenth century, oriented around evolutionism. Evolutionary thinking was, as historian George Stocking remarks, if not the paradigm then the "cynosure" of anthropological inquiry. Indeed, "evolutionism provided the dominant interpretive metaphor and the major focus of theoretical speculation for those anthropologists since regarded as historically significant."[16]

Thinking about human societies rather than nonhuman animals in terms of evolution entailed presumptions that equally contemporary populations represented more or less evolved social forms. As John McLennan stated in *Studies in Ancient History*, "the study of the races in their primitive condition" is one of the "chief sources of information regarding the early history of civil society." John Lubbock, chief Anglophone popularizer of social evolutionary theory, put it more baldly: "The conditions and habits of existing savages resemble in many ways . . . those of our own ancestors."[17] In a revision of the medieval Christian Great Chain of Being—from the Godhead through humans to the lowliest of animals—the "Victorian comparative method" placed groups higher or lower on a newly diachronic *scala natura* according to their putative closeness to civilization. Measurement criteria were a matter of debate, but clustered around technology levels, modes of supernatural belief (with a presumed evolution from pantheism and magic to monotheism and science), and types of gender relations, glossed as "marriage." The Victorian marriage debates involved both figures still well known—such as Herbert Spencer—and others less so—Henry Maine, McLennan, Lewis Henry Morgan, Lubbock, Johann Jakob Bachofen. They both were central to the period's constructions of self and Other, or advanced and primitive, and engaged the imaginations and influenced the later social models of both Karl Marx and Sigmund Freud. Debate centered on how to conceive the marital and sexual component of the *scala natura.* Did "savages" engage in primitive promiscuity—to paraphrase Hobbes, all mating with all? Or, conversely or additionally, was there a period of female rule? Whichever prior state or states one postulated, how could evolution to the civilized present—male-dominated monogamy—be explained?

It is no coincidence that this very heated debate on past sexual and family arrangements took place during the rise of the Victorian woman movement for suffrage, equal education, and access to professional positions. Political stances of key participants varied. Marx and Engels were wholly for equal rights. Influenced by New York railroad lawyer Lewis Henry Morgan's ethnological work on Native Americans and others, they postulated an original state of "primitive communism" in which the sexes were equal, a "world-historical defeat of the female sex" coincident with the rise of private property, and a socialist future in which women's equality would be secured through their participation in public productive labor. Engels even ventured an astute—if, sadly, poorly predictive—assay into the realm of romantic heterosexual love:

> What can we now conjecture about the way in which sexual relations will be ordered after the impending overthrow of capitalist production is mainly of a negative character, limited for the most part to what will disappear. But what will there be new? That will be answered when a new generation has grown up: a generation of men who never in their lives have known what it is to buy a woman's surrender with money or any other social instrument of power; a generation of women who have never known what it is to give themselves to a man from any other considerations than real love or to refuse to give themselves to their lover from fear of the economic consequences. When these people are in the world, they will care precious little what anybody today thinks they ought to do; they will make their own practice and their corresponding public opinion about the practice of each individual—and that will be the end of it.[18]

Bachofen, though hailed by twentieth-century cultural feminists for claiming a prior matriarchy under female supernatural tutelage, actually believed that the victory of the "male principle," and thus of male dominance, was necessary for the future of civilization. McLennan and Spencer both made early equal rights statements that they later disavowed, Spencer most forcefully:

> Two classes of differences exist between the psychical, as between the physical, structures of men and women, which are both determined by this same fundamental need—adaptation to the paternal and maternal duties . . . a somewhat-earlier arrest of individual evolution in women than in men . . . so that both the limbs which act and the brain which makes them act are somewhat less. . . . The mental manifestations have somewhat less of a general power or massiveness; and beyond this there is a perceptible falling-short in these two faculties, intellectual and emotional, which are the latest products of human evolution—the power of abstract reasoning and that most abstract of the emotions, the sentiment of justice—the sentiment which regulates conduct irrespective of personal attachments and the likes or dislikes felt for individuals. . . . Once more, we have in women the predominant awe of power and authority, swaying their ideas and sentiments about all institutions. This tends toward the strengthening of governments, political and ecclesiastical.[19]

Note both Spencer's late-nineteenth-century reflection of the male French revolutionary's deprecation of priest-ridden conservative women who were undeserving of citizenship and his prefiguration of contemporary cognitive psychologist Kohlberg's contention that women do not reach male levels of ethical maturity.

The key point here is not whether Victorian social evolutionism was "a conscious defense of the marital status quo"—Stocking's misguided criticism of feminist historian Elizabeth Fee.[20] The real issue is that gender and sexuality held center stage in Victorian evolutionist debates: constructions of the "primitive woman" were directly linked to notions of proper lives for Victorian ladies—but not, of course, for their female servants. And, except for Marx and Engels and their radical comrades (whose labor theory of value led them to assume women's historic productive role—although they largely missed "primitive" women's extradomestic labor), to a man, the Victorian theorists assumed that the higher the position of women in a society, *not* the more political power they would wield, but the less they would be "made drudges who perform the less skilled parts of the process of sustentation." John Lubbock, whose popularizing works were widely read, adduced as one proof that the "lowest races" had "no institution of marriage" that young men in Australia spoke with praise of the labor that wives could perform. The American O. T. Mason, curator of the Department of Ethnology in the United States National Museum (and commentator on the "forlorn" savage woman in the prologue), claimed that "spirituality," "the genius of progress," characterized "civilized" gender relations: "When, therefore, one reads that a tribe or nation is immoral or brutalizes women, it is equivalent to saying that the guilty one has got out of the great stream of intellectual advancement and drifted into one of the eddies of animal existence."[21]

Stocking rightly stresses the obsession with religion versus rationality that tinged Victorian anthropological debate. He allots a lesser place to but does acknowledge these writers' role in rationalizing Western imperialism: "There can be no doubt that sociocultural thinking offered strong ideological support for the whole colonial enterprise in the late nineteenth century."[22] But clearly, equally important was the Victorian theorists' obsession with what feminists in the 1970s would label sexual politics, an obsession that was threaded, as we have seen, through their varying evolutionary schemes. Thus, gender, sexuality, and race were inevitably woven together in the Victorian mind, linking the savage woman and the Euro-American lady—despite the diverse patterns of that weaving. And thus we return to John Stuart Mill, whose growing convictions concerning women's rights—and relationship with Harriet Taylor Mill—alienated him from his intellectual fellows and marked his departure from elite male consensus in Victorian society.

Mill is widely acknowledged as a major architect of liberal political theory and was a firm abolitionist as well as a women's rights theorist and activist (he introduced the first suffrage bill into British Parliament). But he was also a long-term and ideologically entirely loyal employee of the East India Company—a self-satisfied participant in empire. His arguments for women's rights were hinged on notions of progress: that British (and other European) women's lack of rights was an anomaly, a sign of evolutionary backwardness in largely advanced states:

> The social subordination of women thus stands out as an isolated fact in modern social institutions; a solitary breach of what has become their fundamental law; a single relic of an old world of thought and practice exploded in everything else, but retained in the one thing of most universal interest; as if a gigantic dolmen, or vast temple of Jupiter Olympus, occupied the site of St. Paul's and received daily worship, while the surrounding Christian churches were only resorted to on fasts and festivals.[23]

In addition, Mill assumed that men of the European working classes were even more backward than their bourgeoisies:

> And how many thousands are there among the lowest classes in every country, who, without being in a legal sense malefactors in any other respect, because in every other quarter their aggressions meet with resistance, indulge the utmost habitual excesses of bodily violence towards the unhappy wife, who alone, at least of grown persons, can neither repel nor escape from their brutality; and towards whom the excess of dependence inspires their mean and savage natures, not with a generous forbearance, and a point of honour to behave well to one whose lot in life is trusted entirely to their kindness, but on the contrary with a notion that the law has delivered her to them as their thing, to be used at their pleasure, and that they are not expected to practise the consideration towards her which is required from them towards everybody else.[24]

In this way Mill, despite his dissent on women's rights, was a theorist who worked largely inside the dominant structures of feeling of his times. In his reflexive use of social evolutionism, his demand at every point that evaluation of human behavior be based on a preordained *scala natura* from savagery to civilization, with colonized populations and the domestic poor automatically slotted on the lower rungs of the ladder, he reflected a fundamental Victorian shift from Rousseau's and Wollstonecraft's Enlightenment—one of the key origins of our own complexities.

The Subjection of Women was printed in the United States only months after its British publication. American suffrage leaders considered Mill's the definitive analysis of women's situation, and sold *Subjection* at their conventions. His abolitionist but also bourgeois and racist frame was congenial to the dominant strands in the American woman movement, many of whose most prominent members had been stung to social Darwinian rage at their failure to achieve women's along with black male suffrage with the passage of the Fifteenth Amendment. Elizabeth Cady Stanton, in the very year that Mill published *Subjection of Women,* lectured "American women of wealth, education, virtue and refinement" that "if you do not wish the lower orders of Chinese, Africans, Germans and Irish, with their low ideas of womanhood to make laws for you and your daughters . . . to dictate not only the civil, but moral codes by which you shall be governed, awake to the danger of your present position and demand that women, too, shall be represented in the government!"[25]

No matter what political perspective Gilded Age and Progressive Era commentators took, however—no matter which Others they wished to include in the circle of the we—the epistemic frame of the times was a social evolutionary association of human units, whether "races," genders, or classes, with lower or higher civilizational achievements. The black women's club movement took as its motto Lifting as We Climb. And Anna Julia Cooper, principal of what became the famous Dunbar High School in Washington, D.C., and holder of a Ph.D. from the Sorbonne, wrote in 1892 about gentility and woman's civilizing mission with as much fervor as Elizabeth Cady Stanton a generation earlier. The difference, of course, was that she included herself and other well-educated black women among the women of "virtue and refinement" and scored crude, "low" whites, both men and women, who failed to support black civil rights as failing the test of true gentility:

> Our train stops at a dilapidated station, rendered yet more unsightly by dozens of loafers with their hands in their pockets while a productive soil and inviting climate beckon in vain to industry; and when, looking a little more closely, I see two dingy little rooms with "FOR LADIES" swinging over one and "FOR COLORED PEOPLE" over the other; while wondering under which head I come . . . I cannot help ejaculating under my breath, "What a field for the missionary woman." I know that if by any fatality I should be obliged to lie over at that station . . . that same stick-whittler would coolly inform me, without looking up from his pine splinter, "We doan uccomodate no niggers hyur." And yet we are so scandalized at Russia's barbarity and cruelty to the Jews![26]

Indeed, from the postbellum period through the Progressive Era, the interdigitation of social Darwinism with prevailing Victorian "moral mother" notions—whose descendants we encountered in the last chapter—dictated the hegemony of "relations of rescue" in native-born women's organizations and consciousness. Historian Peggy Pascoe's apt phrase encompasses not only the massive Women's Christian Temperance Union and the multitudinous, heavily supported Protestant women's foreign missionary societies, but also the founding of various settlement houses for immigrants and blacks throughout urban America, homes for orphans, prostitutes, and unmarried mothers, and projects established to "rescue" special regional populations, like Chinese women in San Francisco brothels, Mormon "victims" of polygamous marriages, or Native American women. Common to all these projects, and the women engaged in them, was the presumption that all women "wanted to share Victorian gender values and would do so if placed in favorable circumstances." Native-born, largely but by no means only white, Protestant women engaged in a "search for moral authority"—both over men and over the women and children whom they conceived as needing rescue. And yet these mostly intergroup female-female relations were too often genuinely mutually rewarding to be entirely encompassed with a simple "social control" interpretation.[27] To paraphrase the black women's club movement's motto, genteel American women both lifted their sister Others as they climbed—and themselves climbed upward through placing their feet squarely on those Other female necks.

A special category of this work, for our purposes, is the postbellum foreign evangelical missionizing funded by the burgeoning population of white Protestant middle-class women—and, more often than not, enacted by spinsters from their midst. As Joan Jacobs Brumberg points out, these women, in their very successful missionary magazines—such as *Heathen Women's Friend*—encouraged notions of "characteristic atrocities" against women in non-Christian states. In so doing, they supported the dominant "native women worse off" interpretation (my phrase, not Pascoe's) in Victorian social theory. They also undermined woman movement demands for improving female status in "superior" Christian nations and supported advancing American imperialism in the name of rescuing foreign women. A special focus of this women's crusade—about which more later—was the notion of characteristically "girlless villages" abroad: not villages with no girls, but villages in which "there was no observable period of dependency in which young women capable of reproduction were sheltered and protected by family and community."[28]

Victorian anthropology, then, shared a discourse field with late-nineteenth-century middle-class women's relations of rescue in their mutual assessment of the "forlorn savage woman." But in this early period,

European and American "anthropology" was largely nonacademic, a matter of bourgeois men's armchair speculations on the basis of classical scholars', travelers', and missionaries' reports, of fairs and of exhibits in newly established museums (the major funding source for anthropology prior to World War I, closely tied to the interests of their philanthropic founders), of individuals like Lewis Henry Morgan or Frank Cushing being adopted into Native American populations (Seneca and Zuni, respectively), and taking on the roles of protector and interpreter.[29] Academic institutionalization happened late, and proceeded slowly. Edward Burnett Tylor was not appointed reader in anthropology at Oxford University until 1884.[30] Aside from the evangelical women's dichotomizing the world into Christian and heathen and their proselytizing thrust, the two worlds were overlapping parts of a common, largely nonuniversity public sphere.

And thus they mingled together at the Columbian Exposition, where the young (in status, at least—he was thirty-four) Franz Boas was employed in the Anthropology Building at, among other tasks, measuring visitors to assess their physiological conformation to ideal racial types.[31] Neither he nor his confreres dissented publicly at that time from the use of their growing field for the furtherance of popular imperialist racism and its social Darwinian intellectual rationale. "In turn-of-the-century evolutionary thinking," George Stocking notes, "savagery, dark skin, and a small brain and incoherent mind were, for many, all part of the single evolutionary picture of 'primitive' man, who even yet walked the earth."[32]

But "native woman (and people in general) worse off" coincided contradictorily in the Western fin de siècle mind with the first wave of romantic ethnological antimodernism. Then, as again in the present, transatlantic elites of both sexes shared, and articulated widely, a sense of ennui, of "living life at a remove," an alienation from the social and physical world being created by the maturation of corporate capitalism, the "stale gentility of modern culture." While a fascination with the European Middle Ages and its associated Catholicism and craftsmanship bulked large in this antimodernist wave, for a significant number, immersion in "the primitive" or "the exotic" brought a sense of psychic healing and therapeutic personal integration. Henry Adams, Robert Louis Stevenson, and Paul Gauguin discovered the South Seas. "I have never lived in so unselfconscious a place," Adams exclaimed of Samoa.[33] A fascination with both south and east Asian religions was widespread and connected to ubiquitous interest in the occult and other forms of spiritualism. "Noble savage" depictions of Native Americans, popular since James Fenimore Cooper's and Henry Wadsworth Longfellow's idealizing portraits of the early to mid–nineteenth century, rose to new heights as delegations of Native Americans visited, performed for, and were widely written about by proper white bourgeois and petit bourgeois. Frank Hamilton Cushing, for example, in 1882 took a group of Zuni and Hopi elders for an Eastern tour, including a tea party with enthusiastic Wellesley coeds, who found them "so handsome that they reminded us of Cooper's heroes." Other New England commentators suggested what Curtis Hinsley has labeled the "kinship of spirit and praxis between Zuni and Beacon Street" in assimilating Zuni rituals to then-common parlor seances.[34] Thus was begun American antimodernist "Southwest chic" incorporating both Native American and Latino populations, which, in an unbroken line from Cushing through Mabel Dodge Luhan and D. H. Lawrence, through Ruth Benedict, to silver and turquoise jewelry, kachina dolls, paintings, pottery, and dances for tourists, Tony Hillerman mysteries, "Santa Fe style," and Robert Redford's Sundance Institute, continues to this day.

A significant interpretive thread running through this elite sense of alienage and turn to the primitive and exotic, according to Jackson Lears, was the association of corrupt, weak, and unsatisfying civilization with the feminine and of the primitive, and "more primitive" Western past, with fresh, vital, martial masculinity. "During the 1890s, crusades for physical vigor swept the educated bourgeoisie in both Europe and America," and this vigor was associated with the regeneration of WASP masculinity and thus the turn away from a perceived "feminization" of culture. "The ability to kill became a sign of total virility. Bloodshed marked emancipation from feminine weakness."[35] Such a regeneration would then achieve the disciplining of workers at home and the effective domination of "natives" abroad.

Thus, a therapeutic engagement with the primitive and exotic coincided—as it does in the present—with recurrent crises of masculinity and American state actions against "primitives" both at home and abroad. The fin de siècle was marked, after all, not only by prevalent elite ennui but by the consolidation of federal control over Native Americans—the forced removal of children from families for "civilizing" boarding school education and the parceling of Indian lands for sale to and exploitation by whites—by the violent end of Reconstruction and reestablishment of black peonage in the South, by American martial acquisition of territory in the Caribbean and the Pacific (including the naval occupation that made Mead's Samoa fieldwork possible a generation later) and indirect colonial sovereignty over parts of Latin America, and by an all-out war against native- and foreign-born American industrial workers as they attempted to organize against pitiless exploitation.[36]

It was within the context of this larger, "noble versus nasty savage" American vision and political economy of the primitive and exotic that Franz Boas received his first appointment at Columbia University in 1896. He was promoted to full professor in 1899, and the anthropology department was finally made free standing (it had been part of the psychology department) in 1901.[37] German-born, Jewish, and with a left-liberal scientific outlook (he had originally trained in physics), Boas in 1883–84 had undertaken both geographic and ethnological research among Baffinland Eskimos. His experiences there, George Stocking convincingly argues, were not a "conversion" to cultural relativism but a "confirmation of attitudes . . . he had in fact brought with him."[38] That is, Boas was deeply, romantically impressed with what Marx and Engels would have labeled the primitive communism of the Eskimos: their absolute ethic of sharing. "Where amongst our people would you find such true hospitality?" he asked rhetorically in his journal. But within his larger epistemic frame, he saw Eskimos and Europeans as simply fellow humans, all of whom have to struggle "to give up tradition and follow the path to truth." Boas, whose face carried dueling scars, the results of defending himself against anti-Semitic slurs during his German student years, applied a nineteenth-century idealist humanist measuring rod to each individual: "As a thinking person, for me the most important result of this trip lies in the strengthening of my point of view that the idea of a 'cultured' individual is merely relative and that a person's worth should be judged by his *Herzensbildung.* This quality is present or absent here among the Eskimo, just as among us. All that man can do for humanity is to further the *truth,* whether it be sweet or bitter."[39] And indeed, Boas's measuring project at the Chicago World's Columbian Exposition, an extension of work he had initiated among Wooster schoolchildren while teaching at Clark University, drew from very different presuppositions than those then dominant in American physical anthropology. While still working with notions of hereditary "races," Boas was primarily concerned with process, variation, and the human life course—and thus came to criticize a priori and counterempirical assertions of idealized racial types.[40]

Over the first decades of the twentieth century, Boas's commitment to sweet and bitter truth led him decisively to reject prevailing racist social evolutionary assumptions; and in fact to resign from his position of curator at the American Museum of Natural History (Margaret Mead's later organizational home) when he was unable to prevent his exhibits from being organized according to that epistemic frame.[41] Always searching for funding for his own and students' research, he secured money from the Dilling-

14. Franz Boas, in late career. (Courtesy of the Institute for Intercultural Studies, Inc., New York.)

ham Immigration Commission for a study that documented, contra notions of ideal racial types unmodified by environments, the changing physical characteristics of southeastern European migrants to the United States. (Although his conclusions were progressive in the context of his times, he did also recommend that Sicilians be discouraged from immigrating, as they adapted poorly to American conditions.) Later, in the 1920s, having survived concerted attacks within the profession over his opposition to World War I and his progressive scholarship, Boas presided over the National Research Council's Fellowship Program in the biological sciences, which awarded research grants to his students Melville Herskovits, Otto Klineberg—and Margaret Mead.[42]

MARGARET MEAD, PROGRESSIVISM, AND CONSUMING PRIMITIVE YOUTH

Much has been made of Boas's influence on Mead, not least by Mead herself, whose kindergarten-like account of the mind of "one of those statesmen-scientists who are mapping out the whole course of a discipline" fails to consider Boas's fairly complex theoretical background, his shifting understandings over time, or the political surround, both in Europe and the United States, to which he was always reacting.[43] Derek Freeman, too, belabors the point, in his accounting of the Svengali-like "extreme cultural determinist" Boas's influence on the youthful Mead: "To the twenty-one-year-old Margaret Mead, Boas was the greatest mind she had encountered. . . . [Boas] found in the twenty-three-year-old Margaret Mead the very person to carry . . . out . . . a detailed investigation of hereditary and environmental conditions."[44] For Rosalind Rosenberg, on the other hand, Boas was both the progressive and Progressive enabler of Mead's research, along with the other members of the "sudden wave of women students" whom the older man nurtured in the interwar years. Boas, whose association with Barnard College grew with Columbia University president Nicholas Murray Butler's hostility to Boas's antiwar politics, was moving in the years of Mead's training away from a self-described "over-emphasis on historical reconstruction" toward "a penetrating study of of the individual under stress of the culture in which he lives."[45] And indeed, given psychology's then-high status and its prevalent racism—witness the invention of the intelligence quotient test to "grade" immigrants and blacks—Boas felt compelled to deal with this dominant scholarly ideology on its home ground.[46]

Rosenberg, however, also allowed for the profound influence sociologists William Ogburn and W. I. Thomas had on the young Mead. In those years, both Ogburn and Thomas were concerned with the increased strain on individuals—especially women—in American nuclear families with the capitalist industrialization of the country. Rosenberg as well narrated the particularities of Mead's own family romance, as detailed in her memoir *Blackberry Winter*. In Rosenberg's *Beyond Separate Spheres*, the frustration of Emily Fogg Mead's academic career by the exigencies of Victorian motherhood (she bore five children) and her feminist upbringing of firstborn Margaret play key roles, as does Edward Mead's suffering as an academic social scientist in a larger culture "in which business success still represented the most prestigious attainment in American life." Edward Mead's "doubt had a significant sexual component." That is, a man of his times, he identified scholarship with femininity, ironically enhancing the young Margaret's intellectual self-confidence.[47]

Rosenberg's historical contextualization of Mead's background and training is useful, as is George Stocking's less politically attentive portrait of the romantic "ethnographic sensibility of the 1920s."[48] But neither they nor other commentators on Mead have made the connection between Mead's *Coming of Age in Samoa* and the contemporaneous establishment of the culture of consumption so well documented by American studies scholarship. Nor has anyone actually considered the range of contemporary reaction to *Coming of Age*—though many have made spurious assertions about that reaction. Finally, while she places Mead properly in the context of retreating feminism, expanding professional opportunity, and Progressivism's social engineering mandate, Rosenberg's own hagiographical impulses lead her considerably astray from Mead's actual words. She overinterprets a feminist subtext into the 1928 *Coming of Age,* selectively quotes from the 1935 *Sex and Temperament in Three Primitive Societies,* and cuts her historical narrative cleanly off before the explicitly antifeminist 1949 *Male and Female*—a text that in 1963 led a furious Betty Friedan to spend nearly an entire chapter of *The Feminine Mystique* in detailed attack on Mead. The two phenomena—that Mead appears as a notorious contributor to antifeminism in what is arguably the most famous second-wave feminist text, and the fact that almost no feminist commentator since the 1960s seems to remember this attack—are themselves fascinating acknowledgement of Friedan's assessment of Mead as a "scientific supersaleswoman."[49] Friedan, however, thought that Mead was selling antifeminist femininity. If we consider, as we shall in the following pages, the long history of Mead's changing anthropological politics, we see that feminist or antifeminist, liberal or conservative, what she most consistently sold was the Primitive as commodity—and herself as authoritative anthropological interpreter of the uses of exotic merchandise.

The America of Margaret Mead's coming of age—the first several decades of the twentieth century—encompassed the Progressive Era, World War I, radical organizing prior to and in response to the Bolshevik Revolution, and the technologically modernizing but socially reactionary 1920s. Mead was certainly aware of world political shifts—she writes that her Progressive mother "danced for joy at the outbreak of the [Russian] Revolution." And she was tangentially part of progressive student organizing while an undergraduate at Barnard, attending a mass meeting for Sacco and Vanzetti and making "forays into radical activities, walking on a picket line or stuffing envelopes for the Amalgamated Clothing Workers."[50] But Mead's focal attention lay elsewhere, and in order to contextualize *Coming of Age* properly, we need to understand women and professionalism, "youth," and the commercialization of culture in the 1910s and 1920s.

By the 1920s, according to Peggy Pascoe, American middle-class women's "relations of rescue" were "rendered . . . anomalous" as "rescue homes had come to be regarded as repressive institutions out of step with modern American culture."[51] Multiple factors—the achievement of woman suffrage, the popularization of Freudian notions and thus the sexualization of formerly "passionless" ladies, and, ironically, the success of Progressive woman movement "rescuers" like Jane Addams in forcing government to provide public health and social welfare services (and to hire some women to administer them)—combined to alter public perceptions of women's nature. In a world of female voting citizens, of the "It Girl" and the flapper, of few but highly publicized female doctors, lawyers, professors, cinema stars, athletes—even criminals—notions of women's innately superior morality to men came to seem old fashioned, passé. Jane Addams's arguments that women could do "social housekeeping," that the "mother breast of humanity" would bring about progressive social change, seemed unnecessary. Feminism came to be associated with spinsterhood, the antithesis of the growing ideal of companionate heterosexual marriage for women. Paradoxical, but adding to feminism's unpopularity, was the post–World War I government campaign against "dangerous radicals," which actually targeted not only the Women's Trade Union League but parts of the Parent-Teacher Association as dangerously Bolshevik.[52] Younger, better-off women largely sought the credentials and social positions that had been denied to their mothers, not to be active feminists, not to engage in female relations of rescue, but to be "objective," practicing professionals.

And a young woman *anthropologist* would be all the more likely to wish to stress the distinction between her professional status and that of the former expert on "primitives," the rescuing lady missionary.

"In the early twentieth century," Nancy Cott notes, "diffuse 'professional standards' were being adopted in many occupational areas—even in business and politics—indicating both the growing culture of professionalism and the persuasiveness of this rendering of any occupational group's self-definition and justification for existence."[53] Professional ideology forwarded the notion of scientifically based expertise as the paramount rationale for social authority. And, although few would gain access to "male" professional status, middle- and working-class women in the late nineteenth and early twentieth centuries poured into the professions— teaching and nursing—readily available to them. They pursued college educations en bloc, doubling their proportion of college entrants between 1910 and 1920. The much smaller numbers of women successfully pursuing higher degrees and thus higher status also increased through the 1910s. Women Ph.D.'s reached their proportional apogee (15 percent of all awarded) in the early 1920s—just as Margaret Mead was dedicating herself to anthropology—and slid downward thereafter, returning only in 1950 to 1900 levels.[54]

The growing reign of experts, the American tendency to rely on credentialed authority in all personal and public decision making, intersected with an unprecedented postsuffrage expansion of women's voluntary association. The National American Woman Suffrage Association launched the League of Women Voters. White and black Parent-Teacher Associations, the National Federation of Business and Professional Women's Clubs, and many others were founded in the late 1910s and early 1920s, and membership in the Young Women's Christian Association soared when it abandoned its Protestant Christian requirement for membership. Women's organizations based on ethnic and national groups also grew rapidly. All of these organizations worked, at least some of the time, in alliance with and often subordinated to the prescriptions of newly constituted "expert professionals"—psychologists, sociologists, early childhood educators, social workers—many of them women.[55]

Although women's new civic organizing encompassed all domains of American life, a preponderant focus was the proper care and upbringing, on the part both of parents and of government in its myriad forms, of children and adolescents. And indeed, in this period, despite the demise of "moral motherhood," popular understanding registered an intensification of *maternal* responsibility not only for children's physical but also for

their *mental* welfare.[56] The very category of "youth," meaning both childhood and the long adolescent years, was an invention of this era. G. Stanley
Hall's opus *Adolescence* was published in 1904 and stimulated a flurry of
professional debate about both appropriate activities in this period and the
problems of youth and their proper treatment. Popular and scholarly journal articles on "youth and its problems" increased over the 1920s to twen-
tyfold their representation in the 1910s. And the *New York Times Index* first
listed "youth" as a separate category in 1920.[57]

Material shifts in American life literally created this new category of
humans to be pronounced upon by experts. Progressive Era reforms—
making child labor illegal, extending compulsory schooling, expanding the
population pursuing higher education, raising the age of marital consent—
helped to constitute a class of working-to-upper-middle-class children and
adolescents outside the labor force and with declining family responsibilities. Viviana Zelizer has described the overarching historical shift as one
in which children emerged as "economically 'worthless' but emotionally
'priceless.'"[58]

At the same time, this generation's rebellious leisure activities frightened
professional-class Americans: they feared that their own children would
not adequately reproduce their class status, and that working-class and
impoverished youth unrest would threaten the social order. Youth sexual
experimentation, in particular, set off alarm bells among well-off Americans and their elite advisors. "In the 1920s," Paula Fass has written, "youth
appeared suddenly, dramatically, even menacingly on the scene. . . . Youthful sexuality was at once the sign of social demoralization and a continuing
threat to social order."[59] Kathy Peiss has documented the earlier pursuit of
leisure and sexual experimentation by working-class "charity girls," and
much later bourgeois hysteria was a reaction to the cultural trickle upward
of "low" behavior. W. I. Thomas, with whom Mead worked while at Barnard, wrote an entire study of the "unadjusted girl"—the impoverished or
working-class delinquent.[60]

Thomas noted that female delinquent behavior was usually in reaction
to "an impulse to get amusement, adventure, pretty clothes."[61] But such
impulses are not, despite much "common sense" to the contrary, transhistorical human universals, hardwired components of the second X chromo-
some. Growing rapidly in the closing decades of the nineteenth century
and the first two decades of the twentieth, the commercialization of American culture involved a vastly increased and newly rationalized industrial
output, newly seductive types of retailing sites—such as the department
store—and the rise and institutionalization of the advertising industry to

whip up and to channel consumer demand, to tell people—particularly women—how to navigate in the new "land of desire."[62]

The vast national proliferation of commodities, their urban display in the newly electrified and glassed show palaces of the modern department store, and the institution of a vast industry in itself, advertising, aimed fundamentally at women in their role as guardians of family consumption, are facts without dispute. In this "mingling of sex and sales," Rayna Rapp and Ellen Ross note, women themselves became commodified. Advertising and newly standardized social institutions, such as the beauty pageant, defined female pulchritude as both almost-unattainable female ideal and male object and reward: "women had been trained not only to do the consuming but to be consumed as well."[63]

Scholars have also suggested that American structures of feeling shifted in concert with these changes, older therapeutic modes merging with the new consumption ethic to create an anxious, unfulfilled, passive self peculiarly susceptible to the prescriptive blandishments of merchandising. "Here, after all," writes Christopher Wilson of the tone of the new topical, advertising-filled magazines, "was the pathos of the modern consumer: endlessly enticed and dissatisfied, reminded of one's shortcomings, set 'free'—and yet guided by a 'pseudo-conscience.'"[64] Some, like historian Warren Susman, have discerned a shift in thinking about American selves from theologically driven "character" to psychologically informed "personality." Karen Halttunnen has extended this analysis to spatial symbolism: the transformation of American middle-class interiors from the "moral parlor" to the personality-revealing living room.[65] And, of course, contemporary psychology's prominence among the social sciences conduced to this shift.

Children had great importance in the new culture of consumption. William Leach points out the mutual interests of merchants riding the phenomenal growth in the American toy industry (1,300 percent output increase between 1905 and 1920) and the newly established child welfare experts, who emphasized the role of participating in buying and owning toys, child-size furniture, and other equipment in children's "physical, mental, and social development." Experts even lectured at Macy's in 1928 on "why children should have toys."[66] Thus, the newly defined life cycle stage intersected compellingly with the advertising-stimulated obligation to buy. Finally, Leach also describes the ways in which new commercial forces drew on fin de siècle antimodernism in marketing the "primitive and exotic": he details one curator and merchandiser's "desire to expose Americans to the 'vitality' of the 'primitive' and the 'childlike,' and to find refuge from the 'deadly grind' in preindustrial dreams and fantasies."[67]

Astonishingly, Margaret Mead had more than a ringside seat on the development of the new culture of consumption. Largely absent in both her own account of her upbringing and the uses to which it has been put by enthusiastic feminist scholars is the fact that both her parents (who had met, incidentally, as graduate students at the University of Chicago in 1896, three years after the Chicago World's Columbian Exposition) were professionally engaged in celebrating and analyzing American corporate growth and consolidation and the phenomenal rise and entailments of the advertising industry.[68] Edward S. Mead, who created the Evening School of Accounts and Finance and the Extension School at Wharton, taught corporate finance there. As William Leach notes, he "believed that large corporations were the most efficient economic units and that their 'centralized' structures offered the best means to control the flow of goods and money." "These great organizations," Mead wrote in 1910, naturalizing and celebrating a very contingent historical occurrence, "are like the trees in the primeval forest . . . wide and deep in the necessities of mankind." He recognized and approved the new conglomerates' push to "charge what the traffic will bear . . . to get from the buyer all that the buyer can be induced to pay."[69]

Emily Fogg Mead, despite her professional frustrations, wrote a much-noticed, and reprinted, article both saluting and analyzing the nascent advertising industry. She recognized its inevitable function in stimulating and channeling mass consumer desire in an inegalitarian society: "We are not concerned . . . with ability to pay but with the ability to want and choose," she proclaimed, and she lauded advertising's capacity "to excite desire by appealing to imagination and emotion."[70]

This disregarded element of Mead's family romance by no means proves that she became an enthusiast of commodity consumption at her parents' knees. (And, in fact, Mead, like many intellectuals before and since, rather boasted of personally owning and needing little in the way of material objects.) Rather, it underlines the importance of this shift in American culture during the period of Mead's own coming of age, demonstrates that she cannot have been unaware of it, and suggests that it had an effect on the very structures of feeling behind her intellectual work. The commercialization of American culture, the new professionalism of women, the creation of youth as a construct, the psychologization of cultural interpretations with the rise of "personality," and the new uses of "the primitive" are fused together and instantiated in Mead's own first book. Let us turn, then, to the actual text of *Coming of Age in Samoa*, and to the contemporary response to it.

MARGARET MEAD FINDS HER AMERICA

Mead's introduction sets her stage clearly. Her first sentence—"During the last hundred years parents and teachers have ceased to take childhood and adolescence for granted"—identifies her research problem as youth (not comparative primitive societies, not women or feminism, not liberal political change, not sexuality) and her stance as the professional expert speaking to the American middle-class audience.[71] She then discusses recent psychological work (mentioning G. Stanley Hall) on the inevitable Sturm und Drang of adolescence, notes its historically and culturally limited data base, and introduces her own guild with the air of one announcing the arrival of the cavalry: "But meanwhile another way of studying human behavior had been gaining ground, the approach of the anthropologist, the student of man, in all of his most diverse settings." As anthropology can survey other cultures, it can overcome the methodological problem facing psychologists in the West: "What method then is open to us who wish to conduct a human experiment but who lack the power either to construct the experimental conditions or to find controlled examples of those conditions here and there throughout our own civilisation? The only method is that of the anthropologist, to go to a different civilisation and make a study of human beings under different cultural conditions in some other part of the world."[72]

Anthropology thus both trumps psychology and is defined as the survey of differing billiard balls for the reformist benefit of our own rounded little American globe. So much for ethnological antimodernism, for romantic sensibilities in Mead. Certainly she wrote, throughout the book, lyrically and in the style of children's literature, of the landscape and the daily round: "lovers slip home from trysts beneath the palm trees," "the children are scuttling back and forth, fetching sea water, or leaves to stuff the pig," "a group of youths may dance for the pleasure of some visiting maiden."[73] But while such local color descriptions might seem similar to Henry Adams's enthusiastic announcement that the Samoans "are free from our idiotic cant about work," Mead repeatedly undercuts any romantic idyll by referring to Samoans as "quite simple peoples," "primitive peoples," members of "a shallow society" that cannot produce "great personalities and important art," a "place where no one plays for very high stakes."[74]

No, Samoa is not for Mead a romantic escape from the ordeals of modernity, but a providential experimental setting, a natural laboratory for her professional practice, just as Chicago was (and still is) for the Chicago School social scientists. Mead does not wish to escape modernity's difficulties, but to dissect and taxonomize them, as she wishes to dissect and taxonomize the Samoa of her mid-1920s encounter. The ultimate purpose is to identify bits of Samoan culture which we might wish to use instead of the corresponding bits of our own—something like switching jigsaw puzzle pieces between puzzles. Mead cautions that if "we would reject that part of the Samoan scheme that holds no rewards for us . . . it is necessary to sort out which parts of their practice seem to produce results which we certainly deprecate, and which produce results which we desire."[75] Mead, here truly her mother's daughter, is advertising herself as the authoritative interpreter of the units of "primitive culture" with which we might wish to "excite desire by appealing to imagination and emotion."

Which are Mead's favored units of Samoan culture? While she describes the entire Samoan life course, kinship and social organization, and the division of labor and the specific skills necessary to reproduce daily life, Mead's end focus is child and adolescent psychology. Thus, her recommendations bear on how American institutions might be altered to produce less Sturm und Drang in American youth. First, the family: echoing W. I. Thomas, Mead asserts that "we have developed a form of family organization which often cripples the emotional life, and warps and confuses the growth of many individuals' power to consciously live their own lives." She criticizes the "tiny, ingrown, biological family opposing its closed circle of affection to a forbidding world" and suggests that "a larger family community, in which there are several adult men and women," would "ensure the child against the development of the crippling attitudes which have been labelled Oedipus complexes, Electra complexes, and so on." She also praises the Samoan attitude "towards sex and the education of the children in matters pertaining to birth and death," advocating that adult relatives frankly inform children and not hide from them information about births and deaths of family members, including, for example, the fact that the human dead, like all animate nature, decompose.[76] As to schooling, Mead uses the American and Samoan cases to provide a parallax view, calling for a third path: she repeatedly advocates coeducation, "free and unregimented friendships," and "education for choice":

Education, in the home even more than at school, instead of being a special pleading for one regime, a desperate attempt to form one particular habit of mind which will withstand all outside influences, must be a preparation for

those very influences. . . . this child of the future must have an open mind. . . .
The children must be taught how to think, not what to think. And because old
errors die slowly, they must be taught tolerance, just as to-day they are taught
intolerance. . . . they must come clear-eyed to the choices which lie before them.[77]

Mead, then, is writing as a classic Progressive social engineer, with two
differences. First, she replaces the morally inflected language and material
goals of Progressivism (lighted streets, sewers, government reform) with
the new secular language of psychology and the goal of changing institutions to enhance emotional "adjustment" for most members of a society.
And, of course, Mead the modernist is actually arguing largely for
changes—coeducation, less authoritarian childrearing, youthful sexual experimentation—already in the works in 1920s America. Second, as an anthropologist, she lays claim to expertise on an abstruse but crucial experimental laboratory. Commentators have failed to notice, as well, that more
than a quarter of the text of *Coming of Age* concerns the United States rather
than Samoa. Mead's was the first full-dress "exotic" ethnography in the
now-hoary tradition of the edification and social reform of Westerners
through looking into the mirror of "the primitive." But in so doing she
was by no means a social revolutionary. No, Mead, ironically, used "the
primitive" to sell new, improved *modernity,* to rationalize ongoing shifts in
American culture and society.

A further indication of Mead's modernism is her lack of interest in social
change in Samoa. Both missionizers and romantic antimodernists tended
to be concerned, invested, and activist with reference to local authorities,
their promulgations, the effects of colonial power on native peoples. And
the American presence in Samoa was part of a larger, growing South Pacific
strategy related to Great Power skirmishes in the late nineteenth century—
in this case, among Great Britain, Germany, and the United States. During
the period of Mead's visit, the naval governance of Samoa was apparently
so despotic that the United States Congress found it necessary to appoint
a commission to visit and propose reforms. But according to Mead, the
professional social scientist working with a human society as "natural laboratory," American naval government in Samoa was "tolerant, slow-
moving, and disinclined to meddle unduly with native life."[78]

But what about the dusky maiden? After all, while her overarching subject category was youth, Mead did focus on Samoan adolescent *girls,* a fact
that Derek Freeman and his gleeful supporters have not allowed us to forget. But Mead did so in a remarkably dry, professional, unfeminist manner.
At the outset, she rationalizes her sex-restricted primary group of infor-

mants as a technical issue: "Because I was a woman and could hope for greater intimacy in working with girls rather than with boys, and because owing to a paucity of women ethnologists our knowledge of primitive girls is far slighter than our knowledge of boys, I chose to concentrate on the adolescent girl in Samoa."[79]

Mead's is then an unmarked—in the linguistic sense—generic she: she claims to be studying females for no particular ideological reason. Nor, as we shall see, was Mead criticized or commended (at least explicitly) at the time of publication for her emphasis on female Samoans. Edwin Ardener wrote in 1972 that "no one could come back from an ethnographic study of 'the X,' having talked only *to* women *about* men, without professional comment and some self-doubt. The reverse can and does happen constantly."[80] In fact, that is precisely what Margaret Mead did in 1928. The key is that it *was* 1928, that is, that gender ideology not only shifts over time, but by no means follows a Whig historical upward, democratizing path. In this particular period, Mead could ride the slipstream of the prior woman movement—could lay claim to intelligence and a career—while at the same time she felt it necessary to background her own identity as a woman among women and to ignore any and all contemporary feminist issues. Nancy Cott has documented the exacerbation of "the tension between feminism and professional identity" in the 1920s: "Professional ideology . . . encouraged professional women to see a community of interest between themselves and professional men and a gulf between themselves and nonprofessional women. That angle of vision was counterproductive to feminist practice. . . . the professional ethos encouraged them to see other women as clients or amateurs rather than colleagues in common cause . . . to see a different scope and destiny for themselves than for women in general."[81]

Mead's vision of Samoan women reflected this contemporary professional ethos, this desire to avoid problematizing gender, and yet she also scattered fascinating, and often self-contradictory, points about female Samoan lives through her text. She notes, for example, that "in those social spheres where women have been given an opportunity, they take their place with as much ability as men. The wives of the talking chiefs in fact exhibit even greater adaptibility than their husbands. The talking chiefs are especially chosen for their oratorical and intellectual abilities, whereas the women have a task thrust upon them at their marriage requiring great oratorical skill, a fertile imagination, tact, and a facile memory."[82] On the other hand, she asserts that while adolescent Samoan lives lack the anxieties of their Western counterparts, the Samoan "boy is faced with a far

15. Margaret Mead with Samoan informant, 1925. (Courtesy of the Institute for Intercultural Studies, Inc., New York.)

more difficult dilemma than the girl." The girl, Mead writes, using the schoolroom metaphor, "rests upon her 'pass' proficiency," while "the boy is spurred to further efforts."[83] But Mead's analysis is suspect here, and not only because her observations of girls are from up close, of boys from afar. It is also the case that there is a long Western anthropological (and scholarly generally, and popular) tradition of assuming more complicated, *more political* male lives. Sylvia Yanagisako has nicely labeled this tradition, after Geertz, the provisioning of "thick descriptions" of male kin/political spheres, and "thin descriptions" of their female analogues.[84] Mead is too honest an ethnographer not to report the phenomenon of *moetotolo*, "sleep crawling," or surreptitious rape; nor does she shirk from noting that girls of high *taupo* status may be subject to forced marriage, and formerly were subjected to public defloration.[85] But it does not occur to her that these widespread dangers might cause no little adolescent female anxiety and lead to strategic life choices to minimize pain and horror. Moreover, Mead's primary female informants are mission-connected girls who seem to hold lower rank, and thus fewer possibilities for anxiety-provoking social status, than the boys about whose chances for eventual *matai* status she speculates.

One intriguing, and also unremarked, element of Mead's presentation of Samoan female lives is that she provides an exact counterinstance of the older Protestant women's evangelical, missionizing image of the primitive "girlless village." Mead goes to some length to elaborate the relatively carefree experience of an adolescent Samoan female, released from the baby tending that young girls must perform and not yet expected to marry: "She thrusts away every . . . sort of responsibility with the invariable comment, 'Laititi a'u' (I am but young)."[86] Mead's first husband, Luther Cressman, was a Protestant minister—she herself was a lifelong practicing Episcopalian—and she writes of her period of engagement to him, "a minister's wife was what I wanted to be."[87] I do not think that it is reaching too far to assume that Mead had some familiarity with the women's mission magazines of that period and to speculate that at the back of her mind, during the period of writing *Coming of Age,* was a sense of striking a blow against a kind of theological female moralizing that her 1920s generation stood against. Mead's tendency to downplay male violence against women and girls in Samoa may also have drawn from this source, as well as from the humanistic impetus of Boasian anthropology, and from then-contemporary professional women's ideology that women were not particularly marked as a social group, that their experiences did not differ much from men's. Even apart from any connection to "girlless villages," then, we might see *Coming of Age* as a final popular burial of female relations of rescue, both because the dusky maiden turned out not to need rescuing and because there was no special moral category of human to engage in rescue. From the ashes of the female savior and female victim of male dominance arose the professional/social engineer and the exotic Other who existed to provide data on human variation—both individuals only coincidently female.

But what of Mead's America? How *did* Mead generalize about the society for which she was advocating social engineering? How did gender play a role there? Race and class? To whom was the dusky Samoan maiden contrasted?

First, and most important, Mead employs the truly transhistorical American synecdochic fallacy: she identifies one small portion of the American population with the whole. Mead's America, her circle of the we, is the native-born, white middle, professional, and upper classes. She excludes the recent immigrant wave that so concerned Franz Boas and was the subject of her own master's thesis: "It must be understood that here, as always, when I say American, I do not mean those Americans recently arrived from Europe."[88] Given the demographic realities of the period, Mead was, on the issue of foreign extraction alone, excluding more than one of every five Americans from her analysis of "American culture."[89] If we apply her class lens as well, the proportion shrinks far more. And Mead genuinely means to apply that lens. She describes the "average American home, with its small number of children"—an average then only for the WASP professional classes. She writes of "our young people" who "are faced by a series of different groups which believe different things and advocate different practices." True enough for most Americans, then and now, but her extensive following example assumes universal college attendance—including one relative who spent "two years at Oxford"—professional status, and abundant leisure for reading and engaging in then-elite interests like vegetarianism, writing mystical poetry, and Indian philosophy. This in an era in which only about three quarters of urban whites even finished high school, and in which only 12 percent of college-age Americans attended college.[90]

The only exceptions to this otherwise purely elite portrait of the United States occur late in Mead's text. First, blacks and Asians appear as objects of the white professional-class girl's concern in attempting to make sense of the bewildering moral lessons of her elders: "If she accepts the philosophic premises upon which the Declaration of Independence of the United States was founded, she finds herself faced with the necessity of reconciling the belief in the equality of man and our insitutional pledges of equality of opportunity with our treatment of the Negro and the Oriental."[91]

Then, Mead suddenly includes white working-class youth in her discussion of "education for choice." She does so, however, only to comment on the contradiction between the Horatio Alger myth, "our American theory of endless possibilities," and what most young people can expect: "Careful students of the facts . . . tell us that class lines are becoming fixed."[92] Ever the professional social scientist, she has no quibble with this asserted state of affairs (which was in any event about to be belied by the depression)—only with the "maladjustment" inevitable when millions long for a social mobility they will not achieve.

Most interestingly, Mead in this section also follows the difficulties of "the adolescent girl" with her family: "Because of the essentially pecuniary nature of our society, the relationship of limitation in terms of allowance to limitation of behavior are more far-reaching than in earlier times." Thus, "the importance of a supply of money in gratifying all of a girl's desires for clothes and for amusement makes money the easiest channel through which to exert parental authority." Once the daughter gets a job, "her parents' chief instrument of discipline is shattered at one blow, but not their desire to direct their daughters' lives."[93] The echoes of W. I. Thomas will be clear to the reader. What may be less immediately apparent, however, is that this analysis is an amalgam of Thomas's work on wayward working-class girls and Mead's own frustrations with her father's repeated efforts to direct her life through offering and cutting off money. She even recalls, in *Blackberry Winter*, "When I refused my father's offer of money to travel around the world, instead of getting married, he withdrew his support of my graduate work. But then, in the spring of 1923, I received a note from Ruth Benedict that read: 'First Award No Red Tape Fellowship, $300.'"[94]

Mead's America of 1928, then, has an extremely narrow class and race compass. She is highly aware of her own social and intellectual world, less aware of the working-class Italians among whom both she and her mother worked and of the working-class girls studied by her professors. Within these bounds, she is not lacking in insight, but the problem is that she has no sense that the bounds exist. She was and is by no means alone in this handicap, not only among anthropologists who append unresearched "American contrast" chapters to exotic ethnographies, but also in the culture at large, then and now. It has long been a self-mocking truism among American anthropologists that our scholarly concerns have autobiographical roots. A solipsistic source for scholarly passion, however, should not be at issue. It is when we confuse an autobiographical beginning with a full social analysis that distortion arises, and here Mead the Olympian social engineer links hands across the waters of time with self-concerned contemporary postmodernists who assert the equal relevance of all narratives.

Finally, Mead's partial America, in *Coming of Age* and—as we will see—in all her subsequent work, effaced not only the worlds of race-minority Americans, but of fellow scholars of color. Zora Neale Hurston, for example, also worked closely with Franz Boas, and the Harlem Renaissance of which she was a part was in full swing during Mead's scholarly coming of age. But Mead made no use of her or their work to "find America," nor of that of other white and nonwhite students of Boas—not to mention scholars in other disciplines—who worked on race relations in the United States. Mead would later make specific civil rights gestures: she sat on the board of trustees for the Hampton Institute, for example. But as we saw in her embarrassing "rap" with James Baldwin, Mead's antiracist gestures were undercut by her condescending, self-invented versions of American racial/ethnic history.[95]

Meanwhile, the reviewers of *Coming of Age,* all professional-class white Anglo-Americans themselves, generally found her descriptions of the United States either insightful or unremarkable. She received mostly favorable reviews in both social science and middlebrow journals. But the intellectual framing of these texts—what they thought the book was actually about—and the occasional critical comment reveal not only the falsehood of anachronistic accounts of *Coming of Age,* but the state of 1920s American social science scholarship and of professional-class concerns.

Ruth Benedict, Mead's teacher and friend, focused within the paradigm in the *New Republic* on the necessary use of exotic fieldwork to escape our "pot-bound" measurements of our own society, to envisage "very different possible ways of handling invariable problems." She correctly noted that Mead by no means romantically advocated a wholesale adoption of Samoan mores: "We could recapture [the simplicity of their choices] only at the price of civilization itself." She recommended the book not only to professional anthropologists, but to "the educator and the parent." Most revealing, finally, is Benedict's "selling the primitive" language toward the end of the review, in which she hawks *Coming of Age* as a superior commodity: "Readers who have rejected many accounts of primitive peoples may find this one to their liking."[96]

Well-known *Nation* editor Freda Kirchwey, however, while correctly noting that Mead had not advocated the "expensive simplicity" of Samoan lifeways, failed to notice what she *had* advocated, and spent most of her review ridiculing "our impulses of escape" to "sea, sand, sun, a languorous atmosphere providing freedom and irresponsibility." Kirchway's overmastering concern is the fight against antimodernism: "Most of us . . . will . . . continue . . . to cling to our difficulties and our delights."[97]

H. L. Mencken, in his *American Mercury*, did not misread Mead à la Kirchwey, but nevertheless echoed her concerns in his own inimitable style: "Sex does more damage among us than it does in Samoa, but it also makes for a vastly greater joy. It offers most people their one genuine escape from the slavery of everyday life under civilization. True enough, it usually makes them, in the end, even worse slaves than they were before, but while the flight is on they are happy in a wild, poignant, overwhelming manner that is quite beyond the imagination of a dumb-bell Samoan." Mencken went on to criticize Mead's use of American materials, suggesting she stick to her exotic last: "After all, what she has to say on the former subject has been said before, and very often. But . . . the people of the South Seas live in her precise, scientific pages even more vividly than they live in the works of . . . romantic writers." But Mencken then ends his essay with the classic anthropological gambit, suggesting that Mead's "methodology might be applied to an investigation nearer home" to forward his own antifundamentalist agenda: "We know far more about the daily life of Pueblo Indians than we know about the life of Mississippi Baptists. Whenever, by some accident, light is let into the subject, there is gasping surprise, and even horror. This happened, typically, when a gang of slick city jakes descended upon the primitive mountain village of Dayton, Tenn., at the time of the Scopes trial, and found it full of Aurignacian men clad in dressy mail-order suits, with bibles under their arms."[98]

Other nonscholarly reviewers reflected Benedict's and Mencken's general approbation, with a particular emphasis on Mead's accessible writing and her scientific handling of human sexuality. Walter R. Brooks (author of the *Freddie the Pig* series of children's books), in the *Outlook*, pointed out the "unusual feature" that *Coming of Age* "is exceedingly well written and possesses charm" and commended it "to any reader who does not object to the handling of natural facts with ungloved hands." The *New York Times Book Review*'s anonymous reviewer echoed these sentiments, applauding "Miss Mead's careful scientific work," which "deserves the most earnest tribute"; and describing the book as "sympathetic throughout, warmly human yet never sentimental, frank with the clean, clear frankness of the scientist."[99]

Mead's fellow "clean, clear, frank" scientists had a few quibbles, however. While anthropologist Camilla Wedgwood, in one specialty journal for scholars of the Pacific, found *Coming of Age* "vivid" and illuminating," "B.M." (Bronislaw Malinowski?) of *Pacific Affairs* worried about Mead's actual knowledge of Samoan, given the length of her stay; about her omission "of the consequences of promiscuity . . . social diseases"; and about issues of confidentiality: "Some of the picturesque islands of the Pacific are still smarting from 'true' stories written about them. Surely some day there will appear a searching study of our civilization from the standpoint of another people. Then we will taste the bitterness of the 'native' who finds his personal and stained family laundry is flapping back and forth on a clothesline across another country's Broadway."[100]

Similarly, I. N. Carr in *Social Science* was rather discomposed by Mead's frankness: "The author has certainly discussed questions of sex relations without false modesty." This reviewer, as well, prudishly pretended not to understand Mead's American culture discussion, and ignored all other elements but the one upsetting Mrs. Grundy: "One wonders whether Miss Mead is advocating a reform in America toward questions of sex."[101]

On the other hand, the journal *Social Forces* viewed *Coming of Age* quite positively in an omnibus review, with seven other books—on childrearing! (Mead only two years later contributed the "Adolescence in Primitive and Modern Society" article to a major anthology, *The New Generation: The Intimate Problems of Modern Parents and Children*.) Ernest R. Groves commended the book for its frankness, "extraordinary interest and value," and a "definiteness and vividness which leaves the reader with a feeling he has got below the surface of primitive culture."[102]

Mead, of course, did not assume a singular primitive culture, and anthropologist Robert Lowie reviewed her in the somewhat more sophisticated light of contemporary work in her own discipline. Allowing that Mead had "deliberately set herself a task different from the traditional ethnographer's" and was "dealing with problems incomparably subtler" than the norm, Lowie commended Mead's "solid contribution to ethnographic fact and method. Her picture of child life is among the most vivid I know." He noted her social organizational material, and complimented her for throwing "doubt on a proposition I have hitherto vigorously maintained, viz., the universality of the individual family" (which we now label the nuclear family).

Lowie, however, energetically rejected Mead's "pedagogical sermonizing"—her contrasts between the United States and Samoa—and highlighted the major changes in Samoan girls' lives that resulted from colonial occupation, engaging thereby in a little pedagogical sermonizing of his own: "In other words, it is one thing to have a community treat the individual's sex life as an individual matter when the society is in a normal state; quite another, to find it unconcerned with his amours when abnormal contacts destroy old standards and fail to impose substitutes. The reformer must face the question whether any *normal* society can and will practice the lofty detachment found in Samoa nowadays."[103]

Lowie, then, wished to foreground what Mead had backgrounded: the fact that "Samoan culture" as Mead described it was heavily influenced by European missionizing and imperialism. Lowie also defined then-widespread sexual experimentation among American youth as "abnormal." Rather than consider Samoan and American societies inside the stream of history, Lowie, like Mead, applied a two-stage model to each. It is the content, not the structure, of their models that differs.

Lowie was, nevertheless, a relatively collegial senior reviewer of Mead's text. "I deny nothing; I am asking for information," he graciously appended to a series of doubting queries. Robert Redfield, only four years Mead's senior, felt no such compunction and indicted *Coming of Age* as "not so much an ethnological monograph as a laboratory exercise." "The cultural milieu is hardly sketched," he complained, and he found Mead's American policy analysis equally reprehensible: "The family is evidently to relinquish any lingering claims to being a cultural group and is to become a seminar in ethics." It is astonishing that Redfield denied what every other reviewer, and the public that made *Coming of Age* a best-seller, avowed: Mead's vivid, personalizing treatment. "Miss Mead is interested," Redfield sniffed, "in problems and cases, not in human nature. There is no warmth in her account." Redfield's nasty reaction may be connected to University of Chicago rivalries with Columbia University—he was Robert Park's son-in-law—to professional jealousy, as the younger Mead had beaten him to publication by two years; or to the contrast between his own simultaneously romantic antimodern and social evolutionary vision of patriarchal "folk society" and Mead's resolute antievolutionary modernism.[104]

Whether adulatory or critical, concerned with professional anthropology or American society, or all of the above, Mead's contemporaries all had one thing in common: they saw no particular association between Mead and feminism, or the self-conscious study of gender relations, or a special focus on women and girls. Mead did not in those years—not until the 1970s, and then very ambivalently—see herself that way, and she was not so understood. As late as 1956, a *New Yorker* cartoon (see fig. 16) linked Margaret Mead, the anthropological gambit, and "primitive" men—not a female in sight. Mead's Samoan girls were then more Samoan than girls, more exemplary "youth" for American edification than anything else. In Marx's terminology, they were neither *an sich* nor *für sich*, neither a population really seen in and of itself nor one constituted for itself. Mead's original dusky maiden is thus an anachronistic ghost—a figment of later readers', and a later Mead's, imagination. Ironically, Mead the supersaleswoman herself fell victim to the commodification of American culture: her rather dry social engineering approach was overborne, as decade succeeded de-

"Young men, you've now reached the age when it is essential that you know the rites and rituals, the customs and taboos of our island. Rather than go into them in detail, however, I'm simply going to present each of you with a copy of this excellent book by Margaret Mead."

16. An x is only a y, and only male, too. Representing Mead before the second wave of American feminism. (Drawing by Alain; © 1956 The New Yorker Magazine, Inc.)

cade, by hegemonic market images of exotic brown women redolent of forbidden sexuality. Readers, as I will show, simply could not see her actual texts—neither *Coming of Age* nor successive books.

Later critics have also conflated questions of feminism with sexuality. George Stocking sees the original dust jacket illustration of *Coming of Age*— showing a hand-holding Samoan couple running toward a palm tree—as sexually highly suggestive. Maybe so, but sexual expressiveness does not necessarily engage with questions of women and women's rights. What is far more interesting is that *Coming of Age* cover illustrations maintained the Samoan couple (they seem to be doing the twist, sans palm tree, on the 1949 through 1961 editions) until 1970, a year by which the American feminist movement had made serious headway in popular culture. At this point the Samoan male is dropped, and the dusky maiden appears, beflowered and on her own, on all subsequent covers.[105] Ida Cox's wild woman dates from the 1920s, but Mead's is a product of the American feminist movement of the 1960s.

Book cover designs tell us far more, probably, about publishers' marketing departments than about authors' intentions; but for all that, they do reflect the changing zeitgeist.[106] Before we can consider the recent era and ethnographers' representations of female Others in it, however, we must review the long years of depression, war, and Cold War, and anthropology's growing and changing national role in the political economy of representing self and Other.

PATTERNS OF GENDER IN DEPRESSION AND WAR

The depression years, ironically, were marked by growth and differentiation for American anthropology. Membership in the American Anthropological Association doubled in the interwar years, and by the end of the 1930s there were twenty separate anthropology departments in colleges and universities, most of them founded by students of Franz Boas. A three-pronged, interconnected set of material shifts lay beneath this story of growth. First, added to the tradition of individual philanthropic support for particular anthropological projects were new private research funding consortia, such as the Social Science Research Council, at first funded largely by the Rockefeller Foundation. Margaret Mead, for example, was able to gain funding to spend almost the entire decade in the field—in Nebraska among Native Americans, in New Guinea, and in Bali. Then, individual anthropologists wrote extremely popular books—Mead followed up *Coming of Age in Samoa* with *Growing Up in New Guinea* in 1930 and *Sex and Temperament in Three Primitive Societies* in 1935, while Ruth Benedict's *Patterns of Culture,* published in 1934, was an instant best-seller and sold more than a million copies over the following three decades. Finally, New Deal programs paid off handsomely for archaeologists, who were handed masses of free labor (employees of various Works Progress Administration programs) for use on excavations. To be sure, many anthropologists, like other American academics, felt the economic constraints of the depression years. And until after World War II, contra the impression gained from the globe-trotting Margaret Mead's career, most American anthropological work took place, at relatively low cost, among Native Americans in the United States—with a focus on the Southwest. Nevertheless, the 1930s were growth years for anthropology and for its effects on the American public sphere.[107]

Ruth Benedict's *Patterns of Culture* would certainly be a contender for most influential anthropological text, both in the 1930s and into the present. Even several generations past publication, it is still in print and still assigned in college courses. Benedict, however, unlike her student and close friend Mead, was a seemingly unlikely best-selling author. She was shy and withdrawn, an uninspiring public speaker—all characteristics probably influenced by early deafness. Having in full adulthood finally escaped an unhappy marriage, she spent her remaining years with a series of women companions. (The Society of Lesbian and Gay Anthropologists has established a Ruth Benedict Award in her honor.) She did very little fieldwork on her own, working instead largely with library materials and others' ethnographic accounts.[108]

Benedict was, on the other hand, a passionate, broadly educated intellectual, a close associate of Boas in tune with his desire for *Herzensbildung*, his understanding of the fundamentally political nature of knowledge, who happened also to have a gift for intellectual synthesis and popularly accessible writing. *Patterns of Culture* explicitly extends Boas's lifelong academic battle against social Darwinian racism. Boas's 1911 volume, *The Mind of Primitive Man*, presciently begins with a scientific deconstruction of white racist frames of mind:

> In order to understand clearly the relations between race and civilization, the two unproved assumptions to which I have referred must be subjected to a searching analysis. We must investigate how far we are justified in assuming achievement to be primarily due to exceptional aptitude, and how far we are justified in assuming the European type—or, taking the notion in its extreme form, the Northwest European type—to represent the highest development of mankind. It will be advantageous to consider these popular beliefs before making the attempt to clear up the relations between culture and race and to describe the form and growth of culture.[109]

Benedict in 1934 continues the antiracist battle, made now only more urgent by the rise of European Fascism. But Benedict adds to Boas's dispassionate disaggregation of presuppositions a pointed analysis of how white racism is allowed, encouraged by material circumstances: "Western civilization, because of fortuitous historical circumstances, has spread itself more widely than any other local group that has so far been known. . . . This world-wide cultural diffusion has protected us as man had never been protected before from having to take seriously the civilizations of other peoples; it has given to our culture a massive universality that we have long ceased to account for historically, and which we read off rather as necessary and inevitable."[110]

17. Ruth Benedict, 1924. (Courtesy of the Institute for Intercultural Studies, Inc., New York.)

Writing only half a decade after Mead, Benedict is a far more thorough-going democrat with a strong grasp of the ironies of American racism:

> Contempt for the alien is not the only possible solution of our present contact of races and nationalities. It is not even a scientifically founded solution. Traditional Anglo-Saxon intolerance is a local and temporal culture-trait like any other. . . . In this country [race prejudice] is obviously not an intolerance directed against the mixture of blood and biologically far-separated races, for upon occasion it mounts as high against the Irish Catholic in Boston, or the Italian in New England mill towns, as against the Oriental in California. It is the old distinction of the in-group and the out-group, and if we carry on the primitive tradition in this matter, we have far less excuse than savage tribes.[111]

I have begun our glancing consideration of *Patterns of Culture* with reference to its rather sophisticated anthropological indictment of white racism because, like *Coming of Age in Samoa,* and for similar reasons, this text backgrounds its images of the dusky maiden, merging considerations of gender with a variety of other issues.

Patterns, in fact, performs a number of complicated rhetorical, intellectual, and political functions within the dually restrictive stylistic compass of Nietzschean literary frame and ethnographic portraiture. Asserting the universality of overarching cultural patterning—using then-new Gestalt psychology to argue for cultures as personalities writ large—Benedict uses the ancient Greek labels Apollonian and Dionysian to organize ethnographic material on three societies, focusing on their relative emphases on collectivism, calm, and continuity versus individual efforts, extreme emotions, and social and personal disjunctions.[112] In the process, she argues strongly against the well-respected anthropologist Bronislaw Malinowski's tendency to try to define a homogeneous primitive weltanschauung (based, of course, on the Melanesian Trobriand Islanders, the group among whom he had done fieldwork), making clear how various are the institutions and apprehensions of small-scale societies.

Benedict also relativizes—and thus argues for the merit of—women's equal status, homosexual expression, and a broader sense of "normal" individual psychology. And she does so in a fascinating counterinstance to the anthropological gambit. That is, quite matter-of-factly, without a shred of humor, in stark refusal to acknowledge any sense of inappropriate conjuncture, Benedict discusses features of Pueblo, Kwakiutl, and Dobuan "primitive" culture in the Western high-cultural contexts of Faustian bargains, Don Quixote, William Blake, Plato's *Republic,* Byzantine art, Gothic cathedrals, and the Puritan legacy in the United States. Benedict thus neatly fuses the prestige—the aura—of the ancient Greeks and European high culture, and the high moral aspirations of the Puritans, to the daily lives and artistic and religious productions of "savages." Rather than claiming, à la anthropological gambit, with raised eyebrow, and looking for a laugh, that "an x is only a y," Benedict states flatly, lodging "us" on the same moral and civilizational plane as the Other, "let us consider the prevalence of a among xs and ys."

On the other hand, while Benedict's egalitarianism was far reaching even among anthropologists of her era, she was as little concerned as Mead with the ongoing political economy of her chosen "cultures." She freely used the "natural laboratory" metaphor, unselfconsciously forwarding the notion that Others exist not for themselves, and in long, power-laden interaction with "us" inside the stream of history, but fundamentally for our intellectual delectation, in order that "we" may decide the range and limits of human nature: "Primitive cultures are now the one source to which we can turn. They are a laboratory in which we may study the diversity of human institutions. . . . They provide ready to our hand the necessary information concerning the possible great variations in human adjustments, and a critical examination of them is essential for any understanding of cultural processes. It is the only laboratory of social forms that we have or shall have."[113]

Considerations of comparative women's lives and statuses are thus only a small part of Benedict's agenda in this text, as they were in Mead's. Benedict's treatment of gender relations, though, is more explicit than her younger colleague's. She states baldly, near the beginning of the book, that "adult prerogatives of men are more far-reaching in every culture than women's."[114] Having claimed universally greater social power for men, Benedict then sets about modifying that statement through exploring its varying ramifications in cultures stressing Apollonian versus Dionysian figurations. Most memorable is her description of the calm, orderly, and relatively powerful lives of Pueblo women—the only group in the book among whom Benedict had done fieldwork. Matrilineal and uxorilocal (the married couple resides with the wife's family), Zuni, according to Benedict, make both marriage and divorce smooth transitions in which women have agency equal to or greater than that of men. If a woman is displeased with her husband, she

> will make a point of going to serve at the ceremonial feasts. When she has a tête-à-tête with some eligible man they will arrange for a meeting. In Zuni it is never thought to be difficult for a woman to acquire a new husband. There are

fewer women than men, and it is more dignified for a man to live with a wife than to remain in his mother's house. Men are perennially willing. When the woman is satisfied that she will not be left husbandless, she gathers together her husband's possessions and places them on the doorsill. . . . When he comes home in the evening he sees the little bundle, picks it up and cries, and returns with it to his mother's house.[115]

Since Benedict's study is comparative, her dusky maiden is innately multiple: a series of portraits that give the reader a sense of the possible range of women's lives. Some of these figurations, like the Zuni, seem to represent higher status, greater autonomy, and more freedom for women than in the 1930s United States. Thus we might see Benedict as the first major practitioner of a common feminist ethnographic trope of the 1970s, an argument I have labeled "native women better off." At the same time, as I have noted, her consideration of gender is relativized to her larger narrations of varying cultural patterning, of the ways in which cultures do—and do not—allow individuals with particular predilections to function: "Most human beings take the channel that is ready made in their culture. If they can take this channel, they are provided with adequate means of expression. If they cannot, they have all the problems of the aberrant everywhere."[116]

But the reader concerned with issues of female status would have to draw her own detailed inferences from *Patterns of Culture*: Benedict is far more explicit in dealing with the ways in which other cultures allow for homosexual expression or what Westerners would label mental illness than with gender per se. Like Mead in 1928, Benedict writes within the zeitgeist of her era, one in which struggles for women's rights were marginalized. Also like Mead, she avoids dealing with questions of economic inequality—although this is more surprising in a depression-era text. This second lacuna may be due—aside from the fact that these anthropologists were buffered by class status from real engagement with 1930s poverty—largely to the interwar institutionalization of the "culture and personality" school in American anthropology.

Anthropological "culture and personality" work developed in a period of intellectual fermentation concerning human psychology. The massive influence of Freud and his confreres opened floodgates of speculation concerning early childhood experiences, varying kinds of "coming of age"—for example, Mead's first book—sexual experiences, and altered states such as trance. Mead and her third husband, Gregory Bateson, were instrumental in furthering such work in their field research on trance and dance in Bali. Benedict's treatment of the Native American *berdache* (institutionalized cross-dressing and inversion of gendered roles), of the aberrant statuses of "mild" Kwakiutl and "aggressive" Zuni and her speculations about the possible "normality" of Americans who would be labeled abnormal in another culture were all part of the developing "culture and personality" paradigm. And, of course, the monumental popularity of *Patterns of Culture* helped to further acceptance of that paradigm, and of the notion of its representativeness of American anthropology, while in fact historical ethnological work continued strong, and British structural-functionalism began to gain ground from the 1930s on.[117]

But the "culture and personality" paradigm inherently ignored politics and economy and thus tended to reduce questions about shifting economic and political inequality to questions of individual or group psyche. Class, race, and other social divisions were homogenized, and "cultural snapshots" effaced historical contingency. Eric Wolf has noted that the "culture-and-personality schools . . . made a moral paradigm of each individual culture. They spoke of patterns, themes, world view, ethos, and values, but not of power. . . . the anthropologists's culture of the thirties and forties was 'political economy' turned inside out, all ideology and morality, and neither power nor economy."[118]

Anthropologists working within this mandate tended to make wildly unjustified claims about the connection of personality to social process—as did and still do other scholars and the public at large, in response to the simultaneous commercialization and psychologization of American culture. British anthropologist Peter Worsley complained that "in this sort of anthropology 'culture' tends to be reified. Cultures somehow 'select' or 'choose' social elements which they then combine in some unspecified manner. The spirit of the culture is therefore carefully investigated at the expense of more mundane pressures of, say, an economic or political order."[119]

And, indeed, "the study of culture and personality," Benedict wrote in 1942, "makes it possible to understand our own society in comparison with many others and to answer many questions we need to know in our own embattled democracy. It can tell us under what conditions democracies have worked and under what conditions they have proved socially disastrous. It can tell us under what conditions men have regarded themselves as free men and under what conditions they have regarded themselves as not free."[120]

Such overweening and reductionist pronouncements led to perhaps the most embarrassing moment in the history of the "culture and personality" school—Margaret Mead's postwar espousal of her close friend Geoffrey Gorer's swaddling thesis. Gorer, an English-born psychoanalytically trained writer and anthropologist, claimed, in the 1950 *People of Great Russia*, that the practice of swaddling babies—tying them tightly to cradleboards—explained the "suspicious and despotic" Russian character and thus Soviet policy. Mead, having converted to Freudianism during the 1940s, embraced his crackpot claim with fervor, both in print and at academic meetings, and was in turn ridiculed by scholars as an exponent of "diaperology."[121]

Although Benedict was a chief architect of the "culture and personality" paradigm, she often transcended its intellectual limits, and her sense of her responsibilities as a citizen drew from a broader compass. The subheadings of the last chapter of *Patterns of Culture* give a vivid sense of her attempts to escape the paradigm into a progressive political argument:

Society and Individual Not Antagonistic but Interdependent
Ready Adaptation to a Pattern
Reactions to Frustration
Striking Cases of Maladjustment
Acceptance of Homosexuality
Trance and Catalepsy as Means to Authority
The Place of the "Misfit" in Society
Possibilities of Tolerance
Extreme Representatives of a Cultural Type: Puritan Divines and Successful Modern Egotists
Social Relativity a Doctrine of Hope, Not Despair.[122]

In the meantime, Margaret Mead, back from fieldwork in Papua New Guinea with her second husband, Reo Fortune, published in 1935 her most "feminist" work, *Sex and Temperament in Three Primitive Societies*. It is in this book rather than in *Coming of Age* that Mead makes her clearest arguments concerning the plasticity of human sex role arrangements: "The [ethnographic] material suggests that we may say that many, if not all, of the personality traits that we have called masculine or feminine are as lightly linked to sex as are the clothing, the manners, and the form of head-dress that a society at a given period assigns to either sex. . . . We are forced to conclude that human nature is almost unbelievably malleable, responding accurately and contrastingly to contrasting cultural conditions."[123]

Mead, however, did not use this "human cultural plasticity" claim to argue for the feminist goals of equal political and economic rights for women. Instead, she worked intellectually within the "culture and personality" mandate to discourse on the ways in which differing cultures use differing "innate temperaments"—hardwired biological or near-biological personalities—as bases from which they elaborate settled cultural configurations. Thus, Mead's fundamental moral argument was for an opening of the American cultural configuration to allow for the "normal" operation of varying personality types, not institutions or social roles, then considered deviant.

In making this argument with reference to living societies, Mead used Fascism and Communism as polar opposite, equally repugnant social examples. (Note that in 1934, when Mead was presumably finishing the manuscript, Hitler had already opened concentration camps, but the Moscow show trials had not yet begun.) Fascism represents the turning back of the Western clock to a "strict regimentation of women . . . wasteful of the gifts" of both men and women whose temperaments it does not fit. Communism, on the other hand, represents for Mead in its opening of all occupations to women a "sacrifice in complexity" of culture. Thus,

> The removal of all legal and economic barriers against women's participating in the world on an equal footing with men may be in itself a standardizing move towards the wholesale stamping-out of the diversity of attitudes that is such a dearly bought product of civilization. . . . To the extent that abolishing the differences in the approved personalities of men and women means abolishing any expression of the type of personality once called exclusively feminine, or once called exclusively masculine, such a course involves a social loss.[124]

Having neatly taken a stand *against women's equal rights* for the sake of "rich civilization," Mead then ends *Sex and Temperament* in a vague, psychologically rather than institutionally based call for Americans to recognize "genuine individual gifts as they occurred in either sex": "If we are to achieve a richer culture, rich in contrasting values, we must recognize the whole gamut of human potentialities, and so weave a less arbitrary social fabric, one in which each diverse human gift will find a fitting place."[125]

Many of Mead's positive reviewers ignored her clear stance against equal rights in favor of emphasizing her "gender malleability" argument. Florence Finch Kelly, in the *New York Times Book Review*, articulated this interpretation most strongly: "This Margaret Mead is a dangerous person. She goes down to New Guinea . . . and comes back with a book like a bomb that she drops into the complacent, fundamental conviction of the Occidental world, both scientific and social, that the sexes are innately different in their psychological attributes and that the male is dominant by right of brain and brawn. Her bomb explodes and scatters fragments all over the surrounding area."[126]

Grace Adams, in a squib in *Scribner's Magazine*, asserted that Mead "wonders what effect [the knowledge of the arbitrariness of sex roles] will have upon the future of civilized nations," when of course Mead had not wondered, but clearly preached.[127] Zenka Bartek, in the *Criterion*, interpreted Mead's hostility to equal rights as a stance against "standardization of sex-temperament," while Joseph Wood Krutch, in the *Nation*, emphasized her entertainment value: "Very soon the reader will find himself forgetting anthropology as a science and chuckling with pure delight over a book which combines the charm of 'Gulliver's Travels' and 'Erewhon' with that of 'Alice in Wonderland.'" Krutch also noted that Mead "amusingly demonstrates again how completely absurd was the old assumption that the primitive man was a 'natural man,'" thus stressing the antievolutionist message that primitives 'are as tradition-ridden as any European and at least as far as he from . . . [the] state of nature.'"[128]

Mead also received positive reviews in *Oceania* and *Sociology and Social Research*, but other scholars were strongly critical. Sociologist E. B. Reuter zeroed in on Mead's inconsistency in stressing cultural variation in sex roles while assuming, with no evidence, that there are "innate temperamental differences": "That is, the plasticity and malleability previously assumed is now, by implication, denied." [129]

Anthropologist Richard Thurnwald went much further, giving Mead's text a full-dress critical review, repeatedly (and convincingly) pointing out how much counterevidence to her theoretical claims she provides: "Whatever the author cites in favor of her pattern of equality between the sexes [among the Arapesh] seems to weigh in favor of another hypothesis." He also complained about the brevity of her field experiences, her poor command of native languages, her failure to specify fieldwork conditions and numbers of "aberrant" individuals, and her "attempt to mingle anthropological research with educational planning," "aim[ing] at a moral which would be applicable to modern American society."[130]

It is thus in this period, the depression 1930s, that we see the coalescence of what would prove to be recurrent patterns of scholarly and popular response to Mead. Academic anthropologists appreciated her intrepidity and thorough field reporting but also criticized—in an undifferentiated, soupy manner—her social engineering bent, her sloppy overgeneralizations and self-contradictions, her penchant for popularizing, and even her not-quite-feminist interpretations. Nonacademic readers appreciated her vivid readability and her edificatory homilies and repeatedly misread her texts as far more feminist and progressive than they were intended to be. (Mead would repeatedly object to feminist interpretations of *Sex and Temperament*, and equally repeatedly disavow feminism, until the second wave had already won public acclaim in the 1970s.)[131] Both sorts of readers responded to Mead not just as an anthropologist, but—for good or ill, depending on political perspective—as a woman anthropologist, and Mead was not behindhand in encouraging that response.

Indeed, it was in this period of her life and career that Margaret Mead truly grasped the brass ring of popular acclaim, self-consciously began to sell herself—and she had no moral qualms about using the sensationalist language of the times to do so. In 1934 she sent a memo titled "Dope Which Could Be Used" to an agent, suggesting "Private Life of Cannibals" and "Where Women Fish and Men Dress Dolls" as possible lecture topics, and describing herself as "having lived in parts of the world where no white woman has ever been," and having "lived intimately with people just three years removed from cannibalism and headhunting."[132] For the following four decades, Mead would consistently lay claim to intellectual authority not by virtue of scholarship or hard thinking, but because she had "been anointed"—and specifically as a woman—by arduous, exotic fieldwork experiences.

Mead's personal publicity campaign of the 1930s was highly successful and resulted in a flurry of positive, but rather coy, newspaper and magazine pieces about her. One described Mead as "a slender, comely girl who danced her way into the understanding of the Melanesian people and became an adopted daughter and a sort of princess of the Samoans. When they anointed her with palm oil and indicated that a dance was in order, she did a nice hula and they declared her in—indicating the adaptibility of the modern young women if she just has a chance to step out."[133]

Even more serious pieces on Mead, such as the long profile *Natural History* published in 1939, focused on her own heavily gendered self-descriptions: "There arrived in Pago Pago in the fall of 1925 probably the most unethnical looking ethnologist officials had ever seen. . . . she scarcely looked older and was actually shorter and slighter than the adolescent girls she proposed to study."[134] The two substantive themes of the piece—the utility of primitives as natural laboratories, and the urgent need for "salvage ethnography" among them—strike a false and superficial chord when we consider the disturbing political developments of the late 1930s and the concerns and activities of other anthropologists, many of them Mead's intimates, in those years.

As the Fascist threat deepened over the course of the decade, the elderly Franz Boas abandoned scholarly research to work full-time on his version of Ruth Benedict's "doctrine of hope"—on building a political organization of intellectuals to counter racist and antidemocratic ideology at home and abroad. Working first with the American Committee for Anti-Nazi Literature, Boas soon became frustrated with its inefficiency, and was active in the founding of the University Federation for Democracy and Intellectual Freedom at Columbia. (Boas chaired its Committee on Intellectual Freedom, while Ruth Benedict acted as organizational secretary.) The federation in 1938 initiated a major antiracist, prodemocracy petition-signing campaign whose success exceeded the organizers' wildest expectations. The federation also created a national Lincoln's Birthday program, which garnered, among other media coverage successes, approximately one hundred hours of radio air time. Boas was successful in persuading the American Anthropological Association, which only nineteen years before had nearly expelled him, to adopt a distinctly antiracist resolution including planks asserting that "(2) The terms 'Aryan' and 'Semitic' have no racial significance whatsoever. . . . (3) Anthropology provides no scientific basis for discrimination against any people on the ground of racial inferiority, religious affiliation or linguistic heritage."[135]

From this organizing grew the American Committee for Democracy and Intellectual Freedom, which Boas chaired and in which Benedict was active (and which Karl Wittfogel retrospectively branded in 1951 a "Communist front organization"). From 1939 forward, the committee, with dozens of chapters nationwide, campaigned against the misuse of the term "race" in school curricula, published widely used pamphlets, organized and ran radio programs, and flooded the nation's newspapers with opinion pieces. In New York, the committee fought a scurrilously social Darwinian campaign by the Chamber of Commerce that used the racist claim of southeastern European immigrants' genetic inferiority to argue against publicly funded education.[136]

The flavor of the popular racism that Boas, Benedict, and their comrades were fighting—and failing to vanquish—in the 1930s may be glimpsed in a promotional pamphlet, *Dick Tracy's Secret Detective Methods and Magic Tricks.* This nasty compilation was mailed en masse to children by the Chicago parent offices of Quaker Oats in 1939, the very year Boas's American Committee was founded. The first chapter, "Human Types," asserts "distinguishing characteristics" for different races:

> The Latin group . . . are known for their lively natures and sometimes quick tempers. . . .
>
> Though generally law abiding, the criminals of this group often resort to crimes of passion, revenge, blackmail, kidnaping and extortion. Their weapons at times are the sawed-off shotgun, the bomb, machine gun and stiletto.

The Teutonic group ... are known for their intelligence and strong convictions. ...

They are not naturally criminal minded. ...

The yellow race ... are secretive and clever. ... Those with criminal tendencies have been charged with outer methods of torture, but hardly ever commit a crime outside of their own nationalities.

... Most negroes are a simple, happy folk.

The relatively few negro criminals are those members of the race with the least intelligence and they commit crimes in a blundering fashion.

All nationalities are illustrated by cartoons of men alone. Women appeared only in drawings of "low class" and "high class" criminals—white, of course. The only bow to world news and contemporary concerns in this pamphlet is the complete absence of any reference to Jews. Despite all the work of Boas and the Boasians against racist physical anthropology, the pamphlet still asserted that "anthropology is the study of the cranium or skull."[137] Evolutionary racism, the dominant paradigm of contemporary physical anthropology, coexisted handily with Boasian antiracist ethnology in 1930s America and would maintain the upper hand until the postwar era.

As the 1930s closed and the war years began, progressive anthropologists continued their antiracist work, while the heated-up war economy provided opportunities for the guild as a whole. Ruth Benedict published *Race: Science and Politics* in 1940, an accessible work with distinctly Popular Front sympathies. With verve and originality, Benedict scored then-contemporary racism as "the new Calvinism which asserts that one group has the stigmata of superiority and the other has those of inferiority. According to racism we know our enemies, not by their aggressions against us, not by their creed or language, not even by their possessing wealth we want to take, but by noting their hereditary anatomy. For the leopard cannot change his spots and by these you know he is a leopard."[138]

Late in the text, Benedict follows her antiracist mandate in the direction of economic democracy, commenting both on Europe and the United States:

In Europe ... in the more advanced states ... [those in power] are faced with two alternatives: they must keep down the rank and file by the use of naked force, or they must see to it that the major goods of life are available to a much greater proportion of the population than in earlier European history. We are far from having made economic sufficiency general in America, and essential liberties—opportunity to work, freedom of opinion on moot points, and equality of civil liberties—are far from won. They are, however, not unattainable if we will bend our efforts to achieve them.[139]

Benedict also cowrote (with Columbia University anthropologist Gene Weltfish, who was persecuted in the McCarthy years) a popular pamphlet, *Races of Mankind*.[140] After having sold more than a quarter of a million copies, the pamphlet was banned from distribution as "Communist propaganda" in Army recreation centers by Representative Andrew J. May, chair of the House Military Affairs Committee—because it stated flatly that the Negro and white races were equal.[141] Hortense Powdermaker, Queens College professor, former union organizer, and veteran of fieldwork in the Deep South as well as in the Rhodesian Copperbelt, weighed into the fray in 1944 with *Probing Our Prejudices,* a short, lively book intended to make anthropological understandings of race available to high school students.[142]

Many anthropologists in the 1940s worked instead or in addition in a more uncritical, "have gun will travel" mode for the federal government, selling anthropological expertise as an adjunct to the war effort. Margaret Mead, her husband Gregory Bateson, Ruth Benedict, and many others took positions in federal agencies for the duration. Benedict's famous postwar portrait of the Japanese, *The Chrysanthemum and the Sword,* was a result of one of these federal projects, an effort to do "anthropology at a distance": to write meaningful cultural analyses—on the basis of text and film alone, not participant-observation—of societies with whom the United States was at war. A number of anthropologists even worked uncritically—as technicians of the state, we might say, rather than technicians of the sacred—for the federal government in the western states' internment camps for Japanese Americans. Orin Starn points out that even though there were prominent public protests against internment, most of these anthropologists, despite their intentions to combat racism, "produced a body of literature that legitimized relocation while reflecting and promoting a conception of anthropology as a science of social control. . . . [They] helped preempt reporting on relocation as a measure championed by powerful Central Valley growers who gained the land of dispossessed internees, as an exercise of state power intended to break Japanese-American ethnic identity, and as the largest single violation of civil rights in 20th-century American history."[143] As late as 1969, modernization theory advocate and Berkeley anthropologist George Foster would celebrate the war years as a time providing anthropologists "with an unprecedented opportunity to play a variety of applied roles in government."[144]

Margaret Mead also wrote a "war effort" book, *And Keep Your Powder Dry*, reportedly in only three weeks.[145] *Powder* certainly reads like a three-week project, but is notable for more than mere sloppiness, more than simple failure to master any social science or historical scholarship on the United States. *Powder* is also a revealing transition text, one that on the surface lays out a complimentary analysis of American character while simultaneously both documenting Mead's final jettisoning of any pretense at progressive scholarship on gender and presaging, as does *Sex and Temperament*, her postwar Cold Warrior stance.

First, Mead changed her synecdochic definition of the United States. While in 1928 she had ruled out the new European immigrants as Americans, they were now included—in fact celebrated—but the South was not "American" because "caste is sometimes a directly formative element in developing standards of behavior."[146] But such a stricture, while seemingly liberal and antiracist, denied the prevalence of castelike race relations for blacks, Latinos, Asians, and Native Americans in the non-Southern United States. In addition, Mead failed to apprehend the centrality of the American South to all federal policy—and thus to American culture—since the failure of Reconstruction at the turn of the century.

Further, throughout *Powder*, Mead unselfconsciously uses the generic he, both grammatically and substantively, just as she once used the generic she. Any mention of professional occupations coincides with male occupants. Women appear almost exclusively as mothers, wives, and sweethearts (and this in the era of Rosie the Riveter). The most recurrent scene in the text is the worried (white, middle-class) American mother fussing over "little Johnny's" playground behavior. This shift is all the more astounding in that Mead was at the time of writing a relatively new mother of a daughter. And still the social engineer, Mead now added the Freudian toolkit to her Progressive cultural relativist slide rule:

Or suppose that in a well-organized society it is recognized that ten years from now more doctors will be needed. It would be possible for a totalitarian to select arbitrarily the boys who, on the basis of their school records, will make the best doctors and simply order them to become doctors, the state footing the bill. The democratic state would offer specially good scholarship conditions for boys with the right abilities and advertise these widely.

Must we not become as relentlessly dedicated to the lust for battle as our enemies if we hope to survive? The girls ask: "How is a girl to nourish the love of war in her boy friend who seems curiously reluctant to enlist . . ." The boys ask: "Will marriage before enlistment make a man less free to fight, soften his will, turn his imagination back towards his wife rather than forward towards the enemy?"[147]

At war's end, with the Axis enemy defeated, anthropologists, Mead commented, "took their marbles and went home."[148] But in fact a new era for social scientists—and for anthropologists in particular—was opening: a remobilization of the guild in service to the Cold War. Government War Office jobs may have dried up, but federal funds were flowing, both inside and outside the academy, and they channeled, often indirectly and usually unbeknownst to scholars, the kinds of anthropological work done in that era. The stock of marbles increased considerably, as did the anthropologists gathering them. But at the same time, the discipline, in the process of responding to the new postwar United States political economy, rescientized and remasculinized itself. The Dusky Maiden remained in the ethnographic background, while race and gender became more important than ever before to anthropology's epistemic frame, the often-invisible gesso underneath debates inside ivy walls and in the public sphere.

four

THE DUSKY MAIDEN AND THE POSTWAR AMERICAN IMPERIUM

Never doubt that a small group of thoughtful committed citizens can change the world: indeed it's the only thing that ever has.—*Quote on "Margaret Mead" poster displayed with crystals and incense in import boutique window, Dempster Street*

Interpretations of the Cold War in American popular culture have undergone tumultuous shifts in the past three decades. Generally speaking, the 1960s saw an evolution from fearful silence or gung ho Cold War ideology to increasingly radical questioning of the automatic rightness of American foreign and domestic policy, of the automatically Satanic status of the Soviet Union. In the 1970s, this questioning bore fruit in a cornucopia of popular books, articles, and films—Lillian Hellman's *Scoundrel Time,* Victor Navasky's *Naming Names,* Jessica Mitford's *Fine Old Conflict,* Vivian Gornick's *Romance of American Communism,* and Martin Ritt's movie *The Front,* starring Woody Allen, only skim the surface—that denounced the witch-hunting and its effects on victims' lives and portrayed the civil rights and labor activist work of committed American Communists and fellow travelers sympathetically.[1] The popular press at times admitted the other end of the Soviet paradox: that while it was undoubtedly a cruelly totalitarian regime, it also funded liberation groups in the Third World (while we funded, trained and armed the dictators and torturers). It guaranteed, unlike the capitalist West, a basic level of food, shelter, medical care, and education to all citizens. And, until the successes of the second wave of

Western feminism in the 1970s, Soviet and satellite state women had relatively higher status than their American counterparts. In addition, detailed information about appalling American governmental actions both at home and abroad was increasingly available in the popular press.

With the close of the 1970s, however, and the rightward shift in American and European politics, a narrow, racist nationalism—which could be symbolized by Sylvester Stallone's *Rambo* films—came to characterize popular culture, and Ronald Reagan could succeed in labeling the Soviet Union the Evil Empire. Since the late-1980s dissolution of most Communist governments worldwide, it has been open season in Western popular culture on both Communism and Marxism (with no nuanced distinctions allowed). Reporting on skyrocketing poverty, crime, and the disastrously lowered status of women in all formerly Communist states and in the new "capitalist road" China generally fails to make the obvious connections to newly capitalist economic functioning in those states. Finally, popular cultural "common sense" is selectively blind to United States–based multinational corporate interest in, and American governmental participation in, poverty and endemic warfare in central and peripheral states worldwide.[2]

As we begin to approach the current scene, then, my epigraph citing Galileo's apochryphal, rebelliously muttered response to the pontiff's silencing his heliocentric astronomical theory—"Eppure, si muove"—gains new salience. This interpretation of the recent past may depart from hegemonic contemporary apprehensions, but it moves, anyway.

RACE, EMPIRE, ANGST, AND ANTHROPOLOGY

The cultural history of the postwar period is the history of the reconstruction of American culture on new foundations laid by changes in the world economy in general and the American economy in particular. It is the history of a transvaluation of social values, a reevaluation of cultural signs.—*Serge Guilbaut, How New York Stole the Idea of Modern Art*[3]

The period from the early postwar years to the late 1960s was one of sea change at home and abroad, all related to the colonial decline of Britain and other European states, the rise of the United States as the major world imperial power, the concomitant wave of decolonizations in the Third World, and the development of the American face-off with the Soviet Union in attempting to influence the political structures of these new "nonaligned" states and of war-torn Europe. The shifting entailments of this evolving picture are myriad, both for American political culture and for the practice of American anthropology. Indeed, Eric Wolf has memorably labeled this period in anthropology's history one of "uncertainties and equivocations about power."[4] Here, I deal perforce with issues of race and of gender only as they intersected with postwar American anthropology and popular culture.

The elderly Franz Boas's last utterance, delivered at a wartime luncheon with colleagues, was, appropriately, "I have a new theory of race." Ruth Benedict died following a heart attack in 1948, but not before she had had the opportunity to argue strongly against early McCarthyite persecution of progressive anthropological colleagues, for decent treatment for the American-occupied Japanese, and for strong federal action on postwar Negro civil rights.[5] The real narrative on race in American anthropology, though, shifted in the postwar years to the realm of international abstractions and to the subdiscipline of physical anthropology.

The monumental horror of the Nazi Holocaust and its direct underwriting by "the science of race" put the issue of race squarely on the postwar international agenda. The fledgling and American-dominated United Nations Educational, Scientific, and Cultural Organization (UNESCO) was commissioned to produce the definitive scientific repudiation of racism. Most of the fluctuating original ten to twelve members of the "committee of experts" were anthropologists, including Ashley Montagu, Claude Lévi-Strauss, E. Franklin Frazier, and Juan Comas. Between 1950 and 1967, UNESCO issued four statements on race.[6] The statements established as scientific fact some presuppositions that are now, but were not then, widely accepted, such as the location of racial difference in a dynamic patterning of gene frequencies, not in physiognomy, residence, language, or behavior; and such as the *Homo sapiens* membership of all contemporary humans. (As late as 1954, anthropologist Phillip Tobias actually felt it necessary to publish in the British journal *Man* photographically documented proof that "Bushmen"—Nisa's group—and white Europeans could interbreed and were thus members of the same species.)[7] Other UNESCO contentions, such as the lack of correspondence between racial difference and intelligence, have been challenged repeatedly and are currently under severe attack by a resurgent right-wing, racist "science."[8]

While a recoiling from Nazi racism and an idealistic optimism about building an antiracist postwar society were certainly motivating factors in American-dominated United Nations actions, Cold War realpolitik was also at issue, and far more important than humanitarian concerns to the federal government's domestic civil rights actions. Legal scholar Mary Dudziak has documented American State Department apprehensions of the civil rights issue during the Truman administration. Truman's advisors were deeply concerned that the United States give the appearance of civil equality for Negro Americans in order to counter very successful Soviet propaganda on American racism, propaganda aimed mostly at the newly decolonized nonaligned states whose citizens viewed themselves as non-white. Dudziak notes that "the simple reality of American race discrimination, and the impact of its use in communist propaganda abroad, meant that the United States could not leave these charges unanswered and still succeed with its Cold War international agenda."[9] The United States Information Service released a pamphlet for Third World consumption that untruthfully claimed that racial segregation in public schools was unlawful at least three years before the United States Supreme Court's ruling in *Brown v. Board of Education* in 1954.[10] The United States' amicus curiae brief to the Court on the *Brown* case explicitly named the Cold War imperative as a major reason for outlawing school segregation: "Racial discrimination furnishes grist for the Communist propaganda mills, and it raises doubts even among friendly nations as to the intensity of our devotion to the democratic faith."[11] On the day that the *Brown* decision was made public, the Voice of America was broadcasting the news all over the developing world within one hour of the announcement.[12]

Cold War imperatives were expressed not only in American governmental actions fostering or portrayed as fostering civil rights, but in explicit censorship and harassment of citizens calling attention to their lack. In 1947, the National Association for the Advancement of Colored People filed a petition with the United Nations protesting the treatment of blacks in the United States; in 1951, the Civil Rights Congress, with W. E. B. Du Bois in the lead, took advantage of the 1948 United Nations convention on genocide to file the documented petition, "We Charge Genocide," with the international organization. American governmental pressure in each case led the United Nations, despite an upsurge of postwar lynchings in the American South, to deny the petitioners a hearing. Individuals who attempted to agitate publicly against American racism also found themselves harried at every turn. The entertainer Josephine Baker, for example, having experienced postwar American racism after long residence in France, determined to speak out against ongoing segregation. Her reward was an FBI harassment and disinformation campaign that ruined her American performance prospects, and the successful United States effort to deny her entry into or spoil her publicity in state after state in her planned Latin American speaking tour.[13]

The American Cold War imperative to appear nonracist combined with a number of other postwar phenomena to fuel the vast growth and increasing public importance of anthropology in the ensuing two decades. Among the most important of these developments was the federally funded post-war expansion of American higher education—including the GI Bill and the establishment of the National Science Foundation, increased Ford Foundation grants, and the establishment of Fulbright international fellow-ships. This cash infusion was a direct result of the increased American imperial presence in the Third World, particularly Asia, the Pacific, and Latin America. Finally, new anxieties about the possibility of nuclear anni-hilation led to a more internationalist, existential questioning of values that highlighted the importance of traditional anthropological concerns—the nature of human nature, cooperation versus competition, and cultural dif-ference. Anthropologists actively responded to these openings with con-certed efforts to reorganize and "professionalize" the American Anthropo-logical Association and to increase the discipline's share of the federal and foundation pies.[14] It is telling that in 1958 Berkeley anthropology depart-ment founder Alfred Kroeber and Harvard sociologist Talcott Parsons to-gether published a short piece laying out the distinctions between the study of culture and that of social systems, for all the world like Roosevelt and Stalin sitting down at the Yalta conference table to divide the spoils of war.[15]

Most notable, however, in the race for professional expansion and public acclaim was the new claim of *echt* scientific status—and thus Cold War fundability—for all four fields of anthropology under the National Science Foundation mantle of "behavioral science." And the most successful an-thropological project under the behavioral science rubric was the vast body of heavily funded, Berkeley- and Harvard-based, widely popularized (*National Geographic*, Time-Life books, television and film depictions) set of suppositions labeled "man the hunter."

Developing slowly over the postwar decades and coming into fruition in the 1960s, the "man the hunter" paradigm united the study of human origins, research on nonhuman primates, and contemporary work on small-scale societies in one model. The contentions of the "man the hunter" model were that human speciation was relatively ancient, human raciation relatively recent; that prehuman Australopithecine upright posture, oppos-able thumbs, stereoscopic vision, and relatively large brains were symbioti-cally related to the development of male social communication for band hunting success, and thus to the origin of human culture; that monkey and ape social behavior, particularly that of African savanna baboons, provided a template for inferring that of early humans and prehumans; and that extant human foragers, especially the San peoples of Botswana and what is now Namibia, exhibited probable early human social organization.

Extraordinarily, the "man the hunter" concept simultaneously filled a number of postwar American political and cultural functions and was, like abstract expressionism in painting, a significant actor in the "reevaluation of cultural signs" Guilbaut charts for the period. It redeemed physical anthropology from its racist, brain-weights-and-Master Race heritage, which George Stocking, Michael Blakey, and others have documented. It elevated cultural anthropology through association with high-status postwar "hard science." It spoke to existential nuclear-age anxieties with a soothing model of cooperative, egalitarian, leisured, art-rich, hunting human nature—early humans as the consummate hippies. In addition, it effaced uncomfortable neocolonialist realities by substituting monkeys and apes for "primitives" as representatives of our prehuman past—Trouillot's "savage slot"—while symbolically "evacuating" the postwar African landscape. Focusing on tiny African foraging societies apart from their colonial and neocolonial contexts, apart from the lives of the vast mass of Africans, the "man the hunter" concept spotlighted a romanticized "noble savage" ethnographic vision while evading the political economic realities of the South African apartheid regime, the neocolonial stripping of Africa's natural assets, the exploitation of its labor, and the CIA and European powers' interference, including the assassination of radical politicians, in postcolonial governance.[16]

Finally, "man the hunter" hypostatized postwar male backlash against women's wartime status and agency, making use of animal ethological models (associated, incidentally, with the former Nazi Konrad Lorenz) to claim pan-animal and prehuman gravitas for "natural" male dominance in human societies.[17] Texts and films repeatedly underlined the key social importance of male dominance hierarchies among savanna baboons—middlebrow media were awash with images of threatening male monkeys baring their enormous canines while the much smaller females huddled with infants in arms. The technical term "alpha male" passed into popular cultural parlance, lending itself to an endless series of specious pop analyses of the male corporate world and its stresses. (Remember "type A behavior"?) As we shall see, the very extremity of erasure by the "man the hunter" paradigm of all agency by female actors led to easy rebuttal—and attention to "woman the gatherer," of whom Nisa is an exemplar—in feminism's early second wave of the 1970s.

COLD WAR FEMININE MYSTIQUE

The postwar reimposition of "natural" male dominance—both as brute material fact and as ideology—has been exhaustively researched and represented by feminist scholars and artists. The documentary film *Rosie the*

Riveter gives a vivid sense of the scholarly findings: the deep satisfaction American working- and middle-class women, white and nonwhite, gained in high-paid "nontraditional" wartime jobs and their misery at being thrown out of them and forced to revert to low-paid, onerous service and clerical jobs at war's end. It also portrays the very different wartime and then postwar media campaigns: the first to push women into employment as a civic duty, representing stay-at-home mothers as frivolous bridge players; the second to harry them out of the labor force, ridiculing working women as maladjusted, selfish beings whose children were doomed to juvenile delinquency.

It is now well established, though, that Rosie the Riveter became Rosie the Secretary rather than stay-at-home housewife and mother, and that mass media offered up a fairly complex "bifocal vision," as Joanne Meyerowitz labels it, "of women both as feminine and domestic and as public achievers."[18] Women's labor force participation rose significantly in the postwar years, fueling rather than responding to the feminist movement of the late 1960s onward. And married women were an increasing proportion of those employed. (Black women's employment shifts paralleled white women's at consistently higher levels of participation in the labor force.) Ages at marriage fell, birthrates rose, and Americans moved to suburbs at increasing rates from the late 1940s, creating the "blip" of nuclear family *Ozzie and Harriet* dominance that we then generalized backward in time as the "traditional family form"—but Harriet was as likely, in any case, to be typing the boss's letters as to be baking cookies at home.

Ideological shifts encompassed these realities through a mixture of overwhelming pronatalism with misogyny. Film, fiction, and prescriptive literature represented motherhood as the necessary completion of every woman's life, while popular, although extremist, books like Marynia Farnham and Ferdinand Lundberg's *Modern Woman: The Lost Sex* and Phillip Wylie's earlier *Generation of Vipers* made heavy use of now-hegemonic Freudian arguments to paint mothers as vicious harpies solely responsible for all their children's psychological problems. Finally, the postwar era also saw a revival of the popular sexualization of female public figures, a mandate that women "prove" their femininity.[19] Meyerowitz notes that "while feminine stereotypes sometimes provided convenient foils that enhanced by contrast a woman's atypical public accomplishment, they also served as conservative reminders that all women, even publicly successful women, were to maintain traditional gender distinctions."[20]

Anthropologists as social types began entering public culture in this era, too—not yet at the rate of saturation we saw apparent in the contemporary Halloween costume analysis of chapter 1, but sporadically, and in only a few genres. A particularly telling example of the popular crosscutting of gender-anthropology-"primitiveness" in the early postwar years is the rollicking stage musical turned film *On the Town*.[21]

Filmed in 1949, based on the original Adolph Green screenplay with music by the young Leonard Bernstein, and featuring Frank Sinatra, Gene Kelly, Jules Munshin, Betty Garrett, Ann Miller, and Vera-Ellen, *On the Town* follows three sailors over their twenty-four-hour leave in Manhattan. Each sailor, of course, finds a girl, and the plot is a loosely linked series of song-and-dance routines as they find and lose one another over the day and evening. Frank Sinatra's date is a very forward—and quite overtly Jewish Hungarian—woman cabbie. Gene Kelly pursues "Miss Subway," whom he assumes to be the cynosure of top-drawer New York but who turns out to be a girl-next-door ballet student drawn to New York from his own small town in Indiana. The third sailor, Jules Munshin, is pursued by a woman anthropology student at the "Museum of Anthropological History," where the sailors have gone in search of Miss Subway. "Claire Huddeson" (Betty Garrett) measures and photographs "Gaby" because he "exactly resembles *Pithecanthropus erectus*, a man extinct since six million B.C." (One of the pleasures of this film is its absolutely crackpot paleontology: there weren't even *Australopithecines*, much less any sort of bipedal prehuman, on earth 6 million years ago.) Gaby asks Claire why she studies "anthrowhatsit," and she replies, giving away her upper-class status: "I'd been running around with all kinds of young men, so my guardian suggested I take up anthropology . . . put things on a scientific basis . . . be able to control myself."

Claire then sings "Prehistoric Man" while the entire cast engages in a quite zany production, dressing up in every sort of "primitive" mask and costume, banging tom toms, and jumping about—finally destroying a dinosaur skeleton. Highlights of Claire's cri de coeur include "There are all too few modern males that can measure up to the prehistoric," "I want a happy ape with no English drape . . . jitters, jitters, he never had jitters . . . bearskin [bare skin], I *really love* bearskin . . . no repression, he believed in free self-expression . . . unlike you and me, no ulcers had he, simple and free in the long-ago, prehistoric man."

It takes little deep analysis to note the easy connection the screenplay draws among popular cultural notions of the sexually loose debutante, women anthropologists who *of course*, libido driven, exclusively study sexual customs, and erotically and emotionally free primitive or prehistoric people.

Continuing figurings of the compellingly sexualized dusky maiden, and

"*Practically all my calls come from the 'National Geographic.'*"

18. Sisters under the skin. *New Yorker* cartoon of the 1940s. (Drawing by R. Taylor; © 1944 The New Yorker Magazine, Inc.)

of her relationship to contemporary white Western women, are wonderfully sent up in a *New Yorker* cartoon from the 1940s (see fig. 18). The speaker is obviously gorgeous, equally obviously black African and stark naked (with a strategically placed hatbox). Sitting, ludicrously, among the all-white group of heavily dressed, coiffed, and hatted models awaiting agency appointments, her insouciant identification of *National Geographic* rather than *Vogue* or a couturier as her primary income source simply highlights the "sisters under the skin" anthropological gambit of the drawing. The sexualized, glamorous, postwar white American model is really "just like" her Third World sister whose pulchritude is also subject to the camera lens for corporate profit through the Western gaze. (There is a further grand irony here, as I mentioned in the prologue. According to Lutz and Collins's findings in *Reading National Geographic*, American readers tend to report that the magazine overrepresents Africa in its stories and photographs, while statistical analysis reveals that the magazine has a history of fundamentally neglecting the continent.)[22]

In the same year that *On the Town* appeared on the nation's marquees, Margaret Mead would publish *Male and Female: A Study of the Sexes in a Changing World*. This book fit well the anxious, sexist postwar weltanschauung, and Mead's own statements in publicizing the book reveal her nervous skittering to establish simultaneously her scientific credentials and her inoffensive "femininity," all the while ducking to avoid a stigmatizing sexualization.[23] Mead had already begun this process in 1946, when she published an essay with the Freudian title "What Women Want" in *Fortune*, in which she is described as "a distinguished anthropologist—a woman and a mother."[24]

Male and Female uses all of Mead's Polynesian and Melanesian field experiences and her prior penchant for prescribing "rich culture" and "recognizing diverse human gifts," reinterpreted through the prism of an eclectic Freudianism, and lent existential importance through the invocation of The Bomb: "Upon the growing accuracy with which we are able to judge our limitations and our potentialities, as human beings and in particular as human societies, will depend the survival of our civilization, which we now have the means to destroy."[25]

Mead contended that all societies inevitably reveal the paramountcy of female biological receptivity and male biological activity, potency, in the ways in which maleness and femaleness are construed:

> Our tendency at present . . . is to try to obliterate particular differences that are seen as handicaps on one sex. . . . But every adjustment that minimizes a difference, a vulnerability, in one sex, a differential strength in the other, diminishes their possibility of complementing each other, and corresponds—symbolically—to sealing off the constructive receptivity of the female and the vigorous outgoing constructive activity of the male, muting them both in the end to a duller version of human life, in which each is denied the fullness of humanity that each might have had.[26]

Despite Mead's continued emphasis on cultural variation, her continued crusade against isolated, narrow nuclear families, her maintenance of the notion that women's "gifts" are wasted in American culture and thus her advocacy of professional-class women's being permitted careers—this is simply no longer the anthropologist who wrote in 1935 that "human nature is almost unbelievably malleable." We are a long way from the interwar Boasians, and I don't think we're in Kansas anymore, Toto. In the same year that Simone de Beauvoir, in *The Second Sex*, laid out the fundamentally ideological character of constructions of women as immanent, men as transcendent—quarrying and transforming, as Michele Le Doeuff has pointed out, the misogynist language of Jean-Paul Sartre's existentialism—Mead fervently embraced the Freudian crystallization of that ideology as trans-historical, transcultural truth. She simply layered this crosscutting "innate temperamental difference" on top of the non-sex-based one she had already laid out in the 1930s.[27] Never really a feminist, Mead now joined the official ranks of professional female antifeminists—except for her embrace of careers for better-off women as long as they were "womanly" both at home and at work.

Ironically, in so doing she returned full circle to the "moral motherhood" ideology embraced by her own mother and her Victorian woman movement generation. Indeed, Mead would join other antifeminists in the *Saturday Review*'s panel of experts attacking *The Second Sex* on the occasion of its translation into English in 1953—and specifically because de Beauvoir "constructs a picture in which the only way a woman can be a full human being is to be as much like a man as possible." It is no wonder that Betty Friedan devoted a chapter to Mead's pernicious "super saleswomanship" of the feminine mystique. Among feminist, anthropological, and other commentators on Mead, only Eric Wolf, in his early-1960s textbook, *Anthropology*, noted this shift on Mead's part.[28]

And the reviewers loved her. In the *Nation*, David Riesman pronounced her "brilliant" and was delighted to find her attributing to biology "men's historically greater gift for music and mathematics, as well as their greater interest in ceremonies of initiation." He lauded her description of the differing "sexual styles" that must be balanced in different professions: "Men in professions that are female-dominated find themselves handicapped by styles set by women that are unsuitable to men." In yet another evocation of the Three Bears, he saw Mead as charting the correct middle path between those "surviving feminists who are concerned with proving that women have qualities virtually identical with men" and those "concerned with proving that women are basically dependent creatures."[29]

Bernard Mishkin, in the *New York Times Book Review*, was equally enthusiastic about Mead's antifeminism: "Obviously, Dr. Mead's is not a doctrinaire, egalitarian approach. . . . [her] book has done her own culture an important service. It has come to grips with the cold war between the sexes and has shown the basis of a lasting sexual peace."[30] Other reviewers weighed in positively in the *New Yorker, Social Forces*, the *Atlantic Monthly*, and the *Saturday Review of Literature*. In this last journal, indeed, Chicago psychiatrist Therese Benedek commended "the womanliness of [the book's] author." An illustrated sidebar, based on an interview with Mead, goes to some lengths to reassure the reader as to Mead's femininity: "Dr.

Mead is, additionally, small, plump, and blonde, and women who try to be anything but feminine irritate her. 'I have always worn skirts,' she reports. 'I have always done a woman's job—never a man's.' Ethnologically, that means being admitted to distaff quarters taboo to foreign males. Life in the 'field,' however scientific, is decidedly domestic. Miss Mead sets up a clinic and a household, where she cuddles and cooks for a sampling of youngsters, her metier." The sidebar ends in a reference to "her husband, photographer [*sic*] Gregory Bateson" and Mead's wartime work, when "she wrote OWI pamphlets and interpreted GI's to the British. 'In this country the girl says no; in England the man.' It's just 'knowing who says what.'"[31]

Among anthropologists themselves, Clyde Kluckhohn, in an omnibus review in the *American Scholar*, came to Mead's defense against fellow guild members' criticisms that Mead had "gone psychological" and that she did not adequately support her contentions. Referring to Mead's newly articulated Freudian antifeminism, Kluckhohn magisterially declared, "That she has changed and modified her conclusions in important respects is testimony to her capacity to grow and re-think, and to her freedom from any compulsion to defend to the end of time a position once stated."[32]

Male and Female, however, did attract trenchant criticism, and this criticism made for strange bedfellows. Father Leo J. Trese, for example, in the Catholic journal *Commonweal*, found both Mead's Freudianism and larger anthropological visions religiously offensive, since each, is his eyes, assumes "that the human being is a highly developed animal, and nothing more." The British anthropologist S. F. Nadel as well was annoyed with Mead's Freudianism, because "a great deal in Dr. Mead's evidence requires to be taken on trust . . . greater caution is necessary, even in 'primitive' cultures, when crediting 'womb-envying patterns' and what not with an all-powerful efficacy." Nadel nevertheless approved Mead's new admission of "the weight of physiological factors"—her Freudian sexism. He very much liked her description of the inevitable divergent orientations of males and females, "upon 'acting' and 'doing' in the male and, in the female, upon simply 'being' and fulfilling herself in maternity." And while he was doubtful of the worth of her analysis of "primitive" cultures, he much approved her "final chapters on America"—those based on little scholarship and less fieldwork. He noted, however, that "they make little use of the ammunition carefully prepared in the earlier part of the book," focusing on "the effects of immigration, of social mobility and the creed of success, and of the great equalizers, film and advertisement."[33]

The two most insightful readers of *Male and Female* were the strangest ideological and disciplinary bedfellows of the critical lot. *Partisan Review* political belletrist Diana Trilling brought a dour, lucid Freudian existentialist lens to bear on Mead's abundant self-contradictions.[34] And the British anthropologist D. F. Pocock, relying as well on Trilling's analysis, articulated a much more orthodox British social anthropological response than Nadel's to Mead's work.[35]

Trilling contextualizes *Male and Female* in the light of historical shifts in American modes of conceptualizing sexuality and gender relations. She locates Mead's efforts in terms of the new postwar prestige of social science, the reanimated Progressive assumption that all social goals can be met, and the "intense reaction against the feminism of thirty or forty or even twenty years ago." Trilling sees Mead as caught in the self-contradictions inevitable to "her strenuous effort to reconcile the extra-domestic privileges of her sex which, at the last, turn out still to be her deeply-rooted preference, and the wife-mother character which current sentiment is so eager to establish."[36] She notes that Mead idiosyncratically interprets sex roles as genetically determined or as entirely socially learned, as she pleases or as it suits her rhetorical purpose. As an orthodox Freudian, she criticizes Mead for emphasis on male womb envy and refusal to consider female penis envy. And she indicts her for her benign vision of male homosexuality, which she, Trilling, sees as a neurotic aberration, its increase possibly due to an increase in women's rights. Finally, she most insightfully notes that Mead "does not demand, as she would have in another decade, she merely *asks* that men not exclude women from jobs which are usually designated as masculine . . . indeed, women are to be encouraged to bring to all their activities the special talents of their femininity, the patience, delicacy, and intuition they learn in tending the young and sick. . . . (This is of course a sexual cliché. There is much evidence that these qualities are as often found in men as in women.)"[37] Trilling concludes that "such a prescription for our social salvation is more than a disappointment, it is an embarrassment. We wonder how Dr. Mead can deceive herself that this kind of pious sentimentality will remedy any of the sexual ills of our time, and how she can ignore her own brilliant observations of some of the weaknesses at the base of our social-sexual structure."[38] But Trilling is not pointing here to the need for a revived and militant feminist movement; she is counseling a Freudian-informed acceptance on women's part of the social and sexual status quo: "It is *the* progressive fallacy of our time to suppose that we can rationalize all of life's anomalies. . . . Yet not to take into constant active account the fact that sacrifice and frustration lie at the very core of the personal and social organization—it is the great Freudian truth, of course—is to belie the very nature of the material we wish to shape."[39]

Pocock does not concern himself with these inconsistencies in Mead's work, nor indeed, with issues of women's status at all. He contents himself with pointing the reader to Trilling's review and noting the "controlled interest taken in Margaret Mead's work by intelligent women here and in America." No, Pocock is after Mead as an altogether different sort of character—as a deficient anthropologist, one of those American "cultural" types who cannot understand the need for "primary social analysis." Reading Pocock, we have walked onto the historical stage in medias res. The war is over, the British are passing the world imperialist baton to the Yanks, but British anthropologists (and other academicians) are casting their relations to the ascendant Americans as latter-day defeated Greeks to the imperial Romans—learned tutors whom the brutish, unlettered conquerors must employ in order to gain culture and philosophy.

And in this particular case, the down-at-heels but snooty Brits are quite right. British social anthropology, developing from the 1910s, laid emphasis on ongoing societies and the interrelationships among their many social institutions—kinship, law, religion, politics, &c. A. R. Radcliffe-Brown's marriage of Durkheimian structuralism with Malinowskian functionalism made use of the organic analogy between living societies and living bodies. Institutions were like organs: they functioned symbiotically with one another in furthering the functioning of the organic whole. Thus, the paradigmatic ethnography in British social anthropology gave a chapter to each institution of the particular society studied. (These ethnographies also tended to portray closed, static societies outside the stream of history and without the dynamic of colonial rule.) Mead's Freudian-inflected "culture and personality" paradigm simply ignored most functioning social institutions in favor of overgeneralized observations of childrearing practices and their presumed effects on adult personalities. Where the British social anthropologists derived psychology from institutional structures—and gave it very little houseroom in any event—the American tendency (among "culture and personality" types, not the older-fashioned historical ethnologists) was to focus on psychology *über alles,* and to assume, without any institutional analysis, that they could easily comprehend psychological states in other cultures. Pocock lays out his exasperation with such a mindset in his response to Mead:

> The ways in which we dress, eat or write and so on, form with the values of our society a complex which we call our culture. It is never necessary for us to define culture, as the anthropologist must, as that which in communal life is evident to the senses and which is rendered meaningful by the society. The anthropologist may not assume that any cultural fact observed among an alien people has the

same meaning as a similar fact among his own people. Initially and inevitably he will make such assumptions but he will make it his business to replace them by more refined notions based upon an analysis of the society behind such facts, i.e. he will do what the people themselves never need to do. The psychologist must also have the primary social analysis before him in order to study the mental processes of the people in question. . . . Miss Mead calls herself a cultural anthropologist and so, presumably, feels justified in neglecting the primary social analysis.[40]

Concerning the "gentle" Arapesh, one of Mead's New Guinea groups, among whom she claims "warfare is practically nonexistent," Pocock makes use of information provided by Mead's embittered but undoubtedly accurate former husband, New Zealander Reo Fortune. Fortune points out that the British had suppressed a very much active tradition of warfare among this group only a generation before his and Mead's work among them. Pocock considers the implications of this correction: "If we compare [Fortune's] account with that of Miss Mead we see, for instance, that the woman Amitoa whom she describes as a temperamental deviant is merely a conservative who is behaving in accordance with the expressed social ideals of some sixteen years earlier and still in a traditional manner."[41]

Pocock continues his critique by scoring Mead for failing to make use of the extended case method, then being developed in British social anthropology as a means for establishing the accuracy of observations: "If it is unwise to apply the psychological theories of one society to another, it is a step further in the wrong direction to build up theories in the field based not upon careful case histories but merely upon observation and surmise."[42]

Finally, Pocock returns to the more international anthropological establishment's distaste for Mead's popular treatments of anthropological topics. He is careful, however, unlike many of his confreres, not simply to deride her for popularizing, but to specify what is lost or ignored in Mead's popularizations. He dislikes her tone of "bullying exhortation" but links that dislike to Mead's attempts through its use to claim an organic unity between research findings on "primitives" and observations on American society, between anxiety over humanity's new ability to blow itself up and American sex role dilemmas, between anthropological insights and global ethical certainties. He notes that Mead, through rhetorical sleight of hand, refuses to deal with "the relation of power to ethics," and sadly concludes that such rhetorical evasions are quite successful: "It is obvious and her wide sales testify that she knows her audience well. It is to be deplored that it does not know her better."[43]

Mead was increasingly slapdash in her work, more and more played fast and loose with the necessities of real scholarly work, and was less and less cognizant of developments in the field as the decades rolled on. But so, of course, did and were many male anthropologists who also wrote for popular audiences—Irven DeVore, Robin Fox, Lionel Tiger fairly leap to mind—and they have never been subjected to the severity of well-deserved criticism heaped on Mead's head during and after her lifetime. It was Mead's femaleness and her success at gauging the popular pulse that rankled critics, and rankled them more as anthropology on both sides of the Atlantic remasculinized itself in the Cold War era.

An index of that remasculinization is the pamphlet *The Position of Women in Primitive Societies and in Our Own,* published in 1955 by Oxford University anthropologist Edward E. Evans-Pritchard—the author of the classic *The Nuer*—and based on the Fawcett Lecture he had given at Bedford College, University of London, in the same year. Evans-Pritchard was lecturing not only to women students, but in the name of and paid by funds given by a notable suffrage leader, Millicent Garrett Fawcett. Evans-Pritchard begins rather disingenuously by noting the inherent contradiction: that he is both ignorant of and hostile to the feminist movement. But, he points out, "circumstances, and the climate of opinion, have so changed" that Mrs. Fawcett would no doubt approve his words were she still alive.

Evans-Pritchard then goes on to claim that all early information on gender relations among primitive peoples was tainted by the ideological wars of the Victorian and Edwardian periods, and must be discarded:

> Gone are the days, at least for the time being, of such speculative and uncritical evolutionary theorizing. Gone also are the days of vigorous feminism and anti-feminism which formed a part of that general battle in which the protagonists of all so-called progressive movements and their opponents were mixed up in a general melee. Can any younger person today read Virginia Woolf's *Three Guineas* without wondering what could have been the cause of so much indignation? ... women's status in our own society [has] ceased to be an acute public issue.[44]

According to Evans-Pritchard, we now know enough about primitive societies to make a number of generalizations about primitive women's lives, and about women's status in general. It turns out that all primitive women always marry, that polygyny (he labels it, as it was then termed, polygamy) is almost always allowed, that they all attempt to have as many children as possible, and that all their time is taken up in domestic cares so that they have no interest in public affairs. Nonetheless, the primitive woman does not feel hard done by, because she feels different from, not inferior to men. And we can see surprising parallels between this state of affairs and that which obtained among peasants in preindustrial Europe: "Indeed when we read histories and novels about earlier periods of our history we see that, so far as the vast mass of the population was concerned, woman's position in society and in the home was—certainly in essentials—similar to that of women in primitive societies."[45]

Evans-Pritchard ends in asserting that in fact the recent improvement in women's status is a historical blip, that "there are deep biological and psychological factors, as well as sociological factors, involved, and that the relation between the sexes can only be modified by social changes, and not radically altered by them."[46] He works in a swipe at Mead's 1935 book and de Beauvoir's *Second Sex* and lectures feminists for having dared to consider women's rights when they should have been working for "basic social rights and the dignity of every social being." Lest we imagine Evans-Pritchard was referring here to some sort of social democratic vision, though, he makes it clear that social problems "cannot be solved by an insistence on absolute equality but rather by recognition of differences, exercise of charity, and acknowledgement of authority."[47] This was not, as Ivan Karp has remarked, E-P's finest hour.[48]

I have gone into the argument of this little pamphlet at such length because it indeed captures well the farrago of smug self-satisfaction, easy ethnographic untruths, and wild—and in retrospect embarrassing—claims for a final settling of scores in the gender wars that characterized the Anglophone anthropological consideration of women's status in this era. The reader may as well have noticed that, after having sneered at previous evolutionarily based work on women's status, Evans-Pritchard returned to what was officially structural-functionalist anathema—the use of an evolutionary parallel to describe "primitives." Once again, they're just like our ancestors. Women practitioners were trained in and had to contend with these presuppositions, and we now turn to one such, whose best-known work, published in the same year Evans-Pritchard gave his dreadful lecture, was not an official ethnography but an "anthropological novel" written under a nom de plume.

PASSING THE BATON, HIGH CULTURE, AND THE AMBIVALENT AMERICAN

Return to Laughter, some of whose more unbuttoned expressions we encountered in chapter 1, is Laura Bohannan's elegantly fictionalized account of her fieldwork among the Tiv of Nigeria, work undertaken in concert with that of her husband Paul Bohannan. (Both Bohannan's and the Tivs' identities are disguised in the novel. She writes as "Elenore Smith Bowen," working alone in an unnamed African country.) Just as the wildly popular and long-lived *Coming of Age in Samoa* so well illustrated white, professional-class, Progressive Era American women's weltanschauung, so *Return to Laughter* was received to nearly universal acclaim, became (and still is) a best-selling staple of anthropology and many other classrooms, and reflects almost too neatly all of the postwar shifts I have outlined.

Bohannan, an American trained at Oxford, managed to describe her status, an American anthropologist working in a still-British (Nigeria achieved independence in 1960) anthropological and colonial preserve, in a tone manufactured of equal parts respectful nostalgia and humorous condescension. The baton is passing indeed: "I suddenly realized what a hobble British decorum places on American exuberance."[49] She gives her servants noms de théâtre, Sunday and Monday, of happy colonialist *Robinson Crusoe* inspiration. She gently guys them and herself in a series of classic fables of rapport, as she also indirectly indicts British Blimpishness. "Kako [the headman] gave me that long and incredulous glare with which a brilliant father regards his backward child."[50] Here is the same section I cited earlier, with a little added, in which the reader may now discern a great deal more than upon first reading:

> The sun was high. The tall grass cut out any view and any breeze. Then the carriers began to sing, and my momentary depression vanished. Seeing them file down the path, boxes on their heads, made me feel like something out of an old explorer's book. . . . My relief lasted only through the soup. Then I realized that there was a slit between the thatch and the veranda wall and that, in the lamplight, I was fully displayed. Impervious to the stares of natives, generations of empire-building Englishmen in jungles and deserts have sat down in full evening dress to eat their custard and tinned gooseberries. An American like myself can only feel that she has somehow been tricked into going on a picnic in high heels. In any case, feminine evening fashions are not adapted to mosquito-ridden countries. . . . The coffee was very English. Then Sunday set before me a liqueur glass in which there reposed one pickled onion drowned in gin. I recoiled from it with a gesture of real disgust.[51]

Return to Laughter as a whole is, in fact, one extended fable of rapport—"Far from having docile informants whom I could train, I found myself the spare-time amusement of people who told me what they considered it good for me to know and what they were interested in at the moment."[52] This gives one cause to wonder why this paradigmatic book, unlike the rather arcane, rarely read ethnographic texts upon which the postmodern-ists have expended reams of computer paper, has been nearly untouched by postmodern hands.[53] Perhaps the reason is that the text is as clearly about the existential dilemmas of the white middle-class American in at-tempting to reign over her new global empire, all the while preserving the important fiction that we are not dealing with past European and present American power and profit, with CIA dirty tricks, but with backward peoples who, if we only expend sufficient brain and heart in understand-ing them, will reward us with the fealty we deserve and slowly advance, as did our own ancestors, to our place on civilization's ladder. This evolution-through-the-back-door tack also solves the problem of appearing antiracist in the postwar, post-Holocaust era: these "peasants" simply need our tu-telage.[54]

To this end, Bohannan, for all the world like Allan Bloom or Saul Bellow (but they, of course, seem not to know she ever wrote) repeatedly refers to her loneliness, her Western ennui in the bush, to her recourse to Shake-speare to shore up her sense of the tradition she represents, her true patri-mony: "I was in a party mood, but I could celebrate with them no longer. I should have to do so alone. But not quite alone. I closed my door on Africa and turned to my bookshelves. I wanted good company. Falstaff, I decided."[55] But our canonical texts often betray the "primitive" qualities of our ancestor geniuses who produced them and thus bring us closer to "present-day ancestors." Bohannan continues: "Sack, Falstaff advised, and sack I had, but what I drank would follow native (very small) beer and be followed by a ground nut stew. I mixed a martini, dry and warm, and was soon lost in a roistering England I found vastly preferable to the austere blue-law and red-tape land of my acquaintance. Fat Falstaff rumbled ge-nially, proud Percy glittered defiantly, Ancient Pistol roared—a tremen-dous roar that shook me out of Shakespeare's tavern straight back to the homestead."

When, lo and behold, Shakespearian England comes to life outside her hut:

> I stepped out into the homestead yard, and caught my breath with as-tonishment.
>
> . . . Kako was drunk—for the first time in our acquaintance, gloriously, reelingly drunk—and Kako had a fat stick in his hand. His favorite wife was drunk. She stood with beery concentration before the door of her hut. . . . she would cook whenever and whatever she pleased; if Kako wanted gourd seed sauce instead of okra he could . . . She went into detail. . . . The abuse with which she empha-

sized her first statement was Shakespearian in its gusto. . . . She aimed the cala-
bash, with a slow, drunken windup, and got Kako on the head. Kako just stood
there in amazement. Things like this didn't happen to him. "I'm the chief." His
voice was high with surprise. . . .

I retired to my hut grinning with the unrighteous mirth one feels when a bishop
or anyone pompous slips on a banana peel. As I picked up my book, I almost
thought that the spirits of Falstaff and all his crew, chased from sober England,
had come to do their work here.[56]

Bohannan's plot line allows her a series of denouements, during each of
which she comes to further clarity about Tiv reality and her own. She
comes to see that the "peasantness" of this African group—their casual
cruelty to animals and disabled people, fatalism about human deaths, belief that illness and death result from witchcraft—makes sense in the light
of their harsh living conditions and high death rates. A boys' circumcision
ceremony near the end of the novel offers an opportunity to lay out these
insights: "Men, women and children gathered around to watch and
hearten the lads. Myself pale and shaking from mere watching, I paid full
tribute to the endurance they showed. . . . A few, like Accident, managed
to gasp out faint bawdiness, "Whittle carefully there. Many women shall
judge your work!" No matter how feeble the jest, such sallies were greeted
with great applause. . . . Their courage put me to shame." Again Bohannan
makes the our past/their present parallel: "Vividly, almost blotting out the
sight before me, I saw the old English prints: the patient strapped to the
operating table, the solicitous relatives, the grim surgeon, the bottle that
was the only shield against the shock of pain." Such analogues allow her
to experience empathy, to see the Tiv's responses more clearly, and to question her own quietist tendencies:

No, it was not callousness. Not exactly. Not the callousness of a single heart, but
the callousness of a whole culture, a protection against the pain that had to be
borne. . . . Of all the people there, only I knew it didn't have to be. They had not
learned to cry in their anguish, "This must not be! Surely there must be a way!"
That rebellious cry had encouraged us to find a way. I had been used to mock
at visionaries and reformers. Face to face with the alternative, I was humbled. I
myself was not one who cried, "There must be a way." I had never seen the
need, for I had been born to a pleasant world. . . . here I was forced to consider
the possibility that even my own world might be improved.[57]

Bohannan, however, doesn't particularly think anything about women's
status, among the Tiv or in the West, might be improved. She uses very
much the same frame as Evans-Pritchard in her reactions to Tiv women's

lives. That is, like most postwar anthropologists prior to the renaissance of feminism, she naturalizes and universalizes lower female status, points out significant female feistiness and manipulation within those constraints, and recurs to the evolutionary parallel—how like our ancestors these women are!

Bohannan begins her lesson in describing being forced to go gardening with a group of women, of whom Atakpa teaches her how to weed: "My muscles were aching when she finally let me go. I began to wonder where I could find the oppressed, downtrodden women described by the missionaries. All those I had met were as stubborn and intractable as they looked."[58] She follows up the lesson by relating her discoveries about how much cowives appreciate polygyny, given the constraints of the larger economy and social system: "If, before I came out here, I had expected to feel sorry for anyone in a polygamous household, it was the women. But these women did very well. It was their husband I felt sorry for. We tend to think of the henpecked husband as a rather weak character. But what man can stand up against five united women? If Ava's husband raised his voice to any one of his wives, all of them refused to cook for him. If he bought one of them a cloth, he had to buy four other identical cloths."[59] So Tiv women are like all women, or at least like some selection of present-day and past Western women. Bohannan notes various social types among them: the grande dame, the devoted mother, the giddy matron.[60] She then establishes that Tiv men are not unlike Western ones. After a narrative in which a young cowife's adultery is discovered, Bohannan learns what British anthropologists of the time were labeling the difference between ideal and real social models. Adulterous men are subject to death, but "Cholo snorted, 'That is just what one says at such times. A fight, yes, but it is not a matter for killing.' . . . 'You mean [Bohannan asks] a man doesn't divorce his wife for adultery?' 'Of course not.' Cholo was amused by my question."[61] Bohannan goes on to relate the bull session ensuing from this discussion:

"Mmmm," a brooding voice came in sadly. "The trouble with women is that they run away."

"The trouble with women," Ihugh corrected, "is that women are trouble, and they make trouble between relatives, between friends and between age mates. Yet one must have wives, for without children the homestead perishes, leaving no sign that it has ever been."

"Women . . ." someone else began, and until the truck came, I had to hear my sex thoroughly trounced and defamed.

On reflection, though, Bohannan finds the defamation quite familiar: "Their discussion had been pessimistic, but it also had been what we call a 'civilized' conversation. Cholo had been very much the cynical man of the world; Ihugh's viewpoint was very much like a medieval friar's."[62]

Bohannan also, of course, noticed her own status as female among the Tiv. She begins, over time, to realize that she is being excluded from activities:

> I was rapidly being absorbed in the life of the women and children. All the magic, all the law, all the politics—over half the things professionally important to me—were in the hands of the men, and so far not one man had been willing to discuss such matters with me, not one man had taken me with him to the meetings of the elders which, I knew, often took place. . . . I had been identified with the women: unless I could break that association, I would leave the field with copious information on domestic details and without any knowledge of anything else.[63]

This stalemate is ended in Bohannan's plot through the decision of Yabo, Kako's rival and a reputed witch, to include her and teach her in an effort to gain access to her Western prestige and Western "magic." In other words, she makes a self-conscious Faustian pact with the Devil. By the logic of the narrative, her femaleness leaves her no other road than failure really to be an anthropologist. The narrative's denouement arises through a smallpox epidemic which Yabo, and Bohannan through him, are suspected of causing. The plague section of the text, in which social order breaks down, crowds flee in all directions, and friends and relatives deny one another, is haunting, meant to evoke remembrance of Pepys's *Journal of the Plague Year* and Manzoni's *I Promessi Sposi* in the literary reader. "Terror and death and hate," Bohannan repeats as a *leitmotif*, and refers to the plagues of medieval and early modern Europe, and to the Holocaust, and we are to see this experience as the hell with which Bohannan pays for her alliance with Lucifer.

Resolution comes as a chastened "return to laughter" for Bohannan, who returns to the village, counts the dead, and commends the Tiv for their pragmatism in living under onerous conditions. "If they knew a grim reality, it was because their fate rubbed it into their very souls."[64] The very phrasing of her understanding borrows from Edgar's speech in *King Lear*:

> The lowest and most dejected thing of fortune
> Stands still in esperance, lives not in fear.
> The lamentable change is from the best;
> The worst returns to laughter.[65]

Such is my close reading of the text, for purposes of foregrounding the postwar ethos, Bohannan's treatment of women's roles, and the Tiv as black Africans vis-à-vis white Western "us." (Note that *Return to Laughter* was published the same year that the Supreme Court decided *Brown v. Board of Education.*) What did contemporary reviewers make of it? First, let us get the woman question out of the way: of twelve reviewers, scholarly and middlebrow, American and British (I have considered them since Bohannan was "trespassing" on their colonial turf), not a soul even mentioned her portrayal of Tiv women as women. A couple of male British reviewers commented—rather enviously, it seems to me—on her account of the utilities of polygyny, but that was it. Bohannan's status as a woman was mentioned, but only peripherally, in terms of her intrepidity, &c. Even though her sex is a fulcrum of her plot line, gender is of no more interest to these reviewers than it was to Margaret Mead's in 1928. We are still in the Long Sleep of Denial that followed the Victorian and Progressive woman movement, a good generation prior to the second wave. Brown maidens there are, but they are merely elements, bits of design in the Third World wallpaper that the Western self notices as "he" describes the room of his existential dilemma in the new postwar world.

Otherwise, academic reviewers were mixed but relatively positive. Daniel McCall, in the *American Anthropologist,* took the text on its own terms as a magnificent laying-out of the difficulties of fieldwork: "The anthropologist in the field is the marginal man [!], living in two cultures. Perhaps we might consider this book the most complete description of 'culture shock' available."[66] McCall also notes Bohannan's skill in articulating the workings of polygyny, age sets, and witchcraft accusations for a general reader. "The book presents a clear exposition of the major aspects of a culture—quite as effective as that of a first-rate monograph."[67] He wonders why it is the only one of its kind: "Do professionals regard this sort of effort as beneath their dignity, or is it a question of lack of time, motivation, or perhaps talent?"[68]

Northwestern-trained Afro-American scholar Mabel Smythe, in the *Journal of Human Relations,* does not share McCall's enthusiasms. Not only does she disagree about Bohannan's literary facility: "slow and plodding . . . inclined to put down everything without selecting her details carefully." She also finds her typifying "in many ways the liberal American who wants very much to be capable of bridging the wide gap between cultures—before he comes up against the reality of a primitive situation." While Smythe appreciates Bohannan's attempts, and considers that "her shortcomings are largely faults in us all," she reprobates her repeated use of the term "savage" to describe the Tiv, "a term in severe disrepute among thoughtful liberals and anthropologists alike."[69]

British academic reviewers reacted as variously. It is revealing that anthropologist B. Z. Seligman found Bohannan to be dreadfully *American:* how could she dare to be so emotional about these people? "As an anthropologist I found this book fascinating, interesting and exasperating. . . . To the old-fashioned field worker who was only a sympathetic observer, many of these incidents would not have occurred; others would have been recorded simply without approval or disapproval. . . . It seems doubtful whether accuracy can be combined with such a subjective outlook."[70]

On the other hand, George Craig, in *African Affairs,* entirely approves Bohannan from the unselfconscious perspective of an old colonial hand. He says she understood "'this other and alien world,' with all its simple joys, its dark, pervasive superstitions, its customs and strange inhibitions and fears." He reproduces the drunken Falstaffian scene with deep enjoyment, and then comments in summary that "no attempt is made in this book to deal with the economic or political aspects of this African life; that was not its purpose. It is a picture of something that is a world away from Western civilisation."[71]

Middlebrow journals on both sides of the Atlantic generally took Bohannan at her word as well. From Margaret Mead associate Rhoda Metraux in the *New York Herald Tribune* to anonymous writers for the *New Yorker* and the *Times Literary Supplement,* to regular reviewers for the *Commonweal,* the *Saturday Review,* the *Spectator,* and the *London Magazine,* Bohannan was unusually widely and favorably reviewed.[72] Some, such as R. A. Holzauer in the *Commonweal,* caviled at her bloodless social science epistemology: "Miss Bowen informs us that after her experiences she has undergone a change within herself. Her professional zeal has not abated but it is tempered with that happy fusion of knowledge and experience which allows the newly created Ph.D. to function as a knowledgeable human. The textbooks have been assimilated."[73]

Others, such as the anonymous *Times Literary Supplement* writer, misread Bohannan in a far more vilely Blimpish, imperialist direction than her prose could possibly lead: "The author makes it clear that her Africans are not more stupid, lazier or more superstitious than illiterate peasants elsewhere, nor, once their fairly simple basic ideas are grasped, more difficult to understand. . . . To a sensitive person life as it has to be lived by savages would be unbearable. This is a book which those who wish to know what Africans are really like would do well to read."[74] But in general, writers apprehended Bohannan as she intended, humorously using the anthropological gambit for self-analysis: "Disregarding such secondary mat-ters as heat, inedible food, driver ants, and differences in custom and lan-guage, she finds that it turns out to be a complex of difficult personal relationships, very similar to those in London or New York, except that hostility is attributed to witchcraft, rather than to neurosis."[75] Or taking it in the direction of postwar existential angst: "There may be a sense, too, after the shocking revelation of what happened in Germany, that the primi-tive and the tribal are not buried very deeply in any of us, and that the sooner we realize it the better."[76]

Two final reviewers' readings and concerns are of interest in the context of the parallel growing roles of the United States on the world political stage and of anthropology as a new courtier jostling for the ear of the Prince—or merely as a metaphor, a trope newly used by the real courtiers behind the throne. The *Spectator*'s reviewer notes the broad interest Bohan-nan's *problematique* ought to engender: "An interesting book: partly because the problem with which it deals is one that is common to anthropologists, historians, journalists, politicians, diplomats and itinerant witch-doctors—all those in fact who make a living out of trying to explain or *manage human behavior*—yet is seldom discussed with with the honesty and wealth of detail that one finds here" (emphasis added).[77] That is, ruling Westerners in the brave new world of the Cold War will need the sort of insights Bohannan has to offer, "humanist" as she may seem. We have traced an-other road to the United States State Department, UNESCO, and *Brown v. Board of Education.*

Finally, zoologist Marston Bates, in the *New York Times,* made the con-nection (so obvious to us in retrospect) between the Tiv experience of the smallpox epidemic and the American witch-hunt during the McCarthy era. Bates stakes out terrain to Bohannan's left in doubting her easy dismissal of the possibility of real cross-cultural acceptance. Bohannan writes: "The greater the extent that one has lived and participated in a genuinely for-eign culture and understood it, the greater the extent to which one realizes that one could not, without violence to one's personal integrity, be of it."[78] And Bates responds: "I don't know. Certainly an adult cannot ever wholly belong to a new and foreign culture, but the value of the exposure, it seems to me, lies in the insight thus gained on one's own culture. There is witch-craft in America as well as among Kako's people, and I do not quite see how Miss Bowen managed to keep her integrity so intact or whether this is a 'good thing.'"[79]

After all, if Bohannan was going to write of witch-hunts, and concern herself explicitly and in a literary fashion with her status as a white American citizen vis-à-vis a black African group, and if Arthur Miller's *Crucible,* which made the explicit connection between the Salem witch-hunt and the House Un-American Activities Committee hearings, hit the stage in 1953, how *could* she ignore McCarthyism? I fear that the answer is the same as that to the question of why she ignored British colonial exploitation and American CIA activities in postwar Africa, and the one I have given in general for American anthropologists, except for a few brave radicals: that they were trained to and did find their appropriate place, at home or abroad, safely under the aegis of state power, tidily tucked away from messy political contest.

So where were those brave radicals? Unlike that of the Victorian or Progressive Eras, the real political history of those years in anthropology is yet to be written. We do know that few of Boas's students had his intellectual grasp, political fire, and clarity. There is sketchy evidence that many who sought to consider materialist interpretations of human cultural change in the postwar era turned, as did Leslie White, to circumlocutions like "progressive capture of energy in human history." Others, such as the young Eric Wolf and Sidney Mintz, dedicated themselves to work with Latin American and Caribbean peasantry—sidestepping the more traditional geographic areas—and were thus able to establish their own radical traditions.[80] Oscar Lewis, as we have seen, attempted the same, with more retrogressive results. In addition, many progressive anthropologists were stymied by institutional McCarthyism. Gene Weltfish was summarily fired as a radical by Columbia University in 1952. Boas student Melville Jacobs was brought up before the state of Washington's House Un-American Activities Committee and nearly fired by the University of Washington. Eleanor Leacock, whose radical credentials were equally visibly on her sleeve, was unable to find employment as an anthropologist, despite consistent and well-regarded publication, from receipt of her Ph.D. in 1952 until she was finally hired full-time at Brooklyn Polytechnic Institute in 1963.[81]

Some American anthropologists, on the other hand, cooperated happily with the entity David Price has labeled the National Security State. A number went to work for the CIA. Clyde Kluckhohn, although he had no expertise in the area, was appointed director of Harvard's CIA-funded Russian Research Center and channeled research to secret governmental imperatives. And, of course, much available Cold War–era funding for social science research originated in American military/intelligence interests, thus frequently ensnaring unwitting researchers.[82]

On the other side of the Atlantic, many left-liberal British anthropologists worked in African studies, on labor and urbanization issues in particular. Without overtly opposing hegemonic structural-functionalism, they added key concepts and methods—the developmental cycle of domestic groups, the extended case method, situational analysis—that functioned something like the epicycles orthodox early modern European astronomers added to the earth-centered Ptolemaic system before it was swept away by the heliocentric Copernican revolution. They tried to allow for history, power, and political change without actually jettisoning the epistemological frame that prevented envisioning them. Such work, narrating an urbanizing, decolonizing Africa, labor protest, and new identities, still counts as "classic" anthropology. But it is *Return to Laughter's* portrait of rural, backward and peacefully colonized Africans that has captured a vast popular audience from the 1950s into the present.[83]

The narrative of one postwar radical anthropologist's efforts to take on the hegemonic structural-functionalist and "cultural and personality" paradigms in American anthropology may illustrate the difficulties of crying that the emperor has no clothes in a retrograde era in which the emperor is paying his epigones well and decapitating his critics. Elgin Williams, who held a Ph.D. in economics from Columbia University but shifted fields into anthropology, indicted the first in an *American Anthropologist* piece in 1948, the second in an article (cowritten with Dorothy Gregg) in the same journal the following year. In "Anthropology for the Common Man," Williams cleverly uses the postwar zeitgeist to make crystal clear the contradiction between Ruth Benedict's stated epistemology of total cross-cultural tolerance and her actual political stance:

> For the war period has provided the greatest mass education in "cultural divergences" the world has so far witnessed. Large portions of the world's population have come to learn about "possible human institutions and motives" in exceedingly direct and searching fashion. And the Gold Star Mother (for instance) is going to be reluctant about granting significance to Hitler's culture, the surviving citizens of Hiroshima (for instance) are going to look for their wisdom elsewhere than in a "greatly increased tolerance" toward the divergences of American generals, and the remaining Jews of Europe (for instance) are going to be poor customers for gospels which hold that there are two sides to every question.[84]

Williams notes that "it *is* possible, as Dr. Benedict has made so clear, 'to scrutinize different institutions and cast up their cost in terms of social capital, in terms of the less desirable behaviour traits they stimulate, and in terms of human suffering and frustration.'"[85]

In "The Dismal Science of Functionalism," Gregg and Williams dissect the dominant paradigm of social anthropology, laying out its parallels to neoclassical economics and its utter inability to describe social process nontautologically:

> Thus are caught up all the threads in the functionalist scheme. The mixture of hedonism and organicism, by directing attention from actual behavioral consequences to general "goals" and "motives," precipitates a tautological equilibrium where needs and institutions stand forever in balance. To this selective perception any and every situation appears as one of physiological health ("natural order"). The study of culture-process is reduced to making excuses for the organism whose vagaries, while often brutal, flow from the heart, and to filling in the blanks of an eternally-given paradigm, any change in which is equivalent to the end of society.[86]

These insightful and trenchant critiques did Elgin Williams little good in the face of unremitting FBI harassment for his left-wing activism. Hounded out of teaching positions first at the University of Washington, then Reed College, then North Texas State (he was a native Texan), he was forced to abandon academic work altogether. Oscar Lewis tried to help him find university employment in the face of the blacklist, to no avail. He died still a young man, under extremely suspicious circumstances, only one of thousands of victims of a state-sponsored campaign of terror. Despite the publication of his work in the central journal of the discipline, and despite the fact that his points have become, finally, just anthropological common sense, his name, like those of so many others, has not been resurrected by the new minor industry detailing "the history of anthropology."[87]

THE ANTHROPOLOGIST AS POSTWAR IMPERIALIST HERO

Indeed, pervasive inside and outside the discipline in the 1940s and 1950s was the notion that cross-cultural knowledge was to be harnessed to Cold War imperatives. That radical uses of anthropology were not only newly verboten but unthinkable—and that traditional anthropological expertise was newly valued as Cold War pragmatics—is well illustrated by the publishing sensation of the year 1958. The clear theme of *The Ugly American*, best-seller (twenty printings in the first year of publication), Book-of-the-Month Club choice, and ultimately Hollywood film starring Marlon Brando—was that Americans working for our government abroad were not (and that the Communists *were*) acting sufficiently like anthropologists and must reform themselves to do so, pronto. Focusing, appropriately, on the American presence in Southeast Asia four years after the French debacle at Dien Bien Phu, William J. Lederer and Eugene Burdick, gut-bucket Cold Warriors, devised a linked set of biographical vignettes that satirized the ignorant insularity and luxury-loving actions of Americans working for their government in the Third World and detailed how they were repeatedly hoodwinked by the wily Communists in befriending the "natives," high and low, country and city.

> The first American grain ship arrived two days later in the harbor of Haidho, the capital of Sarkhan [a made-up country]. . . . On each bag of rice there was stenciled in Sarkhanese for every citizen to see and read for himself: "This rice is a gift from Russia." . . . The Americans took pictures of the distribution of the rice and the smiling faces of the now happy people. There were no comments from any of the Americans present. None of them could read or understand Sarkhanese, and they did not know what was happening.[88]

Lederer and Burdick's message was that Americans were dropping the Asian baton that had been passed to them by the various European powers—particularly the French—relinquishing colonial rule. They advised learning native languages, understanding local etiquette, knowing "the people" rather than only native elites, doing as much as possible without luxuries unavailable to most in the society at hand. These are, of course, fundamentally ethnographic practices, and they are the activities of the heroes of the book, including Homer Atkins, the eponymous Ugly American. (It is no coincidence, as well, that this list also characterizes the activities later mapped out by Cold Warrior John F. Kennedy for his "ask what you can do for your country" Peace Corps.)

Providing further proof of the Cold War utility of anthropological practices in the popular mind is the 1963 Dell comic *Brain Boy*, in which a young man with telepathic and transubstantiating powers poses as a mild-mannered anthropology student while working for the Secret Service, dispatching any number of Soviet-inflected monsters (see fig. 19).

As befits the Cold War era jeremiad, there was a proper place for women in these authors' anticommunist schemes: as firm, self-denying helpmeets of their heroic bosses and husbands. The ugly American's wife "Emma, a stout woman with freckles across her nose was, in her way, quite as ugly as her husband. . . . She did not blink when Atkins told her they were moving to Sarkhan. She told Homer that she'd be pleased to move into a smaller house where she could manage things with her own hands, and where she wouldn't need servants. . . . It was a matter of some pride to her that she was as good a housekeeper as most of her [Sarkhanese village] neighbors."[89]

ON A QUIET SIDE-STREET IN WASHINGTON, D.C. MATT PRICE STROLLS NONCHALANTLY, BOOKS UNDER HIS ARM, LIKE THE STUDENT OF ANTHROPOLOGY PEOPLE THINK HE IS.

AND THE NEAT, QUIET BUILDING HE ENTERED SEEMED PERFECT FOR A STUDENT'S AFTER-NOON OF RESEARCH...

BUT ONCE INSIDE, THE ORDINARY YOUNG MAN BECAME SOMEONE QUITE EXTRAORDINARY!

IN THE OFFICE OF CHRIS AMBERS, HEAD OF THE SPECIAL BRANCH OF U.S. SECRET SERVICE WHICH HID BEHIND THE NAME OF "ACTIVE ANTHROPOLOGISTS."

BRAIN BOY...JUST IN TIME! YOUR PLANE LEAVES FOR ANKOOK IN HALF AN HOUR. YOU'LL BARELY HAVE TIME FOR YOUR IN-STRUCTIONS BE-FORE DRIVING TO THE AIR-PORT.

HEY, HOLD IT, CHRIS! ALL YOU SAID ON THE PHONE WAS THAT I WAS IN FOR A **COOL** TIME!

VERY COOL-- THE NORTH POLE! AND I'M **NOT** KIDDING!

CHRIS AMBERS OUTLINED THE CASE: TEN AMERICAN SCIENTISTS HAD DISAPPEARED WITHOUT A TRACE IN THE FROZEN WASTE-LAND NORTH OF THE TINY FRONTIER TOWN OF ANKOOK, JUMPING OFF SPOT FOR SEVERAL AMERICAN SCIENTIFIC EXPEDITIONS.

...THIS IS THE FIRST TIME **ANY** OF OUR SCIENTISTS HAS EVER BEEN LOST. NOW **TEN** DISAPPEAR AT ONE TIME! IT'S FISHY, BRAIN BOY. IT DOESN'T ADD UP. HERE ARE PHOTOGRAPHS OF THE MISSING MEN.

19. Brain Boy, the Cold Warrior anthropologist as hero.

And indeed the new trope of "Anthropologist as Hero," the title of a 1963 Susan Sontag essay introducing and lionizing Claude Lévi-Strauss to an American audience, assumed an apolitical maleness as a precondition for true practice of the discipline. Here we see also the development of a new division between a Mandarin anthropology of quietist contemplation and a larger middlebrow social science (including anthropology) engaged in political pragmatics. For Sontag in the early 1960s, deeply influenced by but seeking escape from Sartre's left-leaning existentialism, "most serious thought in our time struggles with the feeling of homelessness": "The only way to cure this spiritual nausea seems to be . . . to exacerbate it. Modern thought is pledged to a kind of applied Hegelianism: seeking its Self in its Other. Europe seeks itself in the exotic."[90] For Sontag, Lévi-Strauss epitomizes the "*risk* involved in intelligence," his writings case studies of "the unique spiritual hazards to which the anthropologist subjects himself. . . . He is a man in control of, and even consciously exploiting, his own intellectual alienation. . . . Essentially he is engaged in saving his own soul, by a curious and ambitious act of intellectual catharsis [because] field work [accomplishes] that inner revolution that will really make him into a new man."[91]

This religiously tinged act of fieldwork turns out, in Sontag's respectful and accurate reading of Lévi-Strauss, to be a combination of old-fashioned American salvage ethnography—"'Let us go and study the primitives,' say Lévi-Strauss and his pupils, 'before they disappear'"—and the application of a new postwar reductionist, formalizing logic to Others' lives. Structuralism effaces any considerations of biology, of human social relations, even of individual psychology in its discernment of "formal features": "A great cleansing operation is in process, and the broom that sweeps everything clean is the notion of 'structure.' . . . Thus the man who submits himself to the exotic to confirm his own inner alienation as an urban intellectual ends by aiming to vanquish his subject by translating it into a purely formal code."[92]

This process of translation, akin to the postwar game theory/cybernetics movements that swept through American physical, biological, and social sciences, is thus fundamentally concerned with control through the imposition of order. But Lévi-Strauss's control, unlike Oscar Lewis's, is not political, not hands-on. Rather than aspiring to transform and rule the postwar, decolonizing Third World, as did the social science epigones of Cold Warrior politicians, the Lévi-Straussian anthropologist sought to be "'a critic at home' but 'a conformist elsewhere'"—and thus "the anthropologist, so far as his own country is concerned, is sterilized politically": "Anthropology, in Lévi-Strauss' conception, is a technique of political disengagement; and the anthropologist's vocation requires the assumption of a profound detachment. . . . [it is] impossible for the anthropologist to be a citizen. . . . 'Never can he feel himself 'at home' anywhere; he will always be, psychologically speaking, an amputee.'"[93]

Sontag's anthropological hero turns his back on responsibility for the state of the world, assumes the inevitable extinction of the (of course, exotic) people among whom he works, and is thus "not only the mourner of the cold world of the primitives, but its custodian as well. Lamenting among the shadows, struggling to distinguish the archaic from the pseudo-archaic, he acts out a heroic, diligent, and complex modern pessimism."[94]

Structuralism's "modern pessimism" not only counseled political quietism vis-à-vis the tumultuous international politics of the era, but also, in its hieratic formalism, defined gender relations as fixed, immutable. Human social relations, in Lévi-Straussian epistemology, were defined by male communicative exchange, and the most fundamental mutual prestation was "sister exchange," or the male-arranged movement of women as marriage partners between populations. Lévi-Strauss himself recognized the innately illogical character of this claim, its failure to take into account women's human agency: "Woman could never become just a sign and nothing more, since even in a man's world she is still a person, and since insofar as she is defined as a sign she must be recognized as a generator of signs."[95]

Like Margaret Mead, like Laura Bohannan, Sontag established a public intellectual niche in the pre-feminist-renaissance Cold War, was recognized as herself a generator of signs through the avoidance of oppositional commentary on her own existential position as a woman. In her extraordinarily influential *Against Interpretation,* she not only celebrates Lévi-Strauss, but also introduces the French ethnographer and adventurer Michel Leiris (later a subject in James Clifford's *Predicament of Culture*), comments analytically and favorably on homosexual "camp" as modern style, and calls for high-cultural expansion to encompass popular art forms. Thus, in one small package, Sontag helps to further the remasculinization, depoliticization, and Europeanization of American anthropology, heralds the simultaneously liberatory and essentializing discourse on "gay aesthetics," and indexes the post–Frankfurt School American middlebrow and highbrow embrace of pop culture. Sontag's was the first salvo in an intellectual war that was to produce today's flourishing school of cultural studies and the endless apologetics for the status quo of some of its practitioners.

The times were such that even an anthropologist of impeccable left and later feminist credentials like Kathleen Gough, the originator of the phrase "anthropology, child of imperialism," in 1962 coauthored a study of matrilineal kinship with David Schneider that has the air of protesting too much in its careful separation of kin reckoning through females from any taint of female social power or even parity: "The role of women as women [in matrilineal populations] has been defined as that of responsibility for the care of children. I now add that the role of men as men is defined as that of having authority over women and children (except perhaps for specially qualifying conditions applicable to a very few women of the society). Positions of the highest authority within the matrilineal descent group will . . . ordinarily be vested in statuses occupied by men."[96]

In general, indeed—except for the new cohort of women field primatologists so well analyzed by Donna Haraway, who were certainly iconic figures but never thought of as actual intellectuals—female anthropologists, like female "exotics," faded into the public sphere wallpaper in the New Frontier and Great Society era. In Gore Vidal's short comic play *Weekend*, which memorializes the inside-the-Beltway political scene just at the point of President Johnson's 1968 announcement that he would not seek reelection, the senator's disappointing son, who is "studying to be an anthropologist," seems to espouse an unholy combination of Lévi-Straussian structuralism and Desmond Morris–like pop ethology:

CHARLES: It's the new thing. Structure is all.
WILSON: He insists that we read Levi-Strauss.
OLIVE: How interesting!
ESTELLE: He also spends quite a lot of time with animals. Apparently they know something we don't.[97]

Margaret Mead certainly continued to contest for public attention in this period and was quite politically engaged both inside and outside anthropology. In 1955, under the auspices of UNESCO, she published *Cultural Patterns and Technical Change*, a collection of popularized case studies about "how . . . the expert member of an international technical assistance team bring[s] to a people the help they have asked for." The work is a thinly disguised argument for Cold War "development" funding for anthropologists. Mead's rationale is precisely parallel to Lederer and Burdick's later best-seller, although without any reference to fighting Communism: that only an anthropological perspective, a focus on studying the "whole culture," could help "us" to avoid "mistakes" and "to protect the mental health of a world population in transition."[98] She maintained ties with the United States military long past the war years and steadfastly spoke and wrote in favor of a series of imperial and antidemocratic American governmental actions. In 1957, for example, Mead gave a major Cold Warrior speech at the World Federation for Mental Health meetings in Copenhagen in which she claimed that all fear of nuclear contamination from testing was irrational, and that "trade unions are conducting a violent campaign against the dangers of building an atomic reactor [working with] political groups, either Pacifist or Communist."[99] In 1962 she attended an Air Force Systems Command meeting whose purpose was figuring out "how to break the phrase *space is for peaceful purposes.*"[100]

Nevertheless, despite Mead's ceaseless activities, repeated declarations in favor of the Cold War status quo, and never-ending publishing, she failed in these years to command intellectual respect in the public sphere. A 1961 *New Yorker* profile celebrates her as a "character," a nanny-anthropologist, with a perhaps morally—but not intellectually—challenging message for the Western public: "Dr. Mead is now sixty years old, has a rather expansive figure, and radiates the air of authority that comes from many years of telling students, anthropologists, and other people things for their own good. . . . 'The whole world is my field,' she is apt to say cheerfully. 'It's all anthropology.' . . . Dr. Mead is firmly convinced that the understanding gained through the social sciences will someday save the world."[101]

And in 1962 Mead published what we would now call a cultural feminist essay in the *Saturday Evening Post* in which she argued against the then-dominant American pattern of early marriage and high fertility for women because their "intrinsic cherishing role" was thus relegated to their own nuclear families rather than directed outward—as was hers, we are to understand—to public life as well.[102]

Intellectually respectable highbrow anthropology in this period was associated with Lévi-Strauss and structuralism, a world beyond Mead's ken. (She would later attack componential analysis as "discussing how many cross-cousins could dance on the head of a pin.") The major middlebrow anthropological slot was filled first by Oscar Lewis and other novelistic interpreters of the world's poor, and later by Carlos Castañeda as the "technicians of the sacred" costume began upstaging other anthropological raiment in the late 1960s. While Mead attempted to claim psychological expertise as a basis for social policy authority, Catherine Lutz has documented the enhanced military connection and thus masculinization of postwar American psychology: not only was Mead attempting to crash disciplinary boundaries in an era of rigidifying guild membership, she was simply the wrong sex, no matter how Cold Warrior her stance.[103]

Mead's "culture and personality" weltanschauung was taken over by pop psychology, and her interest in sexuality and the life course left her vulnerable to misogynist derogation. In Irving Wallace's sleazy 1963 pot-boiler *The Three Sirens,* for example, a thinly disguised Mead figure, a widow, travels with her disappointing (and, it turns out, murderous) son and a crew of other "experts" to study a hidden South Seas paradise of free sexuality: "She thought of the place: the temperate trade winds, the tall, sinewy, bronze people, the oral legends, the orgiastic rites, the smell of green coconuts and red hibiscus, the soft Italian-like intonation of the Polynesian tongue."[104]

Wallace's plot runs through many nubile young women and men engaged in many sex scenes, but its denouement is the Mead figure's self-castigation for producing her evil son through maternal neglect. The contrast between the two texts—Sontag's high-culture paean to Lévi-Strauss and this piece of tabloid silliness, published within three years of one another—is a neat index of the masculinist temper of the time, of the unlikelihood of public apprehension of a *female* anthropologist (or female anything else) as heroic. In the same year *The Three Sirens* was published, Mead began a monthly column for the women's magazine *Redbook.*[105] In the separate sphere—really the low-status ghetto—of prescriptive women's journalism, she could and did take on the mantle of expert intellectual denied to her in the larger public sphere of the New Frontier and Great Society era. Mead marketed herself consistently across the decades, but in the postwar era, she was forced to lower her price drastically.

SONS AND DAUGHTERS OF THE SHAKING EARTH: POLITICS AND SCHOLARSHIP OF THE 1960S AND 1970S

As the 1960s progressed, developments in Anglo-American anthropology both fed from and inspired the political economic developments of the times. Most small-scale populations by that point had been or were being transformed by colonization and capital penetration into peasants or urbanites of varying sorts. Philip Mayer's well-known monograph, *Townsmen or Tribesmen,* epitomizes anthropological attention to this vast phenomenon.[106] Ethnographers began paying more systematic—and sympathetic—attention to the residents of Third World cities, and this new urban anthropology inspired its First World counterpart.

In addition, anthropologists continued to practice salvage ethnography on remaining small groups, just as they had with nearly decimated Native Americans at the century's beginning. Commentary on the ironies and entailments of "primitive" contact with modern technology—as in Lauriston

20. Ironies of modernization: Kikuyu man and double-decker bus, Nairobi. (© Marc and Evelyne Bernheim—Woodfin Camp and Associates.)

Sharp's 1952 "Steel Axes for Stone Age Australians"—became increasingly common, and photographs of "tribally" dressed men astride motorcycles or stolidly getting off buses became standard textbook fare from the 1960s on.[107]

Coincident with this "ironies of modernization" anthropological vision, however, was a more Rousseauian stance which focused on the strengths of precontact small-scale social life and grew in force over the 1960s and 1970s. This new use of the primitive in critique of modernity—and thus the role of the anthropologist as technician of the sacred—ran parallel to radical Western social movements of the era: ecology/population, antiwar, sexual freedom, gay rights, and feminism. Specific new anthropological subfields arose in complicated symbiosis with these political trends.

Newly defined ecological anthropologists discovered that the shifting horticulture or slash-and-burn methods widely practiced in the tropics, in which people prepared, used, and then abandoned growing sites, both preserved delicate topsoils and provided rich growing media without outside fertilization. Demographic anthropologists found that many small-scale groups seemed to be able to maintain population levels without drastic growth or collapse through the regulation of sexual behavior, lengthy nursing, native contraception and abortifacients and selective infanticide. The Harvard !Kung project that Shostak would later join determined that !Kung foragers maintained highly nutritive diets and good health with a minimal labor expenditure and thus abundant time for leisure activities, findings not coincidently reminiscent of the young Marx's paean to a possible world in which "nobody has one exclusive sphere of activity but each can become accomplished in any branch he wishes, society regulates the general production and thus makes it possible for me to do one thing today and another tomorrow, to hunt in the morning, fish in the afternoon, rear cattle in the evening, criticise after dinner, just as I have a mind."[108]

Economic anthropology and newly labeled peasant studies were influenced by Marxism as well, as McCarthyism waned. Ethnographers working with peasantry in Latin America, Africa, Asia, the Middle East, and Europe newly considered issues of power and economic resources as well as "culture" or "tradition" in mapping lives and social relations.[109] Rural-led peasant rebellions—and successful revolutions, such as China's—inspired respectful as well as romantic consideration of peasant lives. The American involvement in Vietnam heightened the convergence of political and scholarly interest in anthropology as in other disciplines. Eric Wolf, for example, in 1959 published *Sons of the Shaking Earth,* an ethnohistorical and ethnographic account of Mesoamerica and the development of its peasantry's social organization. In 1965, he both helped organize and spoke at the first Vietnam War teach-in, held at the University of Michigan, and in 1969 published *Peasant Wars of the Twentieth Century.* "By showing that Vietnam's history had been shaped by the desires and capabilities of peasants," David Hunt has written, "Wolf achieved a scholarly breakthrough and underscored the futility of U.S. intervention."[110]

It is this tumultuous period, the Vietnam War era, that has fallen down the memory hole of American anthropological history. (Neither postmodern anthropologists nor anthropology bashers outside the guild ever refer to the events or writings of this era.) And yet it was the decade and a half from 1960 to the mid-1970s that set the stage, shaped American anthropology as we know it. And this stage setting had everything to do with the features of the larger American political economy: with the spectacle of obvious inequity and denial of human rights in the midst of breathtaking economic growth and abundance.

In 1960, the American Anthropological Association *Fellow Newsletter* was a small, amateurish booklet worthy of high school journalism; by 1970, it was a slick monthly with high production values. The number of departments offering at least a bachelor's degree in anthropology grew from 87 to 217 over the decade, and four times as many Ph.D.'s were awarded in 1970 as in 1960. (The slope of the curve then leveled off considerably: only double the number of 1970 Ph.D. degrees was awarded in 1980, and only 68 new departments were added over the decade, for a 1980 total of 285.)[111] A veritable cornucopia of funding poured from federal (much of it military related) and private foundation sources for graduate work and professional anthropological research. Enrollments in anthropology courses increased nationwide as left-leaning undergraduates hungry for information on "primitives," human origins, the Third World, and general questions of stratification and exploitation turned to the increasingly visible discipline—and, of course, these burgeoning enrollments helped to spur departmental growth.

American anthropologists in general have never been a particularly radical bunch, but, with and since the Boasians, they have certainly distinguished themselves in the aggregate as significantly more liberal than most other social scientists. The professional association went on record in 1960 for Negro civil rights and reaffirmed its antiracist position in 1961. The executive board issued an "academic freedom" position statement against federal governmental involvement in anthropological research, and in 1966 the business meeting of the American Anthropological Association passed a resolution against the American military use of napalm and a demand that we "proceed as rapidly as possible to a peaceful settlement of the war in Vietnam." (This resolution was passed over the objection of the president-elect that it did not advance the science of anthropology. Michael Harner counterobjected that "genocide is not in the professional interests of anthropologists.")[112]

Academic, and thus relatively toothless, opposition to war crimes was one thing; going public in airing disciplinary dirty linen turned out to be another. Over the course of the decade, anthropologists increasingly turned to extradisciplinary venues to criticize American foreign policy and the complicity of some anthropologists in its enactment. Gerald Berreman decried academic colonialism in the *Nation* in 1969, after having published a caustic essay, "Is Anthropology Alive?" with those of many other anthropologists, including Kathleen Gough, in *Current Anthropology* in 1968. In the same year, Gough herself wrote explicitly about anthropology's imperialist legacy and her vision of anti-imperialist research in *Monthly Review* and elsewhere. Even Lévi-Strauss had been moved to write, in 1966, that anthropology was "the daughter to this era of violence . . . the outcome of an historical process, which has made the larger part of mankind subservient to the other." But the anthropological cause célèbre of the decade occurred in 1970, when Eric Wolf and Joseph Jorgenson published "Anthropology on the Warpath" in the *New York Review of Books*.[113] Wolf and Jorgensen wrote the piece after the Executive Committee of the American Anthropological Association reprimanded them as members of the Ethics Committee for conducting inquiries within the discipline on the extent of anthropological complicity in clandestine military research on Southeast Asia.

"Warpath" made use of documents illicitly acquired from an anthropologist's office by the Student Mobilization Committee to End the War in Vietnam and supplied to Wolf and Jorgensen. The piece both laid out the extent of contemporary anthropological complicity in the American war in Southeast Asia and discussed the larger issue of the evolution of the American military use of social science data on Third World states: "The Thailand episode is only the latest violation of the conscience of anthropology; in retrospect we see that anthropological projects calculated to interfere in the affairs of others have a long, and not entirely visible, genealogy."[114]

Wolf and Jorgensen provided a lightning history of post–World War II military funding and use of social science, particularly anthropology projects: work on "native administration" for the navy in Micronesia, military use of the Human Relations Area Files, the scandalous Project Camelot in Latin America, the Indian government's discovery of American military funding of a Berkeley anthropological project in the Himalayas, and finally documents on widespread anthropological involvement in American military counterinsurgency work in Thailand. They named no names, but this circumspection did them no good: a firestorm of criticism ensued, and they, rather than anthropologists who worked for the American military, were investigated by an ad hoc committee of the American Anthropological Association headed by Margaret Mead (the other two members were William Davenport and David Olmstead).

Mead herself had spent the latter part of the 1960s engaged in rather vague defense of (middle-class) "youth," as long as the actions of the young were countercultural (hippie drug taking) or safely retrospectively sanctified (civil rights protest after the passage of the 1964 Civil Rights Act). Thus, in 1965, in a radio interview with Studs Terkel, she celebrated contemporary young people, in contradistinction to the 1950s "silent genera-tion," for their participation in civil rights and anti-Vietnam protest.

Mead was so widely known for her pro-youth stance that *Hair*, the self-described "American Tribal Love-Rock Musical," included a character who, at least in the earliest versions of the stage play, carried her telltale staff and whose self-representation gently sent up her efforts to affiliate herself with hip young America. She sang "My Conviction," approving male "long hair and other flamboyant affectations," and the song's recitative ended in the exhortation, "Kids, be whatever you are, do whatever you do, just so long as you don't hurt anybody."[115] In 1969 Mead gave Senate testimony on older Americans' hypocrisy in approving liquor and tobacco consumption while decrying youthful marijuana use. She went on to publish *Culture and Commitment*, a short book on the "generation gap" based on 1969 lectures at the American Museum of Natural History.

This qualified embrace of the rising, heavily mass-mediated "youth counterculture" echoed Mead's concerns and prescriptions at the very be-ginning of her career and gained her more respectful public attention than she had received in two decades. The *New York Times Magazine*, for ex-ample, published in 1970 a lengthy, lavish account of *Culture and Commit-ment* and her public intellectual activities, defining her as "a poor man's anthropologist . . . to a society troubled by its own shifting folkways, and hungry for guidance in coping with them":

> To understand the Mead phenomenon, it is helpful to realize that the accelerated changes which society is undergoing in almost every sphere of life, and the speed with which these changes are made public through the mass media, have produced a whole new ball game for the human race. People are understandably anxious about a game in which the rules have been suddenly and drastically revised; and since anthropology is essentially a study of cultural adaptation, Mead the anthropologist has become a social umpire, calling the plays as they happen: At the same time, Mead the popularizer is an effective commentator (or "color announcer") who gives her audiences access to the new, esoteric rules in a language they can understand.[116]

This is a narrative worlds removed from the condescending *New Yorker* profile in 1961.

Mead's hostility to early women's liberation activities, however, is re-flected in Robin Morgan's bitter (and, in retrospect, embarrassing) diatribe against her in a free-form poem at the beginning of her best-selling 1970 anthology *Sisterhood Is Powerful*. Morgan narrates Mead's interruption of a seminar on peace and women in Southeast Asia:

Margaret Mead swept in and yelled at me that
women were perhaps inherently so violent that there's
no evidence we might ever stop if we began to kill.
Therefore, the eminent sister concluded,
this women's revolution must not take place,
we ought not to provoke (dig that) men to be violent
against us, and ought not to unleash our own just anger
at our own oppression

Morgan goes on to record Mead's warning that, in protesting oppression, "blacks, Latins, Asians, but especially women, are provoking fascism."[117] We have seen, before, in Mead's crackpot claims about American race and ethnicity, her tendency to make off-the-cuff and self-contradictory—but almost always politically retrogressive—statements in this era. In addition, she resolutely continued to oppose any infiltration of political self-consciousness or practice into anthropology as a discipline, as her actions during this public crisis attest.

Mead's committee report, presented at the business meeting of the American Anthropological Association's annual meeting in New York on November 20, 1971, exonerated civilian anthropologists of complicity with United States military forces' counterinsurgency work but criticized Wolf's and Jorgensen's lapse of ethics in making their allegations public. Mead was roundly and repeatedly hissed by the overflow crowd of seven hundred. True to her evolving, self-created image as what the *New York Times* labeled "virtually a mother figure of anthropology," she chided the audience, her own professional colleagues, for exhibiting "silly . . . childish behavior." At the end of the four-hour meeting, the membership had voted by overwhelming margins to reject all three parts of the committee's report and to return the matter to the executive board.[118] In an apparent fit of pique, Mead had her committee's files destroyed rather than sent on, and she reportedly spat on Joseph Jorgensen at a private gathering two years later.[119] Eric Wolf remarked to interviewers in the late 1980s that "everyone involved lost a lot of friends in the process."[120]

Margaret Mead, however, rose like the phoenix after this political debacle, reaching her greatest heights of professional and public sphere notice and approval in the handful of years before her death in 1978. So complete was her rehabilitation that, aside from Lenora Foerstal and Angela Gilliam's unabashedly radical *Confronting the Margaret Mead Legacy* and Eric Wakin's monograph on anthropological complicity in the American war in Southeast Asia, none of the proliferating biographies, academic studies, or journalistic pieces on Mead—even those critical of her work or life—now alludes to these Vietnam War–era events. And Mead's public and disciplinary renaissance was inextricably linked to the 1970s rebirth of American, and worldwide, feminism.

American feminist resurgence, as we have seen, drew from many sources. Many have remarked that gender inequities were all the more visible in a historical era so characterized by egalitarian rhetoric and protest. A key cohort of feminist activists emerged from the Civil Rights and antiwar movements: disgusted with sexist mistreatment by male comrades, they organized among themselves. In addition, the baby boom demographic bulge, better off and better educated than previous generations of women, with rising ages at marriage and higher labor force participation rates, found the low status and pay of available "women's jobs" intensely frustrating. The sexual revolution proved paradoxically unliberating for women, as men felt freer to pressure women for sex and abandoned wives and children with little public censure.[121]

Second-wave activists differed from their nineteenth-century predecessors in a number of ways, but most relevant for our discussion was their new emphasis on "sexual politics," or the power-laden encounters between women and men in private life, and their presumption that scholarship in all fields needed to be interrogated in the light of feminist concerns. Anthropology was a central focus in these exciting early years of feminist scholarship, as I have noted:

> Because of American anthropology's historic, cross-cutting four-field emphasis, anthropology seemed to cover women from soup to nuts—from female proto-humans and primates to women in prehistoric societies to a survey of the lives of all contemporary women, whether in the first, second, or third worlds. Feminist anthropologists had a strong sense, as well, that the results of their intellectual work were of key importance to feminist political decision making. Only anthropology, after all, occupied itself with the search for human universals and the documentation of cross-cultural variation. New interpretations of these phenomena seemed likely to aid us in discovering the key factors related to women's secondary status, and thus to determine the Archimedean standpoint from which we could move the male-dominated globe.[122]

Emboldened by a sense of the centrality of their intellectual project, feminist anthropologists of the 1970s, the daughters of the shaking earth, worked rapidly and with intensity on foregrounding and interrogating gender as an analytic category across the various theoretical and substantive schools of the discipline. The two bibles of feminist anthropology, the anthologies *Women, Culture, and Society* and *Towards an Anthropology of*

Women, appeared, white-heat, in 1974 and 1975, respectively, and were widely read inside and outside the academy.[123] Rayna Rapp, editor of the latter volume, served on the *Ms.* magazine editorial board. Even those whose concerns were worlds away from issues of prehistoric origins or the relative statuses of women in non-Western societies attended to new work on "the evolution of sexual asymmetry."

The prevailing "man the hunter" model of the 1960s, as we have seen, addressed gender through the unquestioned assumption that all males—whether nonhuman primate, prehistoric, or contemporary human—must be seen automatically to wield all social power. Feminist anthropologists of the 1970s immediately engaged both this and other fallacies. Insofar as one can deal with this issue without falling into pits of anthropomorphism, the "man the hunter" proponents were quickly set in their place by an avalanche of countervailing data on varying sex-linked behaviors among numerous nonhuman primate species. Given, as well, that "man the hunter" and other schools of thought had already reengaged evolutionary thinking through the "scientific" (heavily quantitative) study of foraging populations like the !Kung and the lavish use of nonhuman primates in the "our primitive ancestors" slot once reserved for "savages," many feminist anthropologists turned to the question of possible evolutionary shifts in gender relations in prehistory.

Two other factors influenced this movement. The first was the keen interest many feminist anthropologists (and anthropologists in general) were taking in Marxist theory with the decline of McCarthyism and the opening of American universities to European and Third World academic leftist influence. Marx and Engels, as I have noted, presumed original gender equality in their Victorian evolutionary schemes and linked the attainment of sex equality in the future to the advance of female labor force participation, the decline of "bourgeois marriage forms" in which women were entrapped and subject to men's power, and, of course, to the achievement of socialism. These analytical connections, and their rhetorical power against "nasty savage" ideology, were powerfully attractive to many feminist scholars. Adopting them provided a unitary theoretical framework for new fieldwork, political activism, and theory that countered common sexist caveman presumptions.

A second factor directed feminist anthropologists' return to evolutionary theory. Westerners dealing with the heightened gender discourse created by the contemporary feminist movement tended to revert to armchair evolutionary speculations and vague reliance on the unequal gender arrangements postulated in popular cultural interpretations of primitive and prehistoric life. From Tarzan repeatedly saving Jane to cavemen (hilariously, right?) cracking cavewomen with clubs and dragging them by their hair, to the Flintstones' more insidiously benign version of *The Honeymooners* minus modern technology, popular culture provided midcentury apologists for sexism with automatic visual and print images legitimizing the status quo through claiming its ancient and thus natural foundation. As feminist anthropologists found themselves positioned strategically to answer popular-culture-based claims for the correctness of male dominance, many were drawn willy-nilly into social evolutionary debate.

I cannot tell the bulk of that scholarly story here—I have done so elsewhere—but we do need to consider the ways in which feminist anthropologists' theoretical choices intersected with shifting images of the "primitive woman." To return to the 1960s and 1970s, with their jostling notions of the "ironies of modernization" versus nouveau "noble savage" ideology—primitives as seasoned ecologists, zero population growth experts, and gay rights pioneers—we can see that both visions coexisted under a generally liberal political umbrella. James Clifford, in fact, has labeled the "set of roles and discursive possibilities" developed by anthropologists in these classic discipline-building decades of anthropology "ethnographic liberalism."[124] Presumptions of cultural relativism and strong advocacy stances for particular populations—as long as they avoid any challenge to state power that might endanger permission to do further research—characterize ethnographic liberalism. For those working with small-scale populations, the prototypical ethnographer's line was not exactly "my group, right or wrong," but something like "my group, understandable, and disappearing anyway." And in fact there was a proliferation of textbooks throughout this era with titles signifying both the "understandableness" of small-scale populations and a wholly unconscious presumption of their (and our) primary maleness: *Every Man His Way* (1968), *Man Makes Sense* (1970), *Man's Many Ways* (1973).[125]

Feminist anthropologists, then, were faced with a conundrum—how to take a critical stance on populations ethnographers were traditionally pledged to uphold? From the outset it was clear that women's lives in at least some small-scale societies were unpleasant even compared to the worst of Western sexism. In other words, ethnographic liberalism could ensure that few modern ethnographers would wish to claim with British Victorian theorist John McLennan that women in small-scale societies were "depraved, and inured to scenes of depravity from their earliest infancy."[126] But feminists might wish to criticize the institutionalized threat of gang rape among the South American Mundurucú or the Pacific Trukese (and

modern ethnographer Ward Goodenough's) acceptance of a man's right to
beat his daughter. Feminist anthropologists, and those who were influenced by them, took a variety of tacks in response to this theoretical tight
spot, each of which had different implications for anthropological and popular visions of "the primitive woman."

One solution available to some ethnographers was to declare "native
women better off." We can see that Shostak was influenced in this direction
in writing about the San. Patricia Draper before her had in 1975 drawn a
strong portrait of autonomous, productive San women whose children
would anxiously scan the horizon waiting for their return from foraging
expeditions. In the same year, Ruby Rohrlich-Leavitt and her coauthors
resurrected the work and reputation of the intrepid Englishwoman Daisy
Bates (not the black American civil rights activist) on the high status and
rich and autonomous ritual life of Australian aboriginal women. Many ethnographers who worked with peasant women also painted similar portraits.

Obviously "native women better off" neatly solved the feminist ethnographic conundrum in advocating both the "primitive" population under
discussion and its gender arrangements as in some way superior to the
anthropologists' own. It also extended the historic "noble savage" vision
in an explicitly gendered direction and opened itself to popular cultural
feminist interpretations of the superiority and wisdom of primitive
women, whether they be contemporary Native Americans, Australian aborigines, or ancient practitioners of matriarchy and goddess worship. Declaring that women in some small-scale societies could offer us "some answers," as did Shostak, however, offered a conondrum: why some primitive
women and not others?

Other feminist anthropologists solved this problem of overgeneraliza-
tion in varying ways. Sherry Ortner simply reversed the logic, marshaling
a scattershot set of ethnographic examples to claim that all women shared
secondary symbolic status to all men. In Ortner's schema, we are all downtrodden and degraded sisters under the skin; "primitive" women are neither better nor worse off. Michelle Rosaldo chose to focus on the relative
distinction between domestic and public domains in any one society, declaring that the more embedded the distinction, the lower would be wom-
en's status. Thus, Rosaldo neatly crosscut the usual primitive-peasant-
urban distinctions of social scientists: the relative separation of public and
domestic neither clearly grows nor diminishes as one moves from "primitive" to "civilized" societies. Victorian Britain and the United States were
characterized by quite rigid ideological distinctions between domestic and

public, but then so were many small-scale societies in the Pacific. In Rosaldo's Weberian scheme, "primitive women" fade as a symbolic construct.
A number of other anthropologists took a different theoretical stand that
had, nevertheless, the same implications for the "primitive woman" image.
Nicole-Claude Mathieu, Penny Brown, and others argued on the basis of
phenomenological reasoning that all cultural translation—attempts to
know other minds—are doomed to failure. Cross-cultural comparisons of
women's lives and statuses, then, would be impossible, and one could not
construct a category that lumped together women in even any two societies, much less one that grandly summed up hundreds.

Finally, feminist anthropologists who returned explicitly to evolutionism
through rereading Marx and Engels ("native woman better off" advocates
often did so implicitly) also took on the nineteenth-century "noble savage"
perspective—but with a difference. Marx and Engels postulated that the
"first class division," that between men and women, occurred with the
evolution of primitive societies from hunting to herding and thus with the
rise of private property. (They assumed that men, presumably because they
were men, monopolized family herding stocks.) Thus Engels wrote of the
"world-historical defeat of the female sex" as an entailment of an inevitable
unilineal social evolution—a defeat that would be abrogated by socialism.
Marxist-feminist anthropologists instead focused on two other phenomena: the relative levels of internal stratification in particular societies together with their entailments, and the consequences of Western colonialism and capital penetration. In "Engels Revisited," Karen Sacks used the
former concern in a return to the Victorian comparative method. She
ranged several contemporary African societies against one another and determined that women's status is the highest within the group that is also
characterized by the least stratification and production for exchange
(rather than production for use). Thus, the Mbuti emerge as contemporary
examples of the sexually egalitarian phase through which Marx and Engels
postulated all societies had moved. For Eleanor Leacock, the key was the
degrading influence of Western colonialism. In a lifetime's careful ethnohistorical work on northeastern Native Americans, Leacock repeatedly un-
earthed evidence of formerly egalitarian populations distorted into male
dominance by Western contact. From the optic of "primitive woman" symbolism, then, "native women better off" and the new Marxist-feminism
converged.

But primitivism, as we have seen, has never been the sole property of
professional anthropologists. During the period in which feminist anthropologists were experiencing the feminist conundrum, crafting escapes

from it, and debating one another and other scholars, the public at large was informed about gendered primitivism from quite other sources. Feminist popularizers of the 1970s like Elizabeth Gould Davis and Elaine Morgan constructed fanciful evolutionary explanations for the rise of male dominance from an ancient base of female power. Drawing, as did Bachofen, on notions of women's greater spiritual capacities (and often drawing on Bachofen himself), they posited former goddess-worshipping matriarchies: "The primacy of goddesses over gods, of queens over kings, of great matriarchs who had first tamed and then reeducated men, all pointed to the fact of a once gynocratic world." The combined efforts of anthropologists and historians to demonstrate that both female monarchs (Elizabeth I, Catherine the Great) and female deities (Kali, the Virgin Mary) can exist quite handily in societies characterized by extreme male dominance has had little effect on the never-ending flood of cultural feminist "goddess" literature, even into the present, as we have seen from the examples of Lynne Andrews, Marianne Williamson, and Trinh Minh-Ha.

PATRIARCHAL BIOLOGY

But this popular cultural goddess-matriarchy vision arose within the context of far more popular, much more widely disseminated notions of natural male dominance, part of the evolving and contested "human nature expert" Halloween costume discussed in chapter 1. Throughout the 1960s and 1970s, Desmond Morris, Robert Ardrey, Lionel Tiger, and others published twentieth-century versions of Sir Henry Maine's Victorian narrative of patriarchy's right and proper and certainly ancient hegemony.[127] These new patriarchs adduced evidence not from "primitive" social structures, but from those of nonhuman primates. Donna Haraway and Susan Sperling have written that with postwar African decolonization and the renaissance of other antiracist movements, the Western use of "primitives" as stand-ins for our ancestors came to be increasingly embarrassing. In their place were substituted apes and monkeys—most importantly the savanna baboons whose "male-dominant" social organization was celebrated in print and film as part of the "man the hunter" complex.[128] Morris and Tiger relied on ethological suppositions based on bad primatology, others on a congeries of crackpot sociology and biology.

With the explicit rise of sociobiology in the late 1970s, E. O. Wilson and other academics strode on stage with texts meant to reach broad audiences with the holy writ of natural selection *über alles*. This first wave of sociobiologists envisioned all male animals, including humans, as packets of DNA self-consciously strategizing to reproduce themselves, and all female animals as insentient objects through which male strategizers realized their goals. Thus, "natural" male dominance was an epiphenomenon of biology. (It took the passage of a further generation of scholars for a school of feminist sociobiologists to arise, a school that sanctified a yuppie vision, as Haraway and Sperling note, of *all* animals as DNA packets strategizing against one another for reproductive advantage.)

Whatever their differences, whether they were scholars or not, all of these "natural patriarchy" writers shared a vision of all contemporary humans as naked apes. As Robin Fox and Lionel Tiger put it in 1971: "We have seen how sexual differentiation is rooted in primate political-breeding processes: the dominant males are the focus of attention and hence cohesion; they dominate by overt strength and by ritualized threat and display; they protect and keep order; they compete in a never-ceasing test of their ability to dominate; but they also combine in coalitions to exercise more effective dominance or to forage and explore." Thus, Fox and Tiger set up a false narrative of the nonhuman primate world. They then continue with a seamless shift to *Homo sapiens:* "The course of human evolution added to this basic pattern all the complexities of the hunting life. Man does not live by bread alone, but how he finds his bread is still important, particularly when it is not bread but meat that matters, and when the hunting way of life persisted for millions of years." [129]

These two popular visions thus heralded the contemporary fissioning of the public sphere with regard to gender relations. The "ancient matriarchy" and "inevitable patriarchy" trains rumble on toward the end of the century on parallel tracks, each with its associated true believers, each claiming anthropological imprimatur, each based on silly falsehoods, each cutting the other dead.

The early 1970s, nevertheless, witnessed an upsurge of popular interest in actual scholarly work on cross-cultural gender relations. Anthropology in particular was of interest, and two deliberately accessible "primitive woman" ethnographies of the early 1970s—both reviewed in *Ms.* magazine, both very popular course-adoption texts, both still in print after two decades—stand for the range of feminist work done in that period, the visions of dusky maidens and of "American women" that evolving anthropological common sense deemed reasonable. [130] Janet Siskind's 1973 *To Hunt in the Morning,* written in a charmingly self-reflexive autobiographical style, details years of fieldwork (from the mid- to late 1960s) among the Sharanahua, a small group of horticultural and foraging South American Indians living just on the Peruvian side of the Peruvian-Brazilian border.

Siskind's intellectual framework, a synthesis of Marxism, emerging feminism, Freudian analysis, and developing ecological anthropology, well illustrates the range of theoretical approaches of interest to younger, progressive anthropologists in that era. Robert and Yolanda Murphy's 1974 *Women of the Forest*, in contrast, is a reanalysis, with gender in mind, of the Mundurucú, the Brazilian Amazonian Indian group about whom senior anthropologist Robert Murphy (with Yolanda Murphy in the classic female helpmeet role) had written on the basis of 1950s fieldwork. Because of this circumstance—restudy in response to the renaissance of feminism in the 1970s—the book as a whole has an unmistakeable "oops, forgot the women" flavor. Siskind and the Murphys overlap in their student-professor relationship, their accessible, popularizing prose, the general cultural area, their interest in ecological issues, and their use of Freud. Their two groups even share a general foraging/horticultural ecological adaptation, patrilineal kin reckoning with uxorilocal residence, the influence of missionaries and traders, and solidary female farming and food provisioning. But Siskind and the Murphys are otherwise fascinatingly different, and were very differently received at the time of publication—as jacket blurbs by Eric Wolf and Robert Carneiro for Siskind, as opposed to Margaret Mead and Ashley Montagu for the Murphys, might indicate.

MARXIAN MAIDENS

The title of *To Hunt in the Morning* is taken, of course, from Marx's famous passage in *The German Ideology* quoted above, and one of Siskind's themes is the general ease, abundance, and aesthetic interest of the daily round for the Sharanaua, male and female. But in keeping with Siskind's adoption of the then-current Marxist evolutionist frame, her epigraph, also from Marx, unromantically casts the Sharanahua to the bottom of the evolutionary ladder (while holding no brief, of course, for the bourgeois West): "Hence in one way the childlike world of the ancients appears to be superior; and this is so, as we seek for the closed shape, form and established limitation. The ancients provide a narrow satisfaction, whereas the modern world leaves us unsatisfied, or, where it appears to be satisfied with itself, is *vulgar* and *mean*."[131]

Siskind's is a thorough—one would now have to say old-fashioned in its rigor—ethnography. She pieces together oral history and extant documents to locate the Sharanahua historically as a migrant remnant of a population decimated by disease. She desribes the tropical forest ecosystem from which they wrest their food, housing, and medicines. She lays out the residential geography of Marcos, the village she studied, the Sharanahua kinship system, the division of labor, the details of foraging and horticultural tasks necessary for survival. She gives a picture of their cosmology, of birth and death practices, of the role of shamans, of ethnomedicine. And she describes the Sharanahua's episodic contact with the outside Peruvian and Western world—with traders and missionaries—and their apprehensions of others' lifeways. She manages all this, and a self-conscious account of her own emotional struggles in the field, her changing apprehensions of human social reality, in the compass of a relatively short and beautifully written text:

> Romance is a form of insanity in which one projects onto another a response to needs unmet and ignores the reality of the other person. The romance of fieldwork is no exception, where needs unmet in our own society for feeling connected to a group of people and experiencing a direct sensation of the physical environment lead one to romanticize primitive life. It is an anthropological mood: the despair of alienation in a cold world which seems to progress only further into dehumanization casts a golden light on the deep greens of the Amazon Basin and one envisons the direct earthly satisfactions of hunting in order to eat, weaving so as to lounge in a hammock, painting one's face in order to make love.[132]

Siskind's title signals not only her fealty to Marx, not only her analysis of the relatively leisured lives of the Sharanahua, but quite specifically her and their obsessions with hunting and with meat. Despite women's success at gathering and horticulture, despite the abundance of food, Sharanahua hunger for meat: "Small children, full of milk and plantains and manioc, scream at their mothers for meat." Sharanahua women, culturally forbidden to hunt, pressure men to do so. Women and men adhere to what Siskind asserts is the "traditional screen of most hunting societies, in which the participants conceive their own system to be that men hunt for women, rather than an exchange of products between the sexes."[133] Moreover, Siskind claims that Sharanahua institutions like the special hunt, in which women ritually send off particular men who are not their husbands to hunt, and in which celebration and sexual expression crown the men's return, prove that Sharanahua conceive "an economic structure in which meat is exchanged for sex. This is neither a 'natural' nor 'rational' exchange, since women produce at least as much of the food supply at Marcos, and a rational exchange would consist of viewing the economy as an exchange of women's production for men's. Certainly there is no evidence that women are naturally less interested in sex or more interested in meat than men are."[134]

Siskind, though, to a certain extent shares with the Sharanahua this "traditional cultural screen" on gendered issues. Despite the Sharanahua's sex segregation of tasks and her status as a woman, she attended to and analyzed male activities far more carefully than those associated with females. Moreover, she asserted a gender differential in Sharanahua lives and consciousness familiar to us from Margaret Mead's apprehensions of the Samoans in 1928. And in so doing, Siskind, in tune with the relatively unsophisticated feminist analysis of her era, simply failed to analyze her own evidence of Sharanahua women's power and strategizing.

Siskind explains that she could not observe men's hunting because of the proscription on women's presence. But she *did* not go gardening with women, perhaps because she avoided the trip as unpleasant, perhaps because Sharanahua "dislike . . . having any but a close kinswoman . . . take part in the harvesting of manioc."[135] Taking part in hallucinogenic drug ritual, however, was purely a male activity among the Sharanahua, and Siskind did so nevertheless. It was not only the case that Siskind believed the Sharanahua to value male activities more, and thus herself attempted to reflect that evaluation in her field research. Siskind also judged Sharanahua women to have uninteresting, vegetative lives with little of the fascinating angst and competitiveness she found among Sharanahua men: "There is no reason for strife between women at Marcos, aside from momentary personal quarrels, which are aired in gossip and tale-bearing. They need only be good daughters, provocative women, antagonistic wives. Their subsistence labor is, perhaps, hard and repetitive, but they are never in a position to fail, and they are secure with their mothers and sisters."[136]

This description uncannily echoes Mead's assertion that the Samoan girl "rests upon her 'pass' proficiency," that the "boy is faced with a more difficult dilemma than the girl." And, as in Mead's early case, Siskind is too good an ethnographer not to include information that the later analyst can use to complexify the image of "native" female lives. Only a year after Siskind published *To Hunt in the Morning,* Jane Collier and Louise Lamphere contributed articles to *Women, Culture and Society* that redrew the map of political anthropology to include domestic concerns, gossip, and kin disputes as key realms through which women across many societies—including our own—can and do express political agency. And indeed, during the period of Siskind's fieldwork, while men alone hunted among the Sharanahua, women not only butchered and cooked the meat, but also made all decisions about food distribution, an arena of high cultural anxiety, diplomacy, constant negotiation, and shifting power plays—in other words, local politics. Even the special hunt bears a different sexual politics interpretation when we consider that its very structure places the burden on women to force men to hunt often enough, where men did not need to bother their little heads about women's sufficient horticultural, child-care, and other labor—women thus appear the more burdened, more adult, more reliable sex. Moreover, women's adult mate choices might be seen to be more rather than less complex and angst-ridden than men's, as they had to decide in terms of hunting prowess and ability to cooperate with their kin (men moved into women's households upon marriage) as well as more personal attractions.[137]

Thus, while Siskind was quite concerned, and in a new, feminist way, with Sharanuhua gender relations, she neither espoused the somewhat romantic "native women better off" line nor engaged in the later style of analysis that assumed women's energetic expression of agency in all cultures. Like Laura Bohannan, Siskind commented explicitly on the limits to data gathering placed on her by her status as a woman: "To the extent that I wished to participate in the everyday activities of Marcos as a familiar equal, I had to accept the limits that Sharanahua culture places on women."[138] Unlike Bohannan, though, she saw gender asymmetry as one of the few bars to her deep pleasure and satisfaction in partaking in Sharanahua culture. Oddly enough, despite her self-consciousness about gender in the field—and the widespread and noisy feminist organizing and consciousness-raising going on in the United States during the period when she was writing *To Hunt in the Morning*—Siskind, as much by silence as by assertion, portrays her status as an American woman unproblematically equal to men, a simple countersign to the Sharanahua and larger Peruvian system. In her writing, Siskind and Sharanahua women are neither quite merged into the anthropological wallpaper nor fully separate from it: they are white American woman and dusky maidens as bas-reliefs.

FREUD IN THE RAIN FOREST

The Murphys, a year after Siskind, do respond explicitly to the American feminist renaissance. They assert that the "depth and magnitude of the modern transformation of sex roles in our own society is greater than most of us are able to perceive," and their last chapter, "Women and Men," comments at length on their perceptions of those transformations in the context of Mundurucú society. Their ethnography, as befits a book written as adjunct to earlier work on the same population, is far more explicitly about women and women's status than is *To Hunt in the Morning*.

The organizing frame of *Women of the Forest* is the assertion of a separate, solidary women's world among the Mundurucú—a world in which the most important work is done, in which young children are socialized, in which women simultaneously police one another's actions and articulate a "pragmatic" rebuttal to male ideology. Unlike the Sharanahua, whose households were cross-gender kin and affine groups, the Mundurucú among whom the Murphys lived organized separate living spaces: those for women and children, and one village men's house. Religious and political power inhered in maleness—special ritual flutes were kept hidden in the men's house—and women who flouted male authority were threatened with gang rape. On the other hand, Yolanda Murphy noted that there were no incidents of male violence against women during their fieldwork. She found that hard work and avoidance of "wanton" behavior was enforced by women themselves through strategic gossiping. Moreover, Mundurucú women were profoundly unimpressed with the "sacred flutes," overtly hostile even to mention of gang rape, openly resentful of men's more leisured lives, and opposed to separate men's and women's houses. Women were actively involved in the general Mundurucú shift from savanna horticultural life to nuclear family riverine settlements, based on male rubber tapping work, under the aegis of the Catholic Church.

Such social organizational material is the skeleton of *Women of the Forest.* The flesh, however, is a resolutely Freudian set of glosses on ethnographic observation. The Freudian themes of the Mundurucú origin myth are "so blatant that they come close to being a parody of psychoanalytic interpretation." The male domicile and rituals are "closely involved with the Oedipal transition and the transformation of the male child to man." Infant feeding on demand "appears conducive to the formation of oral-receptive type personalities"—except for the primal rage created by abrupt weaning to make way for the next sibling.[139] At the same time, however, the Murphys consider women's lives and apprehensions largely through a non-Freudian, middle-range prism that is itself complex and self-contradictory. On the one hand, as I have noted, Mundurucú women are seen as "secular and pragmatic in their orientation": they "cope" with male dominance "as a fact of life."[140] On the other hand, women's preference for the riverine rubber tappers' nuclear family settlements reveals not only a practical desire to escape male-dominant savanna social organization, but also their apparently innately acquisitive and manipulative natures: "But the women have been even more desirous of Western goods than the men. They absolutely need metal pots and pans, having almost forgotten how to make them of pottery; they, too, use knives and axes; and they also have an insatiable desire for clothing, ornaments, perfumes, and other such attractions. . . .

Wives cajole, nag, and even help their husbands—and, in the process, help to get them more deeply into debt."[141] This Old Testament narrative combined with *Femina economicus,* this portrait of the Mundurucú woman as sinful Eve/Delilah merged with the female rational actor, fits well with the story the Murphys have to tell about feminism in the United States.

The Murphy's vision of America is much like Margaret Mead's in 1928— a land inscribed solipsistically, a footnoteless space circumscribed by the analysts' time-, race-, and class-bound personal positions. They repeatedly refer to "the American woman," "the American wife," and the "modern American woman," who "never had such a unity" as the female solidary groups of the Mundurucú—never mind the vast history of women's union struggles, of poor women's mutual prestation, of the ubiquity of nineteenth-century and Progressive Era single-sex bonding. To their credit, the Murphys recognize that American women's increasing labor force participation predates the renaissance of feminism, but they ascribe that growth to "spiralling consumer demands" and see "a curious parallel here with the Mundurucú, whose desires for trade items and involvement in a credit system has also altered the division of labor." They seem entirely unaware of the roles of rising divorce rates and of men's declining real incomes in spurring American women's workplace investment. They declare that "one of the tendencies of an industrial economy is to universalize the labor force," and thus, "women will undoubtedly achieve much of the status of the male, but with it will come depersonalization of their selves and their work." Here, in a single sentence, the Murphys manage two large rhetorical operations. They neatly efface the enormous political struggle begun in the mid–nineteenth century that, even decades after the Murphys wrote, has come nowhere near achieving workplace equality. And they prefigure the Christopher Lasch/communitarian line that we need to return women to the home in order to fight the corrosive effects of industrial capitalism.[142] They add the Freudian-inflected point—as did Lasch—that "the fuller incorporation of women into the labor force will inevitably produce an earlier and more abrupt interruption of the mother-child bond." In contrast to Mead's sanguine Progressive Era recommendation that Americans could borrow bits of culture from the Samoans—could expand their emotional hothouse nuclear families and thus make life easier for children and adolescents—the Murphys see cultural tragedy in the Mundurucú extended kin example: "The extended family child-caring arrangements do teach a child to spread its affect, but these arrangements also teach them to spread it thinly. There is an air of constraint and reserve that shelters every Mundurucú, especially the men, and a kind of personal disinvolvement and distance that permeates their relations with others."[143]

Having declared that "there is room for doubt that [the women's movement] will be an effective means, in the long run, of unifying women," and having pronounced doom upon both stay-at-home and working women, the Murphys briskly change the subject to the sources of male domination. These, in the end, reduce to male Oedipal self-defense in the face of the "terrible bond" to the powerful mother and the "powerful psychic forces that continually press to reverse his advance. . . . Regression poses the ultimate goal of a return to a warm amniotic oblivion." The Murphys sum up this interpretation of male dominance as a merely symbolic psychological screen that hides female power with an offhand remark of Margaret Mead's: "If the men really were all that powerful, they wouldn't need such rigamarole." They end the book with a paean to "woman as custodian and perpetuator of life itself," neatly aligning themselves with the growing women's culture trend in 1970s American life.[144] For the Murphys, male domination is a functional and psychic necessity for men and all children, the epiphenomenon of proper female childrearing and the illusory political carapace over women's "real" power as the reproducers of humanity. Mundurucú and American women are sisters under the skin, seduced by bright commodities from crucial female bonding. Native women sort of better off.

Of the two ethnographies, then, despite a few counterexamples like the Murphys' intelligent, more anthropological consideration of gossip and their clear understanding of the importance of female control over food distribution, *To Hunt in the Morning* is by far the superior book in design and execution. Siskind lays out a vastly more detailed, more carefully historicized ethnographic picture and simultaneously avoids the Murphys' banal and unsupported generalizations about both field site and home. If Siskind is comparatively reticent, it is the reticence of intellectual care. She neither portrays the Sharanahua as exemplary primitives (although they may, in her scheme, evoke some of our ancestors) nor sketches a solipsist's America against which to compare them. She undervalues Sharanahua women's agency but gives us the information with which to make our own interpretations. Reviews of the two books, however, by no means articulated these points. The patterning of the reviews, instead, reflected political contestations inside and outside the academy in the mid-1970s Anglophone West.

Most astonishing is a series of mostly British red-baiting reviews of *To Hunt in the Morning* attacking Siskind for "theoretical confusions" (*Ms.* magazine), "a lack of any theoretical framework" (*Times Literary Supplement*), and for being "strangely naïve" (the *Economist*) and "almost devoid of information" (*New Statesman*). (Siskind probably received so many British reviews because she published with Oxford University Press.) Such statements are obviously purely ideological: whatever Siskind's flaws, her theoretical frame is clear and well argued, and she offers a very thick description indeed of the Sharanahua. These reviewers, though, seem to have slightly different axes to grind beyond their common reflexive anti-Marxism. The journalist Jane Kramer, who praises Siskind for offering "some of the best small portraits of women in a primitive culture that we are likely to get for a long time," forwards an anti-intellectual vision of ideal ethnography as like her own elegant journalism. She seems to object not so much to Marxism's politics as to its demands on the mind. The British reviewers seem motivated at least partly by national chauvinism—the *Times Literary Supplement's* anonymous writer, for example, objects to Siskind's "appalling English usage, of which the publisher should also be thoroughly ashamed." The British reviewers, as well, unanimously exhibit sheer refusal to credit the genre of popular ethnography: Stephen Hugh-Jones in *Man*, for example, complains that "by making her monograph appeal to a non-academic audience, Siskind has also made it rather thin. The account of social structure is inadequate. . . . as a serious monograph on the Sharanahua it is very disappointing." Mary Douglas, as well, in the *New Statesman*, reflects not only her own late-career lurch rightward but also a rooted English distaste for the autobiographical voice and any mention of sexuality in ethnography. Even though Siskind's self-reflexivity is entirely disciplined to her theoretical points, and even though, unlike the Murphys, she barely discusses sex and certainly makes no claims concerning positions, frequency, relative enjoyment, &c., Douglas feels free to brand her with the contemptuous British phrase coined to describe Margaret Mead's overly popular style: "This is in the wind-whispering-in-the-palm-trees tradition of anthropology." The anonymous reviewer for the *Economist*, however, defines Siskind's Marxist political economic analysis as silly maundering outside her proper anthropological purview of "exotic" shamanic ritual: "Outside his [!] field, an anthropologist's view can be strangely naïve. Sharanahua means 'the good people'; and, for Mrs. Siskind, the white man's world around them is virtually made up of 'baddies.' 'The tragedy of Indian cultures is not their vanishing,' she concludes, 'it is the misery of the societies they enter, a tragedy in which we are also trapped.' Quotations from Marx, which begin and end her book, ram the message home."[145]

Siskind also received a few serious, straightforward reviews. Dolores Newton, in the *American Anthropologist*, provides a good précis of the narrative and analysis in *To Hunt in the Morning*, noting especially Siskind's historical understanding of the increased integrative role of hallucinogenic drug taking for in-marrying men in the postplague, migrant social setting. She notes that the text is "intended for a lay audience" and recommends it for both anthropology courses and the general reader. Daniel Gross, in *Reviews in Anthropology,* offers a lengthy appreciation of Siskind's contributions as well as a wrongheaded but collegial argument against her "dialectics." Warwick Bray, in the *Journal of Latin American Studies,* hopes that there will be "a more extensive monograph in the future" but commends *To Hunt in the Morning* as "a rare, sensitive, and personal book" and notes "the amount of information packed into 214 pages."[146]

Looking at the reviews as a whole, negative, positive, and mixed, one thread of interpretation stretches cleanly across the set: insofar as they discuss Siskind's interpretation of gender, all reviewers approbate her. None is the least concerned with her insufficient attention to women's activities and agency. Even the most deprecating of reviewers is willing to "give" Siskind gender. Hugh-Jones labels her analysis of gender relations "one of the most interesting and successful parts of the book." Mary Douglas considers Siskind's description of the sex antagonism of the special hunt, alone of all Siskind's contributions, "worth mentioning."[147]

Despite the similarities between *To Hunt in the Morning* and *Women of the Forest,* the Murphys' reviews were utterly different from Siskind's, and this is in large part because the reviewers themselves were drawn from very different academic precincts and published in quite different venues (there are only three overlapping journals). While Siskind was lacerated by cranky English and anti-Marxist American anthropologists in standard anthropological and some middlebrow journals, the Murphys, having signaled their topic by putting "women" in their title, were considered largely by feminist anthropologists in anthropology—but also sociology and natural history—journals. And these feminists, well versed in contemporary debates, found *Women of the Forest*'s gender analysis distinctly wanting.

Judith Shapiro, now president of Barnard College, then an assistant professor at the University of Chicago, and herself also having done fieldwork among Brazilian Indians, reviewed the Murphys in both the *American Journal of Sociology* and *Natural History.* Shapiro was gracious, praising the Murphys for risking "being charged with subjectivism or ethnocentrism by putting much of themselves into their study" and producing "a particularly moving and thought-provoking analysis of sex roles and sex identity." Nevertheless, in both reviews she scored them for their radical denial of the actualities of Mundurucú male dominance. Referring in the *American Journal of Sociology* to the then-well-known formulation of Marshall Sahlins's, she stated baldly: "I do not think that differences in world view between men and women should be put in terms of an opposition between culture and practical reason." Shapiro laid out her argument more accessibly in *Natural History:*

> This familiar argument, which grants women an inside track on the course toward existential salvation at the same time it denies them a psychic life as complex as that of males, is one that I am reluctant to accept. I have similar reservations about the Murphys' tendency to view culture as an elaborate scheme devised by men to escape from their own insignificence. Do they really mean to reduce the cultural dimensions of human behavior to some kind of psychological defense mechanism? And would they want to have to defend the position that the world view of women is more natural and less culturally determined than that of men? I think not.[148]

Joan Bamberger, in *Science,* made the same point: "Should public displays of sexual antagonism be regarded as merely cover-ups for male fears of inadequacy? Must the men's house and its secret rituals be viewed as fantasies constructed by the men to fool themselves and women into thinking that men are inherently superior beings?" Bamberger also objected to the Murphys' too-facile comparison of Mundurucú and American women: "It does seem specious to assert, when so little is known about the psychology of the Mundurucú woman, that there is a commonality, a 'sisterhood,' . . . between all women which cross-cuts cultural boundaries and is readily identifiable on other grounds, presumably, than biological ones."[149]

Judith K. Brown's criticisms in *Reviews in Anthropology* were even more stringent: Brown scored the Murphys' lack of scholarly citations, bibliography, and index, found their theoretical framework "distinctly anachronistic," complained bitterly about their "heavy-handed psychoanalytic interpretations," and deemed their portrait of American women a set of "unpardonable . . . unsupported generalizations."[150]

Rose Somerville, in *Contemporary Sociology,* provided a specifically feminist sociological critique of *Women of the Forest.* That is, she complained, as did Shapiro, Bamberger, and Brown, about the Murphys' efforts to claim that Mundurucú women really were advantaged compared with the men. But she jibbed especially at their attempts at American comparisons: "Defense of the status quo extends to the American scene. The authors state that in American society where women are moving from the home to the marketplace 'to the extent that the escape from the house is successful, the position of the woman at the affective center of the family will be weakened . . .' There is no suggestion that shared affective roles might enrich the lives of both sexes and have [a] positive impact on offspring."

Even Peter Rivière, in a flippantly nasty review in the *Times Literary Supplement,* complained that "the Murphys' main failing is that they do not tell us how Mundurucú women see, understand and order their social and natural worlds."[151] Only Jane Kramer in *Ms.* and Katherine Weist in *Ethnohistory* found much to favor in the book. Feminist reviewers in general, highly aware of the Murphys' retrogressive and counterempirical interpretation, were unwilling to "give" them gender analysis. And yet such was the confused, broadly amnesiac, and vaguely celebratory spirit of the times that, despite the reviews, the book—since it was written engagingly and accessibly and was about "exotic women"—did extremely well as a course-adoption text for introductory anthropology courses, justifying in 1985 a second edition with additional material.

BORN-AGAIN PROGRESSIVE

Margaret Mead, in publishing her autobiographical memoir *Blackberry Winter* one year after the 1971 American Anthropological Association debacle, was able to capitalize on this fuzzy 1970s zeitgeist to rehabilitate herself, to erase the public record through hitching her wagon to the rising liberal feminist star as other radicalisms of the 1960s slowly faded.[152] Appearing to universal acclaim, *Blackberry Winter,* written with affecting nostalgia and replete with charming period photos of family, friends, and colleagues past and present, effectively determined Mead's public persona for more than a decade until the publication of Derek Freeman's attack in 1983. The amnesiac middlebrow media that would so trumpet Freeman's book on Mead—the *New York Times, Saturday Review, Newsweek,* even the *Wall Street Journal*—published elegiac reviews lauding Mead on her own terms as "everybody's grandmother," "a respected, well-liked international figure," "a woman for mankind." (Among many others, historian Rosalind Rosenberg, biographer Jane Howard, and the filmmakers Ann Peck and Virginia Yans all used the book's structure and material in preparing later accounts of Mead's life.)[153] *Blackberry Winter* fit squarely into a growing genre of popular middlebrow publishing—the prominent older woman's memoir—that took advantage of newly feminist readers' hunger for inspirational literature. Autobiographical texts like Mead's and the writer Lillian Hellman's 1973 *Pentimento* were received as occasions to honor our foremothers, brave women who had succeeded in a man's world and whose insights must be valuable.

Mead's politics in *Blackberry Winter* followed those we have seen her explicate in her dialogue with James Baldwin in 1970 and are a remarkable—and certainly heretofore unremarked—foreshadowing of many contemporary claims to expertise and superior insight on the basis of "positionality." That is, Mead saw herself as having a "correct" line on race and other social issues because of her "proper" Yankee provenance and her parents' social science background:

> When our neighbors in the many places we lived during my childhood behaved in ways that were different from ours and from one another, I learned that this was because of their life experience and the life experiences of their ancestors and mine—not because of the differences in the color of our skin or the shape of our heads. . . . And if the question, "Who is then neighbor unto him?" had not been part of my grandmother's religious experience, it is possible that neither my mother's nor my grandmother's concern for the human race would have made sense to me. And certainly I would not have interpreted in the particular way I did my father's conviction that the most important thing any person could do was to add to the world's store of knowledge.

At the same time, Mead pandered to still-popular youth radicalism—and this took extraordinary chutzpah considering her appalling public behavior only a year earlier—in claiming that her memoir was an analogue to antiwar street protest: "I can try to explain, I can try to lay my life on the line, as you speak of laying your bodies on the line." Mead neglected to lay on that public line, however, her long record as a Cold Warrior—her condemnation of antinuclear protest, her red-baiting of unions, and her postwar promilitary propagandizing, not to mention her efforts to quash protest against anthropological complicity in the war in Southeast Asia—and instead generously larded her text with references to her fellow traveler actions during her college years in the 1920s and with high-minded claims for the Progressive political implications of anthropological research: "I have spent most of my life studying the lives of other peoples, faraway peoples, so that Americans might better understand themselves."[154]

Like the Murphys, Mead in *Blackberry Winter* accommodated herself to new feminist interest in women as women in a male-dominated world but did not actually take the stance that such domination was wrong and should be abolished. Instead, she celebrated herself as a link in a chain of superior, politically progressive intellectuals, largely female—her mother, grandmother, daughter, and granddaughter—in effect melding the cozy warmth of affectionate family memoir with claims to authority through

pioneering status: "I was brought up within my own culture two generations ahead of time. . . . I grew up ahead of my time. . . . Today, young
people, young enough to be my own great-grandchildren, often say, 'You
belong to us.'" Thus, the structure of the book sandwiched middle chapters
on different exotic fieldwork experiences between "family portrait" beginnings and endings. "My Father and Academia," "On Being a Granddaughter," and "The Pattern My Family Made for Me" clustered in part 1, to be
matched with "On Having a Baby," "Catherine, Born in Wartime," and "On
Being a Grandmother" in part 3.[155]

Mead's specific references to issues of Western women's status are fascinatingly revealing, and of two sorts. (Incidentally, she does not refer at all
to the lives or status of "primitive women." As we can see from Robin
Morgan's and the Murphys's references to her off-the-cuff remarks on
"women's nature," Mead remained to the end of her life outside the concerns and scholarship of the new feminist anthropology of the 1970s.) On
the one hand, she narrates a series of autobiographical vignettes in which
dominant males attempted to limit or confine her, vignettes designed to
capture the contemporary public mood, as had been her assurances in the
postwar years that she always wore skirts and never tried to do men's jobs.
Her father, "hoping to get someone to back up his new view that I need
not go to college," called in the local physician, who said, "Look at those
little hands! Never did a day's work in their life and never will! You'd
maybe make a good mistress, but a poor wife. You'd better study nursing."
At DePauw, she rebels against the sexual code: "I neither wanted to do bad
work in order to make myself attractive to boys nor did I want them to
dislike me for doing good work." Later, the anthropologist Edward Sapir
"told me I would do better to stay at home and have children than to go
off to the South Seas to study adolescent girls." Franz Boas himself tries to
dissuade her: "He thought it was too dangerous, and recited a sort of litany
of young men who had died or been killed while they were working outside the United States."[156]

On the other hand, Mead repeatedly undercuts this trope of the rebellious feminist acting against male confinement of female ambition by defining a reduced professional "place" for herself and by stigmatizing feminism itself as proof of emotional instability. Little changed since her
grotesquely antifeminist pronouncements of the 1940s and 1950s, Mead
blithely commends "my anthropological field choices—not to compete
with men in male fields, but instead to concentrate on the kinds of work
that are better done by women." And again and again, she identifies female
anger against male domination as improper, an emotion to which she—

the arbiter of psychological health—succumbed only a few scattered times in the course of her long life. Mead refers to her grandmother admiringly as "unquestionably feminine—small and dainty and pretty and wholly without masculine protest or feminist aggrievement." The doctor's diagnosis of Mead's incapacity for college work catapulted her into "one of the few fits of feminist rage I have ever had." In a discussion of her unhappy year of unpopularity at DePauw, Mead, echoing her earlier condescension to James Baldwin, reveals her rationale for condemning anger against domination, an extraordinary psychologistic dumbing-down of Hegel's master-slave discussion. Inegalitarian social orders, Mead declares, produce "irreversible character damage" among both oppressor and oppressed. While she goes on to proclaim that "today no argument can stand that supports unequal opportunity or any intrinsic disqualification for sharing in the whole of life," Mead, still the Progressive social engineer after four decades, conveniently fails to indicate how gender, race, class, or other inequalities have ever been defeated without large numbers of human beings risking such "character damage"—without widespread anger, organizing, protest.[157]

Never behindhand in robustly declaring for those who had already fought and won, however, Mead spent the remaining years of her life fairly closely identified with then-dominant liberalism and liberal feminism. I saw her appear with left-liberal environmentalist Barry Commoner on the Berkeley campus in 1974. A few years later, she supported Jimmy Carter's centrist Democratic presidential candidacy and sent him an endless stream of advice once he occupied the White House. She was invited to Houston as a special guest speaker for the feminist summit in 1977, introduced as the woman who "began the sexual revolution," and "the grandmother of the women's movement," and proceeded to declare roundly that "the United States . . . is endangering the world most, and it has the greatest chance to save the world." These gestures, nevertheless, did not prevent her from fighting fiercely (and successfully) against a 1976 American Anthropological Association resolution to condemn sociobiology's inherent racism and sexism or, in 1978, from ordering Australian novelist Shirley Hazzard to stop writing and speaking critically of sex discrimination and corruption at the United Nations.[158]

Given this extraordinarily self-contradictory political record, it is no wonder that even Mead's daughter, Mary Catherine Bateson, wrote of her that "in a life lived in an era of introspection and self-doubt, her conviction of undivided motives was distinctive, an innocence that leaves me sometimes skeptical and sometimes awed."[159] Mead, as we have seen, was indeed surprisingly intellectually and politically consistent in certain ways. She never forsook the epistemological frame of top-down Progressive Era social engineering, of the proper political reign of "experts"—thus the grand irony of this chapter's epigraph. Mead's "small group of thoughtful committed citizens" were citizens in the ancient Athenian sense, the tiny group of rulers, never the protesting ruled-over.[160] Nor, once her intellectual twig was bent in a psychologizing direction in the 1920s, did Mead's interpretive interests ever allow her to consider political and economic frames of reference. Mead was indeed, lifelong, the consummate American anthropologist in the public sphere whose statements on "cultural difference" always adroitly avoided contesting—or even admitting—the economic and political power inherent in how that difference is interpreted. More positively, Mead worked for a half-century, and very successfully, for "the spread of the concept of culture as socially learned patterns of thought and behavior," as Marvin Harris told biographer Jane Howard.[161] And however sloppily she may have filled the role, she also stood consistently for the necessity of anthropology's extra-ivory-tower, public sphere role in twentieth-century American politics. Peter Worsley summarized that contribution as playing "a major part in persuading a whole generation that the society we live in is not necessarily the only possible model, let alone the best, or that the apparently bizarre or irrational behavior of people in unfamiliar societies is perfectly rational and understandable, and represents just one more way of solving problems which are common to all human societies."[162]

What Mead, as these chapters have shown in some detail, never stood for—despite widespread popular and anthropological misconceptions—was genuine equality for women and political action to bring it about, whether in the West or in any other society. Nor did she ever interpret her first book to be about women's status, or even the status of Samoan women. For example, not a single one of her five subsequent prefaces to *Coming of Age*, from 1939 to 1972, even mentions these issues. The closest Mead approaches questions of women and change in these texts is the sentimental comment in 1972 that "the little girls whom I studied are buxom grandmothers still dancing light-footed as Samoan matrons do."[163]

Unlike some anthropologists and much of popular culture, Mead was fundamentally unconcerned with the dusky maiden, whether as icon or as living female human being—although she was willing, as we have seen, to exploit popular "noble and nasty savage" imagery to enhance her own public sphere visibility. After her death in 1978, hagiographic misreadings of Mead continued to emanate from scholarly and popular venues. With the coming of the Reagan era, though, new readings of "the primitive woman," of anthropology, and of Mead would rise to contest this relatively stable image. Anthropology would become far more central to popular political culture, even more entwined in contested structures of feeling embedding notions of race, class, and gender—in competing American morality plays prescribing either our proper modernity or our desperate need for antimodernist retrenchment.

EVERY WOMAN HER OWN ANTHROPOLOGIST

Gender, Revanchism, and the Fissioning Public Sphere

Margaret Mead died on November 15, 1978, and was broadly eulogized inside her life's profession and in the wider public sphere.[1] The *New York Times*—noting obsequies from President Carter, United Nations secretary Kurt Waldheim, New York mayor Ed Koch, and Planned Parenthood president Faye Wattleton—devoted two front-page stories to Mead's life and work, stories whose themes closely followed her own self-created personal history. They portrayed Mead as an intrepid polymath always vastly ahead of her time, always under attack as "a woman in a male-dominated discipline" and for "writ[ing] her conclusions in a way that non-specialists could understand and [drawing] bold comparisons between American ways and those of very different cultures." But in fact, as we have seen, 1920s anthropological reaction to *Coming of Age* was largely positive. Certainly no fellow guild member then dismissed the book as "heresy," as the *Times* claimed. It was only after World War II, and despite her increasingly vociferous antifeminism in the 1950s, that Mead really lost caste in a masculinizing profession and larger culture.

Indeed, Mead had attained iconic public sphere status over the course of the 1970s due to her new association with liberal politics on "counterculture" issues. More important, though—despite her lackluster feminism in that era—Mead was adopted by the women's movement and inside anthropology as a respected foremother. The *Times* obituary story rewrote this history with a flourish, describing her as "a general among the foot soldiers of modern feminism."[2] Once again, an empty generation past the era of Jane Addams, Eleanor Roosevelt, and others, it had become possible to lionize women of accomplishment, and Mead had accepted lionization with gusto. Given her New York residence and Museum of Natural History venue, her alliance with the Carter administration (Mead corresponded frequently with Carter, always signing herself "working with you and for you"), and her other Washington connections, she was a particular favorite of the *New York Times* and the *Washington Post.* The *Times* ran an unsigned editorial on her seventy-fifth birthday, celebrating her "sparkling career" and asserting that "her leadership derives from the freshness of her thinking and the breadth of her personality." The *Post* also noted that birthday, sending a young reporter to New York to interview her for a puff piece announcing her "visitation" (like royalty) to give the distinguished lecture at the American Anthropological Association meetings in Washington that year. *Redbook* published a "conversation" between Mead and First Lady Rosalynn Carter the following year.[3]

Mead died at the midpoint of Jimmy Carter's single troubled term, during the period that witnessed the first unravelings of the tenuous power of a centrist liberalism, an unraveling that culminated in the rightist rollback of the 1980 presidential election. This rightward slide has continued and is part of the general weakening of economically egalitarian politics worldwide and the consolidation of the power of global capitalism. As the beginnings of this process took place in conjunction with other demographic and economic shifts, it heralded as well the downswing of American anthropology's institutional (although not symbolic) power and influence. We have come full circle to the contemporary Halloween costume era of anthropology's America and American anthropology, and it is time to catch and reweave these varied political economic and cultural threads.

THE CARTER AND REAGAN YEARS

The post-Vietnam 1970s are a confusing and often ignored period of recent American history, one in which the cultural left and economic right hands often proceeded in partial ignorance of one another. Popular culture and public opinion seemed to indicate a firming-up of a liberal political tilt, especially on social issues—liberal feminism, gay rights, minority rights, ecology—that would later be contained by the "identity politics" rubric. At the same time, the end of the draft and the war eroded the middle-class base of progressive politics, while, as we have seen, federal and state policy encouraged urban job flight, the real estate speculation spiral, and a general deterioration of urban infrastructures and of life chances for working-class and impoverished Americans. Unnoticed in the thrill of the Watergate scandal, Nixon's resignation, and the end of the Vietnam War, real incomes in the United States peaked in 1973 and have declined continuously in the years since.[4]

Jimmy Carter, former Democratic governor of Georgia with a segregationist past, was elected president in 1976 on a platform stressing competence—which translated to cutting social programs in the new "era of limits." While Carter is now remembered by apologists for the rightist surge of the Democratic Party as a gutless liberal who allowed the continued loss of "lunchpail Democrats," his administration's domestic policy was actually more conservative than Richard Nixon's: AFDC cutbacks began under Carter, and it was Carter who refused to fight against the Hyde amendment, which outlawed the use of federal money to pay for abortions for poor women. When, in 1977, a delegation of feminists protested to him the unfairness of denying access to medical services on a class basis, he memorably riposted, "Some things in life are just unfair."[5]

Carter's foreign policy was equally compounded of mixed liberal and conservative intent and ineffectual follow-through. While championing the new international language of human rights, he supported both Nicaraguan and Iranian despots. Lacking, however, the nerve Nixon displayed in bombing Cambodia and in supporting the Chilean generals who assassinated the democratically elected president Salvador Allende in 1973, Carter stood by while the Sandinistas and the anti-Shah protestors won governance of their countries in 1979 (although the administration's diplomatic care of the former Shah led directly to the growth of Khomeini's popularity and to the Iranian hostage crisis that lost him reelection).[6]

In Africa, a complicated intersection of the needs to placate black American voters, to maintain access to Nigerian oil, and to respond to American public outrage over the repression of the Soweto uprising and over Rhodesia's white irridentism led to early Carter administration shifts toward supporting United Nations resolutions attacking the racist regime in South Africa and mandating an arms boycott. The United States also joined other UN states in protesting South Africa's illegal annexation of Namibia (South-West Africa). Nevertheless, Cold War prerogatives took hold with the arrival of Cuban troops to aid Angolan nationalists in the wake of the collapse of Portuguese colonialism: the administration then muffled its criticism of the South African regime's expansionism, massacres, and fundamental denial of civil rights. "The message was clear," wrote William Minter in *Destructive Engagement*, "in the U.S. policy context, the Cuban 'threat' to Africa far outweighted the threat from South Africa."[7]

Inside ivy walls, academics from the mid-1970s on began to experience pressure from the new conservative institutions bankrolled by the New Right—campus newspapers, student spies in the classroom, a barrage of criticism of higher education in mass media. Campus atmosphere shifted due to other developments as well. Within anthropology, quantitative Cassandras warned in mid-decade of the disastrous effect of declining 1960s birthrates on college enrollment figures and thus academic job markets from the 1980s on. In addition, the war's end and anxieties about the economic future cut into undergraduate anthropology enrollments in colleges and universities across the United States: B. A. degrees in anthropology peaked in 1975, moving precipitously downward—with a one-year blip in 1978—to a new nadir in Reagan's second term, slowly rising again toward 1970s levels thereafter.[8] We have returned to the stage of bringing out number and measure in the year of dearth examined in the first chapter.

The radical project in American anthropology also slowed over the last years of the decade. The most important anthologies representing progressive anthropological thought on both sides of the Anglophone Atlantic— Dell Hymes's *Reinventing Anthropology* and Talal Asad's *Anthropology and the Colonial Encounter*—appeared in the early 1970s and were not followed by work garnering equal attention. *Reinventing Anthropology* in particular was subject to widespread criticism—it was certainly a less intellectually rigorous, more various, more hortatory, more intentionally popular collection than its British cousin, which was animated by the common project of reinvestigating ethnography in the light of the political economy of colonizer and colonized at the time of research. In the same years, Diane Lewis published a long essay to the same effect, "Anthropology and Colonialism," in *Current Anthropology,* and Francis Hsu wrote a critical piece in the *American Anthropologist* on the innate racism and parochialism of American anthropology.[9]

Such broadside calls for reform and reanimation faded over the decade as disciplinary economic insecurity became widespread, and energy was drained into local-level wars of position in departments and institutions. (One good indication of this shift is the transformation of the discipline's *Newsletter* over two decades from a raffish site of political contestation into a nervously professional shop journal.) The progressive United States urban anthropologists of the early-decade upsurge, as I have noted, both lost access to the public sphere and to jobs in the discipline as hard times and conservative revanchism took hold with the turn of the decade. Even the major progressive publishing event of the early 1980s, Eric Wolf's *Europe and the People without History,* gained good initial reviews but was then largely dropped both from middlebrow discourse and university curricula.

Two further shifts exacerbated the deterioration of this critical wave in American anthropology. The first, the proliferation since the 1960s of sub-disciplines such as feminist, ecological, economic, development, legal, symbolic, and medical anthropologies was simultaneously a response to intellectual and political shifts and an opportunistic growth in the direction of available research funding and job opportunities. Specialization, at the same time, drew anthropologists centrifugally away from one another and from the substance and politics of the discipline. Eric Wolf, in fact, wrote critically of this fissioning in a *New York Times* editorial in 1980, "They Divide and Subdivide, and Call It Anthropology": "Specialization brought fragmentation, which in turn has raised a troublesome question: What, these days, constitutes the discipline of anthropology? . . . What was once a secular church of believers in the primacy of Culture has now become a holding company of diverse interests, defined by what members do rather than by what they do it for."[10] While it may have been complicit with this larger centrifugal process, anthropological work flying under the feminist flag gained measurably in sophistication and intellectual reach during this period. Three end-of-decade anthologies can stand for this extraordinary scholarly florescence.

Patricia Caplan and Janet Bujra's *Women United, Women Divided* brought together ethnographic work focusing on the social organizational processes channeling solidarity or division among women in a wide variety of cultural and economic settings. This focus, with its inevitable emphasis on hierarchy among women along the lines of generation, status, class, race and ethnicity, nationality &c., provided a strong counter to cultural feminist presuppositions of women's innately nurturant solidarity with one another. Then, Carol MacCormack and Marilyn Strathern's *Nature, Culture, and Gender*, an extended set of anthropological responses to Sherry Ortner's 1974 article asserting the universal human tendency to associate women with nature and men with culture, to the depreciation of women's status vis-à-vis men, both provided important ethnographic material and inaugurated a necessary history-of-thought dimension in feminist work in anthropology. The ethnographic chapters both summarily disproved the notion that nature/culture: female/male is a universal and demonstrated the fact that many societies, in any event, do not construe nature and culture in the dichotomous Western manner. The history-of-thought contributions investigated the European Enlightenment development of "nature" as a category of challenge and development of its complicated gendering, part and parcel of an elite male counter to female efforts to gain power and status in that tumultuous political era. Finally, the contributors to Kate Young et al.'s *Of Marriage and the Market* concerned themselves with an explicitly political economic investigation of the connections among kinship, reproduction, labor, and larger economic change for women in a variety of kinds of states around the globe. Pieces dealt, for example, with Western kinship, female status, and capitalist economic functioning, and with the multiple social effects of multinational corporate establishment of world market factories exploiting Third World women's labor.[11]

In biological anthropology, this new feminist effort to eschew easy, ahistorical answers, really to consider gender in all its contingency, was paralleled by sophisticated work both in evolutionary biology and in primate behavior studies. In addition, Donna Haraway and Misia Landau provided history-of-science contextualizations of the field, pointing out the ways in which, respectively, different primatological and human evolutionary narratives complexly reflected the politics of their eras. Unfortunately, all this research received far less attention, inside and outside the academy, than the rise of feminist sociobiological perspectives, first popularized by Sarah Blaffer Hrdy in *The Woman That Never Evolved*.[12] One simple shift—the presumption of the "agency" and "strategizing" of female as well as male DNA, nonhuman primates, and so on—determined the feminist sociobiological perspective. This vision of universal competition for reproductive success well fit the dog-eat-dog ethos of the Reagan era. As Susan Sperling comments: "Feminist sociobiologists have retold the story of evolution, giving females an active role, but in using the old narrative structures they tell us little about the development of complex behaviors and their context-dependent expressions. The new female primate is dressed for success and lives in a troop that resembles the modern corporation: now everyone gets to eat power lunches on the savanna." Sperling points out that "without a sophisticated grasp of human social behavior [biological anthropologists] have little to offer the social sciences by way of theorizing about biological 'roots' of complex human behaviors."[13] Despite the concerted efforts of many scientists, however, it was the reductionist, anthropomorphizing, demonstrably false sociobiological perspective that won the popularity stakes in the American public sphere of the 1980s and 1990s, largely taking over from the misogynist ethology of the 1960s and 1970s and dominating science reporting in newspapers and magazines as well as television.[14]

Finally, the 1980s rise of postmodernism across the disciplines deflected progressive concerns in anthropology from the realm of the political to the realms of discourse on the political. Useful as some postmodern work may be, its exclusive focus on text and language and its disdain for the strictures of realism have encouraged an anti-intellectual failure both to attend to the

theoretical genealogies of its "discoveries" and to engage with lived material realities at home and abroad. Its antiscientism, as well, has exacerbated
the dominance of bad science in the public sphere. The postmodern world
of pastiche, of appearance, the culture of forgetting, of light-hearted failure
to observe scholarly rigor, provided an extraordinary fit—all the while protesting its radical opposition—for the shell game of American public culture in the Reagan years.

Unlike the short Carter period, the Reagan-Bush decade of the 1980s
has been extensively memorialized in scholarship and popular culture.
There is widespread agreement about the dreadful weltanschauung of the
period: the return of mindless masculinist jingoism, the permission from
above for newly explicit domestic racism, the naked celebration of capitalist exploitation and of the display of wealth in the face of rapidly increasing
want, the public pandering to (and private scorn for) the demands of the
Christian Right for sexual and lifestyle repression.[15]

Less remarked are the actual political economic shifts of the period,
shifts that have reversed the domestic social democratic policies of a half-
century. The Reagan and Bush administrations' tax cuts for the wealthy,
war against unions and working people, gutting of social programs, reversal of civil rights enforcement, and massive military buildup have produced a nation more economically unequal than at any time since 1929,
with the greatest concentrations of wealth and poverty and the smallest
middle class of any contemporary industrial state. The combination of tax
cuts and military expansion also vastly increased the federal deficit, setting
the stage for mean-spirited calls for further social program cuts into the
present.[16]

The emptying-out of the middle sectors of the American class ladder
and the cutting of the never-adequate social safety net have had an intensified effect on white American women and all minority Americans, as we
saw in chapter 2. The male/female pay gap, memorialized in the 1970s in
the feminist "59 cents" buttons, has shrunk considerably, but most of this
shrinkage is due to falling male, not rising female incomes. A few decades
ago, white men with high school degrees earned more than white women
with college degrees; now they earn almost as much. And these men still
earn more than black and Latino women college graduates. While some
women have been able to take advantage of the work and professional
opportunities opened up by second-wave feminist activism, in the mid-
1990s, three-quarters of all working women earned less than twenty-five
thousand dollars annually. (Both white women and minorities of both
sexes who break into middle management positions then fail to be pro-

moted, according to a government-commissioned 1995 report; white men, who in the mid-1990s were 29 percent of the labor force, held 95 percent of all senior management positions in the private sector.)[17]

It is those at the bottom of the class ladder who have been most severely affected by Carter, Reagan, and Bush policies; and it is those Americans who are most vilified in resurgent "blame the victim" ideology—the assertion of "ghetto pathologies"—that denies widely available political economic facts. Minimum wage workers, almost two-thirds of whom are women (and only 15 percent of whom are adolescents) earn about two thousand dollars a year less, in real dollars, than did such workers in the 1960s. For those women with children who are thus unable to work, the real value of AFDC payments plus food stamps shrank by more than a fifth from the early 1970s to the mid-1980s. And housing has become both prohibitively expensive and considerably more scarce. In only the first five years of the Reagan regime, for example, new housing starts financed by the Department of Housing and Urban Development shrank from 183,000 to 28,000.[18] The expanding homeless population, who Reagan actually claimed chose their degradation as a "lifestyle," has been literally created by these policy shifts, shifts whose numbers have the clarity of an elementary school arithmetic lesson. And yet formerly liberal social scientists like Christopher Jencks actually assert that it is the homeless themselves who have created their situation. We have moved, over the past two decades, from a semiwelfare state to a naked free market nation (with increased socialism for the rich)—and a significant *nomenklatura* has shifted its interpretation to suit.[19]

Reagan and Bush administration foreign policy mirrored its domestic face: a fierce war against those unable to fight back. United States forces invaded the tiny Caribbean island of Grenada in 1983, bombed Libya in 1986, invaded Panama in 1989, and carried out the Gulf War against Iraq in 1991. Eric Hobsbawm has argued that the first three acts were "gestures of military power against sitting targets," and were designed more for domestic consumption, to heal the wound of losing the Vietnam War, "rather than as a practical attempt to re-establish the world power balance."[20]

In southern Africa, despite increasing domestic protest throughout the 1980s, the Reagan and Bush administrations pursued the policy of "constructive engagement," that is, reassuring the Pretoria regime, denigrating its opponents as Communists, and funneling money and support to South Africa's surrogates in regional wars. Congressional protest leading to the Anti-Apartheid Act of 1985, effective grassroots campaigns to disinvest state, city, and college funds from firms doing business in South Africa, and dissent from European allies ultimately hobbled this policy. The white government agreed to free elections, and in April, 1994, Nelson Mandela was elected president. American intransigence, however, had bought precious time for the apartheid regime, and the Mandela group inherited a country from which much capital had fled and in which a significant proportion of national industries had been privatized.[21]

It is in this retrograde era that the real fissioning of the American public sphere has taken place. We can track this phenomenon on a number of levels. There is, first of all, the sheer multiplication of what were formerly more unified and limited sets of media units: the competition of cable channels—including non-English programming—with network television, of "lifestyle niche" special-interest magazines with earlier mass-market weeklies and monthlies, of new "niche" radio music programming, of the new computer networks. Books are increasingly marketed to "true believer" rightist or liberal, feminist or antifeminist audiences. Whites and blacks increasingly watch different television programs; magazines increasingly appeal to, and are read only by, Americans in very specific occupational, generational, and interest niches. Right-wing talk radio has proliferated and has its own specific listening market.[22]

This product differentiation process is part of the larger evolution of the "flexible accumulation" of capital that David Harvey documents. Michael Curtin notes that this "reorganization of the culture industries . . . engenders a constant search for narrowly defined and underserved markets. Race, gender, and ethnicity have now joined socioeconomic status as potentially marketable boundaries of difference." The "new entertainment state" is characterized by the globalization/fragmentation dialectic: corporate consolidation across media coinciding with increasingly rapid investment and disinvestment in outlets and labor pools to reach the new niche markets.[23]

Linked to this consolidation and capital's new flexibility is the increasing reliance of the news industry—given the defunding of government-subsidized radio and television and overarching censorship of anticorporate investigative reporting—on the institutions founded by the New Right. The American Enterprise Institute, the Heritage Foundation, the Cato Institute, the Manhattan Institute, and others appear more frequently with each passing year as "reputable" sources of social information. A decreasing number of feminist and progressive outlets, often aided through connection to academic institutions, struggle to maintain an increasingly isolated critical public sphere. This fragile artifact is riven by the partialities of identity politics—the tendencies, for example, of gay and feminist journals to assume middle-class white subjects, or the nationalism inherent in many black outlets. As we approach the second millennium, then, the American public sphere is paradoxically more corporate controlled and less unified than ever before in American history.[24]

Marjorie Shostak's *Nisa* and Derek Freeman's *Margaret Mead and Samoa*, published during Reagan's tumultuous first term, were inevitably received, as are all popular ethnographies, within their contemporary political context. But the fissioning public sphere, the extremity and recency of Reaganite revanchism, and particularly the bitter contestation provided by liberal feminism to that onslaught lent, as we shall see, a uniquely politicized flavor to these two book's receptions. Feminist policy analyst Roberta Spalter-Roth remembers wearing a political button in the 1970s that read "Every Woman Her Own Anthropologist."[25] This feminist twist on historian Carl Becker's 1930s slogan, "Everyman His Own Historian," referred to the grassroots politics and self-help vibrancy of early second-wave feminism. It could also refer, however, to the political environment of the 1980s and 1990s, in which fissioning perspectives, the culture of forgetting, rampant anti-intellectualism, and sheer ignorance or denial of past events and research have become the dominant frame in most discourse on gender—and, for that matter, race, class, and imperialism. Legitimation of the status quo masquerades as populism.

Margaret Mead herself, in misrepresenting anthropology's political history and her own work and actions within it, contributed to this brave new world despite her own self-identification with a positivist science. When every woman is her own anthropologist, when we are forced to live in a postmodern world in which all narratives are equally of interest and assertions are not checked against evidence, there is no accumulated body of knowledge with which to contest hegemony. We find ourselves living in the closed Foucauldian world in which all efforts at resistance merely reconfirm power, in which we end in reforging our own chains.

SISTER UNDER THE SKIN

Let us first consider the actual text, as opposed to the many readings, of *Nisa*. Shostak unselfconsciously introduces her topic, as we saw in chapter 3, in terms of "living ancestors"—a straight-line continuation from the Chicago School's as well as Mead's and Benedict's interpretations of the uses of small-scale societies as "natural laboratories." She makes use of the tradition of the Harvard !Kung project's "man the hunter" assertions, themselves informed by the 1960s development of a "noble savage"–inflected ecological/economic anthropology, not only that the !Kung San represent our early human past, but that foraging societies like theirs are egalitarian, leisured, and culture rich, precisely the opposite of the Hobbesian vision of nasty, brutish, and short primitive lives: "What do we gain from knowing about our gathering and hunting past? Most important, perhaps, is our knowledge that the gatherer-hunter legacy is a rich one. Life for our prehistoric ancestors was not characterized by constant deprivation, but rather by usually adequate food and nutrition, modest work effort, fair amounts of leisure, and sharing of resources, with both women and men contributing substantially to the family, the economy, and the social world."[26]

Shostak further focuses her study, as we have seen, by explicitly stating her concerns with gender—given the burgeoning women's movement in the United States at the time she began fieldwork—and specifying that !Kung women "might be able to offer some answers" to Western feminist questions because "!Kung women's lives . . . today might reflect what their lives had been like for generations, possibly even for thousands of years."[27] In setting up this neo-social-evolutionary feminist framework, Shostak, interestingly, glides over the work of 1970s feminist anthropologists—with their efforts to reconsider social structures through revising Marx, Weber, Lévi-Strauss—and reaches instead back to Margaret Mead's slapdash postwar Freudian universalizing: "In every known society, the males' need for achievement can be recognized." Shostak uses Mead, though, in order yet again to declare the !Kung an ethnographic "anomaly": "Here, in a society of ancient traditions, men and women live together in a nonexploitative manner, displaying a striking degree of equality between the sexes—perhaps a lesson for our own society."[28] Here Shostak rings the changes of the long edificatory tradition in American anthropology. This particular lesson, of course, was one that had already been well argued in rather more nuanced ways in the explicitly Marxist work of Eleanor Leacock, Karen Sacks, and others. Shostak both signals her choice of anthropological lineage and, ironically, turns away from the radical tradition that her senior Harvard colleague on the !Kung project, Richard B. Lee, himself espoused. Most particularly, Shostak, while citing the 1970s feminist bibles in anthropology, fails to make use of any of their lessons—considerations of public and private domains, the political nature of kinship, the roles of gossip, the functions of women's rituals.[29]

But perhaps this is in part because *Nisa* is not a conventional ethnography, but rather an ethnographically informed life history—with abundant accompanying photographs, themselves taken by Shostak. Shostak is at pains to lay out the process through which she came to know Nisa, and through which Nisa—an older !Kung woman all of whose children had died—apparently chose her as amanuensis. She at first disliked Nisa, who made explicit, repeated demands for tobacco and other goods, and compared Shostak and her husband quite negatively to earlier, more open-handed anthropologists. Nisa then alarmed her with a childhood narrative in which she figured as the savior of her just-born baby brother, whom her mother proposed to kill. As her linguistic competence increased, Shostak attempted to establish warm working relations with a series of !Kung women, relations which repeatedly broke down. In the end, she returned to Nisa and discovered in her intelligence, narrative flair, and a business-like firmness about the job to be done: "In Nisa, I finally found what I had been looking for. After she understood the requirements of the interviews, she summarized her life in loosely chronological order; then, following my lead, she discussed each major phase in depth. . . . We were pleasant and friendly and our rapport was easy. She had a determination to make each interview work and seemed to derive considerable pleasure from the entire process. Although she occasionally asked for direction, she led the way most of the time."[30]

Shostak makes clear the collaborative nature of the final life history: while the narratives are Nisa's, their translation and arrangement are Shostak's, as are the "fable of rapport" introduction to the narrative, the beautifully composed (and entirely primitivist—no dresses, no tin cans) *Family of Man* black-and-white photographs, and the anthropological introductions to each narrative chapter. Shostak also very honestly admits that the shape of the final narrative owes as much to her own particular concerns at the times of fieldwork as to Nisa's, but also notes that there is evidence that !Kung women shared her concerns: "My own interest in sexual issues, although substantial in its own right, was probably no greater than and perhaps was even less than theirs."[31]

In addition, Shostak makes clear that Nisa is perhaps an atypical !Kung woman: "None of the other women I interviewed had encountered as much tragedy as Nisa, or had comparable extravagance of personal style." Finally, Shostak addresses the ethical issues involved in changing names and places to preserve !Kung privacy, and in communicating adequately to Nisa the meaning of translating and publishing her life history in English:

> She spun a fantasy of my work—a fantasy that has since proved true. "Yes, you will listen to me and when I say something that makes you laugh, you will laugh aloud and praise me, 'Eh-hey, my aunt! My aunt, I still have you with me, here in my home.' You will feel love for me, because I will be there with you." . . . if they do . . . buy it and you help me, then I will buy a cow." I said, "We will have to wait and see."[32]

Nisa is a beautifully put together book, a fact that undoubtedly spurred its immense popularity. Shostak has a poetic ear for the rhythms of speech and clearly labored over adequate phrasing, words that conveyed the emotive power, the differing colloquial levels of !Kung speech, as she came to understand them. The reader is drawn into the narrative of Nisa's life from the first vignette, a birth scene, that actually precedes Shostak's introduction of herself and her field projects. The emotional thread is constant throughout the chapters, with Shostak's ethnographic introductions providing just enough information to interpret Nisa's narrative. We have seen, as well, how Shostak heightens the reader's identification with Nisa through disclosing their mutual use of kinship terms—"my aunt," "my niece."[33] *Nisa*'s final sentence builds on this emotion and fuses it with second-wave Western feminist locutions: "I will always think of her, and I hope she will think of me, as a distant sister."[34]

But this narrative itself gains its peculiar affective power as much through absence as presence. That is, we never learn about Nisa's specific economic activities—her gathering, hunting, craft skills—how she learned them, how her practices changed over time, or of course the specific skills, such as domestic labor for whites, that she learned in order to wrest a sporadic nonforaging living from the world. (Of course, we do learn, inadvertently, how skilled Nisa has become at wresting goods and services from successive groups of resident anthropologists.) Nor do we gain much sense of the complicated politics of the coming together and parting of different networks of !Kung over Nisa's lifetime, nor of their connections to changing economies and state politics in southern Africa. One reviewer (and one alone) remarked that the absence of all this information from the narrative paints for us a "world composed almost entirely of emotions or actions arising from emotion . . . [which] gives Nisa, who must surely be a capable woman, a curious and rather endearing quality of perpetual, flighty adolescence."[35]

Shostak takes pains to explain that other members of the Harvard !Kung project deal with these issues, and to provide thumbnail sketches of some of their findings. But this material is overwhelmed by her interest in "memories of childhood; feelings about parents, siblings, relatives, and friends; adolescence and experiences with other children; dreams; marriage; the birth of children; childhood sex and adult sex; relationships with husbands and lovers; feelings about death; thoughts about the future."[36] Indeed, she begins *Nisa* with the confessional narrative that "I presented myself to [!Kung women] pretty much as I saw myself at the time: a girl-woman, recently married, struggling with the issues of love, marriage, sexuality, work, and identity—basically, what womanhood meant to me. I asked the

!Kung woman what being a woman meant to them and what events had been important in their lives."[37] But, unnoticed, *work*—including the details of childrearing and food preparation—and the emotional meanings of work to identity drop out of the picture over the course of Nisa's narrative, leaving love, marriage, and sexuality as its burden. *Nisa* thus uncannily echoes *Coming of Age in Samoa* in overarching theme—although Mead actually provided far more information about economic activities. This is the secret of both works, their extraordinary popular drawing power: they are deeply individualizing and psychologistic, characteristics tremendously appealing to a middlebrow American readership that, across the decades, has maintained a profound lack of interest in the economic and political except insofar as they can be personalized, commodified as self-help or scandal. The key difference here is that Nisa, unlike the aggregated Samoans, is deliberately presented to the Western audience as an individual female personality. The Dusky Maiden has stepped free of the wallpaper and stands configured in the round.

Nisa's structure, its first-person account of emotions surrounding life course shifts having to do with sex, reproduction, and dyadic human relationships, offers uncanny parallels to that of Gail Sheehy's 1976 self-help best-seller, *Passages: Predictable Crises of Adult Life*. Sheehy, a psychologically educated popular journalist, is the source of the characterization of Margaret Mead as a "general among the foot soldiers of feminism" in the *New York Times* obituary. And in fact, in *Passages*, Sheehy claims Mead, "the quintessential woman achiever," as her mentor, repeatedly using quotations both from Mead's *Blackberry Winter* account of her life and from her interviews with Mead to lend authority to her psychological generalizations—and to place Mead as the prototype for Sheehy's "having it all" bourgeois feminist model of a properly rich set of female life passages:

> Among all of us who have paid a price for liberation—those who gave birth to themselves as professional women at the cost of not having children, the runaway wives who did not find their latent genius baking clay in Big Sur, and certain celebrity feminists who from time to time, bored and spent with their sexual athleticism, confess to craving one night of zest with an unregenerate male chauvinist pig—among these minions there is still no one quite as self-liberated as Mead. . . . She had it all figured out more than fifty years ago.[38]

This embarrassing, paradigmatic 1970s popular cultural document went through fifteen printings in its first year, was selected for distribution by no fewer than three book clubs, and was excerpted in at least eight magazines. It is probably more responsible than any other single book or film of its times for the dual public sphere vision of Margaret Mead as lifestyle avatar and of Mead's version of anthropology as authoritative interpreter of the world's natural laboratories of "culture" for use in personal and whole-society therapeutic intervention.

Thus, not only their parallel life course organization and focus on individual emotions and sexual relationships, but also their similar use of Mead as feminist authority marks both *Nisa* and *Life Passages*. Nevertheless, *Nisa*, unlike Sheehy's book, and despite Shostak's neglect of anthropological feminist literature, represents serious scholarship: the mastery of a difficult language in the midst of an arduous field experience; the labor of taking, translating, and presenting a life history; the digestion and representation of other scholarly work on the !Kung San. As is the case with any life history, *Nisa* offers less social organization material than would an ethnography, but Shostak attempts to place Nisa's life in the context of other anthropological research on the San. Although she framed *Nisa* in anthropology's edificatory tradition—and indeed, her stance could be described as "native woman complex, and better off"—Shostak is not entirely responsible for the particular lessons readers gleaned from it. It is to that large and varied readership I now turn.

Nisa was widely and favorably reviewed as a specifically feminist—and liberal, anti-Reagan-administration—anthropological work (and it was ignored outside the mass media outlets attending to such politics). Ellen Cantarow, in *Ms.*, asserted that it "wards off the Moral-Majority chill . . . at the cold doorsill of the 1980s." Across both popular and scholarly journals, reviewers focused on Nisa as an exemplar of women's sexual freedom—specifically, freedom to have a number of lovers over a lifetime. (Interestingly, all reviewers ignored Shostak's painstaking presentation of some evidence of violence against women and girls in Nisa's narrative; this was perhaps because, like Margaret Mead, Shostak offered the information but then played it down interpretively.)[39] *Nisa* "naturalized" the increasingly common multiple-partner life pattern of middle-class American women. Cantarow makes this point, and also makes explicit the "sisters under the skin" therapeutic identification by better-off Western women that so boosted the book's middlebrow popularity: "Nisa's childbirths, the deaths of children and husbands, the exquisite pleasures of sex, the pain of illness—aren't easily paraphrased. So I have been reading the book aloud to friends ever since I got it. "Oh!" we exclaim, "so she's felt that, too?" Nisa makes you feel better about yourself; her feelings are so like your own."

The *New York Review of Books* defensively pointed out that "if the narrative is highly charged with sex it is because sex is important in !Kung life."

Nancy Howell, who had also done ethnographic work among the !Kung, noted in the *American Ethnologist* that Nisa "gives details about sexual practices, female orgasm, the how and why of seduction of a new lover. The explicitness is wonderful." Journalist Margo Jefferson, in the *Nation*, agreed, and like most other reviewers, deeply appreciated Nisa as a personality: "Nisa had a great many lovers—a common practice if managed with courtesy, tact and a judicious blend of truth-telling and lying. She holds forth on them and on women, men and sex in a tone that is ironic, provocative, selectively bawdy and jauntily oracular. When she met Shostak, she was married for the fifth time, having survived a third husband and divorced a fourth under painful circumstances." Similarly, Harriett Gilbert in the *New Statesman* approbates Nisa as a latter-day Wife of Bath: "[the book is] a rollicking, picaresque adventure; with Nisa, its unrepentent hero, stealing food from the family food-pouch; cursing 'death to your genitals'; taking lovers; giving birth; suffering the death of her children. . . . The story is not all comedy; but the hunger, violence, and premature death that form its bitter undertaste are sweetened by Nisa's sometimes vicious, sometimes joyful wit, and by the charm of her egocentric, forthright, courageous character." Latin Americanist anthropologist Lisa Peattie, in the *New York Times Book Review,* quoted Nisa claiming little present interest in sex but imagining a future in which "I'll be interested again. Another day I'll think about men. Then I'll wear the beads and powder and I'll be beautiful again, so beautiful that the men will say, 'Nisa, aren't you a lovely one?' I'll smell so good they'll say, 'Why is this older woman who smells so sweetly refusing me?'"[40]

My unsystematic monitoring and that of friends and acquaintances over the past decade indicates that this particular sort of feminist identification with Nisa—most particularly with her active sexuality and her open expressions of fear and sorrow over illness, the difficulties of childbirth, and the death of loved ones—is the most common pattern of reception to the book among American female students, nonanthropological (and some anthropological) faculty, and members of the general public. Nisa is the Reagan and post-Reagan era's benign female Shylock: she asserts that when she is cut, she bleeds. Our (largely white) audience identification with Nisa's pain and pleasures across the divides of color and culture articulates our own humanity both in itself—we are *Ur*-women with Nisa's *Ur*-woman—and through our empathy with a female Other.

This response is an amalgam of the "technicians of the sacred" and the "human nature experts" Halloween costumes: Shostak is both the liminal figure who has touched the hem of that egalitarian culture superior to ours and the scientist who can assure us, on the basis of her work with a "Stone Age" group, that our aspirations for women's freedom are grounded in human nature. Indeed, Shostak has made clear that she invites this reading. In a later essay on the writing of *Nisa*, she retails an early publisher's rejection of the manuscript because "Nisa's voice wasn't interesting enough; she sounded as if she could be 'the woman next door.' . . . That was . . . what I had been hoping for. . . . Her experiences must reflect something universal, after all."[41]

So strongly does Shostak's intention meld with overarching popular feminist ideology that readers literally cannot hear other interpretations. When I gave a talk that included a criticism of Shostak's social evolutionism at an Ivy League university in the late 1980s, for example, an older woman English professor approached me afterward to exclaim nearly tearfully, with presumption of my complete empathy, over her great love for *Nisa*.

Negative reviewers, as well, perceived the book's message to be that the lusty and much-married Nisa offered a feminist lesson for modern American women. They, however, intensely disliked that message. Literary critic James Olney, in the *Yale Review*, gave full vent to that dislike in a long piece nearly unique in the annals of venomous reviewing—and worth looking at in some detail.

Olney begins in deprecating the "jaunty, rather feminist 'beautiful-people' photograph of the author on the back cover" (a photograph, incidently, missing in the paperback edition of *Nisa*). He complains bitterly that the !Kung individuals in Shostak's photographs are not identified, and—entirely failing to take in Shostak's explanations of the need for anonymity—implies that the lack of an identified photograph of Nisa means that Shostak cares only for herself, is really only writing her own autobiography. He seems deeply aggrieved that Harvard University Press has published what to him is the opposite of a properly "staid work of anthropology," most particularly that there is "rather more about the sexuality of !Kung women in *Nisa* than some readers may want to know." He finds the chapter titles, "'Earliest Memories,' 'Discovering Sex,' 'Marriage,' 'Women and Men,' 'Taking Lovers,' and so on," deeply offensive. To Olney, *Nisa* is not actually about Nisa, but a "herstory," an exercise in "gynecology" (leaving unclear whether he realizes that feminists such as Mary Daly had already given new meanings to that word), an example of an anthropologist "studying the face that appears in the mirror" rather than the Other.[42]

Ironically, Olney is rather like those Meese pornography commissioners who couldn't consume enough of what they claimed to despise. He ignores Nisa's extrasexual narratives, and all of Shostak's ethnographic information, in order to quote the erotic material at length. He gives a myth on the male discovery of female genitals and thus heterosexual intercourse in toto, concluding, "Thus Nisa's version of Genesis." He then goes on to cite a "typical opinion-cum-piece of advice from Nisa":

> "Having affairs is one of the things God gave us." In her introductory remarks Shostak, both revealingly and concealingly, adopts the pronoun "one" and the perspective implied by that pronoun to describe all the niceties and necessities of an affair and to tell how a lover and a husband can be managed simultaneously. "It is also important to maintain some emotional restraint in relation to a lover. One's spouse must always come first, no matter how romantic and exciting an affair may be. . . . To succeed at and benefit from extramarital affairs, one must accept that one's feelings for one's husband . . . and for one's lover . . . are necessarily different. One is rich, warm, and secure. The other is passionate and exciting, although often fleeting and undependable. . . . The appeal of affairs, they say, is not merely sexual; secret glances, stolen kisses, and brief encounters make for a more complex excitement."

Olney finishes this diatribe: "I am not aware that *Cosmopolitan* magazine has been in the forefront of the Women's Movement, but this sounds to my ear very like anthropology written to the editorial specifications of Helen Gurley Brown."[43] (He clearly has no ear for style: there is not a single italicized word in the aforementioned passage.) What is most revealing here is Olney's erasure of the fact that much of Shostak's material in this chapter comes from men, and thus that the chapter is as much about male extramarital affairs as female.

The review ends in a blanket condemnation of anthropology, past and present. Olney gives a potted history of the discipline as having shifted from "nasty savage" narratives "for our shuddering fascination and civilized wonderment" to "noble savage" visions "positively recommended to our hypertrophied, rotten civilization," and finally, in the present, "we are now encouraged to see [our society] as simply different—but not even as different if we penetrate to the deeper levels of psychology, biology, and ethology."[44] Olney finds all stances offensive, and the inescapable conclusion is that—like fellow misogynists Allan Bloom and Saul Bellow—he is offended by any and all anthropological attention paid to non-Western societies. At the same time, despite his rather obviously antifeminist distaste for evidences of active female sexuality, Western or other, and despite his sheer self-satisfied ignorance of anthropological history, Olney does put his finger on the problematic, edificatory "natural laboratory" thread in the American anthropological tradition to which Shostak lays claim.

John Leonard, in the *New York Times*, offers a more sophisticated and equivocal reading than Olney's, but one that in the end equally rejects Shostak's vision of the !Kung lesson to Westerners. Leonard accomplishes this rejection by ignoring most of Shostak's ethnographic information and focusing on Nisa alone, whom he finds "difficult," "impossible," "talkative and exasperating and sex-obsessed," selling "shards of her vanishing culture as curios to a stupid tourist." Leonard then judges the !Kung wholesale as cases of arrested psychological development: "If the voluble Nisa is any example, they will die unhappy, still confusing sex with food, still trapped in an emotional economy of scarcity, still wanting to say: 'Ho, ho, daddy! We're going to eat meat!' Still stingy." Sounding remarkably like the *Nation's* Freda Kirchwey commenting in 1928 on *Coming of Age in Samoa*, Leonard ends in implicit rejection of Shostak's feminist themes through his embrace of modernity. Like feminist reviewers, Leonard assumes Shostak's social evolutionism is accurate, that the !Kung are "a culture as old as the human race." But Leonard finds no lesson in our ancestors' lives: he discusses !Kung health problems—"bronchitis, rheumatic fever, and malaria"—and links them to !Kung culture, judging both thoroughly undesirable: "This scrupulous, sad, exciting book suggests that we can't really dream our way out of the bush or history."[45]

Other reviewers, however, found Shostak precisely modern—in fact, postmodern. Or, at least, *Nisa* has seemed appropriate grist for postmodern anthropological mills. Vincent Crapanzano, in an omnibus review in the *American Anthropologist*, considers *Nisa* part of the problematic "life history" tradition in anthropology: "Its reception reflects the ambiguous position of anthropology in 20th-century thought. The life history is more 'literary' than 'scientific'—and yet more 'scientific' than 'literary.' It mediates, not too successfully, the tension between the intimate field experience and the essentially impersonal process of anthropological analysis and ethnographic presentation." Crapanzano goes on to consider the theoretical difficulties of taking and presenting life histories, which he frames as part of the "problems of representation and generalization." He discusses the questions of typicality, and of reliability and validity, but expends most energy on the dyadic enounter between ethnographer and informant and the process of textualizing that encounter in the life history genre. Here he focuses on the variations on and effects of the "arbitrary and peculiar demand from another," the request for a life history narrative. He considers the role of the ethnographer in determining themes of narratives, and wonders how much of Shostak and how much of Nisa is involved in Nisa's specifications of types of proper and improper heterosexual expression.

He considers the possiblities of coercion—given ethnographers' usually greater social and economic power—and commends Shostak's honesty in admitting the overarching role that her gifts, and refusals of gifts, played in her relationship with Nisa. Crapanzano goes on to assert the impossibility of understanding narratives in the absence of information on "how (if at all) the life history interdigitates with other story forms in the subject's culture and how (if at all) the subject makes use of them in negotiations with the anthropologist. We should also like to know something about indigenous notions of authorship, rhetoric, style, and narrative techniques." We should indeed. Crapanzano ably lays out the quite reasonable questions deriving from postmodernist obsessions with the dyadic encounters of fieldwork and with the texts that result from those encounters, and makes us aware that these are questions Shostak does not answer.

Finally, Crapanzano considers the distortions involved when the life history text is "worked over" by the anthropologist using "the literary conventions at his or her disposal," and notes the fact that Shostak "does not include her own interventions in 'Nisa's text.'" He does give Shostak much credit for conveying her relationship to Nisa, and portrays Nisa, rather wonderfully, as "A !Kung version of a Colette, willing to take on memory and the pain of memory—but also . . . an older woman giving instructions to a younger one."

Crapanzano ends in defining the life history text as "a conventionalized gloss on a social reality that, from a strict epistemological point of view, we cannot know."[46] James Clifford, in the *Times Literary Supplement*, takes this assertion of unknowableness a step further in his largely favorable review of *Nisa*.

Clifford insightfully sees *Nisa* as a combination of three distinct discourses. The first is "part of a continuing study of the !Kung, and of hunter-gatherers generally." The second engages Nisa's narrative as a "metaphor of woman's existence—a story that has a strong resonance with many of the experiences and dilemmas highlighted in recent feminist thought." The third is the "story of an intercultural encounter in which two individuals create a specific domain of truth." Clifford begins in approbation of all three discourses, but ends—in fealty to postmodern assertions of the vacuity of grand narratives—in denying validity to the first and affirming only the particularity of textual representation of the dyadic encounter between ethnographer and subject. Thus the title of his review, "A Boswell in Botswana," is uncannily appropriate.

Clifford first notes the value of disabusing antimodernists of their illusions about lives "close to nature." He approvingly cites Shostak's statistics on high mortality rates among the !Kung and the ways in which Nisa's loss of children and husband fit that larger picture. He notes how Nisa's life course narrative allows us to see, contra "classical anthropology's focus on kinship as a set of rules," that kinship and marriage are "a set of contingencies: agreements, separations, the clash of families; individuals learning to love, accepting commitment, misunderstanding each other, being unfaithful, breaking up, reuniting. There is nothing smooth or automatic about marriage in this 'primitive' society."

But at the same time, Clifford finds Nisa's very particularity creates a "truth resistant to the demands of a typifying science." After a long section in appreciation of Shostak's openness about her evolving relationship with Nisa—her "polyvocal construction"—and of the "salutary shock" of realizing how much ethnographic literature tends to omit women's perspectives, Clifford ends in asserting that Shostak should have published Nisa's narrative without ethnographic context: "An insistent tug toward the general is felt through *Nisa*, and it is not without pain that we find Nisa generalized, presented as 'an interpretation of !Kung life.' The book's scientific discourse, tirelessly contextual, typifying, is braided through the other two voices. . . . If such interjections are helpful early in the book, by the end— as Nisa's story gains momentum—we wish that this other voice, neutral, preoccupied with !Kung culture, would no longer interrupt." Clifford ends in describing ethnographic generalization as a kind of spoiler trope: "The scientific discourse functions in the text as a kind of brake on the book's other voices, whose truths are excessively personal and intersubjective. It reinstates, perhaps, an ethnographic authority that has yielded too much to ethnographic desire."[47] This assertion is in line with the tendency of the first wave of postmodernist anthropological writing to prescribe experimental, polyvocal accounts of dyadic ethnographic encounters as the only rhetorical means to destabilize ethnographic authority—and to proscribe all other social scientific methods and accounts. Clifford and Crapanzano are at one here in their assertion of the unknowableness of social reality and therefore the innate falsehood of all typifying ethnographic accounts.

Nonpostmodern anthropologists had no such concerns in their responses to Shostak's work. Eleanor Edelstein, in the *Anthropological Quarterly*, reviewed *Nisa* in a mode parallel to Clifford's, but without his postmodern lexicon and his doubts about representation and social reality. She notes the "three books in one" quality of the work—life history, narrative of the difficulties of fieldwork, and "feminist resource." But she finds no contradiction in these three discourses and finds Shostak's work a "verification of anthropology's function and humanistic goals."[48] Lillian Ackerman, in the *Journal of Anthropological Research,* responds to *Nisa* from a similar midrange anthropological perspective, but far more critically. Ackerman, like Shostak, assumes a unitary, timeless !Kung culture and economic situation, and for that reason takes Shostak to task for contradicting earlier anthropological assertions of !Kung sexual egalitarianism and year-round abundant food supplies—the very departures from "!Kung canon" that Edwin Wilmsen is at pains to praise. She also criticizes Shostak for appearing "to suggest that she is the first to record" incidents of violence among the !Kung, given Richard Lee's previous work in this area.[49]

More recently, *Nisa* served as a bit of a feminist punching bag for contributors to the postmodernist anthology *Writing Culture.* Here Clifford asserts that "*Nisa* is a Western feminist allegory, part of the reinvention of the general category 'woman' in the 1970s and 1980s." George Marcus and Michael Fischer remark on "Shostak's questions deriving from contemporary American feminism," while literary critic Mary Pratt, in a piece (as we shall see) of otherwise extraordinary insight, refers to "current Western conceptions of female solidarity and intimacy" in *Nisa.* I have commented on the self-contradictoriness of this sort of typification, one with which this first wave of postmodern anthropologists had no quarrel:

> How can we understand the theoretical and political short-sightedness of these writers? Why do they insist on holding feminist perspectives at arm's length, insist on feminism's historical contingency, its status as a current intellectual and political movement, while experiencing no difficulty in strongly reprobating, for all time, colonialist, racist mentalities? Imagine Marcus and Fischer referring, in the 1960s, to "Martin Luther King, Jr.'s questions deriving from contemporary American antiracism."[50]

Finally, some readers, both at the time of publication and more recently, have focused on *Nisa* fundamentally as an attempt to inscribe the life of an Other without condescension and with a self-reflexive sense of the Heisenberg effect of researchers' interests on anthropological findings. Such was the main thrust of Margo Jefferson's contemporaneous review in the *Nation,* as well as Harry Lewis's short response in the *Village Voice.* Jefferson commends Shostak's efforts "to stand back and examine the archaic garment of Western womanhood," while Lewis notes that "Shostak allows Nisa the dignity of her own voice."[51]

More recently, in this same vein, anthropologist and filmmaker Leslie Devereaux has discussed *Nisa* as a work that "restores personhood, as we see it, to the ethnographic subject and allows her own account and words

. . . to weave the map of meanings in her life for us. . . . And what Nisa tells us holds our attention, because she is doubly displaced—an illiterate and a woman." Devereaux, rather hyperbolically, likens *Nisa* to the radical Latin American genre of *testimonio,* in which "the intention . . . is political, to render less flagrant the relations of hegemony that are in play and to allow someone who otherwise could not to speak to 'us'—members of the national or international literate culture."[52]

Jefferson, however, is not so certain of the completeness and radical efficacy of Nisa's narrative. She notes that Shostak's search for common ground led to "a good many things [being] obscured by the flowing garment of female universality, draping itself repeatedly about local customs of romance, sex, and marriage." She also points out that most of the "social change" material in *Nisa*—sedentarization, contact with other African populations, !Kung male migration to work in gold mines or for the South African Army—is confined to the epilogue, "and Nisa's reflections [on these phenomena] are brief and scattered."[53]

Mary Louise Pratt, in her mid-1980s essay, also engages with *Nisa's* incompleteness and relative rhetorical efficacy, but from the perspective of some familiarity with the lengthy history of Western discourse on the Bushmen. She points out that the Harvard project of which Shostak is a part "displays direct continuities with a long tradition of writing about the !Kung. . . . What the tradition documents is a long and violent history of persecution, enslavement, and extermination." Pratt's interpretation of some extant colonial documents indicates a shifting discourse on the Bushmen: they were "wild, bloodthirsty marauders" when Europeans desired their lands. But once "the Bushmen definitively lost their struggle against European encroachment on their land and lifeways, they acquire the characteristics that the powerful commonly find in those they have subjugated: meekness, innocence, passivity, indolence coupled with physical strength and stamina, cheerfulness, absence of greed or indeed desires of any kind, internal egalitarianism, a penchant for living in the present, inability to take initiatives on their own behalf."

Pratt points out that Shostak rationalizes her use of !Kung women as emanations of our own past through claiming that their experience of culture change has been recent and subtle. She sourly notes that "'recent' and 'subtle' are not the adjectives that come to mind when one ponders the grim history of the Bushman conquest. This is a history of which Shostak and her colleagues seem at times deeply aware, at times totally oblivious." Pratt ends in asking the question, "What picture of the !Kung would one draw if instead of defining them as survivors of the stone age and a delicate and complex adaptation to the Kalahari desert, one looked at them as survivors of capitalist expansion, and a delicate and complex adaptation to three centuries of violence and intimidation?"[54] That picture now exists, thanks to important recent work by scholars of the Kalahari on both sides of the present Botswana-Namibia border. It allows us to see much more clearly not only the history and present realities of the San peoples, but also the Nisa/Bushmen/*Gods Must Be Crazy* phenomenon in the Reagan and post-Reagan American public sphere, and through it the evolving uses of the Dusky Maiden in American political discourse.

FIGHTING THE GLOBAL POOL HALL

Edwin Wilmsen has written on the prehistory, history, and present-day realities of Kalahari residents living largely within what is now Botswana, while Robert Gordon has published an ethnohistorical account of the complicated political economy of those resident in the territory that is now independent Namibia.[55] Their work, and that of many others, allows us to envision a very different Bushman reality than that espoused by the Harvard Project and Marjorie Shostak.

Wilmsen, summarizing his own and others' archaeological work, asserts that, contra the Harvard group's claims that the San represent "the Stone Age in the present," there is abundant Kalahari evidence of Khoisan-speaking, complex agro-pastoral settlement—including pottery and metalworking—and of trading networks reaching to the Indian Ocean as far back in time as A.D. 600. He elaborates a very complex historical argument, involving waves of capital penetration, black and then white colonization, and a constantly shifting intersection of modes of production on the Kalahari: foraging, herding, horticulture, hunting for the ivory and ostrich feather trade, tourism, begging. Using much documentation, he articulates a vision of the greater or lesser historical domination of Bantu-speaking peoples over Khoisan-speakers (depending upon region in the Kalahari) from prehistory into the present. Spurred by Western capital penetration and settlement, Tswana state making progressed rapidly in the eighteenth and nineteenth centuries, and most (but by no means all) San speakers were integrated into its lower, dispossessed serf class: "It was that San majority . . . who later, in the playing out of the colonial process, became pauperized Masarwa, 'Bushmen.'"[56]

In laying out this long and regionally variegated history, Wilmsen gives us a series of verbal snapshots that destroy the Harvard project picture of the San as pristine foragers unchanged across the millenia. We see young

San speakers, in large numbers, "taken from their homes and transported to established Tswana locations, where they were used as herdboys, milkmaids, domestic servants, and hunters." Later, we see San, often cattle owners, expropriated and forced into cattle herding for Tswana after the Tswana are taxed by the South African government into the necessity of themselves migrating to work in European farms and mines: "Ethnic minorities, San speakers in particular, played a critical role in providing a second-tier labor pool, thereby releasing for labor migration Tswana men who would otherwise have been indispensable for immediate household production."[57]

Marshaling extensive physical anthropological evidence, Wilmsen argues that the smaller stature of contemporary San speakers does not represent their genetically encoded ethnic difference from surrounding populations, but rather "their bodies express their structural position as an ethnically encoded underclass in the political economy of the Kalahari."[58] (One is reminded inevitably of the certainty of many Victorian and Edwardian bourgeois that the scrawny, underfed London Cockney was a race apart from his and her "betters.") Wilmsen reminds us that "as an ethnic label, Bushman/Basarwa/San, alone or in combination, has a history of barely half a century." He points out that economic historical evidence indicates ongoing class formation, with those who manage to accumulate capital and increase their well-being escaping the "Bushman" label. The ethnographers' "Bushman" is the hard-luck descendant of individuals neither biologically nor ethnically different from other Kalahari residents and thus is an individual whose ancestors very likely had experience in herding, farming, domestic service, and begging, even labor in South African mines in addition to hunting and gathering. Wilmsen notes anthropologists' unconscious collusion with white and black oppressor groups in pointing out that "the mystification of San uniqueness [is] a condition imposed on them by other, hegemonically dominant groups." He concludes that "it is useless to speak about "Bushmen"/Basarwa/San as a separate category unless we realize that these terms are class categorizations having nothing to do with ethnic entities or persons and only occasionally relating to a particular, restricted way of life. The first step to this realization leads away from a fixed forager image, a fascination that sets the present of peoples so labeled out of focus and circumscribes any vision of their future."[59]

Robert Gordon has a slightly different intellectual project and covers the Kalahari on the Namibia side of the border, but his findings complement Wilmsen's well. Gordon asserts that "Bushmen," "far from being 'beautiful people living in primeval paradise' . . . are in reality the most victimized and brutalized people in the bloody history that is southern Africa." In his ethnohistorical narrative, the Bushmen

> emerge as one of many indigenous people operating in a mobile landscape, forming and shifting their political and economic alliances to take advantage of circumstances as they perceived them. Instead of toppling helplessly from foraging to begging, they emerge as hotshot traders in the mercantile world market for ivory and skins. They were brokers between competing forces and hired guns in the game business. Rather than being victims of pastoralists and traders who depleted the game, they appear as one of many willing agents of this commercial depletion. Instead of being ignorant of metals, true men [sic] of the Stone Age, who knew nothing of iron, they were fierce defenders of rich copper mines that they worked for export and profit.[60]

Gordon's research documents these assertions in detail. He relates long histories of economic cooperation and even intermarriage with the Ovambo, and of Herero and other populations infringing on Bushman areas after the introduction of European firearms, to be met with bloody, organized Bushman resistance. He lays out the histories of powerful Bushman "headmen" with whom other black Africans and Europeans were forced to negotiate, of long periods of Bushman social banditry against other black populations and Europeans, and of colonial wars of proletarianization and extermination against the population. Gordon's ethnohistorical narrative enhances Wilmsen's assertion of "Bushman" embeddedness in the complicated political economy of the Kalahari.

Vying with the power of his narrative is Gordon's set of photographs gleaned from colonial archives and Namibian newspapers. We see first, in the 1890s, a powerful headman in Western dress with wives and bodyguards; then German colonial-era postcards of indentured farm laborers, of emaciated, starving "wild" Bushmen, of Bushmen hanged from trees by colonial "justice," of Bushmen in chains, starving in colonial jails. Then comes a series of images from 1950s forward, the era of the "discovery" of "the last pristine Stone Age" Bushmen at the point when the population as a whole had been sufficiently exterminated or settled as barely surviving farm laborers for whites and blacks. Here are Bushmen paraded through the streets of Cape Town and exhibited in living zoos by their "protectors," who are working to institutionalize reserves, and here is a Bushman personal servant offering drinks to the smiling rulers of South West Africa. Then, finally, Gordon offers a series of 1970s and 1980s images: of blanket-covered beggars on a reserve waiting for food rations and of Bushman families recruited into the South African Defense Forces (SADF) in their war against the South West Africa People's Organization

21. "Bushman Captain Aribib with wives and bodyguards, photographed by Governor Leut-wein in the early 1890s. Aribib was so powerful that the Germans were forced to sign treaties with him." (This is the caption that appears in Robert J. Gordon, *The Bushman Myth: The Making of a Namibian Underclass* [Boulder, Colo.: Westview Press, 1992.] Photograph courtesy of Robert Gordon. © 1992 by Westview Press. Reprinted by permission of Westview Press and the author.)

(SWAPO).[61] Gordon's century-long photographic history stands as a pro-found indictment of Shostak's glorious celluloid images of pristine !Kung San lacking a single telltale item of Western clothing or technology. In fact, Gordon quotes Nancy Howell, one of the original Harvard anthropologists of the !Kung San—the "Nancy," in fact, whom Nisa held up to Marjorie Shostak as an exemplar of correct generosity—noting in retrospect that she had ignored the paraphernalia of Western "civilization and poverty be-cause we didn't come all the way around the world to see them. We could have stayed at home and seen people behaving as rural proletariat."[62]

Gordon is well justified in his historical, sociology-of-knowledge cri-tique of ethnographic study of "Bushmen":

> For whether we portray them as living in "primitive affluence" or "struggling to survive," the overwhelming textbook image is that they are *different* from us in terms of physiognomy, social organization, values and personality. When we

22. "Bushmen captured by protectorate police in the Keetsmanshoop district for murder and robbery." (This is the original caption of the German-era postcard. Photograph courtesy of Robert Gordon. © 1992 by Westview Press. Reprinted by permission of Westview Press and the author.)

were lounging with a smug sense of ethnocentric superiority in the Victorian era, we saw the Bushmen as the epitome of savagery. But later, in the turmoil of the 1960s, when students were asking serious questions about the nature of Western society, social scientists reified the Bushmen's egalitarianism and generosity, virtues seen to be seriously lacking in Western society. If Bushmen did not exist, we would surely have invented them.[63]

Here Gordon and Wilmsen speak together, both fighting, as did Eric Wolf, the notion of people without history, of human groups envisioned as clean round billiard balls, lacking their own internal divisions and variations, lacking the messiness of the ubiquitous intercultural interactions, the power dynamics of real history. Focusing on the falsehood of the social evolutionary model used to mystify San realities, Wilmsen calls for admitting actual historical political economy:

This is the heart of the matter. San-speaking peoples have not always been as they are now, not even recently, nor have they been as ethnography has depicted them. Their current state is the result of transformations in relations of production involving many other peoples in a social formation that has itself undergone transformation of profound proportions during the last two centuries, and that during the past two millenia has experienced other transformations that we are only now beginning to comprehend. There is nothing to be peeled away to reveal an evolutionary residue that does not exist.[64]

But that mystical evolutionary residue, as we have seen, is ingrained in Western popular political culture. It entered into not only popular feminist response to *Nisa*, but the rather different politics of two films that preceded *Nisa* by only one year: the frequently used ethnographic film *N!ai*, and the wildly popular commercial South African venture, *The Gods Must Be Crazy*.

ETHNOGRAPHY, CINEMA, APARTHEID

N!ai: the Story of a !Kung Woman was shot in 1978 on a Bushman reserve on the Namibia-Botswana border, with a team led by John Marshall and Sue Cabezas Marshall, with Marjorie Shostak and Patricia Draper as official anthropologists.[65] The film has a loosely autobiographical structure, focusing on the now middle-aged N!ai, who describes her idyllic childhood and young adulthood (these experiences are represented by old footage—I recognized bits from the Marshalls' 1958 classic, *The Hunters*) and laments her present in the disorganized camp, where the !Kung San are reduced to quarreling beggars and where N!ai and her family are resented for their relative wealth. Much of the film shows a simple head shot of N!ai playing a thumb piano and declaiming her narrative.

N!ai declares, "Before the white people came, we did what our hearts wanted . . . we were not poor . . . no one told us what to do." The male voice-over observes that the San have been living in southern Africa for twenty thousand years, claims that filming began in 1951 "when the !Kung were an independent people," and represents at length the social evolutionary myth articulated by the Harvard Kalahari project since the 1960s. But N!ai also tells the tale—as did Nisa—of being betrothed against her will as a child. N!ai narrates a long process of disliking her husband, of refusing to sleep with him, of being even more repulsed when he apprenticed himself to learn to cure through trance, of taking another lover, and finally, of coming to terms with him. There is a charming scene in which the two, now middle-aged, tease one another and comment on their bumpy relationship.

The bulk of *N!ai* footage, however, gives us the unsettling picture of !Kung San dependence on white largesse, of white racism and contempt, of !Kung feuding and disorganization. We see nasty white commentary that the !Kung "loaf around all the time," while it is clear that whites are preventing them from hunting and farming. A white doctor blames a sick baby's cough on !Kung domestic dirt and campfire smoke and refuses to treat it; we watch a trance scene for the baby, and hear that it died. There are long scenes of nasty intra-!Kung begging, jealous recrimination, drunken fights, children fighting in mimicry of their elders.

The film ends with the two institutions of religion and the military. There is a church sermon, with commentary afterward by the minister and by N!ai. The minister fatuously explains the symbolism of his parable for !Kung self-improvement. N!ai pours scorn on him and the senselessness of his narrative. Then we see the South African Army recruiting the !Kung for the fight against SWAPO: the promises of benefits, white officers commenting on !Kung military talent, and scenes of military drill and of family farewells for men being trucked away into the bush.

N!ai illustrates the evolution of the Marshalls away from the "pristine hunter" image they parlayed for the Bushmen in *The Hunters* (whose dramatic scenes are the apparent source for House Speaker Newt Gingrich's inane declaration that men are biologically set up to hunt giraffes). *N!ai* indicts the racist South African government and shows us "realistic" scenes of disorderly Bushman life in resettlement camps. But its very realism is extraordinarily familiar to Afro-Americanists. Indeed, the film as a whole provides a remarkable all-in-one parallel to the state of American social science and popular cultural interpretations of poor black Americans' lives in the uncertain 1970s. Its evocative "lost world" of pristine Bushman culture fits the strong "black culture" apologetic present then, a strain of interpretation that has now degraded, as we have seen, into a claim for a nonexistent golden age in the Jim Crow ghetto. Its indictment of the racism of the white professionals, and the positive harm they commit, could have come straight out of Carol Stack's *All Our Kin,* with its portraits of the racism of social workers and hospital personnel. Its scenes of disorder, of drinking and fighting, are classic expressions of the culture of poverty with endless parallels in United States social science, journalism, and popular culture from the 1970s into the present. We even catch a whiff of the later protest against Daniel Moynihan's vile 1960s policy prescription that mass military enlistment—at the key period of Vietnam troop buildup—would solve the problems of "overmothered" ghetto boys. *N!ai* is an extraordinary—really classic—example both of the symbiosis of anthropology and popular culture, and of the continuation of the long Western tradition of recycling the same tropes to represent domestic and exotic Others.

The Gods Must Be Crazy is something else altogether, but has some nearly unremarked connections to *N!ai. Gods,* Jamie Uys's romantic comedy with Bushmen and other black African characters, and two white leads who were well-known figures on the South African stage, was a major international hit, the first ever for that country's nascent film industry. At the same time, the film spurred an international protest and calls for its boycott, and positive reviewers often felt it necessary to reply to the charge that it represented, in Keyan Tomaselli's phrase, "the cinema of apartheid."[66]

The plot of *Gods* traces the intersection of four characters (or groups of characters). The film begins with the now-classic evocation of paradisiacal Bushman life. A "pristine" camp is shown, and a white male voice-over intones: "They must be the most contented people in the world. . . . They have no crime, no punishment, no laws, no police, rules or bosses. . . . In this world of theirs, nothing is bad or evil. . . . They live in complete isolation. . . . they have no sense of ownership at all."

Into this idyll falls a Coca-Cola bottle thrown by a passing prop plane pilot. The Bushmen are represented as puzzled over this object from the "gods." At first, the group discovers exciting uses for the bottle, which ease their craft and food-preparation labor. But then, as the need for the bottle grows, strife appears in the band, culminating in two women fighting over it, and children hitting one another with it. (The notoriously high status of !Kung San women has no place in this film, where they play the classic Western roles of deferential but quarrelsome helpmeets of men.) Xi, the band leader, takes the bottle, vowing to travel to the end of the earth to dispose of this trouble-making object.

The film cuts to a sardonic portrayal of modern white Johannesburg life, focusing on the irrationality of lives determined by timekeeping and technology—classic rat race imagery. A young blonde playing a frustrated newspaperwoman vents her disaffection to her black male coworker, and decides to escape the rat race through going to work as a schoolteacher in Botswana. In the meantime, a young white biologist studying wild game with his mechanically skilled black African sidekick takes on the task of meeting the schoolteacher's bus, even though he has a deep psychological problem: faced with a woman, he loses composure, speech, equilibrium. (Marius Weyers, the actor, is a gifted slapstick comic; he manages to invest each of the endlessly repetitive pratfalls with fresh humor.)

The final plot stream is provided by a group of comically bumbling, unenthusiastic black revolutionaries with a fat, nasty Cuban leader, who fail to assassinate an African head of state and thus embark on a trek cross-country in flight from their pursuers. (The reference here is a pastiche of SWAPO and the Popular Movement for the Liberation of Angola: a swipe against both the legitimate Angolan government's fight against United States–backed guerrillas and the fight for an independent Namibia.)

All characters' lives intersect: Xi is arrested and thrown in jail for stealing stock—he, of course, sees himself as hunting the bounty of nature. Our wildlife scientist and his African sidekick gain his release. The evil revolutionaries kidnap the schoolteacher—with whom the wildlife scientist is already in love—and her black students; Xi, the scientist, and the African sidekick save her, although the credit is claimed by the sleazy white tour operator. Xi throws the Coke bottle off a cliff; the scientist bumbles his way into the schoolteacher's heart. Xi returns home to the wild excitement of his little son and the rest of the band.

The really obscene propagandizing for the apartheid state of this "sweet-tempered" "amiable shaggy-dog story," as reviewers for *Time* and *New York* magazines labeled it, is not very far from its surface.[67] It lies about racial harmony in 1970s urban South Africa, skips light-heartedly over the country's *real* rat race—black life in the townships, arranges the plot so that only black-on-black and black-on-white, but never white-on-black, violence is shown, and elides the brutal and ugly imperialist battle against Namibian independence. The reader already will have noted, as well, the nastiness of the inclusion of !Kung San life as timelessly Edenic at precisely the point when that population was being recruited into the SADF to fight SWAPO. Michael E. Brown points out summarily that "nowhere in all of this does one see evidence of *apartheid*, anything to do with the problems implicit in the political economy of national emergence, indications of the character of the relationship of the South African white regime to the 'homelands' and 'territories,' or the historical decimation of the 'Bushmen' by white invaders and farmers that has left only a few to enact the happy communalism of the primitive."[68]

The film is thus a perfect apologia for the Reagan administration's doctrine of constructive engagement. Ella Shohat and Robert Stam note that *Gods* "relays the colonialist discourse of official White South Africa . . . [through positing] a Manichean binarism contrasting happy and noble but impotent Bantustan 'Bushmen,' living in splendid isolation, with dangerous but incompetent mulatto-led revolutionaries. Yet the film camouflages its racism by a superficial critique of White technological civilization."[69]

In a final irony, it turns out that *N!ai* contains footage of the *Gods* crew recruiting and directing !Kung San in the film. We see the white film crew creating a false bush camp in the middle of the Bantustan. N!xaw, the actor who plays Xi, asks repeatedly for direction, saying of the little boy, "This is my son?" He and the other !Kung San mutter contempt for the crazy, stupid white filmmakers, and their remarks are subtitled for us. For those who have seen *Gods*, this Shakespearian play-within-the-play footage highlighting whites' deliberately turned back on impoverished !Kung San realities is an extraordinarily powerful lesson on the inherently malign nature of "noble savage" social evolutionary visions.[70]

American film reviewers, who could afford to remain happily ignorant of the political economic lies of *Gods*, dealt dismissively with protests and pickets. Richard Corliss of *Time* commented on the "tinge of paternalism" in *Gods* but concluded that the director "seems no racist" because he "tars all his characters, black and white, with the same broad satirical brush." Even the Catholic journal *Commonweal* defended Uys against charges of racism with reference to his "noble savage" message: "The film isn't racist, but primitivist; its hero . . . is a Stone Age Charlie Chaplin, whose benign wisdom subtly underlines the craziness of the technologically superior 'gods' around him. Jamie Uys . . . and 20th Century Fox . . . deserve credit, not demonstrations for bringing N!xaw to us."[71]

The damage wrought by *Gods* was not purely ideological, not merely a matter of helping to moderate Western outrage over South African government human rights violations at home and in South West Africa, slowing progress toward an independent Namibia and a free South Africa. Robert Gordon points out the quite direct ways in which "some films can kill": the success of *Gods* unleashed not only a torrent of hucksterism in Bushmanland, but even influenced the new Namibian government to create a game park in which Bushmen would be allowed to live "traditionally," that is, to starve in the absence of the herding and farming they had always engaged in. Only a major campaign by John Marshall prevented the implementation of this plan.[72]

In many ways, then, *Nisa*, *N!ai*, and *Gods* are all part of the same primitivizing phenomenon, all part of the false representation of "one of the most heavily scientifically commoditized human groups" as a people without history.[73] For each popular phenomenon, there is a different Eden, a different date for the Fall—the 1970s for *Nisa*, the 1950s for *N!ai*, not just yet for *Gods*. But each participates in Johannes Fabian's "provision of temporal distance," each manufactures a "noble savage" for Western therapeutic consumption. The anthropologists' savage clearly engages with feminist hopes for primitive exemplars. *Gods*, just as clearly, does not.

This romantic feminist engagement with a black African population is worthy of note as a counterweight to the nearly hegemonic Western anti-modernist tendency to choose, as Catherine Lutz and Jane Collins note, "bronze" people for approbation and identification: to figure nonblack Latinos, Native Americans, Asians, Mediterraneans and Middle Easterners, and lighter Oceanic populations, worldwide, as model minorities to be held up against the others.

The white Western woman's focus on the heroic black woman, indeed, is a minor theme in American feminist history. Phyllis Palmer has noted its source in the nineteenth-century woman movement's abolitionist roots. Both she and Nell Painter have anatomized its mythologization of Sojourner Truth in substitution for real engagement with the realities of nineteenth-century Afro-American women's lives. Palmer points out the straight-line trajectory of this black-woman-on-a-pedestal tendency into contemporary American feminist symbolism, which figures "heroic black women" as rationale for the escape from the toils of ladylikeness into womanhood while failing to recognize the constricted opportunity structures of most black American women's lives. For Africa itself, Jane Guyer has pointed to the idealized image of the heroic "African female farmer" in Western feminist scholarship, an image that contains false social evolutionary assumptions and prevents "understanding the variety of divisions of labor and their change over time."[74]

With *Nisa*, we have seen in Shostak and many of her feminist readers the wedding of this historical feminist tendency with the "*Ur*-humans" claims of the Harvard Kalahari project: Nisa is at once both our sister, who validates our liberalism, and our ancestress, who proves our normalcy. What the reader fails to see in *Nisa*, because Shostak fails to look for it, is how she and her sisters intersect with the same global economy in which we all are enmeshed—and receive so much less from it.

The grand irony, from the perspective of disciplinary history, is that *Nisa* became a best-seller, probably the work representing anthropology most read by the middlebrow American public, precisely at the point when a flying wedge of well-regarded feminist and other anthropologists was writing directly against this social evolutionary grain, was historicizing with a vengeance. Just as Margaret Mead, after World War II, maintained herself in the public eye but with each passing decade less and less represented actual cutting-edge anthropological work, so Marjorie Shostak's Just-So stories are worlds away from the more theoretically sophisticated feminist "culture and political economy" work published in the same era and into the present. And *Nisa* also indexes the fissioning of the public sphere in this regard: all of the "dusky maiden" ethnographies analyzed in these chapters, save Shostak's, are more or less in tune with the most respected scholarship of their eras. The early Mead, Benedict, Bohannan, Siskind, and the Murphys represented the "culture and personality" school of the 1930s, postwar British structural-functionalism, and the Marxist and Freudian-inflected feminist work of the 1970s.[75] *Nisa* (with *The Paleolithic Prescription,* as I mentioned in chapter 1) placed itself instead out on the anachronistic limb of ahistorical social evolutionary work, work that presumed a scientific grounding but was in fact fairly easily disproven on the basis of empirical evidence.

Finally, Shostak, without using a postmodern vocabulary, concerned herself in the "ethnography as text" mode with ethical questions she construed as "feminist." She focused overwhelmingly on issues of communication in the ethnographic dyadic encounter, questions of how as a privileged white woman to represent the life of an impoverished woman of color in another country and culture. This is, as I have argued, only the micro realm of ethics. In failing to indicate the complicated historical intersection of the San with other populations in the evolving southern African political economy, Shostak fails as well to give her readers a sense of America's foreign policy complicity with the plight of the !Kung San. *Nisa* was written during the years of Carter's backpedaling on Africa policy and became a best-seller in the years of the Reagan administration's "constructive engagement" with the apartheid state. *Nisa's* life narrative thus reflects on us as United States citizens, but Shostak, in the anthropological billiard ball tradition, fails to make that connection. To her credit, however, Shostak does attempt to engage the macro realm in her epilogue, in which she discusses the SADF recruitment of !Kung San and gives the address of a foundation dedicated to working for !Kung San political and economic welfare.

Nisa shared the retrograde 1980s with another popular cultural anthropological phenomenon—but one whose errors were far more grave than the maintenance of a social evolutionary perspective and the constricted reading of ethics in the absence of historical political economy—and whose political effects were far more wide ranging. Let us turn to Derek Freeman's *Margaret Mead and Samoa.*

SPINNING SAMOA FOR THE NEW RIGHT

While *Nisa* certainly received significant press attention, it bears no comparison to the Freeman public sphere phenomenon. (Incidentally, these two early-1980s anthropological works have never been considered together.)

Margaret Mead had lived and died in the glare of eagerly sought publicity. Attacking her image tapped into vast American capacities for lowbrow interest in anthropology. As Roy Rappaport has since pointed out, Mead had attained the status of a Holy Woman toward the end of her career.[76] Desecrating that image created a public frisson akin to catching Mother Teresa in a sexual scandal.

But public reception of Freeman's book, as I have noted, was more importantly about the extraordinary *fit* between his line of attack and newly dominant new rightist politics. Specifically, the neoconservative strategy of focusing away from economic issues and onto "culture" paralleled Freeman's claim that Mead, influenced by her nefarious advisor, Franz Boas, misread the Samoan situation in a "culturally determinist" direction. Thus, *Margaret Mead and Samoa* seemed a heaven-sent opportunity for the press to cavil at the "liberal feminist culture" and "lifestyle experiments" with which it newly identified Mead, conveniently forgetting its fervent paeans to her of only half a decade earlier and celebrating the eminence of its new masters by tying her corpse to the wheels of their imperial chariots. As David Schneider noted, Freeman's book was "a work that celebrate[d] a particular political climate by denigrating another."[77] The scarcely hidden public transcript of the day asserted, "It's human nature, stupid," and Freeman's text offered *the* exemplary excuse for sensationalized press accounts "proving" the inevitability of capitalist, male, white, Western, heterosexual dominance of the world.

Freeman's book, unlike all the other ethnographies considered in these chapters, is poorly written and self-contradictory—a failure on its own terms—and truly parasitic on Mead's reputation and the politics of the times for the interest it excited. The text is repetitious and error ridden and thus far more invoked than studied. In addition, in this case, unlike the rest, others have done most of my job already: The outpouring of popular and scholarly commentary on the Mead/Freeman phenomenon includes such pointed and insightful contributions that there is little reason here to separate précis from interpretation of the text and of its reception.

Key to understanding both the book and its popular reception is Freeman's rhetorical claim to the mantle of true science. He spends more than a fifth of the text in an introductory laying-out of his version of early-twentieth-century American anthropological history. This activity is prefatory to identifying Mead's work with what he sees as Boas's error, the "myth of absolute cultural determinism" as opposed to Freeman's advocacy of "a more scientific anthropological paradigm."[78] It was precisely this stance of scientific disinterestedness that allowed *Fortune* magazine to harrumph that "unlike physical anthropology . . . which has long been recognized as a legitimate science—cultural anthropology gives us only 'soft' data, often of uncertain meaning."[79] But in fact, Freeman not only wraps himself in the "human nature expert" anthropological costume, he also layers over it the clashing raiment of both the technician of the sacred and the raider of the lost ark. Because these several self-contradictory personae correlate with the innate confusions of Freeman's argument, and with the key elements of popular and scholarly reaction to him, let us consider them each in turn.

Freeman's "scientific" account of anthropological developments in the early twentieth century stresses the felt threat of racist eugenics: "Unfortunately for the infant science of anthropology, by the early twentieth century the doctrines of hereditarians like Galton held sway within human biology."[80] He describes Boas and the Boasians as reacting against this development in an unscientific, highly politicized "antipathy to biology, and to genetics and evolutionary biology in particular."[81] Mead's failure, under Boas's heavy-handed direction, to study Samoans as biological beings then becomes the crux of her ethnographic errors.

Let us first get the most general science issues out of the way. Boas, trained in physics, himself engaged in and directed students in explicitly biologically based projects his entire career—including the extensive work on European migrants for the Dillingham Immigration Commission mentioned in chapter 2. In a magisterial piece, Annette Weiner documents Freeman's distortions and omissions of Boas's scientific work, and most specifically Freeman's complete failure to recognize the centrality of *race* to Boas's concerns. In one key article entirely misconstrued by Freeman, "Boas' conclusions are specifically about the relationship between biology and race and not about the absolute separation of culture from biology."[82] Boas's and thus Mead's so-called extreme cultural determinism is therefore a figment of Freeman's imagination.

Moreover, Freeman, as numerous commentators have noted sardonically, presents absolutely no material himself on the biology of Samoans— or of any other human population. Nor does he review any such work in his text. So much for his articulation of the utter necessity of "recognition of both the genetic and the exogenetic and their interaction."[83] Indeed, as Marilyn Strathern points out, Freeman bizarrely attacks American anthropology, which enshrined the four-field approach, for neglecting the biological elements of human behavior: "Yet it was in Britain, not America, that people neglected the 'science of human behavior' in preference for the 'entailments of social customs,' and that can't have been Mead's doing."[84]

George Stocking's review of Freeman's theoretical zigzags over his career helps to explain the extraordinary illogic of his argument. Trained first in 1930s New Zealand in a Boasian framework, he then studied after the war at the London School of Economics and at Cambridge in classic structural-functionalism. In the late 1950s Freeman became hostile to structural-functionalism and converted to Freudian psychoanalysis, then rapidly switched, in the early 1960s, to the application of Konrad Lorenz's animal ethology to human populations, with an admixture of Karl Popper's primitive logical calculus for the testing of scientific hypotheses.[85] During this half-century process of constant epistemic fluctuation, Freeman produced very little—and specifically no extensive work on Samoan ethnography.

Animal ethology, with its behaviorist, observe-from-the-outside stance, hardly provides a theoretical frame from which to consider the issues of human emotion and meaning so central to Freeman's claims. Samoanist Lowell Holmes tellingly notes, for example, Freeman's laughable "experiment" through which he claimed to disprove Mead's contention that, because of differing childrearing practices, Samoan children's ties to biological parents are more diffuse than Americans': "The Freemans had the women of an extended family household walk away from an infant one at a time and recorded the child's response. Freeman maintains that an agitated reaction was forthcoming from the infant only when the separation involved the biological mother. This is pure ethological nonsense, and I have personally observed that adopted children showed no recognition of the biological mother when the two were temporarily reunited."[86] Holmes, among others, also documents Freeman's extensive misrepresentation of historical and ethnographic scholarship on Samoa through highly selective quotation. He notes that while Freeman "cites or quotes my work twenty-six times in *Margaret Mead and Samoa* these are almost exclusively my critical statements concerning Mead's work. He either completely ignores or discounts my statements of corroboration."[87]

Leaving aside his abundant scholarly disingenuousness, Freeman's Popperian stance is, as historian of science Henrika Kuklick crisply notes, "naive and confused": "Philosophers, historians, and sociologists of science have objected to the notion of theory-independent facts on theoretical and empirical grounds, discrediting Popper's assertion that a single counter-example must disprove a theory."[88] But even those who still believe in Popperian falsification, Kuklick points out, "would judge that Freeman has actually proven Mead's argument as he states it—the single case of Samoa showed that American behavioral norms did not derive from biological impulses. For Freeman's Samoans are no more like Americans than Mead's, although their lives are not idyllic but nasty and brutish (we do not know how short)."[89]

Thus, there is literally nothing to Freeman's claim to "scientific argument" disproving Mead's version of Samoa. And, indeed, although no one has yet noted it, actual scientists' reviews of *Margaret Mead and Samoa* were uniformly unenthusiastic. *Scientific American, American Scientist, Human Biology*—even *Ethnology and Sociobiology*—all ranged from lukewarm approval with major reservations to energetic deprecation.[90] "Freeman's scholarship seems to have stopped with the 1960s," noted Thelma Baker of Pennsylvania State University. Paul Alan Cox, a botanist at the University of California at Berkeley with significant experience with Samoa, judged Freeman's a "circumstantial case," and compellingly stated the problem— to which we will return—of the social locations of observer and observed:

> I am not surprised that an investigator who spent nine months with adolescent girls would come back with an image of a gentle and gracious Samoa, nor am I surprised that one who spent several years in the company of chiefs would describe a Samoa of veiled aggression, occasional violence, and the overwhelming importance of rank. Two different investigators studying, respectively, adolescents in Golden Gate Park and corporate executives in the San Francisco financial district would probably reach a similar divergence of opinion concerning the nature of California. Is it possible that cultures other than our own are complex and not easily characterizable?[91]

Scientific American provided a close précis of anthropologist Roy Rappaport's lengthy narrative of Freeman's mistaken accounts of American anthropological history and of Samoan culture, focusing particularly on the nonexistence of cultural determinism in American anthropology and on the partiality of Freeman's elite male lens onto Samoan culture.[92] Only the middlebrow media accepted Freeman's claims to scientific authority—allowed him to wear the "human nature expert" costume. According, then, to other Samoanists, historians of science, and the scientific establishment, Freeman is not a legitimate scientist. He just plays one on TV.[93]

Freeman's claims to the "technician of the sacred" and "raider of the lost ark" statuses are linked—a grand irony, considering their opposing interpretations of primitivism. The juncture is Freeman's contention that his lengthy Samoan fieldwork and male chiefly status—as opposed to Mead's short field stay and femaleness—have given him authority to speak for the "true" Samoa: "I was in an exceptionally favorable position to pursue my researches into the realities of Samoan life."[94] Perhaps the most repeated of Freeman's claims in the short-lived media carnival was that

precisely because of her sex, youth, and small stature, Mead's teenage informants "regaled [her] with counterfeit tales of casual love under the
palm trees."[95] So here Freeman articulates the outrage of some present-day
Samoans who perceive Mead's work—particularly its assertions of adolescent sexual activity—as an insult to national honor. "What would you
think if some foreigner came to your house and started asking about the
sex life of your kids?" exclaimed an elderly woman teacher, according to
the *Wall Street Journal.* "Freeman makes us human, Margaret Mead makes
us unreal—angels and puppets," asserted Le Tagoloa Leota Pita, a member
of the Western Samoan Parliament and a friend of Freeman's, to *Life* magazine.[96]

On the other hand, Freeman's vision of true Samoan life as characterized
by a "primeval rank system" that dictates a "regime of physical punishment" of children and violent "rivalrous aggression" among men, "highly
emotional and impulsive behavior that is animal-like in its ferocity" among
chiefs, and a rape rate "among the highest to be found anywhere in the
world"—would seem hardly to conduce to national pride.[97] And yet Freeman drew this excessive—Dionysian, as George Stocking points out—portrait in order to cast Mead's more "Apollonian" Samoan vision into doubt.
The irony, of course, is that in so doing Freeman locked himself into the
early-twentieth-century "cultural ethos" theoretical frame of Mead's ethnography, a far cry from the disinterested scientific stance he wished to
take. As Robert Levy notes, Freeman's book is "a prisoner of the same ideological conflicts about the moral relation of man [*sic*] to society that generated the nature/nurture opposition in the first place."[98] Jettisoning this
frame involves attending carefully to the conflations across many domains—space, time, polity, text versus reception—practiced by Freeman,
Mead herself, journalists responding to Freeman, and even some anthropologists who were otherwise insightful on the issues involved.

First is the question of which Samoa we are discussing. Pacific specialists have noted the very different colonial histories of American and Western Samoa. Lowell Holmes gives a great deal of detail on the remarkable
differences between Ta'u, the village he and Mead studied in American
Samoa, and Sa'anapu, the village Freeman studied in Western Samoa. The
first site was extraordinarily isolated from Western contact—in terms of
continuation of subsistence agriculture, lack of sanitary, transportation,
and communication infrastructure, and the low number of resident foreigners—at least into the 1960s. Freeman's village, on the other hand, was
early on integrated into cash-cropping, communication, transportation,
and job networks with Apia, the relatively cosmopolitan town on the other

side of its island of Upolu, and the entire region was heavily populated by foreigners from the mid–nineteenth century on.[99]

Then there is the issue of sheer passage of time. Freeman declares an essential Samoa across the decades as across the archipelago, as though, Holmes writes, "it has existed in an absolutely static condition despite its long contact with explorers, whalers, missionaries, colonial officials and bureaucrats, anthropologists and, more recently, educators with Western curricula and television networks."[100] Freeman thus argues for an *Adolescenticus samoanensis*, a tortured, passionate, and repressed creature unchanging in his or her nature from precolonial times to the present—a social type so different from Mead's easygoing portrait as to constitute the primordial model for pubescent Sturm und Drang. The late Eleanor Leacock grasped this point clearly, and her last research work provides the most insightful window onto the key importance of historical change to considerations of adolescence in Samoa and beyond.

Leacock, well known for her theoretical and ethnohistorical work on the relationship between women's status and various histories of colonization, went to Samoa two years after the publication of Freeman's book to investigate conditions affecting the country's adolescents. She was particularly disturbed by the way in which Freeman's ahistorical frame erased the actual lives of Samoan adolescents in the present:

> Nowhere does Freeman make reference to the kinds of problems some Samoans I talked with discussed: disjunctions between traditional mores and contemporary conditions in a poor Third World island nation, the problem of youth unemployment (meaningless in a subsistence economy but a major problem throughout the Third World today), the tragedy of a *rising* rate of youth suicides (a problem of concern throughout the South Pacific as well as in many other parts of the world), and the new phenomena of teenage vagrancy (impossible in the Samoa of the past) and teenage prostitution (a logical spinoff of vagrancy in a port town and a concern in Pago Pago).[101]

Leacock traveled throughout Samoa, spent time with adolescents in a variety of settings, and interviewed large numbers of teachers, social workers, ministers, public health workers, &c. She also consulted missionary and other ethnohistorical records. She found that, contra Freeman's vision of an unchanging harsh Samoan ethos, early records indicate relaxed parental discipline, complaisance over adolescent sexual experience except for girls of *taupo* status, and an adolescent suicide rate growing "from a rare event to a virtual epidemic" only from the late 1960s forward. (Holmes also gives extensive ethnohistorical evidence of well-established institutions of nonviolent conflict resolution in precolonial Samoa.) Leacock made clear the political economic sources of contemporary Western Samoan youth frustration: "Economic difficulties have limited expansion of the job market which cannot accommodate school graduates, and the over supply of labor has depressed wages. Meanwhile, and most important, the New Zealand economy slowed, and American Samoa made it more difficult to enter and go on to the United States, which cut off the option of working for awhile overseas that used to be taken for granted."[102]

Leacock's historicization of Freeman's vision of an essentialized Samoan adolescent emotional state gives us the context with which to interpret the schadenfreude-filled middlebrow on-site reportage—in the *Wall Street Journal* and the *New York Times Sunday Magazine,* for example—on contemporary Samoan poverty, crime, and malaise. When Richard Bernstein sneers about the "strange welfare-state mentality" of Samoans dependent on migrant remittances, or James Sterba refers jokily to adolescent boys "built like Samoan versions of Mr. T" who have to be shifted from rugby to football because of their excessive aggression, their historically grounded commentary, rather than buttressing the critique of Mead's Samoan field-work, actually undercuts the antihistorical ethologist Freeman.[103]

Indeed, while the media uproar over Freeman's attack in general functioned to delegitimate Mead—and with her, American cultural anthropology and the liberal political stance of her last years—individual journalists by no means necessarily signed on as Freeman supporters. The profession simply gravitated to the story, memorably described by Bonnie Nardi as an "ingenious combination of a sensational attack on an internationally famous female scholar with a graphic look at that old standby, sex-in-the-South Seas," as part of its own process of tabloidization in the 1980s.[104] Happily splashing about in the scandal, many members of the Fourth Estate nevertheless took an above-the-fray, "on the one hand, on the other hand" stance: both *Newsweek* and the *Chronicle of Higher Education* cited Emory University Samoanist Bradd Shore to that effect. *Newsweek* sagely concluded, "The truth probably lies somewhere between Mead's and Freeman's views," while *Life* ended its story with a summation from the American Samoan representative to the United States Congress: "I think Mead went too far—Samoans aren't without troubles—but Freeman is too dark, too simple."[105]

The apotheosis of this Grand Guignol media phenomenon came on the Phil Donahue show in Chicago, where Freeman appeared with Bradd Shore and Mead's daughter Mary Catherine Bateson.[106] Donahue, as is his wont, bounced about the studio spouting banalities about how this controversy over "nature versus nurture" had "raised the eyebrows of the entire anthropological community." Freeman, using his Commonwealth accent to the hilt, played the pompously self-assured scientist on TV. "I've got to tell you to go away and get educated," he declaimed to a furious Shore, whose book, he assured the audience, was "cultural determinist to an extreme degree." Responding to Bateson's efforts to tie him to *ad feminam* attacks on Mead, to sociobiology, and to a partial, elite perspective on Samoa, he glibly maintained that "I make not a single personal statement about her"; claimed, truly dottily, to be "very well known as perhaps the most trenchant critic of sociobiology"; and waved away all perspectival concerns with, "I am asking this question: was she right or wrong? That is what science is about." Tying up the issue to his own plummy satisfaction, he declared that "I'm quite sure these two people have never studied Sir Karl Popper. They don't know what science is about."

Freeman's repeated declamations that "I am a scientist" recalled nothing so much as Nixon's protests that he was not a crook. But the studio audience, while enjoying the theatrics of the interplay among Freeman, Bateson, Shore, and Donahue, was largely unconcerned with anyone's status—scientific or anthropological. They exhibited their own frames of reference at the end of the show, frames that revealed the difficulty of arguing any anthropological case in the court of contemporary American public opinion.

Some queries were simply factual: Why had Freeman used Mead's name in his title? Why is Samoa so important, anyway? What about the effect of the different eras in which the studies were done? Could learning itself have a biochemical base? Others were based on religious concerns: "I want to know how you fit God into your studies?" And, from a young priest: "Unless we put in choice, free will, it seems that we're not addressing the question totally." Still others exhibited their articulators' failure to take in the debate among the panelists, or an anti-intellectual skepticism about "experts": "It just seems that you're all agreeing but you won't admit that you are"; "Twenty years from now there will be a new story." One older man was entirely bizarre, ascribing divisions on the panel to the differences between Australian and American culture—but he thought that Australians were more scientific, and Americans engaged instead in salesmanship! (Even Donahue had felt constrained to scold Freeman: "You are difficult, somewhat self-indulgent and intolerant.")

Two queries in particular, in their very naïveté, actually revealed the undercurrents in Freeman's book and the politicized response to it. A woman asked baldly, "If you have two children in your family, they're both raised the same . . . but one goes bad and the other one's good, do you blame genes?" Here in a nutshell is the popular American morality play construction of nature versus nurture: either things are our fault, or they aren't. Either parents determine children's behavior, or biology does— economy, history, larger culture, peers, government policy do not even enter the picture. And then a man put his finger on the silent term—"Don't you feel you could get a better and truer picture of the United States making a survey here rather than going out of the country?"—and received the biggest applause of the day. Absurdly, classically xenophobic as his question is on the face of it, both the media hoopla surrounding Freeman's book and a significant component of Mead's original intervention were of course in fact precisely *not* about Samoa, but about contesting "pictures of the United States" in the public sphere.

AFTER THE BALL IS OVER

Freeman's fifteen minutes of fame are now long past, victim of the increasingly rapid biodegradation of American popular consciousness.[107] His supporters produced a documentary film in 1989, which Adam Kuper and Angela Gilliam have subjected to withering scholarly critique and which has since vanished from the public sphere.[108] I routinely ask both women's studies and anthropology classes if they have heard of Freeman or his book, and very few respond affirmatively, even when they have a niggling sense that there is some sort of blot on Mead's reputation. Only American new rightists remember and believe in Freeman's attack on Mead: a Lexis/Nexis search of all references to the two since 1990 reveals a handful of sneering articles in the *National Review* and the *American Spectator*—and a newspaper column by Pat Buchanan.[109]

Now that Freeman has been returned to the academic wallflower status he so richly deserves, four elements of the Freeman phenomenon, nevertheless, are worthy of note for their significance beyond the Reagan era and into the second millennium. These sequelae, as well, are connected in direct and indirect ways to Freeman's Reagan-era anthropological bookend: the earlier liberal feminist frisson surrounding *Nisa*.

The first element, as I have mentioned, is the extraordinary evidence of fissioning public spheres that the differing receptions of *Nisa* and *Margaret Mead and Samoa* give us. The *Wall Street Journal, Commentary, Fortune,* the *National Review, Forbes,* and the *Economist* certainly paid no attention to *Nisa,* while popular women's magazines and even scholarly feminist and most progressive journals sedulously ignored the Freeman firestorm.[110]

The contrast between the receptions of Shostak and Freeman was indicative of a trend that we can see has since only sharpened: anthropology for me versus anthropology for thee, or the political choice of which sorts of costumed anthropologists to invoke as authority in contestations over public issues.

Connected to this fissioning is the fact that, unnoticed by any commentator, American anthropology was doubly hoist by its own petard in the Freeman affair. That is, the press could happily concur with Freeman's kindergarten-science frame in which we have to decide whether or not Mead "got it right" about Samoa precisely because anthropology itself, in crisis and internally split, has failed to communicate to the public how the understanding that there *are* no "people without history" utterly changes how we envision Others. Similarly, as we have seen, the enduring popularity of *Nisa* among scholarly and popular female audiences indexes widespread belief that we can articulate an essential female nature outside human history. At every turn, the dead hand of the ethnographic present constrains progressive anthropologists from articulating intelligent perspectives on Others'—everyone's—lives. Attempting to counter the horrors of the "raiders of the lost ark" frame, we are forced unwittingly into impersonations of technicians of the sacred, and thus into complicity with an essentializing, ahistorical perspective that leads us right back into the global pool hall with the (often sociobiological) human nature experts. Schooled by American Anthropology Past, the public sphere cannot "read" scholarly commentators' careful historicizations of Others' lives, and so popular representations of Samoa parallel the "timeless" Kalahari and other fictions of "primitive" human lives.

Then, hoist doubly, the discipline itself has been framed through the liminal status of its objects: anthropology is figured by nonanthropological scholars and by the press alike, as I have shown, as timeless, ageless. What anthropologists have done to the !Kung San and Samoans and so many others has been brought home, deservedly, to anthropology. We are Difference, Otherness, Essence, the Once and Future Anthropologists. Never mind that the public recognizes that physical and biological sciences, economics, history, art history, and literary criticism all have their own developmental histories, are unrecognizable now compared with their selves and concerns in the 1920s. Anthropology is always the same, and primitives have no history. We are all Stone Age Nisa, all timeless Samoans—exotics at home.

This dual "exotic" framing directly engages the third key element of the Freeman affair: it marked the new Reagan-era race coding in American public discourse. Freeman certainly articulated no overt racism in *Margaret Mead and Samoa*. He repeatedly, in fact, expressed his admiration for Samoa—even declaring bathetically on the Phil Donahue show that he had arranged to be buried there. Reviewers frequently noted, nevertheless, the racist implications of Freeman's portrait of the "dark side" of the Samoan national character. Nardi, for example, registered the "virulent ethnic slur" of "Freeman's claims that Samoan men have a 'preoccupation' with 'deflowering' virgins and with committing rape."[111] Marvin Harris articulated the logical problem in discussing Freeman's obsession with *moetotolo*—"sleep-crawling"—the Samoan institution of "rape" which may most often be a form of agreed-upon elopement: "Does Freeman believe that Samoans have a gene for sleep-crawling? Does he believe that it is part of human nature to sleep-crawl?"[112] Obviously, if Freeman were to answer yes to the first question, then he would be indisputably a racist as well as in denial of all modern biology. But he has repeatedly declared, as he did on *Donahue*, that Samoans are like the rest of us. This profound logical inconsistency—this flirtation with but never full commitment to the notion of biologically based racial inferiority—is, as we have seen, precisely the trope through which "respectable" racism operates in the post-civil-rights-era United States, extending the Nixon administration's "plausible deniability" into another realm. It was one of the great attractions of Freeman's book in the popular press—and one of the key objections of anthropological critics. But the issue is rather more complicated than it at first appears.

Many critics noted—and some went into great detail in explicating—the racist, eugenicist American political and scholarly climate within which Franz Boas built the Columbia University Department of Anthropology and against which he fought. Citing the evil of the past, however, may be a necessary but is certainly an insufficient counter to that of the present. (Only Lenora Foerstal and Angela Gilliam made the trenchant point that Mead *and* Freeman, lifelong, maintained fundamentally colonialist stances on Pacific peoples.) And we have seen that Freeman, while lacking the righteous antiracist fervor of his critics, did indeed acknowledge the racism of Progressive Era biological anthropology. It was his claim, however, that political interest led Boas and his students astray from the truth: that the Boasians were, in other words, politically correct to the detriment of empirical science. It was exactly this faux magisterial stance that made him for a period the conservative poster boy for the judicious, scientific debunking of liberal claptrap—and that, as we shall see, new rightist Dinesh D'Souza more than a decade later would use as a platform for his explicitly racist arguments.

Shifting constructions of gender in scholarship and in the public sphere are the fourth key element of the Freeman phenomenon with consequences into the present. In parallel to his avoidance of overt racism, Freeman nowhere articulates opposition to feminism or to the study of gender relations. Instead, as we have seen, he insinuates that Mead's very femaleness—and that of her key informants in Samoa—made her scholarship suspect. In Freeman's epistemology, a maiden, dusky or not, is no very worthy thing to be. This indirect attack on the very notion of female intelligence and disinterestedness and thus scholarly accomplishment was certainly taken in by gleeful and horrified respondents alike (although the feminist critique was very slow in arriving—of the vast numbers of those weighing in on the topic within the first year after publication, only Colin Turnbull, Marilyn Strathern, and Bonnie Nardi made this point).[113]

Then, in his portrait of the Samoan ethos, Freeman returns to the worldview of the fin de siècle missionary writings that stressed the ubiquity of "primitive" violence against women—but with *this* end-of-century's twist: instead of using it to justify the need for Western Christian proselytizing, Freeman deploys the existence of Samoan violence against women in multiple and covert ways, as Nardi notes. It functions as a backdoor racist slap—entirely unearned, since Freeman failed to adjust his comparative rape statistics for age and they are therefore so much nonsense. Moreover, as he is "relentless, almost brutal, in his descriptions of sexual violence against women," Freeman's narratives fed Western appetites for such lurid detail and help to explain explosive press attention at the time of publication.[114] But beyond these points, and unnoted by critics, Freeman's obsession with rape in Samoa functions epistemologically in exactly the way all nonfeminist focus on violence against women functions: in highlighting women's potential sexual vulnerability, it rhetorically underlines and reinforces women's already-existing lower status. Thus, the logical and rhetorical structures of *Margaret Mead and Samoa* naturalize *all* women's domination by men—and press reaction at the time was redolent with this meaning.

But Shostak's—and Mead's before her—interpretive focus *away* from violence against women, while offering honest ethnographic reportage of the phenomenon, offers us no aid in escaping Freeman's and the larger culture's false naturalizations. We become locked instead inside the discursive seesaws between noble and nasty savage, between the progressive and retrogressive race and gender essentialisms of identity politics—locked inside the culture of forgetting our own economic, intellectual, cultural histories, to say nothing of their complex intersections with those of Others.

CODA: THE NEW NARCISSAE

One problematic reflection of this ideological inheritance from the Reagan-Bush era is the recent development of a self-described "feminist ethnography." An uneasy amalgam of identity politics and postmodernism, this tendency focuses on the (particularly racial and gendered) self of the fieldworker, the ethics of her relationship with an informant or informants, and on the connections between her chosen textual form and style and these identities and relationships.

The prehistory of this school can be traced to British sociologist Ann Oakley's early contention that women were more empathetic, more ethical, less enamored of positivist methods than men in doing social research. American sociologist Judith Stacey's often-cited 1988 piece "Can There Be a Feminist Ethnography?" then laid out the contradictions in "sisterhood" created by the inevitable use to which even the most feminist researcher puts her female informants. Lila Abu-Lughod followed with an identically titled article very intelligently engaged with these issues but also defining "feminism" very narrowly: in terms only of ethical selfhood in dyadic encounters and in textualization.[115]

Then, however, came the books. In *Translated Woman*, Ruth Behar punctuated a straightforward and fascinating life history of a Mexican woman peddler with her own interweaving autobiography, ending in a claim of identity with the woman:

> I was now lost in a different wilderness, the wilderness of success in the university system, success I myself had striven for. After being the woman who couldn't translate herself, I had suddenly become the woman who translated herself too well. And in the midst of it all, I was planning to turn the tales of a Mexican street peddler into a book that would be read within the very same academy that had toyed with my most intimate sense of identity and then, with even less compunction, bought me out.... In different ways, both Esperanza and I partake of the double-edged identity of a Malinche.[116]

Kamala Visweswaran mused, in *Fictions of Feminist Ethnography*, on her identity as a "halfie," (subcontinental Indian and white American) while skimming lightly across anthropological and literary texts by and about women of color:

> I want to reflect further upon how my particular identity formation influenced not only where but also how I chose to study; to understand, if only partially, how the the anthropological resources available to an American of South Asian

descent might shape a return "home." . . . [Zora Neale] Hurston's move here [in *Tell My Horse*] to posit a strategically unified American womanhood, without invoking the power differentials between different groups of American women, is an important, if problematic one. . . . [Laura Bohannan's] questioning does not stop with the distinction between prejudice and principle but extends to the very nature of self.[117]

Clearly, there is value in such concerns: who we are often channels what we find in research, ethical considerations are always important, and the congealed, passive-verb horror of much social science writing fairly cries out for mandatory textual self-consciousness. But to treat these issues as if they circumscribed the entirety of a feminist anthropological project is simply to mimic the postmodern anthropological gaffe, to elide political economy and history in solipsistic absorption in our personal, unresearched reactions to ethnography and imaginative literature, with the uncertain meanings of textualizing our own dyadic ethnographic encounters. Clifford Geertz has condescendingly scored this stance of a number of postmodern males as "epistemological hypochondria" and endemic "diary disease," a judgment also applicable to their sisters.[118]

Indeed, the "feminist ethnography" school of thought is marked too often by the commission of multiple synecdochic fallacies: taking the part for the whole in feminist research, in anthropology itself, in intellectual history. First, feminism inevitably takes adjectives, and these writers often follow the cultural feminist tendency to ignore all materialist feminist analysis, past and present. Doing so reduces "feminism" to a consideration of differing female selves cut off from economy and history, renders us blind to the most obvious pragmatic points. Visweswaran, for example, who is sharply critical of contemporary "feminists in anthropology [who do not] call into question their own positions as members of dominant Western societies," is nevertheless utterly oblivious to the highly colonialist frame of *Return to Laughter*. She instead sees Laura Bohannan as a pioneer woman anthropologist who should be defended against charges of writing "confessional field literature" that is "inadequate science" because of her "awareness of the integrity and ineffability of difference" and the "profound crises of identity" that she narrates in the novel.[119] Margery Wolf has written compellingly about the problematics of overinvestment in on-the-ground ethical and methodological concerns to the detriment of substantive research and of "get[ting] on with the work of creating a more equitable world." And I have noted the extraordinary fact that no one seems to remember that the ethics/power/methodology domain in social science is simply not at all "feminist" in origin: it was, as we have seen, broached prior to the second wave of feminism by the ethnomethodology/symbolic interaction sociologists.[120]

Then, as I have pointed out, in many contemporary precincts only the recent thin skin of postmodern literature seems to count as "anthropology." Marilyn Strathern's much-cited "Awkward Relationship: The Case of Feminism and Anthropology" is the source of some of these partial frameworks. Although she qualifies her statements, Strathern synecdochically misidentifies anthropology with only postmodern literature, and feminism with only those whose epistemology demands "the construction of a feminist self [and thus] a nonfeminist Other."[121] Such a formulation allows Ruth Behar, for example, to ignore the specific intersections between the peddler Esperanza's life and shifting Mexican and global political economy—and the Mexican, American, and other scholarship on those topics—substituting repeated, affect-laden invocations of the evil of "the border." In addition, she rejects feminist analysis of the woman's life because "she didn't fit the part of the exemplary feminist heroine for whom Western women are always searching among 'native women.'"[122] The culture of forgetting. Every woman her own anthropologist.

There are consummate ironies in this fin de siècle development. Protesting against the rather obvious sexism of the male postmodernists in anthropology, many of these women writers tend nevertheless to cleave unto the narrow and self-defeating postmodern epistemology, denying themselves the contextualizations of historical political economy and cultural and intellectual history. They textualize a very traditional anthropological "America"—an untheorized, unresearched, but privileged "home." (Visweswaran even calls for anthropology to take up "homework.")[123] Instead of identifying with and attempting to contribute to global radical traditions in feminism, in anthropology, or in scholarship and/or activism in general, they yearn toward the status of creative artist and proclaim their "textual innovations" in the place of rigorous analysis of other women's, their own, or anyone's lives.

When it comes to the question of identity, however, many of these writers depart from postmodernism with a vengeance. Rather than accepting the "death of the subject," they proclaim their own gendered and raced subjectivities, implying an isomorphism between status and understanding—the "you see from where you stand" line of identity politics. Mirroring the confusions of the larger culture, they declaim, as British critic Ambalavanar Sivanandan pungently rewrites Descartes: "I am, therefore I resist."[124] But, as we saw in chapter 2, identity politics specifically elides the ways in which particular race, gender, and national subjectivities exist within shifting class relations. And indeed, there is no exit, no escape from the inevitable class privilege of the intellectual, in even these constricted times.

"Going native" in this way, proclaiming *"La* Dusky Maiden, *c'est moi,"* is also going native to, giving in to, embracing some American popular cultural apprehensions of what being an anthropologist constitutes and of the nature of human social reality. The embrace of hybridity, liminality, the celebration of one's exoticism at home, substitutes for the production of actual analyses of the raced and gendered imperial structures of feeling that figure Dusky Maidenhood, that legitimate and enact our increasingly inegalitarian global order. Mead's own self-satisfied, underresearched claims to global understanding—and particularly her articulation of her privileged, omniscient positionality in American life; Freeman's silly "identity" attack on the femaleness of Mead and of her Samoan informants; and Shostak's limited portraiture of white Western feminist ethnographer and Stone Age woman have as their unintended and ironic descendants a body of work that portrays an essentialized world of *all* people with only static and singular identities, without actual material lives in complex intersection in the global economy—without history. Just as the witty British homosexual writer Quentin Crisp finally concluded that There Is No Tall Dark Man, we need to admit a world without Dusky Maidens, neither Others nor ourselves.

six

PATTERNS OF CULTURE WARS

Place, Modernity, and the Contemporary Political Economy of Difference

What can we expect from our cold dispatches which to be clear must necessarily be long? What are they compared to the vivid and interesting accounts of someone who can say: *I have seen?*—*M. de Riquebourg, in Stendhal's* The Telegraph[1]

HEARTLAND PROLEGOMENON

Dempster Street, like Chicago, like America, has altered over the years of this book's composition. The futon store, once a corner grocery, closed suddenly and reopened as a computer games center. A used book store has now transmogrified into the Annapurna Herb Shop. Light of the Moon displays a new sign—"Psychic Today." Down the street, a Starbucks coffee outlet and a fast photo store have opened next door to one another, and the posthippie restaurant across the street has added a bakery. Two new oriental rug stores—one named Tribal Looms—have added themselves to the mix. Billowing incense now mingles with coffee and pastry smells in an ethnic, New Age, and gourmet entrepreneurial synergy. The weekend traffic from the wealthy white suburbs, as evinced by Jaguars and BMWs at the curbs, has intensified. But a thrift store whose profits go to pediatric AIDS care now flourishes around the corner—a store where recently migrant *mexicanas* shop for children's clothes and where a local homeless black woman can often be seen chatting with the workers or catching a nap on the old sofas for sale. Another homeless woman selling *Streetwise*

23. Annapurna Herb Shop, Dempster Street. (Photo by author.)

24. Psychic Today, Dempster Street. (Photo by author.)

25. Tribal Looms, Inc., just off Dempster Street. (Photo by author.)

outside the supermarket and the large young black man in the ice cream store with the peruke and silver feather earring—who waves at me as I pass on my walk to work—now sport Native American dream catcher necklaces. Evolving American and global capitalism—less constrained by the state each year—produces ever-increasing wealth and poverty and continues its juggernaut commodification of objects that offer other-worldly surcease from the anxieties of its privileges and its penury.

At the end of this century in the heartland of America, as at the end of the last, the making of the modern and of the antimodern go hand in hand. In each period, political backlash against progressive change led to sky-rocketing inequalities. In each, American economic and foreign policy stimulated vast global labor migrations. Renascent racism against new-comers and older stigmatized populations distracted and distracts from overarching economic injustice. Simultaneously, as at the last fin de siècle, groups attempt to wrest help for the impoverished and the ill served from the evolving system, organizing the unorganized and drawing labor, cash, and cast-off commodities from the well intentioned.

Some dozen miles down the lakefront, the Field Museum of Natural History, founded for the 1893 exposition and moved north to the Loop area in 1920, reflects the complicated present in which wildly varying represen-tations of race and gender jostle hugger-mugger up against one another. Scattered throughout the halls are large bronze busts and full statues of a panoply of Others—"Zulu Woman," "Ethiopian Man," "Andaman Is-lander," "Vedda, Ceylon," "Bushman Family." They were cast for the 1933 Chicago World's Fair by the intrepid American feminist sculptor and stu-dent of Rodin, Malvina Hoffman, who defied contemporary physical an-thropologists by using bronze instead of plaster—thus erasing skin, eye and hair color differences—and by sculpting real individuals rather than "racial types."[2] Over the ensuing decades, reactions to the bronzes have reflected shifting political sensitivities, different meanings of the modern, the progressive. The depression-era *Federal Writers' Project Guide* revealed its radical Popular Front perspective in the notation that Hoffman's work "indicates that humanity is a single species."[3] In the 1960s, the statues were deemed racially offensive and put in storage; in 1971, many of them were brought back out and relabeled.[4] Today the bronzes stand, with explana-tory material about Hoffman's project, and there is renewed feminist inter-est in her as a struggling, and successful, early-twentieth-century woman artist.[5] But contemporary—and probably mostly youthful—museum visi-tors also have left unmistakable signs of their combined curiosity and condescension: in a veritable counting coup over the Others represented, the statues' knees, noses, mouths, breasts, and genitals have been rubbed shiny.

At the same time, curators of ethnographic materials at the Field Museum, like thoughtful natural history and other museum professionals everywhere, struggle with the objectifying, imperializing heritage of their institutions.[6] They attempt to rework and relabel collections, and to mount different sorts of exhibits—like the small *Body Ornamented* display that underlines human gender malleability as illustrated by counterintuitive cross-cultural jewelry, and the planned *Living Together* project on the human diversity of contemporary Chicago that will use a multiplicity of donated T-shirts and video equipment to allow visitors to "dress" themselves in varying Chicago identities.[7]

Living in the Chicago area during the years of the Hill-Thomas hearings, the Rodney King trial, and the O. J. Simpson media circus—as well as two presidential campaigns and the first and second Clinton administrations—has involved experiencing a virtual flood of race and gender imagery in popular culture. As we have seen, despite some progressive countercurrents, the hegemonic stream of representation in the public sphere shunts off organically connected class relations from its smoothly flowing portraits of American race and gender at the end of this century. As in the flawed "culture and personality" tradition and its postmodern and other inheritors in American anthropology, difference is divorced from power and history, *mentalité* from the material. Public culture makes lavish use of ethnographic fakery to create good and bad Others, model minorities, role model and reprobate dusky maidens—representations that just happen to suit the changing needs of differing fractions of capital in this era of flexible accumulation.

Appalled by the venal and hypocritical Louis-Philippe regime of the early nineteenth-century, Stendhal created the silly "company man," Prefect de Riquebourg, whose bombast on the rhetorical efficacy of firsthand accounts disgusts the young protagonist Lucien Leuwen. At the end of the twentieth century, too many academics—postmodern or middlebrow de Riquebourgs without even his self-conscious cynicism—live inside the ethnographic fallacy with the rest of the public sphere, fetishize the personal encounter, and consider philosophically naive any attempt to hold up dyadic encounter representations to considerations of typicality, of historical context, of political economic connection.

And in those academic precincts still devoted to "cold dispatches," to the quantified empirical and to the life of American cities, where we would expect to find accurate narratives of evolving race- and gender-inflected class relations, the undead hand of the worst of the Chicago School—falsifying, behaviorist, functionalist, and victim blaming—dominates the landscape. We have seen that the University of Chicago's William Julius Wilson (now moved to Harvard) has built, through the counterempirical "underclass" concept, a career and a funding industry based on passive-verb, ahistorical political economy and "blame the victim" sociology. His latest book, *When Work Disappears*, continues this tradition. In a farewell interview with a fawning *Chicago Tribune*, Wilson celebrated himself as the inheritor of the Chicago School, stated that Chicago itself was important only because of its use as a "natural laboratory" by social scientists, and blamed an agentless "deindustrialization" for contemporary black poverty—effacing racism, the widening gulf between rich and poor, and the public policies that have maintained them.[8] Liberal *Tribune* columnist Mary Schmich discovered, as a Nieman fellow at Harvard, that the work of local sociologists Wilson and Christopher Jencks was essential to understanding Chicago "as both the symbol of everything that's wrong in American cities and the source of the solution."[9] The carefully historicized empirical work of other scholars of Chicago—Gary Orfield, David Ranney, Dwight Conquergood, Larry Bennett, James Grossman, Douglas Massey—who fail to portray the "ghetto-specific behaviors" of subhuman Others and whose findings point real fingers of blame at government policy and capital movement for the creation and maintenance of American poverty, somehow cannot manage to attract the same sort of media attention.[10] Sara Paretsky's best-selling series of Chicago-based feminist mystery novels, ironically, offer the narrative of corporate greed, state complicity, and the intertwining of gender and race domination that somehow dares not speak its name in popular "nonfiction" venues.

I observed the rise of "underclass" hegemony in the local and national public sphere, however, from a site a thousand miles to the east of the City of Big Shoulders. I lived and did fieldwork in a working-class neighborhood in New Haven, Connecticut, during the last half-dozen years of the Reagan-Bush era. My ethnographic and volunteer work, and my historical research on scholarly and popular characterizations of the city during the postwar era, heightened my awareness of both the mutability and the material connections of representations of American urban Others.

EASTERN SEABOARD INTERLUDE

New Haven has had a complicated presence in the American imaginary over the course of the twentieth century. It is, first of all, an Ivy League company town: the site of Yale University since the eighteenth century, its center defined by a still-existing village green surrounded by old churches and a commercial area. The Yale campus itself helps to maintain the Anglophiliac fiction of dreaming spires, as its main buildings, including the library, Law School, gymnasium, and many "colleges" (residence halls) are built in the style sardonically labeled "1930s Gothic." That is, their stone pediments, bas-reliefs, and gargoyles are the work of impoverished Italian stoneworkers hired by the university for a pittance during the depression.

These workers are at the center of the second image of New Haven, as a fundamentally white ethnic, blue-collar town—a gritty, redbrick industrial center since the nineteenth century, former home of the Winchester armaments company and dozens of other light and heavy manufacturing concerns. Like most eastern seaboard and industrial Midwestern cities, New Haven experienced landslide migrations first from Ireland in the mid–nineteenth century, and later from southern and eastern Europe until the passage of restrictive federal immigration legislation in 1924. New Haven's white ethnics were overwhelmingly Italian and Irish. The city is the national headquarters of the Knights of Columbus, and there are still a half-dozen "ethnic" Catholic churches. New Haven was immortalized in scholarship as a fundamentally white ethnic town in Irvin L. Child's classic World War II–era essay, *Italian or American?*[11] The city also boasts a long tradition of militant white ethnic unionism, the spillover from which can be seen in Yale's repeated failures to rein in its custodial and maintenance staff, Local 35, and in 35's comradely assistance to its sister union, Local 34, during the notorious, and successful, clerical workers' strike of 1985.[12]

The third, lesser-known layer of this *pentimento* urban portrait is provided by the town's black population, always present but greatly swelled by Northern migration from the Carolina South for Connecticut Valley tobacco cultivation, by wartime industrial employment opportunities in the 1910s and 1940s, and by ongoing flight from the Jim Crow South through the 1950s. Because of the particular demographic character of this migrant stream, the local black population has a distinctive identity. A black radio ad for "Stephanie's Open Pit Barbecue," for example, plays on the slang term for black South Carolinians in its joking end: "And if you don't see little Stephanie, just look for her Dad, Geech." There are also black migrants from other Northern locations, some of whom arrived originally from the Cape Verde Islands, a small number of professional-class in-migrants from all over the United States, and more recent demographic complexity added by migrants from the Francophone and Anglophone Caribbean and by a significant newer population of Puertorriqueños, some of whom identify as black. Because of New Haven's accessibility to New York and New Jersey, black New Haven also has a long tradition of jazz musicianship institutionalized in live music clubs and good local radio.

New Haven's black population intersected with its Yale and white ethnic identity in the 1960s in the course of civil rights organizing and urban unrest, and most particularly during the infamous 1970 trial of Black Panther Bobby Seale. Local politicians and police behaved predictably in defiance of free speech and civil rights, Yale students and some administration figures offered their support, and their left-liberalism (like that of most "radical" campuses), always more apparent than real, was memorialized in Gary Trudeau's *Doonesbury* cartoon series, which itself had begun as a *Yale Daily* feature.[13]

Just before the excursions and alarums of campus Vietnam-era politics, however, Yale political scientist Robert Dahl in 1961 published the book that was to etch New Haven's portrait in stone—to provide the most enduring image of the city to an American audience. *Who Governs?* established New Haven as *the* exemplar of political pluralism, new-style postwar urban democracy, an inclusive win-win politics.[14] *Who Governs?* rapidly became a standard college social science textbook and is still in print and still being assigned nearly four decades after its original publication. Just as Chicago became sociologists' natural laboratory for urban order/disorder issues, New Haven became the political scientists' Holy Grail for "democratic pluralism." The pluralist process that Dahl celebrated in particular was Mayor Richard Lee's town-gown coalition of the 1950s and early 1960s that cleverly gained access to more than $180 million in federal urban renewal dollars—a grotesquely disproportionate amount of federal money expended in all American cities during that period—and transformed the New Haven urbanscape.[15] Demographically speaking, Dahl was also celebrating the working-together of professional-class WASPs and the white ethnics of working-class origin in this process, and of the growth-politics candidates who followed Lee into the mayoralty. And indeed, sixteen of the twenty years of rule between Lee and the inauguration of New Haven's first black chief executive, John Daniels, in 1991, were presided over by two local white ethnics, John Guida and Biagio DiLieto. Dahl did not deal at all with black New Haven's exclusion from this "democratic," successful pluralist process, except in one asterisked bottom-of-the-page admission.

A group of "community power studies" scholars in the 1970s and 1980s challenged Dahl's pluralist model in general and his New Haven case study in particular. William Domhoff demonstrated the "interlocking directorate" of government and corporate capital involved in the Lee enterprise and its siphoning of federal money into private profits. Clarence Stone and Heywood Sanders documented Lee's ultimate failure as politician despite his success as mayor. Norman and Susan Fainstein provided a textured historical account of extraordinary benefits to Yale University and St. Raphael's Hospital and losses for the populace as a whole. Both institutions gained vast tracts of land formerly housing the poor and working classes, while low-income housing was destroyed and not replaced. Fully one in five of New Haven residents—disproportionately black—was displaced. Functioning industry and small business was discouraged, white flight and suburbanization exacerbated, and even the civic centerpieces of Lee's plan—the coliseum, the parking garage, the shopping mall—deteriorated into shabbiness and disuse. The Fainsteins also chronicle the ultimate defeat of 1960s black and white radical organizers through the carrot of co-optation—a handful of public administration jobs and some short-term federal antipoverty money—and the stick of police harassment, including physical violence and widespread illegal wiretapping.[16]

Under Nixon's administration, urban renewal and War on Poverty federal funding was converted into Community Development Block Grants, which were structured to provide even fewer benefits to working-class and poor urban dwellers, irrespective of the intentions of individual urban regimes. Nixon, Ford, and Carter, as we have seen, each further cut federal money flowing to cities, and Reagan shut the spigot off altogether in the early 1980s. National federal enforcement of civil rights laws slowed to near stoppage. Under Reagan and then Bush, the United States experienced significant upward income redistribution, and a variety of indices indicating improvement in minority economic lives began to move in reverse. Nevertheless, the muckraking political economic analysis of the community power scholars failed to enter the public transcript, while a resurgent "blame the victim" structure of feeling captured the American imaginary.

The community power scholars focused on race and class implications of federal and local governmental policies and the ways in which they constrained local-level oppositional politics. They did not deal at all with gendered implications of policies and politics, even though there was considerable feminist activity in New Haven from the late 1960s on, and a short-lived but very active organization of women on AFDC, the New Haven Welfare MOMS.[17] As the 1980s progressed, however, and "underclass" interpretations of changing urban life swamped all others in the public sphere, Wilson's explicitly victim-blaming, male-dominant frame affected even those writers whose self-conscious sympathies lay with their impoverished subjects.

One such example is William Finnegan's well-known two-part *New Yorker* series on inner-city New Haven, published in 1990.[18] Lyrically written, "Out There" focuses on a confused, sixteen-year-old sometime drug dealer from the Newhallville ghetto, in whom Finnegan finds an "eery purity." While Finnegan notes larger political economic forces, the bulk of his narrative retails male youth gang ritual, "Terry's" dysfunctional life choices, and the seemingly irresponsible behavior of Terry's separated parents, particularly his mother. Finnegan spends an inordinate amount of time in Terry's mother's apartment, chronicling her sometime drug use and easygoing neglect of her younger son's nutrition and proper bedtime. Like other recent accounts of the urban poor reviewed by Michael Massing, Finnegan's has a "tendency to champion inner-city kids at the expense of their parents."[19] The overall shape of his narrative allows the reader to imagine a vast gulf between Terry's mother and middle-class American mothers in general, and to suspect that had she only been "properly maternal," New Haven would not have impoverished, segregated schools, atrocious low-income housing, and a double-digit minority unemployment rate. Behind his own back, by both focusing on and neglecting particular topics, Finnegan commits the ethnographic fallacy, and his beautiful writing, so unlike the tedious sociologese of Wilson and his ilk, nevertheless functions to maintain "underclass" ideology.

When Finnegan's piece came out, there was a flurry of interest in New Haven—I even saw a copy at the inner-city adult learning center where I volunteered to teach reading—and especially at Yale. He was repeatedly invited to speak at the university, and many Yale faculty, stirred to interest in the city in which they worked, asked me my opinion. Finnegan had lent to the shabby postindustrial city a new gravitas, a kind of belletristic glamour as a vest-pocket New York, a site of equally interesting and deplorable urban problems in the white middle-class American imaginary.

New Haven, a city of about 130,000, is indeed in many ways a vest-pocket New York, absent the tradition of rent control and with the addition of a tax-avoiding major industry—Yale University—and a more regressive tax structure (state income tax was not enacted until 1991). Over the 1980s, the city experienced the same real estate speculation spiral and then collapse, the same cycles of stalled gentrification, with extraordinary proliferation of scandalous city tax abatements for friends in high places, slumlords, and bank and owner abandonment, the same schizmogenetic emptying out of middle-income occupations and thus residents, the same increase in minority residents. In 1980, New Haven was nearly 60 percent white; by 1990, the majority of the population was black and Latino. Black residents' median household income was only 55 percent of whites', and that of Latinos was even lower.[20] Similarly, each city in this period elected its first black mayor, each of whom had little appetite for mobilizing radical political change, each of whom inherited the combination of inflated expectations and fiscal crisis—and was thus inevitably forced to administer austerity, lose popularity, and be voted out of office.[21] In 1991 alone, New Haven's John Daniels laid off hundreds of city workers, cut recreation programs, and partially shut down the public libraries. The period of my ethnographic present, 1986–1992, captures this boom-to-bust era with its concomitant skyrocketing minority immiseration, burgeoning youth-run drug industry (with an estimated turnover of $1 million a day), and white anxieties over the real estate bust and street crime.[22] One unobtrusive measure of deepening impoverishment: in the nine-month space between my exodus from the state in the fall of 1991 and one return visit in the spring of 1992, three new check-cashing stores and two new pawnshops opened in areas close to my old neighborhood.

The neighborhood in which I lived in New Haven is not yet a ghetto, but a historically working-class area on the margins of immiseration—a site that, I would argue, is a particularly helpful vantage point for viewing shifting urban culture and political economy. The neighborhood lies due west of the Yale campus. Between the two sites is a residential and commercial area, Dwight/Edgewood, that, because of its run-down character and key location near the exit ramps of both freeways, became a prime drug-selling site over the course of the late 1980s. Directly north of the neighborhood is a mixed middle-class and affluent area, Beaver Hills, that has become the major professional-class black residential neighborhood. Perhaps not coincidentally, abutting this integrated neighborhood is Dixwell, one of the three main named New Haven ghettos. Directly south of my neighborhood is The Hill, the second ghetto, originally Italian and Jewish and recently heavily settled by Puerto Ricans. A wooded park provides the natural boundary on the west of the neighborhood. Past the park is Westville, one of the most affluent and whitest residential areas in the city, one of two neighborhoods inhabited by those Yale faculty who do not commute from the wealthy, white shoreline suburbs.

In 1986, the major arterial street bounding the north of the neighborhood boasted a kosher butcher, a Hadassah thrift store, and a number of other clearly Jewish-owned and patronized small businesses, the leftover commercial scaffolding of a prior heavy Jewish settlement now largely suburbanized. By 1991, only Hadassah remained, despite the new settling of a significant group of Hasidim in both my neighborhood and in Westville, which now boasted three *mikvahs* (ritual baths). (Hadassah finally closed in 1997.) The arterial's character altered, ethnicized in a different direction, as several stores and restaurants catering to Caribbean blacks opened. It altered further in 1988 when a local entrepreneur, a "hip capitalist," moved what had been a small, crowded health food grocery in the Edgewood area into a rehabilitated former nightclub, providing the city's first health food supermarket.

The neighborhood's housing stock is largely composed of three-story, wooden, single-family houses built in the 1920s and 1930s, a smaller number of Victorian-era structures, and a few apartment houses of various periods, with small, grassed front yards and mature deciduous trees. Throughout the neighborhood are clusters of homes still inhabited by single owners, while others have been cut up into three-flat rentals. When I moved onto the block in 1986, only one house was still undivided and owner occupied. By 1988, the owner, Dominic, an elderly Italian-American, had divided and rented out the house and moved to a nearby suburb with his ailing wife, leaving his adult blue-collar son, young Dom, sole proprietor of the undivided but tenanted Victorian next door on the corner. The block had originally been mainly Italian and Irish. The elderly sisters of a large Irish family were the owners of my two-flat house before my landlords, a white professional-class couple from out of state, bought and renovated it for rental in a long-term strategy to finance their children's college education. The attic still contained old Christmas decorations and mouldering Catholic school textbooks.

The block in 1986 was all white with the exception of one house, owned since the 1960s by a now-elderly black woman who lived on the third floor and rented the two flats beneath to working-class black couples. By the time I moved out in 1991, most of the houses on the block had some working-class black tenants. The house next door had shifted from all-white to all-black in the period of a year. My landlord, now divorced from my landlady, moved into my apartment, and a black family moved in downstairs. My landlady had only black responses to her rental ad and tried to put the house on the market only to be told that it was currently unsalable.

The number of children on the block fluctuated over the years as renters moved in and out, but the feel of the neighborhood remained small-townish, with yard sales (called tag sales in New England) abundant in season, kids on bikes, black and white, riding on the sidewalks, and heavy pedestrian traffic between the arterial streets that bounded the area to the north and south. On Friday evenings, Hasidim walked to synagogue. On Sunday mornings, St. Brendan's, the Catholic church a handful of blocks away, played dreadful, metallic-sounding fake bell music from a loud-speaker. This idyllic appearance was belied by the high crime rate. My car tape deck was stolen as soon as I moved in, and my downstairs neighbors were mugged at gunpoint in our driveway the following month.

Crime became more serious as the city's immiseration deepened in the late 1980s. All measures of violent and property crime increased markedly between 1985 and 1990.[23] When Adolph Reed moved into my apartment in 1988, his inexpensive compact car was stolen once and broken into three times until I bought him a car alarm, the first in the neighborhood. A work-ing-class black couple moved into the second-floor flat next door in 1990, replacing a white professional couple who moved to New Jersey when the scientist wife was offered a lucrative chemical industry job. Within the first three months, both the new couple's cars had been stolen, and that of a visiting relative was broken into. When the police made major busts of drug customers, though, the bulk of names were recognizably male and white ethnic, their homes in the half-dozen white suburban towns ringing the now-black and brown majority city.

The burgeoning drug industry was still mostly invisible in the neighbor-hood but became increasingly audible, with frequent night gunfire heard from the crack wars a half-mile away. By 1991, the gunfire was a nightly occurrence. In the spring of 1991, there was a shootout between the occu-pants of two jeeps directly in front of my house at ten o'clock on a Tuesday morning. Post hoc analysis indicated that the incident was part of the inev-itable industrial restructuring of the local drug business in the wake of the weekend arrest of the CEOs of one firm in the informal economy. This incident brought home to me, as well, the strength of the iconic representa-tion of "authentic" ethnography as exotically dangerous: my first emotion under fire was de Riquebourg's exhilarated, self-aggrandizing "I have seen."

Another measure, visible to some, of the further impoverishment of the city's poor was the appearance of street prostitution. Largely black and Puerto Rican women, some obviously addicts and others not, they walked slowly through the neighborhood streets at night. They were invisible as prostitutes to many because they were not dressed, shod, coiffed or made up as prostitutes: they habitually dressed very casually, often promenading in sweatsuits and running shoes in the winter months. Car traffic increased as johns, overwhelmingly white men, cruised the streets, frequently accosting black women residents, including middle-class homeowners. When a john stopped and a prostitute got in the car, he would ritually "peel out" as he screeched off to find a place to park and get a blow job. Every few months the local paper would report, straight-faced, the robbery of a motorist who, upon "offering a woman a ride," would find himself facing a man in a wig brandishing a gun.

Here, ironically, our Chicago School inheritance turns out to be of use. That is, Ernest Burgess's 1925 social ecological notions of the inevitable, evolutionary rings of ethnic urban settlement, newcomers pushing out and up from the center city, can be transformed into a vision of the new sexual/ racial economic relation of impoverished New Haven and its surrounding better-off environs.[24] Poor, segregated, minority center-city residents, male and female, increasingly denied jobs and tax revenue through state policy and white flight, are in symbiotic commercial relationship with the stably employed, disproportionately white ethnic men of the outer ring, siphoning off a portion of the male wages no longer available to them. Formerly stable white and minority neighborhoods abutting these new nodes of commerce between city and suburbs experience a plummeting quality of life—one might say a negative externality produced by these new, linked industries.

Another element, a kind of epicycle, of this newly evolving sexual/racial economy was provided by a Yale student's study of a two-block commercial strip, Broadway Street, adjacent to the western edge of the Yale campus. Christiana Lin discovered, through extensive interviewing, that a generation of Yale undergraduates, particularly women, had developed friendly acquaintanceships with the homeless black men who panhandled regularly on the strip.[25] They reported that these men's presence made the area safer at night, providing protection from the predominantly white ethnic local state college men who frequented the area's bars. Thus we can see also the new utility of the old Chicago School notion of the "moral orders" of neighborhoods, appropriately transformed through attention to historical contingency, political economy, and race and gender politics.

Old and new residents on the block perceived and enacted their own senses of the changing city and neighborhood, the slow avalanche of immiseration, and proper spatial moral orders in a variety of seemingly unpredictable ways. Local knowledge, in an advanced industrial society, is presumably in dialectical interaction with mass-mediated information. But in this neighborhood, as I suspect may be true in many others, we were nowhere near the neoclassical economists' assumption of "perfect information." That is, few residents read the provincial, right-wing local newspaper that (until the first black mayor was elected) obsessively recorded street crime while blandly ignoring City Hall graft and corruption. One neighbor and I subscribed to the *New York Times*, but no one else on the block did. The self-consciously "hip," white and black, read the free weekly, the *New Haven Advocate*, which reported local politics with a progressive slant and did "think pieces" on crime issues. Most residents took in news through sporadic attention to television and focused on the national and international "big stories."

A major source of local news might be word of mouth, had residents actually talked to one another. But in this neighborhood the ethnographer served as network star: few people on the block socialized with or even were aware of the identities of neighbors beyond those sharing adjacent apartments in individual houses. My downstairs neighbors, a white progressive Christian couple, made friends with the white, professional-class, single-parent father in the house next door through mutual interest in children and gardens, and with the closeted lesbian working-class white ethnic couple on the other side through shared dog owning. These neighbors, though, spoke to no one else on the block despite many years' residence. Old Mrs. Davidson across the street claimed an idyllic neighborhood past in which she and her now-middle-aged son socialized extensively with the Italian and Irish neighbors, and was certainly an active agent in maintaining a far-flung network of kin and friends and a local social life based on African Methodist Episcopal church membership. But in the present rather than her fond memories, she spoke to no one on the block but her black tenants and the white ethnographer and her black husband. The three black women on the block with whom I worked on life histories knew nothing about one another until I passed on information.

One extraordinary index of imperfect neighborhood and city information was the shootout. As it took place on a weekday morning, only Mrs. Davidson, old Dominic, and Adolph Reed and I were home. Not a single other neighbor with whom I spoke had found out about the incident, which was locally reported, until I told them—including two *New Haven police officers* who were sharing an apartment in old Dom's house. Another measure of imperfect information is the fact that Paul, the white single father, finally figured out that there were prostitutes in the neighborhood when he found discarded condoms in his driveway a full two years after Adolph Reed and I began to attend to the nightly promenade.

On one issue alone, the people on the block had perfect information: they noticed who was white and who was black. Their reactions to racial sameness and difference were, however, various. When I walked over to introduce myself to Patti Hendry, the young working-class black woman who had just moved in next door, she told me how glad she was to meet me because she wanted to get away from black people. She later told me, "I'm not knockin my kind you know, but I never lived with a lot of black people around." Patti was deeply identified with the notion of gentility: her apartment, entirely white and oatmeal, glass and chrome, was the single cleanest and most *House Beautiful*-like living space I have ever been in—and she had a toddler son.

Patti's gentility did not communicate itself to Paul, who, noticing that Patti and James occasionally parked on the sidewalk to load little James into the car during a very snowy winter, leaped to the conclusion that Patti and James were responsible for the deep tire tracks that had appeared recently on his front lawn. Paul confided this opinion to me, not Patti, and after some weeks he realized that the gouges were caused by the newspaper delivery people driving up on lawns in order to throw the papers onto porches clear of the snow. What is most interesting is that the white couple Cathy and Linda, in the same house, had been occasionally parking their cars on the sidewalk to wash them or to unload groceries, but it never occurred to Paul to imagine them responsible for his defaced lawn. (Paul, incidentally, identified as a liberal, and reported not only having been one of the local campus radicals wiretapped in the 1960s, but to have received government compensation for his injury.)

Nor were Cathy and Linda particularly impressed with the high tone Patti and James brought to the house. After the series of car thefts and damage recounted above, Patti put her foot down with the landlord, who had long ago granted Cathy and Linda special parking places on the side of the house. She demanded the same for herself and James, and pointed out that they were paying a much higher rent than the long-term tenants. I wandered over one afternoon to find the landlord and his son cutting down shrubs to make additional space for parking. Linda was on the porch, fuming about the destruction of the garden, the deterioration of the neighborhood, and threatening to move. A year later, when the couple's dog was shot in the leg by a kid, Linda reported that the cop who came in response to their call told them that "the word is out," that the police wouldn't be able to "do anything" because of the new black mayor, and suggested that Linda consider that when she voted in the upcoming mayoral elections. Linda said to me, referring to herself and Cathy, our Christian neighbors, and Adolph and me, "This neighborhood is shot. We're all leaving just in time." When I told Patti about the dog incident, she reacted in terms of her commitment to the neighborhood: "You mean I got to live next door to someone with a gun shooting in the backyard?"

These ethnographic vignettes help us to see how both white and black residents responded to the social changes buffeting them through the prism of hegemonic "underclass" ideology. The neighbors on the block and other working- and middle-class residents, except for professional social scientists, had no particular knowledge of either Robert Dahl's or William Julius Wilson's scholarly interpretations of shifting American political economy. They worked actively, though, with their popular, mass-mediated translation into a morality play. This play scripted progressive white beneficence defeated by both the juggernaut of agentless, blameless, shifting political economy (bearing no relation to corporate profit rates) and the rise of pathological minority behavior ascribed to innate "culture" rather than to political economic constraints. The play's subplot spotlights rising minority male, especially youth violence and increasing female failures to gain access to male income for the support of children, combined with the progressive deterioration of "genteel" female behavior. This subplot neatly effaces the fact that these changing gendered behaviors describe culturewide shifts in the United States, and indeed the world. So pervasive is this script, so "commonsensical," that individual efforts to break free of it often give it inadvertent imprimatur.

One black mode of dealing with the racist presumptions of "underclass" ideology was to narrow the "circle of the we." Although Patti had married endogamously, she tended to identify herself as separate from the rest of black America. When I visited her in 1992, the top flat of her house had turned over again, and now housed a mixed-sex group of white bikers. Patti, pregnant with her second child, was quite tolerant of them, although I couldn't determine whether her approval was due to their whiteness or her general acceptance of the immiseration of the neighborhood: "They be having their bandannas on, Harley-Davidsons across their backs, the girl got a tattoo coming up her leg . . . but they're nice, they're just strange-lookin. They look out for me, help me with the groceries if I'm alone."

Mrs. Davidson talked vaguely about how "some people" didn't want to work, and heavily stressed her northern New England upbringing and her upright family heritage. A black librarian whose roots were in the Cape Verdes and whose children had had drug addiction problems explained that in New Haven "those Southern people spoiled everything for us cause they would work for the low wages," but then contradicted herself by remembering childhood neighbors who grew collards in their front yard and now "own real estate all over town."

The middle-class white neighbors generally avoided talking about crime and immiseration in racialized ways, although we have seen Paul's automatic suspicion of Patti and James. Young Dom on the corner, a blue-collar worker and union shop steward, articulated a class analysis of increased crime: "What they gonna do? They got no money, they wanna go some-where, so they steal a car." He responded to the drug trade similarly: "People don't have nothing to do, they need money to eat."

On the other hand, Dom was extremely hostile to the street prostitutes, calling them "disgusting hookers" and peppering the police with calls complaining about them. He told me that in the period before I moved into the neighborhood, there had been a short-lived rash of prostitution, and that he had "gotten into trouble" because he went out to protect the neigh-borhood with a baseball bat.

Race, class, and gender come together here with notions of spatial moral order. When I took Dom's life history, he told me a bit boastfully that he knew all the black after-hours clubs in New Haven and spent a great deal of time in them. Dom reflects here one historical thread in white American racism: the notion that black residential space appropriately houses illegal commercial entertainment available to visiting white men—drinks after hours, illegal drugs, gambling, sex for sale—but that such activities should not be allowed to spill over into "white" space.

There were other, very different spatial moral orders enacted on the block during my residence. One autumn evening in 1988, I ran downstairs to discover the cause of a tremendous fracas. Once outside, I stood, unseen, and listened to Mrs. Davidson's middle-aged tenant Clifford, himself seem-ingly a bit the worse for wear, engage in a mutual harangue with and attempt to chase away a black wino who must have sat down on the porch or lain on the lawn. For a full twenty minutes, the block was enlivened with Clifford's endlessly repeated injunction: "This is my neighborhood. Go on cross town. You acting ugly." His interlocutor refused to engage the issue, simply shouting at least a hundred times, "I want my fuckin hat." His only variation, after fifteen minutes, was "I *still* want my fuckin hat."

Three years later, and in a significantly poorer and more dangerous neighborhood, Clifford was unlikely to have wasted his time on a mere wino. But one night I ran charging downstairs in response to a woman screaming for help. By the time I got outside, she was gone, apparently having run from door to door down the block. I met two young women roommates from across the street, one black and one white. They had seen men chasing her and called the police, and we could see the squad car two blocks down. I ran to check on her welfare, and had a very unsatisfying conversation with a police officer who implied that the woman, who was probably a local prostitute, was responding to dangers originating in her own mind. The two roommates were Jane and Sarah, both college graduate technical workers with aspirations to make a living at art production. That night and during their life history narratives we discussed sexism, racism, and danger in the neighborhood. Jane had been accosted as a prostitute and was afraid of a former boyfriend who had date-raped her. Sarah discussed her difficulties in biking to work on the arterial road that ran through the drug-dealing area, never knowing whether boys greeting her were friendly or hostile. Both women had heard of my experience of rape four years earlier, ironically when running in broad daylight on an upper-middle-class street in Westville, and this knowledge led to feminist solidarity. Although Jane and Sarah later had a dispute and Jane moved out of the apartment in 1992, the two women shared a sense of the proper spatial moral order: one in which all women, including those forced into prostitution, were defended by other women against male predation.

The final mode of enacting spatial moral order on the block was the series of intra- and interhouse mutual protection agreements and strategies to deter burglary. Most ground-floor dwellers kept dogs, who were then cared for by upstairs neighbors during their owners' absence. During long absences, neighbors took in mail and checked doors and windows. But these contingent practices tended to run along race and class lines, Mrs. Davidson and her tenants watching out for one another, as did the landlord and tenants in Jane and Sarah's building, while the white tenants (plus Adolph Reed) in three houses on my side of the street worked together. As we have seen, Patti failed to make ties with Cathy and Linda. Nor did she approve of the black tenants on the third floor, finally creating an alliance of mutual support with the white bikers who moved into Cathy and Linda's flat.

All the residents on the block were, as Geertz ends his "Local Knowledge" essay, trying to "imagine principled lives they can practicably lead."[26] But they imagined them variously, from social positions of differential access to economic and other resources, and in a context of increasing social stress they were all powerless to alter. "Underclass" ideology distorted their understandings of that context, and of each other. In New Haven, as in Evanston and Chicago, the paradoxically fissioned and corporate-consolidated public sphere channels the maintenance of imperial structures of feeling and their associated images of the various Others against which we define our modern American selves.

THE WORLD IN A GRAIN OF SAND

The years in which I lived and worked in New Haven and then the Chicago area, the years that saw these seemingly self-contradictory shifts in the American public sphere, have also been years of parallel paradox around the globe. These shifting grains of ethnographic sand do indeed reflect the larger world. This recent era recalls Dickens's characterization of the French Revolution, but with the terms reversed: the worst of times, the best of times. That is, while for the first time in history we have effective international labor, women's, environmental, and human rights organizations, extraordinary examples of multinational organizing, yet this is also a post-Fordist period of global capitalist consolidation increasingly free of state controls, and thus of vast, interconnected growth in both wealth and poverty.[27]

Accompanying the maturation of global finance capital—which disguises its movements so much more effectively than did earlier formations—are the uncoincidental defeat of progressive forces working for economic justice in dozens of states around the globe, and racist and misogynist backlashes from Bosnia to Rwanda to Sacramento and Oklahoma City. At the same time, the collapse of Communism, which has clearly allowed for civil liberties long denied, has also opened the former Soviet sphere to the sell-off of national industries and resources to rapacious old and new capital, associated plummeting standards of living for most, and the abandonment of women's former social welfare guarantees, spurring an unprecedented rise in prostitution, sexual harassment and exploitation, and mail-order marriages to men in the United States and other wealthy nations. The turn by the rulers of the People's Republic of China to the "capitalist road" has had similar effects on its national minorities and female citizens.

In addition, the Soviet decline has fueled what the primordialists have labeled a series of tribal wars, which are of course entirely modern in their forms and integrally tied to the new world order. There has also been a negative ripple effect in what we used to call the Third World as progressive forces—particularly those in Latin America and Africa—who were formerly aided by the Soviet Union have been left to twist slowly in the wind. South Africa's African National Congress—better organized and with a broader funding base—is one of the few progressive organizations to have escaped this fate. Worldwide, not just in the United States or the developed world, states are increasingly laissez-faire—or simply complicit—with regard to controlling capital as its velocity increases, and the gap between rich and poor is fast widening.

The complexity and self-contradictions in contemporary American structures of feeling become explicable when we consider them in these multiple contexts. Much ink has been spilled, of course, on changing American self-conceptions with the demise of the Soviet threat. And, as we saw in chapter 2, "American temperament" commentators engage in a variety of rhetorical acrobatics to avoid dealing accurately with race and gender inflections of evolving United States class stratification. The mere existence of civil rights guarantees for Americans of color and white women has been parlayed into the Big Lie that all Americans now compete on a level playing field. (These tropes were in fact introduced in the United States first after Afro-American suffrage/Reconstruction and then after female suffrage, further underlining the parallels across fins de siècles.) As economic anxiety has grown in the West we have seen a harder, more cynical tone evolving in public sphere characterizations of domestic and foreign poverty and violence. A lifeboat ethic has grown as the bulk of Americans increasingly experience relative rather than absolute privilege. In both financial and emotional senses, we are told repeatedly that we "can no longer afford" liberal politics at home or abroad. Spurred by massive New Right investment, the process of rationalizing power with reference to difference has grown exponentially since the 1970s, and the popular political sphere has become increasingly culturalized, "anthropologized."

I have narrated the historical backdrop of these contested American structures of feeling through following American ethnography's Dusky Maiden, as written and as read, over nearly seven decades. In addition, I have charted the patterns of contemporary culture wars through laying out the multiplicity of anthropological costumes in the public sphere; through following the evolution of the "white ethnic community," "women's culture," and "underclass" constructs in American history; through watching the distortions of "underclass" ideology on the ground in New Haven; and through anatomizing American media response to Derek Freeman's attack on Margaret Mead. Let me now shift the optic one final time, and trace this world in a slightly different grain of Blakean sand: the strange fate and increasing salience of one anthropological concept in the American public sphere.

KULTURKAMPF DU JOUR

In the public sphere, the New Right's having hissy fits,
Talking of Boas and Mead and Herskovits.
—*With apologies to T. S. Eliot*

Most commentary on contemporary culture wars has assumed that the battle is joined solely over issues of education, art, and entertainment: multiculturalism and women's studies versus "academic standards" and the "classic canon" in the schools, the morals of rap music and television serials, gay representation in the public sphere, public funding of "obscene" art, the proper messages to be disseminated by museums. But this book documents the dual nature of the culture wars: "culture" as both Arnoldian high culture—"civilization"—and the "other cultures," including domestic ones, thought to be the province of anthropology. Whether Pat Buchanan's Zulus, Saul Bellow's Papuans, or Reagan's "welfare queens" are under consideration, whether domestic "gay depravity" and "unnatural feminism" or foreign "savagery" and "tribal wars" are in question, representations are today—as they were at the end of the last century—thriftily recycled within and beyond our shores.

The conservative uses of contemporary anthropological costuming and the Reagan-era Freeman affair, however, reveal that it is not only "anthropological objects" but anthropologists themselves who have become ubiquitous New Right targets. This point is perhaps clearest in the multiple scathing references to Boas, Mead, Benedict, Herskovits, and a host of contemporary practitioners in Dinesh D'Souza's latest simulacrum of scholarship, *The End of Racism*—which accuses Renato Rosaldo, for example, of advocating head-hunting and asserts that "non-Western cultures have virtually no indigenous tradition of equality."[28] The growing negative cynosure of the New Right's eye, however, is not anthropology as a whole, but the anthropological construction of cultural relativism, or the attempt to envision other cultures from within their own cognitive frameworks. That knackered old war horse of the introductory anthropology classroom is up and running again, stung to seeming life with injections of New Right steroids.

Sheer volume is one good index of cultural relativism's growing importance in the public sphere. A Lexis/Nexis search reveals scattered but increasing—and almost all negative—references to the topic in the popular press through the 1970s and into the mid-1980s.[29] At first, in the Carter years, the references are made by moderates and are used to indict straw people, just off camera, who are "going too far." Christopher Jencks, for example, complains in 1978 in the *Washington Post* of a "kind of spongy cultural relativism that treats all ideas as equally defensible." The *New York Times*, in a 1980 editorial against death by stoning in Khomeini's Iran, thunders, "Cultural relativism has its limits, and at some point tolerance becomes complicity." But then the gloves come off, and all pretense of reasoned debate is abandoned. The *Heritage Foundation Policy Review* announces with horror in 1981 cultural relativism's "deep and lasting inroads into society." Pat Robertson asserts in 1982 that the United States "is a socialist society" because "the courts have embraced cultural relativism." And Leonard Kriegel in 1984 approvingly cites William Bennett complaining of American education that "cultural relativism was in; the traditional literary canon was out," while Phyllis Schlafly's Eagle Forum comes out against "secular humanism and cultural relativism" in the schools.[30] Note the slipperiness of "culture" across these references, the way that appreciating Toni Morrison and failing to judge cruel and unusual punishment (and just exactly where were these Western cheerleaders for Khomeini?) are equated in the new all-purpose rightist indictment.

At mid-decade, with Reagan's second term, the pattern of occurrence takes on the mathematical neatness of the wrentit's call: deliberate notes, each incrementally faster than the last, until all individuality is lost in a buzzing trill of noise. References are not as frequent as those to OJ or Madonna, of course, but from the early 1990s into the present, no week has passed without one or two snide print media swipes at cultural relativism, part of our rodomontade of xenophobic Babbitry.[31] The *New Republic* whined in 1987 that "cultural relativism stops us saying our ways are best." William Pfaff complained in 1988 that cultural relativism allows universities (Orwell is turning in his grave) "to shove truth down the memory hole." Thomas Sowell asserted in 1990 that cultural relativism "says one thing is not better than another." In the *National Review* in 1991, Digby Anderson, not to be outdone, excoriated "repellent cultural relativism" that says "that any culture is as good as any other, you know, black Africans had a Renaissance which outshone the West's, it's just that the West has obliterated it with colonialism." William Henry, in *In Defense of Elitism*, favorably reviewed in the *New York Times*, actually wrote in 1994 that "it is scarcely the same thing to put a man on the moon as to put a bone in your nose." And in 1995, in one of those cute "lifestyle" stories the *New York Times* publishes to attract yuppies for its Barney's and Bloomingdales advertising base, William Honan commented David Letterman–style on the foibles of contemporary college campuses: "Oberlin College recently erected a six-foot slab of marble featuring an optical gimmick designed long ago by the college's namesake, John Frederick Oberlin. If you look at the inset in the column from one angle, you see a bird. From another angle, you see a flower. Do you detect a whiff of cultural relativism?"[32]

For the New Right, obviously, cultural relativism is simply one of the many arrows in its culture wars quiver that successfully reaches its mark—that is picked up across mass media—and so is used again and again. "Secular humanism," for example, which cropped up frequently in the early Reagan years, was found to have no appeal outside the already committed Christian Right and has been largely jettisoned. But newly respectable racism and anxieties about increasingly multiracial America and the diminished place of the United States in the New World Order have com-

bined to give the concept of cultural relativism tremendous negative salience. If "cultural relativism as stigma" were a movie, we'd have to say it's
got real legs.

But what exactly animates those legs? The diatribe against cultural relativism is an extraordinary condensation symbol for a bricolage of New
Right causes. Consider: it links parochial American notions of the heathen
ways of foreigners and domestic racial minorities to the widespread public
sense that, in spawning civil rights, feminism, gay rights, and "entitlement" (economic democracy), the 1960s "went too far," "denied our Western traditions" in favor of a "permissiveness" connected somehow to exactly those heathen ways. The xenophobia/American traditions linkage
engages as well a perverse and fascinating rightist construction of Otherness, history, and—yes—relativism. But first let us consider anthropology's role, as rightist myth and actual historical reality, in the creation of this
powerful political rhetoric.

D'Souza, inspired by Allan Bloom's diatribes against it, sees cultural
relativism as the product of anthropology's early-century dominance by
Franz Boas, whose leftism and Jewishness he finds reasons to mention repeatedly. He uses Derek Freeman's *Margaret Mead and Samoa*—even though
Freeman never mentions the concept—as a broad-based indictment of the
"culturally relativist" work of Boas and all his students, which somehow
also indicts feminism and gay rights (he slyly adds that Mead and Benedict
shared a lesbian relationship). He interprets cultural relativism in typical
kitchen-sink fashion as the heresy that

> denies that race is a meaningful natural category and holds that all cultures are
> equal. . . . group differences are largely the product of environment and specifi-
> cally of unjust discrimination, all attempts to attribute intrinsic qualities to
> groups reflect ignorance and hatred, so that the mission of sound policy is not
> to civilize the barbarians, but to fight racism and discrimination. . . . according
> to the relativist paradigm, the apparently outrageous customs of other cultures
> were to be politely overlooked, or explained as ingenious and necessary adapta-
> tions to the special needs of a particular environment.[33]

Even as rightist parody, this ridiculous set of statements is a mush of three
separate arguments: the modern scientific understanding of biological race
as *at most* contingent gene frequencies, not permanently bounded populations; classic liberal political pluralism; and the radical demand that culture
be considered in the context of wealth and political power. But there is
strategy in intellectual mushiness, and this potpourri of criticisms reani-
mates the dominant Victorian view of race, culture, and civilization.

D'Souza is part of a larger rightist attempt to siphon off diffuse but growing popular nostalgia for the style and certainties of the Victorians and Edwardians—*Masterpiece Theatre, Victoria* magazine, Merchant/Ivory productions—for their own agenda. This is *their* vision of the last fin de siècle. Paul Johnson's call for European recolonialism of the Third World, Samuel Huntington's absurd racist pronouncements about the "coming clash of civilizations," Arthur Schlesinger's trumpeting of Europe as the "unique source" of all liberating ideas in world history, Gertrude Himmel-farb's fervent approval of the starving proletariat and workhouses of the Victorians, Murray and Herrnstein's racist revanchism in *The Bell Curve,* and D'Souza's attempts to rehabilitate the old racist, imperialist traditions of nineteenth-century anthropology and to vilify their twentieth-century anthropological detractors are all part of the well-remunerated rightist campaign.[34] And the delightful reward of reanimating the Victorians, of rehabilitating the "colonial chic" structure of feeling, is the bubbling cognitive cauldron in which notions of biology, culture, and civilization, meld together in the conviction of white, heterosexual, male, Northwestern European superiority, the white man's burden of rule.

This campaign takes place, as it were, with and without footnotes—largely purged of its anti-Semitic base by and for conservative American Jews, or not. Witness the extraordinary parallels between D'Souza and the others and the anonymous filth that showed up in 1995 in faculty mailboxes at Northwestern University (and which also has been circulating on the Internet).[35] "Anti-Semitism—Found" rambles on, through eight tiny-print pages, about Jews as "compulsive liars and unethical to the core," as the "eternal enemy of mankind" who endanger America ("a jewel which shines on the face of this earth with a magnificent light") through their ownership of all mass media and use of them to promote "the Jewish doctrines of race mixing, feminism, homosexual rights etc." "Negroes" and "Mestizo Latinos" are "unfortunate people" who "are expected to handle a civilization which European whites have created.... their frustrations turn to anger and this results in the terrible social problems we have today." Franz Boas stands out in this narrative as "a European Jew who came to dominate the Anthropology Department at Columbia University in 1896 when that science was in its embryonic stages." Boas's students—among them Margaret Mead and Ruth Benedict ("two Gentile ladies whose books and field studies became mandatory reading for a whole generation of educated Americans")—"spread like a cancer across our land and began indoctrinating Americans with their Jewish Liberal point of view." Inherent in this doctrine is cultural relativism, which declares "there can be no objective standards by which any culture can be judged. A skull sucking ab-origine is exactly equivalent to Thomas Jefferson." The only obvious differ-ence between these anonymous fascists and the other rightists higher on the ladder of respectability is simply which national and global popula-tions they strategically include in the circle of the we.

What exactly has cultural relativism meant to anthropologists? The term, like many of those adopted into popular culture from anthropol-ogy—"culture" itself, ethnocentrism, culture shock, ethnography—is a po-litical and historical Rorschach blot. Whimsical popular commentators (and even some anthropologists) gloss it in Cole Porter terms—"Anything goes"—or, for the baby boom set, à la Sly Stone—"Different strokes for different folks." Clearly the term bears some connection to Einsteinian rela-tivity, and to other High Modernist schools of thought recognizing the in-tersubjectivity of knowledge.

But anthropologists have meant, by and large, something rather nar-rower and more technical by the term. Despite popular imaginings, we have seen that romantic visions of "the primitive" have been produced largely outside the discipline, and many anthropologists have warned of the inherent connections between "noble" and "nasty savage" representa-tions. Moreover, in the name of science or of social justice, a significant group of anthropologists has always energetically rejected various defini-tions of cultural relativism, and, in any event, those definitions have shifted over anthropological history in tune with the changing zeitgeist. Finally, the cultural relativist stance is in fact a venerable trope that predates by many centuries the rise of anthropology as a discipline.

Over his long career, Franz Boas certainly expressed respect for non-Westerners, and equally certainly articulated the necessity of evaluating human characteristics and actions in cultural context. Recall Boas's journal entry quoted in chapter 3: "As a thinking person, for me the most impor-tant result of this trip lies in the strengthening of my point of view that the idea of a 'cultured' individual is merely relative and that a person's worth should be judged by his *Herzensbildung*. This quality is present or absent here among the Eskimo, just as among us. All that man can do for human-ity is to further the *truth*, whether it be sweet or bitter."

But, as George Stocking argues, "it could easily be shown that Boas was not a relativist in a consistent sense"—that he imagined cross-cultural study could help us arrive at standards that, as he wrote, "have a greater absolute truth than those derived from a study of our civilization alone." He points out as well that "Boas' cultural relativism was conditioned to a large extent by considerations of anthropological method."[36] These two themes—relativism combined inseparably with foundationalism and the tendency to consider the concept as a fieldwork heuristic alone—have recurred, with variations, in anthropological writing over the decades and into the present.

I have reviewed Margaret Mead's considerable departure from her advisor. A child of the Progressive Era, despite the many twists and turns of her half-century career, she was fundamentally a social engineer who envisioned Others as "natural laboratories" from whom "we"—she explicitly meant the Anglo-Saxon bourgeoisie and petite bourgeoisie—might borrow bits of culture to improve the mechanics of our own civilization. Contra much in-house and popular portraiture, Mead never deviated from a bedrock certainty that "progress" and "Western values" should be paramount in the world. From Samoan youth in the 1920s to American adolescents in the 1960s, from the study of trance in 1930s Bali to the consideration of "modernization" in postwar Melanesia and changing race and ethnicity in 1970s America, Margaret Mead's "cultural relativism" was not at all the antimodernist's worship of non-Western ways—not even the liberal call for contingent suspended judgment—but rather the self-assured modernist's imperial evaluation of the world's cultural wealth for the "benefit of all." Her vision of the larger absolute standards that defined "benefit," of course, shifted significantly over five decades: from Boasian liberalism, to "culture and personality" gestalt, to Cold Warrior Freudianism, and finally to liberal identity politics, a stance Marshall Sahlins has dubbed an "ambiguous combination of cultural relativism and America First."[37]

Ruth Benedict also made use of the natural laboratory model in a creative amalgam with Gestalt psychology and a deeply egalitarian concern. Benedict did, indeed, articulate the notion in the depression years that "the diversity of the possible combinations of culture-traits is endless, and adequate social orders can be built indiscriminately upon a great variety of them."[38] But Elgin Williams—the radical anthropologist whom we met in chapter 4—presciently noted in his postwar piece "Anthropology for the Common Man": "If these statements are ever read for a moment without an investment of benevolent meaning it is just possible that there will be a public hue-and-cry against anthropology."[39]

Williams notes further, though, that "in practice Dr. Benedict views the problem of significance in a totally different light from that which her formal statements would indicate": "Formally she sticks to relativism. Her pragmatism is not so much at the tip of her tongue as bred in the bone. Try as she may to maintain the pose of relativism the test of consequences intrudes." Williams positively analyzes Benedict's simultaneously relativist and pragmatist stance and its implicit "theory of value."[40] That is, Benedict both embraced universal goals of minimizing violence, authoritarianism, and hatred of the body and grasped the nettle of cultural difference in a world of power politics. She adjured us, the powerful West, to recognize that "the world-wide [white] cultural diffusion has protected us as man has never been protected before from having to take seriously the civilizations of other peoples; it has given to our culture a massive universality that we have long ceased to account for historically, and which we read off rather as necessary and inevitable."[41]

Interestingly, one frequently quoted antirelativist passage—which even shows up in introductory anthropology texts—from Kurt Vonnegut's 1968 novel *Slaughterhouse Five*, articulates an anthropology innocent of Benedict's vision and Williams's explicit postwar political analysis, not to mention Mead's social engineering and Boas's antifascism:

> I think about my education sometimes. I went to the University of Chicago for a while after the Second World War. I was a student in the Department of Anthropology. At that time, they were teaching that there was absolutely no difference between anybody. They may be teaching that still.
>
> Another thing they taught was that nobody was ridiculous or bad or disgusting. Shortly before my father died, he said to me, "You know—you never wrote a story with a villain in it."
>
> I told him that was one of the things I learned in college after the war.[42]

Melville Herskovits did write explicitly and repeatedly about cultural relativism. Boas student, founder of Northwestern University's Department of Anthropology and Program in African Studies, and grandfather of contemporary black diaspora studies, Herskovits was less interested than Benedict in the racial dynamics of global politics, more specifically concerned with the detailed ethnography of black societies and cultures of the Old and New Worlds. Herskovits could be considered the discipline's *Ur*–cultural relativist: he wrote in 1948 that "Judgments are based on experience, and experience is interpreted by each individual in terms of his own enculturation. . . . Evaluations are *relative* to the cultural background out of which they arise."[43] But Herskovits explicitly confined this orientation to *fieldwork,* rejecting the "moral relativism" his attackers, primarily philosophers, accused him of espousing.[44]

The Cold War–era, "ethnographically liberal" anthropology that Herskovits represented reflected a specific orientation to politics in a specific historical conjuncture. As we have seen, many American cultural anthropologists, in those Dark Ages and beyond, found their niche in describing "culture," defined in terms of varying human apprehensions of reality—and in defining their disciplinary place beneath the structures of state power. Thus, they connected, safely and uncontroversially, with UNESCO-based, postwar *Family of Man* sensibilities. A major theme of such work was the illumination of alternative cultural logics, ways in which differing languages, kinship systems, notions of health and healing, tribal moot courts, religious cosmologies functioned together in other cultural settings. Rarely engaging with contemporary politics, these anthropologists attempted to describe a benign "culture change" in decolonizing and neocolonizing states—as we saw in Mead's work, in *Return to Laughter,* and in *Men and Women of the Forest*—as if the tumultuous political shifts of the postwar era had little to do with American imperialism and Big Power politics.

Classic "cultural relativism," then, is a fascinating oxymoron, an exercise in powerful powerlessness. In its heyday, it was a toothless liberalism that spoke judiciously, tolerantly of varying initiation rituals, bodily alterations and adornment, polygyny and polyandry, millenarian movements, crop rotation cycles, while remaining largely silent on both the role of Western power in the political economic settings of these shifting practices and the comfortable position of the Western (or non-Western) ethnographer evaluating them. And, of course, given American anthropologists' prevailing ignorance of the history and social relations of their own country, its "relativizing" comparisons to "home" were often both banal and inaccurate. For a form of relativism, in other words, it wasn't very bloody relative.

Even this rather pallid version of humanitarianism, thriving on this simple riff, was subjected to violent onslaught in the scientizing frame of postwar American anthropology, long before the concerted New Right attack. Analytic philosophers, Freudians, scientific materialists, and, latterly, sociobiologists attacked the concept as illogical, unscientific, denying universals of the human mind and human nature. Under such duress, cultural relativism became, as Geertz put it in his 1983 Distinguished Lecture to the American Anthropological Association, a "drained term . . . yesterday's battle cry."[45]

Introductory cultural anthropology texts and encyclopedia entries over four decades reflect practitioners' differing political and intellectual orientations and care in defining the term—and bely critics' widespread claims of an unselfconscious anthropological commitment to the popular interpretation of cultural relativism. Writers, in fact, nearly consistently offered adjectival qualifications to the term. Alfred Kroeber and Clyde Kluckhohn, in 1952, were careful to decry "uncritical acceptance of an immature theory of cultural relativity" while embracing the necessity of its use within the frame of "the best scientific evidence as to the nature of raw human nature."[46] Eric Wolf, in 1964, echoing Elgin Williams's radical critique of Benedict, declared that cultural relativism "remains a prerequisite of objective analysis" while claiming that moral relativism "has been quietly discarded, except as a form of intellectual indulgence among those who claim the privilege of noninvolvement."[47] David Bidney, in the 1968 publication of the *International Encyclopaedia of the Social Sciences,* distinguished among four modes of cultural relativism, ending in the call to "transcend the limitations of both cultural relativism and ethnocentrism through the pursuit of scientific truths concerning facts and values."[48] The multiple-author 1971 text *Anthropology Today* followed Wolf in making the distinction between intellectual and moral interpretations of the term, and Roger and Felix Keesing in the same year raised Elgin Williams's concerns, ingeniously deciding to solve the problem by labeling cultural relativism a necessary stage of anthropological knowledge: "By wandering in a desert of relativism, one can sort the profound from the trivial, examine one's motives and conscience, customs and beliefs. Like all vision quests it can be lonely and dangerous; but it can lead to heightened perceptions of ourselves, of what it is to be human, and of what man could be if he would."[49]

In contrast, Marvin Harris in 1971 cast doubt on cultural relativism's scientific status, branding it "not the only scientifically admissible attitude." Harris's student Konrad Kottak omitted the concept from his mid-1970s introductory text. Conservative ethologist Robin Fox expressed contempt for cultural relativism's "anti–human nature bias" in 1973.[50] But in the 1976 *Encyclopedia of Anthropology,* Klaus-Friedrich Koch followed up Wolf's radical stance in placing the concept in disciplinary and global history and calling for a new orientation in line with a new world order:

There is no doubt that the idea of cultural relativism represents one of anthropology's most significant epistemological contributions to the other social sciences. However, the idealism that originally fostered relativism as the dogma of a value-free study of cultures has recently come under sceptical scrutiny. Anthropologists now understand that the dogma itself is the product of a particular ideological and historical tradition of Western scholarship. The worldwide political changes created first by the imperialist subjugation of tribal peoples, then by the dissolution of colonial empires, and then by the subsequent domination of the new nations in the Third World have challenged anthropologists to rethink this dogma. Once an expression of empathetic tolerance, today cultural relativism can easily turn into detached indifference toward the needs and aspirations of the developing countries as well as those of ethnic minorities in (post-) industrial societies. But if contemporary cultural relativism means to *relate* a people's way of life to national, regional, and even global historical processes, the same knowledge of human nature and culture that enabled anthropologists to reject racism and demolish vicious myths of ethnic superiority should also allow them to evaluate their observations.[51]

Despite this long anthropological history of varying definitions of and disputation about the concept, popular deprecation of cultural relativism from the 1970s forward seems to have put anthropologists more on the defensive, inclined to distance themselves—revealed them, in other words, to be more responsive to public culture than scholars often imagine themselves to be. Carol and Melvin Ember in 1977 located "cultural relativity" in the valued Baby Bear's chair between equally deplored "ethnocentrism" and "noble savage romanticism." But James Spradley and David McCurdy actually attacked the term in the same year as part of a "myth of objectivity." Johnetta Cole in 1988 described cultural relativism as a contested practice of "anthropologists suspend[ing] all their own values," at one end of a shifting pendulum swing. The following year, William Haviland similarly cautioned of the equal "pitfalls of ethnocentrism and cultural relativism." And Herbert Applebaum's 1987 and Paul Bohannan's 1992 introductory texts simply omit the concept.[52]

The history of cultural relativism in anthropology is, then, wholly other from its imagined reality in American popular culture, in New Right bombast, even in some anthropological work. And in fact, contrary to the new conservative apologists for "our humanist traditions"—as in Allan Bloom's hysterical accusation that "a cultural relativist must care for culture more than truth, and fight for culture while knowing it is not true"—cultural relativism is actually the descendant of our own precious Western belletristic heritage, a recurrent trope in the learned armchair essay in cultural criticism.[53]

Michel de Montaigne, in his sixteenth-century essay "On Cannibals," famously adjures us to "take care not to cling to common opinions . . . [to] judge by the way of reason, and not by common report," because "everyone gives the title of barbarian to everything that is not according to his own usage." He relates travelers' reports and his own questioning of Brazilian Indians and concludes that "there is more barbarity in eating a man alive [by then-contemporary European torture] than in eating him dead. . . . We may, then, well call these people barbarians in respect to the rules of reason, but not in respect to ourselves, who, in all sorts of barbarity, exceed them." He achieves Sapir's destructive analysis of the familiar through retailing a vignette in which an Indian visitor is asked his opinion of French society: "They had observed that there were among us men full and crammed with all kinds of good things, while their halves [fellow citizens] were begging at their doors, emaciated with hunger and poverty; and they thought it strange that these needy halves were able to suffer such an injustice, and that they did not take the others by the throat and fire their houses." "But hold on!" Montaigne concludes sardonically of these critically intelligent Indians, "They don't wear breeches."[54]

Rightists, in fact, have long also made use of this venerable Western trope: they simply reverse the evaluative arrows, or split relativist hairs in stigmatizing some while lauding other Others. Faced with ancient Greek slavery and the enormous Euro-American trade in African lives, D'Souza points to indigenous Native American slavery and Arab and black African complicity in the African slave trade.[55] All social thought is innately comparative, finding grounds for emulation and avoidance in the practices of temporal and geographic "other countries." For conservatives, it has always really been a case of cultural relativism for me, but not for thee.

The attack on cultural relativism, then, is of a piece with the entire new rightist program: the hypocritical attempt to rewrite the American morality play, to lay claim to virtue through the shell game of focusing on the mote in Others' eyes while ignoring the beam in one's own. All most anthropologists have ever advocated is the attempt, from the bedrock of one's own enculturation, to empathize with the moral logics of others. It has never been a case of conservative tradition versus present-day license or rebellion, nor of "Western" civilization versus barbarism. We all have histories to extol and to deplore, and, thanks to colonialism, all our histories are intermixed over the last half-millennium. It is their choice of globally produced traditions versus ours.

As the long and bumpy journey of the West's Dusky Maiden has shown, comparative reflections on cross-cultural women's statuses have been central to political discourse for more than two centuries. Whether arguing (relativistically) "native women better off" or (social evolutionarily) "they are brutal to their women," whether using Others to argue for or against greater freedoms and civil rights for particular Western women—or, of course, to argue for women's New Age goddess status—too many practitioners have been alike in their failure to consider the embeddedness of gender relations in any place, at any time, in larger historical political economy. We live inside one another's histories, not only as representatations but as shifting and interconnected practices. Mary Wollstonecraft and John Stuart Mill's oppressed odalisques, David Hollinger's downtrodden Masai women, Marjorie Shostak's self-reliant and sexually explicit Nisa, Margaret Mead's carefree and Derek Freeman's confined Samoan girls: all were limned, billiard-ball-like, as if gender were not part of history, as if the cultures and political economies of the West and the Rest had not long been connected.

A self-conscious, historically informed, politically engaged cultural relativism, then, would involve the intellectual process, as in the reception of art, of willful suspension of disbelief for the purpose of gaining access to alternative ways of apprehending and acting in the universe—because they are there, and because we share the earth, and the United States, with culturally varying human populations. Because we are heirs to long, distinctively but not uniquely Western traditions of stigmatizing Others that need to be unraveled if we are to know ourselves properly. Because Western colonialism has affected even those customs we think of as most Other, and vice versa. Because, in the Latin tag, nothing human is alien to us. Such a process is always partial: as the postmodernists are finally figuring out, relativizing is a liberatory technique that must always arise from a contingent, but nevertheless real, Archimedean standpoint. That standpoint is the investigation of the complex contours of political power for the purposes of furthering economic and political democracy. We need to judge, as Montaigne advised, "by the way of reason, and not by common report." Only in this way can we gain access to Boas's sweet and bitter truth.

AMERICA'S ANTHROPOLOGIES, ANTHROPOLOGY'S AMERICAS

The interweaving of simulacra in daily life brings together different worlds (of commodities) in the same space and time. But it does so in such a way as to conceal almost perfectly any trace of origin, of the labour processes that produced them, or of the social relations implicated in their production.—*David Harvey*[56]

As we move toward an ever-more-unequal millennium, as the anthropologization of politics increases at a frenetic pace, the multiple Halloween costumes donned or foisted upon anthropologists begin to blur, and the American public sphere more than ever resembles the 1893 Chicago World Exposition Midway: "culture" exists, in our vast electronic American carny, under putative anthropological guardianship but not under its control. "Good Others" are widely represented to be consumed therapeutically, whether as political or lifestyle model or as actual commodity. Everybody wears anthropology drag here, and technicians of the sacred run rampant through public culture. The *Utne Reader* dedicates an issue to the solemnly declared "Importance of Being Tribal." Advertising for home furnishings and clothing claim exotic cachet: "The last vestige of tribal culture"; "Our

26. *Utne Reader* cover, July/August 1992. (By permission of *Utne Reader*.)

ethnic decor might be just the change you're looking for"; "That's not tribal drums you're hearing, it's your heart"; "Charm, nostalgia about tribal origins, and comfort come together." Under postmodern conditions of "space-time compression," as David Harvey describes them, we are induced to become transmogrified flaneurs, to consume Otherness, to define our com-

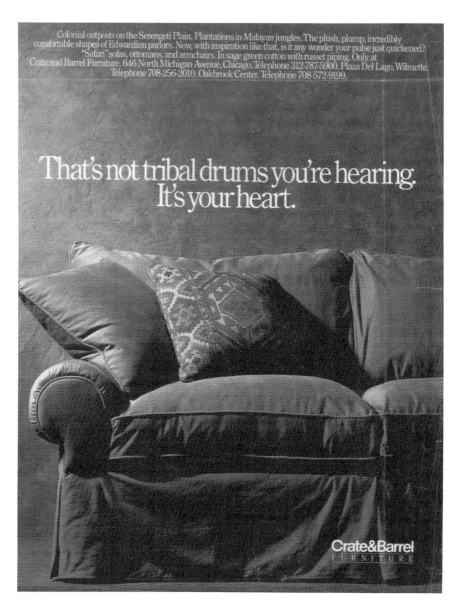

27. Crate&Barrel advertisement, 1990s. (Advertisement supplied by Crate&Barrel.)

plete and benevolent selves, through television, magazines, newspapers, mail-order catalogs, eco-tourism, not to mention Dempster Street boutiques. Even my California art pottery coffee cup carries a label citing "myth, anthropology, literature and nature" as stylistic inspirations.[57]

"Bad Others" tend not to appear in newspaper and magazine ads, catalogs, or lifestyle sections of newspapers. Instead, they headline current events—front pages and top of the news—where their "tribal wars" and "savage crimes," whether at home or abroad, sell not commodities but three-strikes laws, social welfare cuts, unprecedented prison construction, immigration restrictions, an expanded military state, and more favors for arms manufacturers. This is the region of naked power, territory marked by the new rightist think tanks and conservative social scientists, a domain in which anthropologists are rarely allowed a public sphere presence— unless they toe the "underclass" line, as does Philippe Bourgois's recent yellow journalism study of Nuyorican crack dealers, which posits a reified "inner-city street culture" that replaces historical political economic analysis in causal accounting.[58]

Occasionally, front-page and lifestyle sections are juxtaposed. Good and bad Others collide in duelling ideology, as in these letters to the editor ("they are brutish to their women" and "original ecologists") in response to coverage of Joe Kanes's *Savages:*

> I suggest one reason [for the ironic title of the book] might be the treatment most aborigines would give to a woman . . . unless assured of retribution from civilization might well satisfy any definition of savagery. If [she] were young, healthy, and fertile she might last a few years with them, but if she is over the hill (35 or so) they just might play with her for a while before they fed her to the dogs. . . . Bambi biology has confused enough of our generation. Protect us from Alley Oop anthropology.

> It's apparent from [the story about Joe Kane] that he does not think of these people as barbarians. We of this sophisticated, wasteful consumer society have much to learn from them.[59]

Anthropologists, too, appear as heroes and villains in competing national morality plays, Others to be proffered entrepreneurially in furtherance of a variety of ends. I have reviewed ad nauseum the New Right's and faux Left's villainizing of individual anthropologists past and present. Sometimes, however, "the anthropologist" is not a villain, but merely a popular cultural stand-in for "the intellectual nerd," as in Alfred Molina's "Harvard comparative anthropologist" character in the awful film *Species.*

Part of a team of four "experts" brought together to deal with an escaped female alien, Molina helps to articulate the film's sociobiological perspective that the alien is driven to reproduce her kind. He then repeatedly fails—as a clearly non-alpha male—to get a date, and finally falls victim to the alien's erotic wiles. She murders him immediately after the sex act.[60]

In the same year, however, another B movie allowed an anthropologist to play the respectful—and respected—technician of the sacred. Barbara Hershey's archaeologist/ethnologist character in *Last of the Dogmen* is a Cheyenne expert who teams with lost soul cowboy Tom Berenger to search out a remnant group of Indians who have hidden from and defended themselves against whites since the nineteenth-century massacre of most of their population. At first captured and threatened by the Cheyenne, Hershey and Berenger end in saving them from white civilization, and—the ultimate technicians gesture—abandon the West for the Rest for the salvation of their souls.[61]

Less bathetic positive popular cultural attention to anthropologists includes the *San Francisco Chronicle*'s columnist Jon Carroll's humorous attempt to claim cross-cultural sophistication—"Se habla Clifford Geertz!"—and a recent Dear Abby column. Headlined "Feminist Argument a Lesson in Anthropology," Abigail Van Buren allows Soo-Young Chin of the University of Southern California to play human nature expert in countering a male psychotherapist whose letter spouts Desmond Morris–type babble about human females' "perpetually enlarged breasts that dupe the poor hormone-driven, visually addicted human male into unconsciously believing the female is always ready for sex." Chin crisply notes that "cross-culturally . . . the breast . . . is considered that part of the reproductive system intended for babies and children—not grown men."[62]

Most often, though, it is the imago of the anthropologist, rather than the actual figure, that appears in the public sphere. Popular and middlebrow commentators revel in their abilities to play the anthropological gambit, to anthropology-trip (or -trope). *New York Times* columnist Maureen Dowd celebrates her acumen as a peruser of mail-order catalogs—"the shopper as anthropologist"—and declares that Lafayette Park, opposite the White House, "has an anthropology every bit as complex as that of the executive mansion across the way." *Glamour* magazine directs the single woman to "develop your inner anthropologist," as "spending time with married people is not unlike eating in an Ethiopean restaurant for the first time." Humorist Merrill Markoe characterizes Howard Stern's behavior: "When [he] gets too crude with women, it's like you're watching an anthropological study." Heterosexual writer Shane DuBow writes about his accidental evolution from homophobia: "It could have happened to anybody. Anybody clueless, that is. One day I got a job at a cafe. The next day I discovered the cafe was gay. . . . Here was an exotic community, ravaged by disease, famous for erotic excess. To a sporto from the 'burbs, bussing those gay dishes was anthropology."[63]

In the literary world, however, the gambit can carry varying freight. Novelist Bruce Wagner celebrates his use of it: "There's something sexy about Hollywood, and to be an anthropologist in Hollywood may be the sexiest gig of all." (Tell that to Hortense Powdermaker.) English professor Louis Menand asserts in the *New York Review of Books* that "the anthropology" of the Larry Flynt/*Hustler* trial "is a lot more interesting than its jurisprudence." But Terry McMillan, defending herself against charges of black male bashing, argues that the book and film *Waiting to Exhale* "are forms of entertainment, not anthropological studies."[64]

When actual anthropologists are represented in mass media (aside from right-wing attacks), they most often appear to be individuals consumed by the odd, the unusual, the wacky, the titillating—the trivia of human behavior, in other words. Geertz's "merchants of astonishment," they are not represented as intellectual heavyweights or as politically engaged, not as figures we would consult on serious issues of power, policy, and politics— but as figures of fun. Anthropologist Margie Akin, who "has a relative who collects frog stuff," studies "what she calls 'collecting behavior.' . . . 'Collecting seems to be part of a very human urge to put the universe in order.'" "Michael McCabe, a cultural anthropologist . . . is also a tattooist and collector of tattooing paraphernalia." Ilana Harlow, who "obtained her doctorate by collecting tales of banshees and bowlegged corpses in rural Ireland, spends most of her time . . . making friends, gaining confidences and gathering material for a visitor's guide she is preparing on the ethnic enclaves that have entrenched themselves along the elevated line . . . from Long Island City to Flushing." Even television actors feel called upon to send up the guild. Tea Leoni, of NBC's *Naked Truth,* confessed, "I sort of thought I wanted to be an anthropologist. But my father suggested I go to a cocktail party full of anthropologists first. I did. He's a very wise man."[65]

Sherry Ortner wrote in 1984 that "every year, around the time of the meetings of the American Anthropological Association, the *New York Times* asks a Big Name anthropologist to contribute an op-ed piece on the state of the field." But as we have seen, public sphere representations of anthropology are not static, timeless. In recent years, no *Times* invitations have been forthcoming, and no matter how many panels at the annual meetings may deal with war, international human rights, famine, genocide, and other issues of political import, local and national journalists instead find voyeurist "tribal" stories to cover. In 1994, the *New York Times* asserted that "anthropologists are having all the fun," since "these are the guys who were multicultural before it was cool." It suggested that we give anthropologists "credit for realizing that you don't have to go to the Australian outback to find odd cultures and rites" and excerpted some of the more bizarre abstracts for their readers' delectation. In 1996, the *San Francisco Chronicle* headlined its conference story "Happy Campers: Anthropologists Study Seniors on the Road, Find Distinct RV Culture, Rituals, Language."[66]

Even when an anthropologist's research directly engages issues of power, class, and race, that analytic edge seems to get lost in the translation into popular culture. Sidney Mintz, for example, whose careful radical narrative of the linked histories of Caribbean plantation sugar production and the induction of a cultural sweet tooth in the consuming West—particularly the new industrial working classes—is well known to scholars, appears most often in American print media as the foxy old expert on Our Fascinating Foodways.[67] The anthropological gambit reigns supreme on the nation's food pages, where, amid the ads and recipes, food is titillating, delicious, good or bad for you, representative of changing national character—but never connected to hunger and malnutrition, never part of changing global power and economic stratification. Anthropologists can, however, comment on food and national culture and on the meaning of holiday meals:

> "Eating is the single most important activity in which we engage," says Sidney Mintz. . . . "Eating becomes attached to the notion of holidays, which are special days, and what we eat is bound up with . . . our sense of history. . . . our attachment to the people who used to feed us [and] what we eat defines our cultural identity."

> "There are strong moral overtones to the way Americans eat," says Sidney Mintz. . . . "We're a country with a lively appreciation of sin, and our eating behavior appears to be colored by it."

They can note trends in national eating behavior:

> More and more, reports Johns Hopkins anthropology professor Sidney Mintz, people are eating small snack-like meals all through the day, often while walking, driving, or working.

> Food isn't what it used to be. And neither are we. . . . "We don't eat too many potatoes, we eat a lot of potato chips," says Johns Hopkins University anthropol-

ogist Sidney Mintz. "We don't eat a lot of maize, we eat nachos. We now drink more bottled beverages than we do water. Literally."

They can make claims about human universals:

Food metaphors are everywhere and they describe everything. . . . And scholars agree. "For metaphors to work, they must be based on things that are familiar and central to our lives," said Sidney Mintz. . . . "And nothing is more central than sex and food."

And, of course, they can speak on cross-cultural food quirks:

"In Asian culture, you're likely to end a meal with fruit," [Mintz] says. "After a rich, spicy Chinese meal, for example, you don't really have a taste for a sweet dessert like a rich chocolate cake or mousse."[68]

For some anthropologists, however, public sphere presence does have explicit political content. Somewhat separate from benevolent exoticism and anthropology-troping, from voyeur trivialization and Disneyland multiculturalism, even from "nasty savage" new rightism, are two last, interconnected anthropological motifs in contemporary public culture: "the naked ape redux" and "(white male) worlds we have lost." In these arenas, America's anthropology is indeed transposed into a vision of anthropology's America—with specific rightist policy implications.

The naked ape redux is simply sociobiology gone crafty, hiding its retrogressive political epistemology behind a cleaned-up facade of "science," as if prominent opponents of sociobiology's reductionisms and other logical failures were not themselves scientists. Here we see ever more clearly the fissioning of the public sphere: antisociobiology scientists have lost access to most television and newspaper coverage and are increasingly confined to a few prestigious but moderate-circulation journals like the *Nation, Natural History,* and the *New York Review of Books.* Even the formerly liberal *New Yorker,* in the wake of scandals over hazing during Marine Corps training, gave houseroom to sociobiologist Lionel Tiger to claim a universal biologically based "strange passion of young males for stressful testing" and thus to imply the necessity of excluding women from the military. In the popular cultural realm, the appallingly stupid stage play *Defending the Caveman,* whose author argues seriously that "males are basically hunters, whose duty is to guard their territory and protect their females," is a coast-to-coast hit. The *Chicago Tribune* happily editorializes "Blame it on the

Flintstones"—"Thanks are due to prehistoric homo sapiens for explaining away some of our less attractive modern-day foibles and failings."[69]

My close encounter with this newly hegemonic incarnation came when a *Newsweek* reporter phoned in the spring of 1996 to interview me on "the new science of beauty." The narrative of the behind-the-scenes evolution of this story gives us new insight into how anthropology does, and does not, enter the public sphere at the millennium.

The reporter explained that a number of scientists (psychology, ecology, neuroscience) are now claiming that sexual attraction to "symmetry" is a human universal, explicable with reference to "inclusive fitness," and— non sequitur—that across cultures and human history, men are most attracted to women with a particular waist/hip ratio.

I spent an hour or so talking to this woman, long enough to experience amusement, bemusement, frustration, and rage. I cited my own expertise: work on *The Gender/Sexuality Reader* I had coedited with Roger Lancaster.[70] I tried to explain to her that human sexual attraction and mating patterns are extraordinarily various, and connected to human social and political institutions layered over—and not reducible to—biology. I noted that this nouveau sociobiology (unlike E. O. Wilson's original, and embarrassingly silly statements) makes no allowance for ubiquitous human homosexuality. I pointed out that it reintroduces the sexist (and anthropologically absurd) notion of a "bottom line" human nature in which men try to maximize their DNA reproduction through impregnating as many young, nubile women as possible, and women attempt to "capture" male parental support by enhancing their personal attractiveness. I argued that in most of human history we see instead very specific—and widely varying—fertility goals. We have abundant evidence of widespread desires for few, not many, children in many sorts of societies, and that individuals do not make mating decisions as Cartesian monads but as social beings embedded in webs of kin, friends, and neighbors who have enormous effects on sexual and marital choices. I pointed out that attempting to find some "essential" human attractiveness beneath skin and eye color, hair type, nose shape, and body type denied both culturally varying aesthetic systems and the long cultural historical effects of Western imperialism.

Finally, I tried to offer the reporter a sense of déjà vu: that we had already been down this road multiple times, from overtly racist nineteenth-century social Darwinism to 1960s pop naked ape to 1970s sociobiology. All of these explanatory frames laid claim to "tough-mindedness" and high science; all denied their obvious political interests. I told her that I still owned a copy of the ridiculous 1977 *Time* issue whose cover, graced with a white heterosexual couple in half-embrace, dangling from marionette strings, proclaimed, "Why You Do What You Do: Sociobiology: The New Theory of Behavior."[71] I explained that as far as I could tell, these "beauty scientists" were as absurdly reductionist and sexist as ever, differing from older sociobiologists in only two respects: their focus on the issue of attraction/beauty, and their efforts to purge sociobiology of its racist heritage through the specious claim of a "more basic" human perception of symmetry beneath physical variations culturally marked as "racial." I introduced her to the phrase "junk science."

The reporter was sympathetic, identified herself as a feminist, but kept returning to two points: her editor wanted a positive story on this "new science," and didn't contemporary American women's desperate attempts to improve their physical attractiveness through clothing, hair dye, makeup, and surgery despite so many years of feminist activism "prove" that there was a point here? I tried to lay out the contemporary American political economy of gender, but she wasn't really listening. In my frustration, I finally exclaimed, "Look, Wonderbras are *not* genetic!"

The only argument that seemed to have salience was precisely the one I was loath to use: the old ahistorical, natural laboratory, billiard ball use of Other Cultures for our edification. As soon as I edged the !Kung San into sight, the reporter latched onto them like a terrier. I kept trying to hedge cross-cultural comparisons with historical information, but she wasn't having any. Margaret Mead's ghost materialized in my living room as I stared glassily around, trying to figure out what to say in response to the demand that I hand over the appropriate Other Cultures that would "prove the scientists wrong."

The saga continued. Many weeks later, I received a fax of the draft *Newsweek* story and was invited to write a short response for the magazine's Forum section. The story was more appalling than I had imagined possible. It began with kitschy anthropomorphism: "When it comes to choosing a mate, a female penguin knows better than to fall for the first creep who pulls up and honks. . . . choosing among potential mates involves a careful inspection of how closely their left and right appendages match. . . . Is our corner of the animal world different? There's no question that looks count in human affairs."[72] The narrative continued, quoting only the sociobiologists, with no reference to any of the distinguished scientists I had suggested the reporter contact. Opposition arguments were confined to one paragraph, where political essayist Katha Pollitt and I were allowed two sentences each:

> To some critics, the search for a biology of beauty looks like a program for justifying social ills as biological necessities. "It's the fantasy life of American men

translated into genetics," says poet and social critic Katha Pollitt. "You can look at any feature of modern life and make up a story about why it's genetic." In truth, says Northwestern University anthropologist Micaela di Lenardi [*sic*], attraction is a complicated social phenomenon, not just a hardwired response. "People make decisions about sexual and marital partners inside complex networks of friends and relatives," she says. "Human beings cannot be reduced to DNA packets."

The very next paragraph denied that Pollitt and I had a point, and laid out the "naked ape redux" stance of tough-minded disinterestedness: "But no one claims that we're automatons, numb to social forces. The beauty mavens' mission—and that of evolutionary psychology in general—is simply to unmask our biases and make sense of them. . . . Do we have to indulge every appetite that natural selection has preserved in us? Of course not." I also received already-written Forum responses, all wildly positive, from such "experts" as Camille Paglia, the editor of *Allure,* and two sociobiological anthropologists, Melvin Konner (whose *Paleolithic Prescription* we met in chapter 1) and Helen Fisher.

My heart sank. With the deck stacked in this way, there was no real hope of representing an intelligent anthropological perspective. But I girded my loins for the Good Fight, imagining myself at Thermopylae, once more into the breach, good friends, and rode into the valley of the shadow of death. I constructed a more-pop-than-thou response, within the word limit, making the key sociology-of-knowledge point:

> Alas, it's *déjà vu* all over again. First came the 1960s Man the Hunter model with its silly claims of "natural" male dominance in human evolution through analogy with African savanna baboons—some of our most distant primate relatives. Abundant documentation of varying primate behaviors, the importance of plant foods in human prehistory, and greater sex equality in many contemporary small-scale societies shot that one down. Then came 1970s sociobiology, asserting that human class, gender, and race inequalities were genetically hardwired. Scientific and historical refutation killed that one. But no, it wasn't over yet. An academic industry arose that purged sociobiology of its more egregious absurdities, but left its biological reductionism—failure to deal with human history, politics, and culture—intact. Now this ongoing industry has thrown up "scientific" studies of "universal" biological standards of beauty and their connections to sociobiological contentions about mate choice.
>
> Of course we are evolving animals, but we should also be skeptical, intelligent observers aware of the intimate role played by politics in scientific history. Today's "biological truth" is often tomorrow's absurd prejudice. Let's not forget

that Victorian scientists claimed that college education would shrivel women's wombs. *Caveat emptor.*

The denouement was, again, worse than I could have imagined. The *Newsweek* cover displayed a from-the-waist-up naked white heterosexual couple in tangolike embrace, the story's subtitle just covering the woman's profiled nipple. Photos inside showed the same couple measuring one another for "symmetry," and, in an obvious effort to signal nonracism, displayed black actor Denzel Washington's "more symmetrical" face as against white country singer Lyle Lovett's. Not only was my Forum contribution rejected, but the editors altered the text of our critical paragraph. Apparently there was editorial concern that the existence of human homosexuality ought to be mentioned, so Pollitt's and my reponses were reworked to seem to be complaining only about that problematic element of this "new science":

> To some critics, the search for a biology of beauty looks like a thinly veiled political program. "It's the fantasy life of American men being translated into genetics," says poet and social critic Katha Pollitt. "You can look at any feature of modern life and make up a story about why it's genetic." In truth, says Northwestern University anthropologist Micaela di Leonardo, attraction is a complicated social phenomenon, not just a hard-wired response. If attraction were governed by the dictates of baby-making, she says, the men of ancient Greece wouldn't have found young boys so alluring, and gay couples wouldn't crowd modern sidewalks. "People make decisions about sexual and marital partners inside complex networks of friends and relatives," she says. "Human beings cannot be reduced to DNA packets."

The text proceeded to rebut this newly constructed critique to its satisfaction, happily trivializing the lives of homosexuals: "Homosexuality is hard to explain as a biological adaptation. So is stamp collecting. But no one claims that human beings are mindless automatons, blindly striving to replicate our genes. We pursue countless passions that have no direct bearing on survival. If we're sometimes attracted to people who can't help us reproduce, that doesn't mean human preferences lack any coherent design. A radio used as a doorstop is still a radio."[73]

Newsweek did publish two critical Forum texts, by political scientist Jane Mansbridge and by Katha Pollitt, but they accepted too much of the story's argument and—horrors!—used precisely the disproven "primitive woman" claims from which I had been trying to wean the reporter. Mansbridge observed that "our hunter-gatherer days, when these beauty-oriented aspects of our psyches formed, are over." Pollitt, less foolishly, referred to "a lot of small, primitive societies [where] resources are shared and there's a lot of collective caring for children."[74]

As the *Newsweek* saga unfolded, I included its twists and turns in my spring quarter lectures, integrating my points with course material on gender and science and the misuse of cross-cultural data. In the seminar class, I passed around my copy of the 1977 *Time* issue. Only after the term was over did I sit down to reread that historical document. To my shock, the text was very different from my remembrance. *Time's* sociobiology story—in contrast to the 1996 *Newsweek* version—was written relatively seriously and complexly rather than archly and in baby talk. It presented the theory as controversial and noted how well it fit the intimations of backlash, the conservative upsurge of the late 1970s:

> The 1970s have brought with them growing impatience and disillusionment over failed educational and environmental experiments. . . . At such a time the emergence of a doctrine preaching that man [*sic*] is caught in history, able to exercise free will only within the limits set by his genes, may do very well indeed. . . . The fear of many of sociobiology's opponents is that it will prove nothing but leave a heavy political impact anyway. Sahlins fears it will disappear as a science but go on and on in the popular culture.[75]

Finally, unlike *Newsweek, Time* gave much respectful space to critics, including not only Marshall Sahlins but Stephen Jay Gould, Richard Lewontin, and Marvin Harris. The rightist shift and associated deterioration in intelligence from 1970s *Time* to 1990s *Newsweek* parallels the devolution I have traced with the depoliticization of theoretical work and the decline of progressive popular political culture over the last two decades. Sic transit gloria.

The *Newsweek* experience reminded me inescapably of Renato Rosaldo's terrible Reagan-era encounters with the Unification Church–owned *Washington Times* and the *National Enquirer,* both of which horribly distorted his analyses of the cognitive and emotional worlds of the formerly head-hunting Filipino Ilongots.[76] The difference, however, lay not only in relative respectability and impact—the *Washington Times* and the *Inquirer* are well known as scandal sheets, while *Newsweek* is a relatively serious news-weekly. Policy implications, too, were rather different. Rosaldo's journalistic distorters misused his work to promulgate now-classic nasty savagism with only a generalized mean-spirited implication for American foreign policy. The *Newsweek* story, however, helps both to lend credibility to and

to aid funding for silly, biologically reductionist research. It adds yet another brick to the edifice of contemporary American gender backlash. It is
part of the contesting structure of feelings laying claim to the authority of
science for irrational arguments about the fundamental differences in male
and female "basic natures," arguments that just happen to parallel sexist
"common sense." As Stephen Jay Gould notes, "Men are not programmed
by genes to maximize matings, nor are women devoted to monogamy by
unalterable nature. We can only speak of capacities, not requirements or
even determining propensities. Therefore, our biology does not make us
do it."[77]

Those who articulate "(white male) worlds we have lost," however, use
not science, but nostalgia for an imagined past to lend authority to their
arguments. And while sociobiological anthropologists play only a supporting role in the "science of beauty" discourse, an anthropologist stands front
and center in dismantling American affirmative action.[78]

Glynn Custred, a member of the all-white and nearly all-male Hayward
State anthropology department, is a Latin Americanist with an undistin-
guished scholarly record—only second billing on a coedited anthology
and a handful of mediocre scholarly articles to his name in a career of
nearly a quarter-century.[79] Suddenly, in the 1990s, he burst onto the public
scene as the cofounder of the California chapter of the rightist National
Association of Scholars and the coauthor of the misleadingly labeled, and
successful, California Civil Rights Initiative, which outlawed affirmative
action programs in the state.[80] Like other new rightists, Custred lays claim
to the moral high ground. He decries affirmative action as a "phony solution" to discrimination that has given rise to multiple social ills: "Racial,
ethnic and gender preferences . . . encourage fraud and the development
of an ethnic and racial spoils system at taxpayers' expense. . . . [They] also
adversely affect public institutions and public agencies by diluting standards and thus by diminishing the service these institutions and agencies
provide. Moreover, such preferences trammel the rights of those individuals who are passed over in employment and in promotion because of their
race, ethnicity or sex."[81]

Custred, like black neoconservative Shelby Steele—another California
state college system academic with a negligible scholarly record—wraps
himself in the rhetoric of the Civil Rights movement: "These principles [of
the proposed initiative] lay at the heart of the Civil Rights Movement of
the nineteen-sixties." And yet simultaneously he told the *New York Times*
that pre-civil-rights small-town Indiana represented an ideal racial climate,
the "amicable, everyone's-the-same racial climate that he believes charac-

terized Indiana in the 50's." Like Arthur Schlesinger and other "American temperament" commentators, Custred decries the "balkanization" of the present and detests "multiculturalism."[82]

Equally like Steele and Schlesinger, Custred argues by personal anecdote (in this case, of reverse discrimination), and fails to deal with the relevant statistics and other scholarship on his topic. When, in a public debate on the initiative, he was challenged to provide evidence for his claims, he replied, "There is evidence. I don't have it with me tonight." A *Dateline NBC* show exposed Custred and his coauthor, Thomas Wood, for multiple false claims. In the interview, Custred asked rhetorically, "What is the proof that they [women and minorities] are being discriminated against?" The reporter, Josh Mankewizc, then announced gleefully that dozens of careful studies have documented race and gender discrimination in employment, while no study has found significant evidence of reverse discrimination.[83] Nicholas Lemann points out that the California Civil Rights Initiative's literature claims, falsely, that "'the dropout rate for students admitted under affirmative action programs often runs as high as 75 percent.' According to the university, 60 percent of its black students . . . graduate within six years, as against 84 percent of white students. Rather than Berkeley cruelly taking its black students up past their 'level,' it has a black graduation rate 50 percent higher than the national average."[84]

Perhaps most interesting, however, are Custred's perspectives on race and gender in the United States today. Here we see the most egregious ignorance of any historical or contemporary scholarship, any quantitative evidence whatsoever, coupled with an unselfconsciously functionalist optic on nonwhites and women: the "ethnic report card," "model minority," and "women as caregivers" tropes whose history I traced earlier. Speaking to a newspaper reporter from the University of California, Custred revealingly laid out his vision:

> Custred believes one of society's real problems is cultural difference. "For example, Asians focus a great deal of attention to educational achievement and transmit that to their children," he explains. He says that because of this, Asians are no longer minorities. "They've pulled their weight and are doing their job," he says. "But the question is, why aren't the rest?" . . . Although Custred maintains that affirmative action pits different races against one another, his examples are rather effective at doing so as well. "Hispanics," he says, "have lower standards of success which may account for their low academic performance."[85]

An article Custred cowrote with Andrei Simic and published in the *International Journal of the Sociology of the Family* in 1982 reveals the evolution of his perspective on women and families in American life. "Modernity and the American Family" uses sociobiology to claim the biologically based universality of "the family"—a stance very few anthropologists would take—and then posits that "a traditional familial mentality is out of key with the more-recently evolved ethos of modernity." The "associated proliferation of psychological and social pathologies" is then due to "rationalism, universalism, and individualism," evinced, for example, in the "increased orientation of family members away from the home." Although the language is not explicit, the meaning is clear enough: Simic and Custred are arguing (without acknowledging him) a dumbed-down version of Christopher Lasch's 1977 jeremiad against modern industrial life and particularly against women's employment and demands for equality in households. They are also writing against the welfare state: "A circular relationship can be envisioned in which the state is increasingly called upon to fill the void created by the erosion of the family's primary functions, and in so doing further aggravates the situation."[86]

Custred's new rightist nostalgia for a world without Big Government and racial and gender equity is surprisingly similar to the vision explicated in the Unabomber's 1995 manifesto. Although some journalists have attributed the alleged Unabomber Theodore Kaczynski's terrorist violence to his parents' liberalism, his short-term teaching position at the "radical" University of California at Berkeley, even to his very coming of age in the 1960s, the manifesto itself clearly articulates a rightist perspective—and with an unnoted anthropological twist.[87]

"Leftists," writes the Unabomber, "tend to hate anything that has an image of being strong, good, and successful. They hate America, they hate Western civilization, they hate white males, they hate rationality." Feminists fare no better. They are "desperately anxious to prove that women are as strong and as capable as men. Clearly they are nagged by a fear that women may NOT be as strong and as capable as men."

The Unabomber does not come out explicitly against affirmative action, but derides efforts to preserve it in terms similar to those used to argue against the "strident" demands of the Civil Rights movement: "Does it make sense to demand affirmative action in hostile or dogmatic terms? Obviously it would be more productive to take a diplomatic and conciliatory approach that would make at least verbal and symbolic concessions to white people who think that affirmative action discriminates against them." And this from a terrorist!

But the Unabomber assumes that black Americans are so culturally Other that they do not desire access to higher education and good jobs on their own. They are manipulated by a Machiavellian Left: "Many leftists push for affirmative action, for moving black people into high-prestige jobs, for improved education in black schools and more money for such schools. . . . In all ESSENTIAL respects more leftists . . . want to make the black man conform to white, middle-class ideals."

And while the manifesto's intellectual wellspring is a vision of "primitive man," who is not alienated, is at one with nature, is not controlled by Big Brother technology, the Unabomber detests "leftist anthropologists," who "go to great lengths to avoid saying anything about primitive peoples that could conceivably be interpreted as negative. . . . They seem almost paranoid about anything that might suggest that any primitive culture is inferior to our own."[88]

While the manifesto's logic pivots on the vision of unalienated primitive man, its historical ideal is a mythic nineteenth-century American West: "On the growing edge of the American frontier during the 19th century . . . a pioneer settled on a piece of land of his own choosing and made it into a farm through his own effort. . . . American society had an optimistic and self-confident tone, quite unlike that of today's society."[89]

Except for the diatribe against "leftist anthropology" and high technology, the Unabomber's and Custred's new rightist visions of (white male) worlds we have lost are remarkably similar. In both, there is the consistent denial of the facts of race and gender discrimination in the present, the consistent claim that contemporary progressive political action has worsened rather than improved human rights, the consistent evocation of a mythically superior American past—whether forty or one hundred years ago. Like so many other new rightist public sphere figures—Camille Paglia, Shelby Steele, Christina Hoff Sommers, Carol Ianonne, Katie Roiphe, and Dinesh D'Souza, not to mention Newt Gingrich—Custred is an indifferent scholar with no expertise on his chosen topic, catapulted to public sphere attention solely through his embrace of Mean Season politics.

MARGARET MEAD, MODERNITY, THE MILLENNIUM

Glynn Custred may have received his fifteen minutes of undeserved fame, but Margaret Mead, dead two decades now, continues to swamp all other anthropologists, even most scholars, in public sphere recognition. Freeman's attacks have faded, except in the conservative press, and Mead once again stands out as the generic anthropologist in American public culture.[90]

But Mead was a very specific kind of anthropologist, and a slightly different sort over each decade of the American Century. Part of Mead's continued salience is the very timelessness, the fly-in-amber characterization

of anthropology in the public sphere. Another part is, of course, the associated and persistent misidentification of Mead, inside and outside the guild,
as a lifelong liberal feminist. And finally, a great deal of Mead's lasting
appeal derives from her profoundly American psychologization of public
issues and refusal to come to terms with power in history.

Mead is in this way a metonym of American modernity. Her country,
with Virginia Woolf, was indeed the whole world; but Mead, unlike the
socialist Woolf, thought the world was both her natural laboratory and a
domain in need of her American tutelage. Moreover, Mead's knowledge of
her own country—as opposed to opinions about it—like that of too many
American anthropologists, was extraordinarily meager. Mead embodied
the mixed vices and virtues that commentators have long identified as particularly American: she was overly self-assured while underinformed, focused on selfhood to the exclusion of larger social and historical processes,
imperializing, condescending and prescriptive while certain of her own
fairness, and yet also prodigiously hard working, publicly engaged, buoy-
ant, charming, and insightful in many other ways. And another classic
American characteristic: she successfully rewrote her own political and
personal history, re-created her protean self. Margaret Mead, our own Polonius, hortatory, humorless, and happy, has deep appeal to the Therapeutic Culture.

E. M. Forster observed that we should only connect. Mead, with other
anthropologists coming from the "culture and personality" school, made a
series of fascinating and original connections across societies and institutions, looked at human gender, life cycles, art, ritual, and religion in new
ways. But there are a number of key connections that Mead did not make,
or made in partial or mistaken ways. These failures of recognition, ironically, link Mead not only to American popular culture, but to interpretive
and postmodern anthropologists and many cultural studies scholars,
scholars who wouldn't want to touch Mead with a barge pole. And these
connections, unsurprisingly, exist in precisely the scholarship rarely allowed to speak its name in the contemporary public sphere. The leitmotif
of this book has been the advocacy and embodiment of these connections.

First, of course, is a radically reoriented vision of the United States, a
vision containing diversity, multiculturalism—"difference"—but moving
beyond beer-commercial banality to link that difference to power and history within and beyond American shores. *L'abbiamo trovato la nostra
America*, we have found our America in these pages, and it is a site of
shifting identities, of selves constructed in mirrors of imagined Otherness,
linked to political economic histories.

These constructions and reconstructions take place in a public sphere grown simultaneously fissioned and corporate consolidated over the last generation. We have difficulty apprehending the world of public culture—in particular, we frequently fail to recognize its symbiotic relationship with the academy. The popular may be reasonable, partial, or flat-out wrong; it may be aesthetically pleasurable, annoying, or appalling—but it is our public culture, the water in which we all swim, with specific political implications we ignore to our peril.

Mead made herself an important public figure, but she did so not simply through the use of popular language, but also through tailoring her message to the changing cloth of American hegemony. As my *Newsweek* misadventure attests, the real accomplishment is to inhabit the agora despite counterhegemonic avoidance of all anthropological costuming, despite the militant refusal to sell Nasty or Noble Savagism, despite the demand that instead we subvert the culture/power antinomy to reveal the hidden political economic traces in David Harvey's "interweaving simulacra." As Nell Painter adjures her fellow historians, we can "respect the juggernaut of popular culture," while aiming "our investigations toward a . . . public willing to transcend the simplicity of slogans."[91]

Connected to clarity on the linkage of the scholarly and the popular is recognition of the centrality of the sociology of knowledge. Mead's vision of changing knowledge was pure Whig history: continuous progress, ever-increasing scientific knowledge. In some ways, of course, Mead was right, but science does not constitute all of knowledge, and even the very shape of scientific advance is tied to power and politics—from the offshoots of military research to recent shifts spurred by feminist, antiracist, and gay organizing. Alterations in academic common sense, in any event, often represent not progress but retrogression—as with the terminal idealisms of "hard" poststructuralism, the development of "underclass" ideology, the devolution of radical into cultural feminism, the veiling of antiracist and gay-rights critique by identity politics, and the renaissance of sociobiology in the current climate of backlash.

I have tried to provide here a historical sociology of American anthropological knowledge production—largely through the optic of the Dusky Maiden—inside larger American cultural and political history. I have attempted to fill in, to synthesize others' work, and to correct the record—most obviously in terms of Mead's actual writing and politics. These narratives have not been pleasant, but the political past and present are not pretty. Engaging with them fearlessly, rather than ignoring them or trying to reinterpret them positively, is the only means of intellectual emancipation. We may not be doomed to repeat all history because we do not know it, but we are at present doing a fine job of recreating the horrors of the American post-Reconstruction/Gilded Age.

Aiding, alas, in the task of legitimating the nation's rightward turn, the decimation of our never-complete welfare state, and the continuation of our hypocritical and venal foreign policy is the failure to connect dyadic personal experience to other means of gaining knowledge. Some anthropologists' historical illusion that "exotic" societies could be understood without reference to colonial and their own histories has been joined, in the recent past, by desperate anxiety to reverse losses in enrollment, funding, and prestige through claims to the discipline's unique "meaning/experiential" slice of the pie of knowledge. The narrow definition and fetishization of fieldwork deny both social observation beyond the tête-à-tête and other, equally important sources of information, sources that—as in the New Haven example—help to contextualize and interpret ethnographic encounters. They prevent the simple insight that, just as genuine citizenship is innately internationalist, responsible scholarship is innately interdisciplinary (and arduous). They have allowed the development of the new Narcissae in "feminist ethnography." In their antiscientism, they leave the field open for bad science. And they veil the actual unique contributions of an "anthropological vision" to other scholarship and the public sphere: its acknowledgement, no matter what its particular object, of the simultaneously biological, historical political economic, and cultural character of all human life; and its radically democratic demand that we consider all human apprehensions and practices in terms of one another across populations.

Crucially, though, the ethnographic fallacy has led to an open season for ethnographic fakery in the public sphere, an endless series of seemingly authentic narratives of largely urban, largely minority American hearts of darkness, and of Third World and former Soviet sphere "tribal wars and practices." The success of "underclass" and "tribal devolution" ideologies would be impossible without their associated rhetorical "I have seen!" de Riquebourg assertions. Lost in the library and the left press is the quieter, more careful scholarly and journalistic work, work that considers ethnographic material in historical political economic context.

In a related direction, I have argued strongly for attending to, for integrating, two of Haraway's temptations—historical political economy and race and gender analysis—and for refusing the reduction of the material to *mentalité*, or vice versa. Positivism and the turn to language have certainly had their innings in this study: I hope I have demonstrated my convictions that quantifying is important, and that discourse enacts as well as reflects power. But these two temptations have their many champions in the current climate, and political economy few. *Si muove*, nevertheless. Too much postmodern-influenced work on stratified social realities is pure *mentalité*, entirely innocent of knowledge of the actual material lives of raced and gendered subjects and of the economic shifts that channel those lives.

Here Mead in her overpsychologizing, her focus on identities, joins hands with her postmodern inheritors. The central gap in Mead's work, consistent across the decades, was her failure to recognize that we all live in, have varying positions in, changing political economies, and that we cannot claim deep knowledge of any group or society without a political economic accounting. "Translating culture" is necessary but never sufficient; it tells us little in the absence of a larger frame. The historical march of Dusky Maidens across the landscape of American ethnographies underlines the necessity of understanding difference in the context of power over time. Because of these failures of vision—and of labor—in the academy, too much injustice, too many realities of past and present stratification are, like those of the White City, the Midway, and Dempster Street, literally hidden in plain sight.

Finally, and perhaps most obviously, we need to break the antinomy of Here and There, the illusion of the global cultural pool hall. Here and There are not, as Geertz put it, the sites from which "we" depart and to which we travel in order to understand Otherness. Both are arenas of particular evolving economies and particular forms of stratification, sites of contingent and varying daily rounds, cognitive worlds, moral orders. Both have been studied by anthropologists, sometimes not wisely but certainly well, for the entire history of the discipline. And each is intrinsically connected to the other, connected through long histories of exploration, influence, trade, colonialism, and imperialism, through capital and cultural flows, through associated labor migration, through changing state policy.

World War I–era critic Van Wyck Brooks issued a well-known call for the invention of a usable American past: "Discover, invent a usable past we certainly can, and that is what a vital criticism always does."[92] My project has included contributing to the construction of an alternative, more accurate, usable past for my discipline, for larger intellectual life, and for the shifting United States within which they have existed. But a usable past should not imply a usable Other, and I have argued here repeatedly, in a number of ways, for the radical sundering of Time from the Other. That sundering demands, as well, the refusal to view the lives of any Others through a functionalist—or any—optic unless it is widened to include all selves.

From one fin de siècle to the other, despite a century of change, American modernity has been based on imagined Otherness, Otherness that anthropologists have been in the forefront in providing, whether in reputation or in reality. As at the end of the last century, interpretations of the primitive, particularly in its "dusky maiden" aspect, directly concern contemporary crises of masculinity, ruling-class consolidation, and anxieties over global political economic shifts and the changing American imperial role. The very separation of anthropology from history and the other social sciences has fostered the notions that some cultures are without history, that "we" might have such history-less groups within our own borders, and finally, that therefore anthropologists properly study etiolated "cultures"—possessions of exotic and domestic Others—hived off from power, economy, history.

Identity politics, whether of the Left or the Right, is American anthropology's deformed legacy to public culture: the assertion of pure difference sundered from history and economy, coupled with the sole focus on individual selves. Persisting ahistorical notions of culture are associated with, given imprimatur through, postmodern's idealisms and the discipline's public presence. Whether characterized as "rich" or "deficient," these billiard ball "cultures" then veil the economic, political, and historical contexts of individual and group lives. Anthropology-troping is, after all, not so humorous in effect. But far more importantly, it furthers the depreciation of those Others popularly supposed to be anthropology's objects.

Scholarship, like art, cannot stand in for political activism. But academic work, like cultural production, often has political effects in the public sphere. The structures of feeling that constitute American self and Other, American modernity, past and present, are inseparably connected to dominant American anthropological practice, and that practice is based on a fundamental elision of United States history, politics, and economy. American anthropologists need not go home again; we have always been there. But all of us are now moving away from, rather than toward, the harvest for the world—as we were at the end of the last century. It is time really to attend to our country and all its connections to the rest of the globe, time to abandon merchandising the unfamiliar, to exit both the White City and the Midway. It is time to speak truth to, to make demands of power—to doff our costumes, to strip exoticism from Other and self, to put our queer shoulders to the wheel.

Notes

Prologue

1. T. J. Jackson Lears, *No Place of Grace: Antimodernism and the Transformation of American Culture, 1880–1920* (New York: Pantheon, 1981).

2. Jane Addams, "Why the Ward Boss Rules," *Outlook* 57 (April 18, 1892), pp. 879–82, and letter to Alice Hamilton, January 22, 1890, quoted in *American Heroine: The Life and Legend of Jane Addams*, by Allen Davis (New York: Oxford University Press, 1973), p. 72.

3. See Martin Sklar, *The Corporate Reconstruction of American Capitalism: The Market, the Law, and Politics* (New York: Cambridge University Press, 1988); Gabriel Kolko, *The Triumph of Conservatism: A Reinterpretation of American History, 1900–1916* (New York: Free Press, 1977 [1963]); William Appleman Williams, *The Tragedy of American Diplomacy*, 2d ed. (New York: Dell Publishing, 1972); Eric Foner, *Reconstruction: America's Unfinished Revolution, 1863–1877* (New York: Harper and Row, 1988); and Sara Evans, *Born for Liberty: A History of Women in America* (New York: Free Press, 1989), pp. 97–145.

4. Chicago's population in 1890 was nearly 78 percent foreign born or children of foreign born. See Reid Badger, *The Great American Fair: The World's Columbian Exposition and American Culture* (Chicago: Nelson Hall, 1979), p. 34. On Haymarket and Pullman, see American Social History Project, *Who Built America? Working People and the Nation's Economy, Politics, Culture and Society*, vol. 2, *From the Gilded Age to the Present* (New York: Pantheon, 1992), pp. 126–28, 140–43. There are disagreements on numbers of visitors to the fair. William Cronon claims 12 million. See his *Nature's Metropolis: Chicago and the Great West* (New York: W. W. Norton, 1991), p. 343. Robert Rydell is the source for the 27,529,400 figure in *All the World's a Fair: Visions of Empire at American International Exposi-*

tions, 1876–1916 (Chicago: University of Chicago Press, 1984), p. 40. Reid Badger cites an attendance in excess of 21 million; see *The Great American Fair*, p. 131. I have borrowed the phrase "search for order" from Robert Wiebe's classic of that name, *The Search for Order, 1877–1910* (New York: Hill and Wang, 1967). The figures on fair stocks and bonds derive from Rydell, *All the World's a Fair*, pp. 42–43; the description of workers' conditions is from Donald L. Miller, "The White City," *American Heritage*, July/August 1993, pp. 70–87, esp. pp. 78, 80; and Robert Rydell, "A Cultural Frankenstein? The Chicago World's Columbian Exposition of 1893," in *Grand Illusions: Chicago's World's Fair of 1893*, by Neil Harris et al. (Chicago: Chicago Historical Society, 1993), pp. 141–70, esp. p. 166. On Afro-American exclusion and protest, see Elliott M. Rudwick and August Meier, "Black Man in the 'White City': Negroes and the Columbian Expostion, 1893," *Phylon* 26 (1965), pp. 354–61. The source for the quotation from Douglass is Lesley Dunlap, "Red and Black in the 'White City': The Frontiers of Race and National Identity" (senior thesis, Carleton College, 1990), pp. 77–126, esp. p. 101. See also Alan Trachtenberg, *The Incorporation of America: Culture and Society in the Gilded Age* (New York: Hill and Wang, 1982), pp. 208–34.

5. James and Depew are quoted in Badger, *The Great American Fair*, pp. 97, 85.

6. See Rydell, *All the World's a Fair*, pp. 38–71, esp. pp. 40, 56. See also Curtis Hinsley, "The World as Marketplace: Commodification of the Exotic at the World's Columbian Exposition, Chicago, 1893," in *Exhibiting Cultures: The Poetics and Politics of Museum Display*, ed. Ivan Karp and Steven D. Lavine (Washington, D.C.: Smithsonian Institution Press, 1991), pp. 344–65; Trachtenberg, *The Incorporation of America*, pp. 208–34; Cronon, *Nature's Metropolis*, pp. 341–70; Badger, *The Great American Fair*; and Otis T. Mason, "Summary of Progress in Anthropology," in *Annual Reports of the Smithsonian for the Year Ending July 1893* (Washington, D.C.: Government Printing Office, 1894), pp. 601–29, esp. p. 605.

7. On reactions to the Japanese, Javanese, and Samoans, see Rydell, *All the World's a Fair*, pp. 50–51, 66–67; and William Dall, "Anthropology," *Nation*, September 28, 1893, pp. 224–26, esp. p. 225. The phrase "grand sliding scale" is literary critic Denton Snider's. See his *World's Fair Studies* (Chicago: Sigma Publishing, 1895), p. 248. "Thing of beauty" is quoted in Rydell, *All the World's a Fair*, p. 66.

8. Orientalist reference is from Rydell, "A Cultural Frankenstein?" p. 164; Dahomean references are from Julian Hawthorne, *Humors of the Fair* (Chicago: E. A. Weeks, 1893), p. 176; Edward B. McDowell, "The World's Fair Cosmopolis," *Frank Leslie's Popular Monthly* 36 (October 1893), pp. 407–16, esp. p. 415, quoted in Dunlap, "Red and Black in the 'White City,'" pp. 115–16.

9. See Badger, *The Great American Fair*, pp. 78 ff.; Rydell, "A Cultural Frankenstein?" pp. 150–57, esp. p. 157. See also Jeanne Madeline Weimann, *The Fair Women* (Chicago: Academy Chicago, 1981).

10. See Richard Wightman Fox and T. J. Jackson Lears, eds., *The Culture of Consumption: Critical Essays in American History, 1880–1980* (New York: Pantheon,

1983). My rhetorical deployment of the Columbian World's Exposition is, of course, part of a long tradition. See Neil Harris, "Memory and the White City," in Harris et. al., *Grand Illusions*, pp. 1–40.

11. Rydell, *All the World's a Fair*, pp. 52, 60; Weimann, *The Fair Women*, pp. 103–24; Hazel Carby, *Reconstructing Womanhood: The Emergence of the Afro-American Woman Novelist* (New York: Oxford University Press, 1979), pp. 3–6; Badger, *The Great American Fair*, p. 121; *Harper's Weekly: The Magazine of Civilization* 37 (1893), esp. p. x.; Mason, "Summary of Progress in Anthropology," p. 606; Rydell, *All the World's a Fair*, p. 52.

12. Catherine Lutz and Jane Collins, *Reading National Geographic* (Chicago: University of Chicago Press, 1993), pp. 217–58.

13. See Richard Taub, "Differing Conceptions of Honor and Orientations toward Work and Marriage among Low-Income African-Americans and Mexican-Americans" (paper presented at the Chicago Urban Poverty and Family Life conference, University of Chicago, August 23, 1991). Patrica Zavella provides a nuanced discussion of the politics of hiving off particular racial populations as model minorities in "Living on the Edge: Everyday Lives of Poor Chicano/ Mexicano Families," in *Mapping Multiculturalism?* ed. Avery Gordon and Christopher Newfield (Minneapolis: University of Minnesota Press, 1995), pp. 362–386.

14. See James Clifford, *The Predicament of Culture: Twentieth-Century Ethnography, Literature, and Art* (Cambridge, Mass.: Harvard University Press, 1988), p. 228; and Roger Sanjek, "The Ethnographic Present," *Man* 26, no. 4 (1991), pp. 609–28.

15. Rydell, *All the World's a Fair*, pp. 66–67.

16. William Foote Whyte, *Street Corner Society: The Social Structure of an Italian Slum*, 4th ed. (Chicago: University of Chicago Press, 1993 [1943]); Herbert Gans, *The Urban Villagers: Group and Class in the Life of Italian-Americans* (New York: Free Press, 1962); Elliot Liebow, *Talley's Corner: A Study of Negro Streetcorner Men* (Boston: Little, Brown, 1967); Ulf Hannerz, *Soulside: Inquiries into Ghetto Culture and Community* (New York: Columbia University Press, 1969).

17. Eric Wolf, *Europe and the People without History* (Berkeley: University of California Press, 1982).

18. This book, as well, is not a full review of Americanist ethnography—a project not part of its *problematique* that also would have doubled its already considerable length.

19. Arjun Appadurai, "Theory in Anthropology: Center and Periphery," *Comparative Studies in Society and History* 28, no. 2 (1986), pp. 356–61, esp. pp. 357, 358, 360.

20. This is not to deny the power of other states, and of other states' anthropologies. Indeed, I deal in the following pages with both British and French intellectual traditions, as well as much European imperial history. I am signaling, instead, our need to lean against a long tradition of denial of the connec-

tions between American anthropology and American domestic stratification and foreign empire, and against recent postmodernist tendencies to efface, in notions of a new transnational order, the continuing powers of states.

21. See William Roseberry's insightful account of historians' narrow range of appropriations of anthropological traditions, "The Unbearable Lightness of Anthropology," *Radical History Review* 65 (1996), pp. 73–93.

22. David Harvey, *The Condition of Postmodernity* (Oxford: Basil Blackwell, 1989); Micaela di Leonardo, "Otherness Is in the Details," *Nation*, November 5, 1990, pp. 530–36.

23. From "Beach Blanket Book Bingo," *New York Observer*, July 1, 1996.

24. Quentin Bell, *Virginia Woolf: A Biography* (New York: Harcourt Brace Jovanovich, 1972), p. 102.

25. Ann Morse, *Margaret Mead: World's Grandmother* (Children's Press, 1975); Susan Saunders, *Margaret Mead: The World Was Her Family* (New York: Viking, 1987); Edward Rice, *Margaret Mead: A Portrait* (New York: Harper and Row, 1979); "Celebrated Heroines" stamp set, Clearsnap, Inc., in author's possession.

26. Clifford Geertz, *Works and Lives: The Anthropologist as Author* (Stanford: Stanford University Press, 1988), pp. 123, 106, 108, 126, 111, 127.

27. Stendhal [Henri Beyle], *Lucian Leuwen*, trans. Louise Varèse (New York: New Directions, 1950 [1855]), p. 144. "M. Cuvier" is, of course, the same French scientist who figures so prominently in recent literature on the Hottentot Venus; Cuvier measured her and dissected her genitalia after her death. Here, with Stephen Jay Gould, I turn the microscope around. See Stephen Jay Gould, "The Hottentot Venus," in *The Flamingo's Smile* (New York: Norton, 1985), pp. 291–305.

28. Eric Wolf, "American Anthropologists and American Power," in *Reinventing Anthropology*, ed. Dell Hymes, 2d ed. (New York: Vintage Books, 1974 [1973]), pp. 251–63.

29. Clifford Geertz, "Notes on the Balinese Cockfight," in *The Interpretation of Cultures* (New York: Basic Books, 1973), pp. 412–53, esp. p. 452.

30. See Talal Asad's eloquent dissent from the cultural translation tradition in British social anthropology: "My point is only that the process of 'cultural translation' is inevitably enmeshed in conditions of power—professional, national, international." See his "The Concept of Cultural Translation," in *Writing Culture: The Poetics and Politics of Ethnography*, ed. James Clifford and George E. Marcus (Berkeley: University of California Press, 1986), pp. 141–64, esp. p. 163.

31. On multiple publics, see Nancy Fraser, "Rethinking the Public Sphere: A Contribution to the Critique of Actually Existing Democracy," in *Habermas and the Public Sphere*, ed. Craig Calhoun (Cambridge, Mass.: MIT Press, 1992), pp. 109–42. For one cogent analysis of the complex and historically contingent relations between literary form and political expression, see Kenneth W. Warren, *Black and White Strangers: Race and American Literary Realism* (Chicago: University of Chicago Press, 1993).

32. Donna Haraway, *Primate Visions: Gender, Race, and Nature in the World of Modern Science* (New York: Routledge, 1989), pp. 6–8.

Chapter One

1. William Blake, "Proverbs of Hell," from *The Marriage of Heaven and Hell,* ca. 1793, in *William Blake,* ed. J. Bronowski (London: Penguin Books, 1958), p. 96. Saul Bellow is quoted in James Atlas, "Chicago's Grumpy Guru: Best-Selling Professor Allan Bloom and the Chicago Intellectuals," *New York Times Sunday Magazine,* January 3, 1988, pp. 13–15, 25, 31, esp. p. 31.

2. Christina Elnora Garza, "Studying the Natives on the Shop Floor," *Business Week,* September 30, 1991, pp. 74–75.

3. Daniel Goleman, "Anthropology Casts an Eye on the Culture That Made It," *New York Times,* April 2, 1991, sec. C, pp. 1, 9.

4. Philip Zaleski, "Covens and Chaos Groups," review of *Persuasions of the Witch's Craft,* by Tanya Luhrmann, *New York Times Book Review,* June 25, 1989, p. 13.

5. Paul Mattick, "Gross Artistic Product," review of *High Art Down Home: An Economic Ethnography of a Local Art Market,* by Stuart Plattner, *Nation,* June 2, 1997, pp. 26–30.

6. Scott Heller, "Many Anthropologists Spurn Exotic Sites to Work on Territory Closer to Home," *Chronicle of Higher Education,* March 6, 1991.

7. Neil Steinberg, "Strange Tribe Gathers for Professorial Powwow," *Chicago Sun-Times,* November 20, 1991, p. 5.

8. Claudia Deutsch, "Coping with Cultural Polyglots," *New York Times,* February 24, 1991, sec. 3, p. 25; Lucy Suchman, personal communication; Elizabeth Corcoran, "Anthropology, Inc.," *Washington Post,* February 21, 1993.

9. Alden Whitman, "Oscar Lewis, Author and Anthropologist, Dead," *New York Times,* December 18, 1970, p. 42; Oscar Lewis, *La Vida: A Puerto Rican Family in the Culture of Poverty—San Juan and New York* (New York: Vintage Books, 1965); James P. Spradley, *You Owe Yourself a Drunk: An Ethnography of Urban Nomads* (Boston: Little, Brown, 1970); BettyLou Valentine, *Hustling and Other Hard Work: Lifestyles in the Ghetto* (New York: Free Press, 1978); John Langston Gwaltney, *Drylongso: A Self-Portrait of Black America* (New York: Random House, 1980); Carol B. Stack, *All Our Kin: Strategies for Survival in a Black Community* (New York: Harper and Row, 1974); Ulf Hannerz, *Soulside: Inquiries into Ghetto Culture and Community* (New York: Columbia University Press, 1969); Elliot Liebow, *Tally's Corner: A Study of Negro Streetcorner Men* (Boston: Little, Brown, 1967).

10. "Studying the American Tribe," *Time,* December 23, 1974, pp. 54–55.

11. Robin Fox, *Encounter with Anthropology* (New York: Harcourt Brace Jovanovich, 1973), p. 20.

12. Elizabeth Bott, *Family and Social Network: Roles, Norms, and External Relationships in Ordinary Urban Families* (New York: Free Press, 1971 [1957]); Michael Young and Peter Willmott, *Family and Kinship in East London* (London: Routledge and Kegan Paul, 1957); Raymond Firth et al., *Families and Their Relatives: Kinship in a Middle-Class Sector of London* (London: Routledge and Kegan Paul, 1969); Max Gluckman, ed., *Closed Systems and Open Minds: The Limits of Naivety in Social*

Anthropology (Edinburgh: Oliver and Boyd, 1964); Marilyn Strathern, *Kinship at the Core: An Anthropology of Elmdon, a Village in North-West Sussex in the Nineteen-Sixties* (Cambridge: Cambridge University Press, 1981).

13. Franz Boas did extensive physical and cultural research to argue against restrictions on European immigrants—restrictions that were nonetheless legislated in 1924. See his *Changes in Bodily Form of Descendants of Immigrants: Partial Report on the Results of an Anthropological Investigation for the United States Immigration Commission*, 1911, Senate Document 208. Boas as well played a major role in the National Research Council's Committee on the American Negro, assisting funding for antiracist research. See George W. Stocking, Jr., *Race, Culture, and Evolution: Essays in the History of Anthropology* (Chicago: University of Chicago Press, 1982 [1968]), pp. 299 ff.; Franz Boas, *Anthropology and Modern Life* (New York: W. W. Norton, 1928); Zora Neale Hurston, *Mules and Men* (New York: Lippincott, 1935), *Their Eyes Were Watching God* (New York: Lippincott, 1937), and *Dust Tracks on the Road* (New York: Lippincott, 1942); Robert H. Lowie, "Is America So Bad, After all?" *Century Magazine* 109, no. 6 (April 1925), pp. 723–29; Paul Radin, *The Italians of San Francisco*, Cultural Anthropology Survey Monographs, vol. 1, nos. 1–2 (San Francisco, typescript, 1935); Hortense Powdermaker, *After Freedom* (New York: Viking, 1939), and *Hollywood: The Dream Factory* (Boston: Little, Brown, 1950); Elsie Clews Parsons, *The Old-Fashioned Woman: Primitive Fancies about the Sex* (New York: Putnam, 1913); Margaret Mead, *And Keep Your Powder Dry: An Anthropologist Looks at America* (New York: William Morrow, 1965 [1942]), and *Male and Female: A Study of the Sexes in a Changing World* (New York: William Morrow, 1949). Mead also worked with New Jersey Italian-Americans as a graduate student. See her *Blackberry Winter: My Earlier Years* (New York: Washington Square Press, 1972), pp. 132 ff.; and Rosalind Rosenberg, *Beyond Separate Spheres: Intellectual Roots of Modern Feminism* (New Haven: Yale University Press, 1982), pp. 218–19. For pre–World War II anthropology Ph.D.'s, see William L. Thomas, Jr., ed., *Yearbook of Anthropology–1955* (New York: Wenner-Gren Foundation for Anthropological Research, 1955). A count of all United States anthropology dissertations since 1930 reveals a steadily rising single-digit representation for United States non–Native American work until 1978, with proportions hovering around 15 percent thereafter. (In 1989, the listing conventions alter, making percentages thereafter unreliable.)

14. Clyde Kluckhohn, "Anthropology Comes of Age," *American Scholar* 19, no. 2 (1950), pp. 241–56, esp. p. 241.

15. George D. Spindler, ed., *Being an Anthropologist: Fieldwork in Eleven Cultures* (New York: Holt, Rinehart and Winston, 1970). See also George and Louise Spindler's descriptive review essay, "Anthropologists View American Culture," *Annual Review of Anthropology* 12 (1983), pp. 49–78. To their credit, they are aware of Thernstrom's challenge to Warner (see below in text). See also Donald Messerschmidt, ed., *Anthropologists at Home in North America: Methods and Issues in the Study of One's Own Society* (Cambridge: Cambridge University Press, 1981).

16. George Stocking, Jr., "History of Anthropology: Whence/Whither," in *Observers Observed: Essays on Ethnographic Fieldwork*, ed. George Stocking, Jr. (Madison: University of Wisconsin Press, 1983), pp. 3–12, esp. p. 7. Clifford Geertz, "Distinguished Lecture: Anti-anti-relativism," *American Anthropologist* 86 (1984), pp. 263–78, esp. p. 276. Clifford Geertz, *Works and Lives: The Anthropologist as Author* (Stanford: Stanford University Press, 1988), p. 130.

17. Geertz, "Distinguished Lecture: Anti-anti-relativism," p. 275. Clyde Kluckhohn, *Mirror for Man: A Survey of Human Behavior and Social Attitudes* (New York: Fawcett Publications, 1965 [1944]), p. 13. Much ink has been spilled on Habermas's notion of the bourgeois public sphere. See Craig Calhoun, ed., *Habermas and the Public Sphere* (Boston: MIT Press, 1992); Bruce Robbins, ed., *The Phantom Public Sphere* (Minneapolis: University of Minnesota Press, 1993); Terry Eagleton, *The Function of Criticism: From the Spectator to Post-structuralism* (London: Verso, 1984). What I hope to accomplish, in part, in this and subsequent chapters is a project similar to Joan Landes's on the public sphere, gender, and the French Revolution: a detailed historical investigation of shifts in constructions of gender, race, class, and nationality in the American public sphere. See Joan B. Landes, *Women and the Public Sphere in the Age of the French Revolution* (Ithaca: Cornell University Press, 1988).

18. Edith Wharton, *The Custom of the Country* (New York: Bantam Books, 1991 [1913]), pp. 46–47, and *The Age of Innocence* (New York: Macmillan, 1993 [1920]), p. 67.

19. Eric Wolf, *Europe and the People without History* (Berkeley: University of California Press, 1982); Michel-Rolph Trouillot, "Anthropology and the Savage Slot: The Poetics and Politics of Otherness," in *Recapturing Anthropology: Working in the Present*, ed. Richard Fox (Santa Fe: School of American Research Press, 1991), pp. 17–44. For other work on anthropological (and other) constructions of "primitives," see Edward Dudley and Maximilian E. Novak, eds., *The Wild Man Within: An Image in Western Thought from the Renaissance to Romanticism* (Pittsburgh: University of Pittsburgh Press, 1972); Stanley Diamond, *In Search of the Primitive: A Critique of Civilization* (New Brunswick: Transaction Books, 1974); Johannes Fabian, *Time and the Other: How Anthropology Makes Its Object* (New York: Columbia University Press, 1983); Adam Kuper, *The Invention of Primitive Society: Transformations of an Illusion* (London: Routledge, 1988); Roy Harvey Pearce, *Savagism and Civilization: A Study of the Indian and the American Mind* (Berkeley: University of California Press, 1988); and Leroy Vail, ed., *The Creation of Tribalism in Southern Africa* (Berkeley: University of California Press, 1991 [1989]).

20. Bernard Cohn, "History and Anthropology: The State of Play," *Comparative Studies in Society and History* 22, no. 2 (1980), pp. 198–221, esp. p. 199.

21. Fabian, *Time and the Other*, p. 30.

22. Brett Williams, personal communication.

23. George Stocking, Jr., *Victorian Anthropology* (New York: Free Press, 1987), esp. chaps. 1, 2, and 3; Tylor is quoted in Stocking, *Victorian Anthropology*, p. 191.

24. Christopher Herbert, *Culture and Anomie: Ethnographic Imagination in the Nineteenth Century* (Chicago: University of Chicago Press, 1991), pp. 300–301.

25. David Riesman, "Foreword," in *Return to Laughter: An Anthropological Novel,* by Laura Bohannan [Elenore Smith Bowen, pseud.] (New York: Anchor Books, 1964 [1954]), pp. ix–xviii, esp. pp. x, xv; Jennifer J. Laabs, "Corporate Anthropologists," *Personnel Journal* 71, no. 1 (1992), pp. 81–91, esp. p. 88.

26. Stocking, *Victorian Anthropology,* p. 188.

27. Kevin K. Creed, "Wimpy Scientist Quits His Job—to Be a Cannibal!" *Weekly World News,* August 11, 1992, p. 38.

28. Christopher Hill, *The English Bible and the Seventeenth-Century Revolution* (London: Penguin Press, 1993), quoted in Patrick Collinson, "The Sense in the Sacred Writ," *Times Literary Supplement,* April 9, 1993, p. 3.

29. "Drag," of course, properly speaking, contains subversive elements largely absent in the phenomenon I analyze here.

30. I have borrowed this lovely phrase from Jerome Rothenberg's *Technicians of the Sacred: A Range of Poetries from Africa, America, Asia and Oceania* (Garden City: Doubleday, 1968).

31. See Dan Shaw, "If You're Young, Urban, Bourgeois and Bohemian, Here's the Store for You," *New York Times,* July 11, 1994.

32. Colin Turnbull, *The Forest People: A Study of the Pygmies of the Congo* (New York: Simon and Schuster, 1961).

33. Carlos Castañeda, *The Teachings of Don Juan: A Yaqui Way of Knowledge* (Berkeley: University of California Press, 1968; Simon and Schuster, 1973), p. 268. For some considerations of Castañeda's work as fiction, see Richard De Mille, *Castaneda's Journey: The Power and the Allegory* (Santa Barbara: Capra Press, 1976); and Richard De Mille, ed., *The Don Juan Papers: Further Castaneda Controversies* (Santa Barbara: Ross-Erikson, 1980).

34. Jean-Paul Dumont provides a magnificent review and analysis of the Tasaday phenomenon in "The Tasaday, Which and Whose? Toward the Political Economy of an Ethnographic Sign," *Cultural Anthropology* 3, no. 3 (1988), pp. 261–75. See also Gerald D. Berreman's meticulous chronology of the entire Tasaday hoax and its very important connections to the Marcos dictatorship, including the assassination of Elizer Bon, who had publically testified that his relatives were used to "pose as stone-age cave-dwellers," in "The Incredible 'Tasaday': Deconstructing the Myth of a 'Stone-Age' People," *Cultural Survival Quarterly* 15, no. 1 (1991), pp. 3–44.

35. David Maybury-Lewis, *Millennium: Tribal Wisdom and the Modern World* (New York: Viking, 1992).

36. *The Body Shop by Mail* (1993), pp. 12, 30, 29; *PBS Home Video Catalogue* (1993), p. 22. See Caren Kaplan's insightful analysis of the Body Shop phenomenon, "A World without Boundaries: The Body Shop's Trans/National Geographies," *Social Text,* no. 43 (1995), pp. 45–66. In the spirit of full disclosure: one of my own books has been offered in a catalog-like publication, *The Nation Associ-*

ates Newsletter. It is not engaging as an intellectual with market society to which I am objecting (and do we have a choice?), as I hope the following analysis makes clear.

37. Maybury-Lewis, *Millennium,* p. xiii. The noble savage section is on p. 24.

38. T. O. Beidelman, "Millennium," *Cultural Anthropology* 7, no. 4 (1982), pp. 508–15, esp. p. 511.

39. S. Boyd Eaton, Marjorie Shostak, and Melvin Konner, *The Paleolithic Prescription* (New York: Harper and Row, 1988); Jane Brody, *Jane Brody's Good Food Book* (New York: Bantam, 1985), pp. 4–5.

40. And, in fact, many American Indian groups have protested the New Age "continuation of the historic usurpation of Indian land, life and now spirituality, to feed the white man's ego . . . and love of profit." This is one entrepreneurial antimodernism phenomenon exceedingly well reported in the American press. See George Snyder, "Indians Protest Rip-off of Spirituality," *San Francisco Chronicle,* December 25, 1995; "New Agers at Holy Place Arouse Protests by Indians," *New York Times,* June 27, 1994; Dirk Johnson, "American Indians Complain of Cultural Thievery," *New York Times,* June 12, 1993; and David Johnston, "Spiritual Seekers Borrow Indians' Ways," *New York Times,* December 27, 1993.

41. See Robert F. Berkhofer, Jr., *The White Man's Indian: Images of the American Indian from Columbus to the Present* (New York: Vintage Books, 1978), p. 138, for a discussion of the "crying Indian." Ironically, Berkhofer thought he was writing at the *end* of a major period of romantic public interest in "the Indian": "Books about Indians gather on remainder tables" (p. xiii).

42. I deal at some length with the case of the !Kung in chap. 5.

43. Jamie Sams, *Sacred Path Cards: The Discovery of the Self through Native Teachings;* Merlin Stone, *When God Was a Woman* (New York: Dial Press, 1976); Elizabeth Gould Davis, *The First Sex* (New York: G. P. Putnam's Sons, 1971); Lynn Andrews, "Into the Crystal Dreamtime," promotional pamphlet, late 1980s, in author's possession, *Medicine Woman* (New York: Harper Books, 1981), *Jaguar Woman* (New York: HarperCollins, 1985), *Crystal Woman: Sisters of the Dreamtime* (New York: Warner, 1987), *The Mask of Power: Discovering Your Sacred Self* (New York: HarperCollins, 1992), and *Shakkai: Woman of the Sacred Garden* (New York: HarperCollins, 1992).

44. "On the Trail of the Great Goddess," Ana Tours promotional brochure, 1993, in author's possession.

45. Renato Rosaldo discusses imperialist nostalgia in his *Culture and Truth: The Remaking of Social Analysis* (Boston: Beacon Press, 1989), pp. 68–87. See also Elizabeth Traube, *Dreaming Identities: Class, Gender, and Generation in 1980s Hollywood Movies* (Boulder: Westview Press, 1992). Indiana Jones's remark is from *Raiders of the Lost Ark,* directed by Steven Spielberg, 1981.

46. Ivan Karp and Corinne Kratz, "The Fate of Tippoo's Tiger: A Critical Account of Ethnographic Display" (Emory University, Institute of Liberal Arts, unpublished manuscript).

47. *Romancing the Stone,* directed by Robert Zemeckis, 1984. See also here Traube, *Dreaming Identities,* chap. 2.

48. In Edward Said, *Culture and Imperialism* (New York: Knopf, 1993); J. Peterman Company Catalogue (1993), pp. 5, 6, 15, 26, 42; "Booty" catalog is 4th ed. (1994).

49. Said discusses Creighton's role and *Kim* in *Culture and Imperialism,* pp. 132–62.

50. E. E. Evans-Pritchard, *The Nuer* (Oxford: Clarendon Press, 1940); Geertz, *Works and Lives,* p. 50. To identify Evans-Pritchard's colonialist mentality is not, of course, to reject his many accomplishments, any more than anatomizing gender ideology in Dickens indicts his fictional oeuvre. See Ivan Karp and Kent Maynard's appreciative "Reading *The Nuer,*" *Current Anthropology* 24, no. 4 (August–October 1983), pp. 481–503.

51. Laura Bohannan, *Return to Laughter,* pp. xviv, 4, 229.

52. See Linda Nochlin, "Why Are There No Great Women Artists?" in *Woman in Sexist Society: Studies in Power and Powerlessness,* ed. Vivian Gornick and Barbara Moran (New York: Basic Books, 1971), pp. 480–510; Germaine Greer, *The Obstacle Race: The Fortunes of Women Painters and Their Work* (New York: Farrar Strauss Giroux, 1979); and Norma Broude and Mary D. Garrard, eds., *Feminism and Art History* (New York: Harper and Row, 1982).

53. Allan Bloom, *The Closing of the American Mind* (New York: Simon and Schuster, 1987), p. 33.

54. Ibid., pp. 38, 362.

55. Richard Jenkyns, "How Homeric Are We?" *New York Times Book Review,* April 25, 1993, p. 3; Jonathon Barnes, "Like Us, Only Better: Bernard Williams' Theory of the Decline in Ethics Since the Early Greeks," *Times Literary Supplement,* April 23, 1993, p. 3.

56. Judith Rascoe, "A Diagnosis Hits the Mark; the Prescription Misses," *Chicago Tribune,* January 26, 1993.

57. ABC news program *This Week with David Brinkley,* December 8, 1991, official transcript, p. 15; Shula Marks, "Patriotism, Patriarchy and Purity: Natal and the Politics of Zulu Ethnic Consciousness," in Vail, *The Creation of Tribalism in Southern Africa,* pp. 215–40.

58. CNN news program *Crossfire,* February 24, 1992, official transcript, pp. 33–34.

59. Phillips Verner Bradford and Harvey Blume, *Ota: The Pygmy in the Zoo* (New York: St. Martin's Press, 1992), p. 114; V. G. Kiernan, *The Lords of Human Kind: Black Man, Yellow Man, and White Man in an Age of Empire* (Boston: Little, Brown, 1969), p. 222. "Zulu" also has had other, positive meanings, historically, for black Americans. The "Zulus" are one group of Mardi Gras Indians, the now-famous New Orleans black Mardi Gras performance and social clubs. Many cities have a "Zulu Lounge." There is even a brand of "Zulu" condoms.

60. James Wolcott, "On Television: Blows and Kisses," *New Yorker,* November 19, 1993, pp. 107–9, esp. p. 109.

61. Vine Deloria, Jr., *Custer Died for Your Sins: An Indian Manifesto* (London: Collier-Macmillan, 1969). A portion of Deloria's "anthropology" chapter was first published in *Playboy*, giving rise to intriguing thoughts concerning its possible effects on future belletristic anthropology bashers. The remarks on the Prices are from an untitled review of *Equatoria*, by Richard Price and Sally Price, *New Yorker*, December 14, 1992, p. 139. This is an egregiously silly attack, as the Prices' work both here and as a whole is notable both for its antiracism and its self-consciousness about the less attractive threads in anthropological history and in present-day work. See in particular Sally Price's *Primitive Art in Civilized Places* (Chicago: University of Chicago Press, 1989). Marshall Sahlins offers an intelligent critical review of *Equatoria*. See his "Anthropologists Go Home," *New York Times Book Review*, December 13, 1992.

62. Marianna Torgovnick, *Gone Primitive: Savage Intellects, Modern Lives* (Chicago: University of Chicago Press, 1990), esp. p. 8. See also my review of Torgovnick, "Otherness Is in the Details," *Nation*, November 5, 1990, pp. 530–36.

63. Torgovnick, *Gone Primitive*, pp. 4–7, 232, 238; Margaret Mead, *Coming of Age in Samoa* (New York: American Museum of Natural History, 1973 [1928]), pp. 76–84, esp. p. 83. See Clifford Geertz, "From the Native's Point of View: On the Nature of Anthropological Understanding," in *Meaning in Anthropology*, ed. Keith Basso and Henry Selby (Albuquerque: University of New Mexico Press, 1976), pp. 221–39.

64. Torgovnick, *Gone Primitive*, p. 244.

65. Trinh T. Minh-Ha, *Woman, Native, Other: Writing Postcoloniality and Feminism* (Bloomington: Indiana University Press, 1989), p. 52. For an insightful critique of "postcoloniality," see Ella Shohat, "Notes on the 'Post-Colonial,'" *Social Text* 31/32 (spring 1992), pp. 99–113.

66. Trinh, *Woman, Native, Other*, p. 53, 55, 141.

67. Ibid., p. 105. She uses a comment by Denise Paulme (p. 7), considers a (male) response to an article on colonialism and anthropology by Diane Lewis—but not the Lewis article itself (p. 155)—and discusses Zora Neale Hurston as a black woman writer, not as a trained anthropologist (pp. 87, 129). Lest the reader imagine that I am shooting fish in a barrel: Trinh is not a marginal figure. She appears frequently in feminist literature as an expert on race, class, and gender. A piece of this appalling text, for example, is excerpted as "The Language of Nativism: Anthropology as a Scientific Conversation of Man with Man," in *American Feminist Thought at Century's End: A Reader*, ed. Linda S. Kauffman (London: Blackwell, 1993), pp. 107–39.

68. Trinh, *Woman, Native, Other*, pp. 126–27.

69. Edward Said, "Representing the Colonized: Anthropology's Interlocutors," *Critical Inquiry* 15 (Winter 1989), pp. 205–25. I was present at the original session, and remember Ann Stoler's response to Said as particularly trenchant on these issues.

70. Ibid., pp. 208, 214, 217, 224.

71. Ibid., p. 212. Said is here rather sloppily lumping together Wolf, Marshall

Sahlins, and the postmodernist school. I have disaggregated them, and leave the others to mount their own refutation.

72. Eric Wolf, *Anthropology* (New York: W. W. Norton, 1974 [1964]), and *Peasant Wars of the Twentieth Century* (New York: Harper and Row, 1969); Eric R. Wolf and Joseph G. Jorgensen, "Anthropology on the Warpath in Thailand," *New York Review of Books,* November 19, 1970, pp. 26–35; see also the coverage of this fight in the American Anthropological Association *Newsletter,* vol. 13, no. 1 (January 1972), p. 1, and my contextualized account in chap. 4. The final passage is from Eric Wolf, "American Anthropologists and American Power," in *Reinventing Anthropology,* ed. Dell Hymes, 2d ed. (New York: Vintage Books, 1974 [1973]), pp. 251–63, esp. pp. 261–62. For an excellent critical reading of *Europe and the People,* see William Roseberry, *Anthropologies and Histories: Essays in History, Culture, and Political Economy* (New Brunswick: Rutgers University Press, 1989), pp. 125–44.

73. Edward Said, *Culture and Imperialism,* p. 64.

74. Eric Wolf, *Europe and the People,* p. 18.

75. Said, "Representing the Colonized," p. 219.

76. One introduction to this scholarship is William Roseberry, "Political Economy," *Annual Review of Anthropology* 17 (1988), pp. 161–85.

77. Fabian, *Time and the Other,* pp. 30–31; Said, *Culture and Imperialism,* pp. 278, 151, 168.

78. Torgovnick, *Gone Primitive,* p. 9.

79. W. E. B. Du Bois, "The Future of All Africa Lies in Socialism" [1958], reprinted in *W. E. B. Du Bois: A Reader,* ed. Andrew Paschal (New York: Macmillan, 1971), p. 252; Faye Harrison, "The Du Boisean Legacy in Anthropology," *Critique of Anthropology* 12, no. 3 (1992), pp. 239–60, esp. pp. 240–41.

80. Ivan Karp, personal communication; Richard Brown, "Anthropology and Colonial Rule: The Case of Godfrey Wilson and the Rhodes-Livingstone Insitute, Northern Rhodesia," in *Anthropology and the Colonial Encounter,* ed. Talal Asad (London: Ithaca Press, 1975), pp. 173–97, and "Passages in the Life of a White Anthropologist: Max Gluckman in Northern Rhodesia," *Journal of African History* 20 (1979), pp. 525–41; Henrika Kuklick, "The Sins of the Fathers: British Anthropology and African Colonial Administration," *Research in Sociology of Knowledge, Sciences and Art* 1 (1978), pp. 93–119, and *The Savage Within: The Social History of British Anthropology, 1885–1945* (Cambridge: Cambridge University Press, 1991), p. 201; Jack Goody, *The Expansive Moment: Anthropology in Britain and Africa, 1918– 1970* (Cambridge: Cambridge University Press, 1995).

81. Johannes Fabian, personal communication.

82. Phil Donahue, *The Human Animal* (New York: Simon and Schuster, 1985), pp. 8, 10 (the seven anthropologists are Irven DeVore, Melvin Konner, Ashley Montagu, Peggy Sanday, Lionel Tiger, Colin Turnbull, and John Whiting); Amy Linden, "Zap Mama: These Afropeans Are Spreading the Beat around the World," *Mirabella,* April 1993, p. 68; Lance Morrow, "The U.S. Campaign," *Time,* August 31, 1992, pp. 24–27.

83. E. D. Hirsch, Jr., *Cultural Literacy: What Every American Needs to Know* (Boston: Houghton Mifflin, 1987), pp. xvi–xvii; Michael Kammen, *Mystic Chords of Memory: The Transformation of Tradition in American Culture* (New York: Vintage, 1993), p. 17.

84. Dennis Dermody, "Cinemaniac: Moviehouse Anthropology," *Utne Reader*, July/August 1993, pp. 135–37, esp. p. 135; Bruce Feirstein, "New Yorker's Diary," *New York Observer*, July 19–26, 1993, p. 5; Oliver Sacks, *An Anthropologist on Mars: Seven Paradoxical Tales* (New York: Knopf, 1995).

85. Trip Gabriel, "Fifth Avenue, Where Nikes Abound and Guccis Feel the Pinch," *New York Times*, May 14, 1995; Michiko Kakutani, "Getting Drugs, Getting High: Same Old Same Old," *New York Times*, April 8, 1997; Herbert Muschamp, "Gems to Ogle without Acting Rich," *New York Times*, April 4, 1997; Sven Birkerts, "Did Ed Sullivan Die for Our Sins?" *New York Times Book Review*, March 2, 1997, p. 7; Maureen Dowd, "Yada Yada Yuppies," *New York Times*, May 14, 1997.

86. Mary Tannen, "War Paint," *New York Times Sunday Magazine*, August 14, 1994, pp. 42–43, esp. p. 42.

87. Rob Morse, "Blued and Tattooed," *San Francisco Examiner*, August 21, 1994, A3.

88. Glenn Garvin, "How Do I Hate NPR?" *Chicago Reader*, June 25, 1993, pp. 8–9, 28–31, esp. p. 8.

89. See, for example, Christopher Lasch, *Haven in a Heartless World: The Family Besieged* (New York: Basic Books, 1977), chap. 4; Rosenberg, *Beyond Separate Spheres*, chaps. 6 and 8, pp. 147–77 and 207–37; Dorothy Ross, *The Origins of American Social Science* (Cambridge: Cambridge University Press, 1991); on Geertz and the postmodernists, see my review, "Malinowski's Nephews," *Nation*, March 13, 1989, pp. 350–52. For "ethnographizing" sociologists, see Michael Burowoy, ed., *Ethnography Unbound: Power and Resistance in the Modern Metropolis* (Berkeley: University of California Press, 1991); and earlier work of Judith Stacey, "Can There Be a Feminist Ethnography?" *Women's Studies International Forum* 11, no. 1 (1988), pp. 21–27, and *Brave New Families: Stories of Domestic Upheaval in Late Twentieth Century America* (New York: Basic Books, 1990).

90. For enrollment numbers, see *1996–1997 Guide to Departments* (Washington, D.C.: American Anthropological Association), p. 310. For "have gun will travel" ethnography, see Michael Agar, *The Professional Stranger: An Informal Introduction to Ethnography* (New York: Academic Press, 1980); and David B. Givens, "Public or Perish," American Anthropological Association *Anthropology Newsletter* 35, no. 5 (May 1992), p. 1, and "Selling Ourselves," American Anthropological Association *Anthropology Newsletter* 32, no. 7 (October 1991), p. 1.

91. James Clifford, "On Ethnographic Authority," *Representations* 2 (spring 1983), pp. 118–46, esp. p. 143; "Unless we start boasting about anthropology, our public voice may be drowned out by academics and practitioners of sister disciplines who have borrowed 'culture,' 'ethnicity,' 'worldview' and other key

concepts from our lexicon" (David B. Givens, "Selling Ourselves," p. 1). See also Virginia Dominguez's analysis of the problematic relationship between anthropology and cultural studies, "Disciplining Anthropology," in *Disciplinarity and Dissent in Cultural Studies*, ed. Cary Nelson and Dilip Parameshwar Gaonkar (New York: Routledge, 1996), pp. 37–62.

92. See my discussion of these issues in "Introduction: Gender, Culture, and Political Economy: Feminist Anthropology in Historical Perspective," in *Gender at the Crossroads of Knowledge: Feminist Anthropology in the Postmodern Era*, ed. Micaela di Leonardo (Berkeley: University of California Press, 1991), pp. 1–48, esp. pp. 22–27.

93. Eric Wolf, *Europe and the People*, pp. 18, 6.

94. Roseberry, *Anthropologies and Histories*, p. 49.

95. George Marcus, "Ethnography in the Modern World-System," in *Writing Culture: The Poetics and Politics of Ethnography*, ed. James Clifford and George E. Marcus (Berkeley: University of California Press, 1986), pp. 165–93, esp. p. 167.

96. Clifford, "On Ethnographic Authority," p. 120.

97. Roland Barthes, "The Great Family of Man," in *Mythologies*, trans. Annette Lavers (New York: Hill and Wang, 1972 [1957]), pp. 100–102, esp. p. 101.

98. Frank Parkin, *Krippendorf's Tribe* (New York: Atheneum, 1986); Ralph Linton, "Totemism and the A.E.F.," *American Anthropologist* 26 (1924), pp. 296–300; Evans-Pritchard, *The Nuer*, p. 13; Kluckhohn, *Mirror for Man*, p. 197; Laura Bohannan, *Return to Laughter*, pp. 99, 144.

99. Horace Miner, "Body Ritual among the Nacirema," *American Anthropologist* 58 (1956), pp. 503–7, esp. p. 503.

100. James Spradley and Michael A. Rynkiewich, eds., *The Nacirema: Readings in American Culture* (Boston: Little, Brown, 1975); J. McIver Weatherford, *Tribes on the Hill* (New York: Rawson, Wade, 1981), pp. 27, 28, 30, 31; Edward Sapir, quoted and discussed in Richard Handler, "Boasian Anthropology and the Critique of American Culture," *American Quarterly* 42, no. 2 (1990), pp. 252–73; Miner, "Body Ritual," p. 12.

101. Weatherford, *Tribes on the Hill*, pp. 249–53, esp. p. 251. See my discussion of the anthropology and intellectual history of "cross-cultural women's status" in di Leonardo, "Introduction: Gender, Culture, and Political Economy."

102. Michael Moffatt, *Coming of Age in New Jersey: College and American Culture* (New Brunswick: Rutgers University Press, 1989); Micaela di Leonardo, *The Varieties of Ethnic Experience: Kinship, Class, and Gender among California Italian-Americans* (Ithaca: Cornell University Press, 1984), pp. 44, 182.

103. Patricia Zavella, *Women's Work and Chicano Families* (Ithaca: Cornell University Press, 1987); Brett Williams, *Upscaling Downtown: Stalled Gentrification in Washington, D.C.* (Ithaca: Cornell University Press, 1988); Kath Weston, *Families We Choose* (New York: Columbia University Press, 1992).

104. Claude Lévi-Strauss, "We Are We Are You Are You Are We Are You," trans. John and Doreen Weightman, *New York Times*, September 24, 1974, p. 29.

105. James Spradley, *You Owe Yourself a Drunk*; and James Spradley and Brenda J. Mann, *The Cocktail Waitress: Women's Work in a Man's World* (New York: Wiley, 1974); Stack, *All Our Kin*; Constance Perin, *Belonging in America: Reading between the Lines* (Madison: University of Wisconisin Press, 1988), esp. p. 5.

106. Ira Gitler, liner notes for *Dizzy Gillespie: Dizzier and Dizzier*, Victor Jazz, 1996; interview with bop pianist Sadik Hakim in Robert George Reisner, *Bird: The Legend of Charlie Parker* (New York: Citadel Press, 1962), p. 103; jazz historian Carl Woideck, personal communication.

107. Renato Rosaldo, *Culture and Truth*.

108. Ralph Ellison, *Shadow and Act* (New York: Random House, 1964), p. 123.

109. Lee Baker and Thomas Patterson, "Race, Racism, and the History of U.S. Anthropology," *Transforming Anthropology* 5, nos. 1 and 2 (1994), pp. 1–7; Faye Harrison, "The Du Boisean Legacy," pp. 239–60. In 1992, 5.9 percent of full-time American sociology faculty were black, but only 3 percent of anthropologists. In 1995, 7.2 percent of new sociology Ph.D.'s were black, but only 3 percent of anthropology Ph.D.'s. Sociology's record with American Latinos and Asians is also generally, but not as spectacularly, better. Full-time Latino faculty, sociology vs. anthropology, 2.8 vs. 3 percent; Asian faculty, 2.2 vs. 2 percent; recent Latino Ph.D.'s, 3.4 vs. 3 percent; Asians, 11.3 vs. 9 percent. Sources are *1996–97 Guide to Departments*, pp. 304–15, esp. pp. 305, 306; National Center for Educational Statistics, Washington, D.C., *1994 Report*; Havidan Rodriguez, director, Minority Affairs Program, American Sociological Association, personal communication; Patricia Zavella, former president of the Association of Latino and Latina Anthropologists, personal communication.

110. See my review essay, "Boyz on the Hood," *Nation*, August 17/24, 1992, pp. 178–86.

111. Stephan Thernstrom, *Poverty and Progress: Social Mobility in a Nineteenth Century City* (New York: Atheneum, 1972 [1964]), p. 224.

112. Ibid., pp. 229, 228, 230, 231, 101, 111.

113. Ibid., pp. 236, 237, 238.

114. Ibid. p. 239.

115. Ibid., p. 224.

116. di Leonardo, *The Varieties of Ethnic Experience,* p. 96; Stephan Thernstrom, *The Other Bostonians: Poverty and Progress in the American Metropolis, 1880–1970* (Cambridge, Mass.: Harvard University Press, 1973), pp. 173, 140, 169, 174.

117. Thernstrom, *The Other Bostonians,* pp. 203–19, esp. p. 218.

118. Ibid., p. 214.

119. di Leonardo, *The Varieties of Ethnic Experience,* pp. 96–112, 237–42, 102.

120. Stephan Thernstrom, Ann Orlov, and Oscar Handlin, eds., *The Harvard Encyclopedia of American Ethnic Groups* (Cambridge, Mass.: Harvard University Press, 1980), p. ix.

121. See Robert Pear, "Several Reagan Appointees Face Challenges over Fitness for Office," *New York Times*, May 3, 1985.

122. See also my discussions in "Malinowski's Nephews," pp. 350–52, "Introduction: Gender, Culture, and Political Economy," pp. 22–27, and "What a Difference Political Economy Makes: Feminist Anthropology in the Postmodern Era," *Anthropological Quarterly* 66, no. 2 (April 1993), pp. 76–80.

123. Paul Rabinow and William M. Sullivan, "Introduction: The Interpretive Turn," in Paul Rabinow and William M. Sullivan, eds., *Interpretive Social Science: A Reader* (University of California Press, 1979), pp. 1–21, esp. pp. 4–5.

124. Rabinow and Sullivan, "Introduction: The Interpretive Turn," p 6; Perry Anderson, *In the Tracks of Historical Materialism* (London: Verso, 1983), p. 54. Other useful critiques of poststructuralism/postmodernism are Peter Dews, *Logics of Disintegration: Poststructuralist Thought and the Claims of Critical Theory* (London: Verso, 1987); Bryan Palmer, *Descent into Discourse: The Reification of Language and the Writing of Social History* (Philadelphia: Temple University Press, 1990); and Roseberry, *Anthropologies and Histories,* pp. 30–54.

125. See George Marcus and Dick Cushman, "Ethnographies as Texts," *Annual Review of Anthropology* 11 (1982), pp. 25–69; Clifford, "On Ethnographic Authority," pp. 118–46; Clifford and Marcus, *Writing Culture;* George Marcus and Michael J. Fischer, *Anthropology as Cultural Critique: An Experimental Moment in the Human Sciences* (Chicago: University of Chicago Press, 1986); and George E. Marcus, "Afterword: Ethnographic Writing and Anthropological Careers," in Clifford and Marcus, *Writing Culture,* pp. 262–66, esp. p. 266.

126. William Roseberry, "Multiculturalism and the Challenge of Anthropology," *Social Research* 59, no. 4 (winter 1992), pp. 841–58, esp. p. 851.

127. Michel-Rolph Trouillot, "Anthropology and the Savage Slot," p. 37. See Nicole Polier and William Roseberry, "Triste Tropes: Postmodern Anthropologists Encounter the Other and Discover Themselves," *Economy and Society* 18, no. 2 (1989), pp. 245–64, for an excellent critique, including these points and others. On gender and postmodernist anthropology from a postmodern perspective, see Frances Mascia-Lees, Patricia Sharpe, and Colleen Ballerino Cohen, "The Postmodernist Turn in Anthropology: Cautions from a Feminist Perspective," *Signs* 15, no. 1 (autumn 1989), pp. 7–33; my "Introduction: Gender, Culture, and Political Economy"; and my "What a Difference Political Economy Makes."

128. Stephen A. Tyler, "Post-modern Ethnography: From Document of the Occult to Occult Document," in Clifford and Marcus, *Writing Culture,* pp. 122–40, esp. p. 139. On Frankfurt School responses to mass culture, see Herbert Marcuse, *The Aesthetic Dimension: Toward a Critique of Marxist Aesthetics* (Boston: Beacon, 1978); Theodore Adorno, "Television and the Patterns of Mass Culture," in *Mass Culture: The Popular Arts in America,* ed. Bernard Rosenberg and David Manning White (New York: Free Press, 1957), pp. 474–88. See also Mimi White, *Tele-Advising: Therapeutic Discourse in American Television* (Chapel Hill: University of North Carolina Press, 1992).

129. Marcus and Fischer, *Anthropology as Cultural Critique,* pp. 152 ff., esp. p. 155.

130. Final note, an addition to an anthropological pot and kettle collection: Marcus and Fischer end this section with a critique of Margaret Mead's failure really to study American society when comparing it to Samoa's. Her "view of the American practice . . . is static, unambiguous, overgeneralized, and one-sided" (Marcus and Fischer, *Anthropology as Cultural Critique,* p. 159).

131. Sherry Ortner, "Reading America: Preliminary Notes on Class and Culture," in Richard Fox, *Recapturing Anthropology,* pp. 163–90, esp. pp. 167, 169. See William Roseberry's excellent critique of Ortner's "Theory in Anthropology since the 1960s," a piece that apotheosizes the ahistorical billiard ball vision (Roseberry, *Anthropologies and Histories,* pp. 52–53).

132. James Clifford, "Identity in Mashpee," in his *The Predicament of Culture: Twentieth-Century Ethnography, Literature, and Art* (Cambridge, Mass.: Harvard University Press, 1988), pp. 277–346; Paul Rabinow, "For Hire: Resolutely Late Modern," in Richard Fox, *Recapturing Anthropology,* pp. 59–72. George Marcus's uncontextualized contributions to his book with historian Peter Dobkin Hall further prove my point. See George Marcus with Peter Dobkin Hall, *Lives in Trust: The Fortunes of Dynastic Families in Late Twentieth-Century America* (Boulder: Westview Press, 1992).

133. Alvin Gouldner, *The Coming Crisis of Western Sociology* (New York: Avon Books, 1970), pp. 390–95, esp. pp. 391, 394.

134. Eric Wolf, "American Anthropologists and American Power," p. 257.

Chapter Two

1. Frances Fitzgerald, *Cities on a Hill* (New York: Simon and Schuster, 1986).

2. Allan Bloom, *The Closing of the American Mind* (New York: Simon and Schuster, 1987).

3. Russell Jacoby, *The Last Intellectuals: American Culture in the Age of Academe* (New York: Basic Books, 1987).

4. Robert N. Bellah et al., *Habits of the Heart: Individualism and Commitment in American Life* (New York: Harper and Row, 1985), and *The Good Society* (New York: Random House, 1991).

5. Individualism, of course, is a major strand in the history of Western political and social theory. See C. B. MacPherson, *The Political Theory of Possessive Individualism* (New York: Oxford University Press, 1962).

6. William Foote Whyte, *Streetcorner Society: The Social Structure of an Italian Slum* (Chicago: University of Chicago Press, 1943); Herbert Gans, *The Urban Villagers: Group and Class in the Life of Italian-Americans* (New York: Free Press, 1962).

7. John Higham, *Strangers in the Land: Patterns of American Nativism, 1860–1925,* 2d ed. (New York: Atheneum, 1981), p. 67.

8. Ibid., p. 275; Leon Kamin, "Heredity, Intelligence, Politics and Psychology: II," in *The IQ Controversy,* ed. N.J. Block and Gerald Dworkin (New York: Ran-

dom House, 1976), pp. 374–82; Margaret Mead, "Intelligence Tests of Italian and American Children" (master's thesis, Columbia University, 1924).

9. Salvatore La Gumina, *WOP! A Documentary History of Anti-Italian Discrimination in the United States* (San Francisco: Straight Arrow Books, 1973), p. 233.

10. William P. Dillingham, *Reports of the Immigration Commission: Dictionary of Races or Peoples* (Washington, D.C.: Government Printing Office, 1911), pp. 82, 129.

11. Edward Alsworth Ross, *The Old World in the New* (New York: Century Company, 1914), p. 155.

12. Ibid., pp. 156–57.

13. Ibid., pp. 36, 44.

14. David Hollinger, "How Wide the Circle of the 'We'? American Intellectuals and the Problem of the Ethnos since World War II," *American Historical Review* 98, no. 2 (April 1993), pp. 317–33.

15. Susan Okin, *Women in Western Political Thought* (Princeton: Princeton University Press, 1979), p. 10.

16. Madison Grant and Charles Stewart Davison, *The Alien in Our Midst, or, Selling Our Birthright for a Mess of Industrial Pottage* (New York: Galton Publishing Company, 1930); Rosalind Rosenberg, *Beyond Separate Spheres: Intellectual Roots of Modern Feminism* (New Haven: Yale University Press, 1982), p. 194.

17. See Micaela di Leonardo, *The Varieties of Ethnic Experience: Kinship, Class, and Gender among California Italian-Americans* (Ithaca: Cornell University Press 1984), pp. 129–35, for a more extensive critique of the community myth. See also Stow Persons, *Ethnic Studies at Chicago, 1905–45* (Urbana: University of Illinois Press 1987); Higham, *Strangers in the Land;* Oscar Handlin, *The Uprooted* (Boston: Little, Brown, 1951); and Raymond Williams, *The Country and the City* (London: Chatto and Windus, 1973).

18. Robert Park and Herbert Miller, *Old World Traits Transplanted* (New York: Harper and Brothers, 1921), p. 61.

19. Ibid., pp. 62, 237.

20. Ibid., p. 71.

21. Ibid., p. 269.

22. James Barrett and David Roediger, "Inbetween People: Race, Nationality, and the 'New Immigrant' Working Class," *Journal of American Ethnic History* 16, no. 3 (spring 1997), pp. 3–44; Noel Ignatiev, *How the Irish Became White* (New York: Routledge, 1995).

23. Park and Miller, *Old World Traits Transplanted,* p. 264.

24. Ibid., pp. 269–70.

25. Ibid., p. 270.

26. Herbert Gans, *The Levittowners: Ways of Life and Politics in a New Suburban Community* (New York: Vintage, 1967); David Riesman, *The Lonely Crowd: A Study of the Changing American Character* (New Haven: Yale University Press, 1950); William H. Whyte, *The Organization Man* (New York: Simon and Schuster, 1956); Lee

Rainwater et al., *Workingman's Wife* (Dobbs Ferry: Oceana Publications, 1959); Mirra Komarovsky, *Blue-Collar Marriage* (New York: Random House, 1964); Milton Gordon, *Assimilation in American Life: The Role of Race, Religion, and National Origins* (New York: Oxford University Press, 1964).

27. Nathan Glazer and Daniel Patrick Moynihan, *Beyond the Melting Pot: The Negroes, Puerto Ricans, Jews, Italians, and Irish of New York City*, 2d ed. (Cambridge, Mass.: MIT Press, 1970); Michael Novak, *The Rise of the Unmeltable Ethnics: Politics and Culture in the Seventies* (New York: Macmillan, 1971); Andrew Greeley, *Why Can't They Be like Us? America's White Ethnic Groups* (New York: E. P. Dutton, 1971); Richard Gambino, *Blood of My Blood: The Dilemma of the Italian-Americans* (New York: Anchor Books, 1974); Werner Sollors, *Beyond Ethnicity: Consent and Descent in American Culture* (New York: Oxford University Press, 1987), p. 21.

28. Novak, *The Rise of the Unmeltable Ethnics*, pp. 135–36.

29. Nancy Seifer, *Absent from the Majority: Working Class Women in America* (New York: National Project on Ethnic America, American Jewish Committee, 1973), p. 8.

30. Gambino, *Blood of My Blood*, p. 343.

31. Deanna Paoli Gumina, *The Italians of San Francisco, 1850–1930* (New York: Center of Migration Studies, 1978), p. 37.

32. Irving Howe, *World of Our Fathers: The Journey of the East European Jews to America and the Life They Found and Made* (New York: Simon and Schuster, 1976), pp. 170–71.

33. Stephen Steinberg, *The Ethnic Myth: Race, Ethnicity and Class in America*, 2d ed. (Boston: Beacon Press, 1989 [1981]) pp. 218 ff.; di Leonardo, *The Varieties of Ethnic Experience*, pp. 47–151.

34. Douglas S. Massey and Nancy A. Denton, *American Apartheid: Segregation and the Making of the Underclass* (Cambridge, Mass.: Harvard University Press, 1992), p. 33 ff.; di Leonardo, *The Varieties of Ethnic Experience*, p. 129.

35. The following discussion relies on Sara Evans, *Personal Politics: The Roots of Women's Liberation in the Civil Rights Movement and the New Left* (New York: Random House, 1979); Adolph Reed, Jr., ed., *Race, Politics, and Culture: Critical Essays on the Radicalism of the 1960's* (New York: Greenwood Press, 1986); James Miller, *Democracy Is in the Streets: From Port Huron to the Siege of Chicago* (New York: Simon and Schuster, 1987); Dick Cluster, ed., *They Should Have Served That Cup of Coffee: 7 Radicals Remember the 60s* (Boston: South End Press, 1979); Sohnya Sayres et. al., eds., *The 60s without Apology* (Minneapolis: University of Minnesota Press, 1984); John R. Logan and Harvey L. Molotch, *Urban Fortunes: The Political Economy of Place* (Berkeley: University of California Press, 1987); and Barbara Bergmann, *The Economic Emergence of Women* (New York: Basic Books, 1986).

36. See Adolph Reed, Jr., *The Jesse Jackson Phenomenon* (New Haven: Yale University Press, 1986); Martin Shefter, *Political Crisis/Fiscal Crisis: The Collapse and Revival of New York City* (New York: Basic Books, 1985); Norman Fainstein, "The Underclass/Mismatch Hypothesis as an Explanation for Black Economic Depri-

vation," *Politics and Society* 4 (1987), pp. 1–29; Stanley Lieberson, *A Piece of the Pie: Blacks and White Immigrants Since 1880* (Berkeley: University of California Press, 1980; Michael Brown, "The Segmented Welfare System: Distributive Conflict and Retrenchment in the United States, 1968–84," in *Remaking the Welfare State: Retrenchment and Social Policy in America and Europe,* ed. Michael Brown (Philadelphia: Temple University Press, 1988); Frances Fox Piven and Richard Cloward, "Why There Is No Labor Party in the United States; or, Race, Class, and the Democrats," in *With Friends like These: The "New Liberalism" and the New Assault on Equality,* ed. Adolph Reed, Jr. (Boulder: Westview Press, forthcoming).

37. Massey and Denton, *American Apartheid,* p. 49.

38. Michael Brown, "Race in the American Welfare State: The Ambiguities of 'Universalistic' Social Policy since the New Deal," in Reed, *With Friends like These.*

39. Sollors, p. 17. See Carol B. Stack, *All Our Kin: Strategies for Surival in a Black Community* (New York: Harper and Row, 1974); Herbert Gutman, *Work, Culture and Society in Industrializing America: Essays in American Working-Class and Social History* (New York: Random House, 1976); Lawrence Levine, *Black Culture and Black Consciousness: Afro-American Folk Thought from Slavery to Freedom* (New York: W. W. Norton).

40. Andrew Greeley, *Why Can't They Be like Us?* p. 18.

41. Linda Gordon, *Heroes of Their Own Lives: The Politics and History of Family Violence, Boston, 1880–1960* (New York: Penguin, 1988). Gordon is concerned in this study to delineate the racist and sexist ideology of the social welfare establishment, and its hypocrisy in denying the presence of male violence and child abuse among its own kind.

42. Novak, *The Rise of the Unmeltable Ethnics,* p. 35.

43. Stephen Steinberg, *The Ethnic Myth,* p. 219.

44. Margaret Mead and James Baldwin, *A Rap on Race* (Philadelphia: J. B. Lippincott, 1970), pp. 17, 146–47, 150–51. See Stanley Diamond's insightful—and nasty—review "Tape's Last Krapp," in the *New York Review of Books,* December 2, 1971, pp. 30–31. See also my discussion of this and other texts of the era in "White Ethnicities, Identity Politics, and Baby Bear's Chair," *Social Text* 41 (winter 1994), pp. 165–91; and Mead's functionalist, ahistorical "Ethnicity and Anthropology in America," in *Ethnic Identity: Cultural Continuities and Change,* ed. George De Vos and Lola Romanucci-Ross (Palo Alto: Mayfield Publishing Company, 1975), pp. 173–97. For further evidence of Mead's racial insensitivities, see Jane Howard, *Margaret Mead: A Life* (New York: Simon and Schuster, 1984), pp. 398 ff.; and Louise Newman, "Coming of Age, but Not in Samoa: Reflections on Margaret Mead's Legacy for Western Liberal Feminism," *American Quarterly* 48, no. 2 (June 1996), pp. 233–72.

45. di Leonardo, *The Varieties of Ethnic Experience,* p. 222.

46. Ibid., p. 37.

47. Ibid., p. 181.

48. Susan Estabrook Kennedy, *If All We Did Was Weep at Home: A History of White Working-Class Women in America* (Bloomington: Indiana University Press, 1979, pp. 241–42).

49. Herbert Gutman, *Work, Culture and Society in Industrializing America;* Judith E. Smith, "Our Own Kind: Family and Community Networks," *Radical History Review* 17 (1978), pp. 99–120, and *Family Connections: A History of Italian and Jewish Immigrant Lives in Providence, Rhode Island, 1900–1940* (Albany: SUNY Press, 1985).

50. Carroll Smith-Rosenberg, "The Female World of Love and Ritual: Relations between Women in Nineteenth-Century America," *Signs* 1, no. 1 (1975), pp. 1–29.

51. See also my discussion of women's culture, "Women's Culture and Its Discontents," in *The Politics of Culture,* ed. Brett Williams (Washington, D.C.: Smithsonian Institution Press, 1991), pp. 219–42.

52. Elaine Showalter, "Feminist Criticism in the Wilderness," in *Writing and Sexual Difference,* ed. Elizabeth Abel (Chicago: University of Chicago Press, 1982), pp. 9–36, esp. p. 27.

53. Judit Moschkovich, "—But I Know You, American Woman," in *This Bridge Called My Back: Writings by Radical Women of Color,* ed. Cherrie Moraga and Gloria Anzaldua (Watertown, Mass.: Persephone Press, 1981), pp. 79–84, esp. p. 82.

54. Temma Kaplan, "Female Consciousness and Collective Action: The Case of Barcelona, 1910–1918," *Signs* 7, no. 3 (1982), pp. 545–66, esp. p. 543.

55. Gerda Lerner, "Politics and Culture in Women's History: A Symposium," *Feminist Studies* 6, no. 1 (1980), pp. 26–64, esp. p. 53.

56. Carol Gilligan, *In a Different Voice: Psychological Theory and Women's Development* (Cambridge, Mass.: Harvard University Press, 1982). p. 17.

57. Nancy Cott, "Feminist Theory and Feminist Movements: the Past Before Us," in *What Is Feminism? A Re-examination,* ed. Juliet Mitchell and Ann Oakley (New York: Pantheon, 1986), pp. 49–62.

58. Nancy F. Cott, "What's in a Name? The Limits of 'Social Feminism'; or, Expanding the Vocabulary of Women's History," *Journal of American History* 76, no. 3 (December 1989), pp. 809–29; Linda K. Kerber, "Separate Spheres, Female Worlds, Woman's Place: The Rhetoric of Women's History," *Journal of American History* 75, no. 1 (June 1988), pp. 9–39.

59. Alice Echols, *Daring to Be Bad: Radical Feminism in America, 1967–75* (Minneapolis: University of Minnesota Press, 1989), p. 6.

60. Ellen DuBois, "Politics and Culture in Women's History: A Symposium," *Feminist Studies* 6, no. 1 (1980), pp. 28–36, esp. pp. 31, 33; Carroll Smith-Rosenberg in the same issue, pp. 55–64, esp. p. 62.

61. Marija Gimbutas, *The Language of the Goddess* (London: Thames and Hudson, 1989), p. xxi. See also Margaret Conkey and Ruth E. Tringham's thoughtful "Archaeology and the Goddess: Exploring the Contours of Feminist Archaeology," in *Feminisms in the Academy,* ed. Domna Stanton and Abigail J. Stewart

(Ann Arbor: University of Michigan Press, 1995), pp. 199–247. Only two more obvious examples: Riane Eisler, *The Chalice and the Blade* (New York: Harper and Row, 1987), speaks of "those dimly lit Neolithic and Paleolithic Ages when Goddess religions flourished" (cover blurb). Jean Shinoda Bolen, *Goddesses in Everywoman* (New York, Harper and Row, 1984), offers a pre–"running with wolves" Jungian trip through Greek mythology.

62. Sally Gearheart, *The Wanderground: Stories of the Hill Women* (Watertown, Mass.: Persephone Press, 1978); Charlotte Perkins Gilman, *Herland* (New York: Pantheon, 1979 [1915]).

63. Adolph Reed, Jr., "The 'Black Revolution' and the Reconstitution of Domination," in Reed, *Race, Politics and Culture*, pp. 61–96, esp. p. 78.

64. See, for example, Linda K. Kerber et al., "Viewpoint: On *In a Different Voice*: An Interdisciplinary Forum," *Signs* 11, no. 2 (1986), pp. 304–33.

65. Daniel Maltz and Ruth Borker, "A Cultural Approach to Male-Female Miscommunication," in *Language and Social Identity*, ed. John Gumperz (Cambridge: Cambridge University Press, 1982), pp. 196–218, esp. p. 200.

66. Deborah Tannen, *You Just Don't Understand: Women and Men in Conversation* (New York: William Morrow, 1990), p. 42.

67. John H. Cushman, Jr., "Members of an Exclusive Club Attend Monthly Talk on 'Gender Dynamics,'" *New York Times*, March 7, 1992.

68. Susan Gal, "Between Speech and Silence," in *Gender at the Crossroads of Knowledge: Feminist Anthropology in the Postmodern Era*, ed. Micaela di Leonardo (Berkeley: University of California Press, 1991), pp. 175–203.

69. James Scott, *Domination and the Arts of Resistance: Hidden Transcripts* (New Haven: Yale University Press, 1990).

70. Marianne Williamson, *A Woman's Worth* (New York: Random House, 1993), p. 6.

71. Ibid., pp. 15, 120, 137.

72. See Clarissa Pinkola Estes, *Women Who Run with the Wolves: Myths and Stories of the Wild Woman Archetype* (New York: Ballantine, 1992); and John Gray, *Men Are from Mars, Women Are from Venus: A Practical Guide for Improving Communication and Getting What You Want in Your Relationship* (New York: HarperCollins, 1992).

73. Katha Pollitt, "Are Women Morally Superior to Men? Marooned on Gilligan's Island," *Nation*, December 28, 1992, pp. 799–807, esp. pp. 806–7; reprinted in *Utne Reader*, September/October 1993, pp. 101–9.

74. See Gail Bederman's contextualized analysis of Robert Bly and the men's movement in her *Manliness and Civilization: A Cultural History of Gender and Race in the United States, 1880–1917* (Chicago: University of Chicago Press, 1995), pp. 234 ff.

75. Janet Sayers, *Biological Politics: Feminist and Antifeminist Perspectives* (New York: Tavistock, 1982). See also Verta Taylor and Leila Rupp's "Women's Culture and Lesbian Feminist Activism: A Reconsideration of Women's Culture," *Signs*

19, no. 3 (autumn 1993), pp. 32–61, which, in its zeal to defend the "women's culture" construct, implies that only lesbians are feminist activists and claims that drug-abuse therapy and religious groups have the same feminist political status as battered women's and rape crisis groups.

76. Nancy Hewitt, "Beyond the Search for Sisterhood: American Women's History in the 1980s," *Social History* 10, no. 1 (1985), pp. 299–321; Phyllis Palmer, "White Women/Black Women: The Dualism of Female Identity and Experience in the United States," *Feminist Studies* 9, no. 1 (spring 1983), pp. 151–70.

77. See, for example, Moraga and Anzaldua, *This Bridge Called My Back*.

78. Debora Silverman, *Selling Culture: Bloomingdale's, Diana Vreeland, and the New Aristocracy of Taste in Reagan's America* (New York: Pantheon, 1986).

79. See also Marcie Darnovsky's analysis of the advertising campaign, "The New Traditionalism: Repackaging Ms. Consumer," *Social Text*, no. 29 (November 1991), pp. 72–91.

80. "The Glamour Word on . . . Tony 'n Tina's Wedding," *Glamour*, October 1988, p. 175.

81. *Official Columbian Exposition Album* (1893), unpaginated.

82. Elinor Lenz and Barbara Myerhoff, *The Feminization of America* (New York: St. Martins Press, 1985).

83. Mary F. Belenky et al., *Women's Ways of Knowing: The Development of Self, Voice, and Mind* (New York: Basic Books, 1986); Pam McAllister, *You Can't Kill the Spirit* (Philadelphia: New Society Publishers, 1988).

84. Sears Roebuck won the case, although, it is argued, not on grounds of expert testimony. On the politics of this case, see Jon Weiner, "Women's History on Trial" *Nation*, September 7, 1985, pp. 161, 176, 178–80; Rosalind Rosenberg, "What Harms Women in the Workplace," *New York Times*, February 27, 1986; and Alice Kessler-Harris, "Equal Opportunity Commission vs. Sears Roebuck and Company: A Personal Account," *Radical History Review* 35 (April 1986), pp. 57–79.

85. Laura C. Flanders, "MacKinnon in the City of Freud," *Nation*, August 9/16, 1993, pp. 174–77, esp. p. 177.

86. I play here on W. E. B. Du Bois's indictment of the accomodationist politics of Booker Washington, "Of Mr. Booker T. Washington and Others," chap. 3 in *The Souls of Black Folk: Essays and Sketches* (New York: Fawcett, 1961 [1903]).

87. Frances Fox Piven and Richard A. Cloward, *The New Class War: Reagan's Attack on the Welfare State and Its Consequences* (New York: Pantheon Books, 1982); Fred Block et al., *The Mean Season: The Attack on the Welfare State* (New York: Pantheon, 1987).

88. Frank Levy, *Dollars and Dreams: The Changing American Income Distribution* (New York: W. W. Norton, 1988); Doug Henwood, "US: #1 in Poor, #3 in Rich, #8 in Middle Class," *Left Business Observer* 61 (December 13, 1993), p. 5.

89. Michael Katz, *In the Shadow of the Poorhouse: A Social History of Welfare in America* (New York: Basic Books, 1986).

90. William Ryan, *Blaming the Victim*, 2d ed. (New York: Random House, 1976 [1971]).

91. Karl Marx quoted in Tom Bottomore, ed., *The Marxist Dictionary* (Cambridge, Mass.: Harvard University Press, 1983), p. 292, s. v. "Lumpenproletariat."

92. Frances Fox Piven and Richard A. Cloward, *Regulating the Poor: The Functions of Public Welfare* (New York: Pantheon Books, 1971), p. 281.

93. George Russell, "Minority within a Minority: The Underclass," *Time*, August 29, 1977, pp. 14–27, esp. pp. 14, 27.

94. Ibid., p. 17.

95. Ibid., p. 15.

96. William Julius Wilson, *The Truly Disadvantaged: The Inner City, the Underclass, and Public Policy* (Chicago: University of Chicago Press, 1987), p. 13.

97. See Susan M. Rigdon, *The Culture Facade: Art, Science, and Politics in the Work of Oscar Lewis* (Urbana: University of Illinois Press, 1988), for the definitive review of Lewis's life and work.

98. Oscar Lewis, *Five Families: Mexican Case Studies in the Culture of Poverty* (New York: Random House, 1959), *Pedro Martinez: A Mexican Peasant and His Family* (New York: Random House, 1969), *A Death in the Sanchez Family: Autobiography of a Mexican Family* (New York: Vintage, 1963), and *La Vida: A Puerto Rican Family in the Culture of Poverty—San Juan and New York* (New York: Vintage Books, 1965).

99. Oscar Lewis, "The Culture of Poverty," in *Anthropological Essays* (New York: Random House, 1970), pp. 67–80, esp. p. 69.

100. Oscar Lewis, "The Culture of Poverty," pp. 70, 71, 72.

101. Ibid., p. 76.

102. Ibid., p. 77.

103. Ibid., p. 78.

104. Charles Valentine, *Culture and Poverty: Critique and Counter-proposals* (Chicago: University of Chicago Press, 1968), and "Culture and Poverty: Critique and Counter-proposals," *Current Anthropology* 10 (1969), pp. 181–82, responses, pp. 182–201; Eleanor Burke Leacock, ed., *The Culture of Poverty: A Critique* (New York: Simon and Schuster, 1971).

105. George M. Foster, "Peasant Society and the Image of the Limited Good," in *Peasant Society: A Reader*, ed. Jack M. Potter, May N. Diaz, and George M. Foster (Boston: Little, Brown, 1967), pp. 300–323. Margaret Mead, however, weighed in in defense of Lewis, labeling his critics "confused" and extolling the social engineering virtues of the culture of poverty concept. See her response, p. 194, to Charles Valentine, "Culture and Poverty: Critique and Counter-proposals."

106. William Julius Wilson, *The Truly Disadvantaged*, p. 137.

107. Ibid., p. 56.

108. Ibid., pp. 151, 157, 155.

109. Adolph Reed, Jr., "The Liberal Technocrat," review of *The Truly Disadvan-*

taged, by William Julius Wilson, *Nation,* February 6, 1988, pp. 167–70, esp. p. 168, and "Reed Replies" (to letters in response to the review), *Nation,* May 14, 1988, pp. 662, 679, esp. p. 679. See also his "The Underclass as Myth and Symbol: The Poverty of Discourse about Poverty," *Radical America* 24 (January 1992), pp. 21–40; Herbert Gans, "The Dangers of the Underclass: Its Harmfulness as a Planning Concept," in *People, Plans, and Policies* (New York: Columbia University Press, 1991), pp. 328–44; and the articles by Joan Vincent, Andrew H. Maxwell, Ida Susser, and Delmos J. Jones in the special "underclass" issue of *Critique of Anthropology,* vol. 13, no. 3 (1993).

110. William Julius Wilson, *The Truly Disadvantaged,* pp. 10–12.

111. Ibid., p. 15.

112. Stephen Steinberg, "The Urban Villagers: A Critique" (paper presented at the Eastern Sociological Meetings, April 19, 1993).

113. Ken Auletta, *The Underclass* (New York: Vintage Books, 1983), p. 51.

114. Nicholas Lemann, *The Promised Land: The Great Black Migration and How It Changed America* (New York: Alfred Knopf, 1991); Brett Williams, "Aliens in Our Midst," review of *The Promised Land,* by Nicholas Lemann, *Progressive,* June 1991, pp. 40–42, esp. p. 40; William Grady, "A Private Life Becomes a Public Issue," *Chicago Tribune,* January 3, 1994.

115. Alex Kotlowitz, *There Are No Children Here: The Story of Two Boys Growing Up in the Other America* (New York: Doubleday, 1991). The exact figures for 1991: 1.4 percent of AFDC households had "six or more" children (U.S. Department of Health and Human Services, Adminstration for Children and Families, Office of Family Assistance, *Characteristics and Financial Circumstances of AFDC Recipients, FY 1991,* [Washington, D.C.: Government Printing Office, 1991], p. 24, table 6).

116. Chicago Tribune staff, *The American Millstone: An Examination of the Nation's Permanent Underclass* (Chicago: Contemporary Books, 1986).

117. "Children of the Shadows," *New York Times,* 1993, p. 1. Individual reporters did heroic jobs in this series, but their attempts at detailing racism are overridden by the newspaper's editorial frame.

118. Philip Kasinitz, "Facing Up to the Underclass," *Telos* (summer 1988), pp. 170–80, esp. p. 178.

119. Mike Royko, "Don't Shed a Tear for Maxwell Street," *Chicago Tribune,* November 2, 1993.

120. Francis X. Clines, "As Pizza Maker Knows, Sinatra Still Delivers," *New York Times,* October 10, 1993, p. 20.

121. Francis X. Clines, "April: A Little Italy Springs Ahead," *New York Times,* April 2, 1995.

122. Sam Roberts, "Fighting the Tide of Bloodshed on Streets Resembling a War Zone," *New York Times,* November 15, 1993.

123. See Isabel Sawhill, "The Underclass: An Overview," *Public Interest,* no. 96 (summer 1989), pp. 3–15; David Ellwood, *Poor Support: Poverty in the American*

Family (New York: Basic Books, 1988); and Christopher Jencks, *Rethinking Social Policy: Race, Poverty, and the Underclass* (Cambridge, Mass.: Harvard University Press, 1992).

124. Michael Katz, "Conclusion: Reframing the Underclass Debate," in *The "Underclass" Debate: Views from History*, ed. Michael Katz (Princeton: Princeton University Press, 1993), pp. 440–77, esp. pp. 440, 442, 448; and David W. Bartelt, "Housing the 'Underclass,'" in Katz, *The "Underclass" Debate*, pp. 118–57, esp. p. 156.

125. Arline Geronimus and Sanders Korenman, "The Socioeconomic Consequences of Teen Childbearing Reconsidered," *Quarterly Journal of Economics* 107 (1992), pp. 1187–1284, and "Maternal Youth or Family Background? Preliminary Findings on the Health Disadvantages of Infants with Teenage Mothers," research report 91–204 (Population Studies Center, University of Michigan, 1991).

126. See "Who's Poor?" *Left Business Observer* 61 (December 13, 1993), pp. 4–5; Roberta M. Spalter-Roth and Heidi I. Hartmann, "Combining Work and Welfare: An Alternative Anti-poverty Strategy" (report to the Ford Foundation from the Institute for Women's Policy Research, Washington, D.C., 1992); Virginia Morris, "Docs Let Pregnant Whites Off the Drug Hook," *New Haven Register,* April 26, 1990; "Advance Report of New Data from the 1980 Birth Certificate," U.S. Department of Health and Human Services, National Center for Health Statistics, Monthly Vital Statistics Report, vol. 40, no. 12 (April 1992), p. 3; and Claire D. Coles et al., "Effects of Cocaine and Alcohol Use in Pregnancy on Neonatal Growth and Neurobehavioral Status," *Neurotoxicology and Teratology* 14 (1992), pp. 23–33. See also Molly McNulty, "Pregnancy Police: The Health Policy and Legal Implications of Punishing Pregnant Women for Harm to Their Fetuses," *Review of Law and Social Change* 16, no. 2 (1987–88), pp. 277–319; and Arlie Hochschild, *The Second Shift: Working Parents and the Revolution at Home* (New York: Viking, 1989), pp. 248–49.

127. U.S. General Accounting Office, *Teenage Drug Use: Uncertain Linkages with Either Pregnancy or School Dropout* (Washington, D.C.: Government Printing Office, 1991), pp. 16, 17; Andrew Hacker, *Two Nations: Black and White, Separate, Hostile, Unequal* (New York: Scribners, 1992), pp. 234 (high school graduation rates), 95 ff. (returns to education), 182 ff. (crime and arrests); Joleen Kirschenman and Kathryn M. Neckerman, "'We'd Love to Hire Them, But . . .': The Meaning of Race for Employers," in *The Urban Underclass*, ed. Christopher Jencks and Paul Peterson (Washington, D.C.: Brookings Institution, 1991), pp. 203–32; Michael Quint, "Racial Gap Found on Mortgages: Loan-Denial Rate Said to Be Double for Minorities," *New York Times,* October 22, 1993; Saul Hansell, "Shamed by Publicity, Banks Stress Minority Mortgages," *New York Times,* August 30, 1993.

128. Brett Williams, "Poverty among African Americans in the Urban United States," *Human Organization* 51, no. 2 (1992), pp. 164–74, esp. p. 167.

129. See, for example, John Modell, *Into One's Own: From Youth to Adulthood in the United States, 1920–1975* (Berkeley: University of California Press, 1989).

130. George Lipsitz, "The Possessive Investment in Whiteness: Racialized Social Democracy and the 'White' Problem in American Studies," *American Quarterly* 47, no. 3 (September 1995), pp. 369–88.

131. Stephen Steinberg, *The Ethnic Myth*, p. 272.

132. Claire Kim, "Model Minority Compared to Whom?" in Reed, *With Friends like These*.

133. Suzanne Model, "The Ethnic Niche and the Structure of Opportunity: Immigrants and Minorities in New York City," in Katz, *The "Underclass" Debate*, pp. 161–93; Stephen Steinberg, *The Ethnic Myth*, p. 275.

134. Faye Harrison, "The Persistent Power of 'Race' in the Cultural and Political Economy of Racism," *Annual Review of Anthropology* 24 (1995), pp. 47–74, esp. p. 47.

135. John Langston Gwaltney, *Drylongso: A Self-Portrait of Black America* (New York: Random House, 1980), pp. xxx, xviv.

136. Terry M. Williams, *The Cocaine Kids: The Inside Story of a Teenage Drug Ring* (Reading, Mass.: Addison-Wesley Publishing Company, 1989); Lisbeth B. Schorr, "On the Streets Where They Live and Die," *New York Times Book Review*, August 27, 1989, p. 7.

137. See Richard C. Lewontin, Steven Rose, and Leon Kamin, *Not in Our Genes: Biology, Ideology, and Human Nature* (New York: Pantheon, 1984); Susan Sperling, "Baboons with Briefcases vs. Langurs in Lipstick: Feminism and Functionalism in Primate Studies," in di Leonardo, *Gender at the Crossroads*, pp. 204–34.

138. Barbara Myerhoff, *Number Our Days* (New York: E. P. Dutton, 1978), p. 83.

139. Arlie Hochschild, *Unexpected Community: Portrait of an Old-Age Subculture* (Berkeley: University of California Press, 1973).

140. Myerhoff, *Number Our Days*, pp. 3, 9, 10.

141. Ibid., pp. 261, 264. Myerhoff was writing several years after the publication of the key 1970s texts in feminist anthropology, *Women, Culture and Society* and *Towards an Anthropology of Women*. She cites a few articles from the former text but fails to adopt their mandate for the field: comparative social and cultural analysis of gender relations.

142. Jonathan Rieder, *Canarsie: The Jews and Italians of Brooklyn Against Liberalism* (Cambridge, Mass.: Harvard University Press, 1985), pp. 6, 8. For a superficially gentler interpretation of Rieder's work, see Stephen Steinberg, "The Social Context of the White Backlash: A Critique of Jonathan Rieder's *Canarsie*," *Ethnic and Racial Studies* 11, no. 2 (April 1988), pp. 218–24.

143. Rieder, *Canarsie*, p. 7.

144. Ibid., p. 22.

145. Ibid., p. 233.

146. Ibid., pp. 151–52.

147. Benedict Anderson, *Imagined Communities: Reflections on the Origin and Spread of Nationalism*, 2d ed. (London: Verso, 1991 [1983]).

148. Eric Hobsbawm and Terence Ranger, eds., *The Invention of Tradition* (Cambridge: Cambridge University Press, 1983); Michael Herzfield, *Ours Once More: Folklore, Ideology, and the Making of Modern Greece* (New York: Pella Publications, 1987).

149. L. J. Jordanova, "Natural Facts: A Historical Perspective on Science and Sexuality," in *Nature, Culture, and Gender,* ed. Carol MacCormack and Marilyn Strathern (Cambridge: Cambridge University Press, 1980), pp. 42–69; Maurice Bloch and Jean L. Bloch, "Women and the Dialectics of Nature in Eighteenth-Century French Thought," in MacCormack and Strathern, *Nature, Culture, and Gender,* pp. 25–41; Joan B. Landes, *Women and the Public Sphere in the Age of the French Revolution* (Ithaca: Cornell University Press, 1988); Mary Dunham Johnson, "Old Wine in New Bottles: The Institutional Changes for Women of the People during the French Revolution," in *Women, War and Revolution,* ed. Carol R. Berkin and Clara M. Lovett (New York: Holmes and Meier, 1980), pp. 107–43; Darline Gay Levy and Harriet Branson Applewhite, "Women of the Popular Classes in Revolutionary Paris, 1789–1795," in Berkin and Lovett, *Women, War and Revolution,* pp. 9–35.

150. Kumari Jayawardena, *Feminism and Nationalism in the Third World,* (London: Zed Press, 1986).

151. Christopher Herbert, *Culture and Anomie: Ethnographic Imagination in the Nineteenth Century* (Chicago: University of Chicago Press, 1991), p. 208.

152. John Comaroff and Jean Comaroff, *Ethnography and the Historical Imagination* (Boulder: Westview Press, 1992), p. 285.

153. Ibid., pp. 289, 288; Jack London, *People of the Abyss* (New York: Lawrence Hill Books, 1995 [1903]), p. 288. Recently, the *Chicago Tribune Sunday Magazine* published an appalling story ("Beyond Belief," December 12, 1993) about a missionary couple's work among a Latin American Indian population. They later (January 22, 1994) printed no fewer than eight outraged letters complaining about the "destruction of indigenous cultures," the rights of native peoples, ancient knowledge, &c. This in a newspaper noteworthy for the racist virulence of its right-wing "collar county" readership, a newspaper whose daily letters column always contains at least one outraged offering about the depravity of the domestic minority poor.

154. Tom Morganthau, "America: Still Melting Pot?" *Newsweek,* August 9, 1993, pp. 16–25, esp. p. 23.

155. Ellen Messer-Davidow, "Manufacturing the Attack on Liberalized Higher Education," *Social Text* 36 (1993), pp. 40–80; Paul Weyrich, *Cultural Conservatism: Toward a New Agenda* (Washington, D.C.: Institute for Cultural Conservatism/Free Congress Research and Education Foundation, 1987), p. 1.

156. Barbara Epstein, "Political Correctness and Identity Politics," in *Beyond PC: Toward a Politics of Understanding,* ed. Pat Aufderheide (St. Paul: Greywolf Press, 1992), pp. 148–54, esp. p. 153. See also my "White Ethnicities."

157. Robert Hughes, *The Culture of Complaint: The Fraying of America* (New

York: Oxford University Press, 1993). Hughes thanks Arthur Schlesinger because "his own recent book, *The Disuniting of America,* says much of what I say but said it earlier and better" (p. xiii). He said it; I didn't. Key American studies texts on the rise of therapeutic and consumption modes are T. J. Jackson Lears, *No Place of Grace: Antimodernism and the Transformation of American Culture, 1880–1920* (New York: Pantheon, 1981); and Richard Wightman Fox and T. J. Jackson Lears, eds., *The Culture of Consumption: Critical Essays in American History, 1880–1980* (New York: Pantheon, 1983).

158. Arthur M. Schlesinger, Jr., *The Disuniting of America: Reflections on a Multicultural America* (New York: Norton, 1992), p. 15 (first published in 1991 by Whittle Direct Books).

159. Ibid., pp. 134, 127. Schlesinger was preceded in this argument by numbers of new rightist academics. See, for example, classicist and Dean of Yale College Donald Kagan, "The Role of the West," *Yale Alumni Magazine,* November 1990, pp. 43–46.

160. Rogers Smith, "Beyond Tocqueville, Myrdal, and Hartz: The Multiple Traditions in America," *American Political Science Review* 87, no. 3 (September 1993), pp. 549–66, esp. p. 563.

161. Schlesinger, *The Disuniting of America,* pp. 127 ff., 128. For an extensive analysis of how this Western imperialist vision plays out in media, see Ella Shohat and Robert Stam, *Unthinking Eurocentrism: Multiculturalism and the Media* (London: Routledge, 1994).

162. Paul Johnson, "Colonialism's Back—and Not a Moment Too Soon," *New York Times Sunday Magazine,* April 18, 1993, pp. 22, 43–44. See Ann Stoler and Frederick Cooper's excellent response, *New York Times Sunday Magazine,* Letters, May 9, 1993; and also Christopher Hitchens's dissection of Johnson's character and misdeeds, "Minority Report," *Nation,* April 10, 1989, pp. 474–75.

163. Bellah et al., *The Good Society,* pp. 1, 231.

164. Ibid., p. 139.

165. Ibid., pp. 47–48, 129.

166. Harper's Forum: "Who Owes What to Whom?" with Gerald Marzorati, Benjamin Barber, Mary Ann Glendon, Dan Kemmis, Christopher Lasch, and Christopher Stone, *Harper's,* February 1991, pp. 43–54, esp. p. 48.

167. Bellah et al., *The Good Society,* pp. 23, 99, 37. Despite positive reviews in the middlebrow press, *The Good Society* has had a highly critical academic reception. See, for example, responses by Steven Lukes, Frances Fox Piven, and Samuel Preston in *Contemporary Sociology* 21, no. 4 (July 1992), pp. 425–30; Robert J. Myers and Andrew Greeley in *Society* 29, no. 4 (May/June 1992), pp. 70–81; and Susan Dunn in *Partisan Review* 60, no. 1 (1993), pp. 151–61. Interestingly, though, while Frances Piven scores the group for inattention to power, and most respondents note their conflation of social procedures with social goals and the book's total barrenness of empirical or historical data, none of these reviewers engages with the authors' racism or antifeminism.

168. Communitarians have a platform that calls for making divorce more difficult and states flatly that single-parent families should be discouraged. Amitai Etzioni, editor of the communitarian journal, *The Responsive Community,* also disapproves of nonparental child care. See his *The Spirit of Community: Rights, Responsibilities, and the Communitarian Agenda* (New York: Crown, 1993), pp. 253–67, 57 ff. Communitarians have also taken gun control and public campaign financing stands, but these issues predate their movement and certainly do not require their moralizing, antieconomic epistemology.

169. Hollinger, "How Wide the Circle?" p. 335.

170. Ibid., p. 326.

171. Melissa Llewelyn-Davies, *Masai Women,* Granada Films, 1975, and "Two Contexts of Solidarity," in *Women United, Women Divided: Comparative Studies of Ten Contemporary Cultures,* ed. Patricia Caplan and Janet Bujra (Bloomington: Indiana University Press, 1979), pp. 206–37.

172. Raymond Bonner, *At the Hand of Man: Peril and Hope for Africa's Wildlife* (New York: Alfred A. Knopf, 1993), pp. 163–203. Bonner, however, is no more knowledgeable about Masai women than is Hollinger. See p. 166. Reporter James McKinley does, however, recognize the economic bottom line for Kenyan Masai, who are expected to be guardians of game sanctuaries for little benefit. See his "Warily, Masai Embrace the Animal Kingdom," *New York Times,* March 13, 1996.

173. Pottery Barn catalog (1993), p. 6, in author's possession; George Gurley, "The Blueblood Belles, Lost in New York," *New York Observer,* May 12, 1997; Amy M. Spindler, "Taking Stereotyping to a New Level in Fashion," *New York Times,* June 3, 1997; "Chelsea in Tanzania," *Chicago Tribune,* March 26, 1997; Hillary Rodham Clinton, "African Odyssey," *Vogue,* June 1997, pp. 186–99, 280, esp. p. 195.

Chapter Three

1. Marjorie Shostak, *Nisa: The Life and Words of a !Kung Woman* (Cambridge, Mass.: Harvard University Press, 1981); Derek Freeman, *Margaret Mead and Samoa: The Unmaking of an Anthropological Myth* (Cambridge, Mass.: Harvard University Press, 1983). Shostak died in 1996. See Ford Burkhart, "Marjorie Shostak, Who Wrote about Tribal Woman, Was 51," *New York Times,* October 8, 1996.

2. Shostak, *Nisa,* pp. 5–6.

3. Ibid., pp. 6, 16.

4. Ibid., pp. 16, 17.

5. Ibid., p. 13.

6. Freeman, *Margaret Mead and Samoa,* pp. 287, 290, 288.

7. Ibid., pp. 330, 294, 302.

8. I have borrowed the phrase "ourselves undressed" from the late Michelle Rosaldo. See her "The Use and Abuse of Anthropology: Reflections on Cross-Cultural understanding," *Signs* 5, no. 3 (1980), pp. 389–417.

9. Juan Williams and Eric Pianin, "'Women's Place': Silence Greets Reagan's Ad-Libbed Apology," *Washington Post*, August 4, 1983.

10. On Ida Cox and her song, see Daphne Duval Harrison, *Black Pearls: Blues Queens of the 1920s* (New Brunswick: Rutgers University Press, 1988), pp. 9, 110 ff.

11. George Marcus, "One Man's Mead," *New York Times Book Review*, March 27, 1983; Ernest Van Den Haag, "Strange News from the South Seas," *Fortune*, April 18, 1983, pp. 153–56, esp. p. 153; John Leo, "Bursting the South Sea Bubble," *Time*, February 14, 1983, pp. 68–70, esp. pp. 68, 70.

12. Frank Kermode, "Grandeur and Filth," *New York Review of Books* 21, no. 9 (May 30, 1974) pp. 6–9, esp. p. 9.

13. See Barbara Taylor, *Eve and the New Jerusalem: Socialism and Feminism in the Nineteenth Century* (London: Virago Press, 1983); Joan B. Landes, *Women and the Public Sphere in the Age of the French Revolution* (Ithaca: Cornell University Press, 1988); Alice Rossi, ed., *The Feminist Papers: From Adams to de Beauvoir* (New York: Bantam Books, 1974), pp. 25–85; Lynn Hunt, *The Family Romance of the French Revolution* (Berkeley: University of California Press, 1992); Mary Beth Norton, *Liberty's Daughters: The Revolutionary Experience of American Women, 1750–1800* (Boston: Little, Brown, 1980); and Linda Kerber, *Women of the Republic: Intellect and Ideology in Revolutionary America* (Chapel Hill: Univesity of North Carolina Press, 1980).

14. Maurice Bloch and Jean L. Bloch, "Women and the Dialectics of Nature in Eighteenth-Century French Thought," in *Nature, Culture, and Gender,* ed. Carol MacCormack and Marilyn Strathern (Cambridge: Cambridge University Press, 1980), pp. 25–41, esp. p. 31.

15. J. W. Burrow, *Evolution and Society: A Study in Victorian Social Theory* (Cambridge: Cambridge University Press, 1970 [1966]), p. x.

16. George Stocking, *Victorian Anthropology* (New York: Free Press, 1987), p. 286.

17. John Ferguson McLennan, *Studies in Ancient History* (London: Macmillan, 1886), p. 1; John Lubbock, *The Origin of Civilisation and the Primitive Condition of Man,* ed. Peter Riviere (Chicago: University of Chicago Press, 1978 [1870]), p. 1.

18. Frederick Engels, *Origin of the Family, Private Property and the State* (New York: International Publishers, 1972 [1884]), p. 145.

19. Herbert Spencer, *The Study of Sociology* (New York: Appleton and Company, 1929 [1873]), pp. 341, 347.

20. Stocking, *Victorian Anthropology,* p. 205.

21. Herbert Spencer, *Principles of Sociology,* ed. Stanislav Andreski Hamden: Archon Books, 1969 [1876, 1893, 1896]), p. 32; Lubbock, *The Origin of Civilisation,* pp. 50, 52; O. T. Mason, *Woman's Share in Primitive Culture* (New York: D. Appleton and Company, 1894), p. 275.

22. Stocking, *Victorian Anthropology,* p. 237.

23. John Stuart Mill, *The Subjection of Women* [1869], in *John Stuart Mill and Harriet Taylor Mill: Essays on Sex Equality,* ed. Alice Rossi (Chicago: University of Chicago Press, 1970), pp. 125–242, esp. pp. 146–47.

24. Ibid., pp. 163–64.

25. Elizabeth Cady Stanton, "The Sixteenth Amendment," *Revolution*, April 29, 1869, quoted in Ellen Carol DuBois, *Feminism and Suffrage* (Ithaca: Cornell University Press, 1978), p. 178.

26. Anna Julia Cooper, *A Voice from the South* (New York: Oxford University Press, 1988 [1892]), pp. 96–97.

27. Peggy Pascoe, *Relations of Rescue: The Search for Female Moral Authority in the American West, 1874–1939* (New York: Oxford University Press, 1990), p. xxi.

28. Joan Jacobs Brumberg, "Zenanas and Girlless Villages: The Ethnology of American Evangelical Women, 1870–1910," *Journal of American History* 69, no. 2 (September 1982), pp. 347–71, esp. pp. 349, 367.

29. See William Schneider, "Race and Empire: The Rise of Popular Ethnography in the Late Nineteenth Century," *Journal of Popular Culture* 11, no. 1 (1977), pp. 98–109; Raymond Corbey, "Ethnographic Showcases, 1870–1930," *Cultural Anthropology* 8, no. 3 (1993), pp. 338–69; George W. Stocking, Jr., ed., *Objects and Others: Essays on Museums and Material Culture* (Madison: University of Wisconsin Press, 1985), esp. p. 114; Robert Rydell, *All the World's a Fair: Visions of Empire at American International Expositions, 1876–1916* (Chicago: University of Chicago Press, 1984); Stocking, *Victorian Anthropology;* Thomas R. Trautman, *Lewis Henry Morgan and the Invention of Kinship* (Berkeley: University of California Press, 1987); and Curtis M. Hinsley, "Zunis and Brahmins: Cultural Ambivalence in the Gilded Age," in *Romantic Motives: Essays on Anthropological Sensibility*, ed. George W. Stocking, Jr., History of Anthropology, vol. 6 (Madison: University of Wisconsin Press, 1989), pp. 169–207.

30. Stocking, *Victorian Anthropology*, p. 264–65.

31. See Rydell, *All the World's a Fair*, p. 57.

32. George W. Stocking, Jr., *Race, Culture, and Evolution: Essays in the History of Anthropology* (Chicago: University of Chicago Press, 1982 [1968]), p. 132.

33. See T. J. Jackson Lears, *No Place of Grace: Antimodernism and the Transformation of American Culture, 1880–1920* (New York: Pantheon, 1981), esp. pp. 70, 274.

34. Hinsley, "Zunis and Brahmins," pp. 185, 184.

35. Jackson Lears, *No Place of Grace*, pp. 107, 119. See also Gail Bederman, *Manliness and Civilization: A Cultural History of Gender and Race in the United States, 1880–1917* (Chicago: University of Chicago Press, 1995).

36. See Robert F. Berkhofer, Jr., *The White Man's Indian: Images of the American Indian from Columbus to the Present* (New York: Vintage Books, 1978), pp. 166 ff.; Eric Foner, *Reconstruction: America's Unfinished Revolution, 1863–1877* (New York: Harper and Row, 1988); Ronald Takaki, *Iron Cages: Race and Culture in Nineteenth-Century America* (New York: Knopf, 1979); and American Social History Project, *Who Built America? Working People and the Nation's Economy, Politics, Culture and Society*, vol. 2, *From the Gilded Age to the Present* (New York: Pantheon, 1992), pt. 1, "Monopoly and Upheaval, 1877–1914," pp. 7–214.

37. See George W. Stocking, Jr., ed., *A Franz Boas Reader: The Shaping of Ameri-*

can Anthropology 1883–1911 (Chicago: University of Chicago Press, 1982 [1974]), p. 284.

38. Stocking, *Race, Culture, and Evolution,* pp. 133–60, esp. p. 149.

39. Ibid., pp. 149, 148.

40. Ibid., pp. 161–94. See also Vernon J. Williams, Jr., *Rethinking Race: Franz Boas and His Contemporaries* (Lexington: University Press of Kentucky, 1996), for consideration of Boas's influence on Afro-American and white scholars on the meaning of race for black Americans.

41. Ira Jacknis, "Franz Boas and Exhibits: On the Limitations of the Museum Method of Anthropology," in Stocking, *Objects and Others,* pp. 75–111, esp. p. 107. See also Julia Elizabeth Liss, "The Cosmopolitan Imagination: Franz Boas and the Development of American Anthropology" (Ph.D. diss., University of California, Berkeley, 1990), for an interpretation of Boas's failure to appeal to local New York elites through the ideology of a transcendent "science."

42. Stocking, *Race, Culture, and Evolution,* pp. 175 ff., 299–300.

43. Margaret Mead, *Blackberry Winter: My Earlier Years* (New York: Washington Square Press, 1972), p. 137.

44. Freeman, *Margaret Mead and Samoa,* p. 56.

45. Rosalind Rosenberg, *Beyond Separate Spheres: Intellectual Roots of Modern Feminism* (New Haven: Yale University Press, 1982), pp. 207–37, esp. p. 226; Franz Boas, "Some Problems of Methodology in the Social Sciences," in *The New Social Science,* ed. Leonard D. White (Chicago: University of Chicago Press, 1930), pp. 84–98, esp. p. 98.

46. See George W. Stocking, Jr., "The Scientific Reaction against Cultural Anthropology," in Stocking, *Race, Culture, and Evolution,* pp. 270–307, esp. p. 300 ff.

47. Rosenberg, *Beyond Separate Spheres,* pp. 207–23, esp. p. 211.

48. George W. Stocking, Jr., "The Ethnographic Sensibility of the 1920s and the Dualism of the Anthropological Tradition," in *The Ethnographer's Magic and Others Essays in the History of Anthropology* (Madison: University of Wisconsin Press, 1992), pp. 276–341.

49. Betty Friedan, *The Feminine Mystique* (New York: Bantam Doubleday, 1983 [1963]), p. 147. Jane Howard does give the Friedan attack passing reference. See Jane Howard, *Margaret Mead: A Life* (New York: Simon and Schuster, 1984), p. 363 ff.

50. Mead, *Blackberry Winter,* pp. 92, 115.

51. Pascoe, *Relations of Rescue,* pp. 207, 202.

52. See Rayna Rapp and Ellen Ross, "The 1920s: Feminism, Consumerism, and Political Backlash in the United States," in *Women in Culture and Politics: A Century of Change,* ed. Judith Friedlander (Bloomington: Indiana University Press, 1986), pp. 52–61, esp. pp. 53–54.

53. Nancy Cott, *The Grounding of Modern Feminism* (New Haven: Yale University Press, 1987), p. 217.

54. Ibid., p. 218; Barbara Solomon, *In the Company of Educated Women: A History*

of Women and Higher Education in America (New Haven: Yale University Press, 1985), p. 142.

55. Cott, *Grounding*, pp. 85–114.

56. Ibid., p. 167.

57. Paula Fass, *The Damned and the Beautiful: American Youth in the 1920s* (New York: Oxford University Press, 1977), p. 379.

58. Viviana Zelizer, *Pricing the Priceless Child: The Changing Social Value of Children* (New York: Basic Books, 1985). Zelizer's historical frame for the shift begins in the 1870s.

59. Fass, *The Damned and the Beautiful*, pp. 6, 21.

60. Kathy Peiss, *Cheap Amusements: Working-Class Women and Leisure in Turn-of-the-Century New York* (Philadelphia: Temple University Press, 1986); W. I. Thomas, *The Unadjusted Girl: With Cases and Standpoint for Behavior Analysis*, Criminal Science Monograph no. 4 (Boston, 1923; reprint, New York: Harper and Row, 1967).

61. W. I. Thomas, *The Unadjusted Girl*, p. 109.

62. American studies scholars have engaged in vigorous historiographical debate with one another over the timing and exact social entailments of the evolution of the culture of consumption in the United States. It is not my purpose here to enter into that debate, but simply to draw the well-documented contours of historical change and their connections to the larger themes relevant here. See Stewart Ewen, *Captains of Consciousness: Advertising and the Social Roots of Consumer Culture* (New York: McGraw-Hill, 1976); Richard Wightman Fox and T. J. Jackson Lears, eds., *The Culture of Consumption: Critical Essays in American History, 1880–1980* (New York: Pantheon, 1983); Warren Susman, *Culture as History: The Transformation of American Society in the Twentieth Century* (New York: Pantheon, 1984); Simon J. Bronner, ed., *Consuming Visions: Accumulation and Display of Goods in America, 1880–1920* (New York: Norton, 1989); Jean-Christophe Agnew, "Coming Up for Air: Consumer Culture in Historical Perspective," *Intellectual History Newsletter* 12 (1990), pp. 3–21; and William Leach, *Land of Desire: Merchants, Power, and the Rise of a New American Culture* (New York: Pantheon, 1993).

63. Rapp and Ross, "The 1920s: Feminism, Consumerism, and Political Backlash in the United States," p. 56.

64. Christopher Wilson, "The Rhetoric of Consumption: Mass-Market Magazines and the Demise of the Gentle Reader, 1880–1920," in Fox and Jackson Lears, *The Culture of Consumption*, pp. 40–64, esp. p. 64.

65. Warren Susman, "'Personality' and the Making of Twentieth-Century Culture," in Susman, *Culture as History*, pp. 271–85; Karen Haltunnen, "From Parlor to Living Room: Domestic Space, Interior Decoration, and the Culture of Personality," in Bronner, *Consuming Visions*, pp. 157–89.

66. Leach, *Land of Desire*, pp. 85, 371, 328.

67. Ibid., p. 326.

68. Howard, *Margaret Mead*, p. 24.

69. Leach, *Land of Desire,* pp. 160; Edward Sherwood Mead, *Corporation Finance* (New York: Appleton, 1931 [1910]), pp. 361–62, quoted in Leach, *Land of Desire,* p. 17.

70. Emily Fogg-Mead, "The Place of Advertising in Modern Business," *Journal of Political Economy,* March 1901, pp. 242, esp. pp. 227, 221.

71. Margaret Mead, *Coming of Age in Samoa* (New York: American Museum of Natural History, 1973 [1928]), p. 1. Mead never altered her text through multiple editions over half a century. For the reader's convenience, subsequent references shortened to *Coming of Age* are to this easily available edition.

72. Ibid., p. 4.

73. Ibid., pp. 8, 9, 11.

74. Henry Adams cited in Jackson Lears, *No Place of Grace,* p. 274; Mead, *Coming of Age,* pp. 4, 110, 111.

75. Mead, *Coming of Age,* pp. 118, 123.

76. Ibid., pp. 119, 118, 120, 122. As I noted in criticizing Marianna Torgovnick in chap. 1, Mead by no means refrains from discussing Samoan homosexual activities. But for Mead in 1928, all youthful sexual actions are to be considered in terms of how well or how poorly they provide for a "satisfactory sex adjustment" in heterosexual marriage.

77. Ibid., pp. 120 ff., esp. p. 137.

78. See Paul Kennedy, *The Samoan Tangle: A Study in Anglo-German-American Relations, 1878–1900* (New York: Harper and Row, 1978); George Herbert Ryden, *The Foreign Policy of the United States in Relation to Samoa* (New Haven: Yale University Press, 1933), pp. 575–81; Margaret Mead, "Americanization in Samoa," *American Mercury* 16 (March 1929), pp. 264–70, esp. p. 268.

79. Mead, *Coming of Age,* p. 5.

80. Edwin Ardener, "Belief and the Problem of Women," in J. S. La Fontaine, ed., *The Interpretation of Ritual: Essays in Honour of A. I. Richards* (London: Tavistock, 1972), pp. 135–58, esp. p. 138.

81. Cott, *Grounding,* pp. 232, 237–38.

82. Mead, *Coming of Age,* pp. 47–48.

83. Ibid., p. 21.

84. Sylvia Yanagisako, "Family and Household: The Analysis of Domestic Groups," *Annual Review of Anthropology* 8 (1979), pp. 161–205.

85. Mead, *Coming of Age,* pp. 98 ff., 152 ff. Richard Feinberg also makes the point, in an otherwise two-dimensional piece on *Coming of Age,* that Mead does supply the ethnographic material for a Sturm und Drang interpretation of Samoan adolescence. See his "Margaret Mead and Samoa: *Coming of Age* in Fact and Fiction," *American Anthropologist* 90, no. 3 (September 1988), pp. 656–63.

86. Mead, *Coming of Age,* p. 19.

87. Mead, *Blackberry Winter,* p. 88. On Margaret Mead's religious practice, see Howard, *Margaret Mead,* chap. 23.

88. Mead, *Coming of Age,* p. 127.

89. The 1920 census counted more than 13 percent foreign born; 21.5 percent if we include those with foreign-born parents. See John Higham, *Send These to Me: Jews and Other Immigrants in Urban America* (New York: Atheneum, 1975), p. 15.

90. Mead, *Coming of Age*, pp. 117, 112–13. On class differentials in completed family size, see Fass, *The Damned and the Beautiful*, p. 61. On high school attendance, see John Modell, *Into One's Own: From Youth to Adulthood in the United States, 1920–1975* (Berkeley: University of California Press, 1989), p. 77. The college attendance figure is for 1930, cited in James Sloan Allen, *The Romance of Commerce and Culture: Capitalism, Modernism, and the Chicago-Aspen Crusade for Cultural Reform* (Chicago: University of Chicago Press, 1983), p. 82.

91. Mead, *Coming of Age*, p. 114.

92. Ibid., pp. 131–32.

93. Ibid., pp. 133–34.

94. Mead, *Blackberry Winter*, p. 129. Other passages of *Blackberry Winter*, however, can be read as encomia on the progressive educational experiences provided Mead by her parents.

95. See Nathan Irvin Huggins, *Harlem Renaissance* (New York: Oxford University Press, 1971), pp. 129 ff.; David Levering Lewis, *When Harlem Was in Vogue* (New York: Alfred Knopf, 1981); and Henry Louis Gates, Jr., and K. A. Appiah, eds., *Zora Neale Hurston: Critical Perspectives Past and Present* (New York: Amistad Press, 1993).

96. Ruth Benedict, "The Younger Generation with a Difference," *New Republic,* November 28, 1928, p. 50.

97. Freda Kirchwey, "This Week: Sex in the South Seas," *Nation,* October 24, 1928, p. 427.

98. H. L. Mencken, "Adolescence," *American Mercury* 15, no. 59 (November 1928), pp. 379–80, esp. p. 380.

99. Walter R. Brooks, "Margaret Mead's *Coming of Age in Samoa*," *Outlook,* August 29, 1928, p. 717; "Brief Reviews," *New York Times Book Review,* November 4, 1928, p. 18.

100. Camilla Wedgwood, review of *Coming of Age in Samoa,* by Margaret Mead, *Oceania* 1 (1930–31), pp. 123–24; B. M., review of *Coming of Age in Samoa,* by Margaret Mead, *Pacific Affairs* 2 (April 1929), pp. 225–26.

101. I. N. Carr, review of *Coming of Age in Samoa,* by Margaret Mead, *Social Science* 5 (February–April 1930), pp. 246–47.

102. V. F. Calverton and Samuel D. Schmalhausen, eds., *The New Generation: The Intimate Problems of Modern Parents and Children* (New York: The Macauley Company, 1930), pp. 169–88; Ernest R. Groves, "The Sociology of Childhood," *Social Forces* 7, no. 2 (1928), pp. 310–13, esp. p. 310.

103. Robert H. Lowie, review of *Coming of Age in Samoa,* by Margaret Mead, *American Anthropologist,* n. s., 31 (1929), pp. 532–34, esp. p. 533.

104. Robert Redfield, review of *Coming of Age in Samoa,* by Margaret Mead,

American Journal of Sociology, 34 (January 1929), pp. 728–30, esp. pp. 729, 730. See also George Stocking's account of Redfield in *The Ethnographer's Magic,* pp. 301–7.

105. See Stocking, "The Ethnographic Sensibility of the 1920s," pp. 246–47. I have paperback editions of *Coming of Age* for printings of 1962, 1970, 1971, 1973, and 1979.

106. On the production and consumption of academic book covers, see Co-rinne Kratz's insightful "On Telling/Selling a Book by Its Cover," *Cultural Anthropology* 9, no. 2 (1994), pp. 179–200.

107. See George W. Stocking, Jr., "Ideas and Institutions in American Anthropology: Thoughts toward a History of the Interwar Years," in Stocking, *The Ethnographer's Magic,* pp. 114–77, esp. pp. 129–33, and "The Ethnographic Sensibility of the 1920s," esp. pp. 299 ff. Also see Howard, *Margaret Mead,* chaps. 8–13.

108. See Stocking, "The Ethnographic Sensibility of the 1920s"; Margaret Mead, *Ruth Benedict* (New York: Columbia University Press, 1974). For more recent Benedict biography, see Judith Modell, *Ruth Benedict: Patterns of a Life* (Philadelphia: University of Pennsylvania Press, 1983); Margaret Caffrey, *Ruth Benedict: Stranger in This Land* (Austin: University of Texas Press, 1989); and Barbara Babcock, "Not in the Absolute Singular: Re-reading Ruth Benedict," *Frontiers* 12, no. 3 (1992), pp. 39–77.

109. Franz Boas, *The Mind of Primitive Man* (New York: Free Press, 1963 [1911]), p. 21.

110. Ruth Benedict, *Patterns of Culture* (Boston: Houghton Mifflin, 1959 [1934]), pp. 5, 6.

111. Ibid., p. 11.

112. Ibid., pp. 78 ff.

113. Ibid., p. 17.

114. Ibid., p. 26.

115. Ibid., p. 74.

116. Ibid., p. 113.

117. See also George W. Stocking, Jr., ed., *Malinowski, Rivers, Benedict and Others: Essays on Culture and Personality* (Madison: University of Wisconsin Press, 1986), esp. Stocking's introductory essay.

118. Eric Wolf, "American Anthropologists and American Power," in *Reinventing Anthropology,* ed. Dell Hymes, 2d ed. (New York: Vintage Books, 1974 [1973]), pp. 251–63, esp. p. 257.

119. Peter Worsley, "Margaret Mead: Science or Science Fiction?" *Science and Society* 21, no. 2 (spring 1957), pp. 122–34, esp. p. 128.

120. Ruth Benedict, "Anthropology and Cultural Change," *American Scholar* 11, no. 2 (April 1942), pp. 243–48, esp. p. 248. See also Sidney Mintz's commentary on the paradox of Benedict's epistemic frame vs. her larger political vision in *Totems and Teachers: Perspectives on the History of Anthropology,* ed. Sydel Silverman (New York: Columbia University Press, 1981), pp. 141–66.

121. Geoffrey Gorer and John Rickman, *The People of Great Russia: A Psychologi-*

cal Study (London: Cresset Press, 1949); Margaret Mead, "The Swaddling Hypothesis: Its Reception," *American Anthropologist* 56 (1954), pp. 395–409. See also Howard, *Margaret Mead*, pp. 277 ff. Northwestern University historian of science David Joravsky remembers sitting in on a deeply embarrassing 1950s meeting between Mead and a group of scholars of the Soviet Union in which she lectured them on swaddling, and they poured withering scorn on her (personal communication).

122. Benedict, *Patterns of Culture*, p. xiv.

123. Margaret Mead, *Sex and Temperament in Three Primitive Societies* (New York: William Morrow, 1963 [1935]), p. 280.

124. Ibid., 312, 316.

125. Ibid., pp. 321, 322.

126. Florence Finch Kelly, "A Challenging View of the Sexes," *New York Times Book Review*, May 26, 1935.

127. Grace Adams, "Books for Your Library," review of *Sex and Temperament in Three Primitive Societies*, by Margaret Mead, *Scribner's Magazine* 98, no. 1 (1935), p. 5.

128. Zenka Bartek, review of *Sex and Temperament in Three Primitive Societies*, by Margaret Mead, *Criterion* 15 (1935), pp. 565–67, esp. p. 567; Joseph Wood Krutch, "Men and Women," *Nation* 140 (1935), p. 633.

129. E. B. Reuter, review of *Sex and Temperament in Three Primitive Societies*, by Margaret Mead, *American Journal of Sociology* 41 (January 1936), pp. 523–25.

130. Richard C. Thurnwald, review of *Sex and Temperament in Three Primitive Societies*, by Margaret Mead, *American Anthropologist* 38 (1936), pp. 663–67, esp. pp. 664, 665.

131. For one example, see Winthrop Sargent's profile of Mead, "It's All Anthropology," *New Yorker*, December 30, 1961, pp. 31–44, esp. p. 41: "Dr. Mead herself is anything but a feminist, and she was highly irritated by the use to which her conclusions about certain psychological phenomena [in *Sex and Temperament*] were put."

132. Howard, *Margaret Mead*, pp. 167 ff.

133. Ibid., p. 168.

134. D. R. Barton, "Exploring Human Nature: How Margaret Mead Became One of the Foremost Women Explorers; Her Life among Strange Brown People in the Pacific Islands; and How the 'Primitive Experiment' Revises Our Most Cherished Notions of Human Behavior," *Natural History*, November 1939, pp. 246–56.

135. Peter J. Kuznick, *Beyond the Laboratory: Scientists as Political Activists in 1930s America* (Chicago: University of Chicago Press, 1987), p. 188. For a full description of Boas's political career and activities in the 1930s and 1940s, see pp. 176 ff.

136. Ibid., pp. 171 ff., 195 ff. Elazer Barkan also details Boas's political activities in *The Retreat of Scientific Racism: Changing Concepts of Race in Britain and the*

United States between the World Wars (Cambridge: Cambridge University Press, 1992), chap. 6, pp. 279–340. Unfortunately, Barkan is also overly reliant on *Black-berry Winter* and thus repeats the error that Mead was more publicly engaged than Benedict. See pp. 127 ff.

137. *Dick Tracy's Secret Detective Methods and Magic Tricks* (Chicago: Quaker Oats Company, 1939), pp. 1–7.

138. Ruth Benedict, *Race: Science and Politics* (New York: Modern Age Books, 1940), p. 5.

139. Ibid., pp. 144–45.

140. On Gene Weltfish, see her own comments in Sydel Silverman, ed., *Totems and Teachers: Perspectives on the History of Anthropology* (New York: Columbia University Press, 1981), p. 162; and Ellen W. Schrecker, *No Ivory Tower: McCarthyism and the Universities* (New York: Oxford University Press, 1986), pp. 255–57.

141. Ruth Benedict and Gene Weltfish, *The Races of Mankind*, Public Affairs Pamphlet 85 (New York: Public Affairs Committee, 1943). See also the back cover of Ruth Benedict, *Patterns of Culture* (New York: New American Library, 1952); Mead, *Ruth Benedict*, p. 58; and John W. Dower, *War without Mercy: Race and Power in the Pacific War* (New York: Pantheon, 1986), p. 120.

142. Hortense Powdermaker and Helen Frances Storen, *Probing Our Prejudices* (New York: Bureau for Intercultural Education and Harper and Row, 1944). See also the Festschrift issue of the *Journal of Anthropological Research* on Powdermaker, vol. 47, no. 4 (winter 1991).

143. Orin Starn, "Engineering Internment: Anthropologists and the War Relocation Authority," *American Ethnologist* 13, no. 4 (November 1986), pp. 709, 716. See Ruth Benedict, *The Chrysanthemum and the Sword* (New York: Houghton Mifflin, 1946). Although—from the standpoint of a later generation—some of Benedict's language in this text is clearly racist, John Dower points out that in the wartime years in which Benedict was writing, Americans in general espoused a "universal exterminationist" policy against the Japanese. He contrasts Benedict and some other wartime moderates both to popular sentiment and to some of their colleagues—including Margaret Mead. Mead participated in a December 1944 conference that asserted an analogy between Japanese behavior and "the character structure of the American gangster." See Dower, *War Without Mercy*, pp. 55, 132–33. It is also noteworthy that 1950s Japanese scholarly response to *The Chrysanthemum and the Sword* was quite positive, with the exception of a rather sophisticated critique of "culture and personality" ahistoricism and homogenizing tendencies. See John W. Bennett and Michio Nagai, "The Japanese Critique of the Methodology of Benedict's *Chrysanthemum and the Sword*," *American Anthropologist* 55, no. 3 (August 1953), pp. 404–11.

144. George Foster, *Applied Anthropology* (Boston: Little, Brown, 1969), p. 203.

145. Margaret Mead, *And Keep Your Powder Dry: An Anthropologist Looks at America* (New York: William Morrow, 1965 [1942]); Howard, *Margaret Mead*, p. 236.

146. Mead, *And Keep Your Powder Dry*, p. 24. Virginia Yans-McLaughlin interprets this action, and the entire Mead text, very charitably. See Virginia Yans-McLaughlin, "Science, Democracy, and Ethics: Mobilizing Culture and Personality for World War II," in Stocking, *Malinowski, Rivers, Benedict and Others*, pp. 184–217.

147. Mead, *And Keep Your Powder Dry*, pp. 188, 140.

148. From an unpublished Mead draft for *Blackberry Winter*. Quoted in Yans-McLaughlin, "Science, Democracy, and Ethics," p. 214.

Chapter Four

1. Lillian Hellman, *Scoundrel Time* (Boston: Little, Brown, 1976); Victor Navasky, *Naming Names* (New York: Viking, 1980); Jessica Mitford, *A Fine Old Conflict* (New York: Knopf, 1977); Vivian Gornick, *The Romance of American Communism* (New York: Basic Books, 1977); *The Front*, directed by Martin Ritt, 1976.

2. See European Bank for Reconstruction and Development, *Transition Report* (London, October 1994); Doug Henwood, "Bloc Busters: Free Market Fundamentalists Pray for Rain," *Voice Literary Supplement*, no. 133, (March 1995), p. 22.

3. Serge Guilbaut, *How New York Stole the Idea of Modern Art: Abstract Expressionism, Freedom, and the Cold War*, trans. Arthus Goldhammer (Chicago: University of Chicago Press, 1983), p. 8.

4. Eric Wolf, American Anthropologists and American Power," in *Reinventing Anthropology*, ed. Dell Hymes, 2d ed. (New York: Vintage Books, 1974 [1973]), pp. 251–63, esp. p. 252.

5. Boas's last words are recorded by Margaret Mead in *An Anthropologist at Work: Writings of Ruth Benedict* (Boston: Houghton Mifflin, 1959), p. 355. On Benedict's political actions, see Mari Jo Buhle, "Ruth Fulton Benedict," in *The American Radical*, by Mari Jo Buhle, Paul Buhle, and Harvey J. Kaye (New York: Routledge, 1994), pp. 245–51; and Sidney Mintz, "Ruth Benedict," in *Totems and Teachers: Perspectives on the History of Anthropology*, ed. Sydel Silverman (New York: Columbia University Press, 1981), pp. 141–66.

6. E. Franklin Frazier was, of course, nominally a sociologist—but of the Chicago School variety, among whom, in that era, it was impossible really to differentiate between sociologists and anthropologists. See Ashley Montagu, *Statement on Race*, 3d ed. (New York: Oxford University Press, 1972).

7. Phillip Tobias, "On a Bushman-European Hybrid Family," *Man*, no. 287 (December 1954), pp. 179–82.

8. See Richard C. Lewontin, Steven Rose, and Leon Kamin, *Not in Our Genes: Biology, Ideology, and Human Nature* (New York: Pantheon, 1984), chap. 10, "New Biology vs. Old Ideology," pp. 265–90; N.J. Block and Gerald Dworkin, eds., *The IQ Controversy* (New York: Random House, 1976); Montagu, *Statement on Race*, pp. 81–106.

9. Mary Louise Dudziak, "Cold War Civil Rights: The Relationship between

Civil Rights and Foreign Affairs in the Truman Administration" (Ph.D. diss., Yale University, 1992), esp. p. 194. Dudziak also considers Truman administration strategies to gain the northern Negro vote without losing that of the southern whites.

10. Ibid., pp. 126 ff.

11. Quoted in Dudziak, "Cold War Civil Rights," pp. 174–75.

12. Ibid., p. 185.

13. Ibid., pp. 89 ff., 93 ff. See also Mary Louise Dudziak, "Josephine Baker, Racial Protest, and the Cold War," *Journal of American History* 81, no. 2 (September 1994), pp. 543–70.

14. See Walter Goldschmidt, "The Cultural Paradigm in the Post-war World," in *Social Contexts of American Ethnology, 1880–1984,* 1984 proceedings of the American Ethnological Society, ed. June Helm (Washington, D.C.: American Anthropological Association, 1985), pp. 164–76; and George Stocking, "Ideas and Institutions in American Anthropology: Thoughts toward a History of the Interwar Years," in *The Ethnographer's Magic and Other Essays in the History of Anthropology* (Madison: University of Wisconsin Press, 1992), pp. 114–77.

15. A. L. Kroeber and Talcott Parsons, "The Concepts of Culture and of Social System," *American Sociological Review* 23, no. 5 (1958), pp. 582–83.

16. Primary texts on man the hunter include Richard B. Lee and Irven DeVore, eds., *Man the Hunter* (Chicago: Aldine Publishing, 1968); Richard B. Lee and Irven DeVore, eds., *Kalahari Hunter-Gatherers* (Cambridge, Mass.: Harvard University Press, 1976); F. Clark Howell and the editors of *Life, Early Man* (New York: Time, 1965); and Sarel Eimerl and Irven DeVore and the editors of *Life, The Primates* (New York: Time, 1965). Historical interpretive texts include Sally Slocum, "Woman the Gatherer: Male Bias in Anthropology," in *Toward an Anthropology of Women,* ed. Rayna R. Reiter (New York: Monthly Review Press, 1975), pp. 36–50; Donna Haraway, *Primate Visions: Gender, Race, and Nature in the World of Modern Science* (New York: Routledge, 1989), pp. 186–230; and Susan Sperling, "Baboons with Briefcases vs. Langurs in Lipstick: Feminism and Functionalism in Primate Studies," in *Gender at the Crossroads of Knowledge: Feminist Anthropology in the Postmodern Era,* ed. Micaela di Leonardo (Berkeley: University of California Press, 1991), pp. 204–34. On racism and physical anthropology's history, see Michael Blakey, "Skull Doctors: Intrinsic Social and Political Bias in the History of American Physical Anthropology," *Critique of Anthropology* 7, no. 2 (1987), pp. 7–35; and George W. Stocking, Jr., *Race, Culture, and Evolution: Essays in the History of Anthropology* (Chicago: University of Chicago Press, 1982 [1968]).

17. See the entry on Lorenz in the 1977 edition of *Current Biography* (New York: H. W. Wilson Company), p. 277.

18. *Rosie the Riveter,* directed by Connie Field, 1980; Joanne Meyerowitz, "Beyond the Feminine Mystique: A Reassessment of Postwar Mass Culture, 1946–1958," *Journal of American History* 79, no. 4 (March 1993), pp. 1455–82, esp. p. 1459.

19. See Barbara Bergmann, *The Economic Emergence of Women* (New York: Basic

Books, 1986); Elaine Tyler May, *Homeward Bound: American Families in the Cold War Era* (New York: Basic Books, 1988); Stephanie Coontz, *The Way We Never Were: American Families and the Nostalgia Trap* (New York: Basic Books, 1992); Sara Evans, *Born for Liberty: A History of Women in America* (New York: Free Press, 1989), pp. 243–62; Marynia Farnham and Ferdinand Lundberg, *Modern Woman: The Lost Sex* (New York: Harper and Brothers, 1947); and Phillip Wylie, *Generation of Vipers* (New York: Rinehart and Company, 1942).

20. Meyerowitz, "Beyond the Feminine Mystique," p. 1460.

21. *On the Town,* directed by Stanley Donen, 1949.

22. Catherine Lutz and Jane Collins, *Reading National Geographic* (Chicago: University of Chicago Press, 1993), pp. 119–53.

23. Margaret Mead, *Male and Female: A Study of the Sexes in a Changing World* (New York: William Morrow, 1949).

24. Margaret Mead, "What Women Want," *Fortune* 34, no. 6 (December 1946), pp. 172–75, 218–24. Mead's point in this anxiously conciliatory piece—which unconsciously echoes one of John Stuart Mill's—is that if American women are given the "choice" of having careers, and if men are more involved in home affairs, women will more amiably choose to be housewives. Mead tells the nation's fortune wonderfully wrongly: if these changes occur, "a large proportion of women would probably elect homemaking—without outside work—as a full-time occupation for generations to come, unless war or new forms of political organization compelled them to do otherwise" (p. 223). See also her "What's the Matter with the Family?" *Harper's,* April 1945, pp. 393–99, and "Modern Marriage, the Danger Point," *Nation,* October 31, 1953, pp. 348–50, for similar arguments.

25. Margaret Mead, *Male and Female: A Study of the Sexes in a Changing World* (New York: Dell Publishing Company, 1968 [1949]), p. 40.

26. Ibid., pp. 348–49.

27. Simone de Beauvoir, *The Second Sex,* trans. H. M. Parshley (New York: Vintage, 1952 [1949]); Michele Le Doeuff, "Simone de Beauvoir and Existentialism," *Feminist Studies* 6 (1980), pp. 277–89.

28. "The most curious point in the book is the author's absolute failure to recognize anything creative in maternity" (Margaret Mead in "A SR Panel Takes Aim at the 'Second Sex,'" *Saturday Review,* February 21 [1953], pp. 26–31, esp. p. 30). Fellow anthropologist Ashley Montagu, on the other hand, celebrated de Beauvoir's analysis. See pp. 28–29. And, ironically, Clyde Kluckhohn gave it a very positive review. See "A World of One's Own," *New York Times Book Review,* February 22, 1953, reprinted October 6, 1996, p. 22. For Eric Wolf's opinion see his *Anthropology* (New York: W. W. Norton, 1974 [1964]), p. 34. A bit of historical detective work: Eleanor Leacock actually published a very negative review of *Male and Female* in the *Daily Worker* in 1952. She did not, however, see the book as a departure for Mead. Given Eric Wolf's lifetime scholarly radicalism, and Daniel Horowitz's recent disclosure of Betty Friedan's radical Communist Party–

affiliated unionist beginnings, I suspect that Leacock's very interesting piece, which scores Mead as "one of the foremost apologists for the present status of women," may have influenced both of their critical considerations of Mead. See Eleanor Leacock, "Review of Margaret Mead, *Male and Female*," reprinted in her *Myths of Male Dominance: Collected Articles on Women Cross-Culturally* (New York: Monthly Review Press, 1981), pp. 205–8, esp. p. 206; and Daniel Horowitz, "Rethinking Betty Friedan and *The Feminine Mystique:* Labor Union Radicalism and Feminism in Cold War America," *American Quarterly* 48, no. 1 (March 1996), pp. 1–42.

29. David Riesman, "Of Men and Women," review of *Male and Female*, by Margaret Mead, *Nation*, October 15, 1949, pp. 376–78, esp. pp. 376, 377.

30. Bernard Mishkin, "The Sexes in Differing Cultures," review of *Male and Female*, by Margaret Mead, *New York Times Book Review*, October 16, 1949, pp. 7, 38.

31. Review of *Male and Female*, by Margaret Mead, *New Yorker*, November 5, 1948, pp. 133–34; John Useem, review of *Male and Female*, by Margaret Mead, *Social Forces* 28, no. 4 (1950), pp. 444–45; review of *Male and Female*, by Margaret Mead, *Atlantic Monthly*, January 1950, p. 88; Therese Benedek, "Sex Relations—Primitive and Sophisticated," review of *Male and Female*, by Margaret Mead, *Saturday Review of Literature*, October 15, 1949, pp. 10–11.

32. Clyde Kluckhohn, "Anthropology Comes of Age," *American Scholar* 19, no. 2 (1950), pp. 241–56.

33. Leo J. Trese, "Neuter Would Be Better," review of *Male and Female*, by Margaret Mead, *Commonweal*, December 2, 1949, pp. 242–43; S. F. Nadel, review of *Male and Female*, by Margaret Mead, *American Anthropologist* 52, no. 3 (1950), pp. 419–20.

34. Diana Trilling, "Men, Women and Sex," review of *Male and Female*, by Margaret Mead, *Partisan Review* 17, no. 4 (1950), pp. 365–78.

35. D. F. Pocock, "Anthropology and the Lay Reader," review of *Male and Female*, by Margaret Mead, *Scrutiny* 17, no. 4 (1951), pp. 355–59.

36. Trilling, "Men, Women and Sex," pp. 367, 68.

37. Ibid., pp. 373–74.

38. Ibid., p. 374.

39. Ibid., p. 378.

40. Pocock, "Anthropology and the Lay Reader," p. 375.

41. Ibid., p. 375.

42. Ibid., pp. 357–78.

43. Ibid., pp. 356, 359.

44. E. E. Evans-Pritchard, "The Position of Women in Primitive Societies and in Our Own," Fawcett Lecture, 1955–56, Bedford College, University of London, 1955.

45. Ibid., p. 15.

46. Ibid., p. 17.

47. Ibid., p. 18.

48. Ivan Karp, personal communication.

49. Laura Bohannan [Elenore Smith Bowen, pseud.], *Return to Laughter: An Anthropological Novel* (New York: Anchor Books, 1964 [1954]), p. 104.

50. Ibid., p. 16.

51. Ibid., pp. 4, 229.

52. Ibid., p. 38.

53. With the exceptions of a passing reference by James Clifford in James Clifford and George E. Marcus, eds., *Writing Culture: The Poetics and Politics of Ethnography* (Berkeley: University of California Press, 1986), p. 13; and few pages in Kamala Visweswaran's *Fictions of Feminist Ethnography* (Minneapolis: University of Minnesota Press, 1994), pp. 25–27. See my treatment of Visweswaran in chap. 5.

54. In interesting contrast to *Return to Laughter,* which narrates a largely static colonized world with given stratification hierarchies, Laura and Paul Bohannan's *scholarly* publications carefully analyze political economic change among the Tiv over four decades—and focus on women's changing status and issues of trade, new wealth, and new poverty with capital penetration and the monetization of the economy. See Laura Bohannan and Paul Bohannan, *The Tiv of Central Nigeria* (London: International African Institute, 1953); Paul Bohannan, "Some Principles of Exchange and Investment among the Tiv," *American Anthropologist* 57, no. 1 (Februrary 1955), pp. 60–70; Paul Bohannan and Laura Bohannan, *Three Sourcebooks in Tiv Ethnography* (New Haven: Human Relations Area Files, 1958); and Paul Bohannan and Laura Bohannan, *Tiv Economy* (Evanston: Northwestern University Press, 1968).

55. Laura Bohannan, *Return to Laughter,* p. 178.

56. Ibid., pp. 178–80.

57. Ibid., pp. 259–61.

58. Ibid., p. 34.

59. Ibid., p. 128.

60. Ibid., p. 144.

61. Ibid., p. 99.

62. Ibid., p. 99.

63. Ibid., p. 79.

64. Ibid., p. 296.

65. William Shakespeare, *King Lear,* act 4, scene 1, lines 3–6, in *The Complete Plays,* edited by William Alan Nelson and Charles Jarvis Hall (Cambridge: The Riverside Press, 1942), p. 1165.

66. Daniel F. McCall, review of *Return to Laughter,* by Laura Bohannan, *American Anthropologist* 57 (October 1955), pp. 1104–5, esp. p. 1105. Eric Wolf agreed with this evaluation in his *Anthropology,* pp. 90–91.

67. McCall, review of *Return to Laughter,* p. 1105.

68. Ibid., p. 1105.

69. Mabel M. Smythe, review of *Return to Laughter,* by Laura Bohannan, *Journal of Human Relations* 3, no. 4 (1955), pp. 105–6.

70. B. Z. Seligman, review of *Return to Laughter,* by Laura Bohannan, *Man,* September 1954, p. 145.

71. George Craig, review of *Return to Laughter,* by Laura Bohannan, *African Affairs* 54 (January 1955), pp. 66–67.

72. Rhoda Metraux, "High Adventure and Drama," review of *Return to Laughter,* by Laura Bohannan, *New York Herald Tribune,* April 17, 1955, p. 8; review of *Return to Laughter,* by Laura Bohannan, *New Yorker,* May 14, 1955, pp. 174–75; review of *Return to Laughter,* by Laura Bohannan, *Times Literary Supplement,* December 10, 1954, p. 798; R. A. Holzauer, "In Africa," review of *Return to Laughter,* by Laura Bohannan, *Commonweal* 63 (October 14, 1955), pp. 46–47; Seldon Rodman, "Lessons from Aborigines," review of *Return to Laughter,* by Laura Bohannan, *Saturday Review of Literature,* August 27, 1955, p. 19; Thomas Hodgkin, "Anthropologist's Awakening," review of *Return to Laughter,* by Laura Bohannan, *Spectator,* September 17, 1954, p. 346; James Stern, review of *Return to Laughter,* by Laura Bohannan, *A Thing to Love,* by Elspeth Huxley, and *The Moon to Play With,* by John Wiles, *London Magazine* 2, no. 2 (February 1955), pp. 91–92.

73. Holzauer, "In Africa," p. 47.

74. Review of *Return to Laughter, Times Literary Supplement,* p. 798.

75. Review of *Return to Laughter, New Yorker,* p. 175.

76. Rodman, "Lessons from Aborigines," p. 19.

77. Hodgkin, "Anthropologist's Awakening," p. 346.

78. Laura Bohannan, *Return to Laughter,* p. 291.

79. Marston Bates, "What Makes Kako's People Tick," review of *Return to Laughter,* by Laura Bohannan, *New York Times,* April 7, 1955, p. 6.

80. See the Festschrift for Wolf, Jane Schneider and Rayna Rapp, eds., *Articulating Hidden Histories: Exploring the Influence of Eric R. Wolf* (Berkeley: University of California Press, 1995); and Sidney Mintz's *Worker in the Cane: A Puerto Rican Life History* (New York: Norton, 1974 [1960]).

81. See Ruth E. Pathé's entry on Gene Weltfish and Christine Ward Gailey's on Eleanor Burke Leacock in Ute Gacs et. al., eds., *Women Anthropologists: Selected Biographies* (Urbana: University of Illinois Press, 1989), pp. 372–81, 215–21. Melville Jacobs's case is discussed by David Price in "Cold War Anthropology: Collaborators and Victims of the National Security State," in *Identities,* forthcoming.

82. See David Price, "Cold War Anthropology," and "Cold War Funding and the Evolution of Academic Anthropology," in *Universities and Empire,* ed. Christopher Simpson (New York: New Press, forthcoming). See Sigmund Diamond, *Compromised Campus: The Collaboration of Universities with the Intelligence Community, 1945–55* (New York: Oxford University Press, 1992), pp. 65–110, for the material on Kluckhohn and Harvard. Price and Laura Nader, however, tend to treat acceptance of governmental funding as proof of cooptation. Nader goes further, to the outrageous labeling of antiracist, feminist, and gay-rights agendas in an-

thropology as "double-edged landmines" that "displace attention from root problems." See her "The Phantom Factor: Impact of the Cold War on Anthropology," in *The Cold War and the University*, ed. Noam Chomsky (New York: New Press, 1997), pp. 107–46, esp. p. 141.

83. See Ulf Hannerz, *Exploring the City: Inquiries toward an Urban Anthropology* (New York: Columbia University Press, 1980), pp. 119–62; and Richard P. Werbner, "The Manchester School in South-Central Africa," *Annual Review of Anthropology* 13 (1984), pp. 157–85. The Ptolemaic-Copernican analogue is, however, mine.

84. Elgin Williams, "Anthropology for the Common Man," *American Anthropologist* 49, no. 1 (1947), pp. 84–90., esp. p. 85.

85. Ibid., p. 90.

86. Dorothy Gregg and Elgin Williams, "The Dismal Science of Functionalism," *American Anthropologist* 50, no. 4 (1948), pp. 594–611, esp. p. 604.

87. Biographic details are from Brett Williams, personal communication. Williams has her father's papers, including a lengthy correspondence with Oscar Lewis.

88. William J. Lederer and Eugene Burdick, *The Ugly American* (New York: W. W. Norton, 1958; reprint, Fawcett World Library, 1958), pp. 34–35. To my knowledge, no one else has remarked the connection between *Ugly American* Cold War imperatives and ethnographic practice.

89. Ibid., p. 181.

90. Susan Sontag, "The Anthropologist as Hero," in *Against Interpretation* (New York: Farrar, Strauss, and Giroux, 1966), p. 69.

91. Ibid., pp. 70, 72, 74, 75.

92. Ibid., pp. 73, 77.

93. Ibid., p. 74.

94. Ibid., p. 81.

95. Claude Lévi-Strauss, *The Elementary Structures of Kinship* (Boston: Beacon Press, 1969), p. 496. See also my analysis of the pernicious effect of this Lévi-Straussian frame on feminist anthropological theorizing of the 1970s, "Women's Culture and Its Discontents," in *The Politics of Culture*, ed. Brett Williams (Washington, D.C.: Smithsonian Institution Press, 1991), pp. 219–42.

96. David Schneider and Kathleen Gough, *Matrilineal Kinship* (Berkeley: University of California Press, 1961), p. 6.

97. Gore Vidal, *Weekend* (New York: Dramatists Play Service, 1962), p. 14.

98. Margaret Mead, *Cultural Patterns and Technical Change* (New York: UNESCO; reprint, New American Library, 1955).

99. Cited in Angela Gilliam and Lenora Foerstal, "Margaret Mead's Contradictory Legacy," in *Confronting the Margaret Mead Legacy: Scholarship, Empire, and the South Pacific*, ed. Lenora Foerstal and Angela Gilliam (Philadelphia: Temple University Press, 1992), pp. 101–56, esp. p. 128.

100. See Gilliam and Foerstal, "Margaret Mead's Contradictory Legacy," p. 132.

101. Winthrop Sargent, "It's All Anthropology," *New Yorker*, December 30, 1961, pp. 31–44, esp. pp. 31, 32, 43.

102. Margaret Mead, "Return of the Cavewoman," *Saturday Evening Post*, March 3, 1962, pp. 6, 8.

103. Mead quoted in "Studying the American Tribe," *Time*, December 23, 1974, 54–55, esp. p. 55; Catherine Lutz, "The Psychological Ethic and the Spirit of Permanent War: The Military Production of Twentieth Century American Subjects," in *Inventing the Psychological*, ed. Joel Pfister and Nancy Schnog (New Haven: Yale University Press, forthcoming).

104. Irving Wallace, *The Three Sirens* (New York: Simon and Schuster, 1963), p. 45. A young anthropologist, Radhika Parameswaren, tells me that it was through sneaking her father's copy of *The Three Sirens* as a thirteen-year-old in Hyderabad, India, that she learned of Margaret Mead and of the discipline.

105. For a set of selections from these columns, see Rhoda Metraux, ed., *Margaret Mead: Some Personal Views* (New York: Walker and Company, 1979).

106. Philip Mayer, *Townsmen or Tribesmen* (Capetown: Oxford University Press, 1961).

107. Lauriston Sharp, "Steel Axes for Stone-Age Australians," *Human Organization* 11, no. 2 (1952), pp. 17–22.

108. See Andrew P. Vayda, ed., *Environment and Cultural Behavior: Ecological Studies in Cultural Behavior* (Garden City: Natural History Press, 1969); Richard B. Lee, "What Hunters Do for a Living, or, How to Make Out on Scarce Resources," in Lee and DeVore, *Man the Hunter*, pp. 30–48; and Karl Marx and Frederick Engels, *The German Ideology*, ed. C. J. Arthur (New York: International Publishers, 1970 [1844]), p. 53.

109. Key peasant studies work is anthologized in Jack M. Potter, May N. Diaz, and George M. Foster, eds., *Peasant Society: A Reader* (Boston: Little, Brown, 1967); and Teodor Shanin, ed., *Peasants and Peasant Societies* (Middlesex: Penguin Books, 1971). See also William Roseberry, *Anthropologies and Histories: Essays in History, Culture, and Political Economy* (New Brunswick: Rutgers University Press, 1989).

110. Jane Schneider, "Introduction: The Analytic Strategies of Eric Wolf," in Schneider and Rapp, *Articulating Hidden Histories*, p. 5; and David Hunt, "Prefigurations of the Vietnamese Revolution," pp. 108–24, esp. p. 108, in the same volume. On the details of planning the first teach-in, and Wolf's role, see William Gamson, "Commitment and Agency in Social Movements," *Sociological Forum* 6, no. 1 (1991), pp. 27–50. According to Wolf and Jorgensen, Marshall Sahlins invented the concept of the "teach-in." See Eric R. Wolf and Joseph G. Jorgensen, "Anthropology on the Warpath in Thailand," *New York Review of Books*, November 19, 1970, pp. 26–35, esp. p. 26.

111. See American Anthropological Association *Fellow Newsletter* 6 (1960), p. 8; *Guide to Departments of Anthropology, 1970–71*, vol. 3, no. 2, p. iii; *Guide to Departments of Anthropology, 1994–95*, p. 292; *Guide to Departments of Anthropology, 1979–80*.

112. American Anthropological Association *Fellow Newsletter,* vol. 2, no. 10 (December 1961), p. 1; vol. 7, no. 8 (October 1966), p. 1 ff.; vol. 7, no. 10 (December 1966), p. 2. For the Harner quotation, see Gerald D. Berreman, "Is Anthropology Alive? Social Responsibility in Social Anthropology," *Current Anthropology* 9, no. 5 (December 1968), pp. 391–96, esp. p. 391.

113. Gerald D. Berreman, "Not So Innocent Abroad," *Nation,* November 10, 1969, pp. 505–8, and "Is Anthropology Alive?"; Kathleen Gough, "Anthropology and Imperialism," *Monthly Review* 19, no. 11 (1968), pp. 12–27, and "Anthropology: World Revolution and the Science of Man," in *The Dissenting Academy,* ed. Theodore Roszak (New York: Random House, 1968), pp. 135–58; Claude Lévi-Strauss, "Anthropology: Its Achievements and Future," *Current Anthropology* 7, no. 1 (1966), pp. 124–27; Wolf and Jorgensen, "Anthropology on the Warpath."

114. Wolf and Jorgensen, "Anthropology on the Warpath," p. 31.

115. *Hair, the American Tribal Love-Rock Musical,* book and lyrics by Gerome Ragni and James Rado, original Broadway cast recording, RCA Victor, 1968.

116. Excerpts from Mead's Senate testimony are given in the 1981 film on Mead's life from the Public Broadcasting System's *Odyssey* series, *Margaret Mead: Taking Note,* produced, written, and directed by Ann Peck; the Terkel interview is reproduced on the cassette set *Four Decades with Studs Terkel,* HighBridge Company, St. Paul, 1993. See Margaret Mead, *Culture and Commitment: The New Relationships between the Generations in the 1970s* (New York: Natural History Press/Doubleday, 1970); and David Dempsey, "The Mead and Her Message: Some Field Notes on an Anthropological Phenomenon," *New York Times Magazine,* April 26, 1970, pp. 23–102, esp. pp. 23, 75.

117. Robin Morgan, "Introduction: The Women's Revolution," in *Sisterhood Is Powerful: An Anthology of Writings from the Women's Liberation Movement,* ed. Robin Morgan (New York: Vintage, 1970), p. xxxviii.

118. See Israel Shenker, "Anthropologists Clash over Their Colleagues Ethics in Thailand," *New York Times,* November 21, 1971; and American Anthropological Association *Newsletter* 13, no. 1 (January 1972), p. 1.

119. See Eric Wakin, *Anthropology Goes to War: Professional Ethics and Counterinsurgency in Thailand,* monograph 7 (Madison: University of Wisconsin Center for Southeast Asian Studies, 1992), pp. 230, 233–34.

120. See Gilliam and Foerstel, "Margaret Mead's Contradictory Legacy," p. 138.

121. See Sara Evans, *Personal Politics: The Roots of Women's Liberation in the Civil Rights Movement and the New Left* (New York: Random House, 1979), and *Born for Liberty,* pp. 263–314; and Bergmann, *The Economic Emergence of Women.*

122. Micaela di Leonardo, "Introduction: Gender, Culture, and Political Economy: Feminist Anthropology in Historical Perspective," in di Leonardo, *Gender at the Crossroads,* pp. 1–48, esp. p. 3.

123. Michelle Zimbalist Rosaldo and Louise Lamphere, eds., *Women, Culture, and Society* (Stanford: Stanford University Press, 1974); Reiter, *Toward an Anthropology of Women.*

124. James Clifford, *The Predicament of Culture: Twentieth-Century Literature, Ethnography, and Art* (Cambridge, Mass.: Harvard University Press, 1988), p. 78.

125. Alan Dundes, *Every Man His Way: Readings in Cultural Anthropology* (Clifton: Prentice-Hall, 1968); Eugene A. Hammel and William S. Simmons, eds., *Man Makes Sense: A Reader in Modern Cultural Anthropology* (Boston: Little, Brown, 1970); Richard Gould, *Man's Many Ways: The Natural History Reader in Anthropology* (New York: Harper and Row, 1973).

126. John Ferguson McLennan, *Studies in Ancient History* (London: Macmillan, 1886), p. 11.

127. *Elizabeth Gould Davis, The First Sex* (Baltimore: Penguin, 1972), pp. 15–16. See, for example, Desmond Morris, *The Naked Ape: A Zoologist's Study of the Human Animal* (New York: McGraw-Hill, 1967), and *The Human Zoo* (New York: McGraw-Hill, 1969); Robert Ardrey, *African Genesis: A Personal Investigation into the Animal Origins and Nature of Man* (New York: Dell, 1961), and *The Territorial Imperative: A Personal Inquiry into the Animal Origins of Property and Nations* (New York: Atheneum, 1966); and Lionel Tiger, *Men in Groups* (New York: Random House, 1969).

128. Haraway, *Primate Visions*, p. 7; Sperling, "Baboons with Briefcases vs. Langurs in Lipstick," p. 239.

129. Lionel Tiger and Robin Fox, *The Imperial Animal* (Holt, Rinehart and Winston, 1971), pp. 99–100.

130. For reviews of the range of inside-the-guild feminist anthropological work in the 1970s, see my "Introduction: Gender, Culture, and Political Economy."

131. Janet Siskind, *To Hunt in the Morning* (New York: Oxford University Press, 1973), frontispiece.

132. Ibid., p. 18.

133. Ibid., p. 93.

134. Ibid., pp. 103–4.

135. Ibid., pp. 121–22.

136. Ibid., p. 128.

137. I am indebted to several generations of impassioned and insightful "anthropology of gender" students at Oberlin College and Yale University for some details of this analysis.

138. Siskind, *To Hunt*, p. 13.

139. Robert Murphy and Yolanda Murphy, *Women of the Forest*, 2d ed. (New York: Columbia University Press, 1985 [1974]), pp. 120, 121, 194.

140. Ibid., pp. 166, 163.

141. Ibid., p. 208.

142. Ibid., pp. 240–41.

143. Ibid., p. 251.

144. Ibid., pp. 247, 252, 258.

145. Jane Kramer, "Anthropology: Rooting for Cultural Trifles," *Ms.*, June 1975, pp. 44–46, esp. p. 46; "Amazonian Denizens," *Times Literary Supplement*, April 26, 1974, p. 448; "The Shaman Touch," *Economist*, February 9, 1974, pp.

96–97, esp. p. 97; Stephen Hugh-Jones, review of *To Hunt in the Morning*, by Janet Siskind, *Man* 9 (1974), pp. 644–45; Mary Douglas, "Nettling," *New Statesman*, April 5, 1974, pp. 485–86, esp. p. 486.

146. Dolores Newton, review of *To Hunt in the Morning*, by Janet Siskind, *American Anthropologist* 74, no. 3 (1974), pp. 591–92; Daniel Gross, "Dialectics in the Forest," *Reviews in Anthropology* 2, no. 1 (February 1975), pp. 60–68; Warwick Bray, review of *To Hunt in the Morning*, by Janet Siskind, *Journal of Latin American Studies* 7 (1975), p. 344.

147. Hugh-Jones, review of *To Hunt in the Morning*, p. 644; Douglas, "Nettling," p. 486.

148. Judith Shapiro, review of *Women of the Forest*, by Robert Murphy and Yolanda Murphy, *American Journal of Sociology* 81 (January 1976), pp. 981–83, esp. p. 982, and "The Myth of Male Supremacy," *Natural History*, February 1975, pp. 78–81, esp. pp. 80, 81.

149. Joan Bamberger, "Sex Roles in Central Brazil," *Science*, July 18, 1975, p. 213.

150. Judith K. Brown, "Anthropology of Women: The Natural History Stage," *Reviews in Anthropology* 2, no. 4 (November 1975), pp. 526–31, esp. pp. 526, 527, 528.

151. Rose Somerville, review of *Women of the Forest*, by Robert Murphy and Yolanda Murphy, *Contemporary Sociology* 7, no. 4 (July 1978), pp. 471–72, esp. p. 472; Peter Rivière, "Mrs. Mundurucú," review of *Women of the Forest*, *Times Literary Supplement*, September 5, 1975, p. 1000.

152. Margaret Mead, *Blackberry Winter: My Earlier Years* (New York: Washington Square Press, 1972).

153. Jane Howard, review of *Blackberry Winter*, by Margaret Mead, *New York Times Book Review*, November 12, 1972; Caroline Bird, "Everybody's Grandmother," *Saturday Review*, November 25, 1972, pp. 64–66; Edmund Fuller, "Margaret Mead: Formative Years," *Wall Street Journal*, March 7, 1973; Arthur Cooper, "A Woman for Mankind," *Newsweek*, November 13, 1972, pp. 105–6; Rosalind Rosenberg, *Beyond Separate Spheres: Intellectual Roots of Modern Feminism* (New Haven: Yale University Press, 1982); Jane Howard, *Margaret Mead: A Life* (New York, Simon and Schuster, 1984); *Margaret Mead: Taking Note*, directed by Ann Peck; *Margaret Mead — An Observer Observed*, directed by Alan Berliner, produced by Virginia Yans, 1995. See also Bernice Kaplan, "Autobiography," *Science* 180 (May 11, 1973), pp. 618–19.

154. Mead, *Blackberry Winter*, pp. 3, 6, 1.

155. Ibid., pp. 2, 5.

156. Ibid., pp. 90, 107, 9, 139.

157. Ibid., pp. 107, 90, 55, 108. Peter Worsley pointed out of Mead in 1957 that "the problems she deals with can ultimately be tackled and the evils overcome by radical policies which themselves imply transformation of the economic, political, and legal structure of society. To Margaret Mead, however, this is an intolerable notion. The revolutionary, to her, is a 'deviant' or a misfit in

society" (Worsley, "Margaret Mead: Science or Science Fiction?" *Science and Society* 21, no. 2 [spring 1957], pp. 122–34, esp. pp. 129–30).

158. On Mead's support of Jimmy Carter, see Douglas Dillon, "Margaret Mead and Government," *American Anthropologist* 82, no. 2 (1980), pp. 319–39; on Houston, see Ann Peck's film *Margaret Mead: Taking Note;* on sociobiology and the United Nations, see Howard, *Margaret Mead,* pp. 398, 404–5.

159. Mary Catherine Bateson, *With a Daughter's Eye* (New York: William Morrow, 1984), p. 32.

160. Use of this quotation is widespread: an Internet search for Mead turns up three websites parlaying it for promotional purposes for (1) Eugene Eric Kim Technology Consulting, (2) Rutgers University Citizenship and Service Education, and (3) the Montgomery County (Maryland) Green Democrats. It is also printed on the wrapper for Dysan computer diskettes, in author's possession.

161. Howard, *Margaret Mead,* p. 438.

162. Worsley, "Margaret Mead: Science or Science Fiction?" p. 124.

163. Margaret Mead, preface to *Coming of Age in Samoa* (New York: American Museum of Natural History, 1973), p. ix. See also Margaret Mead, *From the South Seas: Studies of Adolescence and Sex in Primitive Societies* (New York: William Morrow, 1939), *Coming of Age in Samoa* (New York: Mentor, New American Library, 1949), *Coming of Age in Samoa* (New York: Modern Library, 1953), *Coming of Age in Samoa* (New York: Laurel, Dell Publishing, 1961), *Coming of Age in Samoa* (New York: American Museum of Natural History, 1973).

Chapter Five

1. See the American Anthropological Association *Newsletter* obituary, January 1979, p. 21: "Margaret Mead created and fostered a public interest in and understanding of anthropology, for some years in the face of scepticism and even scorn from her elitist colleagues." Also see Robin Fox, "Margaret Mead Remembered," *New York Times,* November 19, 1978, p. 20; and the special Festschrift issue of the *American Anthropologist,* vol. 82, no. 2 (1980). For more popular response to her death, see Madeline Lee, "Remembering Aunt Margaret Mead," *Ms.,* February 1979, pp. 57–58.

2. See Alden Whitman, "Margaret Mead Is Dead of Cancer at 76," *New York Times,* November 16, 1978, p. A1; and Boyce Rensberger, "A Pioneer and an Innovator," *New York Times,* November 16, 1978, pp. A1, D18.

3. "Margaret Mead at 75," *New York Times,* December 14, 1976; Henry Allen, "An Attic Afternoon with Margaret Mead on the Eve of Her 75th Birthday and Washington Visitation," *Washington Post Potomac,* November 21, 1976, pp. 12–44; Rosalynn Carter and Margaret Mead, "A Redbook Conversation," *Redbook* 149 (1977), pp. 123–210.

4. See description in chap. 2, and "The Rights-Conscious 1960s," in *Who Built America? Working People and the Nation's Economy, Politics, Culture and Society,* vol.

2, *From the Gilded Age to the Present*, by American Social History Project (New York, Pantheon, 1992), pp. 543–608. On real wages, see Frances Fox Piven and Richard A. Cloward, *Regulating the Poor: The Functions of Public Welfare*, updated ed. (New York: Vintage Books, 1993), p. 347.

5. On the Carter campaign and administration, see Martin Schram, *Running for President 1976: The Carter Campaign* (New York: Stein and Day, 1977); Haynes Johnson, *Sleepwalking through History: America in the Reagan Years* (New York: W. W. Norton, 1991), pp. 19–41; Laurence H. Shoup, *The Carter Presidency and Beyond: Power and Politics in the 1980s* (Palo Alto: Ramparts Press, 1980). For one analysis of the loss of lunchpail Democrats through liberal social policy, see Thomas Byrne Edsall with Mary D. Edsall, *Chain Reaction: The Impact of Race, Rights, and Taxes on American Politics* (New York: W. W. Norton, 1991); and Thomas Byrne Edsall, "Clinton, So Far," *New York Review of Books*, October 7, 1993, pp. 6–9. For a thorough critique of *Chain Reaction*, see Adolph L. Reed, Jr., and Julian Bond, "Equality: Why We Can't Wait," *Nation*, special issue, "The Assault on Equality: Race, Rights, and the New Orthodoxy," December 9, 1991, pp. 733–37. For Carter and the Hyde amendment, see Rosalind Petchesky, *Abortion and Woman's Choice*, revised ed. (Boston: Northeastern University Press, 1990), p. 287.

6. On Carter foreign policy, see Gaddis Smith, *Morality, Reason and Power: American Diplomacy in the Carter Years* (New York: Hill and Wang, 1986); and Haynes Johnson, *Sleepwalking through History*, chaps. 1 and 2. On the hostage crisis and Reagan's election, see Gary Sick, *October Surprise: America's Hostages in Iran and the Election of Ronald Reagan* (New York: Times Books, 1991).

7. William Minter, "Destructive Engagement: The United States and South Africa in the Reagan Era," in *Destructive Engagement: Southern Africa at War*, ed. Phyllis Johnson and David Martin (Harare: Zimbabwe Publishing House, 1986), pp. 281–320, esp. p. 287.

8. See R. G. D'Andrade et al., "Academic Opportunity in Anthropology, 1974–90," *American Anthropologist* 77, no. 4 (December 1975), pp. 753–70; *American Anthropological Association Guide, 1994–95* (Washington, D.C., American Anthropological Association, 1994), p. 292.

9. Dell Hymes, ed., *Reinventing Anthropology* (New York: Random House, 1973); Diane Lewis, "Anthropology and Colonialism," *Current Anthropology* 14, no. 5 (December 1973), pp. 581–91; Talal Asad, ed., *Anthropology and the Colonial Encounter* (London: Ithaca Press, 1975). It is particularly interesting that the postmodern "ethnography-as-text" writers of the 1980s—with the exception of Mary Pratt, who is a literary critic—ignored the Asad school model of investigating the actual political economy of the objects of ethnography in conjunction with critically rereading ethnographic texts. See also Francis L. K. Hsu, "Prejudice and Its Intellectual Effect in American Anthropology: An Ethnographic Report," *American Anthropologist* 75, no. 1 (1973), pp. 1–19. The Nineteenth International Congress of Anthropological and Ethnological Sciences met in Chicago in Sep-

tember 1973 on the theme of the politics of anthropology. The participants were genuinely international and multiracial, and their contributions substantive. The conference volume was not published, however, until 1979, by which time the mood of the discipline had shifted. See Gerrit Huizer and Bruce Mannheim, eds., *The Politics of Anthropology: From Colonialism and Sexism toward a View from Below* (The Hague: Mouton, 1979).

10. Eric Wolf, "They Divide and Subdivide, and Call It Anthropology," *New York Times*, November 30, 1980, sec. 4, p. 9.

11. Patricia Caplan and Janet Bujra, eds., *Women United, Women Divided: Comparative Studies of Ten Contemporary Cultures* (Bloomington: Indiana University Press, 1979); Carol MacCormack and Marilyn Strathern, eds., *Nature, Culture, and Gender* (Cambridge: Cambridge University Press, 1980); Kate Young, Carol Wolkowitz, and Roslyn McCullagh, eds., *Of Marriage and the Market: Women's Subordination Internationally and Its Lessons* (London: Routledge and Kegan Paul, 1981). See also my prècis of this work in "Introduction: Gender, Culture, and Political Economy: Feminist Anthropology in Historical Perspective," in *Gender at the Crossroads of Knowledge: Feminist Anthropology in the Postmodern Era*, ed. Micaela di Leonardo (Berkeley: University of California Press, 1991), pp. 1–48, esp. pp. 14–36.

12. See Donna Haraway, *Primate Visions: Gender, Race, and Nature in the World of Modern Science* (New York: Routledge, 1989); Sarah Blaffer Hrdy, *The Woman That Never Evolved* (Cambridge: Cambridge University Press, 1981).

13. Susan Sperling, "Baboons with Briefcases vs. Langurs in Lipstick: Feminism and Functionalism in Primate Studies," in di Leonardo, *Gender at the Crossroads*, pp. 204–234, esp. pp. 218, 225.

14. Stephen Jay Gould, Richard Lewontin, and others continue to write critically of sociobiology. See Richard C. Lewontin, Leon Kamin, and Steven Rose, *Not in Our Genes: Biology, Ideology and Human Nature* (New York: Pantheon, 1984). For adulation of sociobiology and failure to cover other scientific perspectives, see, for example, Natalie Angier's reporting in the *New York Times*.

15. See Michael Rogin, *Ronald Reagan, the Movie, and Other Episodes in Political Demonology* (Berkeley: University of California Press, 1987); Debora Silverman, *Selling Culture: Bloomingdale's, Diana Vreeland, and the New Aristocracy of Taste in Reagan's America* (New York: Pantheon, 1986); Elayne Rapping, *The Movie of the Week: Private Stories/Public Events* (Minneapolis: University of Minnesota Press, 1992); and Lynda Boose, "Techno-Muscularity and the 'Boy Eternal': From the Quagmire to the Gulf," in *Cultures of United States Imperialism* (Durham: Duke University Press, 1993), pp. 581–616. See also Haynes Johnson, *Sleepwalking through History*.

16. See Edward N. Wolff, *Top Heavy: A Study of the Increasing Inequality of Wealth in America* (New York: The Twentieth Century Fund Press, 1995); Keith Bradsher, "Gap in Wealth in U.S. Called Widest in West," *New York Times*, April 17, 1995; Fred Block et. al., eds. *The Mean Season: The Attack on the Welfare State*

(New York: Pantheon, 1987); Frances Fox Piven and Richard A. Cloward, *The New Class War: Reagan's Attack on the Welfare State and Its Consequences* (New York: Pantheon Books, 1982), and *Regulating the Poor* (1993); and Michael A. Bernstein and David E. Adler, eds., *Understanding American Economic Decline* (Cambridge: Cambridge University Press, 1994).

17. On changes in the wage gap by gender and race, see "The Wage Gap: Women's and Men's Earnings" (briefing paper, Institute for Women's Policy Research, 1995). On corporate racism and sexism, see Peter T. Kilborn, "Women and Minorities Still Face 'Glass Ceiling,'" *New York Times*, March 16, 1995. On working women's wages, see Sam Roberts, "Women's Work: What's New, What Isn't," *New York Times*, April 27, 1995. On changes in the minimum wage, see "Women and the Minimum Wage" (briefing paper, Institute for Women's Policy Research, 1995).

18. On earnings erosion, see Jack McNeil, "The Earnings Ladder," U.S. Bureau of the Census, March 30, 1994. On housing starts, see Jill Quadagno, *The Color of Welfare: How Racism Undermined the War on Poverty* (New York: Oxford University Press, 1994), p. 178. See also Frank Levy, *Dollars and Dreams: The Changing American Income Distribution* (New York: W. W. Norton, 1988).

19. Christopher Jencks, *The Homeless* (Cambridge, Mass.: Harvard University Press, 1994).

20. Eric Hobsbawm, *The Age of Extremes: A History of the World, 1914–1991* (New York: Pantheon Books, 1994), p. 248.

21. See William Minter, "Destructive Engagement"; R. W. Johnson, *How Long Will South Africa Survive?* (New York: Oxford University Press, 1977); Martin J. Murray, *Revolution Deferred: The Painful Birth of Post-apartheid South Africa* (London: Verso, 1994).

22. Stuart Elliott, "Determining Demographics by What's on the Coffee Table," *New York Times*, January 7, 1993; Patricia Leigh Brown, "The World of Shelter Magazines Is Now Turning 'Family Friendly,'" *New York Times*, May 13, 1993; Elizabeth Kolbert, "Racial Gap in Television Viewing Habits Widens," *New York Times*, April 5, 1993; Allan Johnson, "The Difference between Black and White Viewers a Study in Contrast," *Chicago Tribune*, April 18, 1997; Larry Rohter, "Broadcast News: In Spanish, It's Another Story," *New York Times*, December 15, 1996; Stephen Holden, "Listeners Tune Out Top 40 Music on the Radio," *New York Times*, March 23, 1993.

23. David Harvey, *The Condition of Postmodernity* (Oxford: Basil Blackwell, 1989); Michael Curtin, "On Edge: Culture Industries in the Neo-network Era," in *Making and Selling Culture*, ed. Richard Ohmann (Middletown, Conn.: Wesleyan University Press, 1996), pp. 181–202, esp. pp. 182, 190.

24. See Ben Bagdikian, *The Media Monopoly* (Boston: Beacon Press, 1992); Ellen Messer-Davidow, "Manufacturing the Attack on Liberalized Higher Education," *Social Text* 36 (1993), pp. 40–80; Edward Herman and Noam Chomsky, *Manufacturing Consent: The Political Economy of the Mass Media* (New York: Pantheon, 1988); and the special issue of the *Nation*, "The National Entertainment State,"

June 3, 1996, especially André Schiffrin, "The Corporatization of Publishing," pp. 29–33.

25. Roberta Spalter-Roth, personal communication.

26. Marjorie Shostak, *Nisa: The Life and Words of a !Kung Woman* (Cambridge, Mass.: Harvard University Press, 1981), pp. 16–17.

27. Ibid., p. 6.

28. Ibid., p. 237.

29. At the time Shostak was writing, Eleanor Leacock had published, among other pieces, "Women in Egalitarian Society," in *Becoming Visible: Women in European Society,* ed. Renate Bridenthal and Claudia Koonz (Boston: Houghton Mifflin, 1977), pp. 11–35, "Women's Status in Egalitarian Society: Implications for Social Evolution," *Current Anthropology* 19, no. 2 (1978), pp. 247–75; and was working on the anthology Eleanor B. Leacock and Richard B. Lee, eds., *Politics and History in Band Societies* (New York: Cambridge University Press, 1982). Karen Sacks's "Engels Revisited" was printed both in Rayna R. Reiter, ed., *Toward an Anthropology of Women* (New York: Monthly Review Press, 1975), pp. 211–34; and Michelle Zimbalist Rosaldo and Louise Lamphere, eds., *Women, Culture, and Society* (Stanford: Stanford University Press, 1974), pp. 207–22.

30. Shostak, *Nisa,* pp. 22–38, 39, 40.

31. Ibid., pp. 355–56.

32. Ibid., pp. 350, 370–71.

33. Edwin Wilmsen points out, however, that "the use of kin terms is common Zhu practice to indicate affection," so Nisa's intended meaning is not really the same as our reception of it (personal communication).

34. Shostak, *Nisa,* p. 371.

35. Phoebe-Lou Adams, review of *Nisa,* by Marjorie Shostak, *Atlantic,* December 1981, p. 92.

36. Shostak, *Nisa,* p. 21.

37. Ibid., p. 7.

38. Gail Sheehy, *Passages: Predictable Crises of Adult Life* (New York: E. P. Dutton, 1976), pp. 328, 329.

39. See, for example, Shostak, *Nisa,* pp. 112, 114, 156 ff., 311. Interestingly, when Shostak writes self-reflexively about the question of the representativeness of the violence in Nisa's life, she makes no mention of sexual violence.

40. Ellen Cantarow, review of *Nisa,* by Marjorie Shostak, *Ms.,* February 1982, pp. 36–37, esp. p. 36; review of *Nisa,* by Marjorie Shostak, *New York Review of Books,* December 17, 1981, p. 67; Nancy Howell, review of *Nisa,* by Marjorie Shostak, *American Ethnologist* 10, no. 1 (February 1983), pp. 187–88, esp. p. 187; Margo Jefferson, "Field Tripping," review of *Nisa,* by Marjorie Shostak, *Nation,* January 2–9, 1982, pp. 21–24, esp. p. 22; Harriett Gilbert, review of *Nisa,* by Marjorie Shostak, *New Statesman,* November 19, 1982, p. 28; Lisa Peattie, "A Primitive Explains Herself," review of *Nisa,* by Marjorie Shostak, *New York Times Book Review,* November 8, 1981, p. 9.

41. Majorie Shostak, "'What the Wind Won't Take Away': The Genesis of

Nisa — The Life and Words of a !Kung Woman," in *Interpreting Women's Lives: Feminist Theory and Personal Narratives,* ed. The Personal Narratives Group (Bloomington: Indiana University Press, 1989), pp. 228–40, esp. pp. 238–39.

42. James Olney, "Anthropology, Autobiography, Gynecology," *Yale Review* 71, no. 2 (summer 1982), pp. 591–96, esp. pp. 592, 593. See Mary Daly, *Gyn/ecology: The Metaethics of Radical Feminism* (Boston: Beacon Press, 1978).

43. Olney, "Anthropology, Autobiography, Gynecology," pp. 593–94, 594–95.

44. Ibid., pp. 595–96.

45. John Leonard, review of *Nisa,* by Marjorie Shostak, *New York Times,* December 7, 1981, C19.

46. Vincent Crapanzano, "Life-Histories," *American Anthropologist* 86 (1984), pp. 953–60, esp. pp. 954, 956, 957, 958, 959.

47. James Clifford, "A Boswell in Botswana," *Times Literary Supplement,* September 17, 1982, p. 994.

48. Eleanor Edelstein, review of *Nisa,* by Marjorie Shostak, *Anthropological Quarterly* 57, no. 4 (1984), pp. 156–57.

49. Lillian A. Ackerman, review of *Nisa,* by Marjorie Shostak, *Journal of Anthropological Research* 40, no. 2 (summer 1984), pp. 337–38; Edwin Wilmsen, *Land Filled with Flies: A Political Economy of the Kalahari* (Chicago: University of Chicago Press, 1989), p. 305, and personal communication.

50. James Clifford, "On Ethnographic Allegory," in *Writing Culture: The Poetics and Politics of Ethnography,* ed. James Clifford and George E. Marcus (Berkeley: University of California Press, 1986), pp. 98–121, esp. p. 104; George Marcus and Michael J. Fischer, *Anthropology as Cultural Critique: An Experimental Moment in the Human Sciences* (Chicago: University of Chicago Press, 1986), p. 58; Mary Louise Pratt, "Fieldwork in Common Places," in Clifford and Marcus, *Writing Culture,* pp. 27–50, esp. p. 45; di Leonardo, "Introduction: Gender, Culture, and Political Economy," pp. 23–24.

51. Jefferson, "Field Tripping," p. 22; Harry Lewis, review of *Nisa,* by Marjorie Shostak, *Village Voice,* December 23–29, 1981, p. 49.

52. Leslie Devereaux, "Experience, Re-presentation, and Film," in *Fields of Vison: Essays in Film Studies, Visual Anthropology, and Photography,* ed. Leslie Devereaux and Roger Hillman (Berkeley: University of California Press, 1995), pp. 1–20, esp. p. 62.

53. Jefferson, "Field Tripping," p. 23.

54. Pratt, "Fieldwork in Common Places," pp. 45, 46, 48, 49.

55. Wilmsen, *Land Filled with Flies;* Robert J. Gordon, *The Bushman Myth: The Making of a Namibian Underclass* (Boulder, Westview Press, 1992). There has been substantial debate over whether or not the Harvard School authors "really" claimed the San were people outside of history, and over details of Wilmsen's analysis. See Jacqueline S. Solway and Richard B. Lee, "Foragers, Genuine or Spurious?" *Current Anthropology,* vol. 31, no. 2, April 1990, pp. 109–46; Edwin Wilmsen and James R. Denbow, "Paradigmatic History of San-Speaking Peoples

and Current Attempts at Revision," *Current Anthropology*, vol. 31, no. 5, December 1990, pp. 489–524; Richard Lee and Mathias Guenther, "Oxen or Onions? The Search for Trade (and Truth) in the Kalahari," *Current Anthropology* 32, no. 5 (1991), pp. 592–601; and Edwin N. Wilmsen, "On the Search for (Truth) and Authority: A Reply to Lee and Guenther," *Current Anthropology* 34, no. 5 (1993), pp. 715–21.

56. See Wilmsen, *Land Filled with Flies*, pp. 64–129, esp. p. 101.

57. Ibid., pp. 281 ff., esp. p. 287.

58. Ibid., p. 312.

59. Ibid., pp. 280, 317, 289 ff., 325.

60. Robert J. Gordon, *The Bushman Myth*, pp. 10, 11.

61. Ibid., pp. 51, 72, 75, 880, 81, 82, 93, 116, 117, 149, 159, 164, 177, 188, 189. See also Robert Gordon, "The San in Transition: Volume II: What Future for the Ju/Wasi of Nyae-Nyae?" *Cultural Survival*, vol. 13 (July 1984).

62. Robert J. Gordon, *The Bushman Myth*, p. 3.

63. Ibid., p. 217.

64. Wilmsen, *Land Filled with Flies*, p. 322.

65. *N!ai: The Story of a !Kung Woman*, directed by Adrienne Miesmer and John Marshall, produced by John Marshall and Sue Cabezas Marshall, executive producer Michael Ambrosino, 1980.

66. *The Gods Must Be Crazy*, directed by Jamie Uys, 1980; Keyan Tomaselli, *The Cinema of Apartheid: Race and Class in South African Film* (London: Routledge, 1989).

67. Richard Corliss, "A Quartet of Cult Objects," *Time*, February 4, 1985, pp. 83–84, esp. p. 83; David Denby, "The Nothing," *New York*, July 30, 1984, p. 47–48, esp. p. 47.

68. Michael E. Brown, "The Viability of Racism: South Africa and the United States," *Philosophical Forum* 28 (winter–spring 1986–87), pp. 254–69, esp. pp. 256–57.

69. Ella Shohat and Robert Stam, *Unthinking Eurocentrism: Multiculturalism and the Media* (London: Routledge, 1994), pp. 180–81. Even contemporary journalism that dismisses the Edenic aspect of *Gods* uses its false ethnography to maintain grotesque condescension towards San peoples. See Suzanne Daley, "Endangered Bushmen Find Hope," *New York Times*, January 16, 1996.

70. To my knowledge, only Keyan Tomaselli has commented on this extraordinary feature of *N!ai*. see his "Revisualizing the San in the Nineteen-Eighties," *Visual Anthropology* 96 (1993), pp. 97–104, esp. p. 101.

71. Tom O'Brien, "Not-So-Final Battles," *Commonweal*, October 5, 1984, pp. 534–36, esp. p. 536.

72. Robert Gordon, "The Prospects for Anthropological Tourism in Bushmanland," *Cultural Survival Quarterly* 14, no. 1 (1990), pp. 6–8.

73. Robert Gordon, "The Prospects," p. 8.

74. Phyllis Palmer, "White Women/Black Women," The Dualism of Female

Identity and Experience in the United States," *Feminist Studies* 9, no. 1 (spring 1983), pp. 151–70; Nell Painter, *Sojourner Truth: A Life, a Symbol* (New York: W. W. Norton, 1996); Jane Guyer, "Female Farming in Anthropology and African History," in di Leonardo, *Gender at the Crossroads*, pp. 257–77, esp. p. 258.

75. The enduring classroom popularity of *Women of the Forest*, however—given the careful and very negative anthropological reviews it received at the point of publication—could be seen as a phenomenon similar to that of *Nisa*.

76. Roy Rappaport, "Desecrating the Holy Woman," *American Scholar* 55 (summer 1986), pp. 313–47.

77. David Schneider, "The Coming of a Sage to Samoa," *Natural History*, June 1983, pp. 4–10, esp. p. 10.

78. Derek Freeman, *Margaret Mead and Samoa: The Unmaking of an Anthropological Myth* (Cambridge, Mass.: Harvard University Press, 1983), p. xvi.

79. Ernest Van Den Haag, "Strange News from the South Seas," *Fortune*, April 18, 1983, pp. 153–56, esp. p. 153.

80. Freeman, *Margaret Mead and Samoa*, p. 11.

81. Ibid., p. 295.

82. Annette Weiner, "Ethnographic Determinism: Samoa and the Margaret Mead Controversy," *American Anthropologist* 85, no. 4, pp. 909–19, esp. p. 912.

83. Freeman, *Margaret Mead and Samoa*, p. 302.

84. Marilyn Strathern, "The Punishment of Margaret Mead," *Canberra Anthropology* 6 (1983), pp. 70–79, esp. p. 78.

85. See George Stocking, "The Ethnographic Sensibility of the 1920s and the Dualism of the Anthropological Tradition," in *The Ethnographer's Magic and Other Essays in the History of Anthropology*, ed. George W. Stocking, Jr. (Madison: University of Wisconsin Press, 1992), pp. 276–341, esp. pp. 276–77. In this essay Stocking confesses his own role, as a positive referee for Harvard University Press, in the publication of Freeman's book. This position perhaps explains Stocking's extraordinary acceptance of Freeman's statements concerning Mead's and others' work at face value, despite his citation of pieces in which scholars lay out Freeman's misuse of their work, sheer errors of fact, and radical decontextualizations of Samoan life and ethnography. See especially Lowell Holmes, "A Tale of Two Studies," *American Anthropologist* 85, no. 4 (December 1983), pp. 929–35; and Bradd Shore, "Paradox Regained: Freeman's *Margaret Mead and Samoa*," *American Anthropologist* 85, no. 4 (December 1983), pp. 935–44.

86. Holmes, "A Tale," p. 933.

87. Lowell Holmes, *Quest for the Real Samoa: The Mead/Freeman Controversy and Beyond* (South Hadley: Bergin and Garvey, 1987), p. 154. See also Rappaport, "Desecrating the Holy Woman," p. 330.

88. Henrika Kuklick, "Ourselves and Others," *Contemporary Sociology* 13, no. 4 (July 1984), pp. 558–62, esp. p. 560.

89. Ibid., p. 560.

90. I have excluded from this summary statement negative reviews in *Science*,

Natural History, and *Psychology Today,* because they were written by cultural anthropologists rather than "hard" scientists.

91. Thelma S. Baker, review of *Margaret Mead and Samoa,* by Derek Freeman, *Human Biology* 56, no. 2 (May 1984), pp. 402–4, esp. p. 403; Paul Alan Cox, "Margaret Mead and Samoa," *American Scientist* 71, no. 4 (1983), p. 407. See also Peter T. Ellison, review of *Margaret Mead and Samoa,* by Derek Freeman, *Ethnology and Sociobiology* 5 (1984), pp. 69–70.

92. "Untrashing Margaret Mead," *Scientific American* 255, no. 5 (November 1986), pp. 57–59.

93. Mac Marshall, in fact, has analyzed Freeman's rhetoric to this end, pointing out that through lexical choice he lays claim to ethnographic, scientific authority and denies it to Mead. See Marshall, "The Wizard from Oz Meets the Wicked Witch of the East: Freeman, Mead, and Ethnographic Authority," *American Ethnologist* 20, no. 3 (1993), pp. 604–17.

94. Freeman, *Margaret Mead and Samoa,* p. xiv.

95. Ibid., p. 290.

96. James P. Sterba, "Tropical Storm: New Book Debunking Margaret Mead Dispels Tranquility in Samoa," *Wall Street Journal,* April 14, 1983, pp. 1, 23, esp. p. 23; Elizabeth Owen, "Samoa: An Uproar over Sex and Violence in Margaret Mead's Idyllic Isles," *Life,* May 1983, pp. 32–40, esp. p. 40.

97. Freeman, *Margaret Mead and Samoa,* pp. 274, 275, 161, 301, 244.

98. Robert Levy, "The Attack on Mead," *Science* 220, no. 4599 (May 20, 1983), pp. 829–32, esp. p. 831.

99. Holmes, *Quest for the Real Samoa,* pp. 149 ff.

100. Ibid., p. 151.

101. Eleanor Leacock, "Anthropologists in Search of a Culture: Margaret Mead, Derek Freeman, and All the Rest of Us," in *Confronting the Margaret Mead Legacy: Scholarship, Empire, and the South Pacific,* ed. Lenora Foerstal and Angela Gilliam (Philadelphia: Temple University Press, 1992), pp. 3–30.

102. Ibid., p. 185.

103. Richard Bernstein, "Samoa: A Paradise Lost?" *New York Times Sunday Magazine,* April 24, 1983, pp. 48–67, esp. p. 58; Sterba, "Tropical Storm," p. 1.

104. Bonnie A. Nardi, "The Height of Her Powers: Margaret Mead's Samoa," *Feminist Studies* 10, no. 2 (summer 1984), 323–37.

105. Sharon Begley, "In Search of the Real Samoa," *Newsweek,* February 14, 1983, p. 56; Owen, "Samoa: An Uproar," p. 40.

106. *Phil Donahue Show,* March 18, 1983. All subsequent quotations are from the videotape of this show.

107. Except, apparently, Down Under, where playwright David Williamson's sellout at the Sydney Opera House, *Heretic,* represents Freeman as a "lone-wolf eccentric who is savaged by the anthropological tribe when he publishes his 1983 polemic." See Peter Monaghan, "Fantasy Island," *Lingua Franca,* July/August 1996, pp. 7–8, esp. p. 7.

108. *Margaret Mead and Samoa,* directed by Frank Heimans, 1989; Adam Kuper, "Coming of Age in Anthropology?" *Nature* 338 (April 6, 1989), pp. 453–55; Angela Gilliam, "Symbolic Subordination and the Representation of Power in *Margaret Mead and Samoa,*" *Visual Anthropology Review* 9, no. 1 (spring 1993), pp. 105–15.

109. See Nicholas Davidson, "Theoretical Perspectives on Sex Differences," *National Review,* August 20, 1990, and "Was Socrates a Plagiarist? Incorporation of Afrocentrism into Educational Curricula," *National Review,* February 25, 1991; George Sim Johnson, review of *Degenerate Moderns,* by E. Michael Jones, *American Spectator,* November 1993; Fred Siegel, review of *Sick Societies,* by Robert Edgerton, and *The Decomposition of Sociology,* by Irving Horowitz, *American Spectator,* March 1994; Pat Buchanan, "Frauds of the Century Debunking the Work of Freud, Keynes, Kinsey, Marx and Other 'Big Thinkers,'" *Pittsburgh Post-Gazette,* February 7, 1994. The two nonrightist exceptions are a favorable review by Jonathon Benthall of Adam Kuper's *The Chosen Primate* in the *New Statesman,* May 27, 1994; and a relatively reasonable piece by Shannon Brownlee on "noble primitivism," "If Only Life Were So Simple," *U.S. News and World Report,* February 19, 1990, pp. 54–56.

110. With the exceptions of Sharon Tiffany, "In the Steps of Margaret Mead," *Women's Review of Books* 1, no. 11 (August 1984), p. 14–15; and Bonnie Nardi's *Feminist Studies* piece, "The Height of Her Powers." But Nardi's article is actually a Heisenberg effect phenomenon, as I myself commissioned and edited it.

111. Nardi, "The Height of Her Powers," p. 331.

112. Marvin Harris, "The Sleep-Crawling Question," *Psychology Today,* May 1983, pp. 25–27, esp. p. 27.

113. See Colin Turnbull, "Trouble in Paradise," *New Republic,* March 28, 1983, pp. 32–34; Strathern, "The Punishment of Margaret Mead"; and Nardi, "The Height of Her Powers."

114. On age adjustment of comparative rape rates, see Nardi, "The Height of Her Powers," p. 336–37: "If Freeman had controlled for the factor of age, which any graduate student would be required to do even in a term paper, he would have found little difference between the rates of rape in Samoa and the United States."

115. Ann Oakley, "Interviewing Women: A Contradiction in Terms," in *Doing Feminist Research,* ed. Helen Roberts (London: Routledge & Kegan Paul, 1981), pp. 30–61; Judith Stacey, "Can There Be a Feminist Ethnography?" *Women's Studies International Forum* 11, no. 1 (1988), pp. 21–27; Lila Abu-Lughod, "Can There Be a Feminist Ethnography?" *Women and Performance* 7, no. 1 (1990), pp. 7–27.

116. Ruth Behar, *Translated Woman: Crossing the Border with Esperanza's Story* (Boston: Beacon Press, 1993), pp. 335, 20.

117. Kamala Visweswaran, *Fictions of Feminist Ethnography* (Minneapolis: University of Minnesota Press, 1994), pp. 127, 35, 27.

118. Clifford Geertz, *Works and Lives: The Anthropologist as Author* (Stanford: Stanford University Press, 1988), pp. 77, 90.

119. Visweswaran, *Fictions of Feminist Ethnography*, pp. 20, 21, 27, 25.

120. Margery Wolf, *A Thrice-Told Tale: Feminism, Postmodernism, and Ethnographic Responsibility* (Stanford: Stanford University Press, 1992), p. 13, and "Afterword: Musings From an Old Gray Wolf," in *Feminist Dilemmas in Fieldwork*, ed. Diane Wolf (Boulder: Westview Press, 1996); Micaela di Leonardo, "Introduction: Gender, Culture, and Political Economy," and "What a Difference Political Economy Makes: Feminist Anthropology in the Postmodern Era," *Anthropological Quarterly* 66, no. 2 (April 1993), pp. 76–80.

121. Marilyn Strathern, "An Awkward Relationship: The Case of Feminism and Anthropology," *Signs* 12, no. 2 (winter 1987), pp. 276–92, esp. p. 288.

122. Behar, *Translated Woman*, p. 269. The Canadian social scientist Judith Adler Hellman's *Mexican Lives* (New York: New Press, 1994) is a contrasting example of Mexican life history material considered in historical, regional, and political context.

123. Visweswaran, *Fictions of Feminist Ethnography*, pp. 102 ff.

124. Ambalavar Sivanandan, "All That Melts into Air Is Solid," *Race and Class* 31, no. 3 (1990), p. 16.

Chapter Six

1. Stendhal [Henri Beyle], *The Telegraph*, vol. 2 of *Lucien Leuwen*, trans. Louise Varèse (New York: New Directions, 1950 [1855]), p. 168.

2. See David C. Conrad and Karen J. Tillotson, "The Races of Man," *Chicago Reader*, April 16, 1993, pp. 8 ff.

3. *Federal Writers' Project Guide to Illinois* (New York: Pantheon Books, 1983 [1939]), p. 226.

4. Conrad and Tillotson, "The Races of Man," p. 30.

5. See Pamela Hibbs Decoteau, "Malvina Hoffman and the 'Races of Man,'" *Woman's Art Journal* 10, no. 2 (fall 1989/winter 1990), pp. 7–12; Linda Nochlin, "Malvina Hoffman: A Life in Sculpture," *Arts*, November 1984, pp. 106–10.

6. See Ivan Karp, Christine Mullen Kreamer, and Stephen D. Lavine, eds., *Museums and Communities: The Politics of Public Culture* (Washington, D.C.: Smithsonian Institution Press, 1992).

7. I am a consultant on this project.

8. Byron P. White, "On the Record," *Chicago Tribune*, July 7, 1996. Stephen Steinberg points out that Wilson's latest book, *When Work Disappears*, continues to make claims of agentless political economy and black behavioral pathology, even in the face of his own data. See Steinberg, "Science and Politics in the Work of William Julius Wilson," *New Politics* 6, no. 2 (winter 1997), pp. 72–83.

9. Mary Schmich, "No Place like Home, for Journalists Who Wonder, Wander," *Chicago Tribune*, July 5, 1996.

10. Gary Orfield, "The Chicago Study of Access and Choice in Higher Education" (Chicago: University of Chicago Committee on Public Policy Studies Research Project, 1984); Gary Orfield, Albert Woolbright, and Helene Kim, "Neigh-

borhood Change and Integration in Metropolitian Chicago" (report for the Leadership Council for Metropolitian Open Communities, Chicago, 1984); Gary Orfield, Susan Eaton, and the Harvard Project on School Desegregation, *Dismantling Desegregation: The Quiet Reversal of Brown vs. Board of Education* (New York: New Press, 1996); David Ranney and Ann Miller, "NAFTA in Illinois: Who Benefits and Who Pays?" (Chicago: Illinois Fair Trade Campaign Report, April 1996); David Ranney and William Cecil, "Transnational Investment and Job Loss in Chicago: Impacts on Women, African-Americans and Latinos" (working paper, University of Illinois at Chicago, Center for Urban Economic Development, January 1993); David Ranney, Pat Wright, and Tingwei Zhang, "Citizens, Local Government, and the Development of Chicago's Near South Side" (paper presented at United Nations Research Institute for Social Development conference, Istanbul, May 1996); Dwight Conquergood, "Life in Big Red: Struggles and Accommodations in a Chicago Polyethnic Tenement," in *Structuring Diversity: Ethnographic Perspectives on the New Diversity*, ed. Louise Lamphere (Chicago: University of Chicago Press, 1992), pp. 65–94; Larry Bennett, "Harold Washington and the Black Urban Regime," *Urban Affairs Quarterly* 28, no. 3 (March 1993), pp. 423–40, and "Postwar Redevelopment in Chicago: The Declining Politics of Party and the Rise of Neighborhood Politics," in *Unequal Partnerships: The Political Economy of Urban Redevelopment in Postwar America*, ed. Gregory D. Squires (New Brunswick: Rutgers University Press, 1989), pp. 161–77; James R. Grossman, *Land of Hope: Chicago, Black Southerners, and the Great Migration* (Chicago: University of Chicago Press, 1989); Douglas S. Massey and Nancy A. Denton, *American Apartheid: Segregation and the Making of the Underclass* (Cambridge, Mass.: Harvard University Press, 1993).

11. Irvin L. Child, *Italian or American? The Second Generation* (New Haven: Yale University Press, 1943).

12. See Kathryn Oberdeck, "Labor's Vicar and the Variety Show: Popular Religion, Popular Theater, and Cultural Class Conflict in Turn-of-the-Century America" (Ph.D. diss., Yale University, 1991), and her "Religion, Culture, and the Politics of Class: Alexander Irvine's Mission to Turn-of-the-Century New Haven," *American Quarterly* 47, no. 2 (June 1995), pp. 236–79. On the Local 34 strike, see Molly Ladd-Taylor, "Women Workers and the Yale Strike," *Feminist Studies* 11, no. 3 (fall 1985), pp. 465–89.

13. See Norman Fainstein and Susan Fainstein, "New Haven: The Limits of the Local State," in *Restructuring the City: The Political Economy of Urban Development*, by Susan Fainstein et. al. (New York: Longman, 1983).

14. Robert Dahl, *Who Governs?* (New Haven: Yale University Press, 1961).

15. See Fainstein and Fainstein, "New Haven," p. 29.

16. William Domhoff, *Who Really Rules? New Haven and Community Power Reexamined* (Santa Monica: Goodyear Publishing Company, 1978); Clarence Stone and Heywood Sanders, "Reexamining a Classic Case of Development Politics: New Haven, Connecticut," in *The Politics of Urban Development*, ed. Clarence

Stone and Heywood Sanders (Lawrence: University Press of Kansas, 1987); Fainstein and Fainstein, "New Haven."

17. See Heidi Hess, "The New Haven Welfare MOMS: 1969–72," (senior essay, Yale University, Department of History, 1990).

18. William Finnegan, "Out There," *New Yorker*, September 10, September 17, 1990. Heisenberg effect note: Adolph Reed and I strongly urged Finnegan to frame his piece in terms of historical political economy.

19. Michael Massing, "Ghetto Blasting," *New Yorker*, January 16, 1995, pp. 32–37, esp. p. 33.

20. United States Census, 1980.

21. See Adolph L. Reed, Jr., "The Black Urban Regime: Structural Origins and Constraints," *Comparative Urban and Community Research*, vol. 1 (1988), pp. 138–39.

22. Andi Rierden, "Armed Youths Turn New Haven into a Battleground," *New York Times*, May 26, 1991.

23. Josh Kovner and Margaret Costello, "Living in the Echo of Gunfire," *New Haven Register*, May 19, 1991.

24. Ernest W. Burgess, "The Growth of the City: An Introduction to a Research Project," in *The City*, ed. Robert Park, Ernest Burgess, and Roderick McKenzie (Chicago: University of Chicago Press, 1925).

25. Christiana Lin, "The Merchants of Broadway: A Study of Yale and New Haven's Public-Private Partnership, 1958–91" (senior essay, Yale University, Department of Political Science, 1991).

26. Clifford Geertz, "Local Knowledge," in *Local Knowledge: Further Essays in Interpretive Anthropology* (New York: Basic Books, 1983), p. 234.

27. For support of this and the following statements, see David Gordon, "The Global Economy: New Edifice or Crumbling Foundations?" in *Social Structures of Accumulation: The Political Economy of Growth and Crisis*, ed. David M. Kotz et al. (Cambridge: Cambridge University Press, 1994), pp. 292–305; Arthur MacEwen and William K. Tabb, eds., *Instability and Change in the World Economy* (New York: Monthly Review Press, 1989); Nigel Harris, *The End of the Third World: Newly Industrializing Countries and the Decline of an Ideology* (Middlesex: Pelican, 1986); John Walton and David Seddon, "The Politics of Economic Reform in Central and Eastern Europe," chap. 9 of *Free Markets and Food Riots: The Politics of Global Adjustment* (Oxford: Blackwell, 1994); Saskia Sassen, *The Mobility of Labor and Capital: A Study in International Investment and Labor Flow* (Cambridge: Cambridge University Press, 1988); Holly Sklar, *Chaos or Community? Seeking Solutions, Not Scapegoats for Bad Economics* (Boston: South End Press, 1995); Michael Bernstein, "Understanding American Economic Decline: The Contours of the Late Twentieth-Century Experience," in *Understanding American Economic Decline*, ed. Michael A. Bernstein and David E. Adler (Cambridge: Cambridge University Press, 1994), pp. 3–33; Doug Henwood, *The State of the USA Atlas: The Changing Face of American Life in Maps and Graphics* (New York: Simon and Schus-

ter, 1994); Louisa Schein, "The Consumption of Color and the Politics of White Skin in Post-Mao China," *Social Text*, no. 41 (winter 1994), pp. 141–64; United Nations Development Program, *The Human Development Report, 1996* (New York: Oxford University Press, 1996); Barbara Crossette, "U.N. Survey Finds World Rich-Poor Gap Widening," *New York Times*, July 15, 1996; Susan Gal, "Gender in the Post-socialist Transition: The Abortion Debate in Hungary," *East European Politics and Societies* 8, no. 2 (spring 1994), pp. 256–86; Michael Specter, "Plunging Life Expectancy Puzzles Russia," *New York Times*, August 2, 1995; Allesandra Stanley, "Valentines to Russia, Seeking Patient Brides," *New York Times*, February 14, 1997; Tom Hundley, "Eastern European Women Exploited in Sex Business," *Chicago Tribune*, May 7, 1996; and Peggy Simpson, "No Liberation for Women: Eastern Europe Turns Back the Clock," *Progressive*, February 1991, pp. 20–24.

28. Dinesh D'Souza, *The End of Racism: Principles for a Multicultural Society* (New York: Free Press, 1995), pp. 154–55, 357.

29. Actual numbers of citations: 1978, 1; 1979, 0; 1980, 1; 1981, 2; 1982, 2; 1983, 9; 1984, 13; 1985, 7.

30. Christopher Jencks, "The Wrong Answer for Schools Is: b) Back to Basics," *Washington Post*, February 19, 1978; unsigned op-ed, "On 'Understanding' the Abominable," *New York Times*, July 16, 1980; Tery Eastland, "The Prophet Abroad," review of *Solzhenitsyn at Harvard*, ed. Ronald Berman, *Heritage Foundation Policy Review* (spring 1981); David E. Anderson, UPI report on Moral Majority conference, July 27, 1982; Leonard Kriegel, "Who Cares about the Humanities?" *Nation*, December 29, 1984; Constance Holden, "Reagan versus the Social Sciences," *Science*, November 30, 1984.

31. Actual numbers of citations: 1986, 14; 1987, 26; 1988, 19; 1989, 21; 1990, 31; 1991, 43; 1992, 71; 1993, 137; 1994, 95; 1995, 81, 1996, 83 (including my own "Patterns of Culture Wars: The Right's Attack on 'Cultural Relativism' as Synecdoche for All That Ails Us," *Nation*, April 8, 1996).

32. Joshua Muravchik, "What Is to Be Done? A Guide for Anti-Communists," *New Republic*, November 30, 1987; William Pfaff, "In Their Crisis, Universities Can't Shove Truth Down the Memory Hole," *Los Angeles Times*, December 30, 1988; Anne Gowen, "Homage Paid at AEI to Cultural Diversity," *Washington Times*, December 7, 1990; Digby Anderson, "Pate: A Conservative Manifesto," *National Review*, October 7, 1991, p. 45; Roger Kimball, "Some Things Are Better Than Other Things," review of *In Defense of Elitism*, by William A. Henry, *New York Times Book Review*, October 16, 1994, p. 30; William H. Honan, "In Search of the Copacetic Campus," *New York Times*, November 26, 1995.

33. D'Souza, *The End of Racism*, pp. 144, 117, 154.

34. Paul Johnson, "Colonialism's Back—and Not a Moment Too Soon," *New York Times Sunday Magazine*, April 18, 1993, pp. 22, 43–44; Samuel P. Huntington, "The Coming Clash of Civilizations, or, The West against the Rest," *New York Times*, June 6, 1993; Arthur M. Schlesinger, Jr., *The Disuniting of America: Reflections on a Multicultural America* (New York: Norton, 1992); Gertrude Himmelfarb,

On Looking into the Abyss: Untimely Thoughts on Culture and Society (New York: Knopf, 1994); Richard J. Herrnstein and Charles Murray, *The Bell Curve: Intelligence and Class Structure in American Life* (New York: Free Press, 1994).

35. "Anti-Semitism—Found" (1995, typescript), in author's possession.

36. George W. Stocking, Jr., "Franz Boas and the Culture Concept," in *Race, Culture, and Evolution: Essays in The History of Anthropology* (Chicago: University of Chicago Press, 1982 [1968]), pp. 195–233, esp. pp. 231, 230.

37. Marshall Sahlins, "Views of a Culture Heroine," review of *With a Daughter's Eye*, by Mary Catherine Bateson, and *Margaret Mead*, by Jane Howard, *New York Times Book Review*, August 26, 1984.

38. Ruth Benedict, *Patterns of Culture* (Boston: Houghton Mifflin, 1959 [1934]), p. 40.

39. Elgin Williams, "Anthropology for the Common Man," *American Anthropologist* 49, no. 1 (1947), pp. 84–90, esp. p. 85.

40. Ibid., p. 88.

41. Benedict, *Patterns of Culture,* p. 6.

42. Kurt Vonnegut, Jr., *Slaughterhouse Five, or The Children's Crusade, A Duty-Dance with Death* (New York: Dell Publishing, 1971 [1968]), p. 8.

43. Melville Herskovits, *Man and His Works: The Science of Cultural Anthropology* (New York: Alfred A. Knopf, 1948), p. 63. See also his posthumous *Cultural Relativism: Perspectives in Cultural Pluralism,* ed. Frances Herskovits (New York: Random House, 1972), pp. 15, 32.

44. See James W. Fernandez, "Tolerance in a Repugnant World and Other Dilemmas in the Cultural Relativism of Melville J. Herskovits," *Ethos* 18, no. 2 (June 1990), pp. 140–64.

45. Clifford Geertz, "Distinguished Lecture: Anti-anti-relativism," *American Anthropologist* 86 (1984), pp. 263–78, esp. p. 263. Geertz gives a thorough review and taxonomy of these attacks.

46. A. L. Kroeber and Clyde Kluckhohn, *Culture: A Critical Review of Concepts and Definitions* (New York: Vintage, 1952), p. 352.

47. Eric Wolf, *Anthropology* (New York: W. W. Norton, 1964), pp. 21–22.

48. David Bidney, "Cultural Relativism," in *International Encyclopaedia of the Social Sciences* (New York: Crowell Collier and MacMillan, 1968), pp. 543–47, esp. p. 547.

49. Gerald Berreman et al., *Anthropology Today* (Del Mar: CRM Books, 1971), p. 326; Roger Keesing and Felix Keesing, *New Perspectives in Cultural Anthropology* (New York: Holt, Rinehart and Winston, 1971), p. 127.

50. Marvin Harris, *Culture, People, Nature: An Introduction to General Anthropology* (New York: Harper and Row, 1971), p. 139; Conrad Phillip Kottak, *Cultural Anthropology* (New York: Random House, 1975); Robin Fox, *Encounter with Anthropology* (New York: Harcourt Brace Jovanovich, 1973), pp. 19 ff.

51. Klaus-Friedrich Koch, "Cultural Relativism," in *Encyclopedia of Anthropology,* ed. David E. Hunter (New York: Harper and Row, 1976), p. 102.

52. Carol Ember and Melvin Ember, *Cultural Anthropology* (Englewood Cliffs: Prentice-Hall, 1977), 21–22; James P. Spradley and David W. McCurdy, *Conformity and Conflict: Readings in Cultural Anthropology* (Glenview: Scott, Foresman, 1974), pp. 6–7; Johnetta Cole, *Anthropology for the Nineties: Introductory Readings* (New York: Free Press, 1988), p. 10; William A. Haviland, *Anthropology*, 5th ed. (New York: Holt, Rinehart, and Winston, 1989), p. 297; Herbert Applebaum, *Perspectives in Cultural Anthropology* (New York: State University of New York Press, 1987); Paul Bohannan, *We, the Alien* (Prospect Heights: Waveland Press, 1992).

53. Allan Bloom, *The Closing of the American Mind* (New York: Simon and Schuster, 1987), p. 202.

54. Michel de Montaigne, "On Cannibals," in *Selected Essays*, trans. Charles Cotton and W. Hazlitt, ed. Blanchard Bates (New York: Modern Library, 1949 [1580]), pp. 74, 77, 83, 88, 89. Geertz, among many others, cites Montaigne to this effect. See his "Distinguished Lecture: Anti-anti-relativism," p. 264.

55. D'Souza, *The End of Racism*, pp. 71 ff.

56. David Harvey, *The Condition of Postmodernity* (Oxford: Basil Blackwell, 1989), p. 300.

57. *Utne Reader,* July / August 1992; Claude Montana bed linens, Pier One Imports, Crate & Barrel Furniture, and Hush Puppies advertisements, in author's possession; Harvey, *The Condition of Postmodernity;* Klinknerville Design Works label, in author's possession.

58. Philippe Bourgois, *In Search of Respect* (Cambridge: Cambridge University Press, 1995). See also Adam Schatz's insightful negative review, "Among the Dispossessed," *Nation,* December 25, 1995, pp. 836–39.

59. Letters from Walter E. Wallis and Norma P. McGregor, *San Francisco Examiner Magazine,* December 31, 1995, p. 5.

60. *Species,* written by Dennis Feldman, directed by Roger Donaldson, produced by Frank Mancuso, Jr., 1995.

61. *The Last of the Dogmen,* directed by Tab Murphy, 1995.

62. Jon Carroll, "I Live Here, Damn Your Eyes," *San Francisco Chronicle,* September 8, 1995; Dear Abby column, *Chicago Tribune,* October 16, 1995.

63. Maureen Dowd, "Antlers, Boleros, and Crossbows," *New York Times,* November 23, 1995, and "America's Front Lawn," *New York Times Magazine,* January 15, 1994, p. 18; Leslie Dormen, "The Single Woman's Guide to Married People," *Glamour,* June 1995, p. 126; "He Did Her, So Merrill Does Dave," *New York Observer,* December 11, 1995, p. 28; Shane DuBow, "Me and the Boys," *Chicago Reader,* June 16, 1995, pp. 8 ff.

64. Bernard Weinraub, "Stories of Hollywood's Bleak Houses," *New York Times,* August 12, 1996; Louis Menand, "It's a Wonderful Life," *New York Review of Books,* February 6, 1997, pp. 25–29, esp. p. 27; "Whitney Houston, Angela Bassett Share Joys and Pains in 'Waiting to Exhale,'" *Ebony,* December 1995, pp. 24–29, esp. p. 26.

65. Gordon Johnson, "Anthropologist Digs Out Secrets of Collecting," *Chicago Tribune,* July 6, 1995; Rita Reif, "When the Artist's Canvas Is the Body," *New York*

Times, August 27, 1995; Michael T. Kaufman, "Folklorist in Queens Finds a Brimming Melting Pot," *New York Times,* July 26, 1995; Tea Leoni in "Quotables," *Chicago Tribune,* February 4, 1997.

66. Sherry Ortner, "Theory in Anthropology Since the Sixties," in *Culture/Power/History,* ed. Nicholas Dirks, Geoff Eley, and Sherry Ortner (Princeton: Princeton University Press, 1993), pp. 372–411, esp. p. 372; Peter Applebome, "A Trans-narrating, Ethnographic Good Time Was Had by All," *New York Times,* December 11, 1994; Charles Petit, "Happy Campers: Anthropologists Study Seniors on the Road, Find Distinct RV Culture, Rituals, Language," *San Francisco Chronicle,* November 23, 1996. Former American Anthropological Association President James Peacock has noted his own intense frustration with press failure, despite much effort by the association, to attend to serious anthropological reports at the annual meetings (personal communication). There is a notable exception: Bill Hendrick of the *Atlanta Constitution* actually reported the 1994 association's resolution against the racism and bad science of *The Bell Curve.* See his "Anthropology Group Slams 'Bell Curve,'" *Atlanta Constitution,* November 30, 1994.

67. See Sidney Mintz, *Caribbean Transformations* (Chicago: Aldine, 1974), and *Sweetness and Power the Place of Sugar in Modern History* (New York: Viking, 1985); also Sidney Mintz and Richard Price, *The Birth of Afro-American Culture: An Anthropological Perspective* (Boston: Beacon, 1992). A Lexis/Nexis search of references to Mintz from 1990 through the summer of 1996 gleaned 38 "hits." Excluding Canadian and United Kingdom references, and the obituary of Mintz's father, of the remaining thirty-five, twenty-five are of the sort quoted below.

68. Gerri Kobren, "There's No Fighting the Urge to Gorge," *Los Angeles Times,* November 22, 1990; Molly O'Neill, "The Morality of Fat," *New York Times,* March 10, 1996; Marion Cunningham, "Great Home Cooks," *Los Angeles Times,* November 22, 1992; Gressette Felicia, "Where Does Food Come From?" *Des Moines Register,* August 21, 1994; Cara De Silva, "Metaphors for Food and Eating Run All through Our Speech," *Newsday,* June 21, 1995; Sallie Han, "Language of Love Is Laden with Sweets," *Fort Lauderdale Sun-Sentinal,* February 9, 1995.

69. Lionel Tiger, "Hazed and Confused: The Ties That Bind Can Be Cruel," *New Yorker,* February 17, 1997, pp. 7–8, esp. p. 8; Richard Christiansen, "When Everyman Is Caveman," *Chicago Tribune,* March 3, 1994; editorial, "Blame It on the Flintstones," *Chicago Tribune,* September 7, 1995.

70. Roger Lancaster and Micaela di Leonardo, eds., *The Gender/Sexuality Reader* (New York: Routledge, 1997).

71. "Why You Do What You Do: Sociobiology: A New Theory of Behavior," *Time,* August 1, 1977, pp. 54–63.

72. April 30, 1996, draft of "The Biology of Beauty" story, *Newsweek,* in author's possession. The final draft closely matches this quotation.

73. Geoffrey Cowley, "The Biology of Beauty," *Newsweek,* June 3, 1996, pp. 60–69, esp. p. 66.

74. Ibid., pp. 69, 68.

75. "Why You Do What You Do," pp. 58, 63.

76. Renato Rosaldo, *Culture and Truth: The Remaking of Social Analysis* (Boston: Beacon Press, 1989), pp. 64–67.

77. Stephen Jay Gould, "The Diet of Worms and the Defenestration of Prague," *Natural History*, September 1996, pp. 18–24, 64–67, esp. p. 66.

78. For careful analysis of affirmative action's history, rationale, and political entailments, see Stephen Steinberg, *Turning Back: The Retreat from Racial Justice in American Thought and Policy* (Boston: Beacon Press, pp. 164–78); Gertrude Ezorsky, *Racism and Justice: The Case for Affirmative Action* (Ithaca: Cornell University Press, 1991); and Barbara Bergmann, *In Defense of Affirmative Action* (New York: Basic Books, 1996).

79. See Benjamin S. Orlove and Glynn Custred, eds., *Land and Power in Latin America: Agrarian Processes and Social Processes in the Andes* (New York: Holmes and Meier, 1980). Custred started out as a symbolic and folkloric anthropologist. See his "Symbols and Control in a High Altitude Andean Community" (Ph.D. diss., Indiana University, 1973). From 1981 to 1996, Custred's work was cited by other social scientists only twenty-one times. See the *Social Sciences Citation Index*.

80. Stephen Schwartz, "Challenge to Campus Policies," *San Francisco Chronicle,* January 5, 1991; R. Drummond Ayres Jr., "Foes of Affirmative Action Form a National Group," *New York Times,* January 16, 1997.

81. Dan Morain, "Foes Square Off on Affirmative Action," *Los Angeles Times,* April 20, 1995; Glynn Custred, prepared testimony before the U.S. House Judiciary Committee Constitution Subcommittee, April 3, 1995.

82. Custred, in fact, wrote a positive review of Steele's error-littered *Content of Our Character.* See "Tyranny of Old Memories," *Southern Quarterly* 31, no. 1 (fall 1992), pp. 126–30. For an insightful and accurate review of Steele, noting his poor scholarly record, see Adolph Reed, Jr., "The Selling of Shelby Steele," *Nation,* March 4, 1991. Glynn Custred, Judiciary Committee testimony; Nicholas Lemann, "Taking Affirmative Action Apart," *New York Times Sunday Magazine,* June 11, 1995; Glynn Custred, "Multiculturalism Counter to National Integrity," letter to *Heritage Foundation Policy Review,* Winter 1992, p. 94.

83. Morain, "Foes Square Off on Affirmative Action"; *Dateline NBC,* January 23, 1995, produced by Cathy Singer.

84. Lemann, "Taking Affirmative Action Apart."

85. Anh-Minh Le, "Custred's Stand: Glynn Custred and His Initiative," University of California, *Fishrap,* n.d., from World Wide Web (spring 1995).

86. Andrei Simic and Glynn Custred, "Modernity and the American Family: A Cultural Dilemma," *International Journal of the Sociology of the Family* 12, no. 2 (autumn 1982), pp. 163–72, esp. pp. 171, 167, 163. See Christopher Lasch, *Haven in a Heartless World: The Family Besieged* (New York: Basic Books, 1977).

87. For misidentifications of the Unabomber's political perspective, see Ellen Warren, "US Seizes Unabomber: Lonely 'Brain' has Evergreen Park Roots," *Chi-*

cago Tribune, April 4, 1996; and Richard Perez-Pena, "On the Unabomber's Track: The Suspect, A Man Known to Few, and a Mystery to Many," *New York Times,* April 4, 1996, and "On the Suspect's Trail: The Suspect, Memories of His Brilliance and Shyness, But Little Else," *New York Times,* April 5, 1996.

88. Full text of Unabomber manifesto, from the Internet (spring 1996), numbered paragraphs 15, 14, 21, 29, 11.

89. Unabomber manifesto, paragraphs 55, 56, 57.

90. A Lexis/Nexis search in August 1996 indicated 1,680 citations of Mead from January 1990 forward, but only thirteen citations, almost all rightist, of Mead and Freeman together. Custred is cited once in each of 1990, 1991, 1992, 1993, seventeen times in 1994, 203 in 1995, and only twenty-seven in 1996.

91. Nell Painter, *Sojourner Truth: A Life, a Symbol* (New York: W. W. Norton, 1996), pp. 277–78.

92. Van Wyck Brooks, "On Creating a Usable Past," reprinted from the *Dial* [1918] in *Critics of Culture: Literature and Society in the Early Twentieth Century,* ed. Alan Trachtenberg (New York: John Wiley and Sons, 1976), pp. 165–71, esp. p. 169.

INDEX

WITHDRAWAL

MICAELA di LEONARDO is professor of anthropology and women's studies at Northwestern University. She has written *The Varieties of Ethnic Experience*, edited *Gender at the Crossroads of Knowledge: Feminist Anthropology in the Postmodern Era*, and coedited *The Gender/Sexuality Reader: Culture, History, Political Economy*.